THE CAMBRIDGE HISTORY OF
SEVENTEENTH-CENTURY MUSIC

The Cambridge History of Seventeenth-Century Music seeks to provide the most up-to-date knowledge on seventeenth-century music, together with a vital questioning of the way in which such a history can be told or put together for our present purposes. Written by a distinguished team of experts in the field, the chapters not only address traditional areas of study such as opera and church music, but also look at the way this extremely diverse and dynamic musical world has been categorised in the past, and how its products are viewed from various cultural points of view. While this history does not depart entirely from the traditional study of musical works and their composers, there is a strong emphasis on the institutions, cultures and politics of the age, together with an interrogation of the ways in which music related to contemporary arts, sciences and beliefs.

TIM CARTER is the author of the Cambridge Opera Handbook on Mozart's *Le nozze di Figaro* (1987), *Jacopo Peri (1561–1633): His Life and Works* (1989), *Music in Late Renaissance and Early Baroque Italy* (1992) and *Monteverdi's Musical Theatre* (2002). He has also published numerous journal articles and essays on music in sixteenth- and early seventeenth-century Italy; those to 1998 were reprinted in *Music, Patronage and Printing in Late Renaissance Florence* and *Monteverdi and his Contemporaries* (both 2000). In 2001 he became David G. Frey Distinguished Professor of Music at the University of North Carolina at Chapel Hill.

JOHN BUTT is the Gardiner Professor of Music at the University of Glasgow. His book *Playing With History: The Historical Approach to Music Performance* (Cambridge, 2002) was shortlisted for the 2003 British Academy Book Prize and in the same year he won the Dent Medal. He is the author of *Music Education and the Art of Performance in the German Baroque* (1994), *Bach: Mass in B Minor* (1991) and *Bach Interpretation* (1990), all published by Cambridge University Press, and has edited *The Cambridge Companion to Bach* (1997). He is also a highly acclaimed harpsichordist and organist, and has recorded CDs for Harmonia Mundi, France.

THE CAMBRIDGE HISTORY OF

MUSIC

The Cambridge History of Music comprises a group of reference works concerned with significant strands of musical scholarship. The individual volumes are self-contained and include histories of music examined by century as well as the history of opera, music theory and American music.

Each volume is written by a team of experts under one or more specialist editors and represents the latest musicological research.

Published titles

The Cambridge History of American Music
Edited by David Nicholls

The Cambridge History of Western Music Theory
Edited by Thomas Christensen

The Cambridge History of Seventeenth-Century Music
Edited by Tim Carter and John Butt

The Cambridge History of Nineteenth-Century Music
Edited by Jim Samson

The Cambridge History of Twentieth-Century Music
Edited by Nicholas Cook and Anthony Pople

THE CAMBRIDGE

HISTORY OF

SEVENTEENTH-CENTURY
MUSIC

*

edited by
TIM CARTER AND JOHN BUTT

CAMBRIDGE
UNIVERSITY PRESS

CAMBRIDGE UNIVERSITY PRESS
Cambridge, New York, Melbourne, Madrid, Cape Town, Singapore, São Paulo

Cambridge University Press
The Edinburgh Building, Cambridge CB2 2RU, UK

Published in the United States of America by Cambridge University Press, New York

www.cambridge.org
Information on this title: www.cambridge.org/9780521792738

© Cambridge University Press 2005

First published 2005

Printed in the United Kingdom at the University Press, Cambridge

Library of Congress Cataloguing in Publication data

ISBN-13 978-0-521-79273-8 hardback
ISBN-10 0-521-79273-8 hardback

Contents

Contributors

GREGORY BARNETT is Assistant Professor of Musicology at Rice University. He received the MFA and Ph. D. degrees in musicology from Princeton University. Currently writing a book on Italian instrumental music of the late seventeenth century, he has published articles in the *Journal of the American Musicological Society*, the *Journal of the American Musical Instrument Society*, the *Quaderni della Rivista Italiana di Musicologia*, and the proceedings of conferences held by Antiquae Musicae Italicae Studiosi, Como (1999, 2001, 2003). He has also written on tonal organisation in seventeenth-century music theory in *The Cambridge History of Western Music Theory* (2002).

JOHN BUTT is the Gardiner Professor of Music at the University of Glasgow. His book *Playing With History: the Historical Approach to Music Performance* (Cambridge, 2002) led to the award of the Dent Medal from the Royal Musical Association (2003) and was shortlisted for the 2003 British Academy Book Prize. He is the author of *Bach Interpretation: Articulation Marks in Primary Sources of J. S. Bach* (1990), *Bach: Mass in B Minor* (1991), *Music Education and the Art of Performance in the German Baroque* (1994), all published by Cambridge University Press, and has edited *The Cambridge Companion to Bach* (1997). He is also a highly acclaimed harpsichordist and organist, and has recorded CDs for Harmonia Mundi, France.

TIM CARTER is the author of the Cambridge Opera Handbook on Mozart's *Le nozze di Figaro* (1987), *Jacopo Peri (1561–1633): his Life and Works* (New York and London, 1989), *Music in Late Renaissance and Early Baroque Italy* (London, 1992), and *Monteverdi's Musical Theatre* (New Haven and London, 2002). He has also published numerous articles and essays on music in sixteenth- and early seventeenth-century Italy; those to 1998 were reprinted in *Music, Patronage and Printing in Late Renaissance Florence* and *Monteverdi and his Contemporaries* (London, 2000). In 2001 he moved from Royal Holloway and Bedford New College, University of London, to become David G. Frey Distinguished Professor of Music at the University of North Carolina at Chapel Hill.

VICTOR ANAND COELHO is Professor of Music at Boston University. He works mainly in the areas of sixteenth- and seventeenth-century instrumental music, and also has a strong interest in interdisciplinary and cross-cultural issues. His books include *Music and Science in the Age of Galileo* (Boston, 1992), *The Manuscript Sources of Seventeenth-Century Italian Lute Music* (New York, 1995), *Performance on Lute, Guitar, and Vihuela: Historical Practice and Modern Interpretation* (Cambridge, 1997) and *The Cambridge Companion to the Guitar* (2003). He has won awards for his recording (with Alan Curtis) of *La notte d'Amore: Music for the 1608 Medici Wedding* (2004).

PENELOPE GOUK is Senior Lecturer in History at the University of Manchester. She is currently writing about changing medical explanations for music's effects on human nature between the Renaissance and the Enlightenment. Her publications include *Music, Science and Natural Magic in Seventeenth-Century England* (New Haven and London, 1999); she was also the editor of *Musical Healing in Cultural Contexts* (London, 2000), and co-editor (with Helen Hills) of *Representing Emotions: New Connections in the Histories of Art, Music and Medicine* (London, 2005).

BARBARA RUSSANO HANNING is Professor of Music at The City College of New York, CUNY, where she chaired the Department of Music from 1990 to 2002. She is the author of *Of Poetry and Music's Power: Humanism and the Creation of Opera* (Ann Arbor, MI, 1980) and of numerous essays and reviews on topics covering seventeenth-century Italy, musical iconography, and eighteenth-century France. She was co-editor (with Nancy K. Baker) of *Musical Humanism and its Legacy: Essays in Honor of Claude V. Palisca* (Stuyvesant, NY, 1992) and wrote the Norton *Concise History of Western Music* (1998, 2002). She served as President of the Society for Seventeenth-Century Music from 1993 to 1997.

ROBERT L. KENDRICK teaches music history at the University of Chicago, and has worked extensively on issues of sacred music and culture in the seventeenth century. Among his publications are *Celestial Sirens: Nuns and their Music in Early Modern Milan* (Oxford, 1996) and *The Sounds of Milan, 1585–1650* (New York, 2002).

MARGARET MURATA, Professor of Music at the University of California, Irvine, has served as President of the Society for Seventeenth-Century Music and Vice-President of the American Musicological Society. Her research on opera and chamber cantatas in Baroque Rome has led to studies of the transmission of these repertories as *arie antiche* through the nineteenth century into the present. She has written extensively on sources, patronage and performance practices in essays for *Frescobaldi Studies* (1987), *La musica e il mondo: la committenza musicale in Italia fra tardo Quattrocento e primo Settecento* (1993), *Claudio Monteverdi: studi e prospettive* (1998) and *The Jesuits: Culture, Sciences, and the Arts, 1540–1773* (1999), as well as in scholarly journals, conference proceedings and Festschriften. A chapter on court opera is forthcoming in *The Cambridge Companion to Early Opera*.

NOEL O'REGAN is Senior Lecturer in Music at the University of Edinburgh. He is the author of the Royal Musical Association monograph *Institutional Patronage in Post-Tridentine Rome: Music at Santissima Trinità dei Pellegrini, 1550–1650* (1995), as well as of numerous articles on Roman music in the late sixteenth and early seventeenth centuries. He is currently engaged in an extensive study of the role of music in the devotional life of Roman confraternities in this period. He is a member of the editorial board of the New Palestrina Edition currently being planned by the Fondazione Giovanni Pierluigi da Palestrina, and is editing a volume of Palestrina's three-choir music for the same.

STEPHEN ROSE is Lecturer in Music at Royal Holloway, University of London, having previously been a Research Fellow at Magdalene College, Cambridge. His research approaches German Baroque music from various perspectives, including its social and economic contexts, music publishing, popular culture, and performance practice. He has published articles in *Early Music*, *Early Music History*, *Music & Letters* and the *Journal of the Royal Musical Association*, and is currently the Reviews Editor (books and music) of *Early Music*.

LOIS ROSOW, Professor at the Ohio State University, specialises in French opera of the seventeenth and eighteenth centuries. She has published articles on the administrative history and scribal workshop of the Paris Opéra, French music printing, Lully reception, performance-practice issues, and the interplay of dramaturgy with poetic and musical form. Her critical edition of Lully's *Armide* has recently appeared in *Jean-Baptiste Lully: Œuvres complètes*, ser. 3, vol. 14 (Hildesheim, 2004), and she was Guest Editor for *Journal of Seventeenth-Century Music*, vol. 10/1 (2004), devoted to Lully's *Persée* <http://www.sscm-jscm.org/jscm/v10no1.html>.

ALEXANDER SILBIGER is Professor Emeritus at Duke University. He has written on a variety of topics from the sixteenth to the eighteenth centuries, but is best known for his studies on seventeenth-century keyboard music (especially Frescobaldi, Michelangelo Rossi, Froberger and Weckmann) and for his work on early keyboard sources, notations and genres. He has prepared editions of Renaissance polyphony and Baroque cantatas as well as supervising a 28-volume facsimile set of seventeenth-century keyboard music (New York and London, 1987–9); his publications also include *Frescobaldi Studies* (Durham, NC, 1987) and *Keyboard Music Before 1700* (New York, 1995, 2003). Among his special interests are the relationships between score and performance, and the employment of genre and style allusions as elements of compositional discourse. He has also been active as a harpsichordist and as a director of early music ensembles, and is currently Librarian of the *Web Library of Seventeenth-Century Music* <http://www.sscm-wlscm.org>.

Preface

It would be difficult to claim that the idea of a history of seventeenth-century music is a new one. Indeed, some of the first significant attempts at writing a general history of music date from the seventeenth century itself, so writing that century's history today would not be entirely out of sympathy with the attitudes of the time. Nevertheless, Wolfgang Caspar Printz's history of music, *Historische Beschreibung der edelen Sing- und Kling-Kunst* (Dresden, 1690), is profoundly 'unhistorical' by later standards, given that it presents an anecdotal array of traditional knowledge about music, with the primary purpose of justifying and extolling the art. Comparing this sort of history with those of only a century later by writers such as Charles Burney (*A General History of Music from the Earliest Ages to the Present*, 1776–89), John Hawkins (*A General History of the Science and Practice of Music*, 1776) or Johann Nikolaus Forkel (*Allgemeine Geschichte der Musik*, 1788–1801) reveals striking differences of perspective and value; whatever their drawbacks, these later attempts present a sense of critical narrative based on researched material that seems much closer to modern conceptions of what history should do. Thus there would be little virtue in writing an account of seventeenth-century music purely from the historiographical perspective of its time. On the other hand, the differing perspectives of different times, places and beliefs suggest that there is no single 'true' story to tell about any century's musical culture.

There is no shortage of music histories in print today, and these themselves show a variety of approaches. The oldest that is still generally available is the postwar Dent–Norton series, in which music is divided up into stylistic periods rather than centuries – Middle Ages, Renaissance, Baroque etc. – so that only the 'Twentieth Century' does without a label, as if its stylistic category is yet to be processed. The Prentice Hall series follows much the same format, albeit more economical in scale to cater for the mass market of music-history courses. The *New Oxford History of Music* was more ambitious, often dividing the standard periods into more than one volume (distinguished by a specific date-range) or dispensing with some of the traditional stylistic categories altogether (hence *The Age of Humanism, 1540–1630* or *Opera and Church Music, 1630–1750*). But despite *NOHM*'s valiant efforts, 'Renaissance' (which is certainly relevant at least for the earlier part of our period) has undoubtedly proved one of the most durable of the 'standard' labels for the history of Western music, given its application to such a wide range of historical, cultural and artistic phenomena. 'Baroque' is of the most recent application, is the most ambivalent, and has been perhaps the first to be discarded by some historians. Although its etymology is now largely ignored, the word still implies something mannerist and frivolous, standing between the grander-sounding eras of the 'Renaissance' and 'Classicism'.

Some histories devoted to specific instrumental repertories will use 1700 as a cut-off date, such as the histories of keyboard music 'up to 1700' by Willi Apel (1967) or 'before 1700' by Alexander Silbiger (1995). Indeed, Apel also produced a study of Italian violin music (1983) that restricted itself to the seventeenth century alone. One significant general music history, Lorenzo Bianconi's *Il Seicento* (1982), specifically addresses our century shorn of the conventional Baroque epithet or the eighteenth-century appendage of 1700–1750. Might it be that the increasing tendency to divide volumes by date reflects an imperative to neutralise the standard post-war categories, and, in the case of the seventeenth century, to emancipate that century's music from the role of warm-up act to the German giants of the early eighteenth?

Certainly, affirmative action may have played its role in the trend away from stylistic periods and towards centuries. Less positively, one might say that it also betrays a certain failure of nerve, by which we feel reluctant to make any period-division that evidences a value-judgement of some sort; working by centuries is at least clean, neutral and (apart from the usual disputes as to exactly when a century begins and ends) incontestable, even if it is relatively meaningless. But there might be a more urgent, topical reason too: with the recent change of century (and indeed, millennium) we perhaps view century-divisions with more seriousness than might have been the case fifty years ago in the new awakening following a catastrophic war. The seduction of the temporal boundary has, of course, been compounded by other 'convenient' occurrences, namely the collapse of the Eastern Bloc and – most graphically – the events of 11 September 2001. Although comparing such world crises with Western music history must inevitably make the latter seem parochial, it is clear that we frequently look for musically striking events to divide centuries. It has, for instance, often been noted that 1600 conveniently marks the 'invention' of opera and the appearance of the first documentary evidence associated with the 'crisis' of Monteverdi's *seconda pratica*. We should be warned, of course, by the fact that the other end of the seventeenth century does not seem so neat. Yet 9/11 might also help us form important historical questions regarding apparent watersheds: have attitudes and thought processes really undergone a sea-change since that atrocity, and was it itself really that unexpected? Likewise (back in the parish), many have increasingly downplayed the conventional musical break at 1600 in favour either of an earlier start to the new style (by way of a new emphasis on rhetoric and affect in the Italian madrigal of the last quarter of the sixteenth century) or of a later one (the changing role of aria-styles in the musico-poetic discourse of the 1630s). And either way, 'Renaissance' styles and values clearly continued in some major repertories throughout the period. One might also perceive a 'generation gap' from the 1640s to the 1670s by which the narrative threads conventionally linking the early to the late Baroque are at best exiguous and, for some countries or genres, as yet non-existent: it is much easier to construct a coherent story of, say, the sixteenth century than it is of the seventeenth.

It would be disingenuous to claim that the editors and authors of the present volume set out with the idea of a seventeenth-century history entirely independently of the fact that Cambridge University Press was producing similar volumes on the eighteenth, nineteenth and twentieth centuries. There is certainly a pattern to which to conform here, but what would happen if one were to continue the series backwards (sixteenth century, fifteenth century etc.)? It seems likely that here, at least, there would be a strong tendency to revert to conventional periods ('Renaissance', 'Medieval' or just 'Early' music). Perhaps that is to do with the market. Perhaps, however, it is also due to the fact that the sixteenth century, for instance, on its own seems too diffuse, its musical developments too static and comparatively lacking in canonical composers (with the obvious exceptions such as Josquin Desprez and Palestrina). The seventeenth century is clearly richer in terms of famous names whose music is generally both individualistic and diverse – Monteverdi, Cavalli, Schütz, Lully, Purcell, Buxtehude, Corelli and Alessandro Scarlatti – even if these evidently do not match (at least in number) those of the eighteenth and nineteenth centuries. But even if we were to justify our history of the seventeenth century as marking as much the birth of the 'modern' era as it might do in the history of science – we do not – it is the most problematic of the 'useable centuries' in terms of the standard historiographical preconceptions of linear temporality and great, monumental figures. Indeed, it perhaps comes closest to the twentieth century in terms of challenging conventional historical methods and modes of interpretation. If the twentieth century seemed fraught with the splintering of ideologies, styles, and even definitions of what counts as music (not least through the vertiginous opening up of 'world music' and the unpredictable workings of the unfettered market for the popular and the commercial), similar issues seem to be at stake in the seventeenth. Admittedly, the Eurocentric world of seventeenth-century music (and the present book remains, *almost* unashamedly, Eurocentric) seems relatively limited by contemporary standards, but it was undoubtedly the era in which the Scientific Revolution and the rise of the nation-state set the pattern for things to come. There were even the first, tentative glimpses of the world of music beyond the Western tradition (facilitated by colonial expansion and latent in the encyclopaedic approaches of Athanasius Kircher and Marin Mersenne), something that seemed to confirm the superiority of the universalising tendencies of modern Western thought while also opening up the possibility of cultural differences to be recognised, if not necessarily reconciled, within the European context. In short, many of the contradictions, challenges, threats and possibilities that we experience today might be shown to have their roots in seventeenth-century thought and culture, and a history of music in this era must surely be able to play a part in the way in which we understand ourselves.

This last thought renders it abundantly plain that the way in which the present book is constructed is very much a product of our time and its priorities, both overt and covert. The fact that it is not written by a single author (such as a Manfred Bukofzer, Claude Palisca or Lorenzo Bianconi) is in part a question of competence in a time of increasing specialisation, but it also reflects an earnest belief in the value of diversity of approach and opinion. Moreover, we two editors have evolved conceptions that neither would have generated independently, and whatever plans we might have had were inevitably subverted – but hopefully bettered – by the rich variety of authors, all current leaders in the field. This multiplicity, randomness, and contingent editorial synthesis of the contributions seem to chime surprisingly well with the situation in seventeenth-century music, and, of course, it mirrors our own times precisely. It is not the case that strong-willed authorship has entirely disappeared, but that several strong voices can sound simultaneously, any uniformity often coming from 'hidden' factors, such as seemingly innocuous editorial decisions as to order, or what to cut or modify, and from the very format of the volume as determined by the Press.

For the latter, the present volume follows previous Cambridge Music Histories by avoiding music examples and illustrations. This may be a cause for celebration (because many more people, from diverse fields, now read about music), or gloom (because fewer now read music itself, and there is perhaps a general refusal to engage with its inner workings). Certainly, the way in which the entire musicological field has opened out in recent decades, rendering its discourse closer to those of literary criticism and of the other arts, means that music now seems less isolated from the cultural conversations of its time and of ours. There is a sense in which a historian of music can be a 'critic' in much the same way as an 'art critic' might relate to painting or sculpture, as someone who does not necessarily have any expertise in the actual execution of the art. Again, there is something here that resonates with the situation around the turn of the seventeenth century when music became an object of elite public discourse, beyond the day-to-day activities of the profession of practical music. There were also obvious fears about the general 'lowering of standards' as certain composers and performers seemed to circumvent the established rules in the name of some extra-musical imperative. Yet it would certainly be wrong to assert that musical expertise has disappeared (now as then), or that writers deprived of musical examples do not care very deeply for a direct sensual, emotional and intellectual engagement with music.

It remains to be seen whether the tradition of Western art-music can survive in 21st-century society, but it is almost certain that it would die if musicians and scholars battened down their hatches and talked and played only to one another. If this volume undoubtedly loses something with a lessened engagement with the nuts and bolts of music, it also gains much by examining the divers ways in which music interacts with the surrounding culture. Our examination of the seventeenth century can also be an examination of some of the conditions and presuppositions of the present, challenging us to articulate our musical priorities and to define that which makes the classical tradition worth preserving in the first place. By drawing music nearer to the world of letters, we can also lay the foundations for a regeneration of the amateur but sophisticated musical culture that has always been so vital for the health of music within modernity.

Given that our history represents our contemporary conceptions of the seventeenth century, it is worth rehearsing in brief the changes in the reception of seventeenth-century music over the intervening years. Only if our present reception of that era were to be the most accurate or 'true' so far would all earlier reception be rendered worthless. Yet there is clearly no guarantee of truth in this regard, even if our methods of dealing with factual evidence seem more precise than ever (and we should remember that empirical methodology was itself still in its infancy in the seventeenth century). Perhaps a primary question to ask of the history of the reception of seventeenth-century music (and indeed, culture in general) is whether that era has always been viewed with the ambivalence that tends to characterise much of its twentieth-century reception, namely as a period of flux, disorder or even sterility, separating the perfection of the Renaissance from the summits of the high Baroque and Classical periods. Given that it is only in the last 60 years – save some prior flurries of interest in particular composers (notably Monteverdi, Lully and Purcell) – that scholars and performers have developed an extensive concern (whether 'historical' or not) for seventeenth-century music even remotely comparable with that of the two surrounding centuries, has anything changed in our more recent times to render the era seemingly more significant?

The significance of such issues of reception-history has only recently begun to be realised, and much terrain remains to be charted (Haskell offers a start). There certainly seems to be little evidence that the early eighteenth century saw itself to be conceptually severed from the seventeenth. The fact that the most potent political regime of the age, Louis XIV's France, straddled the turn of the century is obviously significant, and indeed the continuity in French performances of Lully's great *tragédies en musique* right up to the Revolution is difficult to ignore. If we examine the historicist habits of the German duo, J. S. Bach and Handel, it is striking that both tended to use seventeenth-century music as if it were their own. Almost all of Handel's 'borrowed' material (except from himself) comes from the immediately preceding generation, and Bach's recently rediscovered 'Altbachisches Archiv' represents members of his family from the entire seventeenth century; many of these pieces show signs of performance in his later years. If this generation of composers who died around 1750 shows a continuity with the previous century, much the same could be said of musical institutions of the time. Most courts continued to employ (or dismiss) their musical employees in much the same way as before; public opera (which had spread to the major centres of northern Europe by the last decades of the seventeenth century) continued wherever it was economically viable; church music and its associated educational institutions were generally unscathed by the change of century. If public performance, unattached to court, church or opera, came into its own in the eighteenth century, this was often an extension of institutions that sprang up in the previous era: the academy, *collegium musicum*, organ recital etc. The only sign of a conscious revivalist culture was in England from around the 1720s: societies such as the Academy of Ancient Music and the Concert of Ancient Music self-consciously performed music by composers of the late sixteenth century up to Purcell. Perhaps this fashion for restoring the past related to the revival necessitated by the Restoration in the 1660s, the Concert of Ancient Music's resolution to play music over twenty years old mirroring the same sort of gap that would have been experienced after the Civil War and Cromwellian eras.

Many of these continuities (even those that made a continuity out of restoration) were of course broken in the latter half of the eighteenth century, when indeed even most of the composers active before 1750 seemed outmoded. It is interesting to note which seventeenth-century repertories continued to survive: the music of Corelli still had classical status throughout the eighteenth century, enjoying an unprecedented number of reprints. Institutions that were not 'progressive' (particularly churches) could still cling to earlier music: obviously significant in this regard is the publication of William Boyce's *Cathedral Music* (1760–73), which did much to maintain the restorative fervour of post-Commonwealth England by implying a continuous tradition of English sacred music stretching back to the era of Tye and Tallis. The new histories of music certainly do not ignore the seventeenth century, although Burney and Hawkins clearly sensed an affinity with the latter half of the previous century but not necessarily with the former.

Whatever continuities seventeenth-century repertory and practice enjoyed in the eighteenth century, the French Revolution and its shockwaves across Europe meant that there was now a sense in which the past was irreconcilably severed. In the nineteenth century, earlier music was rediscovered and re-invented with a fervour that had never pertained before, if also with an unavoidable sense of difference. Nevertheless, it is perhaps here that we see the beginnings of the tendency to overlook the seventeenth century, even against the background of the growing interest in the past: most models that acquired particular prestige (e.g., Palestrina for both Catholic and Protestant traditions, Bach and Handel for German, French and English cultures) tended to come from just before or just after our period. Generally, if seventeenth-century music appeared in nineteenth-century anthologies or specialist publications (e.g., of the Musical Antiquarian Society in England, 1840–47) this was sometimes through a general antiquarian concern for whatever had survived from the past rather than from an interest in the seventeenth century *per se*. 'Arie antiche' (whether real or fake) could subsequently provide fodder for beginning singers, while seventeenth-century keyboard pieces, especially of the more picturesque variety, could grace the music stands of women performers in the salon and drawing-room. The era could also feature in programmes that were devised to show a particular historical progression, such as in the *concert historique* invented by François-Joseph Fétis in Paris during the 1830s. Yet the tendency to view earlier musics as merely a precursor to, or a primitive form of, 'real' music necessarily did them a disservice, not least by inserting them within lines of 'progress' representing just the first steps to the Parnassus of the High Baroque, Classical and Romantic masters. Also, the apparent absence of strong compositional voices, or for that matter of strong biographical presences, tended to relegate early music to a series of 'Kleinmeister', particularly if they came from the seventeenth century.

What is striking is the comparative lateness with which singular national figures of our period made it into the revival industry. Lully began to make an appearance at the Paris Opéra in the 1850s, coinciding with the publication of extracts of several of his dramatic works in vocal score. But only in the wake of the culturally demoralising Franco-Prussian war (1870), and then the battles pro- and anti-Wagner, did he begin to play a significant part in the French patriotic cause, if only by virtue of his association with a great seventeenth-century literary figure, Molière. Lully's (and others') music was soon to be published in editions that attempted to present the entire cultural heritage of the nation, and yet often it was perceived as just that, a 'heritage' to be kept in the museum, rather than to be given life through performance. As Ellis shows, French music of the seventeenth and eighteenth centuries was often deemed to lack a necessary virility, namely that which was demonstrated by the recent vigorous revival of Handel and Bach. It was not until 1930 that an edition dedicated specifically to the complete works of Lully appeared, and even the recent attempt at an *œuvres complètes* has had a somewhat unhappy history. In England, although Purcell was celebrated in performance by the Purcell Club in Westminster Abbey from the middle of the nineteenth century, the Purcell Society which published his works was not founded until 1878 (and the project was not complete until 1965); and the first stagings of his music did not occur until the 1890s. However, the anniversary year of 1895 became an important trigger for the so-called 'English musical Renaissance'. In Germany, the Schütz revival was also surprisingly late. Philipp Spitta pioneered the rediscovery of Schütz's music in the wake of his extensive Bach studies, and he provided the impetus for the complete edition begun in 1885 to celebrate the 300th anniversary of the composer's birth. Perhaps the greatest service to seventeenth-century German music (of the generation from Praetorius to Schütz) was done by Brahms within his programmes as a choral conductor. It may also be that his absorption of some of the rhetorical and motivic elements of this repertory within his own music rendered later generations progressively more accepting of this idiom. Learned through the filter of Brahms, the language of Schütz could become 'modern' once more.

In the early decades of the twentieth century, seventeenth-century music continued to fare relatively poorly in comparison to the German, French and Italian composers of the High Baroque. Indeed, these latter, together with later eighteenth-century composers, were ideal models for the neo-classical climate of the interwar years; earlier seventeenth-century music presumably did not possess enough formal discipline to provide much in the way of models (one significant exception was Richard Strauss's use of Lully's music in his works surrounding *Ariadne auf Naxos*) save, perhaps, in the sphere of expressive intensity and declamatory freedom. The French continued to play an important role. The first 'modern' performance of Monteverdi's *Orfeo* (1904, followed by *L'incoronazione di Poppea* the following year) occurred in a French institution, not an Italian one: namely, the Schola Cantorum that Charles Bordes and

Vincent d'Indy had founded in 1894. Although the primary purpose of this institution was the regeneration of religious music it also presented concert performances of many dramatic works, if in drastically cut versions. It was also in France that Nadia Boulanger pioneered the performance of Monteverdi madrigals in the 1930s, while another Frenchman, Edgard Varèse, presented choral concerts in New York during the 1930s involving music by a wide range of seventeenth-century composers, including Monteverdi, Charpentier and Schütz. By this time, however, a Monteverdi revival had already established itself also in Italy (although there had been sporadic interest from the 1870s on), associated with a national (at times, right-wing) revivalism, a reaction to Romantic excess (whether Wagner or Puccini), a search for cultural roots, and even a sense that modernism might find its anchor in a pre-Classical past. Gian Francesco Malipiero's first complete edition of Monteverdi's works (1926–42) coincided with a particularly ugly period of Italian nationalism. Yet Malipiero's work, and that of many others who followed his lead in the cause of early Italian music, continued unabated after the Fascist era, and for curious reasons, post-war interest in Monteverdi was particularly strong in England.

With the German-based 'Orgelbewegung' from the 1920s, seventeenth-century organ music became more usable, since many surviving instruments contemporary with its composition were now appreciated afresh (the first publications of Buxtehude's organ music date back to 1903). It was also in this period that the music of Schütz became ubiquitous in Germany, coinciding with the Italian rediscovery of Monteverdi. Given that Schütz more or less represented the earliest available repertory of music setting the German vernacular which also conformed to refined, quasi-Renaissance disciplines of composition, his music provided an ideal way of grounding increasingly nationalist sentiment in a 'classical' historical tradition, while also providing music for choral societies to perform (something similar might be said of the German reception of Monteverdi's 1610 Vespers). The English national interest in Purcell also increased between the wars, although it reached its fullest flowering after World War II, particularly with its reworking in the music of Britten and Tippett.

The early-music revival after the war, together with the associated movement in historically informed performance, began to give seventeenth-century music something approaching the attention already given to other centuries. Early pioneers of Baroque opera gave performances that were more (Paul Hindemith) or less (Raymond Leppard) indebted to historical performance, but several works of Monteverdi and Cavalli were well established in the operatic repertory before historical accuracy became more of an imperative (although editions of Cavalli's operas did not appear until the 1960s, and even today we lack proper scholarly ones). If the seventeenth century still seemed to lag behind other forms of early music, perhaps it was partly because the strongest performing personalities in the field specialised either in earlier music (e.g., David Munrow and Thomas Binkley) or in that of a somewhat later period (e.g., Gustav Leonhardt and Nikolaus Harnoncourt). It is also likely, however, that the seventeenth century found itself falling between several stools: its music was not choral enough for the Oxbridge singing-men who did so much for the early-music revival in the United Kingdom, and there was more exotic fun to be gained from picking up (and even making) a medieval rebec than from converting a violin to Baroque use. There was (and for the most part, is) no profit in retrofitting a Stradivarius to its original design and purpose, and even in the 1960s and 1970s performances of Monteverdi's 1610 Vespers still used oboes, clarinets or trumpets rather than cornetts. Singers did not have the voice to beat the throat (at least until Nigel Rogers showed us how to do it), string players did not have the heart to abandon vibrato (not that they necessarily needed to), the harpsichord could only softly clatter in the background, and the recorder and viol were relegated to (and associated with) a sub-Dolmetsch underworld of relentless if spirited amateurism.

Nevertheless, performers were probably in advance of scholars. The British journal *Early Music* showed a pronounced Medieval–Renaissance bias in its first issue of 1973 (although, given its national provenance, the solitary article on Purcell is not out of place). The next few years show a similar partiality, with further obvious English exceptions (such as Dowland and Gibbons). While the late 1970s show an increase in seventeenth-century topics, particularly English or operatic, it is perhaps only in the mid 1980s that one can sense that seventeenth-century music enjoys coverage equal to other 'early' periods. As for the *Basler Jahrbuch für historische Musikpraxis*, founded in 1977, the first issues involve the seventeenth century only if this is relevant to a study of the entire history of a particular instrument. Otherwise, the bias is very much towards the Middle Ages, followed by the eighteenth century; again, it is only in the later 1980s that the seventeenth century seems to gain parity with the others. While the Heinrich-Schütz-Gesellschaft had been covering wider seventeenth-century issues for several years (its journal dates back to 1979), the first society devoted specifically to seventeenth-century music began its (on-line) journal in America in 1995.

It was also in the late 1980s and 1990s that the seventeenth century became a significant subject for some of the newer musicological approaches that were beginning to develop. Whilst the vast majority of authors saw the nineteenth century as their primary playground, the seventeenth also seemed significant owing to its emphasis on text and music, the birth of opera (together with its semantic ambiguity and emerging semiotic codes), the surprising number of distinguished women composers, and the ambiguities of gender in theatrical music (the interest in the castrato also becoming something of an obsession in popular culture). On the other hand, there has also been much new work in a more 'traditional' (or at least post-war) vein, covering specific instrumental repertories and broad genres such as oratorio and French or Italian opera. Although this writing often seems to take a stand against specific 'trendy' approaches, it is significant that most of it brings in far more of the broader cultural contexts than before, often relating music closely to other arts. There has also been a spate of studies relating to specific composers, such as Buxtehude, Corelli, Monteverdi and Purcell, the last two composers receiving significant coverage around the anniversary years of 1993 and 1995.

Obviously, there is no room here to rehearse all the various nuances of the recent culture of historical performance. In many respects, both amateur and professional environments tended initially to favour repertories of the Middle Ages and Renaissance, as reflected in the journals of the 1970s. However, one other noticeable tendency was initially to eschew the more fixed, canonical repertories and favour music such as that of the Baroque that allowed a certain flexibility in relation both to notated text and to performance practice (e.g., in the application of ornamentation or rhythmic inequality). Thus the seventeenth century was an ideal arena for the counter-cultural tendencies in historical performance, so Laurence Dreyfus argues, or even an opportunity to challenge Richard Taruskin's provocative claim that the early-music revival as a whole represented just the last gasp of modernism, and one founded on a fundamentally false premise to boot. It was also soon clear that reconstructing the contextual aspects of seventeenth-century performance meant that one could present spectacles (as in productions of French or Italian opera) that provided a colourful antidote to the sober conventions of traditional concert performance.

Consideration of the recent phenomenal success of the early-music movement inevitably brings in questions of the commercialisation of seventeenth-century music. There is a small but extremely significant selection of 'hits' that have essentially become part of a popular-music culture. These might include Corelli's 'Christmas Concerto', suitable for any establishment wishing to impart an air of sophistication, Dido's Lament, an emblem of tragedy virtually interchangeable with Barber's Adagio, or Albinoni's 'Adagio' (not in fact by Albinoni but by Italian musicologist Remo Giazotto). Most interesting, perhaps, is Pachelbel's 'Canon', something that seems to suit virtually any occasion or atmosphere. This might have something to do with its 'unmarked' serenity, its mesmeric but varied repetitions suggesting a meditative quality. While it is clear that this could easily be related to both New Age and minimalist movements, what is perhaps most significant is the ground bass and the repetitive harmonic pattern this engenders. For it is surely the ground bass (and Dido is significant here, too) that relates it most directly to popular music of the late twentieth century, sharing something of the latter's foundation in dance. Perhaps this is one of the reasons why some seventeenth-century music has become more marketable. Moreover, its early emphasis on text and melody corresponds with the drive to simplicity following the high modernism of the 1950s; the formal structures that developed in the course of the seventeenth century seldom approach the complexity of those of the Classical era and beyond, yet they have a directness easily assimilated by listeners unfamiliar with the more traditional challenges of 'serious' music.

But to say that some seventeenth-century music has become more relevant owing to its 'easy-listening' nature is obviously a rather feeble justification for its place in our culture. Rather, one could look to its plurality, unexpectedness, and dynamic combination of conservative and radical elements in the search for modes of artistic expression fit for its times. Just how this music stems from a culture that shares some of our proclivities while representing a historically alien world is something that the present book must put at centre stage.

Tim Carter   John Butt
University of North Carolina at Chapel Hill   University of Glasgow

Bibliography

Abraham, G. (ed.), *The New Oxford History of Music*, iv: *The Age of Humanism, 1540–1630*. London and New York, 1968

Apel, W., *The History of Keyboard Music to 1700*. Bloomington, IN, 1972
  Italian Violin Music of the Seventeenth Century, ed. T. Binkley. Bloomington and Indianapolis, 1990

Bianconi, L., *Il Seicento*. Turin, 1982; *Music in the Seventeenth Century*, trans. D. Bryant. Cambridge, 1987

Bukofzer, M. F., *Music in the Baroque Era: from Monteverdi to Bach*. New York, 1947

Carter, T., *Monteverdi's Musical Theatre*. New Haven and London, 2002

Chou-Wen Chung, 'Varèse: a Sketch of the Man and his Music'. *Musical Quarterly*, 52 (1965), 151–76

Dreyfus, L., 'Early Music Defended against its Devotees: a Theory of Historical Performance in the Twentieth Century'. *Musical Quarterly*, 69 (1983), 297–322

Ellis, K., *Interpreting the Musical Past: Early Music in Nineteenth-Century France*. New York and Oxford, 2005

Garratt, J., *Palestrina and the German Romantic Imagination: Interpreting Historicism in Nineteenth-Century Music*. Cambridge, 2002

Hancock, V., 'Brahms's Performances of Early Choral Music'. *Nineteenth-Century Music*, 8 (1984), 125–41

Haskell, H., *The Early Music Revival: a History*. London, 1988

Lewis, A., *The New Oxford History of Music*, v: *Opera and Church Music, 1630–1750*. London and New York, 1975

Palisca, C. V., *Baroque Music*. Englewood Cliffs, 1968; 3rd edn, 1991

Silbiger, A., 'Music and the Crisis of Seventeenth-Century Europe'. In V. Coelho (ed.), *Music and Science in the Age of Galileo*. Dordrecht, 1992, pp. 35–44

Silbiger, A. (ed.), *Keyboard Music Before 1700*. 2nd edn, New York, 2003

Taruskin, R., 'The Pastness of the Present and the Presence of the Past'. In N. Kenyon (ed.), *Authenticity and Early Music*. Oxford, 1988, pp. 137–210

Wolff, C., *Johann Sebastian Bach: the Learned Musician*. New York and London, 2000

Renaissance, Mannerism, Baroque

TIM CARTER

It is in the nature of historians of Western art-music to divide their repertories by periods; it is also in the nature of music histories to begin with some
disclaimer about the dangers of such periodisation. These disclaimers conventionally go along one or both of the following lines. First, a period never has a
clear beginning or end. It would be absurd to argue, say, that anything produced
before 31 December 1599 was 'Renaissance' and anything after 1 January 1600
'Baroque'; rather, there are always periods of transition when new currents
start to bubble to the surface and older trends slowly disappear. Thirty or forty
years either way will usually suffice, and may be further enshrined in period
subdivisions (Early, Middle, High, Late). So, the Late Renaissance may somehow overlap with the Early Baroque, but by the time we get to the Middle or
High Baroque, the Renaissance is well and truly over. Secondly, not everything
that happens in a given period will necessarily contain all (or even some of) the
presumed characteristics of that period. Thus not all Renaissance music will be
'Renaissance' by any (narrow or broad) definition of the term, yet if the label
is not to be meaningless save as some vague chronological marker, enough of
the important music produced during the Renaissance period will indeed be
somehow identifiable with the Renaissance in general.

There, of course, lies the rub, or rather, two of them. 'Important' begs all the
obvious questions – to whom, and according to what criteria? – and doubly so
if it is linked to period specificities. Canon-forming processes are contentious
and insidious enough, especially when the value-systems on which they are
based derive from *ad hoc* (or better, *post hoc*) notions of common identity. In our
age of cultural uncertainty and equal opportunity for all, it becomes increasingly difficult to justify the wholesale exclusion of musical repertories just on
the grounds that they do not fit our prejudices concerning a given period,
or about what 'music' might in fact be. More fundamental, however, is the
question of how and why music might be said to belong in the first place to
any period, or to any stylistic category associated therewith. A formalist, for
example, might equally argue that music is an art of and for itself that will certainly have its own history (of genres, forms, styles, techniques and so forth),

although it is a history that works essentially, even exclusively, in musical terms. The counter-argument is to view music-making (which of course broadens the field beyond music *tout court*) as a part of cultural or social practice – 'discourse' is another favourite term – and therefore as somehow reflective of such practice, or even as some kind of determinant thereof. Such an approach is predicated upon the notion that music has always satisfied specific cultural, social and political requirements which have influenced to a significant degree the styles, techniques and genres available to the composer. This approach also seeks to justify the academic study of music as being essential to broader cultural and historical understanding. The careful reader will note, however, that embedding music in an increasingly 'thick' context does not, in fact, solve the chief problem of periodisation: why a given time (age, era) should deserve a given period-label is just another version of the music problem writ large (whose times?).

Perhaps it would be easier to avoid the problem altogether. There has been a trend in the discipline of History to drop period-labels as being too value-laden, narrow, exclusive and somehow distorting: thus 'Renaissance' has been abandoned in favour of 'early modern', although the 'modern' part of that equation is somewhat problematic (is the Renaissance really part of the 'modern' age, even if an early part?). It is probably no coincidence that this terminological shift has occurred as historians themselves have sought to move the 'important' ground of the fifteenth and sixteenth centuries away from the presumed cradle of the Renaissance, the Italian peninsula: it may be possible to speak of a Florentine, Roman or Venetian Renaissance, but it is harder to discern any similar Renaissances in fifteenth-century Amsterdam, London, Madrid or Paris. Another solution is to speak of centuries either in the English or French form (the sixteenth century, the *dix-septième siècle*) or in the Italian (the Cinquecento, Seicento). But this only exacerbates the problem of chronological boundaries – sometimes solved by having 'long' centuries (as with the 'long' nineteenth century from the French Revolution to the start of World War I, i.e., 1789–1914) – and it raises, rather than avoids, the question of whether a chronological span can be a 'period' in some other sense of the term. And even in History, those pesky period-labels remain surprisingly seductive, while Art History still embraces them with a vengeance.

Musicology's use of period-labels has followed on the coat-tails of Art History: the two disciplines obviously have much in common, although the permanence and fixity of the visual art-work remains an obvious difference, and one that is, or should be, troubling for musicologists. But the tendency in the arts in general to adopt these labels seems prompted more by the fear of irrelevance: if we can somehow grasp what it was to be a Renaissance man (woman, peasant, merchant, religious, courtier, prince) by way of the cultural artefacts of the time – if these artefacts somehow contain elements that fashion group identity – then modern dilemmas over the place of the arts in the world become more manageable. It also means that we can counter the tendency of Historians to relegate the arts to the final chapter of their period-surveys as mere icing on the political or social cake. People die, but art survives, and if we can somehow speak of the spirit of an age, then the arts, as a manifestation of the Spirit, are indelible reminders of what it was to be human in dim and distant pasts. Equally, we might feel that we can trace our own roots in art that we can appreciate, however remote its cultural contexts. The art-work offers a window onto some kind of (trans)historical soul, there to be endlessly read, interpreted and even loved.

Or so the Romantics might have us believe. The terminological slippage in the previous paragraph – art(s), art-work, artefact – will already have raised a note of caution: what we choose to call 'art' may or may not have been 'art' in its time. A *Madonna and Child* on the wall of a merchant's house in sixteenth-century Florence is not the same as that *Madonna and Child* in a modern art-gallery; a *concertato* madrigal performed in the ducal palace in Mantua in 1605 is different from that madrigal preserved in our imaginary museum of musical works. Our Florentine merchant may have used the picture for personal devotion, to display his wealth, to instruct his children, or merely to stop a draught; our Mantuan duke may not have cared one jot about the actual music he was hearing, even if he paid some attention to its text, to the manner of performance, or just to the shapely necks of his women singers warbling so seductively. We cannot assume that rapt aesthetic contemplation is the norm in any period (even our own), or that what historians value in the substance of art is what was valued at the time. Nor can we assume, however much we might wish to, that the artistic spirit, even soul, is somehow constant, transcending time and place to speak eternal truths.

But whether the spirit of the times, the Zeitgeist, or if you prefer more fashionable terms (although their meaning is hardly different), the episteme or *mentalité*, is alien or similar to our own, and despite all the caveats raised above (whose spirit?), it remains perhaps the only narrative strategy powerful and plausible enough to enable us to bring sense to our historical constructs, uniting the fractured, fragmented voices that speak, or even sing, from past to present. And although the postmodern historian's tendency is to prefer alienation – to celebrate the 'otherness' of our historical pasts – the art-work somehow resists such othering, accommodating itself to us as we accommodate ourselves to it. Just how one might chart a responsible path through such difficult terrain is a problem that must be posed by the present book.

Renaissance

Historians of different kinds will often make some choice between a long Renaissance (say, 1300–1600), a short one (1453–1527), or somewhere in between (the fifteenth and sixteenth centuries, as is commonly adopted in music histories).[1] The 'short' Renaissance supports the tendency to identify period boundaries with cataclysmic events, the Fall of Constantinople on the one hand, and the Sack of Rome on the other, although 74 years does not seem quite long enough for a period assumed to have been so significant for the formation of the modern European mind, and unmatched in importance until the eighteenth-century Enlightenment. This view of the Renaissance also requires a somewhat jaundiced view of the Middle Ages just as our prejudices in favour of the Enlightenment have tended to downplay the seventeenth century.

Some have preferred to call the Renaissance not a 'period' but a 'movement'. This has the advantage of setting geographical, national and even social limits on who might have partaken of a Renaissance, and it also introduces an element of human agency. The term literally means 'rebirth', and it is generally applied to a sense of revival and renewal in the early fifteenth century prompted in particular by the rediscovery of the arts, sciences and philosophies of Classical Antiquity. As Matteo Palmieri (1406–75) proclaimed in his treatise on 'civil life' (*Della vita civile*):

> Where was the painter's art till Giotto [d. 1337] tardily restored it? A caricature of the art of human delineation! Sculpture and architecture, for long years sunk to the merest travesty of art, are only today in process of rescue from obscurity; only now are they being brought to a new pitch of perfection by men of genius and erudition. Of letters and liberal studies at large it were best to be silent altogether. For these, the real guides to distinction in all the arts, the solid foundation of all civilisation, have been lost to mankind for 800 years and more. It is but in our own day that men dare boast that they see the dawn of better things . . . Now, indeed, may every thoughtful spirit thank God that it has been permitted to him to be born in this new age, so full of hope and promise, which already rejoices in a greater array of noble-gifted souls than the world has seen in the thousand years that have preceded it.[2]

Arts and letters had been great in Classical Greece and Rome, and now, Palmieri felt, they could be great again.

Palmieri had all the right qualifications to be part of a movement: he was Italian and thus purportedly a direct descendant of the Romans; and he was

---

1 Some of the following discussion is drawn from my *Music in Late Renaissance and Early Baroque Italy*. Fenlon (ed.), *The Renaissance*, and Price (ed.), *The Early Baroque Era*, also have much of relevance to the periods under discussion here.

2 Hay, *The Italian Renaissance in its Historical Background*, p. 12.

living in a city (Florence) governed as a republic supposedly along the lines of ancient Greece and Rome in its greatest years, and one with a wealthy merchant-class committed to conspicuous consumption in the arts. His extolling of the 'civil life' did not ignore religion, but it kept it in its place, united with an essentially secularist impulse that saw unlimited possibilities for mankind here on earth rather than just in the after-life. His 'Renaissance', then, was secular, republican, and based on the pillars of Classical thought that, he felt, were now being restored after lying in ruins for centuries. In short, it was Humanist in several senses of the term.

The migration westwards of Byzantine scholars after the Fall of Constantinople, bearing with them Classical texts that had lain unknown in Italy, is what is conventionally regarded as having given the impulse to Humanism in the very specific sense of a grounding in the achievements of ancient Greece and Rome so as to forge a new future. The fact that this ignores the large number of such texts that were known, and very carefully studied, throughout the Middle Ages has until recently been regarded as only a minor inconvenience. More problematic, in historiographical terms, has been the presumed secular, and also republican, nature of the Renaissance. That the age became one of religious upheaval, not least by way of the Reformation, has sometimes been explained by some kind of secular impulse, but this seems misdirected. Luther may have been a Humanist (however defined) but he was scarcely a secularist. His placing the onus on the believer to cultivate faith as the only mechanism for salvation replaced an institutional relationship with God with one grounded in the individual, and challenged the authority of His representatives on earth, not least the Pope. But the Church (both Catholic and Protestant) remained a central force in lives that were more dominated by religion than later historians might wish to believe. For that matter, to see the Catholic Reformation (or Counter-Reformation, as it used to be called), which began with the Council of Trent (1545–63) and extended through the emergence of the Church Triumphant towards the end of the sixteenth century, as sounding the death knell for the Renaissance is somewhat to misinterpret the Renaissance itself.

A little more finesse has been required to deal with the republican issue. Florence may have been a republic in principle, but it was an oligarchy in fact (itself, a mode of government with Classical precedents), and with a *de facto* ruling family, the Medici. Despite periods of exile from the city, the Medici finally returned in 1530 to become dukes, later grand dukes, of Tuscany. Florence therefore succumbed to the predominant pattern of the north Italian states in the fifteenth and sixteenth centuries as duchies under hereditary rule, and fiefdoms of the Holy Roman Empire; by the early seventeenth century, the only republics left on the peninsula were Genoa and Venice, a fact of which the

Venetians, at least, made great political capital. Thus the nineteenth-century Swiss historian Jakob Burckhardt (in his *Die Kultur der Renaissance in Italien* published in 1860) needed to perform a sleight of hand, turning the despotic princes of Italy (and for that matter, of the Catholic Church) into benevolent patrons, working for the benefit of 'the state as a work of art' (to cite the title of the first part of his book). He did so with some reason: in the sixteenth century, the Italian princes distanced themselves from the soldier-class (which is not to say that they did not fight battles) and re-tooled themselves as noble courtiers. They were aided by the chief propagandist for the cause, Baldassare Castiglione, whose famous manual on courtly etiquette, *Il libro del cortigiano* (1528), was widely reprinted and translated through the century and beyond.[3] Machiavelli may have provided the text by which princes might rule (in his *Il principe* of 1513), but Castiglione taught them how to behave, and prominent in that behaviour was an understanding of the arts and music.

The chief difficulties facing notions of a musical 'Renaissance' are of a somewhat different order. Although it was possible to view Greek and Roman ruins and statuary, and to read Classical texts in the original or, increasingly, in translation, no ancient music survived. Certainly one could read what the Greeks and Romans wrote about their music – and they said a great deal about its science and its ethical effects – but one could not hear a note of it. If Humanism in the narrow sense is a defining feature of the Renaissance, then the period-label has only a somewhat limited application to music: settings of Latin odes in a pseudo-Classical homophony adhering strictly to poetic metre; the rather extreme experiments in reviving the ancient chromatic and enharmonic *genera* conducted by Nicola Vicentino (1511–*c*. 1576) and a few others; explorations of different kinds of solo song that would faithfully reflect the form and content of its texts.[4] But alas, the best known of those experiments in monody – by Giulio Caccini in chamber song and by Jacopo Peri in early opera – are conventionally placed by music historians at the beginning of the musical Baroque, despite their obvious Humanist credentials. This is not in itself a problem: Humanism continued long after the Renaissance was well and truly over; indeed, perhaps it has never gone away. But it does make one wonder where it leaves what we call 'Renaissance' music today, i.e., the balanced, imitative polyphony of composers from Guillaume Dufay (*c*. 1400–1474) through Josquin Desprez (*c*. 1440–1521) to Giovanni Pierluigi da Palestrina (1525/6–94). Even if one restricts musical humanism to theory rather than practice – a not implausible

---

3 Burke, *The Fortunes of the Courtier.*   4 Palisca, *Humanism in Italian Renaissance Musical Thought.*

strategy – it elevates a fringe group of theorists beyond their status, and also relegates to the sidelines a great deal of what mattered to mainstream writers on music once, that is, they had made their conventional bows to the wonders of the ancient art.

Another difficulty might seem less troublesome. Dufay and Josquin were from northern Europe, and the style that music historians conventionally associated with the Renaissance is often labelled 'Franco-Flemish polyphony'. If the Renaissance is primarily an Italian phenomenon, this requires another sleight of hand. A good number of Franco-Flemish composers, including Dufay and Josquin, did indeed work in Italy for greater or lesser periods of time: native Italian composers regularly complained of their positions being usurped by foreigners, even as they themselves usurped the Franco-Flemish style for their own musical ends. By the second half of the sixteenth century, too, the influence of the Franco-Flemings was waning as they gradually lost to native musicians their hold over the important Italian positions: Adriano Willaert (c. 1490–1562) was soon to be replaced by Gioseffo Zarlino (1517–90) as *maestro di cappella* of St Mark's, Venice (after Cipriano de Rore's brief tenure in the position), while in Mantua, Giaches de Wert (1535–96) was followed by Giacomo Gastoldi (1554–1609) as Duke Vincenzo Gonzaga's *maestro di cappella*. Yet it is hard to claim that the musical style chiefly associated with the Renaissance is 'Italian' in any significant sense of the term save the geographical location of (some of) its major institutions and patrons.

That problem might be solved by arguing that the Renaissance was, in fact, pan-European. One might also claim that the polyphonic style did indeed share features of other Renaissance arts: the new control of musical space by way of contrapuntal imitation created both a depth and a structure perhaps analogous to the rise of perspective in contemporary painting; the careful control of dissonance brought a new order to musical harmony that might be termed classical, at least in the sense of balance; and the use of this polyphony to express a text allowed the potential for a deeper level of expression that paralleled the moves towards more immediate communication in the other arts. However, the Italian musicologist Nino Pirrotta took the debate down a different path: he suggested, instead, that Franco-Flemish polyphony, and even its Italian imitations, had little or nothing to do with the Renaissance as a broader cultural movement, for all the reasons suggested above. He saw it as essentially a 'public' style, suitable for celebrations of the liturgy and for civic ceremonial but not for the intimate circles of courtly music-making. He viewed it as some kind of last gasp of the Medieval musical tradition. He also suggested that it was a style better associated with Mannerism.

Mannerism

Pirrotta's argument might appear somewhat mischievous, and perhaps mingled
with not a little Italian chauvinism. Yet it is not without a point. Native musical styles linked with Humanism did indeed exist during the Renaissance, he
suggests, but chiefly in the realms of improvisation, as singer–poets declaimed
their epics and sonnets to the lyre (represented in the fifteenth and sixteenth
centuries by the *lira da braccio*). Such improvisatory practices were by definition not a matter of notational record and so have disappeared save for
the vague traces of their existence in contemporary descriptions and in paintings. This improvisatory, Humanist style, Pirrotta argues, surfaced as compositional praxis towards the end of the century in the Florentine 'new music'
(Peri's recitative and Caccini's chamber songs) which, though now viewed as
'Baroque', was, in fact, 'Renaissance' in at least the fundamental sense of its
intentional relation to Classical models.

Pirrotta's association of the Franco-Flemish style with a medievalism on
the one hand, and 'the deliberate adoption of a polyphonic *maniera*' on the
other,[5] is somewhat more controversial. Art historians have broadly adopted
the idea of Mannerism as a style-period separating the High Renaissance from
the Baroque, and brought on by the political, social and economic upheavals
of Italy in the sixteenth century after the French invasions of the peninsula
and the Sack of Rome (in 1527).[6] Mannerism also fits into a new orientation
that is characteristic of at least one major strand of artistic development in the
period: it is an essentially courtly art, where form seems more important than
content, and where the appeal of the art-work lies primarily in an appreciation
of how it effortlessly overcomes self-imposed technical difficulties. For example, Mannerist painting (Parmigianino, Pontormo, Giulio Romano, and some
Michelangelo) revels in intricacies of design and articulation, with figures that
bear little relation to corporeal reality and presented in a manner that seems to
delight in complexity for complexity's sake. The result can seem disorientating,
if impressive and, to be sure, rich in expressive effect.

Mannerism has been called the 'stylish style', and certainly stylishness was
claimed a virtue by many critics in the sixteenth century: thus Raphael criti-
cised Gothic architecture for being 'devoid of all grace and entirely without

5 Pirrotta, 'Novelty and Renewal in Italy, 1300–1600', p. 173. For Pirrotta's views on a more truly
'Renaissance' style, see his 'Music and Cultural Tendencies in Fifteenth-Century Italy'; Pirrotta, *Music and
Theatre from Poliziano to Monteverdi*, chap. 1.
6 The bibliography of Mannerism in art is vast, but a useful introduction to the issues is provided in
Smyth, *Mannerism and 'Maniera'*; an overview (including literature and music) is offered by Shearman,
Mannerism. For music, the most fervent advocacy of the term is in Maniates, *Mannerism in Italian Music and
Culture*. A more measured stance is adopted in Haar, 'Classicism and Mannerism in 16th-Century Music';
see also Haar, 'Self-Consciousness about Style, Form and Genre in 16th-Century Music'.

style [*maniera*]'.[7] Moreover, the merits of grace and *maniera* were directly linked to the courtly ideals of the century as emphasised by Castiglione. The application of the term Mannerism to sixteenth-century music may be a matter of some controversy. But just as Vasari praised rich invention and the reduction of difficulty to facility in painting and sculpture, so did Zarlino admire the 'beauty, grace and elegance' of good counterpoint, praising Willaert for his 'reasoned order of composing in an elegant manner' (*un' ordine ragionevole di componere con elegante maniera*).[8] Certainly, an elegant *maniera* was something to be encouraged in composition. Adrianus Petit Coclico, in his *Compendium musices* (1552), called Dufay and his contemporaries 'musici mathematici', and Josquin and his contemporaries 'musici praestantissimi'. But composers of Coclico's generation were 'musici poetici' who 'compose more suavely, more ornately and with more artifice'.[9] This emphasis on ornament and artifice characteristic of mid sixteenth-century polyphony seems to bring this music into the purview of Mannerism.

The term 'musici poetici' used by Coclico and others in this period has a number of resonances. One is a Humanist association of modern music with the great musician–poets of Classical Antiquity (although Plato would not have approved of suavity, ornateness and artifice); another is a shift of music from the *quadrivium* (with arithmetic, geometry and astronomy) to the *trivium* (grammar, rhetoric and logic), and a consequent reorientation of theory away from the traditional Boethian *musica speculativa* to the art and craft of musical composition, a musical 'poetics' in the Aristotelian sense of the term. It also suggests the emergence of an increasingly close relationship between music and text that has its roots in Renaissance Humanism and also motivates one strand of the early musical Baroque. According to the Ferrarese composer Luzzasco Luzzaschi (?1545–1607)

> Music and poetry . . . are to such a degree similar and so naturally joined together that one could indeed say, speaking of them with some mystery, that they were born as twins on Parnassus . . . Nor do these twins resemble each other only in features and general appearance; in addition they enjoy a similarity of external dress. If one changes garment, so too does the other. For not only does music have as her purpose usefulness [*il giovamento*] and pleasure, most natural features of her sister, but also, grace, sweetness, seriousness, wit, humour, vitality – the garments with which those sisters adorn themselves so charmingly – are worn by the one and the other in so similar a fashion that often the poet resembles the musician and the musician the poet. But since poetry was the first to be

7 In a letter, with Castiglione, to Pope Leo X, 1519, in Shearman, *Mannerism*, p. 17

8 Zarlino, *Le istitutioni harmoniche* (Venice, 1558), p. 2.

9 Coclico, *Musical Compendium*, trans. A. Seay, 'Colorado College Music Press Translations', 5 (Colorado Springs, 1973), pp. 8–9.

born, music reveres and honours her as his lady, to such an extent that music, having become virtually a shadow of poetry, does not dare to move its foot where its superior has not preceded. From which it follows that if the poet raises his style, the musician also raises his tone. He cries if the verse cries, laughs if it laughs; if it runs, stops, implores, denies, screams, falls silent, lives, dies, all these affects and effects are so vividly expressed by music that what should properly be called resemblance seems almost competition. Therefore we see in our times a music somewhat different from that of the past, for modern poetic forms are similarly different from those of the past. Skipping over all those other poetic forms that have changed only in subject matter – such as canzonas, sestinas, sonnets, ottavas, and *terze rime* – I shall say of the madrigal that it seems to have been invented just for music, and I shall speak the truth in saying that in our age it has received its perfect form – a form so different from its former one that, were the first versifiers to return to life, they would scarce be able to recognise it, so changed is it in the brevity, the wit [*acutezza*], the grace, the nobility, and finally the sweetness with which the poets of today have seasoned it. In imitation of their praiseworthy style, our musicians also have tried to discover new ways and new inventions, more sweet and graceful than the usual; from these ways and inventions they have formed a new style [*maniera*], which, not only for its novelty but also for the exquisiteness of its artifice, should be able to please and attract the praise of the world at large.[10]

Brevity, wit, grace, nobility and sweetness were characteristic *maniere* of madrigal verse in the second half of the sixteenth century, especially in the hands of Torquato Tasso (1544–95) and Battista Guarini (1538–1612). So, too, was the search for an artful complexity, as Tasso's contemporaries said:

Tasso . . . understanding that perfect clarity is nothing but superabundant ease towards too sudden understanding without giving the listener the opportunity to experience something for himself . . . with elaborate care sought for his poem [*Gerusalemme liberata*] nobility, strength and excellent grace, but not the greatest clarity . . . He avoided that superfluous facility of being at once understood, and departing from common usage, and from the base and lowly, chose the novel, the unfamiliar, the unexpected, the admirable, both in ideas and in words; which, while artificially interwoven more than is normal, and adorned with varied figures suitable for tempering that excessive clarity, such as caesuras, convolutions, hyperbole, irony, displacement . . . resembles not so much a twisted . . . muddy alley-way but an uphill stony path where the weak are exhausted and stumble.[11]

Music followed suit.

---

10 From the dedication ('ghosted' by Alessandro Guarini) to the Duchess of Urbino (dated 14 September 1596) of Luzzaschi's *Sesto libro de' madrigali a cinque voci* (1596), in Newcomb, *The Madrigal at Ferrara*, i: 118.
11 From Lorenzo Giacomini's oration on the death of Tasso (1595), in Shearman, *Mannerism*, pp. 159–61.

The search for new musical idioms – especially as regards chromaticism and dissonance treatment – to match these developments in contemporary texts did not pass without opposition from conservative theorists. Ghiselin Danckerts (c. 1510–after 1565) noted Willaert's motets approvingly:

> they are not like the harmonies of this said new manner [*nuova maniera*] composed by these novel composers: mournful, lugubrious, disconsolate and without beautiful melody at all, which appear to be always the same song, the same thing and the same progression of consonances without any variation at all, whether in the beginning, the end, or the middle. [This they do] without assigning a determinate proper final to the authentic or plagal modes, as pertains to a good composition by a musician. So they seem truly comparable to a noise or buzzing that the bees make when, chased from their honeycomb, they stray from their natural nest and go meandering in a swarm, lost, without direction, not knowing where they are going. Besides these disorders and errors, these said novel composers proceed in their songs so foolishly by leaping intervals very uncomfortable for voices to sing, without any passage of nice runs of semiminims or *crome*, hewing always to the same manner, in the guise of note against note, as if they were chants for lamentations or for the dead.[12]

Danckerts might be dismissed as a mere pedant. However, his objections to the emphasis on artifice for artifice's sake are not without point: the 'stylish style' could too easily become self-conscious stylisation just for its own sake.

This discussion of the madrigal suggests that Mannerism is not necessarily an all-pervading phenomenon in Italian music (or, for that matter, the arts in general) in the second half of the sixteenth century. There are also other problems in treating Mannerism as a distinct style-period separating the Renaissance from the Baroque period. Mannerism works in counterpoint with accepted norms: for its stylish deviations to be recognised and appreciated, these must be judged by the normative canons of a classical style. Indeed, Mannerism depends on stretching such a style to its limits. Thus Mannerism is perhaps best viewed within, rather than outside, the framework of the Renaissance as a whole. Such an interpretation is reinforced by the geographical limitations of the Mannerist style – largely in northern Italy, excluding the Veneto, and, later, in some art in Rome – and by the restricted socio-political environments in which it flourished. For music, this has the added convenience of permitting the music of, say, Palestrina to adhere to a 'Renaissance' style, if it does, while acknowledging that other music contemporary to Palestrina may move in different directions.

---

12 Danckerts, *Sopra una differentia musicale* (MS, *c.* 1551), in Palisca, 'Towards an Intrinsically Musical Definition of Mannerism in the Sixteenth Century', in Palisca, *Studies in the History of Italian Music and Music Theory*, pp. 315–16.

Baroque

Mannerism has also been linked to Marinism, i.e., to the artful, conceit-laden poetry of Giambattista Marino (1569–1625) and his followers that, in turn, has been regarded as a defining feature of seventeenth-century Italian literature and its north European imitations.[13] Marino's insistence on cultivating the 'marvellous' (*meraviglia*) as the reader wonders at the poet's art certainly fits in with one strand of courtly Mannerism, and the rarefied intellectualism and attenuated eroticism of his verse represent others. By the early twentieth century, if not before, critics such as Benedetto Croce and Francesco De Sanctis had also identified Marinism and all it stood for as but an extreme example of so-called *Seicentismo*, where literature lost its Renaissance purity and natural force, and declined into artistic sterility. The other great Italian poet of the early seventeenth century, Gabriello Chiabrera (1552–1638), gained similar opprobrium for his adherence to formulaic strophic canzonettas derived, Chiabrera said, from the Anacreontic lyric (and thus sanctioned by Classical Antiquity). From the point of view of his later critics, including the Arcadians towards the end of the seventeenth century, Chiabrera's facile verse marked the end of Renaissance lyric and epic traditions. The century has still not recovered from the taint of *Seicentismo* in many literary circles, and indeed some musical ones:[14] countering those prejudices is one concern of the present book.

When first applied to our period, 'Baroque' had similarly pejorative overtones. Thus Jean-Jacques Rousseau, writing from the rather smug viewpoint of the French Enlightenment, claimed that 'a baroque music is that in which the harmony is confused, charged with modulations and dissonances, the melody is harsh and little natural, the intonation difficult, and the movement constrained' (in his *Dictionnaire de musique*, 1768). Here 'baroque' is used in a general sense of extravagant, bizarre, even 'gothic'. The broader notion of the Baroque as a distinct style-period from the mid- or late sixteenth century to the early or mid-eighteenth century gained ground only in the nineteenth century, particularly in Art History by way of Heinrich Wölfflin and Willibald Gurlitt. Wölfflin later expanded his argument to embrace a range of stylistic alternatives that distinguished the Baroque from the Renaissance (painterly rather than linear styles, open rather than closed forms, etc.) and also reflected broad pendular motions within the Western tradition. Various attempts to apply these categories to music have been brave but controversial, but the strength of these notions of the Baroque in Art History established terms that (as Wölfflin

13 Mirollo, *The Poet of the Marvelous*; Mirollo, *Mannerism and Renaissance Poetry*.
14 Take, for example, Tomlinson, *Monteverdi and the End of the Renaissance*.

himself suggested) literary and music historians could scarcely ignore, even if the detail might differ from one field to another.[15]

As we have seen, the search for common factors underpinning the arts of a given period tends to focus either on ill-defined but seductive notions of a 'spirit of the times' or on a more precise articulation of contextual perspectives. Robert Haas's *Die Musik des Barocks* (1928), the relevant chapters of Paul Henry Lang's *Music in Western Civilization* (1941), and Friedrich Blume's entries on 'Renaissance' and 'Barock' for *Die Musik in Geschichte und Gegenwart* variously followed the trend for music.[16] A more autonomous stance was adopted by Manfred Bukofzer in *Music in the Baroque Era: from Monteverdi to Bach* (1947) – focussing on the music's inner stylistic unity – Suzanne Clercx's *Le Baroque et la musique* (1948) and Claude Palisca's *Baroque Music* (1968): here 'Baroque' runs the danger of being treated more as just a label of convenience. However, the past three decades have tended to favour the contextual approach, often influenced by 'soft'-Marxist modes of historical inquiry, as in Lorenzo Bianconi's *Il Seicento* (1982; translated as *Music in the Seventeenth Century*). Yet Bianconi's context is more political and social than artistic: hence he avoids the period-label.

The Baroque era is no less difficult than any other in terms of locating precise dates for the period and its subdivisions. As in the case of 'Renaissance', this depends on notions of congruence between and within the arts, on the features chosen to define a given period, and indeed on the social, political and geographical terrain under discussion. Wölfflin's claims for early, high and late phases in Baroque art (from around 1570, 1680 and 1700 respectively) may or may not square with Bukofzer's division of Baroque music into early, middle and late periods (1580–1630, 1630–80 and 1680–1730). Similarly, it is unclear just how close the parallels might be between, say, Galileo Galilei's arguments for a heliocentric world-view, Battista Guarini's breaking of the rules of tragedy in his pastoral 'tragicomedy' *Il pastor fido*, and Monteverdi's dispute with the Bolognese theorist Giovanni Maria Artusi over the necessity of adhering to the rules of counterpoint, or, in Monteverdi's case, breaking such rules when it served the purposes of text expression.[17] Galileo, Guarini and Monteverdi were all iconoclasts calling into question the status of scholastic precepts and principles on the grounds of empirical experience. Guarini and Monteverdi

---

15 This all-too-brief survey, and much of what follows, owes an obvious debt to Palisca, 'Baroque'. In general terms, I have also found Hauser, *The Social History of Art*, ii: *Renaissance, Mannerism, Baroque*, and Skrine, *The Baroque*, to be useful introductions to the period.

16 Blume's entries are translated in his *Renaissance and Baroque Music*.

17 The comparison is made in Tomlinson, *Monteverdi and the End of the Renaissance*, chap. 1. For Monteverdi, see also Palisca, 'The Artusi–Monteverdi Controversy'; Carter, 'Artusi, Monteverdi, and the Poetics of Modern Music'.

certainly knew each other, and even Galileo had visited Mantua in 1604. But whether any or all of them usher in a period we might call the Baroque is another matter altogether.

The confluence of such iconoclasm, however, does suggest that something different was in the air. The late sixteenth and early seventeenth centuries were characterised by relative political stability both south and north of the Alps. While Protestantism consolidated its gains, the Catholic Church emerged from the rather gloomy self-reflection dominating the period of the Council of Trent (1545–63). In Counter-Reformation Rome, the Jesuit Church of the Gesù, begun in 1568, was finished in 1584, and the Chiesa Nuova was built in 1575–7. Pope Sixtus V (reigned 1585–90) revitalised the city and its institutions, with a radical building programme – including the completion of the dome of St Peter's – and bureaucratic reforms (which also involved reorganising the papal choir). These initiatives continued during the reigns of Clement VIII (1592–1605) and Paul V (1605–21). Such architectural projects emphasising the glories of the Church Triumphant were matched by ambitious endeavours in the visual arts, and also in music. The large-scale polychoral works for various groupings of voices and instruments favoured in Rome (they were by no means a predominantly Venetian phenomenon) offered a powerful reflection of the so-called 'colossal Baroque'.[18] The Church was also quick to exploit for its own ends the rhetorical and emotional powers of the 'new music' for solo voice and basso continuo, whether in the motet or in the dramatic context of sacred dialogues, sacred operas and oratorios.[19] And were an adherence to orthodoxy required, the Church could always take advantage of the music of Palestrina, whose classically balanced polyphony was soon canonised as one 'official' style for church music, counteracting the centrifugal tendencies of the period and representing a golden mean expressing the new-found permanence of the Church and the glory of God.

Church and state could be powerfully intertwined – as the civic liturgies of Venice reveal[20] – and even within the north Italian courts, notions of grandeur, persuasion and orthodoxy (in this case, the orthodoxy of absolutism) were no less effective as guiding forces for the arts. The Medici in Florence had long exploited the politics of spectacle in the context of courtly celebration: the comedies with flamboyant *intermedi* – then later (if briefly) the operas – regularly staged during Medici wedding festivities provide clear examples of the arts being used as propaganda, with lavish displays of wealth signalling the political

---

18 Dixon, 'The Origins of the Roman "Colossal Baroque"'; O'Regan, 'Sacred Polychoral Music in Rome, 1575–1621'.

19 Smither, *A History of the Oratorio*, i: *The Oratorio in the Baroque Era*; Hill, 'Oratory Music in Florence, i'.

20 Moore, 'The *Vespero delli Cinque Laudate* and the Role of *Salmi spezzati* at St. Mark's'; Moore, '*Venezia favorita da Maria*: Music for the Madonna Nicopeia and Santa Maria della Salute'.

and economic health of the state.[21] Court dances (whether or not exploiting some kind of dramatic framework) and tournaments also fostered the social cohesion and distinction of an elite class, not to mention the acquisition of princely skills useful in other contexts (say, on the battlefield). The power of the arts to impress both one's own subjects and foreign visitors also found its counterpart on the more intimate scale of private performance. In the 1580s, the renowned *concerto di donne* of Ferrara supported by Duke Alfonso II d'Este – a virtuoso performing group focussing (but not exclusively) on female voices – was a subject of both admiration and emulation even as the duke attempted to keep its performances and repertory a private *musica segreta*.[22] Many north Italian dukes – not least the Gonzagas at Mantua – similarly prided themselves on their virtuoso singers, instrumentalists and composers.

But for all the importance of church and court for contemporary musicians, music-making could also take place in less formal environments. The mercantile proto-capitalist strategies of the great Renaissance states had fostered an economic environment that granted the nobility and the merchant classes relatively high levels of disposable income that could be devoted to conspicuous private consumption in the arts.[23] Similarly, increasingly urban environments needed to project civic identity. Indeed, the market for which composers potentially catered broadened considerably in the sixteenth and early seventeenth centuries, a broadening that was encouraged, to say the least, by music printing. The need for music for domestic use (the cultured individual singing to the lute, the convivial gathering around the dinner table, moments of family celebration or commemoration), or for the meeting-places of various social groups – including confraternities and academies – remained strong, despite the threat (noted at the time) of excluding such groups from music-making latent in the increasing professionalisation of modern musical endeavour. As in the Renaissance, the academy, whether as a formal institution or more loosely organised as a salon, played an important part in cultural life. For example, early opera in both Florence and Mantua had its roots in this environment, and the remarkable flowering of opera in Venice from the opening of the Teatro S. Cassiano as a 'public' opera-house in 1637 stems from much the same 'academic' context.[24]

These apparent continuities reinforce one theme of this chapter – the difficulty, even undesirability, of enforcing period boundaries – but they also counteract a prevalent trend in historical treatments of the period. The

21 Nagler, *Theatre Festivals of the Medici*; Molinari, *Le nozze degli dèi*.

22 See Newcomb, *The Madrigal at Ferrara*. Useful material can also be found in Fenlon, *Music and Patronage in Sixteenth-Century Mantua*, i.

23 Goldthwaite, *Wealth and the Demand for Art in Italy*.

24 For early opera, see most recently, Carter, *Monteverdi's Musical Theatre*, pp. 17–46, 110–18. However, reference should still be made to Nino Pirrotta's seminal 'Temperaments and Tendencies in the Florentine Camerata'. The academic context of Venetian opera is clearly described in Rosand, *Opera in Seventeenth-Century Venice*, pp. 37–40.

seventeenth century has often been labelled one of 'crisis',[25] embracing political upheaval (the English Civil War), religious turmoil (the Thirty Years War
from 1618 to 1648, which cut swathes through much of northern and central Europe), fundamental shifts of scientific paradigms (Galileo, Descartes,
Newton), plague (for example, in Italy from 1630 to 1632), economic disasters
(beginning around 1620), and even drastic climate change. Only by the last
quarter of the century do things seem to have returned to some kind of stability as Louis XIV's reign in France settled into royal absolutism, as the Italian
and German princely successions proceeded on their hereditary way, and as
England achieved its unique compromise between the crown, parliament and
the Church. For the earlier part of the century, one can speculate on whether
such natural and man-made disasters, and their undoubtedly catastrophic consequences, or these scientific and philosophical paradigm shifts, altered the
pace of change to a degree significantly greater than in previous centuries. But
it is probably more useful to consider why viewing the seventeenth century
in this particular light has proven so attractive in the literature. As we have
seen, the century has tended to receive a bad press from historians and critics,
and not always on reasonable grounds. The predominantly Protestant ethic of
recent historical discourse (at least in Anglo-American circles) – with its aver-
sion to Catholic triumphalism – finds its counterpart in a dialectic of Whig
versus Tory readings of history (the labels emerge in the 1680s) that, from the
Whig perspective, favour an anti-monarchic and anti-absolutist rhetoric. Both
the church and the court, then, become symbolic of outmoded regimes to be
crushed in the inexorable drive towards the political and intellectual liberties
reaching fruition in the eighteenth-century Enlightenment, and then the Age
of Revolutions. The 'crisis' of the seventeenth century therefore inserts itself
within a teleology as old world-orders pass to new, and as 'early modern' society
relentlessly pursues its path towards 'mature' modernity.

Some geographical problems

The emphasis on Italy in the discussion thus far is one often encountered in
the literature. It also raises a broader question similar to that posed earlier
for the Renaissance, but from a somewhat different angle. To what extent is

25 Recent historical studies of the 'crisis' of the seventeenth century take their origin from Aston (ed.),
Crisis in Europe, 1550–1650. The issues have been further explored, and in part reconsidered, in Parker and
Smith (eds), *The General Crisis of the Seventeenth Century*, while revisions of the 'crisis' scenario appear both in
Rabb, *The Struggle for Stability in Early Modern Europe*, where the emphasis is more on the reconfiguration of
European institutions, and in the Marxist interpretations advanced in Kiernan, *State and Society in Europe*.
Important for an economic historian's view of the seventeenth century is de Vries, *The Economy of Europe in an
Age of Crisis*, but compare the revisionist reading in Rapp, *Industry and Economic Decline in Seventeenth-Century
Venice*. For music, see Silbiger, 'Music and the Crisis of Seventeenth-Century Europe'.

the Baroque just an Italian phenomenon, rather than a pan-European one? To be sure, most of the above remarks on music in ecclesiastical, courtly, civic and domestic contexts could be applied, *mutatis mutandis*, to France, Germany, Spain, the Low Countries and England, and even to music in the far-flung reaches of Eastern Europe or the New World. The musical establishment of the Duke of Bavaria in Munich (particularly under Albrecht V, with his passionate if uneven support for Orlande de Lassus) rivalled and indeed surpassed many performing groups in Italy. The French, Spanish, Habsburg and English courts exploited entertainments on a scale no less extravagant than their Italian counterparts. And the burghers of Antwerp, Paris, Leipzig, London or even Mexico City were surely no less interested in civic and domestic music as a sign of urbane accomplishment.

Italian music permeated Europe and beyond, whether by way of music prints, of musicians themselves crossing national boundaries (in various directions), or of broader religious or cultural networks. Italian music prints reached northern Europe through the standard trade routes (not least by way of the Frankfurt Book Fair), and northern printers such as the Phalèse press in Antwerp, Adam Berg in Munich, and Paul Kauffmann in Nuremberg willingly reprinted popular Italian repertories. They made their selection with a keen eye on the local market – music of the avant-garde clearly was not a commercial proposition – and thus appear fairly conservative: the lighter madrigals, canzonettas and ballatas of composers such as Luca Marenzio, Orazio Vecchi and Giovanni Giacomo Gastoldi found striking favour through much of the first half of the seventeenth century. Italian music also found its way to the nascent music printing trade in London, as in the anthologies of madrigals with translated texts such as Nicholas Yonge's *Musica transalpina* (1588; a second book appeared in 1597) or Thomas Watson's *The first sett, Of Italian Madrigalls Englished* (1590). Thomas Morley may have complained in his *A Plaine and Easie Introduction to Practicall Musicke* (1597) of 'the new-fangled opinions of our countrymen who will highly esteem whatsoever cometh from beyond the seas (and specially from Italy) be it never so simple, condemning that which is done at home though it be never so excellent'.[26] But he himself did much to import Italian styles to England by way of his canzonets, balletts and madrigals.

Morley never visited Italy, although his colleague, the lutenist and song-composer John Dowland did, journeying to Venice and Florence in the mid-1590s (he also hoped to meet Marenzio in Rome): the experience presumably

---

26 T. Morley, *A Plain and Easy Introduction to Practical Music*, ed. R. A. Harman (London, 1952; repr. 1966), p. 293.

made itself felt in Dowland's more declamatory lute songs. The Dresden composer Heinrich Schütz paid two extended visits to Venice, the first in 1609–12 – his encounters with Giovanni Gabrieli clearly had a profound effect on his own polychoral settings published in the *Psalmen Davids* (1619) – and the second in 1628–9, when he met and worked with Claudio Monteverdi. The later English madrigalist Walter Porter also claimed to have studied in Italy with Monteverdi. There were close connections between Italy and the Danish court of King Christian IV in Copenhagen, where composers such as Mogens Pederson and Hans Nielsen produced Italianate madrigals (they both studied in Venice with Giovanni Gabrieli). Spanish control of Naples and Milan made for easy commerce between Spain and Italy, and Tomás Luis de Victoria (1548–1611) was neither the first nor the last Spanish composer to study and work in Rome before returning home, taking back Italian styles of sacred music to establish firm roots in Spain and also the New World. Musicians from Italy also headed northward: Giovanni Gabrieli to Munich in the mid-1570s; Luca Marenzio to Poland in 1596–8 (the Roman Giovanni Francesco Anerio was also there in the late 1620s, and Monteverdi had also been temped to make the move); Giulio Caccini and his family to France in 1604–5 (a visit to England was also planned); and Angelo Notari to London in 1610, where he entered court service until the Commonwealth and published an important collection of Italianate solo songs in 1613 which clearly influenced other English composers attempting to emulate Italian styles (such as Henry and William Lawes). These patterns of temporary or permanent migration remained constant through the seventeenth century: Johann Rosenmüller (*c.* 1619–1684) moved from eastern Germany (after a scandal involving choirboys in Leipzig) to take up a career in Venice, while the virtuoso viol player and trumpeter Gottfried Finger (*c.* 1660–1730) left Moravia for a career in London before ending up in Breslau (Wrocław), then Mannheim. With these musicians also travelled music and performance practices, acting as catalysts for stylistic transmission and influence, and as a prompt for musical miscegenation. Purcell's style may seem uniquely 'English', but it also mixes French and Italian elements to varying degrees, and even shows some knowledge of Finger's trumpet writing. The French may have resisted external influence more than most – or so it is commonly asserted – but even here the sought-for *réunion des goûts* was not so much an idealised synthesis as a reflection of a musical reality.

　Much of this movement of musicians across Europe traced routes established by commerce or by lines of political or religious affiliation. The foreigners who came to Italy for training often followed well-developed patterns for broader education, not least through the seminaries and colleges of Rome. And the

Jesuits, with their emphasis on education, established elaborate institutional and individual networks stretching across Europe and into the New World:[27] wherever they extended their influence, they exploited the visual, musical and dramatic arts in the ways they knew best, disseminating Roman confessional, ceremonial and artistic orthodoxies throughout the Catholic communion with only minor concessions to local practice. This suggests some limits that one might choose to place upon notions of a European Baroque, focussing less on its geographical origins than on its religious affiliations. Catholicism was spread widely through Europe, even into Protestant enclaves. In England, for example, an interest in things Italian was prominent in recusant circles – even if it was not quite the marker for recusancy that has tended to be assumed[28] – and although Dowland and other English Catholic musicians (John Bull, Peter Philips) found temporary or permanent employment in safer religious and political environments in northern Europe, Dowland returned to England, and other practising Catholics stayed there (William Byrd is the obvious example). Many Protestants, especially those of a more puritan bent, may have been deeply suspicious of Italian culture: the English pedagogue Roger Ascham (in his *The Scholemaster* of 1570) warned of 'the inchantementes of Circes, brought out of Italie, to marre mens maners',[29] and he was not alone in fearing corruption from an Italian lasciviousness and effeminacy (a common parlance of the time) too redolent of popery. It would also be a mistake to emphasise unduly the differences between Catholic and (at least some) Protestant environments: musicians of either faith could often – with discretion – live and work in either context. Similarly, Protestant and Catholic styles could interact (witness the music of Schütz), even if the mixture of ecstatic vision and a dogmatic adherence to authority typical of the Baroque in its deepest sense was alien to many Protestant world-views. But it is probably true that although the Baroque may not have been an exclusively Italian phenomenon, in its early stages it was essentially a Catholic one, and when Protestant cultures latched on to the stylistic tropes, they sometimes went in different directions. Yet often all it took to sanitise a 'popish' work for general consumption was to give it a different text (i.e., to produce a *contrafactum*), or just to treat it as an abstract instrumental

27 Culley, *Jesuits and Music*, i; Culley, 'Musical Activity in Some Sixteenth-Century Jesuit Colleges'; Kennedy, 'Jesuits and Music'. For missions to the Americas and Asia, and the place of music therein, see O'Malley *et al.* (eds), *The Jesuits*.

28 Compare the myth surrounding Francis Tregian the younger, traditionally associated with the Fitzwilliam Virginal Book (Cambridge, Fitzwilliam Museum, Music MS 168) and with various manuscript collections of Italian music, including London, British Library, Egerton 3665 and New York, Public Library for the Performing Arts at Lincoln Center, MS Drexel 4302, all reputedly copied while Tregian was imprisoned for recusancy in the Fleet from 1609 to 1619. This has in effect been demolished in Thompson, 'Francis Tregian the Younger as Music Copyist'. For the broader phenomenon of English collectors of Italian music, see Hamessley, 'The Reception of the Italian Madrigal in England'.

29 Carter, 'Secular Vocal Music', pp. 181–2. See also Masello, 'Thomas Hoby'.

piece. And in the case of the Lutherans, the musical Baroque eventually found particularly fertile ground given that Luther himself had always stressed the importance of the text, the need for its vivid interpretation, and the intrinsic value of music: the Baroque style brought these together in ways that had not been possible in Luther's own time.

Issues of style

Giovanni Battista Doni, a prominent theorist of the 1630s, called the Renaissance masters 'an abomination from past time'.[30] This suggests that as the musical Renaissance reached its end, something different was emerging, with concepts previously regarded as embodying important truths now (dis)regarded as inadequate, irrelevant or, at best, peripheral. In many music histories, the rise of opera and solo song in Florence in the 1590s – and the emergence of new styles of music for virtuoso voice(s) and basso continuo – are deemed a watershed not just distinguishing the Baroque period from the Renaissance, but also marking the birth of what might be recognised, in however primitive a form, as 'modern' music. In such a context, and in the light of the prejudices exposed above, it is inevitable that historians should tend to favour secular music over sacred, even though most early seventeenth-century audiences probably encountered the newer musical styles more often in church than in any other location.[31] Closely associated with these new styles, so the standard histories would have it, were supposedly new modes of musical thinking, emphasising vertical harmony (witness the basso continuo and its 'figured bass') at the expense of linear counterpoint (which becomes an archaic, and archaicising, device), and a shift from so-called modality to so-called tonality. More recently, the trend has been to locate these 'new' styles in a more traditional context, not least by way of improvisatory and other performing practices common in the Renaissance. Similarly, it is impossible to distinguish so clearly between vertical and linear processes within a given compositional praxis: Renaissance polyphony pays clear attention to vertical sonorities, and the figures used to indicate the inner parts above the continuo bass are often strongly indicative of linear voice-leading (only much later did they alter the basis of harmonic thinking). Certainly matters of style and structure did change from the Renaissance to the Baroque periods, but not always as dramatically as we may have led ourselves to believe.

What is perhaps most striking about the music of the Baroque period is its stylistic variety, ranging from *stile antico* polyphony for four or more voices

30 Blume, *Renaissance and Baroque Music*, p. 28.   31 Carter, 'Music Publishing in Italy'.

to the most up-to-date recitative for solo voice and continuo: this variety can be found even in the work of single composers (for Italy, Monteverdi is the prime example). Such a range of styles doubtless reflects the various contexts in which music was produced, and also a heightened self-consciousness concerning the place of music in changing social and artistic worlds. However, one should be wary of imputing to the Renaissance a single musical style that somehow becomes fragmented towards the end of the sixteenth century, however convenient such a notion might be for ideas of change as Renaissance certainties were replaced by Baroque doubts. Renaissance music clearly had its own languages and dialects – from the studied polyphony of Franco-Flemish Masses and motets to the homophonic simplicity of the Parisian chanson or the Italian *canzone villanesca alla napolitana* and its derivatives – and especially if one takes into account improvisatory vocal and instrumental practices. Nor should the simple presentation of much Renaissance music – dictated largely by the commercial and technical requirements of the music printing industry – mislead us into thinking that this is how the music was actually heard. Imagining a performance of, say, a Palestrina motet with vocal embellishments and instrumental participation – not a necessary scenario but certainly a plausible one in some contexts – may give a better sense of the sounds that perhaps most frequently struck late Renaissance ears.[32] Indeed, what changes as we move from the Renaissance to the Baroque may be not so much musical or performing styles themselves as the fact that these styles are recorded through notation in different ways.

There is no doubt, however, that music now took on different functions. Gioseffo Zarlino's conservative definition of music as 'sounding number' (1558) invoked an external world of order and proportion that was duly reflected in the sounds and silences of day-to-day musical life. The harmony of the spheres – the sounds of a cosmos regulated by the fixed and constant motions of the planets – was audible to God but not, since the Fall, to man. To follow the Boethian trope, this divine harmony (*musica mundana*) found its reflection in the harmony of the well-regulated soul (or the well-regulated state) as *musica humana*, and was imitated by the balanced harmonies and proportions of *musica instrumentalis* (incorporating both vocal and instrumental music), which in turn became a potent metaphor for the harmony both of the soul and of heaven. The whole world was conceived as an interlocking chain of resemblances from the heavenly to the earthly spheres, with each element on one level finding its precise analogy on others, all a product of, and working for, the ineffable dominion of a Divine Creator lauded by choirs of angels, and

---

32 Brown, *Sixteenth-Century Instrumentation*; Brown, *Embellishing Sixteenth-Century Music*.

of men. For all its status as a commonplace, this powerful vision of a world literally in harmony with itself is both mystical and magical, imposing a fervent wish for order to mitigate the fear of chaos.[33] It would also reappear often in the seventeenth century and, indeed, well into the eighteenth.

Chaos was an ever-present threat, as the political and social turmoil of the period constantly revealed. Not for nothing did invocations of harmony take on an incantatory tone, whether in political terms – court entertainments across Europe in the period make the point clear – or within contemporary theoretical speculation on music. Zarlino's emphasis on the perfect numbers and proportions expressed within musical harmony – not least through the *senario*, the number six construed to contain all the rational consonances (the octave, fifth, fourth, third and sixth) – was more than just a theoretical conceit: it also had powerful ideological resonances. And any threat to so ordered a scheme had ramifications far beyond the mathematical note-crunching often typical of *musica speculativa*. When Vincenzo Galilei dismissed the relevance of the *senario* to any practical musical endeavour – given the impurity of the intervals used in contemporary systems of tuning and temperament – Zarlino and his supporters did have one defence: man is *de facto* imperfect and so cannot rise to so ideal a vision of divine perfection. But it was a rear-guard action.

The pages devoted to the matter in contemporary treatises make for dull reading, but there was a crucial issue at stake: the stability of the Renaissance world-view. Galilei, however, had different concerns. His debunking of the *senario* takes second place to the exploration of a new function for music drawing on his own familiarity (and that of his mentors, including the noted Florentine philologist Girolamo Mei) with sources on music from Classical Antiquity.[34] The renowned musicians of Classical myth, and Classical writers on music, offered an alternative, and topically Humanist, message, namely that music exerted powerful ethical and emotional effects upon its listeners. The question now was whether such effects should be both censured and controlled (as Plato argued in his vision of the ideal Republic) or be put to good political and aesthetic use by the virtues of emotional catharsis (an Aristotelian view). As in the Hellenic and Hellenistic periods when such debates were first recorded,[35] the one stance encouraged a conservative retention of the old order, while the other offered a radical defence of the new.

For all the temporal distance between the early seventeenth century and the great thinkers of Classical Antiquity, the conceptual distance had been lessened

33 Tomlinson, *Music in Renaissance Magic*.
34 Palisca, 'Vincenzo Galilei and Some Links Between "Pseudo-Monody" and Monody'; Palisca, *Girolamo Mei*; Palisca, *The Florentine Camerata*.
35 Maas, 'Timotheus at Sparta'.

by the Humanist endeavours of the Renaissance and by the recovery of sources that retained an immediate and considerable presence. However, the new historicism of the sixteenth and early seventeenth centuries prompted a slightly different view of Classical texts. The notion of Plato and Aristotle conveying truths of universal import (at least, once mediated by Christian syncretism) was mitigated by the sense that they were, after all, men like any other men: the ground shifted from universal 'truths' to 'matters for debate', important but with outcomes predicated on their contemporary relevance. Monteverdi, for example, felt it necessary to invoke Plato in his discussion of the *seconda pratica* and the search for a 'natural path to imitation', but Plato, he said, offered only a dim light that was more suggestive than instructive: the composer was left essentially on his own.[36] A new sense of history also affected notions of an *ars perfecta*. Zarlino claimed that the greatness of music in Classical Antiquity had been lost in the Middle Ages but recovered in the Renaissance, not least by his 'new Pythagoras', Adriano Willaert. Monteverdi, on the other hand, was well aware that Willaert existed in a particular historical space, and that his achievement – for all its significance – was essentially transient. Once discovered and articulated, the concept of history as a process of change, rather than as a confirmation of eternal similarity, could not be countered by one great musician, whatever the attempts of theorists – and sometimes institutions (witness the Palestrina 'myth') – to establish a paragon of unsurpassable perfection. For Monteverdi, Willaert certainly marked the peak of the *prima pratica*, but Cipriano de Rore, Willaert's pupil and successor at St Mark's, Venice, had initiated a new practice and new ways of conceiving the relationship between music and word that lay at the heart of a modern text-expressive style.

The discovery of new ways of enabling music to present a text and thereby move the emotions of the listener is normally viewed as one defining feature of the Baroque period. Yet there are other elements in the musical Baroque that might seem, on the face of things, to run counter to it. The most obvious is the rise of instrumental music with its own rhetorical power independent of words; another is the formalist tendency to extol the craft of musical composition as an object of contemplation of and for itself, and thus separate from any other specific function. None of these necessarily contradicts the other: the Baroque aria is a case-study in wordless rhetoric even as it presents a text, and it certainly exhibits formalist traits while remaining able to arouse the emotions. For that matter, little is necessarily new to the Baroque period: the Renaissance had

36 Monteverdi refers to Plato both in his controversy with Artusi (see the documents in Strunk, *Source Readings in Music History, Revised Edition*, iv: *The Baroque Era*, pp. 18–36) and in a letter to Giovanni Battista Doni of 22 October 1633, given in Stevens (trans.), *The Letters of Claudio Monteverdi*, pp. 420–22. For the latter, see also the discussion in Tomlinson, 'Madrigal, Monody, and Monteverdi's "via naturale alla immitatione"'.

its text-painting, its instrumental music, and its formalisms, while the aria's other characteristic, a search for musical *meraviglia* and its potential to inspire wonder, has Mannerist precedents. Yet all these elements come together in new ways that are perhaps the most unique, and certainly the most exciting, aspects of seventeenth-century music.

Bibliography

Aston, T. (ed.), *Crisis in Europe, 1550–1650: Essays from 'Past and Present'*. London, 1965

Baker, N. K., and Hanning, B. R. (eds), *Musical Humanism and its Legacy: Essays in Honor of Claude V. Palisca*. Stuyvesant, NY, 1992

Bianconi, L., *Music in the Seventeenth Century*, trans. D. Bryant. Cambridge, 1987

Blume, F., *Renaissance and Baroque Music*. London, 1968

Brown, H. M., *Sixteenth-Century Instrumentation: the Music for the Florentine Intermedii*, 'Musicological Studies and Documents', 30. American Institute of Musicology, 1973
  Embellishing Sixteenth-Century Music. London, 1976

Bukofzer, M. F., *Music in the Baroque Era: from Monteverdi to Bach*. New York, 1947

Burckhardt, J., *The Civilization of the Renaissance in Italy*. 2nd edn, London, 1945

Burke, P., *The Fortunes of the Courtier: the European Reception of Castiglione's 'Cortegiano'*. Cambridge, 1995

Carter, T., 'Music Publishing in Italy, c.1580–c.1625: Some Preliminary Observations'. *Royal Musical Association Research Chronicle*, 20 (1986–7), 19–37
  'Artusi, Monteverdi, and the Poetics of Modern Music'. In Baker and Hanning (eds), *Musical Humanism and its Legacy*, pp. 171–94
  Music in Late Renaissance and Early Baroque Italy. London, 1992
  'Secular Vocal Music'. In R. Bray (ed.), *The Blackwell History of Music in Britain*, ii: *The Sixteenth Century*. Oxford, 1995, pp. 147–209
  Monteverdi's Musical Theatre. New Haven and London, 2002

Castiglione, B., *The Book of the Courtier*, trans. G. Bull. Harmondsworth, 1967

Clercx, S., *Le Baroque et la musique: essai d'esthétique musicale*. Brussels, 1948

Culley, T. D., *Jesuits and Music*, i: *A Study of the Musicians Connected with the German College in Rome During the 17th Century and of Their Activities in Northern Europe*. Rome and St Louis, 1970
  'Musical Activity in Some Sixteenth-Century Jesuit Colleges, with Special Reference to the Venerable English College in Rome from 1579 to 1589'. *Analecta musicologica*, 19 (1979), 1–29

de Vries, J., *The Economy of Europe in an Age of Crisis, 1600–1750*. Cambridge, 1976

Dixon, G., 'The Origins of the Roman "Colossal Baroque"'. *Proceedings of the Royal Musical Association*, 106 (1979–80), 115–28

Fenlon, I., *Music and Patronage in Sixteenth-Century Mantua*. 2 vols, Cambridge, 1980, 1982

Fenlon, I. (ed.), *The Renaissance: from the 1470s to the End of the 16th Century*, 'Man and Music', 2. Basingstoke and London, 1989

Goldthwaite, R. A., *Wealth and the Demand for Art in Italy, 1300–1600*. Baltimore and London, 1993

Haar, J., 'Classicism and Mannerism in 16th-Century Music'. *International Review of Music Aesthetics and Sociology*, 1 (1970), 55–67

'Self-Consciousness about Style, Form and Genre in 16th-Century Music'. *Studi musicali*, 3 (1974), 219–32

Haas, R., *Die Musik des Barocks*. Potsdam, 1928

Hamessley, L. R., 'The Reception of the Italian Madrigal in England: a Repertorial Study of Manuscript Anthologies, ca. 1580–1620'. Ph. D. thesis, University of Minnesota (1989)

Hauser, A., *The Social History of Art*, ii: *Renaissance, Mannerism, Baroque*. London, 1962

Hay, D., *The Italian Renaissance in its Historical Background*. 2nd edn, Cambridge, 1977

Hill, J. W., 'Oratory Music in Florence, i: *Recitar cantando*, 1583–1655'. *Acta musicologica*, 51 (1979), 108–36

Kennedy, T. F., 'Jesuits and Music: Reconsidering the Early Years'. *Studi musicali*, 17 (1988), 71–100

Kiernan, V. G., *State and Society in Europe, 1550–1650*. Oxford, 1980

Lang, P. H., *Music in Western Civilization*. New York, 1941

Maas, M., 'Timotheus at Sparta: the Nature of the Crime'. In Baker and Hanning (eds), *Musical Humanism and its Legacy*, pp. 37–52

Maniates, M. R., *Mannerism in Italian Music and Culture, 1530–1630*. Manchester, 1979

Masello, S. J., 'Thomas Hoby: a Protestant Traveler to Circe's Court'. *Cahiers Elisabethains*, 27 (1985), 67–81

Mirollo, J. V., *The Poet of the Marvelous: Giambattista Marino*. New York, 1963

Mannerism and Renaissance Poetry: Concept, Mode, Inner Design. New Haven and London, 1984

Molinari, C., *Le nozze degli dèi: un saggio sul grande spettacolo italiano nel Seicento*. Rome, 1968

Moore, J. H., 'The *Vespero delli Cinque Laudate* and the Role of *Salmi spezzati* at St. Mark's'. *Journal of the American Musicological Society*, 34 (1981), 249–78

'*Venezia favorita da Maria*: Music for the Madonna Nicopeia and Santa Maria della Salute'. *Journal of the American Musicological Society*, 37 (1984), 299–355

Nagler, A. M., *Theatre Festivals of the Medici, 1539–1637*. New Haven and London, 1964; repr. New York, 1976

Newcomb, A., *The Madrigal at Ferrara, 1579–1597*. 2 vols, Princeton, 1980

O'Malley, J. W. et al. (eds), *The Jesuits: Cultures, Sciences, and the Arts 1540–1773*. Toronto, 1999

O'Regan, N., 'Sacred Polychoral Music in Rome, 1575–1621'. D. Phil. thesis, University of Oxford (1988)

Palisca, C. V., 'Vincenzo Galilei and Some Links Between "Pseudo-Monody" and Monody'. *Musical Quarterly*, 46 (1960), 344–60; reprinted in Palisca, *Studies in the History of Italian Music and Music Theory*, pp. 346–63

Baroque Music. Englewood Cliffs, 1968; 3rd edn, 1991

'Towards an Intrinsically Musical Definition of Mannerism in the Sixteenth Century'. *Studi musicali*, 3 (1974), 313–46; reprinted in Palisca, *Studies in the History of Italian Music and Music Theory*, pp. 312–45

Girolamo Mei (1519–1594): Letters on Ancient and Modern Music to Vincenzo Galilei and Giovanni Bardi; a Study with Annotated Texts, 'Musicological Studies and Documents', 3. 2nd edn, American Institute of Musicology, 1977

'Baroque'. In S. Sadie (ed.), *The New Grove Dictionary of Music and Musicians*. 20 vols, London, 1980, ii: 172–8

Humanism in Italian Renaissance Musical Thought. New Haven and London, 1985

'The Artusi–Monteverdi Controversy'. In D. Arnold and N. Fortune (eds), *The New Monteverdi Companion*, London, 1985, pp. 127–58; reprinted in Palisca, *Studies in the History of Italian Music and Music Theory*, pp. 54–84

Studies in the History of Italian Music and Music Theory. Oxford, 1994

The Florentine Camerata: Documentary Studies and Translations. New Haven and London, 1989

Parker, G., and Smith, L. M. (eds), *The General Crisis of the Seventeenth Century*. London, 1978

Pirrotta, N., 'Temperaments and Tendencies in the Florentine Camerata'. *Musical Quarterly*, 40 (1954), 169–89; reprinted in Pirrotta, *Music and Culture in Italy from the Middle Ages to the Baroque*, pp. 217–34

Music and Theatre from Poliziano to Monteverdi. Cambridge, 1982

Music and Culture in Italy from the Middle Ages to the Baroque: a Collection of Essays. Cambridge, MA, and London, 1984 (including 'Music and Cultural Tendencies in Fifteenth-Century Italy', pp. 80–112; 'Novelty and Renewal in Italy, 1300–1600', pp. 159–74)

Price, C. (ed.), *The Early Baroque Era: from the Late 16th Century to the 1660s*, 'Man and Music', 3. Basingstoke and London, 1993

Rabb, T. K., *The Struggle for Stability in Early Modern Europe*. New York, 1975

Rapp, R. T., *Industry and Economic Decline in Seventeenth-Century Venice*. Cambridge, MA, 1976

Rosand, E., *Opera in Seventeenth-Century Venice: the Creation of a Genre*. Berkeley, Los Angeles and Oxford, 1991

Shearman, J., *Mannerism*. Harmondsworth, 1967

Silbiger, A. 'Music and the Crisis of Seventeenth-Century Europe'. In V. Coelho (ed.), *Music and Science in the Age of Galileo*. Dordrecht, 1992, pp. 35–44

Skrine, P. N., *The Baroque: Literature and Culture in Seventeenth-Century Europe*. London, 1978

Smither, H. E., *A History of the Oratorio*, i: *The Oratorio in the Baroque Era: Italy, Vienna, Paris*. Chapel Hill, NC, 1977

Smyth, C. H., *Mannerism and 'Maniera'*. Locust Valley, NY, 1963

Stevens, D. (trans.), *The Letters of Claudio Monteverdi*. 2nd edn, Oxford, 1995

Strunk, O., *Source Readings in Music History, Revised Edition*, iv: *The Baroque Era*, ed. M. Murata. New York and London, 1998

Thompson, R. R., 'Francis Tregian the Younger as Music Copyist: a Legend and an Alternative View'. *Music and Letters*, 82 (2001), 1–31

Tomlinson, G., 'Madrigal, Monody, and Monteverdi's "via naturale alla immitatione"'. *Journal of the American Musicological Society*, 34 (1981), 60–108

Monteverdi and the End of the Renaissance. Oxford, 1987

Music in Renaissance Magic: Toward a Historiography of Others. Chicago and London, 1993

2

The seventeenth-century musical 'work'

JOHN BUTT

There is no doubt that a handful of compositions from the seventeenth century have become part of the modern 'classical' repertory. If they are not quite standard concert war-horses owing to their 'unorthodox' scoring, they are nevertheless recognised as 'great works' of early music: Monteverdi's 1610 Vespers and Purcell's *Dido and Aeneas* perhaps come most readily to mind. However, the vast majority of this century's music is still seen as the province of specialist performers, somehow separate from the musical mainstream. It is not the brief of this chapter – or indeed of this book as a whole – to function as a comprehensive critique of current musical values and concert practices, yet some awareness of our own assumptions and prejudices is surely vital in any historical study whatsoever. The question that thus arises is whether musical compositions of the seventeenth century are appropriately described as 'works'. And this leads to a whole string of further questions. Did seventeenth-century composers believe they were writing works? Did those who received these compositions believe them to be works? Or are certain pieces retroactively defined as works – as may be the case with those familiar pieces by Monteverdi and Purcell? And are these defined as works because of qualities latent within them and common to great works of all ages, or is it that they just contain elements that might be seen as conforming to a historically conditioned ideology of what a work should be?

What renders the seventeenth century a particularly dynamic – if frustrating – area of inquiry is the very fluidity of musical practice, something that should make us wary of looking for a definite trajectory towards the full-fledged work of later periods. For instance, even if a piece of music becomes particularly well fixed and transmitted in a notated text (e.g., a *prima pratica* motet) it might not necessarily be so strongly individualised as a 'work' as one of the more celebrated operas of the age. The latter, on the other hand, might not be so exhaustively notated since many aspects of the performance were, by necessity, variable if the opera were to be repeatable and transportable. Even more challenging is the relation of musical canonisation to workhood. As Harold Powers has shown through a study of the Indian *rāga*, it is possible for a cultural canonisation of musical practice to exist without distinct 'works' as such. If, following Powers, we were to define such canonisation as lying in the presence of trained specialists, a body of music theory, a level of autonomy (or at least the detachability of the music concerned from the cultural performance in which it was originally embedded) together with a patron-class professing connoisseurship, it would be relatively easy to identify canonic practice in the seventeenth century.[1] Most obviously, this would lie in the persistence (and skilful modification or extension) of Renaissance counterpoint. Even the most 'modern' composers for their time (e.g., Monteverdi and Corelli, Purcell and Charpentier, Schütz and Buxtehude) show a respect for this canonic practice, yet this does not have to result in specific canonical 'works', however much it might inform their approach to composition in general.

Attempts to define a 'work-concept'

German musicologists such as Carl Dahlhaus and Walter Wiora have wrestled for some time with the historical status of the concept of the musical work.[2] Most in this tradition tend to assume that in any given period there is a phenomenological entity that can be defined as a 'work' so long as our command of language and our intuition of the dynamics of music history are up to the task. In this view, if many works after 1800 did acquire features that gave them a greater claim to autonomy (assuming that this is a useful way of defining a 'work'), this was only a matter of degree rather than of kind. Within the context of the European tradition, there is thus an essential transhistorical unity implied by the work-concept.[3] The Anglo-American tradition of analytical philosophy has attempted the same task from a rather different angle, searching for that which is essential to a musical work without generally considering historical issues of change, development or difference. It was from within – and against – this tradition that Lydia Goehr shocked, or at least irritated, many in the field of historical musicology with her thesis that the work-concept did not develop until around 1800 and that, strictly speaking, no musical works were written before this time.[4]

Goehr's claim would seem senseless if we take at face value Nikolaus Listenius's statement (from the 1530s) that the art of *musica poetica* results in a 'perfect and absolute *opus*' that survives the death of its maker.[5] However,

1 Powers, 'A Canonical Museum of Imaginary Music'.

2 Dahlhaus, *Grundlagen der Musikgeshichte*; Seidel, *Werk und Werkbegriff in der Musikgeschichte*; Wiora, *Das musikalische Kunstwerk* and 'Das musikalische Kunstwerk der Neuzeit und das musikalische Kunstwerk der Antike'.

3 See Strohm, '*Opus*', for an analysis of Dahlhaus's approach.

4 Goehr, *The Imaginary Museum of Musical Works*.

5 Listenius developed this definition from the opening of *Rudimenta musicae* (Wittenberg, 1533) to a fuller version in *Musica: ab authore denuo recognita multisque novis regulis* (Wittenberg, 1537). For a comprehensive survey of these writings and the tradition that they engendered, see Loesch, *Der Werkbegriff in der protestantischen Musiktheorie des 16. und 17. Jahrhunderts*.

according to Heinz von Loesch, Listenius may not be referring exclusively or even primarily to individual pieces of music; Loesch argues that his formulation is one that early Lutheran music theorists adopted from Aristotle and Quintilian to describe the activity of production in general, which could equally result in printed publications or theoretical treatises even if Listenius's formulation was soon to become associated exclusively with musical compositions. Given that the essentially German theoretical tradition of *musica poetica* – of which Listenius was the principal founder – was to die out (together with the theoretical reliance on Aristotle and Quintilian) in the late seventeenth and early eighteenth centuries, it is unlikely that this was a significant step towards later, strong work-concepts.

In tracing the development of musical works in the sixteenth century, much depends on the defining characteristics which one considers necessary for a work. This might involve the identity and portability of notated musical pieces by famous composers as implied by Tinctoris (1477), long before Listenius, or Goehr's open, regulative concept that requires a broad combination of conditions such as the separability of musical works from extra-musical environments, 'free' and original composers, disinterested contemplation on the part of the listener, bourgeois concert-hall practice, and copyright. One way out of this impasse might be to take as a starting point Gretel Schwörer-Kohl's distinction between a broader (and weaker) sense of 'work' and the narrower sub-category of 'opus-work'.[6] The broader concept would cover compositions resulting from 'creative activity of the highest order', some form of self-contained formal structure, and some historical durability. The concept of the 'opus-work' demands notational fixity, attribution to a specific author, and some degree of originality within the context of the age. The broader concept of work could be applied to a wide range of music, including much non-Western music, while the 'opus-work' would refer mainly to a Western tradition lasting from the mid-fifteenth century to the mid-twentieth and to only a limited number of non-Western traditions.

Nevertheless, Schwörer-Kohl's distinction is not without its problems. Reinhard Strohm notes that the term 'opus' has a longer genealogy than has normally been assumed (his evidence dates back to Kraków in the 1430s and 1440s).[7] But while this suggests the transfer of work-concepts from other artistic fields, it does not necessarily evoke the strong, individualised and unique connotations of Schwörer-Kohl's definition. Moreover, her inclusion of 'creative activity of the highest order' as a principal definition of the broader sense of 'work' begs the question of relative quality that cannot be answered

---

6 Schwörer-Kohl, 'Zum Werkbegriff in der Ethnomusikologie und in der historischen Musikwissenschaft'.

7 Strohm, '*Opus*', pp. 5–6.

objectively; it also raises the issue of whether the judgement is made from the standpoint of the composer's environment or of later reception. Perhaps the broader definition should be liberalised to include *any* musical entity (be it an event, a musical text, or just an idea) that can be perceived, remembered or discussed. Yet this would make the term 'work' virtually synonymous with 'music' and thus more or less superfluous. The word 'work' works to the extent that it carries some sort of charge that 'music' would not otherwise hold. My question here, then, is whether something of that charge is present in seventeenth-century musical culture. Indeed, it may well be that the seventeenth century is signally important in bringing many of these issues to the fore.

So significant is the notion of workhood to the Western tradition that, to many, it is imperative to trace the roots of its corollary, compositional thinking, to its earliest stages and follow these through the subsequent centuries. Workhood can thus be thought of as something that develops in tandem with the very concept of Western civilisation and the universality that this brings.[8] Strohm makes the point that there has always been a 'cohabitation' of functional elements with 'work-like significance' in music; thus it is a mistake to take the absence of a specific functional role as a crucial factor in defining any particular piece as a work.[9] From this perspective it is eminently possible to see the seventeenth century as playing its part in the process towards 'full' workhood in the nineteenth. Indeed, Strohm and Anthony Newcomb suggest that much was in place before the seventeenth century even began.[10] They note Tinctoris's assertion (1477) that composers found fame in their works, and also that commentators of the next generation likened the finest music of the Josquin era to the great works of pictorial and verbal art. While this latter point suggests, incidentally, that music culture does not lag so far 'behind' the other arts as we are often told, it does raise the question of whether even the contemporary objects in other arts should be considered works in the strong sense. In all, though, it is clear that the idea of a musical work as something that could enjoy a public trajectory and bring fame to a composer without him necessarily being present greatly expanded during the sixteenth century. Strohm and Newcomb also observe a growing sense of canon formation and the predominance of single-author collections; this would suggest the notion of a 'great' composer standing above the merely skilled musician. Strohm notes that Orlande de Lassus's *Magnum opus musicum* (Munich, 1604) was a representation of the composer's complete motets, produced by his immediate family for the delectation of a whole host of connoisseurs and amateurs, and thus

8 Strohm, *The Rise of European Music*, pp. 1–5, 412–88.
9 Strohm, 'Looking Back at Ourselves', p. 139.
10 Newcomb, 'Notions of Notation and the Concept of the Work'.

showing how a broad culture of patrons and consumers was complicit in the stronger profiling of the composer.[11] To this one might add the example of Johann Caspar Kerll, who, in his *Modulatio organica* (Munich, 1686), appended a thematic catalogue of his other keyboard works.[12]

Newcomb proposes that the degree to which composers moved towards the idea of works depended on whether the genre concerned approached the two poles of a composer- or a performer-related type (one could perhaps also call this a division of musical pieces into reified abstractions on the one hand, and events on the other). Of the composer-oriented type, the ricercar for instruments was a particularly significant example, by which the 'old style' was thematically manipulated with an increasingly rigorous structural logic. The use of open score implied that this was primarily music for visual study, an object for analysis, and not inviting improvisational input from the score-reading performer. The height of abstraction is suggested when keyboard pieces were presented in partbook format, as in the first editions of ricercars of the Venetian school before *c.* 1590; incidentally, this same practice was still evident in Michael Praetorius's publication of his solo organ music within the partbooks of his vocal music in 1609.[13] This is something that would seem positively to mitigate against ease of performance (although keyboard players clearly did play from partbooks as a matter of course in performing vocal music, at least around 1550).[14] Even some genres specifically geared towards performance, such as the repertory of the *concerto di donne* at Ferrara in the 1580s, show evidence of the performers obeying the letter of the notation, diminutions and all,[15] although here it is almost as if the *concerto* was being celebrated for its unusual practice of *not* improvising embellishments.

It is possible to extend Newcomb's argument to cover developments later in the seventeenth century: the *stile antico* as retained in the ricercars of Girolamo Frescobaldi and Johann Jacob Froberger; the preservation of the 'Palestrina' style in some areas of Catholic practice; the German Lutheran 'learned' school of organists raised in the Sweelinck tradition; the purposeful espousal of old styles in the wake of the English Restoration. There was also a steady solidification of musical form in vocal genres – that notional 'third practice' which superseded (or at least co-existed with) the *seconda pratica* (that itself had so forcefully advocated the supremacy of text over music).[16] And there was obviously a continued growth in single-author collections, in both manuscript and print.

11　Strohm, 'Looking Back at Ourselves', p. 150.
12　Butt, 'Germany and the Netherlands', pp. 201–2.
13　Rose, 'Music, Print and Authority in Leipzig during the Thirty Years' War', i: 179.
14　Owens, *Composers at Work*, pp. 48–9.
15　Newcomb, *The Madrigal at Ferrara*, i: 25–6, 55.　　16　Carter, '*Possente spirto*'.

Nevertheless, it may be too crude to view the century as a single, seamless whole, in which various trends underwent a continuous development. Alexander Silbiger observes that Burney and Hawkins, writing in the later eighteenth century, felt an affinity with music after 1650 while remaining distinctly cool to music of the Monteverdi generation.[17] Burney rejoiced in the 'great improvement' brought about by Carissimi, Rossi, Cesti and Stradella, and compared Corelli to his own contemporary, Haydn. Silbiger then infers that the first half of the century could be more profitably connected to the end of the previous one, the Thirty Years War being only the most obvious feature of a general period of crisis stretching back to the Reformation: 1650 thus marks the beginning of a period of relative stability, one to which some eighteenth-century historians believed themselves to be still connected. Silbiger is certainly right to observe that many genres in the later seventeenth century came to be based on longer, more consistent and more individual musical utterances, and therefore gained a substance and a stability (or instability within stability) that might warrant the label 'work'. The sonata, suite and concerto – and their constituent movements – were established in their recognisable 'modern' forms, as was the recitative–aria format, which was to survive well into the nineteenth century and beyond. Moreover, the tonal system became increasingly prevalent, influencing the entire structure of extended compositions. Something approaching the modern orchestra also dates from around this watershed, as does the development of opera as a specifically public entertainment. To Silbiger's points one could also add the evidence of contemporary writers who show a greater awareness of the individuality of pieces of music as objects of study *per se* (rather than merely as models for imitation). Thomas Mace's *Musick's Monument* (London, 1676) is primarily addressed to the practice of the lute and viola da gamba. Yet it contains general points to be observed by both composers and performers: one needs to pay particular attention to the consistency of 'fugue' throughout the course of a piece (loosely meaning the continued use of the opening theme); to the basic form of the piece (whether free, such as Prelude or Fancy, or a specific dance); and the Humour to which it corresponds.[18] In short, the development of all these issues after 1650 suggests a way of thinking that regarded pieces of music as individual entities with their own internal laws, character and consistency (most previous modes of analysis – if there be any such thing – related either to contrapuntal procedures or to the musical use of rhetorical figures). Uniqueness, individuality and originality were not necessarily at a premium, but this analytical concern with the interior of pieces of music at least rendered such considerations possible.

---

17 Silbiger, 'Music and the Crisis of Seventeenth-Century Europe'.

18 T. Mace, *Musick's Monument; or A Remembrancer of the Best Practical Musick* (London, 1676; repr. New York, 1966), p. 123.

There is clearly a difference between Silbiger's and Newcomb's conceptions of what counts as essential to the development of the work. For Newcomb, the crucial point is the autonomous musical process and product determined by a structural logic dictated by the materials at hand; for Silbiger, it is the hardening of musical forms into recognisable, replicable patterns. In both cases, however, matters might not be as clear-cut as either model suggests: abstract composerly thinking extends well beyond the rigorous counterpoint of the ricercar, while even so hardened a musical form as the concerto or the da-capo aria might often be the platform for what is essentially a performance-based genre.

Some problems

The distinction between composer- and performer-related genres – between 'work' and 'event' – suggests that if music took a step towards a stronger work-concept in one sense, it took a step backward in another. Indeed, with the splitting of styles around – and often away from – the *prima pratica* (itself immediately recycled as a *stile antico*), there was in sum a considerable loosening of the perfected rules of late sixteenth-century composition. Ironically for those looking at the seventeenth century as a necessary step towards later work-concepts, the contrapuntal rigour of Renaissance music that was to become so essential to the pedagogic background of nineteenth-century music was precisely that element which was so often subverted in the seventeenth century.

Furthermore, the very development of opera as a public institution tended to render the music subservient even while elevating its function as a major vehicle of public entertainment. Ellen Rosand has argued that, in the context of Venetian opera, there was more public focus on the librettist (considered *l'autore*) than on the composer.[19] The fact that it was the libretto, and not the music, that was printed and distributed contributed to this; moreover, more than half the librettos printed between 1637 and 1675 contain no reference to the composer concerned. Rosand also points to the considerable social presuppositions that librettists were writers whose words had a traditional claim to immortality while composers were seen more as artisans of a service profession. Librettos were expected to have dramatic coherence and literary integrity, while the music was a contingent, and impermanent, element, dependent both on the libretto and on the performers involved. If this is true, it would suggest that literature had something closer to a work-concept than did music at this time; however, it also proves that a 'work-like' thinking was possible, something that could thus conceivably be applied to music. Nevertheless, the very adaptability demanded of operatic production meant that musical texts (and,

---

19 Rosand, *Opera in Seventeenth-Century Venice*, pp. 198–220.

indeed, authorship) were more fluid than they had been in previous years (and continued to be in the case of church music, where it was the norm for texts to be much more stable). Perhaps, then, if we follow Rosand, a fixed and perfected conception of musical works would have been entirely anathema within the context of seventeenth-century Italian opera.

Could it be, though, that the entire production connected with an opera was in itself something collectively memorable, spectacular and imbued with its own sense of individuality (poetic or otherwise)?[20] Moreover, it would be an exaggeration to claim that celebrated operas had no identity that remained consistent when the production moved from place to place, even if the site of this identity remains difficult to locate. It is also clear that Monteverdi himself considered that his services as an opera composer were best employed when he himself was moved by a story that thus led him to write an integrated composition with an effective climax; otherwise the music might as well have been composed by the individual singers and the commissioner could dispense with the services of 'a single hand'.[21]

The case of Lully and his relation to the absolutist practice of Louis XIV's court also suggests that Rosand's view of Italian public opera is not necessarily valid throughout Europe. Jean-Baptiste Lully's split with Molière almost certainly owed something to the latter's sense that the music was beginning to dominate the text. Moreover, Lully owned most of the equipment and costumes for his productions at the Palais Royal, ran his company like the standing army of an absolutist monarch, and was able to direct elements of dance and drama. Here, then, there was both a fixing of musical text and performance, and the dominance of the composer over the entire production. On the other hand, Lully was quite content to leave certain elements of the compositional tasks to others; he was clearly more interested in wielding control over all aspects of the production than in striving for total purity in terms of the authorship of a notated text.

In all, then, virtually every premonition of workhood in the seventeenth century seems to be accompanied by some factors that point in the opposite direction (and vice versa). This is especially true of technological influences, such as print culture, that gave a composer the opportunity both to reach a wider audience and to work towards a definitive version of the musical text. Yet print did not necessarily enjoy a greater prestige than manuscript transmission. As Thomas Elias observes for late sixteenth-century England, print carried a stigma for its association with 'lower' forms of music such as

---

20 Strohm, '*Opus*', p. 15.
21 Monteverdi to Alessandro Striggio, 9 December 1616, in Stevens (trans.), *The Letters of Claudio Monteverdi*, pp. 108–11.

ballads and monophonic psalms.[22] Within literary circles, print was considered to threaten the exclusivity of the elite learned culture, inviting criticism and discussion by an uncontrolled and undiscriminating public. Tim Carter shows that this is exactly what happened in the Italian musical field: the reification of pieces in print for all to see, together with the widening market, generated the need for a public discourse on the nature of composition. Now 'professionals and intelligent amateurs could partake of critical discourse on musical composition and performance', something for which traditional theory was entirely inadequate.[23] Thus, a new public conception of music arose as a by-product of print culture, but not necessarily through the intentions of the composers, printers and publishers concerned.

If print did allow composers to exert some form of authorial control over multiple copies, this same development diluted the sense of individuality and the personal presence of the composer that a manuscript within an institutional performing context might have evoked. Composers such as William Byrd and Giulio Caccini followed conventions that had developed in literature by adopting an apologetic stance towards their publications, claiming that they were necessitated by the number of inaccurate copies in circulation.[24] One especially common use of print throughout Europe was to commemorate a specific event such as a court celebration or funeral.[25] Here the edition was normally designed as a reflection of something that was effectively unrepeatable, a way of distributing the aura of that event to a wider audience, but certainly not as a record of an enduring 'work' or as a prescription for later performance. Something similar might apply to the more extravagant prints of early seventeenth-century Italian secular music (opera and monody), where composers may have sought the kudos of print while still retaining 'ownership' of their music by, in effect, disabling rather than enabling performances outside their control.[26] This was clearly one significant way in which the advantages of print were used towards ends entirely antithetical to any concept of autonomous, repeatable musical works.

If print did eventually separate itself from the contingencies of manuscript culture, the acquisition of work-like qualities was the accidental by-product of a number of independent factors, few of which operated with a specific teleology in mind. Musicians undoubtedly feared the loss of their social status by

22 Elias, 'Music and Authorship in England', p. 18.

23 Carter, 'Artusi, Monteverdi, and the Poetics of Modern Music', p. 192.

24 Elias, 'Music and Authorship in England', p. 80; Carter, 'On the Composition and Performance of Caccini's *Le nuove musiche*', p. 209.

25 Bianconi, *Music in the Seventeenth Century*, p. 74; Rose, 'Music, Print and Authority in Leipzig during the Thirty Years' War', pp. 91–120.

26 Carter, 'Printing the "New Music"'.

transferring their exchange away from their patrons and more towards their paying public, and if they enjoyed greater control over the production of printed texts, this in turn lessened their control over performances.[27] But however much print culture might ultimately have contributed to the fixing of musical texts in the sixteenth century, much worked against this as the seventeenth century progressed. Publishing activities declined precipitously, especially in Italy, in the wake of the economic crisis at the end of the second decade.[28] This meant that musicians still retained a sense of the universality of sixteenth-century styles owing to the survival and reprinting of a large number of earlier publications (indeed, Monteverdi ordered six volumes of *a cappella* Masses for St Mark's, Venice, in 1614, shortly after his arrival).[29] Moreover, the production of printed church music actually rose in relation to secular publications. This may have resulted from the comparative standardisation of the Roman liturgy after the Council of Trent, which rendered church music far more transferable and stable than it had been before.[30] But the newer publications could be unashamedly modern in style, so that the church may well have been the principal venue in which one could hear both old and newer styles together. In all, though, there was a far less comprehensive view of music from closer generations: the culture of musical transmission and influence became far more local and fragmentary, something that undoubtedly confirmed the impression of the *prima pratica* as the foundation, or perhaps the counterbalance, for the more ephemeral genres of the present. Another reason for the comparative marginalisation of print culture was the fact that partbooks, the most common format of production, were increasingly unsuitable for the more modern forms of concerted music (with the possible exception of purely instrumental music).[31] In sum, then, if we accept that the later seventeenth century saw a greater concretisation of individual, formally structured pieces, this was clearly something distinct from the comparative notational fixity formerly achieved through print, especially given that publications that did present a comparatively 'finished' version of the music, such as Corelli's celebrated prints, often appeared well after the music had been formed in manuscript and by way of multiple performances.

   Some would account for the rather contradictory nature of seventeenth-century developments in musical transmission by acknowledging that the progress towards the reification of musical works was not a continuous, linear process. The same could be said for the developments of genres and styles,

27 Elias, 'Music and Authorship in England', pp. 104, 124–34.
28 Bianconi, *Music in the Seventeenth Century*, p. 77; Carter, 'Music Publishing in Italy'.
29 See Fabbri, *Monteverdi*, trans. Carter, pp. 132–3.   30 Carter, 'Music Publishing in Italy', pp. 21–3.
31 Bianconi, *Music in the Seventeenth Century*, pp. 78–9; Rose, 'Music, Print and Authority in Leipzig during the Thirty Years' War', pp. 51–7.

thus accommodating, for instance, the 'zig' of the ricercar with the 'zag' of opera within the broader cultural progress towards the musical work. We still might wonder, though, whether it is correct to see the 'strong' nineteenth-century concept of the musical work as a product of progress, or even process, and thus to view the seventeenth century as merely provisional or transitional. Karol Berger senses more an alternation of priorities over the course of several centuries, by which the bias towards formal, autonomous, internally coherent works of art (regardless of their immediate function) alternates with a more mimetic, functional, populist approach. His model thus replaces the notion of progressive development with a succession of paradigm shifts. He senses such a shift from around the 1550s away from a more abstract conception of music towards a more mimetic one, the latter relating both to verbal text and to the underlying passions. With the dominance of mimetic music, its emphasis on the performer's art and 'the popular mode of hearing in which the listener passively identifies with the personage at any given moment', Berger suggests that abstract music did not become 'modern' again until Bach's seemingly anachronistic music was adopted as a model of compositional practice after 1800.[32] If Berger's very general heuristic scheme is plausible, it would suggest that we would be wrong to concentrate on a linear progression in the development of the work-concept. Abstraction and formalism (admittedly, only two of several possible defining characteristics of the 'strong' musical work) are always a potential in Western culture, but enjoy particular esteem only at certain junctures. Thus it was not the case that they were entirely displaced or went underground in the seventeenth century; rather, they just did not have the upper hand. In this light, the increasing technical control within the abstract ricercar tradition would seem to be a rearguard action (and needless to say, it accounts for only a relatively small proportion of the music actually produced at the time).

Is it possible to form a conclusion from these various readings of the work-concept in the seventeenth century? We have the choice of seeing our period as one in which the concept continued to develop, or one in which it declined; or one in which internal structural logic declined simultaneously with a solidification of outward form. But are these contradictions to be seen as a sort of dialectic leading to the grander synthesis of the late eighteenth and nineteenth centuries? Or might not many be mistaken in assuming there to be a long-term historical process of any kind in relation to musical works? The suspicion will already have arisen that the decision as to how and whether a piece of music can be defined as a work depends on the point of view at hand. I would now

---

32 Berger, A Theory of Art, pp. 133–4.

suggest that while the foregoing discussion may have made complexities of the situation more readily evident, the status of musical works and the various developments of the era need to be examined from the broader perspective of seventeenth-century culture, looking beyond the way in which pieces of music are instantiated.

Artful artefact or social construction?

One of the most productive implications to emerge from these debates is that we should be discussing not whether works as actual objects or idealised embodiments of pieces of music existed at one time or another, but whether the interaction between ideas held about music and the various musical objects or events at hand *together* generated the various notions of the musical work. If some tend to assume that musical works are fixed objects that are inherently stable in character, others have gone too far in the opposite direction of social construction and have assumed that pieces of music exist only by virtue of the attitudes of a particular society – that there is nothing essentially 'there' beyond the cultural norms at hand. Here I am very much influenced by Bruno Latour's attitude towards the findings and 'facts' of science: rather than opting for a natural order 'out there' on the one hand, or total social construction on the other, he sees a constant circulation between the human and the non-human.[33] Facts and natural objects obviously have to be constructed in order to be accessible to the human understanding, yet they also acquire some little autonomy in return, influencing both what appears as, and how we conceive of, the world around us.

By this token, pieces of music – whether remembered, composed in the mind, notated or sounded – are obviously human constructions through and through, but they also instantaneously acquire an element of autonomy. We cannot necessarily predict how we are going to react to (or conceive of) them at any point in the future. If we are somehow changed through our encounter with music, the music must surely somehow be 'there' and not merely be something constructed by us on the spur of the moment. But what the argument for social constructivism does indeed show us, is that what is 'there' is not a stable entity that endures regardless of the energy we bring to it.

In examining the possibility of work-concepts before the nineteenth century, most music historians tend to look for similarities linking one age to another. But some who are sceptical of an earlier work-concept, namely Goehr herself, look for differences. To her, apparent similarities, such as the perfection of a notated musical text or a canon of commendable pieces of music, hide profound

---

33 Latour, *Pandora's Hope*.

differences in culture by which the meaning of a perfected text or commendable exemplar was entirely different. It is clear that Goehr tends to homogenise the extremely complex and varied attitudes to pieces of music before 1800, ignoring factors that in some respect come close to elements of the later work-concept, but certainly there is sense in her suggestion that we examine backwards rather than forwards the concepts we ourselves hold dear.[34] Indeed, most forms of significant artistic influence result from the intentional activity of the receiver drawing on the past and from ideas already at hand. But we cannot simply assume that any innovation of a past era was made with anything close to the aim we might now attribute to it.

This anti-teleological point is, of course, one of the central – if unsung – elements of Darwinian evolution.[35] The concept of evolution, however, is more popularly associated with a process that is progressive and developmental, one in which there is some ideal end in mind even if earlier actors were not aware of this. This relates to the so-called Whiggish approach to history, in which aspects of the past are highlighted for their foreshadowing of a more perfect and enlightened present. There is absolutely nothing wrong with finding resonances between past and present – this is, after all, one of the crucial functions of history, which serves to enhance our own sense of belonging to a broader culture of humanity. But this should not be confused with a notion of the past anticipating the developments of the future. The Whiggish approach also tends to undervalue aspects of the past that do not conform to its particular model of progress; it may well render us ignorant of alternative concepts, events, styles or pieces from which we might be able to learn. This is especially pertinent in our study of music in the seventeenth century, when the very instability of concepts of music led to a degree of experimentation that was possibly unprecedented. Many pieces from this time would be undervalued or ignored if we judged them according to whether they were 'hot' or 'cold' in relation to a game of work-hood hide-and-seek. As is already obvious, the seventeenth century provides a particularly fascinating lesson in revealing how the development of later concepts was not necessarily achieved in a straight line; the necessary conditions obviously had to occur (and endure) at one stage or another, but they almost always originated in entirely different purposes.

The seventeenth century as contradiction

The contradictory nature of the early seventeenth century is central to William J. Bouwsma's analysis of 'the waning of the Renaissance'. He notes many aspects

---

34 Goehr, '"On the Problems of Dating" or "Looking Backward and Forward with Strohm"'.
35 Dennett, *The Intentional Stance*, pp. 319–21.

of Renaissance thought that encouraged a sense of human individuality crucial for a culture that could conceive of unique, individual authorship and unique, individual artistic products. Thus far, then, he seems to provide substantiation for Strohm's and Newcomb's observations of musical practice in the fifteenth and sixteenth centuries.

Yet this era also brought with it a profound degree of reaction that attempted to restore the old certainties of scholastic thought. The traditional concept of the self saw human reason as somehow parallel to God's, and considered everything else – the will, passions and the body – as laid out below reason in a hierarchy, and fundamentally corrupted by sin. Under this scheme, anything that cultivated individuality or originality was seen, at best, as mistaken, and at worst, as a form of heresy against the only true Creator. Of course, there were alternative views, some of which became more dominant during the Renaissance. Most important among these was the Augustinian sense of the heart as giver of life, will and the passions; now it was possible to conceive of the self – as did Montaigne – as a single, mysterious unity, somehow unique given the countless permutations of passions and wilful urges. Indeed, works of art could be just as various as humans themselves. This move evidently parallels the Humanist desire for music that related directly to the passions. For many, now it was the supposedly rational intellect that erred. Sidney (1580) even claimed that the poet, with divine inspiration, could transcend that which was already given in nature.[36] As Tim Carter notes, Monteverdi's 'natural path to imitation' was, in reality, a use of art to improve upon nature.[37]

Nevertheless, if we follow Bouwsma, we would be unwise to underestimate the hostile reaction to this neo-Augustinian sense of self. There was a growing pressure to re-establish order and the old hierarchy governed by reason; many condemned invention as a form of hypocrisy; and even thinkers as profound as Bacon inveighed against the over-use of imagination.[38] It was, of course, the fear of disorder that also motivated Giovanni Maria Artusi (1600) in his condemnation of Monteverdi's compositional licences,[39] a polemic that was still very much alive in German disputes over compositional practice fifty years later. In this respect, the movement towards seemingly autonomous *stile antico* composition was more reactionary than progressive.

While scholastic forms of rationalism had seen rationality as somehow corresponding with all other elements of creation, Descartes almost unwittingly inaugurated a new rational tradition by throwing all forms of sensation and

---

36 Bouwsma, *The Waning of the Renaissance*, pp. 21–3, 30.
37 Carter, 'Resemblance and Representation', p. 134.
38 Bouwsma, *The Waning of the Renaissance*, pp. 140, 165, 169.
39 Strunk, *Source Readings in Music History, Revised Edition*, iv: *The Baroque Era*, pp. 18–36.

subjectivism into doubt, initiating a long-lived divorce between mind and body. As Arthur C. Danto has noted:

> the first famous meditation in which everything is darkened by the shadow of doubt is really a strategic move by someone anxious that doubt be cast on matters ordinarily regarded as certain beyond sane question, in order to abort a spontaneous contrast between them and matters ordinarily construed as abstruse, as items of mere faith and orthodoxy, like our immortality and the existence of a perfect being, which in fact, he contends, are luminously secure.[40]

This was also the age of Neoplatonic academies, reinforcing order in those very sciences and arts that had threatened anarchy. Bouwsma's point is not, of course, that all the charisma and freedom unleashed by the Renaissance were simply reversed, but, rather, that these continued to develop in the wake of an increasingly organised opposition. Thus it would be wrong to consider the sixteenth century (in music or in broader culture) as a sort of golden age and the seventeenth as an era of reaction: it was the very conflict between the systems that generated one of the most fertile centuries, a conflict that was central to the birth of modernity. It was also the reworking of rationalism in an era of uncertainty that ultimately heralded the familiar musical work of the classical tradition. But rationality as it stood in the seventeenth century was hardly hospitable ground for notions of artistic individuality or for the separation of musical works from the everyday world of human experience. If Descartes's mind–body distinction is frequently blamed for creating the cerebral abstractness of the so-called classical canon, he would doubtless have conceived of music as an element of mathematical and natural certainty rather than as a potentially unique form of human achievement.

Individuality within a culture of imitation

Given that almost all speculative music theorists of the seventeenth century continued to see music as something intimately connected to the structure of the universe, it remains to be seen how composers could assert their individuality, and how pieces of music could readily be distinguished from one another. Of course, it may well be that theory characteristically lingered behind practice, and that elements of originality and uniqueness were appreciated more in the 'practical' realm of composition. One way in which theory and practice may have coincided was in the sense that notation could embody the most perfect representation of a piece of music; this was something implied by theorists

---

40 Danto, *The Body/Body Problem*, p. 194.

working in the German *musica poetica* tradition inaugurated by Listenius.[41]
But such perfection usually related to contrapuntal integrity (and thus to a
comparatively narrow area of the repertory), and not to the individuality of
the piece concerned. Perfection or fixity of text thus does not automatically
guarantee 'work' in the stronger sense.

The concept of compositional perfection as held at the outset of the seventeenth century thus tended to work against the idea of the composer as original
genius. Lodovico Zacconi in 1591, for instance, mentions originality as a feature of style – indeed he is one of the first to allow several different categories
of compositional style – but his main concern is with the traditional rhetorical
task of establishing exemplars worthy of imitation.[42] In other words, while it
is undoubtedly correct that Renaissance composers gained more fame through
the autonomy their compositions enjoyed, they may not necessarily have been
admired specifically for their originality. And even if composers did indeed
gain a measure of originality by creatively breaking rules for special effect, such
was the culture of imitation that these licences were themselves soon rendered
part of the general language, and thus no longer original.

From the outset of the seventeenth century, theorists and critics had the
choice either of condemning transgressions (e.g., Artusi) that went beyond
the traditional norms of 'reason', or of somehow accommodating them within
or beside the older conceptions of music by allowing for a plurality of styles.
Adriano Banchieri divided music basically into that which conformed to the
norms of Zarlino and that which attempted to portray the affections; in other
words that which followed the heart rather than the traditional dictates of
reason.[43] This sense of plurality was to be developed by numerous theorists,
all tending to assume that stylistic differences in music had inevitable affective
consequences. Christoph Bernhard, writing around the middle of the century
in Germany, may have managed to prolong the ancient belief that music corresponded to the natural world by asserting that all modern styles are grounded
in the 'natural' style of the *prima pratica*, a point that is also latent in earlier
Italian writing,[44] but it was something of a rearguard action.

Perhaps the most significant attempt at accounting for a new sense of human
individuality without dropping the notion of music representing an objective
reality was Athanasius Kircher's, half-way through the century (in his *Musurgia
universalis* published in 1650). The *stylus impressus* relates to the way in which

---

41 This is covered extensively in Loesch, *Der Werkbegriff in der protestantischen Musiktheorie des 16. und
17. Jahrhunderts*.

42 Elias, 'Music and Authorship in England', p. 48.

43 Collins, 'The *Stylus phantasticus* and its Expression in Free Keyboard Music of the North German
Baroque', pp. 8–9.

44 Carter, '"An Air New and Grateful to the Ear"', p. 129.

music has different effects on people of different temperaments, and the *stylus expressus* to the calculated stylistic characteristics of the composition itself; the latter comprises Kircher's version of the plurality of stylistic categories. Most striking for our purposes is Kircher's definition of the *stylus phantasticus* which, superficially, might seem to offer a free rein to the composer's imagination – it is 'an extremely free and uninhibited method of composition particularly suitable for instrumental music' – therefore giving rise to the notion of the musical work untrammelled by style, function and context.[45] Yet freedom to Kircher is merely freedom from the constraints of a cantus firmus, text or dance: he continues to insist that the composer adhere to the perfection of compositional rules. Kircher thus effectively justifies the cultivation of *stile antico* keyboard works, arguably the closest genre to absolute music during the early Baroque. But this is clearly quite different – in terms of the intentions behind it – from the absolute music of the nineteenth century. No genre went further to efface the individuality of the composer. What counted was his skill in realising the potentials according to a naturalised norm.

Another irony is that music of the *prima pratica* was later seen as the most perfected genre, its rules of dissonance and voice-leading classicised in the music of Giovanni Pierluigi da Palestrina. Yet at least some of this music was originally performed with levels of improvised ornamentation that would have wrecked the notated perfection (at least according to the rules of strict Renaissance counterpoint). Quite possibly Palestrina would not have objected: he may well have thought of ideal, paper music and sounding, performed music as two intersecting but not coterminous forms of music.[46] The calls for a control on ornamentation come not just from conservatives like Artusi but also from 'modern' composers such as Caccini, anxious that the expressive arsenal improvised by performers be adequately captured and controlled to present the textual affects correctly.[47] Yet this call to compositional attention comes from a composer who, by the standards of strict counterpoint, was barely composing at all, reducing the principal lines to two and exploiting dissonant licences to expressive effect. With the development of improvised accompaniments and figured bass, the music's fixity was essentially lessened, its identity on paper rendered less precise (at least in terms of prescribed pitches and rhythms). And although composers sometimes insisted on the proper use of ornaments, this was perhaps more for preserving an assumed connection with objective passions than necessarily an assertion of the individuality and uniqueness of a work. If Caccini seems to insist on his authorial prerogatives, this might relate more

---

45 Bianconi, *Music in the Seventeenth Century*, pp. 49–50.   46 Butt, *Playing with History*, pp. 119–20.
47 Carter, 'On the Composition and Performance of Caccini's *Le nuove musiche*', p. 209.

to his reputation as a skilled, flamboyant performer than to his desire to fix the music eternally in notation. Moreover, it is highly likely that some of the most spectacular solo numbers, such as Monteverdi's 'Possente spirto e formidabil nume' (*Orfeo*, 1607) and Arianna's lament (*Arianna*, 1608), were heavily influenced by the styles of the singers involved; they might even partially be records of what the singer actually did.

The erosion of contrapuntal integrity continued, even in church music, and was much lamented by Heinrich Schütz, who, like his student Bernhard, tried to shore up the increasing laxity by maintaining that the new style was firmly grounded in the old.[48] Yet the dominance of thorough-bass thinking grew to the extent that, by the end of the century, German Lutheran theorists tended to see it as the fundamental grounding of harmony rather than as something to be adopted as a shorthand, only after the true laws of composition had been absorbed. In this tradition at least, counterpoint thus became something of an optional 'finishing school'.

If composers settled on a style and developed a compositional method somewhere between the traditional rules of intervallic counterpoint and the more modern practice of thorough-bass, how did they themselves view the task of producing a new piece of music? The key concept spanning both sixteenth- and seventeenth-century compositional thought was 'imitatio', the imitation of admired models. This generally aimed more towards greater perfection of the art in general than greater individuality.[49] Given the ubiquity of this attitude to musical composition (shared in literary composition, too), it would be incorrect to infer that the veneration of canonic models was evidence of an emergent work-concept, as has recently been proposed.[50] It was something essential to the Classical world that had survived – and had been periodically revived – well into the seventeenth century (after which it receded). As Thomas Mace mentioned in 1676, invention is the 'Great, and Principal Matter of a Composer', one that is no better learned than through reading discourses on composition and studying choice musical examples.[51]

The veneration of past authorities, using imitation as a spur to invention, was central to the Classical rhetorical education (and practised within the commonplacebook tradition) that persisted through to the eighteenth century. Nevertheless, there was a move in the direction of originality, directly parallel to the increased individuation of the thinking subject. Not surprisingly, it was Descartes who most forcefully expressed the rejection of the assumption that past authorities were automatically to be followed; authority was now to be

48 Butt, 'Towards a Genealogy of the Keyboard Concerto'.
49 Berger, *A Theory of Art*, p. 117; Brown, 'Emulation, Competition, and Homage'.
50 White, '"If it's Baroque, Don't Fix it"'.   51 Mace, *Musick's Monument*, 138.

located in the individual, reasoning subject. As Cervantes had already written in the prologue to *Don Quixote* (1605), he contrived 'a story filled with thoughts that never occurred to anyone else'. He wondered, in irony, how the public would receive this tale

> wholly lacking in learning and wisdom, without marginal citations or notes at the end of the book when other works of this sort . . . are so packed with maxims from Aristotle and Plato and the whole crowd of philosophers as to fill the reader with admiration and lead him to regard the author as a well read, learned, and eloquent individual[.][52]

We may thus infer that composers were pulled in several directions: to conform to an established canon of model musical textures; to capture an assumed natural connection between music and the affects; and to produce an element of novelty, paralleling the growing sense of individual identity. Even in the late seventeenth century, young composers seem to have pursued a rather unsystematic approach to learning composition. They were probably pedagogically conditioned to devise their own 'heads' (i.e., categories of useful elements to imitate), their own way of learning all they could from what was lent by the authority of the past. All previous styles – whether strict or free – could be seen through the magpie eyes of the Baroque as other characters to impersonate, other costumes to be worn. One would study musical grammar for refinement and stylistic etiquette, but – if the quality and originality of the best music is anything to go by – much of the work was done intuitively and almost unconsciously.

'Disenchantment' and 're-enchantment'

Whatever new sense of individuality did indeed evolve during the course of the seventeenth century, this was against the background of an overriding belief that music was still grounded in natural and universal rules governing all musicians regardless of their local differences. However wary we might be of the dangerous assumptions that can hide under the word 'natural', many, if pressed, would probably opine that the mimetic, seemingly spontaneous music of the *seconda pratica* is in some sense more 'natural' than the restrictive dissonance rules and affective neutrality of the *prima pratica*. Yet to its adherents of the time (and perhaps some today), late Renaissance polyphony embodied assumed natural laws that connected music directly to the rest of creation; all systems belonged together under a sort of supernature.[53] At best,

---

52 Cervantes, *The History of Don Quixote de la Mancha*, p. xiii.
53 Chua, 'Vincenzo Galilei, Modernity and the Division of Nature', p. 18.

the aspect of nature embodied in the passions would have been a lesser one. At worst, the emphasis on the heart rather than the mind was the beginning of a slippery slope towards anarchy. This point demonstrates very clearly the way in which seemingly abstract *prima pratica/stile antico* music was so fundamentally different in conception from the more 'absolute' branches of music in the nineteenth century. The abstractness of perfected Renaissance counterpoint was testimony to its contiguity with the whole chain of being, which, after all, had never been immediately evident to the naked eye. The abstractness of later, stronger work-concepts, on the other hand, was testimony to the very separation of the world conjured by art from the world itself.

There is obviously no hard-and-fast way of explaining the general change in thinking that was beginning in the seventeenth century itself, and of which music was both symptom and partial cause. Foucault's theory of the move from a system of knowledge based on resemblance to one based on representation is perhaps the most widely known approach to these issues. Tim Carter develops this in the musical field by observing that music's affective codes became increasingly stylised in the seventeenth century, dictated more by convention than by literalistic mimesis. This could obviously relate to the increasing degree of structural control over the music, that hardened into recognisably 'modern' forms in the latter half of the century. Carter also notes that the 'distance' cultivated between the means of representation and the thing represented is balanced by an increasing verisimilitude on the part of the representing voice (with each now more likely to represent a single, consistent character).[54] This might reflect a growing sense of the subjective differentiation and uniqueness of each individual, and the need for human rationalised constructs as a way of controlling an increasingly alien natural world.

The related theoretical conception of 'disenchantment' is particularly relevant to the discussion of the development of the concept of works. Theories of disenchantment, first formulated by Max Weber, highlight the gradual move from the veneration of past ancestors and authorities, and reliance on beliefs in a wider religious order, towards materialism, control of nature and bountiful information; one becomes alienated from the objects disenchanted, precisely as these become more familiar and comprehensible within a rationalised taxonomic system.[55] 'Works' in the strong sense might serve to shore up this loss by providing alternative worlds where wholeness still pertains. Willem Erauw draws attention to a particular point made in Goehr's thesis concerning

---

54 Foucault, *The Order of Things*; Carter, 'Resemblance and Representation'; Carter, '"Sfogava con le stelle" Reconsidered', p. 164. For a counter-argument, see Karol Berger's review-essay on Tomlinson, *Music in Renaissance Magic*, in *Journal of Musicology*, 13 (1995), 404–23.
55 Chua, 'Vincenzo Galilei, Modernity and the Division of Nature'.

the development of musical works around 1800, namely that cultural activities assumed the transcendental function that a declining religious practice could no longer provide.[56] He sees essential practices in reception, such as the motionless concert audience and reverence for the musical score, as being specifically religious in nature. From this viewpoint based on reception, it is possible to see why there is at least a conceptual problem in considering earlier music as instantiating works in the strongest sense.

The increased emphasis on subjectivity and individuality in the seventeenth century – and by extension, on some notions of workhood – can also be seen as a compensation for the increasing uncertainty of the natural order. It is therefore plausible that an increasing sense of individuality in musical composition does indeed parallel a stronger conception of human individuality and subjective presence. Yet this – almost paradoxically – does not necessarily reflect a deeper confidence in the human condition, but more a reaction to a loss of security within the wider order of things. Descartes's famous move was to advocate the total certainty of the thinking – or rather, doubting – mind, compensating for the absolute uncertainty of everything else. The whole of nature is swapped for the unshakeable nature of one's own existence. Reason, no longer at one with surrounding nature, becomes a tool to dissect the world. Hobbes represents the other wing of this disenchantment with nature, by which human order no longer has an unmediated connection with the raw, natural order of the world. While he is careful not to disbelieve in miracles, he is sceptical as to whether we can distinguish a true miracle from the products of our own ignorance or imagination; enchantment is, more often than not, 'imposture and delusion wrought by ordinary means'.[57]

From the very outset of Hobbes's *Leviathan* (1651), the 'art' of man consists in constructing artefacts in imitation of nature, which are in essence no different from the given automaton of the human body, as already created by God. The human creation of the state is but a further fabrication of this kind. If such a common power is not constructed, man reverts to a kind of war and famously experiences life as 'solitary, poor, nasty, brutish and short'. It is not so much that there is brutish nature on the one hand and human civilisation on the other, but that humans need to construct order out of the various conflicting natural orders at hand (which, unchecked, represent the condition of 'mere nature' in which all would recklessly pursue absolute liberty and thus bring about a condition of anarchy and war). Men avoid the condition of 'mere nature' by following rational precepts that are themselves the 'laws of nature'.[58] Hobbes's

56 Goehr, *The Imaginary Museum of Musical Works*, p. 157; Erauw, 'Canon Formation'.
57 Hobbes, *Leviathan*, pp. 137, 189.   58 Ibid., pp. 85–9, 159.

principal departure from the old thinking of mankind as part of a broader chain of being is that the human must take a more active role in ordering nature. The artificial is as necessary as the natural and is indeed part of a more refined aspect of nature. Something of this attitude is evident in the way in which musical instruments rose in importance in the course of the century: the fascination with describing and cataloguing instruments may well be part of the wider view of using artifice to improve nature and extend human capabilities.[59] Another development was noted by Max Weber, in his linking of the move away from 'natural' tuning towards tempered systems within the broader process of 'rationalisation'.[60] Human capabilities are greatly enhanced by the imposition of an ordered, rational system that patently ignores the 'natural purity' of musical intervals in order to extend the tonal system. Music thus moves out of the natural world into a seemingly richer one of its own.

The rationalism so central to the scholastic tradition is resurrected as an abstract form of reason no longer directly connected to everything else. To arch-rationalists like Descartes and Spinoza, the passions are to be understood in painstaking detail in order that they can be mastered by reason. History and commonplace truths are now to be mistrusted, and each subject has to form itself with its own intentions and desires. The political corollary of this is, of course, the rise of the absolutist monarch in which the will of the individual subject is complicit. According to Hobbes, the sovereign's power comes from the authorising power of the subjects, a newly charged sense of authorship working hand in hand with a new transcendental sense of subjectivity and will, of which the sovereign is a representation.[61] Political and social behaviour were regulated no longer by the assumption of a natural order, but more by the concept of an abstract, transcendental position of subjectivity.[62] Hobbes's sense of authority also suggests that a circulating process is involved, one by which authority itself depends on the will of those in an apparently passive position. In the context of art, this would suggest that while the concept of individual authorship is elevated, this is at the same time dependent on the collective will of those who receive the work composed. We might also recall the example of Lully here, strongly complicit in authorising his monarch's power, but also creating his own authority within the same hierarchy. A stronger seventeenth-century concept of the musical work thus corresponds to a stronger concept of human subjectivity that, in turn, coincides with the rise of absolutism (a 'modern' development despite its seemingly retrograde political direction).

59 Austern, "''Tis Nature's Voice'", pp. 44–5.
60 Weber, *Die rationalen und sozialen Grundlagen der Musik.*
61 Hobbes, *Leviathan*, p. 100.   62 Cascardi, *The Subject of Modernity*, p. 43.

One exceptionally illuminating theory of the role of art in this period is Lukács's of the novel: to Lukács, Cervantes's *Don Quixote* is the first true novel, in which the old epic practices no longer connect to the surrounding totality. The form of the novel thus compensates for the actual disenchantment of the surrounding world by its very irony. According to Lukács, Cervantes was writing at a time 'when man became lonely and could find meaning and substance only in his own soul, whose home was nowhere; when the world, released from its paradoxical anchorage in a beyond that is truly present, was abandoned to its immanent meaninglessness'. The period was that 'of the last, great desperate mysticism . . . a period of a new view of the world rising up in mystical forms; the last period of truly lived but already disoriented, tentative, sophisticated, occult aspirations'.[63] The autonomy of the novel, its formal re-enchantment within its fictional world, its very inessential yet vital place in its culture, thus show the beginnings of crucial traits in a new conception of art, that 'raised the most confused problematic into the radiant sphere of a transcendence which achieved its full flowering as *form*'.[64] This sense of distance from the world, this consciousness of the autonomy of art, clearly resonates with the strong concept of the musical work as it reached its full flowering in later centuries. However much this type of art resembles aspects of the surrounding world, there is no longer a process of direct imitation, an uncomplicated correspondence between the world pictured and the world from which we read. To Lukács our consciousness of the disintegration and inadequacy of the world is the precondition for the existence of high art and of its becoming conscious and autonomous. Cervantes, incidentally, also raises the stakes for the concept of authorship, first by feigning ignorance of authorities to quote, then by quoting spurious sources and by handing the narrative over to a fictional Arab author. The very play with the concept of authorship thus solidifies Cervantes's own self-constructed subjectivity. On the one hand, workhood is strengthened by the effacement of a concept of simple possessive authorship ('work' thus corresponding to a greater degree of autonomy); on the other, authorship is elevated through its very artificiality, as something somehow appearing behind the feigned authorities of the narrative – indeed, as a factor of the text itself ('work' thus corresponding to a new, richer, but ultimately uncertain sense of author).

If Lukács is right, then there *are* actual traces of struggle, irony, distancing, disenchantment and re-enchantment within artefacts that should be described as 'works' in the strong sense. The work-concept may indeed widely reside in the culture of reception but it also leaves its tell-tale traces in the artefacts

63 Lukács, *The Theory of the Novel*, pp. 103–4.   64 Ibid., p. 130.

concerned. In this somewhat demanding conception, Goehr may well be correct to doubt the existence of musical works long before 1800. It is clear that seventeenth-century music did not generally enjoy that degree of transferability and detachment from its contexts that literature was beginning to experience. One can, of course, point towards developments in compositional practice that do show a sense of abstraction – most significantly an increasing interest in musical form, even in genres, such as opera, where the music was assumed to serve other functions. One might even be able to find examples where musico-dramatic works become self-reflexive, directly commentating on their contrivance and necessary detachment from the world. As Chua observes, it is perhaps no accident that early operas so frequently concentrate on music in the form of the Orpheus myth as a medium of re-enchantment, a nostalgia for an ancient age in which music actually had magic power.[65] Operas that interrogate the nature of political power and the responsibilities it brings (e.g., *L'incoronazione di Poppea*) might also come closer to the notion of disenchantment. However, there is no certain way in which this evidence of disenchantment within a few opera texts is paralleled in the music, save by treating music as itself a disenchanting (i.e., alienating) force, or by attributing to it the capacity for irony. Indeed, such is the complexity of issues of authority, commission, intention and collaboration in early opera, that disenchantment – if there is such – is the net result of these factors and not easily to be attributed to a single composer or librettist. It is precisely the ambiguity as to what music represents or reflects, and by whose authority, that renders seventeenth-century music so fascinating. Perhaps this was even one of the few eras in music history when it was possible for music simply to represent itself, a form of pleasure fortuitously falling between a former age of conformity to hidden natural order and later ones of supercharged authorial will.

This brings us back to the question of pieces that exploit a particular issue of compositional theory. Can these pieces really be 'works' if they presuppose a continuity between the fabric of the music and the structure of the world? Indeed, this would seem to suggest that they reflect the survival of a form of musical thought that is yet to be disenchanted, and thus considerably more distant from the 'strong' work-concept than might at first seem apparent. In some cases, perhaps, they may approach 'full' workhood if they integrate theoretical concerns into a piece that is formed through other considerations (e.g., following an external structure such as a dance), or if they are in some way detached from the technical task by a form of irony (e.g., Frescobaldi's keyboard *capriccio* based on the call of a cuckoo). The fact remains, though,

65 Chua, 'Vincenzo Galilei, Modernity and the Division of Nature', pp. 25–6.

that most music-making was still connected to traditional institutions such as church and court, and, intellectually, the assumption of a connection between music and the natural order was slow to erode – indeed, it was hardly in musicians' interests that this should be allowed to happen. While there is some evidence of a decline in the status of traditional *musica theorica*, particularly in France, and a general move of music from the scientific *quadrivium* to the human arts of the *trivium* (thus continuing a Renaissance tendency as encapsulated by the Florentine Camerata),[66] there were equally strong movements towards restoring the relationship between music and mathematical nature in the latter half of the century.[67]

In all, we should be very cautious in assuming that pieces approaching musical autonomy were autonomous in the same way as later works, and were not intended to preserve some sense of the hidden chain of being. I am not trying to argue that no music from the seventeenth century can be treated, elevated or 'retrofitted' as a 'work', since the very concepts of workhood are inherent not just in a musical manifestation in sound or on paper, but in the circulation between these and the wider concepts both held in the period and evolving through reception. It might also be relevant that some Baroque music designed for religious worship transferred particularly easily into nineteenth-century aesthetics, in which music and the formal experience of the concert became a sort of substitute religion. But while it is extremely important to note that certain aspects of thought and culture developed in the seventeenth century would eventually become crucial in the construction of the stronger work-concepts, we should never presume that the earlier period ever had the latter in mind.

Bibliography

Austern, L. P., ""'Tis Nature's Voice": Music, Natural Philosophy and the Hidden World in Seventeenth-Century England'. In Clark and Rehding (eds), *Music Theory and Natural Order from the Renaissance to the Early Twentieth Century*, pp. 30–67

Berger, K., review-essay on G. Tomlinson, *Music in Renaissance Magic: Toward a Historiography of Others* (1993). *Journal of Musicology*, 13 (1995), 404–23

A Theory of Art. New York and Oxford, 2000

Bianconi, L., *Music in the Seventeenth Century*, trans. D. Bryant. Cambridge, 1987

Bouwsma, W. J., *The Waning of the Renaissance 1550–1640*. New Haven and London, 2000

Brown, H. M., 'Emulation, Competition, and Homage: Imitation and Theories of Imitation in the Renaissance'. *Journal of the American Musicological Society*, 35 (1982), 1–48

66 Fend, 'Seventeenth-Century Criticisms of the Use of Analogy and Symbolism in Music Theory'; Chua, 'Vincenzo Galilei, Modernity and the Division of Nature', p. 28.

67 Rivera, *German Music Theory in the Early Seventeenth Century*, p. 29; Austern, ""'Tis Nature's Voice"'.

Butt, J., 'Germany and the Netherlands'. In A. Silbiger (ed.), *Keyboard Music before 1700*. 2nd edn, New York, 2003, pp. 147-234

Playing with History: the Historical Approach to Musical Performance. Cambridge, 2002

'Towards a Genealogy of the Keyboard Concerto'. In C. Hogwood (ed.), *The Keyboard in Baroque Europe*. Cambridge, 2003, pp. 93-110

Carter, T., 'On the Composition and Performance of Caccini's *Le nuove musiche* (1602)'. *Early Music*, 12 (1984), 208-17

'Music Publishing in Italy, c.1580-c.1625: Some Preliminary Observations'. *Royal Musical Association Research Chronicle*, 20 (1986-7), 19-37

Artusi, Monteverdi, and the Poetics of Modern Music'. In N. K. Baker and B. R. Hanning (eds), *Musical Humanism and its Legacy: Essays in Honor of Claude V. Palisca*. Stuyvesant, NY, 1992, pp. 171-94

'"An Air New and Grateful to the Ear": the Concept of *aria* in Late Renaissance and Early Baroque Italy'. *Music Analysis*, 12 (1993), 127-45

'*Possente spirto*: on Taming the Power of Music'. *Early Music*, 21 (1993), 517-22

'Resemblance and Representation: Towards a New Aesthetic in the Music of Monteverdi. In I. Fenlon and T. Carter (eds), '*Con che soavità*': *Studies in Italian Opera, Song, and Dance, 1580-1740*. Oxford, 1995, pp. 118-34

'"Sfogava con le stelle" Reconsidered: Some Thoughts on the Analysis of Monteverdi's Mantuan Madrigals'. In P. Besutti, T. M. Gialdroni and R. Baroncini (eds), *Claudio Monteverdi: studi e prospettive; atti del convegno, Mantova, 21-24 ottobre 1993*. Florence, 1998, pp. 147-70

'Printing the "New Music"'. In K. van Orden (ed.), *Music and the Cultures of Print*. New York and London, 2000, pp. 3-37

Cascardi, A. J., *The Subject of Modernity*. Cambridge, 1992

Cervantes, M. de, *The History of Don Quixote de la Mancha*, trans. S. Putnam. Chicago, 1952; repr. 1993

Chua, D. K. L., 'Vincenzo Galilei, Modernity and the Division of Nature'. In Clark and Rehding (eds), *Music Theory and Natural Order from the Renaissance to the Early Twentieth Century*, pp. 17-29

Clark, S., and Rehding, A. (eds), *Music Theory and Natural Order from the Renaissance to the Early Twentieth Century*. Cambridge, 2001

Collins, P., 'The *Stylus phantasticus* and its Expression in Free Keyboard Music of the North German Baroque'. Ph.D. thesis, National University of Ireland, Maynooth (2001)

Dahlhaus, C., *Grundlagen der Musikgeschichte* (1977), as *Foundations of Music History*, trans. J. B. Robinson. Cambridge, 1983

Danto, A. C., *The Body/Body Problem: Selected Essays*. Berkeley and Los Angeles, 2001

Dennett, D. C., *The Intentional Stance*. Cambridge, MA, 1987

Elias, T. P., 'Music and Authorship in England 1575-1632'. Ph.D. thesis, University of Cambridge (2000)

Erauw, W., 'Canon Formation: Some More Reflections on Lydia Goehr's *Imaginary Museum of Musical Works*'. *Acta musicologica*, 70 (1998), 109-15

Fabbri, P., *Monteverdi*, trans. T. Carter. Cambridge, 1994

Fend, M., 'Seventeenth-Century Criticisms of the Use of Analogy and Symbolism in Music Theory'. *Miscellanea musicologica: Adelaide Studies in Musicology*, 17 (1990), 54-64

Foucault, M., *The Order of Things: an Archeology of the Human Sciences*. London, 1970; repr. 1989

Goehr, L., *The Imaginary Museum of Musical Works: an Essay in the Philosophy of Music*. Oxford, 1992

'"On the Problems of Dating" or "Looking Backward and Forward with Strohm"'. In Talbot (ed.), *The Musical Work*, pp. 231–46

Hobbes, T., *Leviathan, or Matter, Form, and Power of a Commonwealth Ecclesiastical and Civil* (1651). Chicago, 1952; repr. 1994

Latour, B., *Pandora's Hope: Essays on the Reality of Science Studies*. Cambridge, MA, 1999

Loesch, H. von, *Der Werkbegriff in der protestantischen Musiktheorie des 16. und 17. Jahrhunderts: Ein Mißverständnis*. Hildesheim, 2001

Lukács, G., *The Theory of the Novel: a Historico-Philosophical Essay on the Forms of Great Epic Literature* (1916), trans. A. Bostock. Cambridge, MA, 1971; repr. 1999

Newcomb, A., *The Madrigal at Ferrara, 1579–97*. 2 vols, Princeton, 1980

'Notions of Notation and the Concept of the Work, 1550–1640'. Paper presented at the conference *Musical Improvisation, Description, Notation, 1570–1620*, London, British Academy, 19–21 April 2002

Owens, J. A., *Composers at Work: the Craft of Musical Composition 1450–1600*. New York and Oxford, 1997

Powers, H. S., 'A Canonical Museum of Imaginary Music'. *Current Musicology*, 60–61 (1996), 5–25

Rivera, B. V., *German Music Theory in the Early Seventeenth Century: the Treatises of Johannes Lippius*. Ann Arbor, 1980

Rosand, E., *Opera in Seventeenth-Century Venice: the Creation of a Genre*. Berkeley, Los Angeles and Oxford, 1991

Rose, S., 'Music, Print and Authority in Leipzig during the Thirty Years' War'. 2 vols, Ph.D. thesis, University of Cambridge (2001)

Schwörer-Kohl, G., 'Zum Werkbegriff in der Ethnomusikologie und in der historischen Musikwissenschaft'. In C.-H. Mahling (ed.), *Ethnomusikologie und historische Musikwissenschaft: Erich Stockmann zum 70. Geburtstag*, 'Mainzer Studien zur Musikwissenschaft', 36. Mainz, 1997, pp. 313–24

Seidel, W., *Werk und Werkbegriff in der Musikgeschichte*, 'Erträge der Forschung', 246. Darmstadt, 1987

Silbiger, A., 'Music and the Crisis of Seventeenth-Century Europe'. In V. Coelho (ed.), *Music and Science in the Age of Galileo*. Dordrecht, 1992, pp. 35–44

Stevens, D. (trans.), *The Letters of Claudio Monteverdi*. 2nd edn, Oxford, 1995

Strohm, R., *The Rise of European Music 1380–1500*. Cambridge, 1993

'Looking Back at Ourselves: the Problem with the Musical Work-Concept'. In Talbot (ed.), *The Musical Work*, pp. 128–52

'*Opus*: Aspects of the History of the Musical Work-Concept, and a Post-Modern Antidote to Anxieties over the Beethovenian Prototype' (MS, 2003)

Strunk, O., *Source Readings in Music History, Revised Edition*, iv: *The Baroque Era*, ed. M. Murata. New York and London, 1998

Talbot, M. (ed.), *The Musical Work: Reality or Invention?*. Liverpool, 2000

Weber, M., *Die rationalen und sozialen Grundlagen der Musik*, appendix to *Wirtschaft und Gesellschaft* (written 1911, pub. 1921), trans. as *The Rational and Social Foundations of Music*, ed. D. Martindale, J. Riedel and G. Neuwirth. Carbondale, IL, 1958

White, H., '"If it's Baroque, Don't Fix it": Reflections on Lydia Goehr's "Work-Concept" and the Historical Integrity of Musical Composition'. *Acta musicologica*, 69 (1997), 94–104

Wiora, W., *Das musikalische Kunstwerk*. Tutzing, 1983

'Das musikalische Kunstwerk der Neuzeit und das musikalische Kunstwerk der Antike'. In H. Danuser, H. de la Motte-Haber, S. Leopold and N. Miller (eds), *Festschrift Carl Dahlhaus zum 60. Geburtstag*. Laaber, 1988, pp. 3–10

3

Music in the market-place

STEPHEN ROSE

Professional musicians must make a living, and thus their activities are bound by economic forces and by society's various demands for their craft. The seventeenth century was a time of such social and economic upheaval that musicians could scarcely escape unscathed. There were civil wars in England and Germany; outbreaks of plague and famine across Europe; and the shape of society was changed by the rapid growth of cities and the rise of absolutist monarchs. The first half of the century was a period of particular instability, which may well have contributed to a notable fragmentation of musical styles in contrast to the international *lingua franca* of polyphony so characteristic of the Renaissance period. Europe was becoming more polarised – with marked differences emerging between nations, between town and country, and between governments and governed – and music was also diversifying. Many new genres were developing and becoming identified with different outlets for musical activity.

One major change in musical life was a move to performances by virtuosos before an audience. Such a trend can be seen in opera, in its chamber equivalents of solo song and cantata, and later in the century in the instrumental concertos performed in Bologna and Rome. A distance between performer and listener had already begun to emerge in virtuosic court repertories at the end of the sixteenth century, notably the music of the *concerto di donne* of Ferrara and the 'luxuriant' style of the madrigals of Luca Marenzio (1553/4–99) and Luzzasco Luzzaschi (?1545–1607). Courts continued to seek to dazzle and amaze an audience in their festivities throughout the seventeenth century. A similar mode of performance was adopted by the new public and commercial venues, such as the opera-houses of Venice and the concert rooms of London.

Any such changes, however, tended to be local and may not have had the impact that some scholars have assumed. Although increasing urbanisation created new markets for music, the rise of princely absolutism also made some patrons more powerful than ever. Music-printing collapsed in some regions such as Lutheran Germany, but thrived in others such as Restoration England. The result by the end of the century was a variety of localised, and somewhat fragmented, musical arenas. In London or Amsterdam, say, the public market was predominant, while in Paris, Dresden or much of northern Italy (save Venice), the court prevailed. Only the emerging hegemony of Italian opera across the theatres of Europe – despite staunch resistance in England and France – brought some potential cohesion to a rapidly changing musical world.

The pace and variety of change posed many challenges to professional musicians. In England, the decline of courtly employment led musicians such as Henry Purcell (1659–95) to turn instead to London's theatres for work. As musicians moved from being live-in servants to professional freelances, they had to fashion a new social identity and foster new skills to get work. Rather than offering service, loyalty and an honourable name to a patron, they had to act more as entrepreneurs and to negotiate their contracts and fees. Throughout Europe, the traditional hierarchies of the profession were challenged by the rise of new performing and compositional skills, and there were bitter disputes over the terms that might define professional competence. Yet this time of change also opened new opportunities, particularly for virtuoso singers and instrumentalists. A few women musicians also saw their careers flourish and were among the highest-paid performers of the century. In sum, this was a period of social and economic regrouping, with musicians affected by every change.

The demand for music

Professional musicians faced multifarious demands for their services. Their performing skills were required by courts, churches, public venues and private individuals. Sometimes they would write pieces for these outlets. Compositions were also required by amateurs and by professional performers who were unable or disinclined to write their own repertory. And tuition was required by amateurs and aspiring professionals. Equally varied were the financial arrangements by which the market operated, which ranged from traditional client-patron relationships to straightforward monetary transactions.

Courts were a traditional source of patronage. Some court music, such as trumpet salutes, had ceremonial origins, while other such music – whether sacred (in a princely chapel) or secular (in a court theatre) – articulated and projected notions of power and prestige. But much was designed for amusement. Noble courtiers expected to while away the hours with witty conversation and music. Banquets were invariably accompanied by music, and the provision of 'table music' was often the first item on the contracts of court musicians. Music was also needed for dancing, which was a major social event and an opportunity for stylised courtship, displays of good breeding, and even quasi-military training.

Whether or not court patronage stemmed from any real love of music, it was a means of asserting senses of identity and obligation. Princes had always needed music worthy of their rank, and in the seventeenth century (as before) they also used music as political and ideological propaganda. The cultural policies of Louis XIV of France (ruled 1661–1715) epitomise the role of music in an era of increasingly centralised, absolutist power. He developed the agencies of government to focus all authority on himself and pursued an aggressive foreign policy, repeatedly invading neighbouring countries. His lavish patronage of art, architecture and music was another means of asserting power and exercising diplomacy. The magnificence of the French court conveyed his éclat and power; the vast new palace at Versailles displayed splendour and wealth, and its distance from central Paris signalled regal aloofness.[1] Louis cultivated musical styles that were distinctively French and thus reinforced the national identity centred upon him. His favourite entertainment was the *ballet de cour*, a multi-media spectacle that embodied his love of dance and usually featured a hero such as Hercules or Alexander the Great who would be a model for the king and might be acted by him. Meanwhile, dynastic or military celebrations were marked with settings of the *Te Deum*, whose rich martial effects provided a musical counterpart to the assertive national spirit. *Grands motets* gave solemnity and richness to sacred ceremonies that honoured regal as much as divine power. And even Jean-Baptiste Lully's (1632–87) *tragédies en musique* were pressed into political service by way of their prologues and apotheoses, and also by their canonisation. Louis's image-making through patronage was so successful that it was emulated by other rulers, notably Emperor Leopold I of Austria and King Charles II of England, and musicians were sent to the French court to learn its distinctive styles.

Court music was characterised by its exclusivity. Even the largest spectacles were usually solely for invited guests and diplomats; ordinary people were further excluded by the trend towards staging entertainments within indoor theatres or at night. The nearest that many of Louis's subjects came to his festivities was seeing the fireworks at a distance. Printed descriptions of court festivities thus played a major role in transmitting such spectacles to a wider public arena. Yet despite being intended for a select audience, court music could be extremely expensive. At least twenty musicians were needed for a decent ensemble, and they could account for 2–5 per cent of a court's entire salary expenses. For much of the century, the English court had 70–100 musicians;

---

1 Burke, *The Fabrication of Louis XIV*.

similar if not greater numbers were retained by the French court and by the Saxon electors at Dresden, although it must be remembered that such numbers could be inflated by honorary appointments or by payment in perpetuity to aged, infirm or inactive musicians.[2] Courts also devoted considerable resources to lavish musical effects at dynastic celebrations. The 1634 festivities in Copenhagen for the wedding of Christian V of Denmark cost about two million *rigsdaler*.[3] As Kristiaan Aercke has explained, such spectacles functioned in a symbolic economy where overwhelming expenditure earned esteem by showing that princely magnificence had no earthly end.[4] Sometimes the strategy backfired: Luigi Rossi's *Orfeo*, performed at the French court in 1647, was so lavish that its extravagance, and its testimony to the Italian influence at court, provoked riots that helped to bring down the government.

The other traditional patron of elite music was the Church. In Catholic countries, many church musicians were clerics or belonged to a monastic order, whether out of religious vocation or, more often, for reasons of social or professional pragmatism. In Protestant areas such as Lutheran Germany or the Dutch republic, churches were usually controlled by town councils and the musicians were civic employees. Churches could use music as a component in regular services of worship. Sometimes these services were without a congregation and were for the ears of the musicians and God alone: a benefaction for a Requiem Mass, for instance, would pay for a regular service praying for the soul of the departed to ease the transition through Purgatory. In Lutheran countries, music was seen as an aid to devotion and a means of bringing sacred words to the believer's heart. Catholic communities, with the burgeoning of Counter-Reformation spirituality, used music to suggest the mystery of God. Both denominations exploited sacred dramas and oratorios to bring biblical stories to life before the laity. Of course, many other motives existed for church music. Town councils derived prestige from the music in their churches, particularly in trading centres such as Hamburg and Leipzig where services were attended by visiting merchants. And wherever a church service was held, individual listeners brought their own interests and preoccupations. Samuel Pepys, English civil servant and diarist, attended some services mainly for the music. Visiting St George's Chapel in Windsor, he was given cushions to sit upon and a copy of the anthem to follow: 'And here, for our sakes, [the choir] had this anthem and the great service sung extraordinary, only to entertain us'.[5]

2 Spink (ed.), *The Blackwell History of Music*, iii: 2; Munck, *Seventeenth-Century Europe*, p. 331.
3 Wade, 'Triumphus nuptialis danicus', p. 278.   4 Aercke, *Gods of Play*.
5 Latham and Matthews (eds), *The Diary of Samuel Pepys*, vii: 58 (26 February 1666). I am grateful to Richard Luckett for sharing his notes on Pepys's diary.

Music thrived in private homes for a variety of reasons. Its sensual and restorative powers were widely acknowledged: as Pepys said, 'Music and women I cannot but give way to, whatever my business is'. He played privately to calm himself before and after work, and he found that his page's lute-playing made his 'mind' 'mighty content' before bed.[6] Musical skills were also an accomplishment allowing participation in social discourse. Pepys often met with friends to sing, and was keen that his wife should learn music so she would be an asset at such gatherings and 'become very good company for me'.[7] Sometimes music was cultivated as an ostentatious symbol of refinement. Molière satirised the unquestioning pursuit of all the arts in *Le bourgeois gentilhomme*, and we may perhaps detect a similar aspiration to musical knowledge when Pepys had his servant read Descartes's 'Compendium of Musick' to him, though 'I understand [it] not, nor think he did well that writ it'.[8] Consequently there was a rich domestic market for tuition, instruments and sheet music. Lessons could be expensive: Pepys's teacher charged £5 a month for elementary tuition in composition, at a time when the going rate for a domestic servant was £3 a year plus board.[9] Many tutors assembled manuscript anthologies for their pupils: Cesare Morelli provided Pepys with collections of songs selected to suit his voice.

Although singing was the most common form of domestic music, instruments were symbols of wealth and refinement. Pepys's harpsichord was said to be one of the finest in London, even though he was not a keyboard player himself. This piece of musical furniture was an object of conspicuous consumption, something to be enjoyed just as Pepys relished his coach and horses or the gold lace on his sleeves. Dutch and English paintings of the period suggest a high rate of ownership of musical instruments in cities such as Amsterdam and London; and according to Pepys, one in three boats fleeing the Great Fire of London had possessions including a pair of virginals.[10] However, inventories of the time indicate that less than a tenth of London households owned instruments; perhaps they are over-represented in paintings and elsewhere, owing to their prestige and iconographical significance.[11]

Domestic music was richest in towns, where the population also provided a market for many other types of music. Pedlars sang ballads on the streets and sold the words as broadsheets. Court and church musicians also looked to the urban market to supplement their official income. A proud citizen might hire professional musicians as a special treat or for a familial commemoration. As a

---

6 Ibid., vii: 69–70 (9 March 1666); ix: 401 (25 December 1668).   7 Ibid., viii: 205–6 (8 May 1667).
8 Ibid., ix: 401 (25 December 1668). Descartes's *Compendium musicae* was written in 1618; there were several printed editions from 1650 on.
9 Ibid., ii: 37 (27 February 1662); ii: 53 (26 March 1662).
10 Ibid., vii: 271 (2 September 1666).   11 Earle, *The Making of the English Middle Class*, p. 296.

periodic piece of self-flattery, Pepys paid to be woken with a salute from the King's Trumpeters.[12] In Königsberg and Leipzig, wealthy burghers commissioned pieces to mark their weddings and funerals. Urban musical activity was further encouraged by the instrumentalists salaried by the council (in Germany, Stadtpfeifer; in England, waits) whose duties were a mixture of the functional and the ceremonial. The town band might be expected to keep watch, to signal the approach of hostile armies or to warn of fire, but they also played flourishes in honour of visiting dignitaries and at civic festivals. Councils sometimes used music to edify or entertain their citizens: Dutch cities such as Leiden often employed an organist to give recitals in an attempt to keep citizens away from the inns and taverns.

The biggest innovation in urban music was, of course, the opening of opera-houses to paying audiences, starting with the Teatro S. Cassiano in Venice in 1637. Many similar opera-houses then began in other Italian towns, bringing opera to a much wider audience than had hitherto been possible through the court. The audiences were still from the elite – in Venice, opera tickets did not come cheap[13] – but were no longer by invitation only. North of the Alps, opera generally remained the preserve of courts, but public outlets opened in Paris (1671), Hamburg (1678) and Leipzig (1693). In the seventeenth century, London lacked an opera-house, but music dramas were presented to the public by the city's two licensed theatrical companies (the Duke's Company and the King's Company) principally at the Lincoln's Inn Fields and Dorset Garden Theatres.

Public concerts also developed. One of the first examples was a lunchtime concert series that Jacques Champion de Chambonnières started in 1641 in Paris, with a group of ten musicians. They called themselves the Assemblée des Honnêtes Curieux (Assembly of the Honourable and Interested), giving a veneer of dilettante respectability to what was in fact a commercial enterprise. But it was in London that a lasting culture of public concerts emerged, in part as a result of the decline of courtly and religious patronage in the political crises and secularisation of mid century. Court and church music had in effect been dissolved during the Civil War, and the musicians who did not flee abroad either made a living by teaching amateurs or gathered in music meetings such as the weekly one at William Ellis's house in Oxford. Such activity continued even when the court music and church choirs were reinstated in 1660. As the economy grew and towns expanded, an urban 'middle class' emerged with a disposable income for music and other entertainments. Thus the convivial

---

12 Latham and Matthews (eds), *The Diary of Samuel Pepys*, vii: 421 (27 December 1666).
13 Bianconi and Walker, 'Production, Consumption and Political Function of Seventeenth-Century Opera', p. 227.

music meetings evolved into concert rooms that charged for admission; these were places, like the coffee-houses and clubs, where the middle classes could meet socially and spend their leisure. In 1672 in London, John Banister started commercial concerts 'in alehouse fashion', using court musicians who were moonlighting to augment their stipends. Entry cost one shilling (the same as the cheapest ticket at the theatre) and you could 'call for what [tunes] you pleased'.[14] Other concert series were for narrower social circles. The small-coal merchant Thomas Britton began a close-knit meeting in his premises at Clerkenwell, while nobility and gentry attended the concerts in the grand surroundings of the York Buildings. This new public market came into its own when court music was pared down in the 1690s, and figures such as Henry Purcell instead sought employment in London's theatres and concert rooms.

Public opera and concerts had somewhat different modes of operation from court music. Although many opera-houses still relied on aristocratic subsidy or other support, their commercial basis required new tactics to entice an audience. Whereas court operas were expensive one-offs the audience of which was small and obliged to attend, public opera-houses had to build a repertory that drew regular custom. Consumers were to be enticed with the new forms of publicity developing for the urban market such as handbills and advertisements in newspapers. Regular audiences were vital for a constant income, so promoters encouraged opera-going as a social habit. Although some opera-goers were drawn by the music or the chance to see vocal stars on stage, others were attracted by the opportunity to meet friends, to conduct romantic liaisons, to be seen socially, and to gaze voyeuristically at celebrities in the audience. In Paris as in Venice, it was common to go several times to the same opera.[15] Impresarios invited subscriptions for boxes, thereby securing their cash-flow and also encouraging attendance by allowing audience members to create their own social space in the theatre. Subscriptions were a new way of paying for music and suited those members of the middle classes who were not rich enough to be individual patrons but who collectively constituted a powerful market-force.

Some people found it a shock to have to pay to attend a performance. In Paris, nobility and members of the royal household expected to be admitted to places of entertainment free of charge, usually accompanied by their retinue of footmen. When Pierre Perrin established a public opera-house in 1671, there was brawling as pages and footmen tried to force their entry without paying. The following year, Lully relaunched Perrin's enterprise as the Académie

14 Wilson (ed.), *Roger North on Music*, pp. 302, 352.
15 Wood and Sadler (eds), *French Baroque Opera*, p. 36.

Royale de Musique, obtaining a royal privilege that specified that all persons had to pay for entry regardless of their status, and that armed guards would be stationed on the doors.[16] Fee-paying performances were a new *modus operandi* for musicians, too, and were among the challenges that the profession faced in the new economic climate of the century.

Polarisation and professionalisation

The newer styles of music in the seventeenth century tended to be characterised by a widening gap between performers and their audiences. In an opera-house as in a concert-room, solo performers sought to captivate and control an audience like an orator and a magician. Genres that were performed as chamber music, with the performers as the only listeners, were looking increasingly old-fashioned. In Italy during the second quarter of the century, commentators such as Pietro della Valle and Giovanni Battista Doni noted how the serious polyphonic madrigal had declined in favour of performances by soloists.[17] Later in England, Roger North observed that the viol fantasia had been ousted by violin music played by a soloist.[18] Under the new order, an audience sought intense emotional arousal and allowed itself to be moulded like wax by the performer-cum-orator. Monteverdi's *Arianna* (1608) was famous for having moved its female audience-members to tears with the heroine's lament. Much later in the century, a woman attending Parisian opera could expect to feel 'emotional stirrings in her heart' as 'all the senses are aroused'.[19] Such tropes of wonder, amazement and emotional arousal may have been highly conventional, but they still reveal something of what contemporaries wanted to believe about the performances they heard.

The polarisation of listeners and music-makers was of great importance for the formation of the profession. Professionals were increasingly distinguished by their virtuosity and skill at musico-rhetorical delivery. And this move to virtuosity encouraged musicians to specialise in particular repertories or styles. Formerly many professionals had been expected to be competent on several instruments or to hold non-musical skills, and in more traditional environments such expectations still persisted. Keyboard players were often also copyists or instrument-repairers, while in German towns the Stadtpfeifer had to be able to shift within and between the wind and string families of instruments. At Lutheran churches the organist was often also in charge of the accounts – as

16 La Gorce, 'Lully's First Opera', p. 311.
17 Carter, *Music in Late Renaissance and Early Baroque Italy*, pp. 241–2.
18 Wilson (ed.), *Roger North on Music*, pp. 222, 314.
19 Wood and Sadler (eds), *French Baroque Opera*, p. 39.

with Dieterich Buxtehude (*c.* 1637–1707) in Lübeck – while the cantor was expected to teach Latin as well as music.

Increasingly, however, the new virtuoso performances required specialists dedicated to a particular voice-type or instrument. Performers needed to perfect the skills of affective ornamentation and the rhetorical delivery and good memory of a stage actor; all this demanded years of practice and experience. The best example of such specialisation is the castrato, which John Rosselli has shown to be a phenomenon above all of the seventeenth century.[20] Solely for the sake of a prized voice, castratos underwent a painful operation that also required them to forsake procreation and accept their alterity. Often they would undergo a lengthy specialist training, perhaps at one of the conservatoires discussed in more detail below. This distinctive breed arose mainly to meet the demand for singers in courtly and urban opera-houses, and in church, where in most Catholic countries women were unable to perform save in certain special contexts (such as convents).

Equally dramatic was the rise of the virtuoso string or keyboard player. In the Renaissance, instrumentalists had traditionally been regarded as humble mechanics, little above travelling minstrels. Instrumental repertories were also low in the pecking order of musical styles. To be sure, exceptions were made for instruments and their players sanctioned by Classical precedent and courtly utility (witness Baldassare Castiglione's emphasis on the lute and viol) or by ceremonial requirements (the trumpeters and kettledrummers whose military duties put them among the best paid of musicians). By contrast, the seventeenth century saw the increasing emergence of repertories specific to one instrument, notably the violin sonata. For the first time, leading composers made their reputation primarily, sometimes solely, through instrumental music: the roll-call includes Heinrich von Biber (1644–1704), Dario Castello, Arcangelo Corelli (1653–1713), Johann Jacob Froberger (1616–67), Marin Marais (1656–1728) and Biagio Marini (1594–1663). Myths circulated about the performances of the finest soloists: Girolamo Frescobaldi (1583–1643) supposedly attracted 30,000 listeners on his first appearance in Rome, while Corelli's eyes were reported to 'turn as red as fire' when he played.[21] Although such anecdotes can rarely be proven, they testify to the rising fame of instrumental soloists.

In the Protestant cities of northern Germany, musical life was increasingly dominated by organists rather than choir-directors. Organists such as Buxtehude and Johann Adam Reincken (1643–1722) were renowned for their lavish improvisations and solo recitals; as continuo players they were involved with the modern vocal concertos and hence stood at the forefront of musical

20 Rosselli, *Singers of Italian Opera*, pp. 35–8.   21 Allsop, *Arcangelo Corelli*, p. 53.

innovation. In Lübeck, Buxtehude and Franz Tunder (1614–67) inaugu-rated the ambitious series of Abendmusik concerts. Meanwhile in Hamburg, Matthias Weckmann (?1616–1674) started a *collegium musicum*, and Reincken was pivotal in the founding of the opera-house. In 1666 Reincken rejected the multi-tasking that was traditionally associated with his post at the Cathari-nenkirche, resigning the duties of church clerk because he saw them as incom-patible with his 'profession'.[22]

Virtuoso vocalists and instrumentalists enjoyed great economic rewards. Violinists such as Biber and Corelli were highly sought after, while Reincken was the best-paid musician in seventeenth-century Hamburg. Opera singers were in huge demand for their celebrity, skill and rarity; their fees were pushed up by the international nature of the market. Enticing a troupe of Italian singers to London in 1667, Charles II's staff noted that they should be paid 'not less than they get in Germany'; each singer received £200, as much as the Master of the King's Musick and more than four times the salary of an ordinary court musician.[23] As this example indicates, the remuneration of such virtuosos was not shared by rank-and-file musicians. Indeed, the century saw the rise of orchestras that institutionalised the differences between leader, soloist and ordinary player. In the opera-houses of Italy, a solo singer could be paid between twenty and forty times what an orchestral member received for providing the accompaniment.[24]

The success of the virtuosos could arouse disquiet and envy in the rest of the profession, particularly because they often seemed to jeopardise estab-lished methods of performing or composing. Nowhere was this more evident than in Germany, where traditionally the *Kapellmeister* was at the head of the musical hierarchy for his indisputable skills in counterpoint, composing and directing.[25] In newer styles, however, such knowledge of vocal polyphony might count for little. Tensions had already emerged at the start of the cen-tury with the growing importance of instrumentalists in court ensembles. At Stuttgart, the instrumentalists challenged the directorial authority of Leonhard Lechner (*c.* 1553–1606), accusing him of ignorance about their craft because he had risen from among the ranks of singers. Such accusations may have held some truth, given that Lechner's surviving output consists exclusively of vocal polyphony.[26] Later there was widespread incomprehension of Italianate

22 Krüger, *Die Hamburgische Musikorganisation im XVII. Jahrhundert*, p. 163; Edler, 'Organ Music within the Social Structure of North German Cities in the Seventeenth Century'.
23 Ashbee (ed.), *Records of English Court Music*, viii: 174–5.
24 Bianconi and Walker, 'Production, Consumption and Political Function of Seventeenth-Century Opera', pp. 224–5, 230.
25 J. Kuhnau, *Der musicalische Quacksalber* (Dresden, 1700), pp. 503–4.
26 Sittard, *Zur Geschichte der Musik und des Theaters am württembergischen Hof*, i: 30.

performing techniques. Many German organists could not realise a figured bass or even read staff notation until the second half of the century (traditionally, they performed from keyboard tablature), while few string-players understood the bowing needed for Monteverdi's avant-garde *Combattimento di Tancredi e Clorinda* (1624), as Heinrich Schütz (1585–1672) noted in his *Symphoniarum sacrarum secunda pars*, op. 10 (Dresden, 1647). Furthermore, anxiety at such novel techniques could breed envy of the successful Italians. In Dresden in the 1650s, the German musicians resented the preferential treatment given to newly arrived Italian singers: Christoph Bernhard (1629–92) complained that he was not receiving 'respectable advancement', while the elderly Schütz disliked working alongside an Italian 'three times younger than I and castrated to boot'.[27] And in 1700 Johann Kuhnau published a satirical novel, *Der musicalische Quack-Salber*, where the central figure is an incompetent German musician who tries to disguise his deficiencies by pretending to be that most marketable of commodities, an Italian virtuoso. The moral to fellow musicians and audiences is clear: do not be hoodwinked by a superficial display of the latest foreign fashions. Indeed Kuhnau ended the novel with a list of the attributes of a 'true musician', stressing the value of older contrapuntal knowledge and including a catty attack on 'castratos who affect the title of the most splendid singers and yet know nothing of composition'.[28]

The reconfiguration of the musical profession also prompted criticism from the wider public. Practical music had always struggled to appear respectable, but the lifestyle and success of opera musicians aroused particular charges of immorality. Castratos were regarded with a mix of suspicion and innuendo; censure was also directed at those who combined church posts with operatic work. Not for nothing did many take objection to the licentious life of Antonio Cesti (1623–69), who both worked in the opera-house and was a friar. In a satire on music, the artist Salvator Rosa wrote that 'By night castratos play girls' parts on stage / and in the morning serve as priests in church'.[29] More thoughtful commentators complained that the new order excluded amateur performers and deterred serious music-making. Such complaints were articulated with particular finesse in England, where the tumultuous changes of the Restoration led to a sudden reconfiguration of musical life. Roger North wrote nostalgically of the old days when a performance of a polyphonic madrigal or viol fantasia embodied the 'respùblica among the courtiers' in which all parts (and people) were equal. Now there was an 'unsociable and malcreate . . . violin spark that thinks himself above the rest . . . It is enough for the underparts to be capable

27 Spagnoli, *Letters and Documents of Heinrich Schütz*, pp. 19–21; see also Schütz's letter of 21 August 1653, given in Müller (ed.), *Heinrich Schütz*, p. 238.
28 Kuhnau, *Der musicalische Quacksalber*, p. 506.   29 Scott, *Salvator Rosa*, pp. 80–81.

of waiting on him.'[30] North grasped the political and social implications of the new order: a communal recreation of gentlemen had been replaced by a 'them-and-us' relationship between soloist and accompaniment. He also complained that the newer styles drove a wedge between professionals and amateurs. In the first half of the century, a fine musician such as the viol player John Jenkins (1592–1678) could spend a fulfilling career in the households of provincial gentry, giving tuition and playing fantasias with members of the family. By the end of the century, however, new genres such as solo violin sonatas were too advanced for amateurs. 'Now it is come to pass', wrote North, 'that few but professors can handle [music], and the value is derived upon high flights and numbers of capitall performers'.[31]

While the violin symbolised all that North disliked in the new musical order, other amateurs found that new techniques such as figured bass were their own particular stumbling-block. Pepys could not realise a bass and had to get court musicians to write it out for him. Gentlemanly amateurs were also deterred by the increasingly commercial basis of music-making, for they would never be so mercenary as to accept money for a performance. At least one music meeting in London folded when admission charges were introduced for listeners, and the gentleman players withdrew in horror.[32] Some commentators also argued that the emerging cult of the virtuoso, and the larger public audiences for music, acted to the detriment of attentive listening. Thomas Mace was wary of the new concert venues that were emerging in London, and in 1676 he proposed an alternative 'Musick-Roome' where the audience could not see the performers. The musicians were to sit around a table, enjoying the eye contact and intimacy of chamber performance; the listeners would sit in separate cubicles, with the disembodied sound conveyed to their seat by speaking-tubes. Mace's design thereby eliminated the temptation of the visceral and 'all inconveniences of Talking, Crowding, Sweating and Blustering'.[33] His ideal venue, indeed, bore many resemblances to the private and studious atmosphere in which the social elite of the 1630s listened to viol fantasias.[34]

Although amateurs such as North felt excluded from the new and professionalised styles, there nonetheless remained distinct repertories intended for domestic or genteel performance. In France these included the airs of Sebastian Le Camus (c. 1610–1677) and Michel Lambert (c. 1610–1696), printed in elegant books by the Ballard press. The equivalent books in German lands were the *Arien* of Heinrich Albert (1604–51) or Johann Rist (1607–67) that set a mix of

30 Wilson (ed.), *Roger North on Music*, p. 222.   31 Ibid., p. 314.   32 Ibid., p. 352.
33 T. Mace, *Musick's Monument; or A Remembrancer of the Best Practical Musick* (London, 1676; repr. New York, 1966), p. 240.
34 On practices in the 1630s, see Pinto, 'Music at Court', p. 28.

secular and devotional texts. Meanwhile, in London the market of middle-class amateurs was supplied with printed songbooks by John Playford. Other genres specifically for amateurs included simple instrumental pieces such as the 'lesson' for keyboard or for recorder. Another role also emerged for the amateur, as a collector of music. In earlier centuries, collecting had typically been the privilege of the ruling classes who created cabinets of curiosities as symbols of their acquisitive power and all-encompassing knowledge. By the seventeenth century, men of lower birth such as clerics, lawyers and doctors were also assembling collections that might include musical texts, perhaps as the trophies of a 'grand tour'. The English apothecary and botanist James Sherard accumulated manuscripts of German church music (now in the Bodleian Library, Oxford) which he probably never performed; Pepys's library (now at Magdalene College, Cambridge) included a fourteenth-century music manuscript and printed editions of French opera. Margaret Murata observes a similar phenomenon among the aristocrats of Rome, who sometimes collected manuscripts of cantatas.[35] These functioned as souvenirs of performances or perhaps as tokens of a prestigious repertory. Murata argues that many of the collectors could no longer afford household musicians, given the high fees now commanded by virtuosos; for such aristocrats, music became an object in the library rather than a live performance in the chamber.

Patterns of dissemination

The changing relationship between musical producers and consumers was accompanied by new patterns for disseminating notated music. Most prominent was a decline in music-printing in Italy and central Europe. Whereas much polyphony was printed in these lands between 1560 and 1630, by the middle of the seventeenth century there was a greater use of manuscript. The shift has been demonstrated statistically,[36] and it can also be seen in the careers of composers: whereas Claudio Monteverdi's (1567–1643) published output included one opera, nine books of madrigals and three of sacred music, and Schütz had fourteen major publications to his name, later figures such as Alessandro Scarlatti (1660–1725) or Buxtehude kept the majority of their music in manuscript. The immediate causes for the decline in music-printing included the international economic crisis of the 1620s, the outbreaks of plague in northern Italy around 1630, and the devastation wrought by the Thirty Years War in

---

35 Murata, 'Roman Cantata Scores as Traces of Musical Culture and Signs of Its Place in Society'.

36 Bianconi, *Music in the Seventeenth Century*, p. 76; Carter, 'Music-Publishing in Italy'; Rose, 'Music, Print and Presentation in Saxony during the Seventeenth Century'.

central Europe. But the underlying reason was that newer musical styles often seemed unsuitable for wide dissemination in print.

The success of music-printing in the sixteenth century reflected the sheer versatility of its product. A typical edition contained polyphonic pieces presented in partbook format (one book for each performing part) and in as neutral a form as possible, usually in their contrapuntal bones. They could be realised in many ways to suit numerous social contexts and degrees of technical ability: amateurs might perform the notes as written; professionals might add ornamentation; a vocal piece could be performed with instrumental doubling or substitution, or in some kind of arrangement. Additionally, some purchasers might regard the book as a token of prestige rather than as performing material. Newer styles and genres, by contrast, were more specific in their instrumentation and more varied in their textures. Such specificity and heterogeneity were difficult to capture in print and also split the market into numerous niches. The florid roulades and short note-values of solo lines or keyboard toccatas were hard to represent in the movable type that had been used throughout the sixteenth century. Engraving was better able to accommodate such complexities – as seen in Frescobaldi's two books of toccatas (1615, 1627) – but it remained expensive and limited to the upper end of the market. Furthermore, the newer styles of music, and their varied textures, were often unsuitable for partbook format, and scores increasingly became a necessity to coordinate the complexities of performance. Avant-garde collections published in partbooks, such as Monteverdi's Eighth Book of madrigals (the *Madrigali guerrieri, et amorosi* of 1638), must have caused headaches to printers and users alike: its variety of textures led to a set of partbooks of widely different lengths, while some pieces (the *Combattimento di Tancredi e Clorinda* and the *Lamento della ninfa*) had to be given in full score in the continuo partbook.

The newly dominant genres such as opera and solo song had an ambivalent relationship with print. These genres could not be published in their bare essentials in the same way as the madrigals and canzonettas of the previous century. Furthermore many such pieces were not intended for use outside a particular time, place or set of performers. Most of the earliest court operas were staged as one-offs and although some appeared in print and were even reprinted (such as Monteverdi's *Orfeo*), the editions seem to have been intended not so much as a template for further performances as souvenirs communicating the courtly event to those not lucky enough to be invited. As opera started to become a commercial product, there was even less reason to disclose pieces in print: opera companies sought their profit through productions rather than books. By the end of the century, Italian composers such as Alessandro Scarlatti never saw their operas in print.

Solo song also had a problematic relationship with print. There was a boom in editions of Italian monody at the start of the century but, as Tim Carter has shown, the purposes of these elegant and expensive books can be enigmatic.[37] Sometimes the musical contents were beyond the grasp of amateurs or were specific to a single professional singer. The preface (by the printer) of Jacopo Peri's (1561–1633) *Le varie musiche* (1609) described the notated contents as inferior to the composer's own rendition: 'it would be necessary to hear the composer play and sing them himself to fully appreciate their perfection'. Peri certainly did not need the printed edition for his own performances, which he would presumably deliver from memory; instead, the book perhaps served as an upmarket record of his performances and as an advertisement of his abilities. The cachet of the 'new music' made it imperative for singer-composers and their patrons to prove in public print that they had mastered such a style, or even to claim that they had invented it. But once such jostling for precedence was over, solo song gradually reverted to manuscript. By mid-century the cantata repertory of composers such as Luigi Rossi (d. 1653) and Giacomo Carissimi (1605–74) was circulating largely in handwritten texts.

In short, musical dissemination was fragmenting into niche markets that reflected the diversification of genres and styles. A sense of this fragmentation can be gained from those bibliographical curiosities of the second half of the century, the partly printed editions. Schütz's *Historia der freuden- und gnadenreichen Geburth Gottes und Marien Sohnes, Jesu Christi* (1664; his 'Christmas Story') consists of recitatives interspersed with grand 'intermedia' depicting scenes of the nativity. The recitatives were printed but the intervening *intermedi* could only be obtained in manuscript from Schütz's agents, because their larger textures 'would not attain their proper effect except in princely chapels'. The technical difficulty and lavish instrumentation of the *intermedi* restricted their market and made scribal transmission the most feasible option. Other examples of partly printed editions, such as Schütz's *Schwanengesang* (1671) or François Couperin's (1668–1733) *Pièces d'orgue* (1690), had a printed title-page but hand-written music. Here the title-page partook of the prestige of print, but there seems to have been insufficient capital or demand for the music to be printed.

The move towards manuscript set limits on broader musical knowledge and encouraged localisation, as is evident from the inventories of churches in central Germany. Many of these institutions had similar stocks of printed books dating from the earlier part of the century, including collections by Giovanni Gabrieli (d. 1612), Johann Hermann Schein (1586–1630) and Schütz. For music from the 1650s on, however, modern pieces such as vocal concertos circulated in

---

37 Carter, 'Printing the "New Music"'.

manuscript, and churches possessed only the pieces that their music-directors could obtain through personal contacts. Whereas around 1600 the circulation of printed editions had allowed composers such as Schein to learn Italian styles without leaving Saxony, the transmission of the latest styles soon depended far more on the movements of individual musicians and their agents. Schütz was only one of many northern European musicians who travelled to study in Italy, and some such as Johann Rosenmüller (*c.* 1619–1684) made their careers there.

The move to manuscript also conspired to exclude amateurs from the professional repertory. Most amateurs lacked the contacts or status to participate in the exchange of scribal copies. When Pepys wanted copies from court musicians, he had to win their favour by buying them drinks.[38] The conventions of scribal circulation could also leave Pepys feeling powerless: whereas in a bookshop he could peruse sample copies before purchase, he found it hard to know whether a manuscript was worth its price. When a visiting viol master played some pieces, 'I was afeared to enter too far in their commendation for fear he should offer to copy them for me, and so I be forced to give or lend him something'.[39] Equally an amateur might be told that notated copies were unavailable. In 1676 an admirer of Lully's operas asked how he could get copies of his favourite tunes; the answer was to find someone who sang them well.[40]

However, there are also counter-narratives against the story of the decline in music-printing. It must be remembered that the intensity of music-printing during the sixteenth and early seventeenth centuries was largely a phenomenon limited to Italy, Germany, the Low Countries and (to some extent) Paris; in Spain or England, for example, local repertories mostly circulated in manuscript. Indeed in England there was a gradual, if unsteady, rise in music-publishing through the seventeenth century. At the outset, professional repertories such as cathedral music circulated in manuscript; the relatively few printed editions (compared, at least, with Continental outputs) contained secular madrigals – often modelled blatantly on Italian settings – and lute-songs, and thus repertories intended for the gentry who also enjoyed musical editions imported from Antwerp and Venice. From the 1650s, however, John Playford pioneered inexpensive printed music for the growing market of middle-class amateurs. His books rarely cost more than a cheap seat in the bear-pit or a medium-priced theatre ticket. Many of his ventures seem to have been wholly commercial, for some of his books lack dedications, and he published pieces without the composer's consent, as Henry Lawes (1596–1662) complained in his *Ayres & Dialogues* of 1653. English music publishers also began marketing

38 Latham and Matthews (eds), *The Diary of Samuel Pepys*, ix: 271 (3 August 1668).
39 Ibid., v: 25 (23 January 1664).   40 Turnbull, 'The Sources for the Two Versions of *Psyché* ', p. 352.

their books with the same tools that sold opera to the urban public, namely newspaper advertisements and subscription schemes. A notice in the *London Gazette* of 28 May 1683 invited subscriptions for Purcell's *Sonatas of III Parts* (printed 'for the author' and sold by Playford); remaining stock or copies from a new impression were advertised in *The Post Man* of 12 May 1702. Such schemes anticipated the retail techniques that would be used by John Walsh in London and Estienne Roger in Amsterdam during the resurgence of music-printing in the early eighteenth century.

Even as music-printing dwindled to a shadow of its former self (on the Continent) or was reconfigured to cater for new markets (in England and elsewhere), it could still hold a residual status for composers and patrons. We have already seen how Italian musicians and patrons used editions of monody to assert their claims to have invented or mastered the new style. In Germany throughout the century, music was printed to mark weddings and funerals, and for composers such as Buxtehude these occasional pieces were their only vocal compositions to reach the press. According to Roger North, the violinist Nicola Matteis discovered that he could engrave books of violin pieces and present 'them, well bound, to most of the [music] lovers, which brought him the 3, 4, and 5 ginnys'.[41] Such private presentations were no doubt more lucrative for Matteis than going via middlemen such as bookdealers; even so, he also offered these books to the general public in an advertisement in the *London Gazette* (11 December 1676). Other composers and patrons on occasion also provided the necessary capital for an edition, especially if a commercial printer could not be persuaded to take it on. Frescobaldi committed 300 *scudi* towards the printing of his 1615 *Toccate*, part of which sum was loaned by his patron.[42] Schütz overcame the apparent indifference of booksellers towards his music by acting as his own publisher, with help from the Elector of Saxony as he acknowledged in his *Symphoniarum sacrarum tertia pars*, op. 12 (Dresden, 1650).

The prestige of printed music is evident in the practice of presenting copies. Most books had a printed dedication paying homage to a current or prospective patron, who would typically be presented with copies by the composer. Sometimes the patron would send these gifts to a local musician for valuation before deciding whether to reward them. In Nuremberg in the 1620s, Johann Staden assessed printed editions that had been presented to the town council by Samuel Scheidt (1587–1654) and Schein; in Dresden, Schütz executed a similar task for the Elector of Saxony. Presentation copies were often also sent to institutions or individuals not named in the printed dedication. Schütz sent out at least twelve copies of his *Psalmen Davids* (1619) to town councils

41 Wilson (ed.), *Roger North on Music*, p. 356.   42 Hammond, *Girolamo Frescobaldi*, pp. 49–50.

and cathedrals across central Germany, and doubtless further presentations are not documented. Often the institution would reciprocate with a reward of cash, precious metal or alcohol. Yet these German editions were not solely for private presentation, with most also being listed in the wholesale catalogues of booksellers at the Leipzig and Frankfurt fairs. Authors and printers would want to distribute copies via all possible avenues, and even books intended for a specific patron could sometimes hold interest for general readers.

Throughout the century, composers used publications as a means to showcase their output and broadcast their name. Schein spoke in his first book (the *Venus Kräntzlein* of 1609) of the necessity of putting his music before public judgement. Many Italian composers, and a good number of north European ones, started their careers with an 'opus 1' madrigal book, which displayed their skill at counterpoint and word-setting in a widely respected genre. Printed editions could also be useful in job applications. In 1609 Monteverdi told an organist aspiring to a post at the Mantuan court that 'you do not have anything in print about which an opinion can be given concerning your worth'.[43] Much later, in Bautzen in 1680, the value of print was shown when the brass-player Johann Pezel (1639–94) was accepted as principal musician without an audition and on the strength of his published pieces alone.[44]

Some composers seem to have perceived print as fixing their work on the page, creating a repertory that could partake of (or even contribute to) emerging notions of a musical canon. The Hamburg musician Hieronymus Praetorius (1560–1629), for instance, concluded his career by looking over his previously published collections and reissuing them as a five-volume *Opus musicum* (1616–25). Somewhat similarly, Schütz was determined to see his pieces into print, even at the relatively old age of 65. As he told his patron in 1651, he wanted to be freed from his performing duties so he could 'gather together and complete what remains of the musical works that I began in my youth and have them printed for my remembrance'.[45] Even if this was a disguised plea for retirement, in the previous four years he or his colleagues had already published three major collections of his music. Print also placed composers in a public forum where they might display authorial authority. The *Modulatio organica* (1686) of Johann Caspar Kerll (1627–93) included a thematic catalogue of his keyboard output and a complaint about copyists who failed to credit his authorship.

Kerll had good reasons for lamenting that scribal copying obscured the composer's name: surviving manuscripts such as the Lowell Mason Codex (Yale University Library, LM5056) misattribute some of his pieces to such figures

---

43 Stevens (trans.), *The Letters of Claudio Monteverdi*, p. 63.
44 H. Biehle, *Musikgeschichte von Bautzen* (Leipzig, 1924), p. 35.
45 Müller (ed.), *Heinrich Schütz*, p. 213.

as Alessandro Poglietti (d. 1683). But manuscript dissemination was not necessarily detrimental to all composers: the music of Lully, for instance, was
so firmly associated with the French court that its copying remained under
institutional control and it gradually became a canonic repertory. In the case
of public opera, however, scribal transmission often conspired to diminish
the income and exposure of the composer. Whereas the librettist could make
money by selling printed text-booklets to audiences, the composer usually had
to cede the score to the company and rarely had further control over its use.
It is indicative that Monteverdi's last operas – *Il ritorno d'Ulisse in patria* (1640)
and *L'incoronazione di Poppea* (1643) – survive in manuscripts that do not bear
his name. The fragility of manuscripts and their limited circulation also made
it harder to preserve operatic repertories for posterity. In the *London Gazette*
of 9–13 October 1701, the Theatre Royal in London advertised a reward of 20
guineas for the return of its copy of Purcell's *Fairy Queen*, the manuscript 'being
lost by his death'. And nowadays we know Schütz almost entirely through his
church music, because all his music dramas and most of his secular songs stayed
in manuscripts which are no longer extant.

Musical training

The training of musicians showed a mix of older and newer procedures. Many
professionals continued to be trained by the traditional method whereby they
joined the household of a master musician. Pupils from musical families might
initially be taught by their father; children who were born outside the profession needed to find a master who would become their metaphorical father. The
emphasis on the master made this a somewhat patriarchal system; it also bore
strong similarities to the apprenticeships that operated in crafts such as car-
pentry or metal-working. In music as in these crafts, the trainee would expect
to perform domestic chores and aid the master in his own work. Indeed town
musicians and brass-players often had a formal system of apprenticeships regulated by guilds that enforced the professional hierarchy by imposing strict moral
and financial restrictions on apprentices. In London, the Musicians' Company
stipulated that apprenticeships should last a minimum of five years, and banned
apprentices from marriage, fornication and gaming.[46] At more advanced
levels, there were fewer restrictions on the pupil's conduct, but the patriarchal
element remained, with a master of wide repute taking on what might almost
be termed disciples. Giulio Caccini (1551–1618) housed and trained a series of
singers, including castratos, for the Medici court and other Italian princes. The

---

46 Spink (ed.), *The Blackwell History of Music in Britain*, iii: 31.

Amsterdam organist Jan Pieterszoon Sweelinck (1562–1621) taught a series of pupils sent to him by German courts and towns, including Samuel Scheidt, Heinrich Scheidemann and Jacob Praetorius II; Andreas Düben studied with him for six years, funded in part by the Leipzig council.

Pupils seem to have been educated via sheer immersion in the master's professional routine and by imitating the examples of his performances. To be sure, some pupils copied books from their master's library, and for keyboard repertories this was the main route by which compositions were transmitted within the profession. But the main point of an apprenticeship was to gain knowledge not readily available on paper. As singing treatises often said, the art of performance was best learned by hearing a master rather than by following a book. Moreover, ornamentation and improvisation were techniques in which the master's example would be invaluable. Some pieces may also have been communicated aurally. As late as the eighteenth century, François Couperin (in his *L'art de toucher le clavecin* of 1716) spoke of the value of the pupil learning pieces by memory rather than from the book. Brass players probably learned their field-pieces and military signals by rote, for this repertory and its distinctive tonguing were not written down until the late eighteenth century by Johann Ernst Altenburg.

Partly because of the importance of unwritten knowledge, some masters gained the reputation of jealously hiding the secrets of their art from their pupils. Thomas Mace wrote of lutenists who were 'extreme Shie in revealing the Occult and Hidden Secrets of the Lute'.[47] Johann Gottfried Walther (1684–1748) experienced similar concealment while studying with the learned organist Johann Heinrich Buttstett in 1702: Buttstett gave obfuscating accounts of topics such as modality, and made Walther pay to see the rare books in his library.[48] Although by the eighteenth century such secrecy was mocked by musicians who sought to open up their art to the wider public, it indicated the sheer value of the professional knowledge being imparted by the master. This value was also apparent in the cost of professional training. In 1613 Sweelinck charged the equivalent of 200 guilders for a year's lessons to Augustus Brücken, a figure put into relief by Brücken's annual living allowance of only 186 guilders.[49]

Musicians were also taught within institutions. Some church and court choirs were famed as training-grounds for professional musicians. Most of the leading composers of Restoration England, for instance, had been choirboys at the Chapel Royal, including Pelham Humfrey (1647/8–1674), John Blow (1649–1708) and Henry Purcell. Here, as in most choirs, the education of the trebles

---

47 Mace, *Musick's Monument*, p. 40.   48 Walther, *Briefe*, pp. 68–9.
49 Sigtenhorst Meyer, *Jan P. Sweelinck en zijn instrumentale muziek*, p. 68.

was the responsibility of the master. Henry Cooke (*c.* 1615–1672) was Master of the Chapel Royal in the 1660s and presumably had a busy household, full of pupils receiving lessons as well as assisting with the music-copying and rehearsals. The training offered in a choir was therefore usually an extension of the traditional master–pupil relationship.

Of greater significance was the development of conservatories in Venice and Naples. These grew out of charitable foundations for the orphaned, sick and helpless, which by the start of the century were using music to raise their profile and income. In Venice, the fine choirs and orchestras in the chapels of the orphanages attracted the public and led to a plentiful supply of bequests. Music tutors were employed not only to run these ensembles but also because music was deemed to be a useful skill. Given the demand from opera-houses for singers and instrumentalists, a musical training allowed foundlings to perform a productive role in society. Thus in 1633 the Conservatorio dei Poveri di Gesù Cristo in Naples had specialist teachers of string and brass instruments, and in 1675 it hired a castrato to teach singing. Similar developments in Venice paved the way for Antonio Vivaldi (1678–1741) to spend much of his career as a violin teacher at the Ospedale della Pietà, a girls' orphanage. By the end of the seventeenth century, the conservatories were attracting fee-paying pupils from wealthy families. The development of such institutionalised training was a response to the riches that could potentially be won by specialising in a lucrative skill such as opera-singing or virtuoso instrumental playing.

Many musicians found that their working life was shaped by family ties and by the contacts they had made during their training. In the case of civic musicians, an apprentice might expect to be helped into a post through his master's connections. Sometimes a trainee married the master's daughter, took over his 'business' and provided for his retirement. Something similar could also happen in court contexts: when Monteverdi moved to join the musicians of the Gonzaga court at Mantua in 1590 or 1591, he was lodged with the string-player Giacomo Cattaneo, married his daughter Claudia (a singer), and had to deal with problems over Cattaneo's estate in the 1620s. Marriage also allowed outsiders to enter a local circle of musicians: in Lübeck, for instance, the organist who succeeded Buxtehude had to marry his daughter. The importance of blood ties was strongly evident in Thuringia, where the Bach family was a dynasty occupying numerous posts in towns and churches. It acted as a network through which musical information could circulate and younger members could be sent to a relative for training or work. Similar functions were served by the guild of civic instrumentalists founded in Saxony in 1653 (the Instrumental-Musicalisches Collegium). The guild gave order, security and hierarchy to the profession. It sought to protect the livelihood of musicians by banning competition between members and by restricting entry to the profession through a system of onerous apprenticeships. It also upheld the standing of its craft, not only by legislating against incompetent or fraudulent practitioners but also by imposing strict moral standards. Musicians had to avoid coarse behaviour and dishonourable instruments such as the bagpipes, and prospective apprentices had to prove their good birth before starting their training.[50]

Although patriarchal structures shaped the training and career of many musicians, some women still managed to enter the profession. The first obstacle that a woman had to overcome was the association between public performance and sexual availability: to sing or play before an audience could imply that her body was also somehow on offer, whether in theory or (in the case of Venice's well-known courtesans) in practice. Hence women's careers, such as they were, usually developed under the protection of an institution, a patron, or a musical father. The conservatories of some Italian cities were one space where women could develop musical skills to a high level. At court, too, many daughters of musicians enjoyed the same opportunities for training and performance as sons – the renowned singer–composers Francesca and Settimia Caccini, are obvious examples, as is the keyboard player Elisabeth-Claude Jacquet de la Guerre (1666/7–1729) – but usually only if they could be kept within the court by way of marriage, often to other court musicians. Both Caccinis were married to instrumentalists in Medici service, while Jacquet de la Guerre wedded an organist. Other women 'musicians' in court occupied non-musical positions such as ladies-in-waiting, or were granted a status of semi-nobility, or achieved it again through marriage: this had already been the pattern with the renowned *concerto di donne* of Ferrara in the late sixteenth century.

Convents provided a further space where women's musical talents could flower more or less without hindrance. Nuns in some parts of Italy enjoyed significant musical opportunities, although even here some ecclesiastical authorities tried to curb music-making in the convents. It would be wrong to assume that all nuns of the period were happy with their lot: the increasing number of girls taking the veil was above all a result of bridal dowries being inflated beyond the pockets of many parents. But convents allowed musical women to sing services, play the organ, direct choirs and compose. Nuns in Bologna, Milan, Naples and Siena were sometimes permitted to have lessons from male teachers and to invite secular musicians to perform in their chapels.[51] Some nuns even had their music published: Lucrezia Vizzana's (1590–1662) *Componimenti musicali* (1623) contained new-style motets, while in the 1640s several

50 Regulations reprinted in Spitta, *Johann Sebastian Bach*, i: 144–52.
51 Kendrick, *Celestial Sirens*; Reardon, *Holy Concord within Sacred Walls*.

books of *concertato* motets appeared by Chiara Margarita Cozzolani (b. 1602). Later in the century, one of the most published Italian composers was Isabella Leonarda (1620–1704), a nun from a minor noble family in Novara. It is intriguing that these cloistered women were allowed to release their works to the public; Craig Monson suggests that Vizzana's convent may have sponsored the printing of her music to increase its profile in the wider world.[52]

The changes in the profession nonetheless allowed a few women to make musical careers outside the court or the cloisters, notably as virtuoso singers in the opera-house. Views on women performing on stage varied across Europe: the practice was forbidden in Rome and the Papal States, but in other parts of Italy female actresses were already accepted by the middle of the sixteenth century. The origins and training of these virtuoso singers tend necessarily to be obscure: the renowned soprano and composer Barbara Strozzi (1619–77) may or may not have been the illegitimate daughter of her adoptive father, the Venetian poet Giulio Strozzi, and she may or may not (depending on which contemporary pamphlet one reads) have practised as a courtesan as well as a musician. The early career of Anna Renzi, perhaps the greatest virtuoso of the Venetian opera-houses in mid-century, is equally shadowy, although she was associated with and perhaps also trained by the Roman composer Filiberto Laurenzi. Somewhat similarly, the training of Lully's leading soprano, Marie Le Rochois, is unknown but she was brought to his notice by his father-in-law, Michel Lambert. As these examples suggest, the new operatic divas still required patriarchal protection from a family (father or brother), a patron, a husband or a lover. They faced many obstacles and inequalities, and were usually regarded as fair game by the men titillated by their performances. But they enjoyed a greater power in the musical market-place than ever before, and a consequent financial independence that granted them a position hitherto inconceivable for women.

Servants, employees and entrepreneurs

An ambitious musician could pursue various avenues for advancement, each offering different opportunities and requiring different strategies for self-promotion. Church employment was probably the most stable and conventional, with a regular round of duties, and at least a reasonable expectation that pay would be received on time. Mobility up the profession (e.g., to a more important institution or one with a richer musical establishment) could depend on networks or on patronage, but was primarily achieved by way of merit, to

---

52 Monson, *Disembodied Voices*, p. 121.

be demonstrated by audition or other evidence of talent. Here, the main threat to job security was antagonising present or future colleagues, but even then, it took some effort to get rid of a recalcitrant member of a chapel once an appointment had been confirmed.

Court musicians relied largely on their personal relations with a single patron; by contrast, a town musician – whether or not employed in a church – might have dealings with several patrons and also might entrepreneurially develop the urban market for music. Both needed to perfect skills of self-presentation, whether humbly requesting a patron's protection or launching ventures in the public market-place. Court musicians had to build a strong relationship with their prince. Flattering language helped, as did proximity to the ruling family. Here musicians had an advantage among court servants: although they did not have quite such intimate access to the ruler as a dresser, midwife or surgeon, many performed music in the private chamber. Further-more, the affective power of their performances was reputed to sway patrons in unique ways. In Jakob von Grimmelshausen's novel *Simplicissimus* (1669), the protagonist uses his musical skills to captivate a succession of patrons and move upwards in their service. In Italy, virtuoso singers were envied for the easy advancement that they supposedly received. As Rosa wrote in his satire, 'The whole court's tuned to music, nothing else. / The rising sing *do, re, mi, fa, sol, la*. / The falling sing *la, sol, fa, mi, re, do*.'[53]

The career of Jean-Baptiste Lully demonstrates how skilled dealings with patrons could lead to spectacular advancement. He was the son of a Florentine miller and came to France as a scullion in a minor household. He entered royal service in 1652 as a dancer and rapidly became the favourite of Louis XIV, who was just a few years younger. The two men danced together in the *Ballet de la Nuit* (1653) and their shared enthusiasm for dancing enabled Lully to build a close relationship that he then exploited to the full. Already in the 1650s Lully was granted a musical power-base at the court in the form of his own band (the *Petits violons*) with which he could bypass existing court ensembles. When Louis began his personal rule in 1661 he declared Lully *Surintendant de la Musique de la Chambre*; the next year Lully married the daughter of Michel Lambert, the senior musician in the Chambre. Having thus consolidated his position, Lully deprived rivals such as Robert Cambert (*c.* 1628–1677) or Marc-Antoine Charpentier (1643–1704) of opportunities at court. In 1672 he gained the royal privilege for opera in Paris, taking advantage of the bankruptcy of the exist-ing patent holders and then excluding his former collaborator, the dramatist Molière, from royal productions. Already holding a monopoly over France's

---

53 Scott, *Salvator Rosa*, pp. 80–81.

musical life, he entered the highest rank of the peerage when he was declared *Secrétaire du roi* in 1681; he requested this office after having charmed the king by dancing in a revival of *Le bourgeois gentilhomme*. Lully's rise to complete musical power was facilitated by the cultural centralisation that accompanied Louis's political absolutism. With artistic resources focussed upon the court and the formation of state-sponsored *académies* to promote the arts, it was possible for a single musician to become very powerful indeed. Nonetheless, Lully deserves particular credit for having overcome the stigma that had adhered to Italians at the French court since the days of Cardinal Mazarin. His rise was a testimony to his skilful manoeuvring, back-stabbing and bribery, and also his strong rapport with the king.

The considerable opportunities for a court musician included many non-musical privileges and duties. A musician sent abroad to get scores and recruit singers for the court was often also entrusted with diplomatic work. Nicholas Lanier (1588–1666), Master of the King's Musick, went to Italy to buy paintings for the Stuart court; Agostino Steffani (1654–1728) spent most of the 1690s as an envoy for the House of Hanover; while other court musicians acted as spies or informers. Many used their contacts to gather lucrative sinecures, such as ecclesiastical benefices creating an income to be enjoyed for life. Some musicians at the English court dabbled in trade: Alfonso Ferrabosco (II; *c.* 1575–1628) and the flute-player Innocent Lanier had a monopoly to dredge the Thames, which entitled them to a penny on every ton of strangers' goods imported or exported.[54]

It was not surprising that most musicians coveted positions in court, where often the most exciting and innovative musical developments took place. For instance, in central Europe the latest Italian styles and opera were found at such courts as Dresden and Innsbruck. A musician at a court did not have to liaise with conservative, interfering institutions such as churches and town councils. Some patrons encouraged enterprise and innovation by funding foreign study: in the 1600s northern musicians were regularly sent to Italy by Landgrave Moritz of Hesse-Kassel, by the Elector of Saxony and by Christian IV of Denmark. Perhaps most important, court service promised unequalled status and pay. In the ordinances regulating social status in Halle, the *Kapellmeister* at the nearby Weissenfels court was in the third out of nine orders of society, while the rank-and-file court musicians took fifth place, above even the trumpeters and kettle-drummers who usually earned prestige from their ceremonial duties.[55] Pay at the German courts was also good. Schütz at Dresden earned 400 gulden a year in the 1620s, when Schein's basic salary as Leipzig Thomaskantor

54 Holman, *Four and Twenty Fiddlers*, p. 49.   55 Braun, *Die Musik des 17. Jahrhunderts*, p. 27.

was 100 gulden. Admittedly the figures are hard to compare, because Schein received free board and lodging, numerous gifts from the town council, and extra income from funerals and weddings. It is unclear whether Schütz also received food, clothing and housing, and as we shall see, his wages often went unpaid; but on paper, at least, he was undoubtedly one of the best-remunerated musicians of his day.

Yet court employment had its own peculiar disadvantages. It bound a musician completely to the prince, curbing personal autonomy and (save by special request) freedom for private projects or travel. This subjugation was also evident in how court posts were filled: whereas most town musicians were recruited by way of competitive audition, those at court were sought out by talent-scouts and then summoned to the lord's service. Few dared to defy that call. The musician then promised to serve that prince exclusively and to seek no other patron. Looking for another post could arouse princely displeasure: in 1717, Johann Sebastian Bach was imprisoned by Duke Wilhelm Ernst of Weimar for requesting release from his service. Furthermore, the compositions written during courtly service were often regarded as the patron's property. In the 1560s the Duke of Bavaria tried to keep the motets of Orlande de Lassus (d. 1594) exclusive to the Munich court, until a copyist smuggled a manuscript to the outside world. At Wolfenbüttel, Michael Praetorius (1571–1621) was not allowed to publish his court compositions without his patron's consent.[56] And when the Medici family wanted a copy of Monteverdi's *Arianna* after its Mantuan première, they asked the Mantuan court rather than the composer.[57]

Musicians' letters suggest that court employment was highly insecure: as Monteverdi noted, court incomes could 'dry up on the death of a duke or at his slightest ill humour'.[58] In reality, however, courts varied widely in their treatment of their employees. Monteverdi's cynicism must be read in the context of the Gonzagas at Mantua, who were volatile masters, and also, perhaps, of his own refusal to adhere to the system. Following the death of Duke Vincenzo in 1612, many court servants were laid off; Monteverdi remained for several months but was then dismissed for reasons that remain unclear, although he may have incurred displeasure by hinting that he could get work elsewhere. By contrast, the Medici court could offer veritable sinecures, paying salaries for life and sometimes to the musician's heirs as well. Even here, however, musicians could be summarily dismissed on the death of their patron, and the band at any court could be dispersed during periods of mourning or when princely taste changed. We have already seen how music at the English court was reduced

56 Deeters, 'Alte und neue Aktenfunde über Michael Praetorius', p. 103.
57 Stevens (trans.), *The Letters of Claudio Monteverdi*, p. 89.
58 See Monteverdi's letter to Alessandro Striggio of 13 March 1620, in ibid., p. 192.

after the accession of William and Mary in 1689, forcing composers such as
Purcell to turn to the commercial theatres for work. Because court music was
so prone to interruption and change, musicians often ended up moving around
so as to fill these temporary periods of unemployment.

Court salaries were high on paper, but were not always paid in full or on
time. Sometimes the princes who were the keenest music-lovers had little
eye for future prudence and were perpetually short of cash. The letters of
Monteverdi and Schütz are full of appeals for arrears to be paid. In 1611, at a
time of relative economic and political stability, most of the musicians at the
Dresden court were owed between 3 and 22 months of back-pay.[59] Conditions
deteriorated markedly as the Thirty Years War took its toll. In August 1651,
Schütz complained to his patron that the musicians had received only nine
months' wages in the past four years. One bass was 'living like a sow in a
pigsty, has no bedstead, sleeps on straw, and has already pawned his coat and
doublet'.[60] Schütz himself was not too badly off (in the same year he bought
a house in Weissenfels, and at other times he loaned substantial sums to the
towns of Erfurt and Pirna), but his repeated petitions to the Elector of Saxony
paint a bleak picture of the state of the Dresden musicians. He claimed to be
finding court employment so wretched that he rhetorically declared, 'I for my
part . . . would, God knows, rather be a cantor or organist in some small town
than stay any longer in such circumstances'.[61]

Schütz's outburst resonates with some of Monteverdi's dissatisfaction over
courtly service. As Monteverdi became more aware of his own worth, he increasingly disliked being subjugated to the whims of the Gonzagas. He refused to
compose hastily or badly, taking up to a week to compose a madrigal, and he
regularly complained about having to write to princely command. His letters to
his patron became increasingly forceful (although still larded with the conventional formulas of supplication), and in 1608 he audaciously requested his own
dismissal.[62] This request was not granted, but after he was removed from the
court in 1612 he became *maestro di cappella* at St Mark's, Venice. Although this
was far from the small-town job rhetorically envisaged by Schütz, Monteverdi
valued the security of his church post and was also able to tap the urban market
for music. In a letter of March 1620 he recounted the opportunities available to
him in Venice: besides his job at St Mark's, he could earn money from outside
engagements at other churches and private houses. Unlike a court composer,
Monteverdi was here paid separately for writing pieces and for directing performances.[63] One also assumes that he was paid for his work for the newly

59 Munck, 'Keeping up Appearances', p. 228.   60 Müller (ed.), *Heinrich Schütz*, pp. 224–5.
61 Ibid., p. 224.   62 Stevens (trans.), *The Letters of Claudio Monteverdi*, pp. 44, 51.
63 So Monteverdi reported to Alessandro Striggio on 13 March 1620; see ibid., pp. 190–94.

opened public opera-houses in Venice, which he undertook even when he was in his seventies.

Musicians in other towns also found a wide range of opportunities. In Lutheran cities such as Nuremberg or Königsberg, the upper social stratum often commissioned new pieces for their weddings and funerals. In Leipzig during the 1620s, Schein presented printed copies of such pieces to the citizenry, asserting his presence in civic society and creating a demand for his services. Pamphlets of occasional music were exchanged among the elite to affirm friendships and cultivate allegiances. As Schein noted in *Israelis Brünlein* (1623), he often had to write occasional pieces at short notice and more hastily than he would have liked, but such commissions doubtless gained him healthy fees and useful contacts. As we have seen, the earliest public concerts are another instance of musicians cultivating the urban market for music. In Lübeck, the organists Franz Tunder and Dieterich Buxtehude established the evening concert series known as *Abendmusik*. These concerts required immense work not only in writing the music and marshalling the performers but also in raising sponsorship from the town council and support from merchants. Although there was no charge for entry, money was made by selling printed booklets containing the texts, and encouraging some dignitaries to subscribe for their seats.[64] Whereas concert series in other cities were often initiated by impoverished musicians seeking to supplement their income – as with the ill-paid London court musicians under John Banister in 1672 – Tunder and Buxtehude seem to have used the *Abendmusik* as an outlet for their ambitious projects in composition and performance.

Yet town musicians often cast longing looks at the prestige attached to the courts. Monteverdi was a prime example. In 1615, after only two years in Venice, he sent a supplicatory letter to Mantua when it looked likely that Muzio Effrem would receive court commissions. He continued to compose for the Gonzagas and other north Italian dukes, and in the 1620s he began negotiations to enter service at the Polish court and perhaps also at Vienna.[65] In part these were the wiles of a musician keen to retain every chance of work and to play off prospective and current employees. But doubtless Monteverdi was also tempted by the honour and status carried by court service, as well as by the flattering knowledge that his name and music could enhance the prestige of some of the most powerful princes of Europe.

64 Snyder, *Dieterich Buxtehude*, pp. 56–72.
65 Saunders, 'New Light on the Genesis of Monteverdi's Eighth Book of Madrigals'; Parisi, 'New Documents Concerning Monteverdi's Relations with the Gonzagas'.

The musician in society

The practical musician had an ambiguous place in society. Although some composers won respect for their output and learning, their craft remained separate from the intellectual mainstream and lacked the undeniable status of theology or law. Part of the problem was that the profession was tarred by its association with itinerant musicians whose status was no higher than beggars and vagrants. In Germany wandering musicians were classed as dishonourable (*unehrliche*) along with hangmen, jailers, prostitutes and the like.[66] Hence the guild of civic instrumentalists in Saxony founded in 1653, mentioned above, made strenuous efforts to prove the honour of its members and to distinguish them from itinerant players. Even elite musicians could be irked by the associations of dishonour, with Tobias Michael (Thomaskantor in Leipzig during the 1630s) quoting the following proverb in his *Musicalischer Seelen-Lust ander Theil* (Leipzig, 1637):

> Wiltu reich werden und geehrt
> Vor gschicht gehalten und gelehrt,
> So laß die Music ungeacht
> Sonst wirstu selber werdn veracht.

[If you want wealth and honour / or to be adroit and learned, / leave Music well alone / or you'll be despised yourself.]

As proof of such a proverb, Schütz's family – a line of well-off innkeepers and civic officials – tried to dissuade their son from becoming a professional musician and would have preferred him to enter the law like his brothers.

The ambiguous status of musicians perhaps also reflected a fundamental rootlessness in their lives. They could ply their trade to all social classes but sometimes that very mobility prevented them from putting down roots. Schein was indispensable to the elite of Leipzig in his capacity as Thomaskantor, writing and performing compositions that could boost the reputation of the town and of its leading individuals; and he managed to get some of the most distinguished citizens to be godparents to his children. Yet he also worked at lower levels, writing lewd drinking songs for students; and when he came to choose his second wife, he aligned himself with a middling class by marrying the daughter of a decorative painter. Many professionals seem to have spent a life betwixt and between, belonging to no other class than that of musician. This impression is strengthened by the tendency of musicians to marry within the profession. When they did marry into a non-musical family, they could rarely reach higher than the daughters of minor officials. Even lesser nobility

66 Danckert, *Unehrliche Leute*.

were firmly out of reach: in 1589 the Mantuan *maestro di cappella* Giaches de Wert (1535–96) was forbidden to continue an affair with Tarquinia Molza, a lady-in-waiting and singer at the Ferrarese court.

The relative wealth of musicians is hard to determine, partly because hard currency was not the most important economic measure in the period. More-over the fortunes of individuals could fluctuate markedly: war or plague could destroy the richest family, and bad harvests could lead to soaring grain prices and famine. Some musicians died paupers. Others, however, left substantial estates, such as Francesco Cavalli (1602–76) whose cash investments alone were worth more than the annual music budget at St Mark's, Venice. More typical was the variety of incomes of musicians in Dresden and London. At the Dresden court, Schütz earned for his work as *Kapellmeister* as much as an assistant preacher, and probably only slightly less than his brothers earned as lawyers. The other Dresden musicians received a range of salaries similar to those of well-paid kitchen staff.[67] For London, Ian Spink has estimated that a rank-and-file court musician might expect to be paid the same as a better-off member of the clergy, a military officer, or someone in the liberal arts. Lesser musicians such as town waits were closer to shopkeepers or minor tradesmen in their income, while a street musician might be indistinguishable from a beggar.[68] But it must be remembered that the nominal wages of musicians might go unpaid or might equally be augmented by freelancing, and that fringe benefits (such as allowances for housing, clothing and food) could make a significant difference to an annual income.

Although music was a risky choice for a child of a well-off family such as Schütz, it could also offer remarkable economic and social advancement to those of modest birth. We have already seen how Lully rose from being a miller's son to holding high noble rank in France; similarly, Giulio Caccini was the son of a carpenter and yet achieved the ability to move freely through the Medici court. Musical skills had always allowed those of humble origin to enter and influence privileged circles. The commercialisation of opera increased the opportunities for those with musical talent, and we have seen how the orphanages of Venice taught music to foundlings as a skill that allowed them to make their own way in the world. Castratos perhaps furnish the best example of music as a means of advancement. Just as many Italian parents sent their children into monasteries and convents in order to save the costs of marriage and rearing a family, it was common for families in the Kingdom of Naples to have one or more of their sons castrated and then enrolled in a conservatory. At the least, the son might

---

67 Munck, 'Keeping up Appearances', pp. 26–7.
68 Spink (ed.), *The Blackwell History of Music in Britain*, iii: 33.

gain the security of a church post; at the best, he might make a fortune from opera. The castrato would have no children of his own to raise – setting limits on the dispersal of the family patrimony – but would instead be devoted to his career and to making an income that might support his parents in their old age.

Yet the act of composing and performing cannot always be reduced merely to matters of economic or social survival. In the same way that amateurs were drawn to music, some professionals felt a commitment to their craft that defied reason or need. Schütz persisted with music against his parents' wishes, devoting 'continuous study, travel and writing' to the craft.[69] Not all of his output was written for his duties or for immediate pecuniary advantage. In 1655 one of his colleagues published Schütz's *Zwölff geistliche Gesänge*, a collection of modest pieces that Schütz had written in his 'spare time' (*Neben-Stunden*) for the Dresden choirboys. Even if this claim is discounted as the typical false modesty in statements of authorship, there exist other pieces that Schütz seemingly wrote for private reasons. Upon the death of his wife in 1625, he composed a heartfelt *Klaglied* and also completed a book of simple psalm-settings, the Becker Psalter, written partly for his own domestic use and 'to draw greater comfort in my sorrow'. Here the very act of composition seems to have been a therapeutic act to structure and dissipate his grief. Schütz's sense of a musical vocation may also be evident in his later desire to revise and publish his music, even if here he was also concerned to maintain his professional identity in print.

And although most music was an accompaniment to ceremony, liturgy or social gatherings, it was doubtless still possible for practitioners to get personal satisfaction from their playing and composing. Whatever the patron had commissioned, musicians could include details to raise a knowing or appreciative smile between performers. Musicians were subject to economic and social forces, but their achievements in the musical styles and genres discussed elsewhere in this book cannot be seen solely as functions of these forces. Music could be a family trade, a courtier's skill, a connoisseur's pleasure or a means of advancement, but it was a craft that demanded and rewarded quality workmanship, despite the many uncertainties of a profession racked by change.

Bibliography

Aercke, K. P., *Gods of Play: Baroque Festive Performances as Rhetorical Discourse*. Albany, NY, 1994

Allsop, P., *Arcangelo Corelli: 'New Orpheus of Our Time'*. Oxford, 1999

Ashbee, A. (ed.), *Records of English Court Music*, viii: *1485–1714*. Aldershot, 1995

Bianconi, L., *Music in the Seventeenth Century*, trans. D. Bryant. Cambridge, 1987

---

69 See his petition of 14 January 1651 given in Müller (ed.), *Heinrich Schütz*, pp. 212–13.

Bianconi, L., and Walker, T., 'Production, Consumption and Political Function of Seventeenth-Century Opera'. *Early Music History*, 4 (1984), 209–96

Biehle, H., *Musikgeschichte von Bautzen*. Leipzig, 1924

Braun, W., *Die Musik des 17. Jahrhunderts*, 'Neues Handbuch der Musikwissenschaft', 4. Wiesbaden, 1981

Burke, P., *The Fabrication of Louis XIV*. New Haven and London, 1992

Carter, T., 'Music-Publishing in Italy c. 1580–1625: Some Preliminary Observations'. *Royal Musical Association Research Chronicle*, 20 (1986–7), 19–37

Music in Late Renaissance and Early Baroque Italy. London, 1992

'Printing the "New Music"'. In K. van Orden (ed.), *Music and the Cultures of Print*. New York and London, 2000, pp. 3–37

Danckert, W., *Unehrliche Leute*. Berne, 1963

Deeters, W., 'Alte und neue Aktenfunde über Michael Praetorius'. *Braunschweigisches Jahrbuch*, 52 (1971), 102–120

Earle, P., *The Making of the English Middle Class*. London, 1989

Edler, A., 'Organ Music within the Social Structure of North German Cities in the Seventeenth Century'. In P. Walker (ed.), *Church, Stage and Studio: Music and its Contexts in Seventeenth-Century Germany*. Ann Arbor, 1990, pp. 23–42

Hammond, F., *Girolamo Frescobaldi*. Cambridge, MA, 1983

Holman, P., *Four and Twenty Fiddlers: the Violin at the English Court 1540–1690*. Oxford, 1993

Kendrick, R., *Celestial Sirens: Nuns and their Music in Early Modern Milan*. Oxford, 1996

Krüger, L., *Die Hamburgische Musikorganisation im XVII. Jahrhundert*. Strasbourg, 1933

La Gorce, J. de, 'Lully's First Opera: a Rediscovered Poster for *Les fêtes de L'Amour et de Bacchus*'. *Early Music*, 15 (1987), 308–14

Latham, R. C., and Matthews, W. (eds), *The Diary of Samuel Pepys*. 11 vols, London, 1970–83

Monson, C., *Disembodied Voices: Music and Culture in an Early Modern Italian Convent*. Berkeley, 1995

Müller, E. H. (ed.), *Heinrich Schütz: Gesammelte Briefe und Schriften*. Regensburg, 1931

Munck, T., 'Keeping up Appearances: Patronage of the Arts, City Prestige and Princely Power in North Germany and Denmark 1600–1670'. *German History*, 6 (1988), 213–32

Seventeenth-Century Europe. London, 1990

Murata, M., 'Roman Cantata Scores as Traces of Musical Culture and Signs of Its Place in Society'. In A. Pompilio, D. Restani, L. Bianconi and F. A. Gallo (eds), *Atti del XIV congresso della Società Internazionale di Musicologia: 'Trasmissione e recezione delle forme di cultura musicale' (Bologna, 27 Agosto – 1 Settembre 1987; Ferrara–Parma, 30 Agosto 1987)*. 2 vols, Turin, 1991, i: 272–84

Parisi, S. H., 'New Documents Concerning Monteverdi's Relations with the Gonzagas'. In P. Besutti, T. M. Gialdroni and R. Baroncini (eds), *Claudio Monteverdi: studi e prospettive; atti del convegno, Mantova, 21–24 ottobre 1993*, 'Accademia Nazionale Virgiliana di Scienze, Lettere e Arti: Miscellanea', 5. Florence, 1998, pp. 477–511

Pinto, D., 'Music at Court: Remarks on the Performance of William Lawes's Works for Viols'. In *A Viola da Gamba Miscellany: Proceedings of the International Viola da Gamba Symposium, Utrecht 1991*. Utrecht, 1994, pp. 27–39

Reardon, C., *Holy Concord within Sacred Walls: Nuns and Music in Siena 1575–1700*. New York and Oxford, 2001

Rose, S., 'Publication and the Anxiety of Judgement in German Musical Life of the Seventeenth Century'. *Music & Letters*, 85 (2004), 22–40

'Music, Print and Presentation in Saxony during the Seventeenth Century'. *German History*, 23 (2005), 1–19

'Mechanisms of the Music Trade in Central Germany 1600–1640'. *Journal of the Royal Musical Association*, 130 (2005), 1–37

Rosselli, J., *Singers of Italian Opera*. Cambridge, 1992

Saunders, S., 'New Light on the Genesis of Monteverdi's Eighth Book of Madrigals'. *Music and Letters*, 77 (1996), 183–93

Scott, J., *Salvator Rosa: his Life and Times*. New Haven and London, 1995

Sigtenhorst Meyer, B. van den, *Jan P. Sweelinck en zijn instrumentale muziek*. 2nd edn, The Hague, 1946

Sittard, J., *Zur Geschichte der Musik und des Theaters am württembergischen Hof*. 2 vols, Stuttgart, 1890

Snyder, K. J., *Dieterich Buxtehude: Organist in Lübeck*. New York, 1987

Spagnoli, G., *Letters and Documents of Heinrich Schütz, 1656–1672: an Annotated Translation*. Ann Arbor, 1990

Spink, I. (ed.), *The Blackwell History of Music*, iii: *The Seventeenth Century*. Oxford, 1992

Spitta, P., *Johann Sebastian Bach*. Engl. edn, 3 vols, London, 1884–5

Stevens, D. (trans.), *The Letters of Claudio Monteverdi*. 2nd edn, Oxford, 1995

Turnbull, M., 'The Sources for the Two Versions of *Psyché*'. In J. de La Gorce and H. Schneider (eds), *Jean-Baptiste Lully: actes du colloque Saint-Germain en Laye, Heidelberg, 1987*. Laaber, 1990, pp. 349–56

Wade, M. R., '*Triumphus nuptialis danicus*': German Court Culture and Denmark. Wiesbaden, 1996

Walther, J. G., *Briefe*, ed. K. Beckmann and H.-J. Schulze. Leipzig, 1987

Wilson, J. (ed.), *Roger North on Music, Being a Selection of his Essays Written during the Years c. 1695–1728*. London, 1959

Wood, C., and Sadler, G. (eds), *French Baroque Opera: a Reader*. Aldershot, 2000

4

Music in new worlds

VICTOR ANAND COELHO

Imagine that during the last week of December around 1600, a Portuguese vessel leaves Goa, the magnificent capital of the Portuguese Asian empire located 350 miles south of Bombay, for the six-month return to Lisbon. The bottom two layers of the four-deck ship are devoted to storing spices – mainly pepper, but the return cargo also includes cinnamon, ginger, nutmeg, cloves, indigo and Chinese silk bought from Moorish traders. With the remaining two decks reserved for official cabins and the storage of privately owned chests, little room is left for the 100 sailors and a chicken coop.[1] Crossing the Indian Ocean during the most pleasant time of the year, the ship docks briefly at the Portuguese possession of Mozambique (settled 1507) and arrives a month later at the Cape of Good Hope. But instead of rounding the Cape and sailing north up the coast of West Africa, past the Portuguese settlements of Benin (1485), the Congo (c. 1480), Sierra Leone (1460), the archipelago of São Tomé (c. 1471), and the Cabo Verde islands (1444), which lie along the route that brought them to India, the Portuguese crew sails due west into the heart of the Atlantic bringing the ship almost within sight of the Brazilian coast before its sails catch the easterly winds that will allow it to tack north towards the Azores, the last stop of the over 10,000-mile round trip before reaching Lisbon. Along the way, descriptions and opinions of native instruments and musical styles are logged into diaries: a Congolese lute, xylophones from Mozambique, cymbals, drums and bells, and reed instruments.[2]

Had this ship continued on to Brazil, where the Portuguese had settled in 1500, our musically minded crew would have noticed that the music performed in some of the larger churches there involved the same or similar repertory to what they had heard 7,000 miles away in the Sé Catedral in Goa, which, in turn, was the music, including chant, used in countless Catholic churches in Portugal and across Europe. This observation will certainly come as a surprise for readers accustomed to the European map on which we have plotted the main itineraries

---

1 On the itineraries and personnel, etc., of Portuguese vessels, see Domingos, 'Vaisseaux et mariniers'.
2 For a summary of these accounts, see Brito, 'Sounds of the Discoveries'.

of our early-modern music histories. We are so used to working on this narrow geographical scale – for example, considering how quickly Josquin's music was disseminated throughout Europe, or the speed at which musicians in northern Germany kept abreast of developments in Baroque Italy – that we may be startled at how swiftly and comprehensively repertories, instruments, performance styles and ceremonial practices were transmitted along the routes of exploration in the sixteenth and seventeenth centuries, allowing the Oriental, Old and New worlds to share common musical experiences at roughly the same time. To give but two examples: non-European sources show that the music of Francisco Guerrero (1528–99) was heard during the late sixteenth century not only in Spain (and, to be sure, in other parts of Europe), but also in Guatemala as well as in the Philippines. And we find near-contemporaneous sources of dances of African origin in the Congo/Angola, Brazil and Portugal, some of which later found their way into the European guitar repertory.[3]

Interest in the transmission of mainstream European repertories (or at least styles) across continents and cultures has emerged as a fertile area within musicology in recent years, not least because of its relevance to the discipline's ongoing re-examination of its methods and canons. The topic has shed light on the colonial and political – what used to be considered 'ambassadorial' – roles of music, as well as on the self-awareness (or not) of 'dominant' cultures, and on the nature of and reasons for musical export itself.[4] In many ways, work in this area is symptomatic of, if not a cause of, the new rapprochements between musicology, ethnomusicology, literature, critical theory and cultural studies. Colonial and post-colonial studies have inspired fresh examinations of opera and its subtexts, ranging from orientalism and missionary conquests of Asian 'others' in the seventeenth century, to an increased interest in New World sources, non-Western influences, and politics (both sexual and institutional).[5]

On the other hand, traditional methodologies such as documentary and source studies remain fundamental for any assessment of the global history and politics of cross-cultural repertories during the sixteenth and seventeenth centuries. The voluminous archival work on Jesuit documents by scholars such as Joseph Wicki and Carlos Leonhardt, for example, are rich with information about music's function along the routes of Asian and New World missions respectively, and its context in terms of evangelical and institutional politics.

---

3 Budasz, 'The Five-course Guitar (*Viola*) in Portugal and Brazil in the Late Seventeenth and Early Eighteenth Centuries', pp. 148–56. See also Budasz's study and edition of musical references in the works of the seventeenth-century Brazilian poet, Gregório de Mattos (1636–96): *A Música no Tempo de Gregório de Mattos*.
4 Baumann (ed.), *World Music, Musics of the World*.
5 Dellamora and Fischlin (eds), *The Work of Opera*; Maehder, 'The Representation of the "Discovery" on the Opera Stage'.

In his work on the Philippines, William Summers has also noted the detail and frequency of discussions about music in Jesuit correspondence.[6] Similarly, archival research conducted in Japan, Paraguay, Brazil, Mexico, Bolivia and Guatemala – again, mostly dealing with Jesuit missions – has raised important issues concerning both the installation of European music in conquered territories, and the culturally embedded politics within that music.

Not surprisingly, despite the dispassionate and objective pretexts of archival work, post-colonial history has revealed its own subjectivity through the mounting tension between European and non-European perspectives that is part of the complexity that overwrites post-colonial identities to the present day. In other words, scholars have split, interpretatively speaking, along culturally grounded lines that are often in conflict. The result is a re-opening of the past that has allowed non-Western scholars to reclaim their own history, apart from, and on different terms from, their inherited tradition of Western historiography. After all, as Gerard Béhague has remarked, colonialism is 'a premeditated act of transfer and imposition of the cultural/musical values of the colonising group. In this, it differs from more natural situations of contact.'[7] Ever since the publication of Edward Said's *Orientalism* challenged the post-colonial attitudes embedded in literary and artistic representation, many recent methods for understanding colonised cultures have appeared across the academic spectrum, though with varying degrees of success at escaping the gravitational pull of the West.[8] According to Dipesh Chakrabarty, who has examined several post-colonial models for the study of Indian history, much of the newest work produces a situation in which even with a concerted effort to amplify the voices of subaltern others, the end-result remains predominantly Eurocentric: so long as the history remains a discourse 'produced at the institutional site of the university . . . Europe remains the sovereign'.[9] Third-World historians feel a need to refer to works in European history, Chakrabarty continues,

> but historians of Europe do not feel any need to reciprocate. Europeans produce their work in relative ignorance of non-Western histories, and this does not seem to affect the quality of their work. This is a gesture, however, that Indians cannot return. They cannot afford an equality or symmetry of ignorance at this level without taking the risk of appearing 'old fashioned' or 'outdated'.[10]

In sum, Indian history, when filtered through a Western genre of history (for example, colonialism, Jesuit histories, determinism, Marxism or Manifest

6 Summers, 'The Jesuits in Manila', p. 666.

7 Béhague, 'The Global Impact of Portuguese Music and Musical Institutions', p. 75.

8 Among the most successful challenges to earlier post-colonial models is Mignolo's *The Darker Side of the Renaissance*, which proposes new paradigms for studying 'hybrid' cultures and identifying the syncretic relationships that evolved between coloniser and colonised that were ignored in previous historical accounts.

9 Chakrabarty, 'Postcoloniality and the Artifice of History', p. 1.   10 Ibid., p. 2.

Destiny), is but a variation on a master European narrative. This may be inevitable, given that it is difficult to present any form of history as we understand the term without some recourse to Western structures of historical thought. However, the situation prompts some circumspection. Accordingly, my essay will examine the geographical reach of seventeenth-century music and its political and cultural ramifications by considering both sides of the colonial dialogue. If by the word 'politics' we can understand a web of interacting relationships involving authority, power and influence, music becomes an important source of information as both cultural product and mode of political discourse. Since music outside Europe during the sixteenth and seventeenth centuries was mainly managed by missionaries, religious orders, viceroys, diplomats, merchants, and soldiers in the service of Christianity and nation, our sources are mostly European, ecclesiastical, diplomatic – not to mention written and therefore targeted at an audience – and so inescapably prejudiced and Eurocentric. But I have endeavoured to approach this material in a critical fashion, also acknowledging non-European voices and perspectives. Beginning with analyses of source studies and patronage in order to identify musical repertories and their context, I will proceed to the connections between global politics through a case-study of music as it was exported to and developed within the Portuguese colony of Goa from the arrival in the city of the first Jesuit, Francis Xavier in 1542, to the decline of Goa's role as the capital of the Portuguese empire in the late seventeenth century. I will also discuss some of the cross-cultural travels of instruments and instrumental music during the seventeenth century, which will permit some further observations about the role of music within the politics of culture.

Quomodo cantabimus canticum domini in terra aliena?

'How shall we sing the Lord's song in a foreign land?', wrote the Italian Jesuit Rudolf Acquaviva (quoting Psalm 137) during his celebrated mission to the heart of the Mughal Empire in India.[11] Source studies and documents have played a crucial role in identifying the global range of European musical transmission, music's institutional setting and users, and the relationship between genre and ceremony. The most precise information concerning European musical exports comes from earlier in the sixteenth century, when Spanish, Portuguese and English colonial missions to the New World, Africa and Asia

11 Letter from Fr. Rudolf Acquaviva to Fr. Nuno Rodrigues, 10 September 1580. For a translation of this letter, see Correia-Afonso (ed.), *Letters from the Mughal Court*, pp. 87–91. This book contains the complete correspondence dealing with the Jesuit mission to Fatehpur Sikri.

quickly established a musical infrastructure for use in liturgical services, diplomatic missions and military operations, thus necessitating the exporting of music books, choir directors, singers, trumpeters, drummers and occasionally string players. In essence, this was an installation of a prefabricated European musical tradition bound to its function, a co-ordinated system of ritual designed mainly to overwrite indigenous sacred and ceremonial practices, analogous to the manner in which Christian churches in India supplanted razed temples and mosques on the very same locations. The importance placed on music throughout early European colonialism betrays its role as both a superior language and a replacement of existing ones. Prior to coming to India, the Portuguese Vicar-General Miguel Vaz produced a 41-point plan that wrote into law extremely harsh measures meant to secure the conversion of the natives.[12] Shirodkar writes that 'Hindus in Goa were to be deprived of all human rights, idolatry was to be outlawed, temples to be destroyed, idols in no form to be made' – although Hindu idols were indeed replaced by crucifixes – and 'Hindu festivals to remain uncelebrated'.[13] In political terms, the penalty of violating any of these rules was harsh. King D. Sebastião II of Portugal banned even the domestic display of idols, and set severe limits upon temple festivities and ritual, marriage and cremation ceremonies, all of which normally called for elaborate and explicit musical expression.[14] Punishments were meted out in the form of economic disenfranchisement in which violators lost their estates to the Church.[15] Many other cases and laws could be cited to document further how indigenous practices involving music were both obliterated and comprehensively replaced by ready-made colonial values.

Thus the success of evangelical missions to both Asia and the New World was predicated to a large degree on a concomitant musical colonisation deriving from the transplanting of traditional representational ceremonies such as those of the Mass and Office, as well as of processions and feast-days. These rituals imposed a new cultural grammar through sight, sense and sound. In his study of music and death rituals in sixteenth-century Mexico, Wagstaff shows how the elaborate tradition of Processions of the Dead re-enacted by the Spanish in Latin America 'served a pedagogical purpose because they provided a moment when the new "journey" of Christianity could be solidified in the new converts' minds'.[16] In a similar fashion, the native dances and music in Corpus

---

12 For a full account of the suppression of Hindu practices, see Priolkar, *The Goa Inquisition*, pp. 114–49.

13 Shirodkar, 'Evangelisation and its Harsh Realities in Portuguese India', p. 81, which provides a concise summary from a Hindu scholar's perspective.

14 Pearson, *The Portuguese in India*, p. 117.

15 Shirodkar, 'Socio-Cultural Life in Goa during the 16th Century', p. 33.

16 Wagstaff, 'Processions for the Dead, the Senses, and Ritual Identity in Colonial Mexico', p. 169.

Christi processions from colonial Cuzco were intentionally programmed by the Spanish elite as a way for Andeans 'to "perform" their indigeneity and thereby act out the role of the defeated Other in the triumph of Christianity over native religion'.[17] By 1545, musical training and its attendant ceremony in Goa had become institutionalised as part of a pedagogical system for the parochial schools that all boys were required to attend. On the other side of the world, the Spaniards of Guatemala, only a decade following their conquest of 1523–4, had built a cathedral, providing a theatre for such rituals to evolve within a mixed community; this was soon followed by the installation of a permanent organist, and also of a *chantre* 'who must always be expert enough to sing and conduct chant at the choirbook stand'.[18]

On a more local level, missionaries in the field in Mexico and Goa were instructed to use chant, then polyphony, to assist in the conversion process. Polyphony, in fact, was introduced in Goa explicitly as a means for the musical seeding of villages and to increase the number of 'heathen' baptisms. The pedagogical success of the enterprise – in musical training if not necessarily in conversion – is borne out by the testimony of Joseph di Santa Maria from the last quarter of the seventeenth century, reporting on his visit to Goa:

> In that city I enjoyed many times listening to very beautiful music for feasts, especially that of St Ignatius Loyola, which was celebrated with seven choirs and the sweetest *sinfonie* in the Professed House of the Fathers of the Society [the Basílica do Bom Jesus], where the body of St. Francis Xavier is found; and in saying that it was like being in Rome, I was told that I was not mistaken, because the composition that had been brought to that place was by the famous Carissimi. I cannot believe how musically proficient are the Canarini [Goans], and with what ease they perform.
>
> There is no Christian hamlet or village that does not have in its church an organ, harp, and a viola, and a good choir of musicians who sing for festivities and for holy days, Vespers, Masses, and litanies, and with much cooperation and devotion . . .[19]

Amerindian choirs in Mexico had also become highly accomplished in singing polyphony and as copyists of European music.[20]

17 Baker, 'Music at Corpus Christi in Colonial Cuzco', p. 364.

18 Stevenson, 'European Music in 16th-Century Guatemala', p. 343.

19 Letter from Joseph di Santa Maria (Giuseppe Sebastiani), in the *aggiunta* to Vincenzo Maria Murchio, *Il viaggio all'Indie orientali del padre F. Vincenzo Maria di S. Caterina da Siena . . . con le osservationi, e successi nel medesimo, i costumi, e riti di varie nationi . . . con la descrittione degl'animali quadrupedi, serpenti, uccelli, e piante di quel mondo nuovo, con le loro virtu singolari. Diviso in cinque libri . . . Con la nuova aggiunta della seconda speditione all'Indie orientali di monsignor Sebastiani* (Venice, 1683), iii: 105.

20 S. Sadie and J. Tyrrell (eds), *The New Grove Dictionary of Music and Musicians*, 2nd edn, 29 vols (London, 2001), xvi: 543 (*s.v.* 'Mexico').

Repertory and transmission

Along all of the roads of exploration, the documentary and musical sources, whether associated with the cathedral or with the village parish, reveal an extraordinary level of musical proficiency, both Euro-insular and syncretic. As I have already noted, the early repertories brought to the New World and to Asia are remarkable both for their similarity to European music, and for their contemporaneity with it. The Guatemala and Puebla manuscripts studied by Snow and Borg dating from between the 1580s and the early seventeenth century, for example, contain a large and significant repertory of polyphonic Mass, motet, Magnificat, hymn and Holy Week settings by Spanish and Portuguese composers. Some of them were émigrés, such as Gaspar Fernandes; but other works are by the likes of Isaac, Josquin and Mouton, reflecting the 'classic' and retrospective – even canonical – tastes revealed by Spanish sources of the period.[21] Other New World manuscripts from Bogotá and Mexico reveal trans-Atlantic concordances with works by the greatest Iberian composers of the age – Morales, Guerrero, Victoria and Lobo – alongside works by émigrés.[22]

Similarly, Summers has shown how Spanish polyphonic sources in Manila reflect how the city's celebratory life 'was densely intertwined with the bifocal projection of Spanish colonialism, that worldwide enterprise undertaken by the inextricably interlocked institutions of the Roman Catholic church and the Spanish crown'.[23] Virtually all of the major Catholic orders – Dominicans, Augustinians, Franciscans and especially, of course, the Jesuits – were responsible for the cultivation of music and the teaching of musicians. The first books of polyphonic music, as well as the first *chantre* and organ, were brought to Manila not from Spain but from Mexico, where the parent tradition had presumably proved its ability to operate in a new context. An early seventeenth-century inventory of a Manila book merchant lists Guerrero's first book of motets (Venice, 1570), leading Summers to speculate that his music was well known in Manila alongside much other polyphony, some of it by native musicians. The genres represented included virtually every type of music: Mass cycles, motets, *villancicos*, canzonettas, and polyphonic settings for Vespers, for the *Salve* service, and of the *Te Deum*.[24] The performance styles described by the

---

21 See Snow, 'Music by Francisco Guerrero in Guatemala', and his splendid edition of one of the Guatemala manuscripts: R. Snow (ed.), *A New World Collection of Polyphony for Holy Week and the Salve Service: Guatemala City Cathedral Archive, Music MS 4* (Chicago, 1996). See also Borg, 'The Polyphonic Music in the Guatemalan Music Manuscripts of the Lilly Library'.

22 For general descriptions, see Stevenson's indispensable *Renaissance and Baroque Musical Sources in the Americas*, and the checklist contained in Sadie and Tyrrell (eds), *The New Grove Dictionary of Music and Musicians*, xxiv, *s.v.* 'Sources, MS, §IX, 23: Renaissance polyphony: South and Central American MSS', which also lists more specialised studies.

23 Summers, 'The Jesuits in Manila', p. 659.   24 Ibid., pp. 663–4.

sources – for example, *alternatim* performance between singing and instrumental sections played by loud winds, drums and bells – may prove to be valuable indications of European tastes as well. As a technique used in all colonial outposts, the polychoral style may also have had broader pedagogical and ideological aims. A report from Angola around 1620 mentions that a polychoral Mass was sung accompanied by instruments, with thirteen black musicians divided into three choirs for sonic effect.[25]

The presence of the Jesuits in Paraguay from 1609 contributed to much the same type of New World musical culture.[26] The main activity remained the teaching of music as part of training missionaries for their work in the field and for the deployment of larger musical forces for processions and ritual. Indigenous music was initially tolerated, but soon native musicians, such as the highly-skilled Guaraní, were retrained. As for the specific repertory in Paraguay, little concrete evidence has surfaced prior to the residence there of the Jesuit composer Domenico Zipoli from 1717 to his death in 1726; his works are well documented in the Archivio Musical de Chiquitos in Concepción. However, Herczog believes that Spanish polyphony is likely to have been used by the Jesuits, though probably not before 1614. Between 1617 and 1639 a solid infrastructure of musical training, both vocal and instrumental, was created through the arrival of two professional Jesuit musicians, the Belgians Jean Vaisseau and Louis Berger, which initiated what has been described as a 'Flemish-Iberian' musical style.[27] Documents show that in just a few years, polyphonic, polychoral Masses were given with frequent participation of instruments. In addition, organs and harps, among other instruments, were manufactured locally, examples of which are extant in Bolivian collections.[28]

The documentation for India is similar in that it provides only a few details of any specific musical works, and other than Carissimi as noted by Sebastiani, no other composer is named. But references to motets and *cantigas* are ubiquitous, as are numerous instances of polychoral performance, perhaps involving *alternatim* practice, along with the singing of Vespers. Frequently, Indian instruments were used along with the voices and organ. The political and evangelical purpose of such extravagant and pluralistic music is made very clear. Francesco Pasio, a key figure in the Japanese missions of the Society of Jesus, writes from Goa in 1578 that in the Colégio de São Paulo

25 Stevenson, *Portuguese Music and Musicians Abroad to 1650*, p. 17; Brito, 'Sounds of the Discoveries', p. 13.
26 On music in Paraguay under the Jesuits, see Herczog, *Orfeo nelle Indie*.　　27 Ibid., pp. 165–87.
28 Szarán and Nestosa, *Música en las reducciones Jesuíticas de América del Sur*. Some of these instruments are reproduced in Herczog, *Orfeo nelle Indie*.

the Divine Office is celebrated in this church with as much solemnity and perfection as there can be, because to make the gentiles dismiss their own ceremonies and to make them seize the important meaning and affection of our Christianity and divine cult, the Fathers celebrate the Offices very solemnly, singing the Mass of the principal feasts with a deacon and sub deacon, and Vespers with five Fathers with copes, employing very good music [performed by] orphans and new converts, who, numbering a little less than 100, remain in one part of the College, playing the organ and other instruments of the land.[29]

The only sources that have come to light so far in Goa are two books, probably dating from no earlier than the 1690s, containing *villancicos*, *chacotas* and *cantigas* from the Convento das Mónicas, built between 1609 and 1627. Some of the texts, including a play, are to be sung to formulas, while others, intended for St Michael's day – to which a *villancico* in Guatemala and a Mass in Bolivia are also dedicated[30] – are scored polyphonically with parts for harp and viola.[31]

Instrumental diplomacy

One of the richest areas of study towards evaluating the (inter)relationships among colonial cultures (and their post-colonial ramifications) involves the history and transmission of musical instruments. As a barometer of cross-cultural influence, instrumental families have long been central sources for ethnomusicologists (including scholars of popular culture): they bear witness to a long history of multi-cultural appropriation, and they are also indicators of status and class, and, to use Bourdieu's term, of 'cultural capital'.[32] Within the matrix of colonial or state politics, instruments are often pressed into service as symbols of national identity, whether through representations in art, through pre-meditated export, or through their subsidised production. Needless to say, the topic is immense and extends far beyond the scope of this discussion. But a few examples illustrating the cultural and political dimensions of instrumental transmission will, I hope, give an indication of how fertile this area can be to the topic at hand.

Ian Woodfield's important study on the global itineraries of English musicians delineates the role of music and instruments in cross-cultural encounters,

29 Wicki (ed.), *Documenta indica*, xi: 358–9.

30 Stevenson, 'European Music in 16th-Century Guatemala', p. 347. On the *Missa S. Miguel*, see Herczog, *Orfeo nelle Indie*, figs 17–18.

31 For a study, albeit superficial, of the texts, see Castel-Branco, 'The Presence of Portuguese Baroque in the Poetic Works of the Sisters of Santa Monica in Goa'.

32 For a broad look at cross-cultural itineraries and guitar history, see Coelho, 'Picking through Cultures'. For a more anthropologically oriented study that underscores the guitar's role within class hierarchies, see Reily, 'Hybridity and Segregation in the Guitar Cultures of Brazil'.

particularly after the establishment of the East India Company in 1600. This ranged from traditional gift-giving (still crucial in the mating dance between Western and Asian business executives today) and the use of trumpets for signalling and military manoeuvres, to anaesthetising the prick of foreign cultures (such as by allowing a native to 'have a go' at a Western instrument to promote cooperation and friendship),[33] as well as, of course, for ceremony and ritual. Here, politics, diplomacy and etiquette are allied concerns, with instruments used as olive branches to make inroads to the other side. If only they had organs, singers and other instruments, an Italian missionary in Japan wrote to Rome, it would take only a year to convert the populations of Kyoto and Sakai.[34] By 1601 a school of organ craftsmen was making instruments with bamboo pipes, initiating a decade during which Japan's cultural sympathies were officially bound to the West.[35] In this same year, the first clavichord arrived in China, beginning almost two centuries of use of Western keyboard instruments in the royal courts: brought by the famous Jesuit missionary Matteo Ricci, the instrument stimulated the acculturation in, and teaching of, Western idioms, and was even used for accompanying Mass.[36]

Continuing a convention well established by explorers, Portuguese traders of the sixteenth century routinely bartered portable organs with native leaders, presenting such instruments as wonders of European technology. The first organ probably arrived in India in 1500 in this manner, and both organs and harpsichords were carried as gifts on Portuguese expeditions from Goa to Ethiopia.[37] Intended initially as a traditional diplomatic overture, the gift-giving of instruments planted the seed for unexpected musical developments. The use of the harmonium in India, for example, is an outgrowth of the introduction of organs from this period, its fixed-pitch keyboard remaining a peculiarly Western element at odds with Indian variable-scale instruments and singing techniques. In 1550, Francis Xavier brought as gifts to Japan musical instruments which have been variously described as a 'monacordio', 'vihuelas de arco' and a 'clavicordio'.[38] Examples of Japanese art-works during the early seventeenth century reveal the extent to which the Jesuits promoted the representation of instruments as part of their pedagogy, as in the case of those Japanese paintings showing instruments mentioned in the Psalms (trumpets,

33 Woodfield, *English Musicians in the Age of Exploration*, p. 112.

34 See Waterhouse, 'The Earliest Japanese Contacts with Western Music', p. 38, which also contains an account of the famous European visit from 1582 to 1586 of four *samurai* musicians that was arranged by Valignano, during which they performed in Portugal, Venice and Rome on keyboard and stringed instruments, and were painted by Tintoretto.

35 Ibid., p. 42.

36 Lindorff, 'Missionaries, Keyboards and Musical Exchange in the Ming and Qing Courts', pp. 403–5. On Jesuit music in China in this period, see also Picard, 'Music (17th and 18th Centuries)'.

37 Woodfield, *English Musicians in the Age of Exploration*, p. 96.   38 Ibid., pp. 183–4.

harp) or associated with angels (lutes, viols, vihuelas).[39] Guitars (synonymous with the Portuguese *viola*) are listed in Brazilian inventories of 1614 and 1615, and a 1676 inventory from a monastery in Chile lists a guitar and two vihuelas (whether *da mano* or *de arco* is unclear). There exist two seventeenth-century New World guitar manuscripts: the so-called Códice Saldivar no. 2 from Mexico, which contains a work by the Spanish guitarist Gaspar Sanz plus pieces for cittern with New World titles; and a Peruvian manuscript dating from 1670–1703 copied by a Franciscan. This has led James Tyler to speculate that by the end of the seventeenth century, 'it seems that the guitar was as much a part of everyday life in the New World as it was in the homeland'.[40]

By the middle of the seventeenth century, lutes and vihuelas begin to be mentioned in Goa. Pietro della Valle wrote from India that the Portuguese captain Manoel Pereira de la Gerda 'entertain'd us with Musick of his three daughters, who sung and play'd very well after the *Portugal* manner upon the Lute';[41] archival sources frequently mention the playing of the 'bihuela' in domestic settings; and John Fryer's *A New Account of East India and Persia* (London, 1698) describes (pp. 152–4) the women of Goa as being 'extraordinarily featured and compleatly shaped' and as 'plying themselves wholly to devotions and the care of the house' – 'they sing and play on the lute, make confections, pickle *achans*'.[42] In sum, it is no exaggeration to say that the strong Western classical tradition of music in Goa, formed within the Indo-Portuguese cultural crucible of the seventeenth century, is of a piece with the sentiment and temper of the period of exploration. Covert Christian communities in Japan, sent underground as a result of anti-Christian exclusion laws after 1614, nevertheless kept many Western traditions alive and even fostered them through contact with the Dutch up until the renewed interest in the West during the eighteenth century.[43]

Goa: a case-study in Portuguese expansion and Jesuit patronage

The first European settlers in Goa were the Portuguese, who with the landing of Vasco da Gama in 1498 opened up the spice routes between Europe and

39 See the reproduction of a *nanban* screen showing a Japanese female musician playing a vihuela (not a lute, as stated in the catalogue) in Cooper *et al.*, *The Southern Barbarians*, p. 166. On the representation of Western instruments in Japan, see also Minamino, 'European Musical Instruments in Sixteenth-Century Japanese Paintings'. On viols in Japan, as well as the visit there of some young Goan musicians skilled in chant and polyphony, see Kambe, 'Viols in Japan in the Sixteenth and Early Seventeenth Centuries'.

40 Tyler and Sparks, *The Guitar and its Music from the Renaissance to the Classical Era*, p. 151; for a list of other New World guitar sources of the eighteenth century, see p. 163. On cross-cultural aspects of the Baroque guitar, see Russell, 'Radical Innovations, Social Revolution, and the Baroque Guitar', pp. 171–81. On the Portuguese guitar and its presence in Brazil, see Budasz, 'The Five-Course Guitar (*Viola*) in Portugal and Brazil in the Late Seventeenth and Early Eighteenth Centuries', pp. 24–8. For the Chile inventory, see Aguilera, 'Music in the Monastery of La Merced, Santiago de Chile, in the Colonial Period'.

41 Grey (ed.), *The Travels of Pietro della Valle in India*, i: 181.

42 Fryer may be talking about the guitar, or even a hybrid instrument.

43 Waterhouse, 'The Earliest Japanese Contacts with Western Music', p. 46.

India.[44] Goa came under Portuguese political rule in 1510, when Afonso de Albuquerque captured the city and overcame the Muslim domination of the area. (One could say that Jawaharlal Nehru 'recaptured' Goa with his march into the city 450 years later, leading to Goa's official – and bloodless – independence from Portugal in 1961.) Under Albuquerque, Goa became one of the main cosmopolitan centres in all of Asia, a magnet for traders and sightseers, and the jewel in the crown, both architecturally and culturally, of the Portuguese empire, as well as its episcopal and administrative hub. Documents mentioning books of chant (*canto chão*) appear from 1512, with some of them, like a 'livro grande de canto', intended for the early Goan church of Santa Catarina (1513–30).[45] In the first few decades of Portuguese rule, Masses and the Office were sung by as many as ten clerks, who were probably not trained musicians since they were noted as singing 'as best as they can'.[46] Thus in Goa as well as in Cochin and Cananor, an infrastructure was established very early on for using plainchant, although the precise liturgies are difficult to reconstruct given that the earliest extant chant books in Goa (located mainly in the chapter archives at the Sé Catedral) date mostly from the eighteenth century. By the mid 1540s, polyphony is specified (*canto d'orgão*) in correspondence and in the Annual Letters between Goa and Portugal, which required the importing of trained singers, and much debate ensued over the efficacy of using polyphony to attract new Christians.[47]

The most important role in the teaching of music and the development of polyphony in Goa was taken by the Jesuit Colégio de São Paulo, founded in 1542 (50 years before the Jesuit Colegio de San Ignaçio in Manila began to fulfil the same function). The College, which included the first Jesuit church in Asia, offered throughout the seventeenth century a comprehensive musical

---

44 The fundamental work in this area, and still the starting point, is Danvers, *The Portuguese in India*. For a more inclusive, less hegemonic approach to Indo-Portuguese history, see Pearson, *Coastal Western India*. For documentary and post-colonial approaches to music in sixteenth- and seventeenth-century Goa, see Coelho, 'Connecting Histories' and 'Music in Portuguese India and Renaissance Music Histories'. On the relevance of Goan literature and music to its colonial history, see Coelho, '*Saudades* and the Goan Poetic Temper'. For a synoptic view of music in Goa in the service of exploration, see Woodfield, *English Musicians in the Age of Exploration*, pp. 219–48.

45 Silva Rego (ed.), *Documentação para a historia das missões do Padroado Português do Oriente*, i: 127, 431.

46 Ibid., i: 250: 'Os cleriguos: cantam as misas e ofiçios honde ha hy livros, e hande os nom temos, dizemos emtoado, no milhior modo que se pode.'

47 There is some debate regarding the definitions of the term *canto d'orgão* in a colonial context. Given the amount of discussion over its replacing of chant as an enticement to Catholic conversion, the term could hardly denote simply organ-accompanied, unison chant, as Harich-Schneider (*A History of Japanese Music*, p. 473) has suggested in relation to Jesuit reports from sixteenth-century Japan. Woodfield (*English Musicians in the Age of Exploration*, p. 227), has persuasively explained that the term, as used in Goa, was at least evocative of simple polyphony or harmonisations, and occasionally for polychoral performance. In any case, some evidence that the polyphonic style may have resembled something akin to simple harmonisations, perhaps in relation to a borrowed melody, comes from a late seventeenth-century account by the Capuchin Martin de Nantes, who wrote that the Cariri Indians of Brazil sang the rosary of the Virgin every night, divided into two choirs 'à la maniere Portugaise fort agréablement avec une espece de faux bourdon'; see Castagna, 'The Use of Music by the Jesuits in the Conversion of the Indigenous Peoples of Brazil', p. 651.

training directed towards the formation of a native clergy, and it became Goa's main centre of musical activity and patronage.[48] The influence of the Jesuits in Goa also led to the building of the two most important churches in the city, the Sé Catedral (1562–1631), the architecture of which was strongly influenced by the Jesuit design of the Chiesa del Gesù in Rome, and the Basílica do Bom Jesus (1594–1605), built by the Jesuits as a symbol of their power and to house Xavier's body.[49] Raised in 1946 to the status of a Minor Basilica by Pope Pius XII, Bom Jesus is as venerated a shrine on the pilgrim's itinerary as Compostela, Assisi or Vézelay.

The significant expense undertaken by the Jesuits to support music was justified by their reasoning that polyphonic Masses could be more effective than spoken or chanted ones in attracting new converts to Christianity. For the same reason, Masses at the Colégio de São Paulo increasingly included the participation of Indian instruments, a practice that conformed to one of the more successful Jesuit methods, of adopting local customs, language and dress. Documents of musical events at the College frequently mention the use of harpsichords, trumpets, flutes, shawms and organs alongside instruments 'of the land' ('instrumentos da terra'), all in conjunction with the singing of motets and *cantigas*.[50] In Goa, polyphony was generally not an everyday practice, but was used mainly for Mass on Sundays and particular feast-days ('todos os dominguos e festas . . . se fere missa cantada'),[51] often with instruments. Otherwise, services were celebrated in chant. The principal feasts cited in the documents are the Assumption of the Blessed Virgin (15 August), Corpus Christi, the Feast of the Circumcision (1 January), the Feast of the Conversion of St Paul (25 January), Holy Week, and the Feast of 11,000 Virgins (or Feast of St Ursula; 21 October), which was the main feast of the Colégio de São Paulo involving 'muytos generos de instrumentos, assi come charamelas, atables, trombetas, frautas, violas d'arco, e cravo'.[52] As was the case with recorders and reed instruments in New World polyphony, wind instruments may have been used to reinforce the lower voices. Other religious ceremonies called for instruments as well: for a baptism in 1567, for example, Fr. Gomes Vaz mentions 'trumpets and other instruments, with a gathering outside of a procession of singers'.[53]

As a Jesuit enterprise, the education at the College was rigorous and modelled on the strict curriculum – the *ratio studiorum* – of the Jesuit schools in

---

48 Today only the façade remains, following the demolition of the College in 1829. For a reconstruction of its ground-plan and a discussion of its function, see Kowal, 'Innovation and Assimilation'.

49 Kowal, 'Innovation and Assimilation'; Hibbard, '*Ut picturae sermones*'. A good architectural summary of the churches of Goa is in Hutt, *Goa*. A more detailed, though somewhat pedantic, approach is in Pereira, *Baroque Goa*.

50 See, for example, Wicki (ed.), *Documenta indica*, viii: 87, 89.   51 Ibid., viii: 432.

52 Ibid., iii: 189; see also p. 735 for a similar account.   53 Ibid., vii: 402.

Rome. Most feast-days were celebrated at the College with unusual extravagance, involving singing, dramatic presentations, processions, and the playing
of instruments. In Goa, both chant (*canto llano* or *canto chão*) and polyphony
(*canto d'orgão*) were taught along with grammar, the arts and theology, the
aim being to instil in the students not just virtue and morality, but also kin-
ship with a Christian, European tradition. Musical training was also regarded
as a necessary tool for the arduous future of these students as missionaries.
The introduction of polyphony was facilitated through the many debates that
appear in the documents regarding the appropriateness of sung Masses versus
those that were spoken, with the general consensus that sung Masses (in chant
or in polyphony) were much preferred by newly converted Christians as well
as by the Portuguese. The topic was important enough to merit discussion in
a long letter from Antonio Criminalis to Ignatius Loyola, the founder of the
Jesuit Order, regarding the suitability of either chanting or intoning parts of
the Mass and Office.[54]

The emotional and spiritual benefits of a sung, rather than spoken, Mass
are also emphasised in a particularly revealing letter written by Padre Mestre
Belchior from Cochin in 1561, which appears to summarise the relationship
between the Jesuit missionary enterprise and musical aesthetics. Belchior's
letter also provides valuable information about the motivation for using
polyphony in churches, and the flexibility of musical styles encountered in
a Goan service:

> I preach here in this house of the Mother of God, where there is so much
> devotion among the people of Cochin who, for a greater part of the year, during
> all the Sundays and Holy Days of the year come here without any expense to
> celebrate our Masses with polyphony, flutes and shawms. At Vespers on feast-
> days, they come here with much solemnity, and whenever a voice is missing
> and they cannot have polyphony, there is never lack of chant.
>
> During the first two years I was here, we said our Masses in prayers [i.e.,
> spoken], and since there are in this city many churches and monasteries, it
> seemed that for a greater number of these people, they were not satisfied with
> the feast if the Mass was not sung; so it was necessary to meet the needs of the
> church-goers and to introduce a sung Mass at other church Offices, thus not
> only increasing much devotion among the Portuguese, but also enabling the
> native people [*gente da terra*], as well as Christians and Hindus, to show greater
> reverence to the Divine Mysteries.
>
> It is for this very reason that in the principal feasts that the Holy Church
> celebrates for the mysteries of our Redeemer, we want them to be solemn feasts,
> for on Christmas Day, the mystery of the Nativity was celebrated with much

54 Ibid., i: 20.

devotion among all the people and with much solemnity in the Divine Offices, which were sung with many instruments, and there were many *prosas e jubilos* [tropes, interpolations to existing chants, or additional cantus-firmus settings?] on the birth of the child Jesus. And during the Feast of the Circumcision, the solemnity was heightened for the love of the Church and for all the other things that might increase spiritual joy; for beyond the Mystery they celebrated the name of Jesus which is that of our Society, with as many means of devotion as they could gather, even having entertainment and dances of the school-children, with such songs that they were much more a rejoicing of the spirit than mere children's amusements.[55]

Despite the boost given to the missionary campaigns by polyphony, multi-choir performance and the participation of instruments, the cold wind of the Tridentine reforms had reached the colonies by the early 1570s. Although only descriptions of Goan polyphony have survived, and not the actual music, it is clear that the Council would have found much to change in Goa. For one thing, the cross-cultural exuberance of the processions and celebrations that are mentioned by every visitor to sixteenth- and seventeenth-century Goa was infiltrating the services themselves, and also spreading to other parts of Portuguese India – in Travancore the *folías* was danced for the feast of the Assumption in 1577[56] – threatening Tridentine aims and thus coming under criticism. In addition, the increasing use of 'loud' wind instruments such as shawms (*charamelas*), along with flutes, trumpets, indigenous instruments and drums, during Mass and other services, plus the presence of secular music, was seen as distracting and disrespectful, even though the practice of *villancicos* within Matins and Mass was much cultivated in Portugal and Spain during the Tridentine period.[57] Clearly, what happened at home was one thing, and in the colonies another, and there were strong attempts to have music in Goan churches restrained by Counter-Reformation austerity, even if such radical reforms met with some resistance.

But there was a deeper political motivation for these changes. By the early seventeenth century it had become clear that the Jesuits were falling far short of their goal in converting Indians to Christianity. At the same time, where music was traditionally used by missionaries as an evangelical technique – frequently the students of the Colégio de São Paulo would even walk through the streets singing the Credo – the extravagance of music was becoming a profession unto itself, rather than an activity strictly in the service of missionary training. The debates make interesting reading. The die-hard reformers Francisco Cabral

55 Silva Rego (ed.), *Documentação para a historia das missões do Padroado Português do Oriente*, viii: 464–5 (31 December 1561).
56 Ibid., xii: 390.   57 Nery, 'The Portuguese *Villancico*'.

(*fl.* 1581–94) and Claudio Acquaviva, respectively the Provincial and the General (1581–1615) of the Society of Jesus, proposed that many facets of music-making should be discontinued altogether. On the other hand, Alessandro Valignano (1539–1606), one of the great Jesuit cultural pluralists, strongly supported the need for musical training and was persuasive in his attempts to keep it alive for the sake of proper education.[58] Valignano was convinced of the power of music to aid the Christianization of India and, especially, Japan, the country that held his strongest interest. Addressing the difficulty in teaching native boys to sing measured music in Latin, Valignano admitted Portuguese boys to the part of the Colégio de São Paulo intended for natives only, in order to help out with the choir. This was challenged by Acquaviva; he included music among his general reforms of abuses at the College, and sought to reduce the number of boys who were contracted to furnish liturgical music, with the eventual aim of abolishing the practice completely. The Jesuit historian Joseph Wicki concluded that this was 'a wise decision'.[59] Valignano, however, insisted that liturgical music should not be suppressed in an area such as India, in which music had a very strong impact, and he was therefore against reducing the number of boys at the College. But a lack of finances was often cited in support of the reforms. Francisco Fernández wrote to Acquaviva in 1589 that it was unnecessary to have so many 'ministriles' – a designation for performers of secular songs (such as *villancicos*) rather than simply instrumentalists[60] – at the College, and likewise 'moços', the latter perhaps referring to young slaves, whose mention in the same breath as minstrels suggests musicians as well. This corresponds closely with Jesuit musical culture in Manila around 1600 in which the earliest documented orchestra consisted of nine slaves playing flutes and reeds (*chirimiras*) that were brought to the Philippines along with an organ and music books from Mexico.[61] This was one of several indigenous ensembles in Manila that performed for church services, and it had a significant influence on many local musical traditions within the native population.

For a brief time, the reforms were uncompromising: Acquaviva himself soon disallowed even organ music in the new Professed House of the Society of Jesus. His proactive approach was clearly an exaggerated response to the complaints he was receiving from all sectors of the Jesuit establishment. In 1591, Fr. Nuno Rodrigues wrote him a letter highly critical of an instance when instrumental music and 'cantigas' had been performed at the Saturday morning service ('sinco horas de la mañana') at the College, including 'other vulgarities, which in Portuguese is called *chacota*, and similar instruments such as guitars, citterns

58 Ross, 'Alessandro Valignano'.   59 Wicki (ed.), *Documenta indica*, xvi: 25.
60 Zayas, 'Les *ministriles* et leur rôle dans l'interprétation de la polyphonie espagnole du Siècle d'Or'.
61 Summers, 'The Jesuits and Music in Manila', pp. 660–61.

and the like'.[62] Taste aside, Rodrigues succeeded in leaving us with one of the most revealing documents in the Jesuit correspondence about cross-cultural music making and the spread of Portuguese popular culture through the indigenous community.

By the early seventeenth century, writes Wicki, 'singing and instrumental music were not in favour in the Society of Jesus'.[63] A close reading of the documents suggests that the reasons go beyond musical style. Aquaviva became further inflamed through his correspondence with Francisco Cabral, a veritable crusader against excesses in the church. But he was also racially prejudiced, vehemently opposing the admission of Japanese to the Society, and even the use of silk for Jesuit robes.[64] (For his part, even Valignano, who was sympathetic to 'white skinned' Japanese, dismissed the intelligence of the darker-complexioned Africans, Malay and Indians.[65]) In a letter of 1594, Cabral urged Acquaviva to end the practice of singing Mass and the Offices in the College.[66] He gave three reasons: first, that in order to sustain the tradition, a Father or a brother of the Society was always needed as choirmaster and to teach singing, but these were not always dependable or available, nor was it economical; secondly, although singing was originally cultivated in order to assist in conversion, few new converts actually came to church, and therefore music was not making its intended impact; thirdly, singing was originally introduced to attract faithful and honourable people to church, but this had not proved to be the result.

All of this had little to do with music *per se*. By foregrounding music in the context of missionary directives, it was inevitable that it would share the blame for the larger failures that occurred in the missionary campaigns. What is interesting about Cabral's letter is that in having to justify the specific use and expense of music, he reveals information about the Society's mission that is often silenced. The discourse was normally constricted by position and station, but when entering into a dialogue over musical issues, these authors exposed their cultural and aesthetic beliefs.

(Re)Writing colonial history in seventeenth-century Rome: Kapsberger's *Apotheosis*

Even as the Jesuit missionary project in India no longer seemed so certain, weeks of festivities took place in Rome following the canonisation in 1622 of the first two Jesuit saints, Francis Xavier and Ignatius Loyola. Of the three Jesuit

---

62 Wicki (ed.), *Documenta indica*, xv: 721–2.   63 Ibid., xvi: 7.
64 Bailey, *Art on the Jesuit Missions in Asia and Latin America*, p. 61.
65 Ross, 'Alessandro Valignano', p. 347.   66 Wicki (ed.), *Documenta indica*, xv: 852–4.

dramas mounted for the occasion, the most elaborate was Giovanni Girolamo Kapsberger's *Apotheosis sive consecratio SS. Ignatii et Francisci Xaverii*, a mixed-genre propaganda piece in which a feminised India, as one of the characters, willingly submits to the Catholic Church. Elsewhere I have examined this work in detail from the point of view of the Other, and as an example of a gendered colonial revisionism.[67] India's conversion was neither total nor willing, but Kapsberger's drama, replete with themes of procreation and church paternalism, redefines the Jesuits as conquerors and India as their progeny. It will come as no surprise that modern Jesuit scholars see things differently. Musicologist T. Frank Kennedy, who has produced a splendid recording and translation of the work, proposes looking at the libretto not as a didactic tool, as many non-Jesuit scholars – myself included – would have it, but as an affirmation of a '*human* experience' that addresses 'sweeping transcultural issues that move beyond to reconcile all people of all time'.[68] But it is difficult to view it in such idealistic and egalitarian terms, devoid of any political subtext, particularly given the way in which the different countries represented are judged by the Church according to their acquiescence to conversion. It seems clear that the *Apotheosis* aimed to address the decaying situation in Asia by displacing those countries that had refused Xavier's ministrations.

By the early seventeenth century, the missionary map had been redrawn considerably. While missionaries continued to be disappointed by Indian resistance – particularly after the establishment of the Inquisition in 1561 that caused many Indians to flee to Muslim territory, beyond the missionary perimeter – there were a number of at least symbolic victories.[69] Peruschi's account of the Jesuit missions to the court of Akbar the Great (Abu'l-Fath Jalal Ad-Din Muhammad Akbar (1543–1605)) at Fatehpur Sikri (near Agra) is particularly relevant here.[70] The Jesuits saw Akbar's eventual conversion as necessary for the Christianization of the entire Mughal Empire. But even after lengthy visits by missionaries, and despite Akbar's keen interest in Christian art and liturgy (he celebrated the Feast of the Assumption in 1580–83), he did not convert. Nevertheless, Jesuits remained at the court until 1803, and Pastor writes of 'twenty parishes with 70,000 Christians on the peninsula of

---

67 Coelho, 'The *Apotheosis* . . . of Francis Xavier and the Conquering of India'.

68 Kennedy, '*Candide* and a Boat', pp. 319–21. A more extensive discussion appears in his liner-notes to *The Jesuit Operas: Operas by Kapsberger and Zipoli*, Ensemble Abendmusik, directed by James David Christie, Dorian 93243 (2003). Quotations from the libretto in the present text are based on Kennedy's translation in the CD booklet.

69 The main targets of the Goa Inquisition were not primarily the non-converted Hindus or Muslims, but 'New Christians', i.e., descendants of Iberian Jewry forcibly converted to Christianity in Spain in 1492 and in Portugal in 1497; see Boyajiyan, 'Goa Inquisition'.

70 G. B. Peruschi, *Informatione del regno et stato del Gran Re di Mogor . . .* (Rome, 1597); see also Welch, *India*, pp. 146–64.

Salsette near Goa; ten in Ceylon . . . [and] another 60 parishes in Manar and Travancore'.[71]

In China and Japan, however, the Christian effort was decaying rapidly, and the persecution and execution of Jesuits were becoming commonplace. This might explain the hierarchy of nations in the *Apotheosis*, where these countries play roles subsidiary to India. In fact, China receives a paternal scolding as being Xavier's ultimate destination yet unable to receive him because Xavier had died on a nearby island waiting for a boat to complete his voyage: 'I am denied such glory of great praise', China states on her entrance in Act IV, 'as that of our parent Xavier's chaste bones embraced by my great blessed bosom . . . While Xavier was trying to approach my realm, but was repulsed by unexpected death that indeed sought to halt my progress, I have been cheated in my undertaking to honour the sacred spoils of the deceased Father in a poor land'. Thus China, 'cheated' by its failure to receive Xavier who was so close to her shores, yearns for union with the Church. But reports during the first decade of the seventeenth century confirm the difficulty of the missionary efforts in China. Although the Jesuit Matteo Ricci adopted Chinese customs and learnt the language, he could count only some 2,000 conversions over 25 years of work.

Even as the Portuguese empire in India began to collapse in the seventeenth century, however, the Colégio de São Paulo remained active in its use of the arts as a source of identity and as a consolidation of Jesuit power commensurate with the close relationships the order was forging with the popes in Rome. The festivities accompanying the 1622 canonisation in Rome were echoed on a lavish scale a few years later in Goa, as Pietro della Valle described in detail.[72] From his account of processions, music and drama, it is clear that the musical austerity envisaged by Cabral and others was very much a passing phenomenon. Moreover, the itemised College accounts for the last two decades of the seventeenth century show regular payments for an organist, as well as for viol and harp strings, a combination of instruments capable of accompanying small- and large-scale genres that was used in Spanish and Portuguese churches at home and abroad.[73] But mid seventeenth-century reports attest to Goa's steady decline as a city and cultural centre in the face of rising competition from the maritime expansion of the English, Dutch and French. In 1672, Abbé Carré, visiting 'this large and once flourishing city of Goa, could hardly find a shadow or vestige of its former splendour'.[74] He found no worshippers in the Sé Catedral, nor a church open for prayer on Christmas Day, while 'other

71 Pastor, *The History of the Popes*, xxvii: 147.

72 Grey (ed.), *The Travels of Pietro della Valle in India*, ii: 402–13.

73 Some of these documents are listed in Coelho, 'The *Apotheosis* . . . of Francis Xavier and the Conquering of India', p. 47 nn. 62, 63.

74 Fawcett (trans.), *The Travels of the Abbé Carré in India and the Near East*, p. 214.

churches, both of the parish priests and of the regulars, are ill-suited, and in most of them the Mass and divine service are no longer sung for want of priests and monks'.[75]

Placing seventeenth-century music in this colonial context permits the cultural and missionary subtexts embedded within European musical styles and training to come into sharp focus. Music was seen as a powerful political medium both in Europe and beyond, and it was very much part of the cultural and political imperatives of both the Portuguese and the Jesuits. Because this music was imposed on cultures that were bound to much older, unwritten traditions, and was used as ambassadorial and evangelical tools, studying it in the broader context of the colonial enterprise teaches us a great deal about the role of music in constructing and defining political, social and cultural hierarchies whether outside Europe or, for that matter, within.

Bibliography

Aguilera, A. V., 'Music in the Monastery of La Merced, Santiago de Chile, in the Colonial Period'. *Early Music*, 32 (2004), 369–82

Bailey, G., *Art on the Jesuit Missions in Asia and Latin America, 1542–1773*. Toronto, 1999

Baker, G., 'Music at Corpus Christi in Colonial Cuzco'. *Early Music*, 32 (2004), 355–67

Baumann, M. P. (ed.), *World Music, Musics of the World: Aspects of Documentation, Mass Media and Acculturation*. Wilhelmshaven, 1992

Béhague, G., 'The Global Impact of Portuguese Music and Musical Institutions: a Preliminary Sketch'. In Castelo-Branco (ed.), *Portugal e o mundo*, pp. 71–80

Borg, P., 'The Polyphonic Music in the Guatemalan Music Manuscripts of the Lilly Library'. Ph.D. thesis, Indiana University (1985)

Borges, C., and Feldmann, H. (eds), *Goa and Portugal: Their Cultural Links*. New Delhi, 1997

Borges, C., Pereira, O., and Stubbe, H. (eds), *Goa and Portugal: History and Development*. New Delhi, 2000

Boyajiyan, J. C., 'Goa Inquisition: a New Light on [the] First 100 Years (1561–1660)'. *Purabhilekh–Puratatva* [Journal of the Directorate of Archives, Archaeology and Museums, Panaji, Goa], 4 (1986), 1–40

Brito, M. C. de, 'Sounds of the Discoveries: Musical Aspects of the Portuguese Expansion'. *Review of Culture* [Instituto Cultural de Macau], 26 (1996), 5–22

Budasz, R., 'The Five-Course Guitar (*Viola*) in Portugal and Brazil in the Late Seventeenth and Early Eighteenth Centuries'. Ph.D. thesis, University of Southern California (2001)

A Música no Tempo de Gregório de Mattos: Musica Ibérica e Afro-Brasileira na Bahia dos Séculos XVII e XVIII. Curitiba, 2004

Castagna, P., 'The Use of Music by the Jesuits in the Conversion of the Indigenous Peoples of Brazil'. In O'Malley *et al.* (eds), *The Jesuits*, pp. 640–58

---

75 Ibid., p. 216.

Castel-Branco, M., 'The Presence of Portuguese Baroque in the Poetic Works of the Sisters of Santa Monica in Goa'. In Borges, Pereira and Stubbe (eds), *Goa and Portugal*, pp. 248–57

Castelo-Branco, S. (ed.), *Portugal e o mundo: o encontro de culturas na música*. Lisbon, 1997

Chakrabarty, D., 'Postcoloniality and the Artifice of History: Who Speaks for "Indian" Pasts?'. *Representations*, 37 (1992), 1–26

Coelho, V., 'Connecting Histories: Portuguese Music in Renaissance Goa'. In Borges and Feldmann (eds), *Goa and Portugal*, pp. 131–47

'The *Apotheosis* . . . of Francis Xavier and the Conquering of India'. In Dellamora and Fischlin (eds), *The Work of Opera*, pp. 27–47

'Music in Portuguese India and Renaissance Music Histories'. In T. R. de Souza (ed.), *Vasco da Gama and India*. 3 vols, Lisbon, 1999, iii: 185–94

'*Saudades* and the Goan Poetic Temper: Globalising Goan Cultural History'. In Borges, Pereira and Stubbe (eds), *Goa and Portugal*, pp. 319–25

'Picking through Cultures'. In Coelho (ed.), *The Cambridge Companion to the Guitar*, pp. 1–14

Coelho, V. (ed.), *The Cambridge Companion to the Guitar*. Cambridge, 2002

Cooper, M. (ed.), *The Southern Barbarians: the First Europeans in Japan*. Tokyo and Palo Alto, CA, 1971

Correia-Afonso, J. (ed.), *Letters from the Mughal Court: the First Jesuit Mission to Akbar (1580–1583)*. Bombay, 1980

Danvers, F. C., *The Portuguese in India*. 2 vols, London, 1894; repr. New Delhi, 1992

Dellamora, R., and Fischlin, D. (eds), *The Work of Opera: Genre, Nationhood, and Sexual Difference*. New York, 1997

Domingos, F. C., 'Vaisseaux et mariniers'. In M. Chandeigne (ed.), *Lisbonne hors les murs, 1415–1580: l'invention du monde par les navigateurs portugais*. Paris, 1992, pp. 56–70

Fawcett, M. E. F. (trans.), *The Travels of Abbé Carré in India and the Near East, 1672 to 1674*. London, 1947–8; repr. New Delhi, 1990

Grey, E. (ed.), *The Travels of Pietro della Valle in India, from the Old English Translation of 1664*. 2 vols, London 1892; repr. New Delhi and Madras, 1991

Harich-Schneider, E., *A History of Japanese Music*. London, 1973

Herczog, J., *Orfeo nelle Indie: i Gesuiti e la musica in Paraguay (1609–1767)*. Lecce, 2001

Hibbard, H., '*Ut picturae sermones*: the First Painted Decorations of the Gesù'. In R. Wittkower and I. Jaffe (eds), *Baroque Art: the Jesuit Contribution*. New York, 1972, pp. 29–49

Hutt, A., *Goa: a Traveller's Historical and Architectural Guide*. London, 1988

Kambe, Y., 'Viols in Japan in the Sixteenth and Early Seventeenth Centuries'. *Journal of the Viola da Gamba Society of America*, 37 (2000), 31–67

Kennedy, T. F., '*Candide* and a Boat'. In O'Malley *et al.* (eds), *The Jesuits*, pp. 317–22

Kowal, D. M., 'Innovation and Assimilation: the Jesuit Contribution to Architectural Development in Portuguese India'. In O'Malley *et al.* (eds), *The Jesuits*, pp. 480–504

Leonhardt, C. (ed.), *Cartas anuas de la Provincia del Paraguay, Chile y Tucumán, de la Compañia de Jesús (1615–1637)*. Buenos Aires, 1929

Lindorff, J., 'Missionaries, Keyboards and Musical Exchange in the Ming and Qing Courts'. *Early Music*, 32 (2004), 403–14

Maehder, J., 'The Representation of the "Discovery" on the Opera Stage'. In C. Robertson (ed.), *Musical Repercussions of 1492: Encounters in Text and Performance*. Washington, DC, and London, 1992, pp. 257–87

Mignolo, W. D., *The Darker Side of the Renaissance: Literacy, Territoriality, and Colonization*. Ann Arbor, 1997

Minamino. H., 'European Musical Instruments in Sixteenth-Century Japanese Paintings'. *Music in Art*, 24 (1999), 41–50

Murchio, V. M., *Il viaggio all'Indie orientali*. Venice, 1683

Nery, R. V., 'The Portuguese *Villancico*: a Cross-Cultural Phenomenon'. In Castelo-Branco (ed.), *Portugal e o mundo*, pp. 103–24

O'Malley, J. W., et al. (eds), *The Jesuits: Cultures, Sciences, and the Arts, 1540–1773*. Toronto, 1999

Pastor, L., *The History of the Popes*, trans. E. Graf. 40 vols, London, 1938

Pearson, M. N., *Coastal Western India: Studies from the Portuguese Records*. New Delhi, 1980

The Portuguese in India. Cambridge, 1987

Pereira, J., *Baroque Goa: the Architecture of Portuguese India*. New Delhi, 1995

Picard, F., 'Music (17th and 18th Centuries)'. In N. Staendart (ed.), *The Handbook of Oriental Studies: Christianity in China*, i: 635–1800. Leiden, 2001, pp. 851–60

Priolkar, A. K., *The Goa Inquisition, Being a Quatercentenary Commemoration Study of the Inquisition in India, with Accounts Given by Dr Dellon and Dr Buchanan*. Bombay, 1961

Reily, S. A., 'Hybridity and Segregation in the Guitar Cultures of Brazil'. In A. Bennett and K. Dawe (eds), *Guitar Cultures*. Oxford, 2001, pp. 157–78

Ross, A., 'Alessandro Valignano: the Jesuits and Culture in the East'. In O'Malley et al. (eds), *The Jesuits*, pp. 336–51

Russell, C., 'Radical Innovations, Social Revolution, and the Baroque Guitar'. In Coelho (ed.), *The Cambridge Companion to the Guitar*, pp. 153–81

Shirodkar, P. P., 'Evangelisation and its Harsh Realities in Portuguese India'. In T. R. de Souza (ed.), *Discoveries, Missionary Expansion and Asian Cultures*. New Delhi, 1994, pp. 79–84

'Socio-Cultural Life in Goa during the 16th Century'. In Borges and Feldmann (eds), *Goa and Portugal*, pp. 23–40

Silva Rego, A. (ed.), *Documentação para a historia das missões do Padroado Português do Oriente*. 12 vols, Lisbon, 1947

Snow, R., 'Music by Francisco Guerrero in Guatemala'. *Nassarre: revista aragonesa de musicologia*, 3 (1987), 153–202

Stevenson, R., 'European Music in 16th-Century Guatemala'. *Musical Quarterly*, 50 (1964), 341–52

Portuguese Music and Musicians Abroad to 1650. Lima, 1966

Renaissance and Baroque Musical Sources in the Americas. Washington, DC, 1970

Summers, W., 'The Jesuits in Manila, 1581–1621: the Role of Music in Rite, Ritual, and Spectacle'. In O'Malley et al. (eds), *The Jesuits*, pp. 659–79

Szarán, L., and Nestosa, J. R., *Música en las reducciones Jesuíticas de América del Sur: colleccíon de instrumentos de Chiquitos, Bolivia*. Asunción, 1999.

Tyler, J., and Sparks, P., *The Guitar and its Music from the Renaissance to the Classical Era*. Oxford, 2002

Wagstaff, G., 'Processions for the Dead, the Senses, and Ritual Identity in Colonial Mexico'. In L. P. Austern (ed.), *Music, Sensation, and Sensuality*. New York and London, 2002, pp. 167–80

Waterhouse. D., 'The Earliest Japanese Contacts with Western Music'. *Review of Culture* [Instituto Cultural de Macau], 26 (1996), 36–47

Welch, S. C., *India: Art and Culture, 1300–1900*. New York, 1985

Wicki, J. (ed.), *Documenta indica: missiones orientales*. 18 vols, Rome, 1948–88

Woodfield, I., *English Musicians in the Age of Exploration*. Stuyvesant, NY, 1995

Zayas, R. de, 'Les *ministriles* et leur rôle dans l'interprétation de la polyphonie espagnole du Siècle d'Or'. In J.-M. Vaccaro (ed.), *Le concert des voix et des instruments à la Renaissance*. Paris, 1995, pp. 657–70

5

Music and the arts

BARBARA RUSSANO HANNING

In many ways, the arts in the seventeenth century were shaped by the same aesthetic principles that had held sway during the sixteenth: the Humanist belief that a work of art had the ability, through imitation, to portray psychological, moral and other realities, and the power, through rhetorical means, to make those realities present to others.[1] Writers from antiquity to the present have recognised these dual goals as common to the 'sister arts', by which they usually mean painting and poetry. The phrase connotes a certain rivalry that was based on Horace's famous dictum *ut pictura poesis* – as is painting so is poetry – a comparison much discussed during the Renaissance, with the result that painting acquired the status of a liberal art in the sixteenth century and was deemed to deserve serious consideration equal to that given to poetry.[2] But the beliefs and goals that were shared by the sister arts of painting and poetry also propelled developments in architecture, sculpture, theatre and music in the Renaissance and Baroque periods. In fact, early-modern writers on music, particularly those who relied on Plato and Aristotle for their understanding of the educational ideals of Greek culture, stressed the inseparability of music from poetry. For our purposes, then, music was indeed one of the sister arts and this chapter will suggest ways in which it participated, both in theory and in practice, in the various aesthetic dialogues that characterise the age.

It may be helpful to understand these dialogues – the antithetical trends and tendencies that mark the seventeenth century – as a series of dichotomies or tensions which animated all the arts. The international style that was later called 'Baroque' is thus a dynamically unstable fusion of contrasts: between the real

All of the paintings mentioned in this chapter may be seen in full colour via one or more of the virtual art galleries on the world-wide web such as <http://www.Artcyclopedia.com>, <http://gallery.euroweb.hu> and <http://cgfa.sunsite.dk> (there are many other examples as well). Furthermore, the on-line *Grove Dictionary of Art* (<http://www.groveart.com>) may be accessible through university and other research libraries; here, entries on individual artists also provide links to websites where the artist's works are available for viewing. For Versailles and the Boboli Gardens, see respectively <http://www.chateauversailles.fr/EN/100.asp> and <http://www.photo.net/photo/pcdo800/boboli-grotta-grande-80>.

1 On the influence of Aristotle's theory of imitation on painting and poetry in the sixteenth century, see Lee, '*Ut pictura poesis*', pp. 9–16; I discuss its influence on music further, below.

2 Lee, '*Ut pictura poesis*', p. 3.

and the ideal; between high and low, serious and comic; between heroic and prosaic, elevated and fallen; between light and dark, pleasing and disturbing; between passionate movement and noble calm, stirring drama and still life. This list could be greatly expanded. Among the most revealing of these dialectics is that between the ancients and the moderns, or between classicists and innovators, whose ongoing debates drew the battle-lines particularly clearly in art and music. Other binaries that will be evoked in the discussion below include order and disorder, action and reaction, naturalism and illusion, and drama and stasis. It may be argued that these categories are overly simple and artificial; to be sure, they are at the same time incomplete and overlapping. Some debates were inherited from trends in the preceding age, though extended and intensified through confrontation with new issues; others were genuinely new, spurred by the scientific exploration and discovery unique to the new century. Nevertheless, naming and categorising these binaries helps to call attention to some of the distinguishing features common to all of the sister arts in the period.

Ancients and Moderns

Tension has always existed between new and old, between what is deemed *au courant* or fashionable and what is considered old-fashioned and dated. But this tension became exacerbated in the debates fuelled by Humanist scholars of antiquity in the sixteenth century and resulted in the wholesale rejection by some writers, artists and composers of received artistic practices. Moreover, the opposition of 'old' and 'new' took on more complex nuances because 'old' became equated with 'antique' or 'classical', and its qualities were championed as ones that 'new' or 'modern' artists and musicians should adopt. In other words, the 'ancient' arts became privileged over the hitherto 'modern', perhaps for the first time in history. In music this attitude fostered a virtual revolution in style at the end of the sixteenth century – not only in the sound of music but even in its very appearance on the page – from polyphonic part-music written in individual, separate parts requiring precise coordination by the performers, to solo song, written in score, consisting of a single melodic line with a simple harmonic outline each needing discreet and flexible elaboration.

In his *Dialogo della musica antica, et della moderna* ('Dialogue concerning ancient and modern music', 1581), Vincenzo Galilei, father of the famous physicist and astronomer Galileo, both followed the trend and set the tone for the next century by contrasting the practices of his contemporaries with the ideals of the ancients. Unlike the situation in the visual arts, where marble sculpture and architecture from antiquity had been discovered and imitated during the Renaissance, the musical practices of the ancient Greeks could only be inferred from written texts. Nevertheless, Galilei compared the legendary expressivity of ancient monodic music to the intricate web of vocal polyphony produced by the madrigal and motet composers of his time, and he found this polyphony wanting in its ability to deliver the emotional message of the text. Invoking the art of oratory as a model, he urged modern composers to imitate the manner in which effective actors declaimed their lines on stage:

> in what range, high or low, how loudly or softly, how rapidly or slowly they enunciate their words . . . how one speaks when infuriated or excited; how a married woman speaks, how a girl . . . how a lover . . . how one speaks when lamenting, when crying out, when afraid, and when exulting with joy. From these diverse observations . . . one can deduce the way that best suits the expression of whatever meanings or emotions may come to hand.[3]

Indeed, Jacopo Peri heeded Galilei's advice in devising a new style of singing (recitative) specifically for theatrical purposes (in the first operas, *Dafne* of 1598 and *Euridice* of 1600); and Giulio Caccini applied similar principles to the composition of his solo songs (in *Le nuove musiche*, published in 1602), complete with a new style of ornamented singing tailored to the nuanced expression of the words.

In music, the subject of text expression became the *locus classicus* for the debate between the conservatives and the moderns. The prime example is provided by the famous polemic initiated in the late 1590s by the Bolognese theorist Giovanni Maria Artusi against the madrigals of Claudio Monteverdi, including some published in the composer's Fifth Book of 1605. Giulio Cesare Monteverdi defended his brother Claudio's unorthodox use of dissonance and apparent indifference to the rules of counterpoint by appealing to the desire for a vivid interpretation of the poetry, which in turn meant following a freer, more casual 'second practice'. This *seconda pratica*, which embodied 'The Perfection of Modern Music', distinguished itself from the traditional *prima pratica* – upheld by the conservative Artusi in his commentary on the 'Imperfections of Modern Music' – precisely by privileging text over music.[4] Monteverdi and 'the moderns' believed themselves to be in agreement with ancient values, whereas the music approved by Artusi, while 'modern' in chronological terms, in fact now belonged to the conservative madrigal and motet composers (and their partisans) from Monteverdi's generation and earlier. Their works were invested with the authority handed down in the rules of counterpoint, rather than with the imperative of text expression. In actuality, the two styles – conservative and modern, *stile antico* and *stile moderno, prima* and *seconda pratica* – coexisted well

---

3 Quoted and translated in Weiss and Taruskin (eds), *Music in the Western World*, pp. 167–8.
4 Weiss and Taruskin (eds), *Music in the Western World*, pp. 171–3.

into the eighteenth century. By the mid seventeenth, the composer and writer Marco Scacchi, in his *Breve discorso sopra la musica moderna* ('Brief discourse on modern music', 1649), acknowledged that both styles had equal validity but differing functions whether in the church, chamber or theatre, and that each such location could avail itself of either style.[5] The productive tension between the two styles had already begun to dissipate.

In other fields the 'quarrel' of Ancients and Moderns over the extent to which arts and letters ought to imitate or even rival Classical examples also became an issue of conservatives versus innovators. The Moderns extolled the painter Rubens over the Greek Apelles, the playwright Racine over Euripides, and the thinker Newton over Aristotle, whereas the Ancients – adherents to the principles of Classicism – struggled to uphold the values of ancient art, the knowledge of the ancient philosophers, and the themes of sacred and profane history and mythology. One of the principal manifestations of this dichotomy in the seventeenth century was the debate over 'design' (*disegno, dessein*) versus 'colour' (*colore, couleur*) in painting, which played out mostly in France, though there were parallel camps in Italy and Spain as well. (During the sixteenth century, a similar discussion comparing the virtues of Raphael and Titian had taken place between partisans of Florentine design and Venetian colour; indeed, Raphael remained the paragon for those seventeenth-century critics who upheld the superiority of design, and hence drawing.)

The French Académie Royale de Peinture et de Sculpture (Royal Academy of Painting and Sculpture, formed in 1648) laid down strict rules for the training of its students which involved learning to draw by copying paintings of the accepted masters – be they Raphael or the greatest French painter of the age, Nicolas Poussin (1594–1665) – and by drawing figures from casts of ancient Roman sculpture.[6] Through this process students were expected to learn the proportions of the human body and to judge what was truly beautiful in nature. The Academy's doctrine held that design was the true basis of painting because it appealed to the mind, whereas colour, which only appealed to the eye, was of lesser importance. Poussin, who had settled in Rome where he was inevitably surrounded by antique sculpture, went so far as to fashion miniature statues in clay, arranging them in a three-dimensional diorama in preparation for painting his history canvases.[7] This method of working is reflected in the 'stagey' poses and gestures of some of the figures in his *The Rape of the Sabine Women* or *The Judgement of Solomon*, for example. The anti-Poussinistes, the partisans of

---

5 Bianconi, *Music in the Seventeenth Century*, pp. 47–8.

6 This paragraph is largely based on Blunt and Lockspeiser, *French Art and Music since 1500*, pp. 17–18.

7 A detailed description of Poussin's working method is given by his contemporary biographer, Joachim von Sandrart; see Pace, *Félibien's Life of Poussin*, p. 25.

colour, proclaimed their allegiance to Peter Paul Rubens (1577–1640), a painter of Flemish origin who achieved enormous success as both painter and diplomat at the courts of Italy, the Netherlands, England and Spain. The Rubénistes challenged the supremacy of ancient sculpture and argued in favour of colour, light and shade, which they deemed capable of producing a more complete imitation of natural objects than drawing alone. Rubens's *The Rape of the Sabine Women* and *The Judgement of Paris* provide interesting comparisons with Poussin's paintings on the same or similar subjects.

Order and disorder

The seventeenth century was one of taxonomies, of ordering and objectifying everything from the passions of the soul (as in the case of Descartes, discussed below) to the senses of the body (as in Giambattista Marino's image-oriented verse, which names long lists of objects and describes in exquisite detail things seen, heard, tasted etc.). But an opposing current also surfaced, the liking for an arranged disorder, not exactly chaos but something that had the semblance of spontaneity, or indeed grew out of a practised improvisation.

The penchant for order has already been suggested by the classification of musical styles and functions mentioned above. In the preface to his Eighth Book of madrigals, the *Madrigali guerrieri, et amorosi* ('Madrigals of war and love', 1638), Monteverdi tried to summarise the musical conventions at his disposal.[8] There was a staggering array of options, including the relaxed, moderate and excited styles (*molle, temperato, concitato*); the ranges of the voice (*bassa, mezzana, alta*) that connote different affections (*umiltà, temperanza, ira*, i.e., humility, equanimity, anger); and the various functions of secular music (chamber, theatre, dance) that may be couched in any one of a number of musical languages. Monteverdi also divided the collection into *canti guerrieri* and *canti amorosi*, and he further identified some pieces as being in the *genere rappresentativo*. It was as though he needed to make sense for himself and for others of the bewildering variety in this book and in his previous collection, the Seventh Book of 1619, which was a jumble of madrigals and other types of song (*altri generi de canti*) for one, two, three, four and six voices with continuo, all gathered under the rubric *Concerto*.

We find similar tendencies in instrumental music, too: the ordering of dances into suites and of suites into tonal cycles (see, for example, Denis Gaultier's *La rhétorique des dieux* of 1652), or the regular patterning of movements (slow–fast–slow–fast) into sonatas and the grouping of sonatas into collections for church

---

8 Hanning, 'Monteverdi's Three *Genera*', pp. 146–9.

or chamber (compare Arcangelo Corelli's opp. 1–5). There were centripetal forces that held pieces together, such as ostinato basses, underlying harmonic patterns, recurring *tutti* sections; and centrifugal forces that pushed them apart, such as the improvisational impulse behind a stream of fantasy-like sections in a toccata or canzona, or the expansion of a series of such divergent sections into the separate movements of a sonata. Eventually, such antipodal elements were acknowledged and codified into pairs of contrasting pieces: toccata and fugue, allemande and courante, sarabande and gigue, or even – in vocal music – recitative and aria.

The dichotomy between order and disorder, control and freedom, is also mirrored in the architectural forms of the century and in their ancillary manifestations, such as landscape design. On the one hand, the gardens at the royal palace of Versailles show the rhythm and order of classicism, with symmetrically positioned forms and fixed modules. On the other, the grottoes and *grotteschi* of the Boboli Gardens behind the Medici's Palazzo Pitti in Florence reveal the irregular forms and surprising shapes of Bernardo Buontalenti's (1531–1608) fanciful imagination. Buontalenti was also a set designer and director of theatrical productions at the Florentine court who created special machinery for transformation scenes and other spectacular effects on stage. The nobility must have delighted in such escapist retreats as these cool, man-made caverns, antidotes to the grandly magnificent, carefully patterned open spaces that publicly symbolised their owner's centrality and importance in the universe. But just as every extreme may be seen to harbour within it the seeds of its opposite, so, too, does the formal landscape of Versailles – with its tree-bordered alleys, canals, and geometrical terraces punctuated by sculptures and fountains – contain its antithesis, the Petit Trianon. Like the Boboli Gardens' grottoes, this is a private park within a park, where Marie Antoinette later played at being a shepherdess in less artificial, more 'natural' surroundings.[9]

In Jacobean and Caroline England, there were the court masques and antimasques of Ben Jonson (1572–1637) and others. Antimasques were antic or grotesque interludes and, as such, served as disintegrating forces that contrasted with the formality of the masque and resorted to comedy, personal satire and topical allusion: 'The antimasque world was a world of particularity and mutability – of accidents; the masque world was one of ideal abstractions and eternal verities'.[10] Jonson himself credits Anne of Denmark, Queen Consort of James I, with the idea of including a 'foyle, or false-Masque' in *The Masque*

---

9 About gardens in this period, see the brief section in Bazin, *The Baroque*, pp. 306 ff.
10 Orgel, *The Jonsonian Masque*, p. 73.

of Queenes that might precede her own grand masquing dance. Antimasque elements continued to exert strong influence on the Restoration stage, as the witches in Purcell's opera *Dido and Aeneas* (1689) attest.

One of Jonson's disciples in poetry was Robert Herrick (1591–1674), who published his collection *Hesperides* just months before the execution of Charles I in 1649. It includes a telling little poem in praise of feminine disarray, in which women's dress is but a means of exploring the relationship between nature and art. *Delight in Disorder* opens with the couplet

> A sweet disorder in the dress
> Kindles in clothes a wantonness.

After succinctly describing the attributes of certain carelessly worn items such as shawl, petticoat, ribbon and shoestring, Herrick concludes that these articles

> Do more bewitch me than when art
> Is too precise in every part.

In a footnote to 'precise', the modern editors of this poem point out that the word was used satirically to describe the Puritans – their name itself signifying disparagement – who were of course responsible for the king's downfall.[11] But Herrick's *Delight in Disorder* also conjures up the swirling folds of drapery on Bernini's statue of *The Ecstasy of St Teresa* (see below), whose disarray is suggestive not of 'wantonness' but, rather, of turbulent emotion.[12]

Motion and emotion, action and reaction

Expressing emotion was at the core of the Baroque aesthetic, and emotion was a function of motion. The dynamic movement so characteristic of the painting and sculpture of the seventeenth century has its parallels in the active bass lines so typical of its music. These, in turn, could be linked to what modern scholars have called the Doctrine of the Affections (*Affektenlehre*) that, so it is argued, influenced all the arts of this period. Given the Aristotelian notion that human nature in action is the proper object of imitation among artists, the sister arts had each come to be regarded as capable, through imitation (*mimesis*), of representing or expressing the emotions, and therefore of moving or affecting one's actions or behaviour. Aristotle's theory about how this happens in music was best stated in his *Politics* (viii: 5.1340a):

---

11 See Abrams and Greenblatt (eds), *The Norton Anthology of English Literature*, i: 1646.
12 The comparison is suggested by Praz, *Mnemosyne*, pp. 120–21.

Rhythm and melody supply imitations of anger and gentleness, and also of courage and temperance, and of all the qualities contrary to these, and of the other qualities of character, which hardly fall short of the actual affections, as we know from our own experience, for in listening to such strains our souls undergo a change.[13]

These ideas on emotional arousal were further strengthened by the scientific discoveries of the era. Galileo's observations through the telescope, and his deductions from the laws of mathematics and physics, had demonstrated that the senses as well as reason were instruments for learning.[14] Placed in the service of human knowledge, then, eye and ear could certainly be conduits through which to influence emotions and behaviour. A new emphasis on the sense of hearing, in fact, may account for the sudden plethora of paintings that include musical instruments – as signs of the ear's potency – in the seventeenth century.

By the middle of the century the mathematician and philosopher René Descartes announced, via the publication of his treatise *Des passions de l'âme* ('On the passions of the soul', 1649), that he had located the actual seat of the passions in the human body.[15] At that point, the hypothetical link between the senses and the soul became a reality because the soul, having a corporeal presence in the body, could be affected via sensory perceptions conveyed there by the movement of the 'animal spirits'. Descartes's treatise set forth in all its mechanistic simplicity the principle that had been lurking behind theories of the affections since the late sixteenth century: for every *action* in the physical universe there is an equal and opposite *reaction*; and for every *motion* stimulating the human body there is a resultant *emotion* evoked in the soul. Action and reaction, motion and emotion – these words underlie the basic imperative of the sister arts in this period and help to explain the mimetic resolve to move the emotions and stir the passions.

Painters of this period frequently concentrated on subjects involving physical action and psychological reaction. The *Boy Bitten by a Lizard* (*c.* 1597) painted by Michelangelo Merisi da Caravaggio (1573–1610) should be called 'Boy *Being* Bitten . . .' because it captures the precise moment at which the youth's finger is pierced by the reptile emerging from the vase of flowers and fruit. (Of course, the titles themselves were often bestowed on paintings retrospectively and are usually merely convenient descriptions of the subject or action depicted.) But Caravaggio is interested in the reaction as well as in the action, and he depicts the boy's face contorted in painful surprise, his arm straining to pull

---

13 *The Works of Aristotle*, x: *Politics*, trans. B. Jowett (London, 1952).
14 The son of a musician (see above), Galileo himself had a lively interest in the arts; see Panofsky, *Galileo as a Critic of the Arts*.
15 The relevant passages are given in Weiss and Taruskin (eds), *Music in the Western World*, pp. 212–17.

away from the source of the pain. Another example is Artemisia Gentileschi's powerful *Judith Slaying Holofernes* (*c.* 1620), in which Judith is shown decapitating her victim and in the same instant recoiling with loathing from his gushing blood. It is telling that the first operas were also about a single significant action (often merely narrated) and the reactions prompted thereby, be it Apollo's response to the metamorphosis of Daphne, or Orpheus' to the death of Eurydice.

In music, a motion intended to represent and ultimately stimulate an emotion could be encoded in many ways, the most obvious being by means of rhythm. For example, the rapid repetition of a pitch, often in semiquavers as in Monteverdi's *concitato genere*, was appropriate for bellicose, heroic or angry sentiments or actions because it mimicked the agitated or excited utterances of someone in the throes of those emotions. Decades before he actually coined the term in the preface to his *Madrigali guerrieri, et amorosi* (1638), Monteverdi had already imitated the accents of such speech in his treatment of some lines in the *Lamento d'Arianna* (from the opera *Arianna* of 1608). Here, the abandoned heroine's long monologue ranges over a broad gamut of emotions, but in the fourth section, overcome with rage at Theseus' desertion, she rails at him in semiquavers, virtually spitting out the syllables in a torrent of unbridled emotion. But motion could also be encoded in a series of pitches, such as the doleful descending tetrachord of the opening phrase of Dowland's *Lachrimae* pavan or the ground-bass of Monteverdi's *Lamento della ninfa* ('Lament of the nymph') in his Eighth Book, in which the drooping four-note figure captures the quintessential gesture of sorrow. As such, it has been called an 'emblem of lament'.[16]

In this period, emblems were simple designs or images accompanied by an explanatory motto or description; both the image and the text were intended to convey a moral lesson or to represent a real or abstract truth in the form of a coded message. The first collections of emblems, an artistic genre that came to be known as emblem books, appeared during the sixteenth century and were related to the fashionable idea of *ut pictura poesis*. With the help of the printing press, they proliferated at an enormous rate during the seventeenth century, in keeping with that era's proclivity for naming and classifying all things knowable. Thus there were emblems that depicted images of the gods, and others that allegorised earthly pursuits, some that personified virtues and vices, and still others that represented human passions and affections. Moreover, the emblem book also satisfied the age's desire for the union of sense and reason in art by joining the visual and the verbal, the picture and the word.

16 Rosand, 'The Descending Tetrachord'.

Giambattista Marino (1569–1625), perhaps the poet who had most influence in the seventeenth century, eloquently described the symbiotic relationship of painting and poetry in this way: 'one imitates with colours, the other with words; one imitates chiefly the external, that is the features of the body, the other the internal, that is, the affections of the soul; one causes us almost to understand with the senses, the other to feel with the intellect'.[17] Although his remarks are not specifically about the emblem, they do help to elucidate the peculiar efficacy of that device, stemming from its fusion of icon and word. To pursue Marino's line of thought, a musical emblem, then, is one that imitates in sound, with or without words, a bodily feature (or gesture) and/or an affection of the soul. This causes a feeling or emotion, such as grief or lament, to be 'understood through the senses', in this case, hearing.

Among other things, emblem books were intended to be useful to artists and poets alike, providing a source of suggestions for depicting all manner of subjects. They generated, in effect, a lingua franca of symbols in the arts. They influenced the description of emotions and their bodily expressions in treatises on painting, such as Charles Le Brun's *Méthode pour apprendre à dessiner les passions proposée dans une conférence sur l'expression générale et particulière* ('Method of learning to draw the passions as proposed in a lecture on expression in general and in particular', 1698), wherein the author renders a variety of emotions – anger, fear etc. – both in minute verbal descriptions and in drawings of the corresponding facial expressions.[18] Although not published until late in the century, Le Brun's treatise mirrors the practice of artists such as Poussin, who selected his poses and gestures to express the feelings of the participants caught up in the momentous events of his history paintings. If Poussin's figures at first seem artificial or their poses stilted – for example, in his *Israelites Gathering Manna in the Desert* – we must remember that he was telling the story without the benefit of words and must therefore have felt the need to exaggerate the gestures and actions in emblematic fashion in order that the viewer might easily recognise 'those who are languishing from hunger, those who are struck with amazement, those who are taking pity on their companions' and so on.[19] On another level, Poussin's treatment of the executioner in his *Massacre of the Innocents* parallels the personification of Choleric Temperament – the most violent of the four temperaments – in Cesare Ripa's *Iconologia* (1603), one of the earliest and most widely circulated of the emblem books: 'Pacing menacingly about is a muscular, half-naked man with wild hair and an angry expression

17 The quotation is from the first essay of Marino's *Dicerie sacre* (Vicenza, 1622); see Hagstrum, *The Sister Arts*, pp. 94–100.
18 Excerpts appear in Holt, *A Documentary History of Art*, ii: 159–63. The drawings are printed there as fig. 7, following p. 186.
19 Blunt, *Nicolas Poussin*, p. 223.

on his face . . .' Ripa's description further relates that the choleric has a flame emblazoned on his shield and gives off a great deal of heat when enraged, a connection which Poussin perhaps makes by draping the naked torso of his executioner in red.[20]

Seventeenth-century poetry included a pictorialist tradition that was closely related to the emblem. Marino's interest in painting reveals itself prominently in all his poetry – his epic poem *Adone* (1623) is consciously imagistic, with its long and virtuosic descriptions – but the most obvious expression of this interest was his collection of iconic poetry published under the title *La galleria del Cavalier Marino* (1620).[21] Emulating the art galleries he saw in noble houses and royal palaces in Italy and France, he created a series of brief poems on individual paintings, such as Caravaggio's *The Head of Medusa* or Titian's *Magdalene*. But these poems are more than mere descriptions of the works to which they correspond; instead they respond verbally and autonomously to the emotion graphically expressed by the painting – raw horror in the case of the unseeing, open-mouthed, detached head of Medusa, or contrition in the sweet face of the penitent prostitute – and re-present that emotion poetically. In effect, they are verbal emblems which cause us 'to feel with the intellect' just as their visual counterparts cause us 'to understand with the senses'. Marino's poetry and his claims for the interrelationship of the arts exerted a powerful influence on Poussin, who spent many years in Rome, as well as on English poets such as John Milton (1608–74).

In England, the popularity of emblems spawned a generation of 'emblematic poets' like George Herbert, whose sole collection of iconic poems, *The Temple* (1633), is in effect a denuded emblem book (that is, without the accompanying engravings). Many of its poems contemplate a single image ('The Altar') or emotion ('Affliction'), and some actually take the shape of the image evoked by the subject: the verses of 'Easter Wings', for example, first decrease and then increase in length, resulting in a butterfly shape that outlines a pair of wings.[22] In a still different way, John Milton's companion poems *L'Allegro* and *Il Penseroso* elaborate the concept of the emblem.[23] Their Italian titles, alluding to the humoral theory of the ancients as well as to the emblematic tradition that helped sustain it, name respectively the sanguine, cheerful person and the melancholy, contemplative one. In presenting the contrasting qualities or temperaments personified by these characters, Milton not only celebrates their different values and lifestyles but also renders a psychological portrait of each. The scholarly and introspective Penseroso forms a convincing

---

20 See Plate 107 in the facsimile of the Hertel Edition (1758–60) of Ripa's *Iconologia* (New York, 1971).
21 Hagstrum, *The Sister Arts*, pp. 100–104.
22 *The Norton Anthology of English Literature*, i: 1595–1615.   23 Ibid., i: 1782–90.

poetic counterpart to Dürer's famous engraving of Melancholy. But Milton's verbal portraits are even more closely related to the seventeenth-century character-book, a genre distantly inspired by the Greek writer Theophrastus. Characters, or verbal sketches describing general types of persons and behaviour, are close cousins of the emblem and succeed it in the conduct-literature of the period. Perhaps the most famous example is Thomas Overbury's *Collection of Characters* (1614), which included his own witty poem, *A Wife*.[24]

Understanding how emblems and characters encoded an affection or represented a particular temperament sharpens our appreciation for the great portrait painters of the century, such as Rembrandt (1606–69) and Anthony Van Dyck (1599–1641). Similarly, the increasing respect for pictorial expressivity is reflected in the phenomenal success of Van Dyck in seventeenth-century England: his early self-portraits proclaimed him to be a refined genius and gentleman cavalier – rather than a prosaic craftsman from Antwerp – thus prophesying the knighthood he would eventually receive from Charles I. He created a new type of royal portrait which minimised the defects of nature without falsifying them, and which imparted to his subjects a relaxed air of dignity and instinctive sovereignty by their graceful, almost casual elegance.[25]

In discussing portraiture we may seem to have digressed far from the music of the period, yet the aria, a set-piece which evolved towards the middle of the century along with Venetian opera, was effectively a type of portraiture. Its subject, however, was not the physiognomy of a particular character but, rather, the affections of the person's soul, which were revealed when whatever events or psychological developments leading to that point in the drama called for the character to react in song. One function of the aria was precisely to stop the action and allow the listener to perceive and be moved by the psychological state or emotions of the personage represented by the singer. To this end, composers developed an emotive vocabulary – a musical lexicon of motives and figures that communicated and then evoked those emotions in the listener with some particularity. Arias became in effect a series of emblematic elaborations, each of a different passion – rage, lament, desire, joy etc. – with each passion associated with a certain set of musical attributes, much like the gestures and colours that conveyed expression in painting. Action and reaction, motion and emotion – these are the dialectic agencies that are common to the sister arts of the period and summarise their *modus operandi*.

24 Reprinted as *The Overburian Characters*, ed. W. J. Paylor (Oxford, 1936); see Braider, *Refiguring the Real*, p. 132.
25 Levey, *Painting at Court*, pp. 124–33.

Naturalism and illusion

Painting and poetry were united by their common ability to achieve verisimilitude: to give a convincing *representation* of the truth was as important a goal for the Baroque artist as it had been through antiquity and the Renaissance, and music was not exempt. In a way, the innovations already discussed of both Monteverdi in music and Rubens, his contemporary, in painting were directed towards this same artistic purpose, naturalism: they both imitated, represented and enhanced their 'texts', the one by way of unorthodox dissonances and similar harmonically 'colourful' devices that rendered the text more convincing, and the other by way of colour, light and shade, which, for their proponents, were more effective than design in rendering a subject in a more convincing fashion.

In music at the beginning of the seventeenth century, the new *stile rappresentativo* (the 'representative' or 'representational' style) promulgated by the early opera composers may be seen as a manifestation of naturalism. This is especially true of recitative, that species of the *stile rappresentativo* which most partook of the goals of naturalism because it imitated speech, which, in turn, was presumed to be (along with gesture) a natural means of human communication. Recitative was opera's most radical innovation because it sought to eradicate altogether the distinction between speaking and singing, between words and music, between nature and art. It did so by synthesising the two elements into an inseparable whole, creating a language which was *sui generis* – more than speech but less than song, as Peri explained it – a language able to communicate simultaneously to both mind and body. Furthermore, the new style of solo song, of which recitative was only the most extreme example, was cultivated as a spontaneous vehicle for imitating, expressing and arousing the emotions, emotions that inhere in the rhythmic patterns and melodic inflections of the 'natural' voice. (Recall Galilei's admonition to composers to learn about good text expression by listening to actors declaim in the theatre.) Similarly, it is no accident that the earliest protagonists of opera – the gods and demigods of the first pastoral plays to be entirely sung – were chosen because singing was in their very nature: Apollo, god of music, and Orpheus, legendary musician and Apollo's offspring, who by virtue of his powerfully eloquent lyre was able to retrieve Eurydice from the Underworld. At least initially, then, the musical style of opera, the art form *par excellence* of Baroque Europe, steadfastly pursued a naturalistic course, even while at the same time its elaborate sets and stage machinery embraced the conventions of illusion.

However important verisimilitude was as an artistic goal, truth nevertheless had to be tempered by beauty, especially for certain classicising academicians who believed in modelling their work on previous works of art judged to be near perfect, rather than copying directly from nature in the raw. Poussin, for example, sought to render an idealised abstraction, a beauty superior to anything in nature. It is not surprising, then, that some seventeenth-century art critics reacted adversely to the style of Caravaggio, who pioneered so aggressive a naturalism that his works were seen as vulgar, lacking in decorum, and somehow indecent in their realism. His *Death of the Virgin*, now in the Louvre, was pronounced unacceptable because the figure of the Madonna 'imitated too closely the corpse of a woman'.[26] Caravaggio rejected graceful invention for its own sake, and instead sought to enhance the expressive content of his paintings by forcefully contrasting light and dark, by merging his subjects with their environment, and by generally sacrificing clarity and explicitness of form to pervasive, disturbing and disruptive emotions. In addition to the works already cited (*Boy Bitten by a Lizard*, *The Head of Medusa*), examples include *The Musicians*, *David and Goliath*, and *The Cardsharps*. His themes were not always elevated ones: Caravaggio was also drawn to representations of street life, including drunken brawls, gambling dens, and young men carousing with prostitutes.

Among the many artists influenced by Caravaggio was the court painter, Diego Velázquez (1599–1660), who not only produced intimate portraits of the Spanish royal family but also chronicled (in works called *bodegones*) a subheroic world of vernacular experience, of humble subjects pursuing ordinary activities, in the ultra-realistic manner popularised by Caravaggio. Dutch painting in the seventeenth century experienced a 'golden age', partly as a result of the Italian influence exercised by Caravaggio and his followers. Among other Netherlands artists, Rembrandt adopted various features of the style: the magical dark brown and golden hues of many of his paintings, known as 'tenebrism', and his concern for naturalistic detail both stemmed from Caravaggio.[27] Just as, in music, Monteverdi had made the irregular use of dissonance acceptable for expressive purposes, disturbing the smooth surface of the art of counterpoint with crude 'imperfections', so too did Rembrandt make ugliness acceptable in art by choosing models from among the most ordinary and coarse specimens of humanity and daring to show them as they were, even if marred by warts and wrinkles (as in his own self-portraits).

The vogue for naturalism in painting led to the 'art of genre', a type of subject in which Northerners excelled. For example, the Dutch master Jan Steen (1626–79) produced hundreds of tavern scenes, 'merry companies', brothel

---

26 The comment was made by Giovanni Pietro Bellori (1613–96), one of Caravaggio's greatest detractors, who wrote a biography of the artist among many others (*Le vite de' pittori, scultori ed architetti moderni*, 1672); quoted in Enggass and Brown (eds), *Italy and Spain*, p. 76.

27 Braider, *Refiguring the Real*, pp. 199ff.

settings, musical gatherings, village fairs, and the like. Steen himself was a tavern keeper, and his canvases are painstakingly peopled – indeed, teeming – with characters from all walks and conditions of life, captured in contrasting states of hilarity and dejection, drunkenness and sobriety, brawling and trysting, playing and working, as they register the multifarious, unexpurgated and (despite painting's proverbial muteness) *noisy* experience of their world. Governed by conventions roughly corresponding to those of comic drama, which also came into its own during this period, Steen's art is diametrically opposed to that of history painting and the ideal, illusionist world portrayed by Poussin, or by the tragedies of Corneille and Racine, which in turn resemble the exalted and artificial universe of Lully's stage works or of Italian *opera seria*. And Steen's Characters (with an uppercase 'C'), although stereotypes of fallen humanity who in some settings readily evoke the Parable of the Prodigal Son, are a far cry from the noble heroes of the Bible, or the enduring valiants of mythology and epic poetry.[28] Take, for example, his *Doctor Feeling a Young Woman's Pulse* or his numerous variations on the theme of the *Merry Company*.

The pursuit of naturalism led inevitably to the Baroque cultivation of illusion. These terms are not contradictory: in achieving verisimilitude the artist deceives the audience into believing that it is observing nature when of course it is seeing only a representation of nature (a marble sculpture painted into a fictive landscape) or hearing only a representation of mournful speech (a lament on the operatic stage). These conventions of illusion go hand-in-hand with the concept of *meraviglia* (the marvellous, the unexpected, the extraordinary), which the Baroque artist must discern in nature and then reveal to the viewer, even while outdoing nature by creating something new. In Baroque literature, *meraviglia* is also frequently equated with the kind of response aroused by the artist's or poet's virtuosity or technical prowess. When Marino says 'del poeta il fin la meraviglia' ('The aim of the poet is the marvellous'), he means that a successful poem should elicit wonder and delight, making people *marvel* at the poet's wit (broadly defined as virtuosic ingenuity) or, by extension, at the artist's impressions of beauty, and the dramatist's flashes of insight.[29] Thus *meraviglia* is the hidden operative in the complex relationship between nature and art, and between art and illusion.

Drama and stasis

The seventeenth century was the Golden Age of European drama, beginning with William Shakespeare (1564–1616) and closing with Jean Racine (1639–99). But it was also an age in which the doctrine of the sister arts, *ut pictura poesis*,

---

28 Ibid., pp. 135ff.   29 See Mirollo, *The Poet of the Marvelous*, pp. 117–18.

reached its consummation in opera, where painting, poetry and music (not to mention other arts) were united. The theatre, being both a visual and a literary mode of representation, was the perfect medium for the 'speaking picture', while the new proscenium-arch stage (in the Venetian opera-houses, for example) created a picture-plane that transformed the dramatic scene into a sounding image. At the same time, Baroque painting and sculpture became intensely and explicitly theatrical; along with music, they shared theatre's rhetorical status as a kind of show, a *rappresentazione*, designed to move and persuade their beholders.[30] Roger de Piles (1635–1709), one of the most influential art theorists of the century, was unequivocal in this matter: 'One must think of painting as a kind of stage on which each figure plays its role'.[31] Elsewhere he tells us that the 'principal end' of the painter is 'to imitate the mores and actions of men'.[32] The first opera composers had said as much for music. And at the very beginning of his career, Descartes, taking the physical world as his starting point, had begun his treatise on music with a revolutionary definition: 'The object of music is *sound*', he says (my emphasis), and not number, as Renaissance theorists had believed: 'Its end is to delight and *move the affections* in us'.[33] By adopting rhetorical goals, the sister arts had all, each in its own way, become dramatic.

The theatricality of Baroque art is compounded by the tendency in the seventeenth century for art to contemplate itself. Painters often portrayed art within art: statuary, architecture, musical instruments, even other paintings – all are richly represented, suggesting that the exaltation of art was an important theme. Perhaps this phenomenon was a reaction on the part of Counter-Reformation Europe to the Protestant attack on sacred images in particular, and to the condemnation in some quarters of painting, music, and the stage in general.[34] Not confined merely to painting, examples of such self-reflection abound in and across all the arts: Dryden's odes to St Cecilia are a poetic testament to the power of music; Bernini's marble sculpture of *The Ecstasy of St Teresa* places the Spanish nun's private vision of her mystical union with the heavenly bridegroom before a fictive, almost voyeuristic audience; and Monteverdi's *Lamento della ninfa* transforms the traditional texture of a polyphonic madrigal into a dramatic *scena* that unfolds within the framework of the piece.

30 Braider, *Refiguring the Real*, pp. 151ff.

31 From *Abrégé de la vie des peintres* (1699), quoted in Braider, *Refiguring the Real*, p. 156.

32 From *Cours de peinture par principe* ('The principles of painting', 1708), excerpts of which appear in Holt, *A Documentary History of Art*, ii: 176–86.

33 See his *Compendium of Music*, which deserves to be better known. Written in 1618, it was Descartes's first scholarly discourse but remained unpublished until 1650, after his death; there is an English translation by W. Robert in 'Musicological Studies and Documents', 8 (American Institute of Musicology, 1961).

34 Hagstrum, *The Sister Arts*, p. 204 n. 55.

These last two examples are particularly instructive because in each of them the work itself, in effect, becomes the stage.

The *Lamento della ninfa*, probably written in the 1630s, is a kind of proto-cantata. The central section, a trend-setting lament for female voice and continuo, is composed over a relentlessly repeating four-note ground, suggestive of an emblem in that its stepwise descent through a minor tetrachord (from tonic to dominant) connotes a mournful gesture (see above). But what is remarkable here is that this section is framed by a trio of male voices that sets the stage for us by drawing back the curtain, as it were, to reveal the disconsolate nymph and, as her lament progresses, by commenting on her plight. Like onlookers at a theatrical performance, the trio functions as an audience placed on the 'set', serving to draw our attention to the main 'action', taking on the role of narrator and choral commentary, and highlighting the nymph's emotional distress. Thus, Monteverdi's work unfolds to our ears and under our contemplative gaze at the same time as the nymph spins out her complaint to the attentive ears and watchful gaze of her male observers. As with Bernini's *The Ecstasy of St Teresa* (discussed further, below), Monteverdi's nymph is at once the subject and the object of art within art. (In the text excerpted here, the words in italics are sung by the male trio, the rest by the solo female voice.)

Non havea Febo ancora	*Phoebus had not yet*
recato al mondo il dì	*brought daylight to the world*
ch'una donzella fuora	*when a maiden emerged*
del proprio albergo uscì.	*from her dwelling place.*
. . .	
Amor, *dicea,* il ciel	Love, *she said,* skyward
mirando, il piè fermò,	*gazing, her feet arrested,*
Amor, dov'è la fè	Love, where is the faith
che 'l traditor giurò?	that the traitor promised?
Miserella . . .	*Unhappy maid . . .*

The notion of the theatrical extended even to the city and its physical spaces. Rome in effect provides the backdrop for the art of Gianlorenzo Bernini (1598–1680), the outstanding sculptor of the century. In addition to St Peter's Basilica, and fountains, piazzas and sculpture all over the city, he designed a side chapel within the church of Santa Maria della Vittoria at the request of the Cornaro family that was to be dedicated to St Teresa of Avila.[35] The commission gave Bernini the opportunity not only to create a sculptural group as the chapel's

35 Wittkower, *Gian Lorenzo Bernini*, pp. 24–6. A famous essay by Mario Praz ('The Flaming Heart: Richard Crashaw and the Baroque', in Praz, *The Flaming Heart*, pp. 204–63) juxtaposes Bernini's sculpture with an iconic poem by the Englishman Richard Crashaw ('The Flaming Heart upon the Book and Picture of the Seraphicall Saint Theresa'), who may or may not have known Bernini's version.

altarpiece, but also to plan the details of its setting, which he fashioned as though it were a theatrical performance. The figures of St Teresa and the angel enact her mystical vision above the altar, bathed in the warm glow emanating from the chapel's hidden window of yellow glass above them – an architec- tural feature contrived to throw a 'spotlight' on the scene. Bernini stunningly reinforced the theatrical aspect of the tableau by depicting members of the Cornaro family seated high along the side walls of the chapel, on the same hor- izontal plane as the statue, in pews that resemble theatre boxes, as though they were attending a command performance of this dramatic mystery. Like the male trio in Monteverdi's *Lamento della ninfa*, the images of the Cornaro family here function as a surrogate audience, and by identifying with these onlookers, we are drawn in, physically and emotionally, to contemplate St Teresa, who is both the object of our gaze and the subject of her own dramatic vision, and thus, once again, an example of art within art.

The passionate movement implied by the swirling drapery of Bernini's statue and the relentless motion of the ground bass in Monteverdi's madrigal have their antithesis in the beautiful stillness and meditative quality of other seventeenth-century works. Poussin's output remains unusual by exhibiting both these opposing traits: overwhelming dramatic power, in keeping with the heroic magnification of his history paintings; and restrained lyrical intro- spection, expressed in his pastoral subjects (such as *Et in Arcadia ego, c.* 1655). However, the artist whose works most obviously make stillness an expressive virtue is Johannes Vermeer (1632–75), who excelled in the 'art of describing' that was so characteristic of his Dutch countrymen.[36] Most famous for his small-scale interior scenes, Vermeer captured the intimate details of quotidian existence. But unlike the 'noisy' and boisterous canvases of his contemporary, Jan Steen, Vermeer's are quiet and understated observations of inconsequential activities that nevertheless unveil a universe of concrete reality. By turning a magnifying lens on the most ordinary of genre settings, he makes *looking* the Cartesian equivalent of *thinking*: his world exists because he pictures it.[37] At the same time his graceful meditations invite us to contemplate the deeper meaning of the reality he so skilfully portrays.

The Music Lesson is a case in point. Presumably, it belongs to a genre associating music with courtship that was popular during the seventeenth century. A well- dressed young woman, her face reflected in a mirror, stands in a beautifully lit and windowed room in the presence of a gallant gentleman, who observes her from a respectful distance. The meticulously rendered keyboard instrument

36 The phrase is the apt title of a book by Alpers, *The Art of Describing*.
37 Braider, *Refiguring the Real*, p. 189.

which the woman appears to be touching, with her back to the viewer, is exactly like a virginal made by the famous Ruckers firm in Antwerp. Its open lid reveals the inscription *Musica letitiae comes . . . medicina dolorum* ('Music is the companion of joy . . . and the remedy for sorrow'). Another musical instrument (a viol) and an empty chair in the middle of the room's marble-tiled floor suggest the possibility of a duet, and hence a courtship. But as in so many Vermeer paintings, there are several mysterious elements that remain indecipherable, despite the governing conventions and intellectual assumptions of Dutch art in general. What *is* the relationship between the man and the woman at the virginal: is he her teacher, her suitor, or both? What are we to make of the disparity between the 'real' woman, visible only from the back, and the reflection of her face, held at a different angle, in the mirror? How can we reconcile the precision of Vermeer's descriptive art to the distortion of this reality? What bearing should the inscription have on our interpretation of the painting: do the words deepen or merely extend the painting's meaning? What is the significance of the presence of musical instruments: are they a variation on the topos of art within art, or do they symbolise the power of the sense of hearing? And if the latter, do they exalt music as domestic harmony or denigrate it as fleeting pleasure? These questions may be unanswerable, but the mere fact that we can pose them demonstrates the participatory nature of artistic contemplation in this period.

The contrast between the dramatic and heroic on the one hand and the introspective and intimate on the other parallels the difference in seventeenth-century musical developments between, say, the grand concerto, exemplified by the Venetian polychoral motet, and the small-scale concerted motet or vocal chamber piece written by Italian and Lutheran composers; or between *opera seria* and the chamber cantata. Although the last two went in separate directions, they both promoted and harboured within them the same formal structure that became the musical epitome of static introspection: the da-capo aria of the late seventeenth and early eighteenth centuries. With its rounded form, minimal text, and unified content, the da-capo aria by its very nature is expressively inert. Like a Vermeer painting, it circumscribes a finite and static world, one in which nothing 'happens' except for the depiction of a solitary, unremarkable event (in the genre painting) or the communication of a single affection resulting from a typically quite remarkable event (in the *opera seria*). Generally considered to be merely a virtuosic vehicle, the da-capo aria is also a compositional device which permits a lyrical moment to be arrested and expanded outside of the diegetic time of the work; but it ends where it began, usually without effecting any change in the personage who presents it or in the outcome of the action. Thus the da-capo aria functions much like a cinematic close-up, or like a musical portrait of an emotion or Character in the seventeenth-century sense.

Despite the antithetical and competing currents we have noted, there is something in the very nature of Baroque expression that seems to have fostered the association of the arts in seventeenth-century Europe, and, as Marino would have us believe, even their interpenetration. *Ut pictura poesis* had placed the sister arts on equal footing as valid interpreters of human experience. Their combined powers – such as the sculpture, architecture and lighting brought together in Bernini's Cornaro chapel, or the music, poetry and theatre synthesized in a Cavalli opera – immeasurably enhanced their individual effect. And after all, the wondrous effect – *meraviglia* – was everything. Infinitely more important than didactic or rational suasion, emotional suasion was seen as key. Thus artistic expression in the seventeenth century apotheosized the emotions, and the goal of moving the affections licensed painters, sculptors, poets and musicians to transcend palpable reality, and to imitate and penetrate the invisible wonders of the soul.

Bibliography

Abrams, M. H., and Greenblatt, S. (eds), *The Norton Anthology of English Literature*. 7th edn, 2 vols, London and New York, 2000

Alpers, S., *The Art of Describing: Dutch Art in the Seventeenth Century*. Chicago, 1983

Arasse, D., *Vermeer: Faith in Painting*, Princeton, 1994

Bailey, A., *Vermeer: a View of Delft*. New York, 2001

Bazin, G., *The Baroque: Principles, Styles, Modes, Themes*, trans. P. Wardroper. Greenport, CT, 1968

Bianconi, L., *Music in the Seventeenth Century*, trans. D. Bryant. Cambridge, 1987

Blunt, A., *Nicolas Poussin*. New York, 1967

Blunt, A., and Lockspeiser, E., *French Art and Music since 1500*. London, 1974

Braider, C., *Refiguring the Real: Picture and Modernity in Word and Image, 1400–1700*. Princeton, 1993

Chatfield, J., *A Tour of Italian Gardens*. New York, 1988

Enggass, R., and Brown, J. (eds), *Italy and Spain, 1600–1750: Sources and Documents [in the History of Art]*. Englewood Cliffs, NJ, 1970

Hagstrum, J. H., *The Sister Arts: the Tradition of Literary Pictorialism and English Poetry from Dryden to Gray*. Chicago and London, 1958

Hanning, B. R., 'Monteverdi's Three *Genera*: a Study in Terminology'. In N. K. Baker and B. R. Hanning (eds), *Musical Humanism and its Legacy: Essays in Honor of Claude V. Palisca*. Stuyvesant, NY, 1992, pp. 145–70

Hazlehurst, F. H., *Gardens of Illusion: the Genius of André Le Nostre*. Nashville, TN, 1980

Holt, E. G., *A Documentary History of Art*. 3 vols, Garden City, NY, 1957–66

Lavin, I., *The Genius of the Baroque: Essays on the Sculpture of Gianlorenzo Bernini*. London, 2000

Lee, R. W., '*Ut pictura poesis*': the Humanistic Theory of Painting. New York, 1967

Levey, M., *Painting at Court*. New York, 1971

Maser, A. (ed.), *Cesare Ripa: Baroque and Rococo Pictorial Imagery; the 1758–60 Hertel Edition of Ripa's 'Iconologia'*. New York, 1971

Mirollo, J. V., *The Poet of the Marvelous: Giambattista Marino*. New York and London, 1963

Orgel, S., *The Jonsonian Masque*, Cambridge, MA, 1965

Pace, C., *Félibien's Life of Poussin*. London, 1981

Panofsky, E., *Galileo as a Critic of the Arts*. The Hague, 1954

Praz, M., *The Flaming Heart: Essays on Crashaw, Machiavelli, and Other Studies in the Relations between Italian and English Literature*. Garden City, NY, 1958

Studies in Seventeenth-Century Imagery. 2 vols, Rome, 1964–74

'Milton and Poussin'. In *Seventeenth-Century Studies Presented to Sir Herbert Grierson*. New York, 1967, pp. 192–210

Mnemosyne: the Parallel between Literature and the Visual Arts. Princeton, 1970

Rosand, E., 'The Descending Tetrachord: an Emblem of Lament', *Musical Quarterly*, 65 (1979), 241–81

Scott, K., and Warwick, G., *Commemorating Poussin: Reception and Interpretation of the Artist*. Cambridge and New York, 1999

Spear, R., *From Caravaggio to Artemisia: Essays on Painting in Seventeenth-Century Italy and France*. London, 2002

Stratton, S. L., *The Cambridge Companion to Velazquez*. Cambridge and New York, 2002

Weiss, P., and Taruskin, R. (eds), *Music in the Western World: a History in Documents*. New York, 1984

Wittkower, R., *Gian Lorenzo Bernini: the Sculptor of the Roman Baroque*. London, 1966

Wolf, B. J., *Vermeer and the Invention of Seeing*. Chicago, 2001

6

Music and the sciences

PENELOPE GOUK

The relationship between music and the sciences during the seventeenth century is normally characterised as a movement away from music being classified as a mathematical discipline – typically, part of the *quadrivium* with arithmetic, geometry and astronomy – towards its association with the verbal disciplines, the *trivium* of grammar, rhetoric and logic, and, above all, the art of poetry.[1] It is certainly true that a new literature on musical poetics emerged around 1600, in which the effects of music were grounded in rhetorical rather than mathematical principles. From this point onwards, composers increasingly aimed to move the passions of their audiences, their express goal now being to portray or represent the gamut of human emotions through the effective union of words and music. That Diderot unhesitatingly located music among the fine arts in his *Encylopédie* (1751) shows just how much Western sensibilities had altered in the two centuries since Zarlino himself identified music as a mathematical science in his *Istitutioni harmoniche* (1558).[2]

From the perspective of music history, this generalised account of music's transformation from a scientific discipline to a poetic art serves well enough. Put simply, the tradition of *musica speculativa* cultivated by learned fourteenth- and fifteenth-century theorists was irrelevant to musicians trying to please audiences within what was becoming an increasingly secular and commercial marketplace. However, even though this concentration on the professionalisation of music as a practical art is understandable, it tells us nothing about the fate of the scientific tradition that was supposedly rejected. With a view to broadening what might be said about 'music and the sciences', this chapter starts from the premise that, far from becoming separated, these apparently distinct domains could be as close in the seventeenth century as they had ever been. The crucial difference was that now, for the first time, 'science', just like music, was becoming increasingly understood in terms of its practice rather than simply denoting a theoretical system. To appreciate the significance of this

---

1 Palisca, *Humanism in Italian Renaissance Musical Thought*; Moyer, *Musical Scholarship in the Italian Renaissance*.
2 Gozza (ed.), *Number to Sound*, p. 10.

conceptual shift, and why music had anything to do with it, it is necessary to understand what 'science' used to mean before it took on a more recognisably modern guise.

Changing definitions: science, art and philosophy

Briefly, up to the seventeenth century 'science' (i.e., knowledge) could simply mean theory, or a body of written doctrine on a particular subject. 'Philosophy' (i.e., wisdom), was a higher form of learning which went beyond scientific knowledge because it involved understanding the fundamental causes of things; it was normally divided into its moral, natural, epistemic and divine aspects. The category of 'natural philosophy' (explanations about the natural world) can be seen as roughly cognate with the physical and life sciences today, although founded on very different assumptions and methods. The term 'natural philosopher' was broadly similar to our term 'scientist' in that it denoted an individual committed to understanding and explaining the natural world. Yet the occupational category of 'scientist' did not exist before the nineteenth century, and before the seventeenth century, the idea that 'science' or even 'natural philosophy' was a powerful practice, that it should constitute an activity based on mathematical analysis and empirical observation, was unthinkable. Natural philosophy as taught in the universities (scholastic physics), focussed on the sensible (i.e., manifest to the senses) qualities and properties of bodies, and was a completely separate discipline from the quadrivial sciences, the latter occupying an inferior place in the curriculum. Sound constituted a part of physics as the object of hearing, but this was not always directly connected to the arithmetics of pitch relationships. Moreover, although Aristotle identified in his *Physics* a category of 'mixed mathematics', including optics, harmonics, astronomy and mechanics, he left no actual writings on the subject, and so it played only a minor role in the scholastic tradition.

While the term 'science' broadly indicated theory, the term 'art' broadly signified practice, and was used to denote a body of applied knowledge, or technical skill, acquired through human endeavour. Obviously, music was recognised as an art, but so too were other practices which are now more associated with science and technology, including the mixed mathematical disciplines already mentioned above. Somewhat less obviously – since it now conspicuously lacks intellectual credibility – magic was also recognised as an art and a science. What distinguished its practice from other applied forms of knowledge was not so much that it was forbidden – all magic being formally condemned by the Church – as that its effects were achieved through the manipulation of occult (i.e., hidden or secret) forces in nature, albeit supposedly only impersonal ones not relying on demonic agency. This is important because it helps to explain why during the sixteenth and early seventeenth centuries it was the natural magician who was more often associated with experimental procedures than the natural philosopher. Indeed, the magician, just like the musician, was capable of bringing about marvellous effects (physical as well as psychological) through the manipulation of forces and the application of practical techniques. It was only after Francis Bacon (1561–1626) openly challenged the methods of scholastic natural philosophy, and Galileo Galilei (1564–1642) vaunted the power of his new, experimentally based science of motion, that empirical knowledge began to be regarded as an essential part of philosophy. Within less than a hundred years, Bacon's vision of a new, experimental philosophy became increasingly established as a viable alternative to traditional natural philosophy, while natural magic declined in status.[3]

This provides an essential context for three main questions raised, if not definitively answered, in this chapter. The first concerns the 'science' of music itself: how the field of musical knowledge was defined, classified and understood in the seventeenth century – not so much by practitioners who earned their livelihood through music (few of whom wrote on the subject), but by individuals who had the necessary education, leisure and interest to pursue its theory. The second question is where music fitted into classifications of the arts and sciences more generally. The third, and I believe the most interesting, is how music – as an art, a body of skill, and a practice – contributed to changing understandings of 'science' and the 'sciences' during the seventeenth-century 'Scientific Revolution', an astonishing period of intellectual transformation during which it is generally recognised that 'the conceptual, methodological and institutional foundations of modern science were first established'.[4]

Music and the Scientific Revolution

What the seventeenth century understood by the science of music was approximately equivalent to modern musicology as most broadly defined: it might encompass every branch of knowledge that aids the understanding of what music is, including what it is made of, how it works, what its purpose is, and why it affects people. And just as it is now accepted that aspects of musicology can be studied by people who neither compose nor perform music, this was also accepted of musical science in the seventeenth century. There was, however, a broad distinction made between the category of knowledge (and its theoretical codifications) thought to be essential for practical music, and

---

3 Dear, *Revolutionizing the Sciences*; Henry, *The Scientific Revolution and the Origins of Modern Science*.
4 Henry, *The Scientific Revolution and the Origins of Modern Science*, p. 1.

the rest, namely speculative music. Speculative music constituted the kind of philosophical knowledge that intellectuals might be expected to possess about music – a body of doctrine that was usually produced by graduates, especially those with higher academic qualifications. And although speculative music had been dropped from the arts syllabuses in most European universities by this time (Oxford and Cambridge being notable exceptions), the influence of Boethius's *De musica* as a set text still lingered. Indeed, with the recovery of such ancient treatises as Euclid's *Elements* and *Sectio canonis* (*c.* 300 BCE) and Ptolemy's *Harmonics* (2nd cent. CE), the Pythagorean harmonic tradition gained even wider currency.[5] The subsequent retrieval of Aristoxenus' *Harmonic Elements* (late 3rd cent. BCE) and other Greek texts which dismissed Pythagoreanism as an inadequate basis for musical practice did not so much replace this tradition as provide a starting-point for debate on the division of the musical scale and its proper foundations in nature and art.[6] In short, speculative music was effectively the same in the seventeenth century as it had been in the Middle Ages inasmuch as it was philosophical learning, and focussed on the underlying mathematical and physical principles governing the nature of musical sound, and the causes of its effects.

The context in which this speculative learning was being generated, however, was very different, for a number of reasons. First, there had been a significant expansion in the European university population since the middle of the sixteenth century, including an increase in the numbers taking higher degrees in law and medicine. Second, there was a remarkable transformation in social attitudes towards music making, which meant that practical music was viewed as an indicator of gentility and therefore could be cultivated without opprobrium. In short, although it remained the case that few professional musicians went to university, there was a growing pool of educated men who not only had the right academic qualifications to write on the science of music, but also were musically literate and intellectually curious about the instruments and techniques involved in its practice. Far from diminishing in importance, therefore, the field of musical science arguably expanded during the seventeenth century, just as the map of knowledge itself was being completely transformed around it.[7]

Some sense of this expansion and interconnection can be gained from looking at two of the most influential works of musical science to appear in the seventeenth century: Marin Mersenne's *Harmonie universelle* (Paris, 1636–7), and Athanasius Kircher's *Musurgia universalis* (Rome, 1650). As their titles indicate,

---

5 Gouk, 'The Role of Harmonics in the Scientific Revolution'.
6 For an introduction to these issues, see Mathiesen, 'Greek Music Theory'.
7 Kelley (ed.), *History and the Disciplines*; Dear, *Revolutionizing the Sciences*, esp. chaps 2, 7, 8.

both works aspire to universality, in terms not just of encompassing everything known about music, but also of music's capacity to encompass the whole universe. Both Mersenne and Kircher provide, in effect, an encyclopaedic survey of seventeenth-century musical science. From the perspective of mathematics alone, these texts show how far scholars had moved from treating musical intervals simply as an arithmetical problem; now the subject required a sophisticated grasp of the mathematics of continuous quantity, using geometry and the recently developed tools of logarithms and decimals.[8] Even more significant, however, is how these tomes reflect the new approach towards natural philosophy that Galileo and Bacon had already demanded in their very different critiques of scholastic learning. Not only do Mersenne and Kircher take for granted that the harmonics of pitch are empirically grounded in physics, but they also reveal that within this field there is now emerging a new science of sound (i.e., acoustics), in which the properties of musical sound can be investigated experimentally.

A significant body of literature addressing the relationship between music and science during the late sixteenth and seventeenth centuries has appeared since Claude Palisca published his influential article on scientific empiricism in musical thought (1961).[9] This material draws attention to the striking number of 'scientists' who also wrote on music during this critical period between Renaissance and Enlightenment.[10] Apart from Galileo, the most famous are Johannes Kepler (1571–1630), Marin Mersenne (1588–1648), René Descartes (1596–1650), Christiaan Huygens (1629–95), Robert Hooke (1635–1703) and Isaac Newton (1642–1727); Newton's demonstration that all bodies were governed by the same universal laws was to provide a powerful model for Rameau's system of fundamental bass.[11] The emergence and institutionalisation of a distinctively new kind of science in this period – characterised by its emphasis on the value of instruments and observation as a means of generating useful and powerful knowledge about the world – was intimately connected with the emergence and institutionalisation of a radically new kind of music. Around 1600 these new practices and experimental ideologies (in both science and music) were mostly limited to princely courts. By 1700 they had moved into the public realm, the creation of the first formal scientific institutions dedicated to experimental philosophy coinciding precisely with the purpose-built theatres and music rooms that began to cater for a growing urban gentry class.

8 H. F. Cohen, *Quantifying Music*, pp. 45–74.   9 Palisca, 'Scientific Empiricism in Musical Thought'.
10 Dostrovsky, 'Early Vibration Theory'; Walker, *Studies in Musical Science in the Late Renaissance*; H. F. Cohen, *Quantifying Music*; Coelho (ed.), *Music and Science in the Age of Galileo*; Kassler, *Inner Music*; Gouk, *Music, Science and Natural Magic in Seventeenth-Century England*; Gozza (ed.), *Number to Sound*.
11 Christensen, *Rameau and Musical Thought in the Enlightenment*, esp. chap. 1.

Galileo Galilei and the 'Two New Sciences' (1638)

Galileo Galilei (1564–1642) is justly regarded as a leading figure of the seventeenth-century Scientific Revolution. The publication of his *Discorsi e dimostrazioni matematiche intorno à due nuove scienze attenenti alla mecanica et i movimenti locali* in 1638 effectively marks the transition from Aristotelian to modern physics.[12] Here Galileo presented his first law of the pendulum, together with the law of falling bodies and inclined planes, and showed how these discoveries were the result of precise measurement and meticulous experimental procedures. Galileo's contribution to the development of modern physics is important to this chapter not least because the roots of his new experimental method are partly to be found in instrumental techniques of musicians in this period, including skilled lutenists such as Galileo's father, Vincenzo, his younger brother Michelagnolo, and, of course, he himself.[13] Also, the *Discorsi* helped to disseminate a new theory of consonance which was based on the relative frequency of vibrations striking the ear rather than abstract mathematical ratios.[14] Finally, Galileo's new, empirically based science was promoted in precisely the same courtly milieu in which his father and other members of the Florentine Camerata had already developed their new, affective ideology of music as a powerful language of the emotions.

According to Stillman Drake, Galileo could not have created his motion experiments without the musical training that gave him the ability to measure small, equal divisions of time accurately. (This was several decades before pendulum clocks were invented, a technological advance dependent on Galileo's discovery.) One of his experiments, for example, involved rolling a ball repeatedly down an inclined plane, around which a series of frets were tied. These frets were gradually adjusted so that the bumping sounds that occurred when the ball went over them finally came at regular half-second intervals, precise units of time which Galileo calculated to within 1/64th of a second. The idea of using adjustable frets was most likely to occur only to a lutenist or viol player. More significantly, however, Galileo's experiment relied crucially on the musician's internalised 'clock' (or 'metronome', more anachronistically) as a means of marking small, equal units of time over a sustained period. Drake argues that from this experiment later came Galileo's idea for a timing device which used the weight of water flowing during the swing of a pendulum to establish the rule that doubling the length of the pendulum quadruples the duration

---

12 G. Galilei, *Two New Sciences Including Centers of Gravity and Force of Percussion*, trans. S. Drake (Madison, WI, 1974).
13 This claim is powerfully argued in Drake, 'Music and Philosophy in Early Modern Science'.
14 H. F. Cohen, *Quantifying Music*, pp. 75–8.

of its swing, leading to his founding the law of the acceleration of falling bodies.[15]

Galileo treats the properties of pendulums in the 'First Day' of his *Discorsi*, at the end of which appears a discussion of music. 'Salviati' (Galileo's mouthpiece in the text, named after Filippo Salviati) is asked to deduce good reasons for the phenomenon of resonance (sympathetic vibration), and also for the musical consonances and their ratios. The purpose is to give Salviati/Galileo another opportunity to demonstrate the superiority of his 'new science' over university physics, which treated mathematics as inferior. Salviati starts by stating the three properties of a swinging pendulum, the third of which he invokes to explain resonance, and he then extends this explanation to demonstrate that pitch is not only determined by frequency, but is also proportional to it.[16] As D. P. Walker was the first to realise, none of the experiments which Salviati describes in support of his argument could have been carried out.[17] However, Galileo was right to the extent that the propositions which his imagined experiments demonstrated were valid, and it is clear that he derived his intuitive understanding of vibration from using musical instruments as scientific apparatus.

At this point Salviati/Galileo goes on to explain his theory of consonance, namely that it is produced by the coincidence of sonorous impulses striking the eardrum, a motion which is then transmitted inwards to the brain (Galileo did not hypothesise about this inner mechanism). The more frequently the pulses of sound coincide with each other, the more pleasing the consonance. Despite the obvious problems (such as the subsequent inability of Galileo's theory to account for the ear's acceptance of temperament), the coincidence theory opened up a whole new range of questions about the production, transmission and reception of musical sound that preoccupied succeeding generations. Again, we must credit Galileo's practical training as a musician, and his sharp ear, for the empirical direction that his new science was taking.

There was, however, a further dimension to Galileo's musical experience without which he might never have performed any pendulum experiments at all. As Palisca has explained, it was his father who inadvertently initiated the exercise in the context of his long-standing debate with Zarlino over the

---

15 Drake, 'Music and Philosophy in Early Modern Science', p. 15.

16 The three properties are: (1) that the duration of one complete vibration is always the same (isochronism; which Galileo wrongly claimed to be exact for any arc); (2) that the lengths are inversely proportional to the square of the numbers of vibrations; and (3) that every pendulum has a natural vibrational duration, or period, of its own. See H. F. Cohen, *Quantifying Music*, pp. 87–90.

17 Walker, *Studies in Musical Science in the Late Renaissance*, chap. 3; see also H. F. Cohen, *Quantifying Music*, pp. 92–4.

true causes of consonance.[18] Some time in the late 1580s, while Galileo was staying with his parents in Florence, Vincenzo Galilei actually tested the experiments Pythagoras was supposed to have made in the course of discovering the correspondence between the consonances and the ratios of the first few integers (described, for example, in Gaffurius's *Theoria musicae* of 1492). Through repeated trials, Galilei ascertained that a variety of ratios other than those using the numbers 1 to 4 and their multiples could cause consonances in pipes, glasses and strings. Furthermore, in an unpublished essay written just before his death in 1591, he described experiments showing that pitch can be varied not just by the length or tension of a string, but also by changing its thickness or the material out of which it is made. Here for the first time, a 'real' musical instrument (Galilei's lute), rather than one with little practical application (the monochord), was made the subject of theoretical analysis, in effect becoming a piece of laboratory equipment.

The controversy which led to Vincenzo Galilei's 'scientific' discoveries had its origins in the correspondence he began with Girolamo Mei in 1572 comparing modern music with that of the ancient Greeks, an initiative prompted by the Florentine Camerata's desire to create a new way of making music based on Classical models. As is well known, members of the Camerata felt that prevailing musical techniques were inadequate for moving the emotions of the listeners, and they were receptive, at least in principle, to Mei's scholarly conclusions that the Greeks had achieved their marvellous effects through use of a single melody which exploited the naturally expressive different pitch levels of the voice. They began to experiment with new types of solo writing, and also with new musical instruments (including the chitarrone) to produce new musical styles and genres. Yet while the artistic consequences of the Camerata's experiments are familiar to music historians, their parallels with, and long-term consequences for, scientific method are less well appreciated. As Ruth Katz has pointed out, the Camerata's activities might be compared to those of modern research institutes in that they involved a collaborative process of targeted problem-solving by a group whose members possessed a diverse mix of practical and theoretical skills, the costs of implementing their results (i.e., the staging of *intermedi*, opera etc.) being met from noble coffers.[19] However, their goal was not just to create new knowledge, but also to arouse wonder, delight and strong emotions. Even if the Camerata did not so much resemble as prefigure the modern research institute, it remains significant that elite patrons were subsidising experiments to discover and harness sources of musical power

---

18 Palisca, 'Was Galileo's Father an Experimental Scientist?'; see also Walker, *Studies in Musical Science in the Late Renaissance*, chap. 2.
19 Katz, 'Collective "Problem-Solving" in the History of Music'.

decades before Bacon articulated his ideology of collective public science, just as Vincenzo Galilei conducted the first 'scientific' musical experiments decades before Galileo presented his in the *Discorsi*.

Francis Bacon, natural magic and the experimental philosophy

Unlike Galileo, the English nobleman, statesman and lawyer Francis Bacon did not perform any important experiments; nor did he achieve any scientific breakthroughs. He was a philosopher of science rather than a practising 'scientist'. Nevertheless, Bacon was an influential figure in the development of experimental science, which he argued was a powerful collaborative means of generating new knowledge for the benefit of the state and of society. He was also the first to identify 'Acoustica' or the 'Acoustique Art'. What is less appreciated, however, is just how many procedures previously identified with natural magic were simply taken over by the new experimental science.[20]

The broad contours of Bacon's acoustical programme were elaborated in two of his most popular works, *New Atlantis* and *Sylva sylvarum* (both published posthumously in 1626). In the fictional *New Atlantis*, the narrator is shipwrecked on the eponymous island and is taken to its technologically advanced city of Bensalem founded by 'King Solamona' 1900 years earlier. He is allowed to visit 'Solomon's House', a publicly funded research institute dedicated to the co-operative study of God's works, the aim of which was 'knowledge of Causes, and secret motions of things; and the enlarging of the bounds of Human Empire, to the effecting of all things possible'.[21] Thus as well as dealing with causes (which are addressed more fully in *Sylva sylvarum*), Baconian philosophy also has an operative side concerned with harnessing the secret forces of nature and producing marvellous effects. Among the most striking marvels in Solomon's House are the musical and acoustical wonders displayed in its 'sound-houses, where we practise and demonstrate all sounds, and their generation'.[22] Although part of a Utopian dream, many of the aural effects which Bacon invokes were not fanciful, but were real examples of wonders that musicians, engineers and other skilled practitioners were already creating for the delectation of the most powerful patrons in Europe. As part of England's social elite, Bacon had privileged access to the musical (and visual) effects that were an essential part of early Stuart court culture. In addition to the newly invented

20 On Bacon's acoustics and natural magic, see Gouk, *Music, Science and Natural Magic in Seventeenth-Century England*, pp. 157–70.
21 Spedding, Ellis and Heath (eds), *The Works of Francis Bacon*, iv: 254.
22 'New Atlantis: a Worke Unfinished (1626)' in ibid., iii: 162–3.

instruments and musical genres that members of the king's Private Music were introducing at the English court (in imitation of French and Italian fashions), Bacon was also familiar with the hydraulic organs, speaking statues and musical automata that the engineers Salomon de Caus and Cornelius Drebbel had recently introduced into the gardens of the English nobility (in imitation of the famous gardens of Tivoli and Pratolino created for the Este and Medici families respectively). Like Bernardo Buontalenti, who designed the stage effects for the 1589 Florentine *intermedi* as well as the gardens at Pratolino, these engineers claimed to go beyond the marvels described in Vitruvius' *Ten Books on Architecture* (1st cent. BCE) and Hero of Alexandria's (*fl.* 62 CE) *Mechanics*. This active, manipulative approach to nature is now accepted as characteristic of experimental science and technology, but in Bacon's time it was most closely associated with natural magic.

Indeed, Bacon himself described his new method as a 'higher' form of natural magic, which was 'the science which applies the knowledge of hidden forms to the production of wonderful operations'.[23] The speculative side of acoustics, the investigation into the causes of sounds, is addressed most comprehensively in *Sylva sylvarum*, a work comprising 1,000 'Experiments' divided into ten 'centuries' (acoustics is covered in the second and third centuries). This collection of observations was Bacon's way of demonstrating the process of accumulating 'natural histories' (i.e., registers of facts about everything in the world) which would provide the basis for his new inductive method. The section opens with a characteristically provocative statement about the inadequacy of scholastic philosophy and the merits of bringing the contemplative and active parts of music together. Paradoxically, although Bacon generally attacked scholasticism, his challenge here relied on a Humanistic understanding of music which was essentially Aristotelian in orientation. Furthermore, most of the acoustical 'Experiments' he proposed were borrowed from earlier literary sources, notably the pseudo-Aristotelian *Problems*, and the *Magia naturalis* (1589), a best-selling work by Giambattista della Porta (1535–1616), which contained recipes, 'experiments' and other investigations into the 'secrets of nature' that Porta's Accademia dei Secreti carried out in the 1570s.[24]

The scope of Bacon's proposed science of acoustics was extremely wide ranging. Of most relevance here are his demand for systematic investigation into the properties of musical instruments as a basis for discovering the causes of harmony; his injunction to mount a similar enquiry into the nature of voice and speech; and above all, his recognition that music's power to affect the passions

23 Spedding, Ellis and Heath (eds), *The Works of Francis Bacon*, iii: 366–8.
24 Eamon, *Science and the Secrets of Nature*.

was closely akin to rhetoric. The causes of all these phenomena were rooted in the operation of the *spiritus* (vital spirit) in both animate and inanimate bodies.[25] Musical instruments seemed to offer the best starting-point for an empirical investigation into harmony, which Bacon thought preferable to an unquestioning acceptance of Pythagorean theory (at the time of writing *Sylva sylvarum*, the quantitative relationship between pitch and the frequency of a vibrating string was not yet common knowledge in England, as it was to become once the works of Galileo and Mersenne were published). And although Porta's *Magia naturalis* was the major literary inspiration for Bacon's suggested experiments into the 'great secret' of numbers and proportions, he also drew on his familiarity with musical instruments to suggest experiments that might reveal how the materials used in their construction, together with various other factors, determined qualities such as pitch and timbre. He was particularly interested in the new types of stringed instrument developed by court musicians such as Daniel Farrant (*fl.* 1607–40) that exploited sympathetic resonance, as well as their experiments using different consort groupings to achieve pleasing harmonies and effects.

Bacon was certain that his experimental method could uncover the cause of 'sympathy', of which the simplest instance is where a musical tone produced by a string on one lute or viol causes a string on another instrument (if tuned at the unison or octave) to vibrate – a motion which, if not immediately detectable, can be made visible by laying a straw on the resonating string.[26] In scholastic natural philosophy this vibration was an occult 'action at a distance' in that its causes were not manifest to the senses and therefore not susceptible to physical explanation. Indeed, within natural magic the fact that the occult sympathy between two strings could be demonstrated empirically, supported the view that there were other sympathies and hidden forces operating throughout nature. But by identifying it as a topic for investigation, Bacon began the transfer of what might have seemed just a magical curiosity into the domain of natural philosophy. By the time John Wallis published his account of the discovery of nodal vibrations in 1677, sympathy had apparently lost its associations with magic and had become a scientific demonstration of the complex motion of strings.[27]

Bacon's writings had a demonstrable influence on later seventeenth-century experimental research. However, Bacon himself was far from carrying out the kind of inquiry he recommended to others. The first person who really did embark on such a programme was Marin Mersenne. Unlike Bacon, Mersenne

---

25 Bacon, *Sylva sylvarum*, no. 114; Gouk, 'Some English Theories of Hearing in the Seventeenth Century'; D. P. Walker, 'Francis Bacon and *Spiritus*'.
26 *Sylva sylvarum*, no. 278.
27 'Dr Wallis's Letter to the Publisher, Concerning a New Musical Discovery, Written from Oxford March 14th 1676/7', *Philosophical Transactions of the Royal Society*, 12 (1677), 839–44.

rejected natural magic on orthodox religious grounds, and also unlike Bacon, he believed that mathematics had a crucial role to play in uncovering the secrets governing musical harmony.

Mersenne: experimental science and music

Mersenne's emphasis on experimental and mathematical methods for discovering the rational principles of nature, coupled with his efforts to establish an international philosophical academy, identify him as a key figure in the emerging 'new science'. Music played a central role in his philosophical and experimental endeavours, which not only had a profound impact on scientific practice and theory but also changed prevailing understandings of music.[28] Mersenne's *Harmonie universelle* (1636-7) was intended as a compendium of 'everything a true musician should know', and it offered an essentially new classification of the divisions of musical knowledge. The first volume deals with the physical and mathematical properties of musical sound, the second with voice, composition and performance, and the third with instruments and 'the utility of harmony and other parts of mathematics', in which music is treated as central to all mathematical studies. Mersenne's works devoted to music represent about one-sixth of his published output, which also include substantial texts on other branches of mathematics (notably optics, mechanics and ballistics) as well as a series of treatises defending Catholic natural philosophy against heretical doctrines. Mersenne tirelessly promoted the innovations of Galileo, Descartes and other champions of the new philosophy. At the same time, he was a vociferous critic of occult philosophy, especially the writings of Robert Fludd (1574-1637). Together with Kepler, he launched (around 1619-20) a vehement attack on Fludd's conception of universal harmony, and his attempt to eradicate the occult from the sphere of natural philosophy appears to mark a watershed in seventeenth-century attitudes towards magic.[29] As this prodigious output might suggest, Mersenne was not a professional performer or composer, but a scholar–priest who spent most of his life in the Minim Friar monastery in the Place Royale, Paris.

Despite his doctrinal opposition to the magical tradition, Mersenne's worldview still had much in common with it, and his intellectual goals were also similar to Bacon's. For example, he wanted to establish a pan-European academy devoted to the construction of the 'whole Encyclopaedia', and although nothing like this was created in his own lifetime, Mersenne successfully ran his

28 H. F. Cohen, *Quantifying Music*, pp. 75-114; Dear, 'Marin Mersenne'.
29 Gouk, 'The Role of Harmonics in the Scientific Revolution', pp. 229-33.

own informal academy, and an international network of scholarly exchange, from his monastic cell in Paris. As his correspondence reveals, he was in close touch with leading European intellectuals of his time, including Descartes and Giovanni Battista Doni.[30] This network provided him with up-to-date information on a variety of subjects, including everything he could learn on musical matters. Proximity to the French royal court also meant that he was able to consult some of the foremost musicians of his day for details of current practice. Yet while we value his observations for what they can tell us about actual music of the seventeenth century, they were part of his metaphysical agenda: Mersenne regarded music as a means of achieving a true understanding of God, not merely as a human aesthetic activity.

Mersenne believed the universe to be constructed harmonically, as is the human soul, and that these cosmic proportions also govern the principles of musical practice. This was in essence a Platonic view which, in Mersenne's case, was also grounded in the teachings of St Augustine.[31] Within this conceptual framework, harmony (i.e., the ordering of numerical ratios) constituted the highest manifestation of divine wisdom. But rather than simply asserting these harmonies as incontestable truths, Mersenne believed that the best available insight into the mind of God was gained through accurate measurement of physical phenomena, and the observation and quantification of external effects.

Mersenne's contribution to seventeenth-century acoustics and musical science can hardly be overestimated. During the 1620s and 1630s he engaged in a comprehensive investigation into the behaviour of sound. Musical instruments provided him with experimental apparatus for investigating many different properties of sound, not just pitch. Like Bacon, Mersenne believed that makers and performers could aid philosophers' searches for the causes of particular acoustical phenomena by providing descriptions of the structure and properties of the instruments they built and played. He also drew on published works, notably Michael Praetorius's *Theatrum instrumentorum* (1620), one of the most important sources of information on sixteenth- and early-seventeenth-century instruments. Mersenne's publications, however, were unparalleled in their breadth of coverage and depth of detail about the structure, properties and tunings of specific instruments, thus providing us with a vital source of information for the reconstruction of seventeenth-century performance practice.

From the perspective of the history of science, Mersenne's most significant contribution was his discovery of the rules governing the vibration of musical strings and pendulums. In modern terminology, he established that frequency

---

30 Waard *et al.* (eds), *Correspondance du P. Marin Mersenne*.   31 Dear, 'Marin Mersenne', pp. 287–8.

is proportional to the square root of string tension, inversely proportional to string length, and inversely proportional to the square root of the string's thickness; he also discovered independently of Galileo that the frequency of a pendulum is inversely proportional to the square root of its length. 'Mersenne's laws', as they are known today, provided a powerful model for other natural philosophers searching for quantitative laws in the physical world, above all Newton.[32] Mersenne himself also recognised that they might have practical applications, some of which were eventually realised after his death. For example, he suggested that the pendulum might prove useful to musicians for maintaining standards of pitch and time (evidence for musicians keeping time with pendulums dates from *c.* 1660, shortly after Huygens developed the pendulum clock). Similarly, he thought that the pendulum might prove useful to physicians measuring the human pulse (the first pulse watches, rather than pendulums, appeared in the 1690s). These inquiries constituted part of a more general search for a universal measure that could be applied to the physical world.

The harmonic laws that Mersenne discovered also provided for a new theory of consonance, one that Galileo also promoted, possibly under his direct influence. The theory was based on Mersenne's observation that the pitch of a musical sound is determined by the frequency of its vibration or pulses. He argued that these regular pulses are communicated in a wave-like fashion through the air, and strike the drum of the ear, where they are perceived as a single note. Consonance is the result of the relative coincidence of the vibration of two notes striking the ear. Mersenne's thoroughly mechanistic explanation of consonance proved pertinent to the new mechanical philosophy that was currently being developed by Descartes as an alternative to Aristotelianism; Descartes's unified system, in which all phenomena, from the motion of planets to people's emotions, might be explained mechanistically in terms of moving particles of matter, was elaborated most extensively in his *Traité de l'homme*, drafted in the early 1630s but only published posthumously in 1664.[33]

Mersenne's own view was that the power of music, especially rhythm and metre, stems from the similarity between sound waves and the motion that is imprinted on the eardrum. This action creates a corresponding motion in the animal spirits that flow through the nerves, which in turn stimulate the vital spirits in the blood to move towards or away from the heart, the seat of the passions.[34] Indeed, Mersenne regarded music as a natural language of the passions,

32 Gouk, 'The Role of Harmonics in the Scientific Revolution', pp. 235–9.
33 On Descartes, see H. F. Cohen, *Quantifying Music*, pp. 172–5, but for alternative theories of sense perception, see Gouk, 'Some English Theories of Hearing in the Seventeenth Century', and Kassler, *Inner Music*.
34 Gouk, 'Music, Melancholy and Medical Spirits in Early Modern Thought'.

superior to spoken language because it used the accents of the passions and not an arbitrary relationship between words and what they represent.[35] However, he also recognised the close links between music's powers and those of speech (especially oratory), compared the structure of musical compositions with the structure of language, and linked both of these to the mathematics of combinatorial analysis. Mersenne used the same combinatorial method in trying to discover the best possible musical composition as in attempting to develop a universal system of rational communication. The underlying assumption was that both music and speech can be broken down into a finite number of elements that can be reconstituted in a variety of ways. He also thought that the elements of speech could be explored through the imitation of the voice by musical instruments, a direct consequence of the assumption that the natural mechanisms of the body (including those responsible for voice, hearing and perception) operate under the same laws as artificial mechanisms and instruments. Of course, this sympathy between bodily and musical instruments was a central tenet of natural magic, but Mersenne distanced himself from this tradition and presented his experimental method as the better alternative. His powerful rhetoric against magicians such as Fludd, who believed in false correspondences between numbers and things rather than trying to establish the real harmonies discoverable in nature, did much to discredit magic among later seventeenth-century natural philosophers.

Kircher, natural magic and the harmony of the world

Natural magic, however, continued to be an important category in the seventeenth-century field of knowledge, especially in relation to music. This was in large measure due to Athanasius Kircher (1601–80), one of the most famous polymaths of his age.[36] Kircher's work must primarily be seen as more or less the formal expression of the syncretic world-view of the Jesuit order, something purporting to be both up-to-date and religiously unassailable. Rather than seeking to create new knowledge, Kircher spent his academic life assembling knowledge of everything already known, and also of what might have been forgotten, overlooked or hidden. This theme of hidden knowledge runs throughout his voluminous publications (some 40 in all), such as *Oedipus Aegyptiacus* (1652–4) on Egyptian hieroglyphics, *Polygraphia nova* (1663) on cryptography and universal language, *Mundus subterraneus* (1664–5) on the geocosm

---

35 Duncan, 'Persuading the Affections'.
36 Godwin, *Athanasius Kircher*; Gouk, 'Making Music, Making Knowledge'.

beneath the earth's surface, and *China illustrata* (1667) on the marvels of Chinese nature and art. The same theme was embodied in Kircher's famous museum at the Collegio Romano in Rome, a cabinet of antiquities, curiosities and wonders that was designed to lead the visitor to contemplate the hidden system of correspondences and harmonies operating within the cosmos. The museum's collection of automatic machinery – which included magnetic, mathematical and catoptric devices as well as hydraulic organs, musical clocks and aeolian harps – was not just to teach mechanics, but also to arouse wonder and awe at the marvels of God's creation.

As a secret and powerful art, the reservoir of magical knowledge was of extreme interest to Kircher, something which he traced back to the ancient Egyptians. While Mersenne had taken the view that all magic was wrong, Kircher's objective was to show that good natural magic was the practical part of natural philosophy; only illicit magic was superstition and idolatry, and should not be practised, even if it might be the subject of erudite discussion. Working within the Aristotelian framework to which Jesuits were required to adhere, Kircher's study of preternatural phenomena (natural effects that were exceptional or rare) was designed to give privileged insights into normally hidden natural processes, the investigation of which was also an important topic in the new scientific academies.

To Kircher, music's extraordinary power to affect the mind and body had to be magical. This was because although these psychological and physiological effects clearly existed, their causes were hidden and could not be accounted for in terms of conventional scholastic physics. The ninth book of *Musurgia universalis* is therefore devoted to the 'magic of consonance and dissonance'. The action of automatic musical instruments and composition machines also falls into this preternatural category because their various sources of power (e.g., sunlight, wind, water, weights and springs) are concealed from view. Although Kircher did not explicitly classify these devices as magic, how they fit into his magical world-view was mapped out in Caspar Schott's *Magia universalis naturae et artis* (1657–9), a work based on material that Kircher had been intending to publish but turned over to his student instead. Here 'acoustics' comprises the second branch of natural magic (the others being optics, mathematics and physics), and each of its books focusses on a branch of acoustical magic. Thus 'phonurgical magic' (Book 4) considers mysterious effects on bodies that can be produced by sympathetic sounds, 'phono-iatrical magic' (Book 5) focusses on the therapeutic powers of music, while Books 6 and 7, on 'musical magic' and 'symphonurgical magic', discuss marvellous instruments, most of which had already appeared in *Musurgia universalis* and which were to reappear in *Phonurgia nova* (1673), Kircher's own comprehensive treatise on acoustics. Even critics of Kircher's magical agenda found these compilations of acoustical and musical marvels worth studying, not least because of the lavish illustrations and fine engravings that were such a distinctive feature of his writings.

Kircher's *Musurgia universalis* achieved a much wider circulation, and in some ways was more influential, than Mersenne's *Harmonie universelle*. Like all of Kircher's publications, *Musurgia universalis* also gained world-wide distribution through Jesuit networks, with hundreds of copies ending up in European academic libraries as well as in private collections of savants such as Robert Hooke. Long after Kircher's posthumous reputation declined, men of letters continued to plunder his work as a repository of musical facts, images and opinions. Thus his taxonomies of the various affective or emotional states that music imitates, of all the different musical rhythms of the human pulse, and of the musical preferences contingent upon national or personal character, continued to be influential well into the eighteenth century.

From the viewpoint of medical history, the significance of *Musurgia universalis* lies in its being the first scholarly treatise to deal extensively with the therapeutic properties of music, as well as trying to uncover the hidden mechanisms responsible for its powerful effects on the body, mind and soul. Now that the idea of listeners being strongly affected by music was becoming taken for granted, it is not surprising that natural philosophers should begin theorising about it. That music had an effect on the passions of the mind, and could cure melancholy, was not a new concept.[37] But Kircher's work, like Descartes's treatises on the passions, offered a way of explaining mental and physical responses to music in instrumental terms, by which the body was the soul's instrument, with 'sympathy' accounting for the actions of the nerves and spirits.

The first part of the book, on the 'magic of consonance and dissonance', relies extensively on Mersenne's laws and theory of consonance, but with a view to showing that natural magic can not only account for the marvellous effects created by contemporary musicians, instrument-makers and engineers, but also most of the other wonders that Kircher has read about. Among the examples discussed at length are David's cure of Saul's melancholy; the story of a Danish king aroused to frenzy and murder by his court musician; the use of music in divination and prophecy; and tarantism, a mysterious affliction confined to Apulia that could only be cured through dancing and music. These cases provided Kircher with an opportunity to show that most miraculous cures, altered states of mind, and strange diseases associated with music are a result neither of supernatural intervention nor of demonic action. Like other

---

37 See, for example, Timothy Bright's *A Treatise of Melancholy* (London, 1586).

acoustical wonders they can be explained in terms of natural powers, secret correspondences and technological mastery, which if improperly understood can give rise to superstition.

The epitome of Jesuit scholarship, Kircher was one of the most important natural philosophers of his age, something testified by his scholarly output and by the number of princes, popes and emperors he counted among his patrons. The breadth of his musical erudition was unparalleled, and his scientific method was equal to any of his time. He performed 'experiments', engaged in priority disputes, and did much to establish the field of acoustics. Yet while Mersenne is counted among the early modern scientists, Kircher tends to be seen as an occult philosopher, more concerned with arcane wisdom than practical knowledge. His reputation inevitably declined during and after the establishment of the Enlightenment ideology of science as an open, public endeavour to advance learning for the benefit of society.

Performance practice and public science

The founding of two influential scientific societies in the 1660s marked a turning-point in the status of experimental philosophy, which now increasingly moved into the public sphere. The Royal Society of London (1660) and the French Académie des Sciences (1666) both claimed Bacon's Solomon's House as their inspiration. The Royal Society presented itself as a public research institution, free from sectarianism and theoretical bias, whose members sought to establish reliable 'matters of fact' through the witnessing of 'experiments' (a term which had not yet stabilised as a technical expression).[38] The success of this public science relied on a few 'virtuosi' (a word used in English first to denote natural philosophers rather than musicians) to entertain and edify an essentially passive if critical audience. It is no coincidence that Restoration London was also one of the first sites for public concerts requiring no less critical a musical audience.[39] Indeed, the same upheavals that forced England's top musicians to resort to new methods of making a living also lay behind moves to promote experimental philosophy in the public sphere. Gresham College, where the Royal Society conducted its earliest meetings, was the most prominent location for this new kind of public science, but the experimental method was soon being marketed to a wider audience in and around the heart of the capital.[40]

38 Henry, *The Scientific Revolution and the Origins of Modern Science*, pp. 47–53.
39 On the overlap between the experimental philosophy and new musical practices, see Gouk, *Music, Science and Natural Magic in Seventeenth-Century England*, pp. 23–65.
40 Stewart, *The Rise of Public Science*.

The essential background to these parallel innovations in music and science lies in the turbulent years of the Civil War. It is well known that royal musicians introduced the custom of playing consort music with university scholars when they took up residence with the king at Oxford in December 1642. Up to this point the genre had mainly been confined to court circles. After Charles I's defeat in 1646 the practice became disseminated among a wider public, since not only the royal musicians but also those in Oxford and Cambridge colleges lost their positions and were forced to find different markets for their skills. At the same time as William Ellis's public music meetings became part of the Oxford social scene (these being weekly occasions where academics and other gentlemen paid for the privilege to make music with professionals), the city became the focus of a new kind of scientific practice, for quite similar reasons. William Harvey arrived in Oxford as a royal physician, and pursued his career there until the Parliamentarians took the town. Over these years, with a small group of friends (mainly physicians) who were college fellows, Harvey pursued a type of experimental research into anatomy and embryology that he had learned as a medical student in Padua.

Although Harvey left Oxford, the kind of informal experimental gathering he promoted continued to flourish in the city during a period of relative stability under Parliamentary control. During the 1640s and 1650s, a scientific 'research community' developed in the city, whose members engaged in regular, informal meetings, variously held in wardens' lodgings, student rooms, coffee houses and taverns, just as did the music meetings. They were similarly intimate occasions where were taught and practised intensively technical procedures and skills such as those required for the correct deployment of surgical or mathematical instruments, or of chemical apparatus. Although not a formal part of the curriculum, the culture of experiment became part of university life, and most of the founder members of the Royal Society had been participants in these Oxford meetings. Some individuals, notably Anthony Wood, participated in both musical and scientific meetings from the time of their instigation, and both types of meetings continued in Oxford long after the Restoration.

A few years later in London, music and scientific meetings continued to evolve in a similar way. In 1672 John Banister inaugurated the modern type of concert with professional performers and a paying audience, and directly thereafter, commercial concert rooms were established in many parts of London and other towns. By the 1690s, these spaces were also being used by mathematical practitioners for giving public lectures on experimental philosophy (York Buildings, as a venue for regular concerts and lecture demonstrations, being a case in point). By the early eighteenth century, London had become the largest single market-place in Europe for experimental science as well as for music.

The Royal Society, whose membership constituted a rather more exclusive 'public' than those of the lecture-demonstrations, aspired to the status of a national research institute. Weekly meetings provided a forum for Fellows to witness experiments and to engage in wide-ranging discussions that were systematically recorded by Henry Oldenburg, the Society's Secretary. Oldenburg also maintained a network of international contacts (an institutionalised version of Mersenne's) and founded the *Philosophical Transactions*, the earliest scientific journal.[41] By drawing on this and other archive material – as well as the diaries of Pepys, Evelyn and Hooke, all early Fellows – a comprehensive picture of the range and extent of interest in acoustics and the science of music in the early Royal Society emerges.

Despite receiving a royal charter in 1662, the Society failed to attract funding from the crown. Its status as an amateur body depending entirely on members' subscriptions was in marked contrast to the Académie des Sciences established in Paris by Louis XIV. This institution was lavishly endowed with purpose-built facilities, and its research staff (limited to around twenty individuals) was made up of salaried public servants. However, record-keeping was neither systematic nor complete at the Académie, and details of its activities before 1700 were only retrospectively published in a set of twelve volumes between 1727 and 1733, making the task of reconstructing its earlier activities surprisingly problematic.[42] Nevertheless, Cohen and Miller's study of the Académie's archives indicates that as far as musically related topics were concerned, its members showed an interest in roughly the same subjects as their English counterparts, for the most part following categories already mapped out above: general acoustics (e.g., the speed of sound, properties of echoes, physics of vibration), tuning systems and temperaments, musical instruments and other inventions (e.g., speaking and hearing trumpets, non-Western instruments), the anatomy of voice and ear, comparisons of music and language, the curative powers of music (especially its effects on tarantula bites), and music of the ancients compared to the modern. Although hardly adding up to a systematic programme of inquiry, these topics constituted a significant proportion of the activities of these institutions, especially during their earliest years.

The most concentrated period of activity relating to music in the Royal Society was during the early 1660s. Between 1662 and 1664, several papers by John Birchensha, Pepys's music teacher, were read before the Society (his

41 For full details of musically related topics addressed by the early Royal Society, see Gouk, *Music, Science and Natural Magic in Seventeenth-Century England*, pp. 184–91, 199–221; Miller and Cohen, *Music in the Royal Society of London*; Miller, 'Rameau and the Royal Society of London'.

42 Cohen, *Music in the French Royal Academy of Sciences*. For a checklist of surviving records, see A. Cohen and Miller, *Music in the Paris Academy of Sciences*.

low social status precluded him from membership).[43] Birchensha's support of Pythagorean intonation led to a discussion of the true grounds of consonance, and the suggestion that Mersenne's experimental results needed to be verified. Hooke embarked on a dramatic series of demonstrations over the summer of 1664. Birchensha was then summoned to appear before the Society to determine 'how near the practice of music agreed with the theory of proportions'. It is striking that immediately after having witnessed this performance a number of Fellows went on to a concert of Birchensha's music at the Post Office (the Black Swan in Bishopsgate), just a short walk away from Gresham College.[44] The last occasion before the end of the century when musical and scientific practice overlapped so clearly was in October 1664, when the 'Arched Viol' which comprised 'both an organ and a conceit of 5 or 6 viols' formed part of the Society's entertainment.[45]

One reason for the Royal Society's early concentration on musical subjects was that its first president, Viscount William Brouncker, was, in addition to being a gifted mathematician, also a keen patron of music and himself a skilled performer: he was the anonymous 'author' of *Renatus Descartes's Excellent Compendium of Musick and Animadversions by the Author* (1653). Other early Fellows also known to have played music were Lord William Brereton, Sir Robert Moray and, of course, Pepys. Fellows not known for performing music themselves but who nevertheless exhibited knowledge of its theory included Walter Charleton, William Holder, Hooke, John Pell, William Petty, John Wallis, Thomas Willis and Christopher Wren. Between them, they possessed an impressive number of academic and professional qualifications in the fields of mathematics, natural philosophy and medicine. This shared expertise and professional orientation probably explains why certain topics (e.g., the mathematics of pitch) crop up in Society records more frequently than others.

In France, where the number of fellows was small and membership was explicitly based on professional expertise in mathematics and physics, this emphasis is even more pronounced. The Dutch mathematician Christiaan Huygens, the Académie's only foreign founder member, is known to have been musically trained. However, although Huygens had already written on music by the time of his appointment (in his manuscript treatise of *c.* 1661 on the division of the monochord), and continued doing so, he never made it part of his work for the Académie in the way of his contemporaries Gilles Personne de Roberval (1602–75) and Claude Perrault (1613–88).[46] Indeed, the full extent

43 Miller, 'John Birchensha and the Early Royal Society'.
44 Latham and Mathews (eds), *The Diary of Samuel Pepys*, v: 238: 'I found no pleasure at all in it'.
45 Ibid., v: 290. The archiviol was similar to the 'Geigenwerk' invented by Hans Hayden which is described in Michael Praetorius's *Syntagmatis musicis tomus secundus* (Wolfenbüttel, 1618), section XLIV and plate III.
46 A. Cohen, *Music in the French Royal Academy of Sciences*, pp. 6–16.

of Huygens's writings on tuning and temperament (especially the division of the octave into 31 equal steps) and on intervals and the modes, as well as his attempts to establish absolute frequency, only became known in the 1940s.[47]

A similar discrepancy between public and private spheres can be seen in the case of Hooke, who, like Huygens, was chiefly responsible for launching his institution's research programme. Although Hooke presented musical experiments at Royal Society meetings, and explicitly related these to other investigations into the physics of vibrating bodies, most of his writings on music were unpublished. Recent research has established that the underlying goal of his experimental programme was to prove his theory that the entire universe was composed of vibrating particles of matter which acted like musical strings, following Mersenne's laws: those with the same 'bigness, figure and matter' vibrated in sympathy with each other, accounting for their coherence or congruity, while those with different sizes and frequencies did not.[48] In his *Micrographia* (1664), Hooke used this musical model to try and explain the forces of magnetism, light and gravity, while his *Lecturae de potentia restitutiva* (1678) used the same insight in the context of his law of springs. In other unpublished work he extended this vibrational model to suggest that the brain's function as the internal organ of perception and memory relied on resonance for its capacity to receive, store and transmit impressions. Hooke's speculations distinctly recall Kircher's 'magic of consonance and dissonance', but his demonstrations of the properties of strings and other vibrating bodies were presented to the Society as neutral 'matters of fact'. Hooke's method started with the certainty of Mersenne's laws to ground his hypothesis that the same laws operated in realms which lie beyond the range of the unaided human senses. It was Newton, of course, who systematically worked out the implications of this insight in the context of his unified theory of matter.[49]

Music all but disappeared from the Society's experimental agenda after 1664, although Hooke was privately working on the subject between 1672 and 1676. His diary records discussions with Wren and Holder about the vibrational nature of sound, and in 1681 Hooke demonstrated a brass-toothed wheel to the Society which proved the correctness of identifying interval with relative frequency (a similar device was invented by Huygens around 1682). Nevertheless, Fellows were kept abreast of relevant theoretical and practical work through the *Philosophical Transactions*.[50] From the early 1670s, short notices and reviews began to appear for books such as Pietro Mengoli's *Musica speculativa*

---

47 H. F. Cohen, *Quantifying Music*, pp. 205–30.

48 Gouk, *Music, Science and Natural Magic in Seventeenth-Century England*, pp. 193–223; Kassler, *Inner Music*, pp. 124–59.

49 Gouk, *Music, Science and Natural Magic in Seventeenth-Century England*, pp. 224–57.

50 For a complete list of relevant articles, see Miller and Cohen, *Music in the Royal Society of London*, pp. 47–64.

(Bologna, 1670), Salmon's *Essay to the Advancement of Music* (London, 1672), North's *Philosophical Essay* (London, 1677), Wallis's edition of Ptolemy's *Harmonics* (Oxford, 1682), and Holder's *Treatise on the Natural Grounds and Principles of Harmony* (London, 1694). More substantial articles notably included Wallis's account of the discovery of nodal vibration by two violinists at Oxford (1677), Narcissus Marsh's 'Proposals for the Improvement of Acousticks' (1684), Francis Robartes's comparison of the trumpet and *tromba marina* and their overtones (1692), and Wallis's essays on canonic composition, the problems of organ tuning, and a comparison of the effects of ancient and modern music (1698).

Joseph Sauveur: a reassessment

By way of a coda on music and sciences in the seventeenth century, let me turn finally to the mathematician Joseph Sauveur (1653–1716), who in 1701 claimed to have founded a new science that would be 'superior' to that of music, and for which he coined the term 'acoustique', in the mistaken belief that he was the first to do so. Although not as original as he thought, Sauveur's contribution to this field was extraordinarily influential, first because it appeared in a highly respected scientific publication, and secondly because of its perceived relevance as a foundation for practical music.[51] In a series of five papers published in the *Mémoires de l'Académie Royale des Sciences* between 1701 and 1713, Sauveur sketched out a five-stage process necessary for the comprehension of sound, one which still appears appropriate today – i.e., its production, transmission, reception by the ear, interpretation by the brain, and psychological effect on the soul or mind (*l'âme*). He also presented findings from his own experimental investigations.

Writing after Sauveur's death in 1716, Bernard le Bovier de Fontenelle claimed he was the first person to determine the absolute frequency of pitch (*son fixé*) using the phenomenon of beats, and to develop a logarithmic division of the octave for classifying temperaments and comparing pitches, plus a practical scale based on logarithmic division for measuring the sizes of intervals and the duration of sounds. Sauveur clearly understood the phenomenon of overtones, including the nature of partials, and introduced a terminology to describe them that is still current today (*son fondamental, sons harmoniques, nœuds, ventres*). He explicitly stated that harmonics are components of all musical sounds, and suggested that the relative consonance or dissonance of a given interval may be partly due to the nature and number of beats it produces. He

---

51 A. Cohen, *Music in the French Royal Academy of Sciences*, pp. 24–9. See also Dostrovsky, 'Early Vibration Theory'; Cannon and Dostrovsky, *The Evolution of Dynamics*.

also attempted to calculate the auditory limits of the human ear and to develop precise mathematical formulas for expressing a string's frequency. In 1713 he succeeded in deriving the absolute frequency of a string by treating it as a compound pendulum. From a practical point of view, Sauveur recommended a new system of solmization that corresponded to his logarithmic scale of 43 *merides* to an octave, explained the relevance of his knowledge of overtones for the construction of organ pipes, and also designed a series of monochords that would be useful to musicians for tuning their instruments.

It will be clear from this chapter that Sauveur's work had been anticipated in almost every respect, not least by Mersenne in terms of the scope and extent of his acoustical programme. There are also other claims for priority: Newton had developed a logarithmic measure for the scale as early as 1666, and he was the first to analyse the propagation of sound mathematically in 1687; both Hooke and Huygens developed methods for calculating absolute frequency; Wallis and Robartes had already described nodes in 1677 and 1694; and Brook Taylor discovered another method for deriving absolute frequency in exactly the same year that Sauveur reached his solution (1713).

This chapter has also shown that speculative music, that aspect of seventeenth-century music theory often considered least interesting today, served natural philosophers as one major point of departure in constructing a new approach to what is now called 'science'. With the new tools of the Scientific Revolution, Sauveur pulled his work together into the unified theory of acoustics that Rameau adopted as a scientific foundation for his theory of harmony.[52] Rameau saw himself reconnecting practical music theory to science by demonstrating that the 'nature' of music was grounded in physics. What neither he nor Sauveur realised was that the harmonic laws they took as natural had first been discovered as a result of philosophers using musical instruments and techniques for the purpose of discovering hidden truths about nature. On the one hand, 'science' at the end of the seventeenth century was understood quite differently from how it had been understood at the beginning, due in substantial part to inspiration drawn from practical and theoretical music. But on the other, in consequence of the rise of 'modern science', the foundation of music theory was no longer an abstract theory of number but a concrete theory of physics.

Bibliography

Cannon, J. T., and Dostrovsky, S., *The Evolution of Dynamics: Vibration Theory from 1687 to 1742*. New York, 1981

Christensen, T., *Rameau and Musical Thought in the Enlightenment*. Cambridge, 1993

---

52 Christensen, *Rameau and Musical Thought in the Enlightenment*, pp. 133–68.

Christensen, T. (ed.), *The Cambridge History of Western Music Theory*. Cambridge, 2002

Coelho, V. A. (ed.), *Music and Science in the Age of Galileo*. Dordrecht, 1992

Cohen, A., *Music in the French Royal Academy of Sciences: a Study in the Evolution of Musical Thought*. Princeton, 1981

Cohen, A., and Miller, L. E., *Music in the Paris Academy of Sciences 1666–1793*. Detroit, 1978

Cohen, H. F., *Quantifying Music: the Science of Music at the First Stage of the Scientific Revolution, 1580–1650*. Dordrecht, 1984

Dear, P., 'Marin Mersenne: Mechanics, Music and Harmony'. In Gozza (ed.), *Number to Sound*, pp. 267–88

Revolutionizing the Sciences: European Knowledge and its Ambitions 1500–1700. Princeton, 2001

Dostrovsky, S., 'Early Vibration Theory: Physics and Music in the Seventeenth Century'. *Archive for the History of Exact Sciences*, 14 (1974–5), 169–218

Drake, S., 'Music and Philosophy in Early Modern Science'. In Coelho (ed.), *Music and Science in the Age of Galileo*, pp. 3–16

Duncan, D. A., 'Persuading the Affections: Rhetorical Theory and Mersenne's Advice to Harmonic Orators'. In G. Cowart (ed.), *French Musical Thought 1600–1800*. Ann Arbor and London, 1989, pp. 149–75

Eamon, W., *Science and the Secrets of Nature: Books of Secrets in Medieval and Early Modern Culture*. Princeton, 1994

Godwin, J., *Athanasius Kircher: a Renaissance Man and the Quest for Lost Knowledge*. London, 1979

Gouk, P., 'Some English Theories of Hearing in the Seventeenth Century: Before and After Descartes'. In C. Burnett, M. Fend, and P. Gouk (eds), *The Second Sense: Studies in Hearing and Musical Judgement from Antiquity to the Seventeenth Century*. London, 1991, pp. 95–113

Music, Science and Natural Magic in Seventeenth-Century England. New Haven and London, 1999

'Music, Melancholy and Medical Spirits in Early Modern Thought'. In P. Horden (ed.), *Music as Medicine: the History of Music Therapy since Antiquity*. Aldershot, 2000, pp. 173–94

'Making Music, Making Knowledge: the Harmonious Universe of Athanasius Kircher'. In Stolzenberg (ed.), *The Great Art of Knowing*, pp. 71–83

'The Role of Harmonics in the Scientific Revolution'. In Christensen (ed.), *The Cambridge History of Western Music Theory*, pp. 223–45

Gozza, P. (ed.), *Number to Sound: the Musical Way to the Scientific Revolution*. Dordrecht, 2000

Henry, J., *The Scientific Revolution and the Origins of Modern Science*. 2nd edn, Basingstoke and London, 2002

Kassler, J. C., *Inner Music: Hobbes, Hooke and North on Internal Character*. London, 1995

The Beginnings of Modern Philosophy of Music in England with Francis North's 'A Philosophical Essay on Music (1677)' and the comments of Isaac Newton and Roger North. Aldershot, 2004.

Katz, R., 'Collective "Problem-Solving" in the History of Music: the Case of the Camerata'. *Journal of the History of Ideas*, 45 (1984), 361–77

Kelley, D. (ed.), *History and the Disciplines: the Reclassification of Knowledge in Early Modern Europe*. Rochester, NY, 1997

Latham, R. C., and Mathews, W. (eds), *The Diary of Samuel Pepys*. 11 vols, London, 1970–83

Mathiesen, T. J., 'Greek Music Theory'. In Christensen (ed.), *The Cambridge History of Western Music Theory*, pp. 109–35

Miller, L. E., 'John Birchensha and the Early Royal Society: Grand Scales and Scientific Composition'. *Journal of the Royal Musical Association*, 115 (1990), 63–79

'Rameau and the Royal Society of London: New Letters and Documents'. *Music and Letters*, 65 (1984), 19–33

Miller, L. E., and Cohen, A., *Music in the Royal Society of London 1660–1806*. Detroit, 1987

Moyer, A. E., *Musical Scholarship in the Italian Renaissance*. Ithaca and London, 1992

Palisca, C. V., 'Scientific Empiricism in Musical Thought'. In H. H. Rhys (ed.), *Seventeenth-Century Science and the Arts*. Princeton, 1961, pp. 91–137

Humanism in Italian Renaissance Musical Thought. New Haven and London, 1985

Studies in the History of Italian Music and Music Theory. Oxford, 1994

'Was Galileo's Father an Experimental Scientist?'. In Coelho (ed.), *Music and Science in the Age of Galileo*, pp. 143–51

Spedding, J., Ellis, R. L., and Heath, D. D. (eds), *The Works of Francis Bacon*. 14 vols, London, 1857–74

Stewart, L., *The Rise of Public Science: Rhetoric, Technology and Natural Philosophy in Newtonian Britain*. Cambridge, 1992

Stolzenberg, D. (ed.), *The Great Art of Knowing: the Baroque Encylopaedia of Athanasius Kircher*. Stanford, CA, 2001

Waard, C. de, *et al.* (eds), *Correspondance du P. Marin Mersenne*. 13 vols, Paris, 1932–77

Walker, D. P., 'Francis Bacon and *Spiritus*'. In A. G. Debus (ed.), *Science, Medicine and Society in the Renaissance*. New York, 1972, pp. 121–30

Studies in Musical Science in the Late Renaissance. London, 1978

7

The search for musical meaning

TIM CARTER

In 1488 or thereabouts, the renowned poet and Humanist Angelo Poliziano attended a banquet held by Paolo Orsini in Rome. The occasion included music, which Poliziano described enthusiastically to Pico della Mirandola, noting in particular the performance of the host's son, the eleven-year-old Fabio:

> No sooner were we seated at the table than [Fabio] was ordered to sing, together with some other experts, certain of those songs which are put into writing with those little signs of music, and immediately he filled our ears, or rather our hearts, with a voice so sweet that . . . as for myself, I was almost transported out of my senses, and was touched beyond doubt by the unspoken feeling of an altogether divine pleasure. He then performed a heroic song which he had himself recently composed in praise of our own Piero dei Medici . . . His voice was not entirely that of someone reading, nor entirely that of someone singing: both could be heard, and yet neither separated one from the other; it was, in any case, even or modulated, and changed as required by the passage. Now it was varied, now sustained, now exalted and now restrained, now calm and now vehement, now slowing down and now quickening its pace, but always it was precise, always clear and always pleasant; and his gestures were not indifferent or sluggish, but not posturing or affected either. You might have thought that an adolescent Roscius was acting on the stage.[1]

In discussing Fabio's performance 'with some other experts' of what one assumes were notated polyphonic songs, Poliziano notes the sensuous qualities of the music transporting the listener by a pleasure akin to the divine. But in the case of the song in praise of Piero de' Medici, he focusses on a different set of issues: here was a declamatory style, not quite singing or speaking, responding flexibly to the demands of the words and displaying significant rhetorical power.

As Nino Pirrotta has noted, Poliziano's account is important for a number of reasons. It provides early evidence of an alternative style to the one now considered typical of 'Renaissance' music – Franco-Flemish polyphony ('those songs which are put into writing with those little signs of music') – and one

1 Pirrotta, *Music and Theatre from Poliziano to Monteverdi*, p. 36.

with impeccable Humanist credentials: the link between Fabio's 'heroic song' and the reputed power of the music of antiquity is cemented by Poliziano's reference to Roscius, the Roman actor praised by Cicero for his rhetorical powers. This style was also one that depended on a solo voice delivering a text clearly and effectively. Poliziano's account offers a striking anticipation of the Florentine recitative and monody that emerged a century later, which in turn drew their roots from a Humanist-inspired tradition (so the likes of Jacopo Peri and Giulio Caccini claimed), formalising in the early Baroque period various improvisatory techniques that had lain underground during the Renaissance as a powerful, if unwritten, tradition.

More significant for present purposes, however, is Poliziano's implied distinction not just between different musical styles and performance practices but also between modes of listening. His reference to 'an altogether divine pleasure' invokes the well-worn trope of *musica divina*, the harmony of the spheres of which *musica instrumentalis* (vocal and instrumental music) was but a pale echo. By listening to earthly music, we catch a glimpse of something denied us since the Fall, the sounds of paradise. As St Augustine pointed out in his *Confessions*, however, the danger was that such divine musical pleasure could also become a distraction, seducing the mind from the demands of worship. Fabio's 'heroic song', in contrast, engaged the human faculty of reason, and not just the senses, to persuade and move by virtue of the effective and affective delivery of the text. Such song would not just delight but also profit the listener, thus supporting Horace's classic precept that the poet 'who has managed to blend profit with delight [*qui miscuit utile dulci*] wins everyone's approbation, for he gives his reader pleasure at the same time as he instructs him'.[2] However pleasurable the Humanist style might be, it could also convey other messages of import to the listener, be they the heroic attributes of a Florentine prince or the spiritual truths of the Word of God.

The two elements of the Horatian precept – instruction and pleasure – might or might not be able to co-exist: the potential conflict between them animated the arguments in the sixteenth century over the place of music within the Church on the one hand, and on the other, over the power of polyphony, rather than solo song, to move the mind to higher things. At the heart of the matter lay two simple questions: what might music mean, and how might such meaning be achieved? The answers to those questions were complex, however, and were predicated upon philosophical presumptions that might or (more often) might not receive articulation. They were also subject to challenge by new discoveries

---

2 *Ars poetica*, ll. 343–4. Compare also ll. 333–4: 'Poets aim at giving either profit [*prodesse*] or delight [*delectare*], or at combining the giving of pleasure with some useful precepts for life'. These passages were regurgitated regularly in Renaissance poetics.

concerning the science of music, and by new (or newly discovered old) aesthetic principles.

For example, the claim that music reflected divine harmony by virtue of its containing rational proportions ('sounding number', as Zarlino called it in 1558) – 2 : 1 for the octave, 3 : 2 for the fifth, etc. – might or might not be theoretically sound, but as Vincenzo Galilei and others pointed out, it did not reflect the pragmatics of current tuning systems where pure intervals were rendered impure so as to extend the gamut of earthly harmony, even at the expense of 'divine' ratios. Galilei also argued that while a mixing of high and low pitches, and slow and fast rhythms, was typical of polyphony, Plato's claim that different pitch-levels and rates of movement invoked different emotional and other states therefore meant that counterpoint was *de facto* unable to represent such states, the ear constantly being confused by the tussle of opposites. Zarlino would no doubt have countered that the impurity of modern tuning was a practical incidental rather than a theoretical fundamental; he would also have said that earthly imperfection should not cast doubt on divine perfection. As for defending counterpoint, he would have claimed that to limit music to just high or low notes, or to just a single voice, denied music's historical progress towards the sonic richness of an *ars perfecta*: surely the angels sing in polyphony, just as the celestial spheres move at different speeds around the earth.[3]

It is relatively easy to discern in these types of debates the emergence of a polarisation of apparent opposites – soul versus body, reason versus sense, theory versus practice, form versus content – the relative configuration of which might, in turn, help distinguish 'Baroque' from 'Renaissance' views on music and the other arts. More striking, however, is the fact that such debates – and there were many – emerged so strongly towards the end of the sixteenth century and into the seventeenth; these binary oppositions somehow became essential to the thought of the day. Of course, theorists had long had their controversies, and even in the Middle Ages and Renaissance, *musica speculativa* was not always so rarefied, and thus impractical, as has sometimes been assumed. Yet the theoretical ground was now shifting away from music's substance to its effect. Whether one views this as a consequence of emerging notions of the composer as artist rather than artisan, or of new demands being made upon theory by the broadening market for music (aided not least by various aspects of 'print culture'), the ramifications are clear. Musical meaning became less a matter of universals than something contingent upon time and place; music was to be justified not by what it is, but by what it does as a particular event in

3 For these and other issues placed in broader scientific and philosophical contexts, see Palisca, *Humanism in Italian Renaissance Musical Thought*.

time. Musical science was never forgotten, but the study of the art and craft of music also expanded into a different area, that of musical poetics.

There is one caveat worth making in any preface to a historical discussion of musical meaning, where one might reasonably ask the question, 'Whose meaning?'[4] On the one hand, this invokes the standard debate of historicism versus transcendentalism, and therefore of different notions of authenticity: how might a 21st-century reader most plausibly, and responsibly, approach issues of meaning in the music of historically distant times and places? On the other, it is clear that even seventeenth-century readers would have construed musical meanings in multiple ways and on various levels. Some of the more arcane structural and stylistic issues to be discussed below were matters purely of professional interest, if that, for those concerned with musical practice (whether composers or performers): a singer or instrumentalist might (or might not) understand, and even take pleasure in or be intrigued by, some clever compositional device or performance problem, but it has no bearing on the listening experience. At the other extreme, no doubt for many seventeenth-century listeners music's meaning lay more in its decorative immediacy than in any depths hidden or otherwise: so long as this music was, say, 'beautiful', 'sweet', 'regal' or 'loud' according to circumstance, it fulfilled its ritual and other purposes. Musicologists normally direct their findings to 'competent' readers well enough informed, able and willing to acknowledge the import of the various issues under discussion. Whether such competence is a historical given, rather than just a self-projecting fantasy, is another matter altogether.

Poetics and taxonomies

While my discussion thus far has concerned the responsibilities of the modern historian, there is also a question of the extent to which historical awareness made its impact upon seventeenth-century musicians, and what any consequences might have been. There is no doubt that the powerful preserving force of print expanded the chronological frame of musical knowledge to a significant degree: Monteverdi wrote a parody mass – the *Missa 'In illo tempore'* (1610) – on a motet by Nicolas Gombert first published in 1538, and in 1627 he oversaw a new edition of Arcadelt's *Il primo libro de madrigali a quattro voci* written almost a century before. Composers could be classified as *antichi, vecchi* and *moderni* – as became common in contemporary treatises[5] – and the *moderni* could see themselves within, and therefore potentially outside, the context of one or more

4 My arguments here build on Murata, 'Scylla and Charybdis'.
5 Owens, 'Music Historiography and the Definition of "Renaissance"' and 'How Josquin Became Josquin'.

musical traditions. Reifying the art-work on the printed page also prompted a shift on the part of contemporary theory away from arcane mathematics in favour of a more humane criticism, catering for the musically sophisticated audiences that printing itself had done so much to create.[6] A shift from the whats and hows of musical creation to the whys and wherefores of musical perception exposed the need for a poetics of music, of the art and craft of modern musical expression, and thus for a critical language to explore notions of value in contemporary musical art.

The emerging focus in the sixteenth century on the poetics of music fostered a range of new analytical and critical tools for approaching musical works of art. It responded to various needs felt, for example, by composers left unsure of the place of music in changing political, religious and social worlds, or by musical consumers (performers or, increasingly, listeners) seeking to systematize, and therefore validate, their aesthetic and other perceptions of an ever-widening range of musical activity. It also drew on broader trends in later sixteenth-century thought – and in the 'new science' of the early seventeenth century – where apparent disorder was reduced to order by classifying and categorizing all areas of artistic and other endeavour. This emphasis on taxonomies might serve various agendas, be they Humanist, philosophical, scientific or religious; it could also be oppressive, establishing rigid categories with hard-and-fast boundaries, or liberating, analysing past achievements so as to provide an impetus for the present and the future. In either case, however, such taxonomies needed to be based on both reason and principle, if only for the sake of appearances. In perhaps the most emblematic literary controversy of the late sixteenth and early seventeenth centuries, over Battista Guarini's controversial pastoral play *Il pastor fido*, Guarini worked harder than he might have needed to justify his invention of the hybrid 'tragicomedy' by way of Classical precedent and of an approach to theories of genre that was reasoned, if not always (depending on one's point of view) reasonable. Similarly, in a musical controversy with some important parallels to the one over *Il pastor fido*, the composer Claudio Monteverdi sought to persuade his opponent, the Bolognese theorist Giovanni Maria Artusi, that he could defend the *seconda pratica* 'with satisfaction to the reason' and not just 'to the senses'.[7] Artusi's objections to the modern style were based on an appeal to the time-honoured rules of counterpoint, which he had

6 Haar, 'A Sixteenth-Century Attempt at Music Criticism'; Carter, 'Artusi, Monteverdi, and the Poetics of Modern Music'.

7 Monteverdi's comment is made in the statement on the *seconda pratica* in his Fifth Book of madrigals (1605) that was then glossed by his brother, Giulio Cesare, in the 'Dichiaratione' in Monteverdi's *Scherzi musicali . . . a tre voci* (Venice, 1607); for the materials, see Strunk, *Source Readings in Music History, Revised Edition*, iv: *The Baroque Era*, pp. 18–36. The similarities between controversies over *Il pastor fido* and the *seconda pratica* (and also the Galilean revolution) are explored in Tomlinson, *Monteverdi and the End of the Renaissance*, chap. 1.

already 'reduced' into schematic tables in his primer *L'arte del contraponto ridotta in tavole* (1586); Monteverdi, on the other hand, sought justification both in the Classics (Plato explicitly, and Aristotle implicitly) and in the musical imperative to represent a text and arouse the emotions. One might argue over the extent of Monteverdi's knowledge of, and adherence to, Classical thought, but whatever the case, he over-trumped Artusi in his recourse to the authority of the past.

The Bolognese theorist Adriano Banchieri sought to reconcile the extreme positions adopted by Artusi and Monteverdi, and also to establish new criteria for assessing musical achievement. In his *Conclusioni nel suono dell'organo* ('Conclusions on playing the organ', 1609), Banchieri distinguishes between the 'osservanza' and the 'inosservanza' of the traditional rules of counterpoint, claiming that observance is appropriate in works without words (instrumental toccatas, ricercars) and in pieces where the text does not require 'unobservance', whereas to 'express' a madrigal, motet, sonnet or other kind of poetry, the musician must be free to exploit unobservance so as to proceed by 'imitating the affections with the harmony'. These incipient notions of genre- and function-specific styles are taken further in the preface to Monteverdi's Eighth Book of madrigals, the *Madrigali guerrieri, et amorosi* (1638), which elaborates a schematic taxonomy of two- and three-fold categories based on genre and function (*musica da camera, da teatro* and *da ballo*), genre and style (*canti senza gesto* and *opuscoli in genere rappresentativo*; *madrigali guerrieri* and *amorosi*), and style and expression (the three *generi* – *concitato, temperato* and *molle* – which in turn match the ranges of the voice and the 'passions or affections of the soul').[8] His analysis of modern music has also revealed a potential for new invention: 'In all the works of the former composers I have indeed found examples of the "soft" [*molle*] and the "moderate" [*temperato*], but never of the "agitated" [*concitato*], a genus nevertheless described by Plato'.[9] Monteverdi then proceeds to describe his discovery of the *concitato genere* and its present popularity in music for church and chamber.

A still more complete musical taxonomy was offered by the Italian composer and theorist Marco Scacchi, *maestro di cappella* at the Polish court from 1628 to 1649.[10] Scacchi distinguishes between three classes of music: church (*ecclesiasticus*), chamber (*cubicularis*), and scenic or theatrical (*scenicus seu theatralis*). The church style divides into Masses, motets etc. without organ for four to eight voices – i.e., the *a cappella* 'Palestrina' style that still remained a required norm

---

8 Hanning, 'Monteverdi's Three *Genera*'.

9 From the preface to the *Madrigali guerrieri, et amorosi*, given in Strunk, *Source Readings in Music History, Revised Edition*, iv: *The Baroque Era*, pp. 157-9.

10 Scacchi's *Breve discorso sopra la musica moderna* (Warsaw, 1649) is translated in Palisca, 'Marco Scacchi's Defense of Modern Music (1649)'.

for certain liturgical and ritual environments – plus motets with organ or for several choirs, and vocal music *in concerto* (with instruments and in the modern style). The chamber style is made up of (unaccompanied) madrigals sung round a table (*da tavolino*), vocal pieces with continuo, and those with instruments. The theatrical style consists of 'speech perfected by song, or song by speech'. Scacchi's divisions established important precedents for later theorists such as Christoph Bernhard and Angelo Berardi. They also supported his powerful plea (in the *Breve discorso sopra la musica* of 1649) for tolerance in accepting the multiplicity of styles available to the modern composer. Like Monteverdi and Banchieri, Scacchi had learnt perhaps the most important lesson of the early seventeenth century: that different groups of composers, regardless of their orientation, were already coexisting in relative equanimity within a pluralist musical context.

Such taxonomic endeavours had further ramifications to be discussed below (for example, the fixing of musico-rhetorical 'figures'). But in essence, they facilitated (at least for 'competent' listeners) some notion of decorum – that specific things were to be expected in specific contexts – enabling seventeenth-century musicians and their audiences to chart their paths through the varied terrain of modern music. Such a notion hinged on an awareness of the contextual contingency of musical genre, style, function, and even, as the period developed, national identity. It also set constraints upon notions of compositional invention, wherein 'originality' was not necessarily a desideratum in the context of composing out particular genres, styles and structures.

Words and music

The influence of Classical poetics on the emergence of musical poetics was guaranteed in part by Humanist precedent: not for nothing were Galilei's arguments presented in the context of a 'dialogue' on ancient and modern music (the *Dialogo della musica antica, et della moderna* of 1581). It was also a result of the fact that musical thinkers, finding scant help for their task in conventional music theory, looked for other models in closely related fields. The common purpose of the arts easily permitted such transfers, while music's evident links to poetry urged them in specific directions. Just as Horace's equating of poetry and painting in the dictum *ut pictura poesis* could become a catchphrase of art criticism in the sixteenth century, so might *ut musica poesis* have found similar favour.

The primacy of poetry as a model for all the arts was encouraged by Classical texts (not least, Aristotle's *Poetics*), but it was also a result of the role of the word as a rational means of communication that distinguished man from beast.

Poetry might 'paint' a picture, but the best pictures would also 'tell' a story. Similarly, poetry might be 'musical' (by virtue of rhyme, metre and assonance), but music could gain its perfection only by virtue of its association with a text. Here Zarlino and Galilei would have broadly agreed: through the word (or in sacred music, the Word), music could engage the faculty of reason in ways more tangible than some abstract perception of mathematical order. In this sense, textless music was essentially meaningless, and here Galilei was happy to give counterpoint its due, to be appreciated for its artful craft but appealing only to older beliefs about musical harmony as reflecting hidden cosmic order.

The issue was just how music might best reflect, represent and convey the word. Galilei objected to the literal word-painting typical of the sixteenth century (for example, in settings of the Credo of the Mass a falling line for 'descendit de caelis', a rising one for 'et ascendit in caelum', etc.) and similar so-called madrigalisms. He also (and perhaps surprisingly, given the modernist role in which he is often cast) complained about harsh dissonances and other 'outlandish' devices used to express words denoting, say, the pains or suffering of love.[11] His point – and here, too, Zarlino might have agreed – seems to be that such word-'painting' is supererogatory: if a text already presents its meaning, then music does not need to re-present it. Rather, music's role is more supportive, making the listener's mind receptive to the message of a text that was best delivered clearly. But the medium was not itself the message. Here we have perhaps the first genuine definition of music as a rhetorical art, something used to deliver, embellish or subvert meaning, but not to be confused with the semantic function of verbal discourse.

In the arguments over the *seconda pratica*, Monteverdi (and his brother, Giulio Cesare) granted more force to inherently musical devices in support of text expression. As Banchieri put it (see above), 'unobservance' of the rules of counterpoint was justified in the service of text expression: thus harsh, even irregular, dissonances were appropriate for 'harsh' texts. Monteverdi also contradicted Galilei on the role of madrigalisms: even in his late works, we find obvious instances of word-painting, where the musical sign directly imitates concepts within the text. In part, this is just an extension of the notion of *mimesis*, that art should somehow 'imitate' nature. In part, however, it also reflects mechanistic theories of emotional stimulation: if our emotions are 'moved' quite literally by way of the movement of the bodily humours (blood, phlegm, choler, melancholy), then the direct physicality of specific musical gestures could assist in generating such motion. The *concitato genere* is one of several

11 For Galilei's remarks on madrigalisms and on dissonance, see the passage from his *Dialogo della musica antica, et della moderna* (1581) in Strunk, *Source Readings in Music History, Revised Edition*, iii: *The Renaissance*, pp. 186–7.

examples fulfilling both mimetic and humoral requirements: this 'aroused' style not only reflects the arousal of battle, but it also arouses in us an appropriate physical response. In Monteverdi's *Combattimento di Tancredi e Clorinda* (1624), later published in the *Madrigali guerrieri, et amorosi*, we do not just hear the sounds of war, but our bodies are also made to feel as though we are right in the thick of things.

Effective text delivery, on the one hand, and emotional arousal, on the other, were central to the art of rhetoric. The theoretical and practical exploration of music's potential links with rhetoric (and therefore its shift from the *quadrivium* to the *trivium*) by way of word-tone relationships had been noticeable at least from the second quarter of the sixteenth century on: indeed, some would see it as a defining feature of 'Renaissance' music. Increasingly, however, these links became formalised into various systems. Countless manuals in the period drew on the great Classical rhetoricians – Aristotle, Cicero and Quintilian – to demonstrate how the perfect orator might invent, organise and deliver an argument so as to persuade an audience and arouse it to some kind of action. Once more, music drew on a sister art, borrowing both the ideals and at times the actual principles of oratory to fulfil its musico-rhetorical mission. In his *Musica poetica* (1606), the German theorist Joachim Burmeister established a theory of music predicated directly upon rhetoric and its associated system of tropes and figures: the lesson is emphasised by a 'rhetorical' analysis of a motet by Orlande de Lassus, 'In me transierunt'.[12] Similarly, another German, Athanasius Kircher, in his *Musurgia universalis* (1650), spoke of 'musurgia rhetorica' and identified Giacomo Carissimi as the composer who 'surpasses all others in moving the minds of listeners to whatever affection he wishes'.[13] Kircher discusses part of Carissimi's oratorio *Jephte*, also finding within the works of Carissimi and others a series of musical devices comparable to rhetorical figures: sequential repetition as *anaphora*, a stark dissonance or false relation as *parrhesia*, a rising line painting words denoting ascent as *anabasis*, etc. But rhetoric had more influence than just by way of figures used according to principles that early twentieth-century (German) musicologists – heavily influenced by Wagnerian leitmotiv theory – would categorize as 'Figurenlehre' (the doctrine of musical figures) or 'Affektenlehre' (the doctrine of the affections). Rhetorical thinking rationalised the processes involved in bringing an oration to fruition, fixing the structures by which it might be organised. It also defined the styles (plain, middle, grand) appropriate to specific types of oration, and thereby once

---

12 Palisca, '*Ut oratoria musica*'.
13 *Musurgia universalis* (Rome, 1650), i: 603, cited in Palisca, *Baroque Music*, p. 126. See also Smither, *A History of the Oratorio*, i: *The Oratorio in the Baroque Era*, pp. 215–46, illustrating the application of rhetorical figures in Carissimi's oratorios. For definitions, see Buelow, 'Rhetoric and Music'; Bartel, *Musica poetica*.

more generated intersecting taxonomies that linked genre, style and function. Finally, rhetoric recognised the utility of its apparent rigidities – once rules were fixed, they could be broken for special effect – and acknowledged its own transience (formerly novel figures could become commonplaces, therefore demanding still more novelty). For all its appeal to systems, rhetoric was inherently transgressive. The lessons for music were obvious.

The ideal composer – and for that matter, performer – became some manner of orator, delivering a text effectively and invoking a response in the listener that involved both reason and the emotions. Thus composition, performance and listening were all enfolded within the creative act. Accordingly, one can reasonably take a piece of seventeenth-century music and analyse its presentation, elaboration and generation of meaning by way of such musical oratory. The seven-part *Gloria in excelsis Deo* published in Monteverdi's *Selva morale e spirituale* (1640–41) – perhaps intended for performance in 1631 at the celebrations for the cessation of the plague in Venice[14] – might seem to be a straightforward example (see Table 7.1). It is in an avowedly modern style, for voices, two violins and continuo (although the solo tenor of the opening seemingly invokes the plainchant intonation found in old-style polyphonic Masses). Monteverdi breaks the text down (very conventionally) into syntactic units variously articulated in the music as sections or subsections by way of cadential markers, the introduction of new musical ideas, contrasts of pace and scoring, etc. Some of the text-setting involves quite literal word-painting: the 'high' scoring for 'in excelsis Deo' or the 'low' homophony for 'et in terra pax'. Other aspects are more generally evocative, as with the repetitive paeans of 'Gloria' or the homophonic declaration 'Gratias agimus tibi'. Elsewhere, Monteverdi's concerns seem more purely musical: once he has begun a new section at 'Laudamus te' (by way of a new motive in the violins) – quite appropriately in syntactical terms – he then moves into a long section based on an ostinato bass pattern (a cadential figure stated on different degrees of the scale) that serves to link the short invocations 'Laudamus te. Benedicimus te. Adoramus te', and therefore to maintain the musical flow. In general, the approach seems quite sectional – which is not at all unusual for Gloria and Credo settings (and later in the century, the sections would start to become separate movements) – although Monteverdi takes advantage of textual parallelisms to prompt musical repetition that might be viewed as contributing to an architectonic whole, as with the repetition of the opening 'Gloria' roulades at '[propter magnam] gloriam tuam'. The whole opening is also repeated at the end of the movement, at '[Cum

---

14 Moore, '*Venezia favorita da Maria*'; but compare Kurtzman and Koldau, '*Trombe, Trombe d'argento, Trombe squarciate, Tromboni*, and *Pifferi* in Venetian Processions and Ceremonies of the Sixteenth and Seventeenth Centuries', para. 43.

Table 7.1 *The opening of Monteverdi's Gloria in excelsis Deo (1640–41)*

Section	Text	Translation	Musical setting
1a	Gloria in excelsis Deo.	Glory be to God on high,	**C**: tenor begins with quasi-intonation; rising scales and then roulades with voices in thirds suggest angelic choirs; text is set emphatically.
1b	Et in terra pax hominibus bonae voluntatis.	and in earth, peace, good will towards men.	**C**: slower pace, low textures and homophony paint 'earth' and 'peace'.
2a	Laudamus te. Benedicimus te. Adoramus te.	We praise Thee, we bless Thee, we worship Thee,	**C**: two violins mark start of new section and then provide interjections; voices move predominantly in duets; bass line consists of repeating cadential patterns.
2b	Glorificamus te.	we glorify Thee,	**C**3/2: shift to triple time; duets and repetitive bass continue.
3a	Gratias agimus tibi	we give thanks to Thee	**C**: slower pace and low homophonic chords . . .
3b	propter magnam gloriam tuam.	for Thy great glory . . .	. . . picking up speed at 'propter magnam'; 'gloriam' prompts repetition of initial roulades (on 'Gloria'); voices in groups juxtaposed in blocks.

etc.

sancto spiritu, in] gloria dei patris. Amen' ('with the Holy Ghost, in the glory of God the Father. Amen'). The location of this last repetition quite significantly disrupts the syntax of the text for the purpose, it seems, of providing a strong musical conclusion. As for the opening sections, however, the only apparent oddity is the shift to triple time at 'Glorificamus te', which might be explained by the accentuation of the word (*Glo*-ri-fi-*ca*-mus) had not Monteverdi in fact misaccentuated it by starting on an up-beat (Glo-*ri*-fi-*ca*-mus). In another era, the triple time might be read as a reference to the Holy Trinity; here, however, it appears to invoke glorification through some kind of 'song' or dance, which is what triple time most often seems to represent in this period.

Monteverdi's manipulations of the text, and also his focus on musical development, is not perhaps what one might expect from his claims for the *seconda pratica* (where the words should be the 'mistress' of the music). This might be explained by way of this being a piece of sacred music and not secular, for public ceremonial and not for a private chamber, and setting words well known to all. But it is not, in fact, untypical of the composer even in his most obvious *seconda pratica* mode, where the treatment, and supremacy, of the text is often not quite what modern scholars of this period would have it. However, this does raise an important question: for all the emphasis on the word in this period, just how 'musical' is any setting of a text allowed to be? Inevitably, the answer would seem to vary. Operatic recitative, for example, may not seem very musical at all, given its intended proximity to some kind of speech. Arias, on the other hand, may seem very musical indeed, whether or not they serve some kind of expressive purpose. I shall return to this point below.

Modal types and tonal categories

The focus on text setting at least in the early part of this period did not only reflect apparent priorities on the part of composers; it also allowed non-musicians to participate in musical discourse. Even if one was not aware of music's technicalities, one could still appreciate the refinement of a poem and of a musician's response to it within a literary world that we should try to understand.[15] One can detect a similar strategy in many modern accounts of this music, where the treatment of the text comes high on the agenda, no doubt because it is the easiest matter to broach, and because it allows us to escape Romantic ideologies of 'absolute' music. Such accounts often make one wonder whether, in fact, one needs to delve into other music-theoretical issues at all, be they couched in seventeenth-century terms or modern ones. But that

15 Freitas, 'Singing and Playing'.

does an injustice to musical works that are often highly sophisticated in design and construction. It also avoids some difficult questions, in particular concerning whether we are not, in fact, selectively blind or deaf to other important aspects of this music.

Monteverdi's *Gloria* discussed above is in what to all intents and purposes might be called 'G major', a key that elsewhere in the composer's output is associated with the *concitato genere* (as in the *Combattimento di Tancredi e Clorinda*) and also with love-songs (in, say, *L'incoronazione di Poppea* of 1643). Although these different associations might be grounded by way of some kind of proximity (the 'martial' fanfares of the angelic hosts praising God; love as a 'battle' between two hearts and minds), it is clear that 'key' is not yet so precise an extra-musical signifier as it could be in, say, Handel's da-capo arias, Bach's cantatas, or even Mozart's operas. Eric Chafe, however, is quite prepared to transfer meanings from one context to another on the basis of common keys: the final piece in *L'incoronazione di Poppea* ('Pur ti miro, pur ti godo', for Nerone and Poppea) is not quite the simple love-duet most would assume, given that it is in a key (G) associated with 'the victory of Love over Virtue and Fortune', with Love as 'a force allied to the predominant key of the Book Eight *guerriero* style'.[16]

For seventeenth-century music, issues of tonal structure are complex and have yet to be fully resolved.[17] The traditional view has the period marking a transition from Renaissance modes (Dorian, Phrygian, Lydian, Mixolydian, Aeolian, Ionian) to the major–minor tonalities of the Classical period (C major or minor, C sharp major or minor, etc.). Each mode comprises a species of fifth, from the final up to the 'dominant', and a species of fourth, from the dominant to the upper final: the fifth-plus-fourth division explains the alterations associated with 'tonal' answers in contrapuntal expositions long after the demise of the modal system. In 'authentic' modes, the fifth is beneath the fourth, whereas in 'plagal' modes (Hypodorian, Hypophrygian etc.), the position is reversed; therefore in authentic modes, the final is the lowest note of the scale, whereas in plagal modes, it is in the middle. Although the Renaissance modes are conventionally construed by way of the keyboard (as 'white-note' scales starting on D, E, F, G, A and C), they are not pitch-specific: rather, they are made up of the distinct sequences of tones (T) and semitones (S) that also distinguish the different species of fifth and fourth: so, for the authentic Dorian mode on 'D', the

---

16 Chafe, *Monteverdi's Tonal Language*, p. 324. For this, and also the question of whether the duet is in fact by Monteverdi, see Carter, *Monteverdi's Musical Theatre*, p. 233.

17 The following draws on Dahlhaus, *Untersuchungen über die Entstehung der harmonischen Tonalität*; Allaire, *The Theories of Hexachords, Solmization and the Modal System*; Meier, *Die Tonarten der klassischen Vokalpolyphonie*; Powers, 'Tonal Types and Modal Categories in Renaissance Polyphony'; Chafe, *Monteverdi's Tonal Language*; Collins Judd, 'Modal Types and *Ut, re, mi* Tonalities'.

fifth-plus-fourth is TSTT/TST, and for the Phrygian on 'E', STTT/STT, etc.[18] In terms of their notated representation, modes can be transposed down a fifth by turning B-*mi* (B♮) into B-*fa* (B♭) and therefore adopting a one-flat signature: thus G-Dorian preserves the tone–semitone sequence of D-Dorian by virtue of its B♭. Further transpositions downward by a fifth (adding one flat each time) are possible, as (later in the seventeenth century) are upward transpositions by a fifth (adding one sharp each time). But even if each mode began on the same sounding pitch (say, C), it would reach its upper octave by a different route. Therefore the six modes (twelve if one counts both authentic and plagal versions) sound very different one from the other, and cultivating an aural sensitivity to such difference is an important aspect of coming to understand Renaissance music.

In Classical tonality, there are only two 'modes' distinguished by their sequence of tones and semitones: the 'major' scale has TTST/TTS (the sequence of the Ionian mode), and the 'minor', TSTT/STT (the Aeolian).[19] These two modes can each occur on every degree of the chromatic scale, but they will be transpositionally equivalent (so, C major contains the same sequence of tones and semitones as C sharp major, D major, E flat major, etc.), at least within an equal-tempered system where the octave is divided into twelve equal semitones. Thus C major should not sound any different from C sharp major (although we shall see that it does), and in terms of scale-type, tonality is in principle less rich than modality. However, this limitation makes it easier to move through tonal space defined by pitch centre. Renaissance modes have their finals and dominants, and pieces based on such modes will normally start and end on their final (the Phrygian mode is always a special case because of the difficulty of creating a 'perfect' cadence given the diminished triad on the dominant). But the different degrees of the scale are not so much distinguished by priority; nor do they exist in a strong hierarchical relationship. Notions of modal propriety also militate against changing modes within a given piece (shifting from, say, Dorian to Lydian), and when this occurs (e.g., in cases of modal 'mixture'), it is often a matter of introducing new patterns of tones and semitones rather than changing the final. In the tonal system, however, certain notes

18 There are four species of the fifth (STTT, TSTT, TTST, TTTS) and three of the fourth (STT, TST, TTS). Thus in an eight-mode system, the four authentic modes (Dorian, Phrygian, Lydian, Mixolydian) each have a different species of fifth. The twelve-mode system does not preserve this distinction (the Aeolian mode contains the 'Dorian' fifth, and the Ionian mode the 'Mixolydian' one), which is one reason why the twelve-mode system did not always find acceptance in contemporary theory.

19 This is the so-called 'natural' minor, as distinct from the 'melodic' and 'harmonic' minors. But one should also be wary of assuming that the Ionian mode was the direct progenitor of the major scale, and the Aeolian the minor: these two modes do not exist within an eight-mode system, and shifting to a twelve-mode system was not an essential precursor for tonality. Indeed, as we shall see, major and minor scale-types tend to get inflected by way of various associations with a number of former modes.

of the scale and the chords built upon them (tonic, subdominant, dominant etc.) have priority over others and have a hierarchical relationship between themselves. Similarly, major and minor modes that involve the same altered pitches (relative to a white-note scale) are construed as related: thus C minor is the 'relative minor' of E flat major because they both require B♭, E♭ and A♭ and therefore have the same key signature. This creates a field of pitch-centres relative to the tonic to which one can 'modulate'. Such modulation need not involve a change of mode (C major and G major are both major) – although it will when modulating from major to minor or the reverse – but, rather, will depend upon tonicization so that what was once, say, a dominant now becomes a temporary tonic, even if it remains somehow perceived as not the 'real' tonic.

Even so detailed a summary as in the previous two paragraphs does not do justice to the issues. And if it is so hard to define 'pure' modality and 'pure' tonality, any transition between the two, if such there be, is doubly difficult to explain. One problem is caused by the fact that theories of mode in the Renaissance sought to apply to polyphony models designed essentially for monophonic repertories (plainchant). While this might be important as a post-compositional classificatory tool – for example, to enable a psalm delivered in chant in a given tone to be matched with a polyphonic antiphon-setting in an appropriate mode – modal theory, at least in one view, did not always under-pin compositional praxis save in the most basic terms. It also interacted with other means of perceiving pitches and their relationships which were of more immediate impact at least for (vocal) performers. From Guido of Arezzo on, the gamut (the full range of possible pitches) had been structured by way of the hexachord, the six-note scale solmized as *ut–re–mi–fa–sol–la*, comprising a sequence of two tones (*ut–re*, *re–mi*), one semitone (*mi–fa*) and two tones (*fa–sol*, *sol–la*); it is the location of the *mi–fa* semitone that is most important (given that everything else follows from it). In order to progress from the bottom to the top of the gamut, one had to change hexachords, in the first instance on *fa*. Thus if one starts on Guido's lowest note, gamma-*ut* (say *G*, for present purposes, although the system is, again, relational and not pitch-specific), one can commence a new hexachord on *fa-ut* (*c*), and then another new hexachord on the *fa* created by this second *ut* (*f*). The *re* of this third hexachord (*g*) can itself become an *ut* (it is an octave above gamma-*ut*), and so on and so forth. The second hexachord (beginning on *c*) interlocks with the first as C-*fa-ut*, D-*sol-re*, E-*la-mi*, and with the third hexachord (on *f*) as F-*fa-ut*, and then with the fourth (on *g*) as G-*sol-re-ut*, A-*la-mi-re*. However, the interlocking of the third and fourth hexachords involves a problem: in the hexachord on *f*, A-*mi* leads to B-*fa*, a semitone above *mi*; continuing the hexachord on *g*, A-*re* leads to B-*mi*, a semitone below C-*fa*. This enables the system to include both B♭ and B♮; the distinction between B-*fa* and B-*mi* also explains the use in some languages of different letter-names for B♭ and B♮ (in German, B and H respectively). Other 'black' notes (to follow the keyboard) must be generated by 'feigned' hexachords (thus, F♯ as *mi* in a 'feigned' hexachord on D), or by way of 'accidental' alteration according to the principles of *musica ficta*, e.g., to raise leading-notes at most cadences, to avoid tritones, or to flatten a neighbour-note above *la*.

Solmization is primarily concerned with intervallic relationships and not notated pitches. Its relationship to such pitches is defined by a (normally) five-line stave where a clef indicates the position of what can be a hexachordal *ut* (hence, the G-clef, C-clef, and F-clef, each of which can be placed on more than one line of the stave), and if necessary, a flat-signature marks the use (and location) of B-*fa*. In the case of purely vocal music, these notated pitches have no necessary relationship with sounding pitches: a notated *G* need not sound as the *G* on the keyboard but, rather, can be pitched at any convenient level so long as all the notes related intervallically to that *G* within the piece fall within a range that can be embraced by the vocal ensemble. Problems only arise when singers (who read staff notation primarily by way of intervals) are joined with instrumentalists, who read staff notation by way of a direct correlation between a pitch, a position on the instrument, and, according to the tuning, a fixed sound. Combining voices and instruments therefore required that the instruments conform to a standard pitch (so that when the players saw a notated *a*, they each produced the same sounding note), and it defined where the singer should locate specific notes (the notated pitch that the singer read as an A-*la-mi-re* must sound as an A in the correct octave). Given that using voices with instruments was a prominent feature of the new styles of the early seventeenth century (not that it was unheard of before), one can see why theory needed to change to accommodate practice. But solmization continued to be discussed through the late sixteenth and seventeenth centuries, even if it was acknowledged that the system needed simplification (as with Thomas Morley's insistence that everything can be solmized with *fa*, *sol* and *la*) and/or expansion (Adriano Banchieri's addition of a seventh syllable for the seventh degree of the scale). Solmization's currency is also apparent in the continuing use of solmization 'puns' – where text syllables equivalent to, or sounding like, solmization syllables prompt a given musical setting ('Amor *mi fa* mor*ire*', 'Love makes me die', is a classic example) – and also techniques in learned instrumental ricercars etc. such as pieces built around a solmization-based cantus firmus, or the so-called 'inganno', where a theme can be manipulated by retaining its solmization syllables but variously changing the hexachords in which those syllables are situated, thus altering the theme's actual intervallic content.[20]

The three hexachords on C (the 'natural'), G ('hard') and F ('soft') operate within the systems of *cantus durus* (with B-*mi*) and *cantus mollis* (B-*fa*). By way of 'feigned' hexachords, these two systems can also be transposed: *cantus durus* sharpwards with the successive addition of sharps by fifths, and similarly *cantus mollis* flatwards (leading to two-flat, three-flat etc. systems). The hexachords also intersect with the modes, which, as we have seen, are defined by their combinations of distinct species of fifth and fourth each distinguished by the position of the semitone (in hexachordal terms, *mi–fa*). However, hexachord, system and mode are three different things serving three different purposes: mixing them without due caution can all too easily produce analytical accounts of this music that may claim some kind of historical authenticity (by virtue of using contemporary, rather than modern, theory) but are in fact both spurious and flawed.

Given that hexachords are six-note scales, and modes seven-note ones, singing up a modal scale requires hexachordal mutation to complete the octave. And given that it is the position of the *mi–fa* semitones that distinguish one mode from another, this position will also fix the point in the hexachord where at least the species of fifth of a given mode will start (the species of fourth also has its *mi–fa* fixed, but the *mi* may be reached by different mutations). Thus as Cristle Collins Judd has noted, one might equally well speak of *ut-*, *re-* and *mi-* modes – beginning TTS, TST and STT respectively – as of Ionian/Mixolydian, Dorian/Aeolian, and Phrygian ones.[21] In this way, the modes start to boil down to three, and thence, one assumes, to two: *ut-*modes starting with a major third between *ut* and *mi*, and *re-*modes with a minor third between *re* and *fa* (although this is, again, an oversimplification). The *mi*-mode (formerly Phrygian) remains problematic – its chief vestige is the so-called, if misnamed, 'Phrygian' cadence – and it has to be represented in different ways, whether by scales starting on *mi* but not preserving the STT opening (e.g., E minor and its upward-fifth transpositions, B minor and F sharp minor), and/or (by the late seventeenth century) an emphasis on the flat supertonic (the 'Neapolitan') to replicate the Phrygian's initial *mi–fa*; prominent Neapolitan tendencies remain common in F sharp minor pieces through to the nineteenth century. But these pseudo-Phrygian keys are not the only example of seventeenth- (and eighteenth-)century tonality retaining some modal characteristics. For example, the tendency to notate

20 Jackson, 'The *Inganni* and the Keyboard Music of Trabaci'; Harper, 'Frescobaldi's Early *Inganni* and Their Background'.
21 The Lydian, a potential *fa*-mode, becomes problematic because of the tritone F–B♮, i.e., *fa–mi*, and thus it often tends to get treated as an *ut*-mode, with B♭, or in modal terms, as transposed Ionian.

minor keys with a signature containing one flat fewer than the modern norm, and major keys with one sharp fewer, relates to their modal ancestry: 'D minor' is associated with D-Dorian with a no-flat signature (its B♭ is therefore incidental),[22] and 'G minor' with transposed (downward) D-Dorian with a one-flat signature, etc.; 'G major' is associated with G-Mixolydian with a no-sharp signature (its F♯ is therefore incidental),[23] and 'D major' with transposed (upward) G-Mixolydian with a one-sharp signature. It also relates to the pairings associated with *ut*- and *re*-modes: Ionian/C major and Mixolydian/G major are both *ut*-tonalities and therefore have the same signature (none), and similarly Dorian/D minor and Aeolian/A minor as *re*-tonalities.

Although hexachords might be viewed as a matter of a musical mechanics that became more and more outdated, system (*cantus durus* with no, one, two or three sharps; *cantus mollis* with one, two or three flats), mode and pitch-centre may contribute to musical meaning, not always in entirely consistent ways. In the Renaissance, the modes were given generic (and not always uniform) affective characteristics drawing upon comments by writers from Classical Antiquity on the very different ancient Greek modes.[24] These characteristics did not always square with emerging notions of the difference between the major and the minor third (recognised by Zarlino), and hence the sense that modes with their species of fifth divided into a major third plus minor third (*ut*-modes) are somehow happy, and those with their species of fifth divided into a minor third plus major third (*re*-modes) are somehow serious or sad.[25] Similarly, any gradual association of *cantus durus* with the major ('Dur' in German) and *cantus mollis* with the minor ('Moll') conflates system and mode in ways that are inappropriate, given that mode is not system-dependent. Monteverdi's seemingly different G majors in his *Gloria*, the *Combattimento di Tancredi e Clorinda* and *L'incoronazione di Poppea* reveal something of the problem. For Artusi (1600), the Mixolydian mode was 'lascivious' and suited to words which suggest threats, anger and upsets: this may reconcile the G major of the *concitato genere* (threats, anger and upsets) with that of a 'lascivious' love-duet. For Scipione Cerreto

22 As it is often found in D-Dorian pieces where the flattened submediant (B♭ rather than B♮) often derives from the rule of 'fa supra la' (one note above *la* – A in the Dorian mode – is to be sung as *fa* rather than *mi* in specific circumstances) or else from the need to avoid the F–B♮ tritone.

23 Although again, it is not uncommon in G-Mixolydian, where the raised leading-note provides for a 'perfect' cadence.

24 Carter, *Music in Late Renaissance and Early Baroque Italy*, pp. 53–6.

25 See, for example, Salomon de Caus's *Institution harmonique* (1615) cited in Steblin, *A History of Key Characteristics in the Eighteenth and Early Nineteenth Centuries*, p. 28: 'Let some notes be placed in the diapason [= octave] of C sol, fa, ut, and then let similar intervals of notes be placed [in] the diapason of D la, sol, re: it is evident that the first example will be an entirely different kind of melody than the second, as a result of the major third being in the lower part of the fifth in the first example; and in the second example, the minor third is at the bottom of the fifth . . . This different movement carries with it a change of character in the music. For it can be easily grasped that the nature of the first example is much gayer than the second, which is grave.'

(1601), however, the Mixolydian was 'much prouder than the other modes, and even most cheerful', which is appropriate for the text of a Gloria. The G major of the *concitato genere* may owe something to its association with a 'hard' *cantus durus*, while a love-duet and a Gloria might just prompt a 'happy' major rather than a 'sad' minor. Of course, given the presence of violins in the *Gloria*, Monteverdi may just have chosen a key to suit that instrument.

In his discussion of Carissimi's *Jephte*, Kircher pointed to 'mutation of mode' as a crucial technique through which Carissimi achieves contrast between different emotional effects: the reference is to Carissimi's use of G major and C major for the festive, joyful opening of the oratorio, then shifting to A minor for its sad, lamenting conclusion.[26] Even if modes or keys *per se* may or may not be significant in this period, composers have to start and finish somewhere, and how one gets from beginning to end, exploiting modal or tonal contrasts along the way, can still be significant. We might reasonably assume that if a seventeenth-century composer moves strongly sharpwards or flatwards – e.g., through multiple transpositions of *cantus durus*, with C♯s, G♯s and D♯s, or of *cantus mollis*, with E♭s, A♭s and D♭s – then those regions are intended to express some kind of emotional extreme, even if *cantus durus* may not always be 'hard', especially if combined with the 'soft' minor (F sharp minor is again a case in point). Such extremes are particularly striking in the case of non-equal-temperaments, where moves to three sharps or three flats and beyond will start to sound very exotic, if not 'out of tune'. Yet one still needs to be careful over granting affective significance to gestures (and to modulations) that might simply derive from standard syntactical procedures. For example, Purcell will often juxtapose major and minor versions of the same 'key' on the basis of tonic equivalence (F major and F minor, say, are both colourings of F); the transition is aided by the preference for the *tierce de picardie* in minor-key cadences. In such cases, it is difficult to determine whether the minor has specific affective significance.

The problem of when we are dealing with syntax versus when with semantics is always hard to resolve, especially in the context of a (modern) aesthetic value-system that tends to demand semantic richness even from the most normative syntactical process. For example, given that Renaissance modes and their seventeenth-century counterparts are strongly determined by the intervallic content of their species of fifth, projections of a descent through this fifth (and ancillary descents through the corresponding fourth) often serve to generate larger-scale structures in this period. Middleground (and even background) melodic 5–4–3–2–1 descents are very common, and each note within such descents can itself be prolonged by subsidiary fifth descents (in effect,

---

26 Palisca, *Baroque Music*, pp. 126–7; see also Stein, 'Between Key and Mode'.

creating temporary modal mixture).[27] The 5 tends to be harmonised as the fifth, or sometimes the third, of a triad; and the 2 and 1 tend to be treated as a fifth and a root respectively (producing a V–I cadence) save where a cadence is avoided. Degrees 4 and 3, however, can be treated in various ways: some of the possibilities are apparent in such stock melodic-harmonic formulas as the Romanesca and Passamezzo. If 5, 4, 3 and 2 are each the fifth of a triad, this produces consecutive fifths that might or might not be mitigated by foreground elaboration: this explains the consecutives typical of canzonetta and related styles in the early part of the period. Degree 4 is also interesting in other ways: its possible consonant supports are the triads on the supertonic, subdominant and flattened leading-note; its potential treatment as the seventh of a dominant seventh does occur (most famously, in Monteverdi's 'Cruda Amarilli, che col nome ancora' in his Fifth Book, at 'ahi *las*-so', i.e., 'alas') but only in contravention of the standard rules of dissonance treatment. This explains why pieces in, say, G major, can often move quite quickly to a local A minor (supporting 4), and thence back to G major, or perhaps to E minor (supporting 3): such local shifts are probably not affective or significant in any way other than revealing a conventional procedure.

This use of the supertonic and submediant (compare Kircher's comments on G and C major versus A minor in *Jephte*) stands in contrast to the later tendency to favour the dominant both as a chord and as a tonal region; it also is one reason why much seventeenth-century music can seem somewhat fluid and directionless when analysed in fully tonal terms. And it is probably true to say that in the course of the seventeenth and early eighteenth centuries, keys, and the practices associated with them, tended to become stabilised. What is most intriguing, however, is that the system managed to recuperate some of its losses arising from the reduction essentially to two modes (major and minor). As we have seen, within equal temperament, C major and C sharp major should 'sound' the same, yet as any instrumentalist knows, they certainly 'feel' different by virtue of their different technical demands (e.g., in terms of fingering); they also 'sound' different depending on the acoustical properties of the instrument. Most non-keyboard instruments tend to favour keys in different ways by way of their 'open' notes (for example, G major and D major work well on the violin because of its 'open' strings, g, d', a', e''; the treble recorder is pitched in F and therefore works best in that key). In the case of brass instruments unable to modify the sounding length of the pipe, the available pitches will be limited to the harmonic series above the pipe's fundamental: a natural trumpet (without

27 McClary, 'The Transition from Modal to Tonal Organization in the Works of Monteverdi'; Chew, 'The Perfections of Modern Music'; Carter, '"An air new and grateful to the ear"'.

finger holes or valves) cannot play a full diatonic scale in tune save in its upper register (and then only by 'lipping'), and is extremely limited in its range of chromatic movement; a natural horn in D is similarly limited, and it cannot play in, say, E flat major without changing the length of the pipe (e.g., by way of a crook). Before the invention of valves in the nineteenth century, the trombone was the only fully chromatic brass instrument (given that the length of its pipe is changed by way of the slide). This is one reason why the standard 'brass' ensemble of the sixteenth and seventeenth centuries comprised sackbuts (the early version of the trombone) and cornetts, the latter in fact, an instrument made of wood (but with a cup mouthpiece like a brass instrument) and with finger holes to enable a diatonic and chromatic range similar to a recorder.

Thus keys that in principle sound the same were treated differently because of how they work on different instruments. But similar differences can be discerned even on equal-tempered keyboards. In part, this is by virtue of association with non-keyboard instrumental gestures; in part, it reflects the continuing, if increasingly tenuous, association of pitch-specific scales with former modes (discussed above). The two books of Bach's *Well-Tempered Clavier* (the '48' preludes and fugues) offer a lexicon of musical styles and gestures that are in some way key-specific, and therefore serve to give a D major piece a very different character from, say, an E flat major one. These differences, and the tropes that ensue, had already been acknowledged towards the end of our period, and they recur throughout the eighteenth century and into the nineteenth. For example, the *Méthode claire* (1691) by the virtuoso viola da gamba player and singing teacher Jean Rousseau seeks to articulate them even while he struggles with the systemic and terminological confusions that have bedevilled my foregoing discussion. Rousseau asks the question why keys are transposed:[28]

> The second reason is to find the keys [*Tons*] suited to express the different passions which one meets according to the different subjects treated. For although the manner of sounding the music is the same in the transposed keys as in the natural ones, the modulation is nevertheless quite different.[29] There are keys suited to serious subjects, as are D *la re* minor and A *mi la* minor, which are natural keys. There are those for gay things and for denoting grandeur, as are C *sol ut* major which is natural, and D *la re* major which is transposed. There are those for sadness, like G *re sol* minor which is natural, and there are those for tenderness, as are E *si mi* minor and G *re sol* major, which are transposed. For complaints and all subjects of lamentation, there are no keys more suitable than C *sol ut* minor and F *ut fa* minor, which are transposed, and for devotional pieces or church songs, F *ut fa* major which is natural, and A *mi la* major, which is transposed, are very suitable.

28 Steblin, *A History of Key Characteristics in the Eighteenth and Early Nineteenth Centuries*, pp. 31–2.
29 By 'modulation', Rousseau means 'character' or 'way of proceeding', using the term in a sense rather similar to earlier and contemporary notions of 'air'.

It seems clear that late seventeenth-century instrumental composers (Corelli, for example) sought to mix sets of pieces in different keys in their individual collections – usually ranging from three sharps to three flats, and combining major and minor – not just for the sake of technical variety, but also to allow the exploration of the different affects increasingly associated with each key.

Signs and symbols

The would-be 'reader' of seventeenth-century music is in not so different a position from the reader of, say, seventeenth-century poetry. Shakespeare or Racine can make relative sense to their modern English and French counterparts, but the syntax often seems quaint or unclear, and one must be wary of words that do not always mean what one assumes. Such issues of grammar and vocabulary need not always have a significant impact on modern perceptions of meaning, at least on the broadest scale, but, rather, may be more a matter for philologists and linguisticians. One might say something similar for the foregoing discussion of modality and tonality, which will impinge directly on the listener only when there is an apparent mismatch between what a piece does and (anachronistic) modern expectations thereof, as with, for example, a funeral march in a 'happy' – *recte* 'grand' – major key (as in Handel's *Saul*) rather than a 'sad' minor one. However, the subtleties may need further consideration. It would no doubt be impish to argue that the last piece that Dido sings in Purcell's *Dido and Aeneas*, 'When I am laid in earth', is not, strictly speaking, a 'lament', given that while it is certainly in a 'sad' (to cite Rousseau) G minor, it is not in one of the keys suitable for 'complaints and all subjects of lamentation', e.g., C minor (the key of Dido's 'Ah Belinda, I am prest' in Act I of Purcell's opera). It also raises the question of just which theory might be matched with which music. Yet the point does provide an incentive for some exploration of the composer's tonal practices and their possible (or not) affective associations.

Objectors might reasonably argue that while Dido's 'When I am laid in earth' may or may not be in the 'right' key, there are enough other textual and musical signs in the piece to mark it as a 'lament'. This is in effect to argue that tonal allegory, if there be any such thing, is but one of a range of possible signifiers in this music working (ideally, at least) in tandem. Or to put the point another way, seventeenth-century music (like much other music) tends to be information-rich to the point of redundancy: such redundant overload was no doubt useful to ensure the apprehension of meaning on the part of as wide a range of listeners as possible. Thus musical meaning might be more transparent than an obscure discussion of hexachord, system, mode and key would suggest. There is nothing particularly subtle about most word-painting, or for that matter, about the *concitato genere* and other such instrumental *mimesis*

Table 7.2 *The* intermedia *of Schütz's* Historia der freuden- und gnadenreichen
Geburth Gottes und Marien Sohnes, Jesu Christi *(1664)*

Intermedium	Subject	Voice(s)	Obbligato instruments
I	The angel speaking to the shepherds in the field	S	2 'violette'
II	The chorus of angels in heaven praising God	SSATTB	2 violins, 1 bassoon
III	The shepherds resolving to go to Bethlehem	AAA (or AAT)	2 'flauti' (recorders), 1 bassoon
IV	The Three Wise Men coming from the East	TTT	2 violins, 1 bassoon
V	The High Priests and Scribes telling Herod where it is prophesied that Christ will be born	BBBB	2 trombones
VI	Herod ordering the Three Wise Men to go to Bethlehem	B	2 'clarini' (trumpets)
VII, VIII	The angel twice telling Joseph to flee	S	2 'violette'

(as in the 'Frost' scene in Purcell's *King Arthur*). Keyboard works called 'The
Cuckoo' will invariably include a musical representation of that bird-call, and
vocal pieces about the pains of love will usually pile on the dissonances to add
spice to the experience. Here, at least, the signs are clear, almost to the extent
that we take them for granted as conventional gestures not directly confined
to the seventeenth century (the musical means for representing the sound of
the cuckoo scarcely changed from Janequin to Delius), and so we are more
surprised by their absence than by their presence.

Even if the principles cannot be intuited, they are easily learnt. For example,
Heinrich Schütz's *Historia der freuden- und gnadenreichen Geburth Gottes und
Marien Sohnes, Jesu Christi* (partly published in 1664) tells the story of Christmas
by way of a narrating Evangelist (in recitative) and eight episodes (each labelled
'intermedium') for different voices to represent the various actors; the whole
is also framed by two choruses as an introduction and conclusion. The vocal
scorings are clear (a soprano for the angel, a bass for King Herod, etc.), and are
reinforced by instruments used with conventional associations (see Table 7.2).
Angels are represented by strings (violins or 'violette', the latter an obscure term
that may mean small violas), the shepherds by recorders (a pastoral instrument

by virtue of the association with pan-pipes), the High Priests and Scribes by pompous trombones, and King Herod by typically 'regal' trumpets. The only slight oddity is the instrumental scoring for the Three Wise Men – two violins and bassoon – but then, in this period there is hardly any conventional musical sign for exotic Others, and Schütz may have been constrained by his available instruments.

These kinds of instrumental associations hark back to the sixteenth-century theatrical *intermedi* (the Florentine set of 1589 is the classic example) and continue through seventeenth-century opera and beyond. One can say much the same of voice types and particular styles of vocal writing. Although the design and casting of an opera would depend on the singers available, as a general rule of thumb (to which one will always find exceptions), female sopranos represent goddesses, nymphs, or lovers; male soprano-castratos are heroic lovers, villainous tyrants, or noble youths; female mezzo-sopranos represent tragic queens; female (or transvestite male) altos can be comic characters (nurses and the like); male altos and tenors are shepherds (although there are some examples of 'heroic' tenor roles, as in Monteverdi's rather oddly scored *Il ritorno d'Ulisse in patria*); basses are gods, wise old men, or comic figures. Gods and other supernatural beings can have elaborately ornate vocal writing to denote 'magical' powers; shepherds and other low-class characters can sing songs, as can noble lovers provided it does not offer too much of a threat to verisimilitude (an issue to which I shall return, below).

Within seventeenth-century opera, there also emerge topical scene-types that become conventional on the stage: the love-duet, the sleep scene (including a lullaby), the incantation scene, the lament.[30] Such scenes are often linked to particular types of poetic and musical signifiers. For example, incantation scenes in Italian opera (appeals to the gods; representations of white or black magic) often use *versi sdruccioli* (lines with the accent on the antepenultimate syllable rather than the more normal penultimate). In Act III scene 9 of Cavalli's *Giasone* (1649; libretto by Giacinto Andrea Cicognini), the vengeful Medea appeals to the Furies (italic indicates the position of the main stress in each line):

> L'armi appres*ta*temi,
> gelosi *fu*rie,
> infuri*a*temi,
> gelidi *spi*riti,
> . . .

[Give me weapons, jealous furies, inspire me to rage, cold spirits . . .]

30 Rosand, *Opera in Seventeenth-Century Venice*, chap. 1.

The strong–weak–weak line endings of these *quinari sdruccioli* have an obvious effect on the musical setting. So conventional do such scenes become that they are also open to parody as opera gained the maturity to make fun of itself.

Musical signifiers range from the literal (as in word-painting) to the conventional, where the musical sign stands as an emblem representing the thing being imitated without bearing any obvious resemblance to it. This latter category of signs is the most interesting, because it suggests the emergence of musical codes that need to be 'learnt' by an audience, rather than merely apprehended on the basis of similarity.[31] Such signs will also tend to become culture-specific, and hence can cause misunderstanding if assumed to apply too widely. One classic case of the conventional signifier has been identified by Ellen Rosand: the descending tetrachord (a four-note descent from tonic to dominant) appears as an 'emblem of lament', whether used melodically (as at the opening of John Dowland's 'Flow, my tears' and of his *Lachrimae* pavan) or in a bass line.[32] Early in the seventeenth century, lament scenes were usually set in a dramatic recitative: Monteverdi's *Lamento d'Arianna* from his now-lost opera *Arianna* of 1608 is a totemic example.[33] However, Monteverdi's *Lamento della ninfa* (included in his Eighth Book of madrigals of 1638) is very different in style (see also the discussion in chapter 5): in its central section, the abandoned nymph laments her fate in a free-flowing aria-style (some might prefer to call it *arioso*) over a repeating ground-bass consisting of the four-note descent, *a–g–f–e*. The piece seems to have established, or at least confirmed, a pattern: such ground-bass laments start to appear frequently in Italian opera (there are many in the works of Cavalli) and even in their French and English counterparts. This emblematic tetrachord may be presented diatonically (as in the *Lamento della ninfa*) or chromatically (*a–g♯–g–f♯–f–e*), and with or without a cadential completion. This is, of course, the chief reason why Dido's 'When I am laid in earth' is conventionally construed as a lament, given that Purcell uses just such a chromatic ground-bass (in G minor). There is nothing particularly verisimilar about a lamenting queen singing in triple time over a repeating bass pattern, yet few would deny this music its power. Not only do we suspend disbelief (as conventionally occurs in the theatre), but we also engage a different belief, that this music can somehow stand as a representation of deep emotional expression.[34]

Again, however, some caution may be in order. Bass lines formed of such descending tetrachords (whether or not as a ground) are also found in what

---

31 Tomlinson, *Music in Renaissance Magic*, chap. 7; Carter, 'Resemblance and Representation'. The tendency has been to associate these different types of signs with Foucault's 'Renaissance' and 'Baroque' epistemes, although the enterprise is trounced in Karol Berger's review-essay on Tomlinson's book in *Journal of Musicology*, 13 (1995), 404–23.

32 Rosand, 'The Descending Tetrachord'.   33 Porter, '*Lamenti recitativi da camera*'.

34 Tomlinson, *Music in Renaissance Magic*, p. 243.

are, strictly speaking, non-lamenting contexts: Monteverdi uses them (with the diatonic tetrachord in D minor) to represent love's 'sweet delights and sighed-for kisses' ('i dolci vezzi, e sospirati baci') in his madrigal 'Altri canti d'Amor, tenero arciero' at the head of his Eighth Book; the major descending tetrachord appears in the bass lines of love-duets in *L'incoronazione di Poppea*; and the minor descending tetrachord underpins the final love-duet in Cavalli's *Calisto* (1651). Similarly, Purcell's G minor version of the trope is anticipated by Hecuba's despairing invocation of the Underworld spirits in Act I scene 8 of Cavalli's *Didone* (1641). It may be but a short step from love, or invocation, to lament, but the comparisons suggest that, like most conventional signs, this one can be somewhat slippery, with its meaning needing to be fixed by way of contextual determinants.

Such contextual determinacy also raises another question. Few would deny the passion of Dido's lament, and most would probably feel that Monteverdi's lamenting nymph has some kind of a serious message to convey. In general, we tend to trust our immediate responses to music of this period, however much we might accept the need for caution in reading unfamiliar codes. If the music sounds, say, tragic, then all other things being equal, we are inclined to take it thus. Of course, all other things are not always equal: when a comic nurse or servant sings a ground-bass lament, we will suspect some kind of humorous parody given the mismatch between the character and the musico-rhetorical register. But even when the case seems clear, things might not be what they appear. What for one reader is the passionate outpouring of a lamenting nymph could, for another, be ironic exaggeration for comic effect. The problem is clear in Monteverdi's *L'incoronazione di Poppea*, Act II scene 3, where Seneca prepares to commit suicide on command of the emperor. Three 'famigliari' (members of his household) implore him not to carry out the deed in a trio based (at its opening) on the intense contrapuntal working out of an ascending chromatic theme. Monteverdi had already used this passage in a six-voice motet published in 1620, 'Christe, adoramus te' (linking it with the Crucifixion), and in a strophic canzonetta in his Eighth Book of 1638, the trio 'Non partir, ritrosetta'. Clearly the motet is serious; equally clearly, the canzonetta is parodic (and also very funny). So which reading is appropriate in the case of Seneca? The obvious answer, 'serious' (according to the subject matter), might in fact be subverted in the light of contemporary Venetian views on the historical Seneca, and also by the cultural values seemingly embraced by Monteverdi's opera as a whole.[35]

As we shall see below, one might reasonably argue that these potential and actual readings rest not so much within the musical text (as fixed in the score)

35 Carter, *Monteverdi's Musical Theatre*, pp. 282–6.

as in its performance on the one hand, and in the way we choose to read that performance on the other. But there is another point. Meaning may be conveyed by signs and symbols, but those signs and symbols also play with meaning according to a ludic impulse that may itself be one chief 'meaning' of the semiotic game. The seventeenth century would have identified this ludic impulse with 'wit', and it offers the possibility of a different interface between reason and the senses, between thinking on the one hand, and feeling on the other.

Wordless rhetoric

Whatever the nature of seventeenth-century musical signs and their potential meanings, they become conventionalised to the extent that they can operate without any verbal text with which they might originally have been associated. The Renaissance would have denied instrumental music the power to convey any significant meaning above and beyond its functional or aesthetic self precisely because it lacked words and thus could not appeal to the faculty of reason. Instrumentalists were also relatively low down the pecking order of the musical profession. Thus the organist Girolamo Frescobaldi was the butt of theorist Giovanni Battista Doni's typical disdain: 'he is a very coarse man, although he plays the organ perfectly and may be excellent for composing fantasies, dance music and similar things; but for setting the words, he is extremely ignorant and devoid of discrimination, so that one can say he has all his knowledge at the ends of his fingers'.[36] During Frescobaldi's lifetime, however, instrumental music was acquiring a new status and even some notion of eloquence, such that a violin, say, could move the listener on a par with the voice.

Instrumental music continued both to draw on vocal models and to rely on sixteenth-century styles and genres. Broadly speaking, the repertory divides into imitative pieces (ricercars, canzonas), dance movements, and quasi-improvised works (toccatas, preludes) that, in turn, may be less or more precisely notated. But these broad categories are not mutually exclusive, and they can be combined both within pieces – as in a toccata that contains dance-like and/or imitative episodes – and by movements in sequence (in nascent forms of the suite). This fluidity also prompts a flexible approach to generic labels which may or may not have precise meanings: a 'sonata', for example, is a work that involves instrumental sounds (from the Italian verb 'suonare'; compare the Greek-derived 'symphony') rather than having a specific form; and at least for the early part of the period, a 'concerto' ('sounding together', from

---

36 For Doni's remark on Frescobaldi (made in a letter to Marin Mersenne, 22 July 1640), see Hammond, *Girolamo Frescobaldi*, p. 85.

'concertare') need not play off a solo instrumentalist (in a solo concerto) or a group thereof (in the *concerto grosso*) against a larger body in some kind of competition (as in the Italian 'consertare', meaning to intertwine or to vie). Indeed, 'concerto' can also be used in its sense of 'sounding together' for pieces that combine voices and instruments (hence, 'in concerto' or the somewhat later coinage, *concertato*).

The sixteenth-century canzona and imitative ricercar have been variously linked to vocal models (respectively, the French chanson and the contrapuntal working out typical of sacred polyphony). By the early seventeenth century, if not before, the ricercar embraced, and also signified, a 'learned' style that was also identified with the *stile antico*, the canonised Palestrina-style that now stood in opposition to the *stile moderno*. Such pieces allowed instrumental composers to display their artifice by way of the complex working out of contrapuntal ideas. Canzonas had long lost their direct associations with the chanson (although the long–short–short opening typical of chansons remained conventional within, and a marker of, the genre). In both cases, contrapuntal techniques, or the juxtaposition of contrapuntal and homophonic blocks, solved the chief problem facing instrumental music: how to provide structure in the absence of the structural force of a text. A similar impulse is apparent in the adoption of ground-bass techniques in the early seventeenth century, with pieces over stock bass patterns (also used in vocal music) – the Romanesca, *passamezzo* (*antico* and *moderno*), *aria di ruggiero*, *passacaglia* and *ciaccona* – or popular tunes (*La monica*, *La folia*), and also in the emergence of variation sets. Failing such form-giving techniques, instrumental composers tended to let their music fall into short, contrasted sections defined by cadential articulations, only gradually solving the problem of how to work on a larger scale through sequences and 'modulation'.

Although instrumental music began to claim an affective power akin to vocal music, it is not always clear how this might be achieved save by a generic appeal to contrasts of pacing and texture, or to particular types of writing (virtuosic flamboyance, chromaticism, dissonance etc.). When musical signs fixed in vocal music are transferred to instrumental music, the conventional meaning of those signs might or might not pass with them: the sixth (G minor) sonata in Purcell's *Ten Sonata's in Four Parts* (1697) involves a mammoth ground-bass movement based on the descending minor tetrachord that hardly seems an emblem of 'lament' in this context. Even where a piece bears an emblematic title, the issue is not always clear. Heinrich von Biber's *Rosary Sonatas* (or *Mystery Sonatas*) are for violin and continuo, with the violin often using non-standard tunings (*scordatura*) so as to enable unusual timbres and multiple-stopped sonorities. Each of these highly virtuosic sonatas – all but the last divided into movements (variously including dance-types such as the 'Allamanda', 'Sarabanda', 'Courente' and 'Guigue') – is associated with one of the fifteen mysteries of the rosary, providing a set of meditations on events in the life of the Blessed Virgin and hence of Christ (the Annunciation, the Visitation, the Nativity etc.); there is also a concluding 'Passagalia'. Some of the instrumental gestures are directly mimetic, such as the sounds of whipping in Sonata 7 ('The Scourging [of Christ] at the Pillar') or the hammering of the nails and the earthquake in Sonata 10 ('The Crucifixion'). Elsewhere, Biber relies on indirect textual associations, as when he quotes the plainsong hymn 'Surrexit Christus hodie' ('Christ was risen today') in the second movement of Sonata 11 ('The Resurrection'). For the most part, however, the music is evocative rather than descriptive: it usually relates (or at least, can be related) to the atmosphere or mood of the event described by the title, but in the absence of the title, one would be hard-pressed to identify this event.

This lack of specificity is not surprising: even the most directly program-matic nineteenth-century instrumental music has relatively limited semiotic power. The question, however, is whether this is a weakness or a strength. Kircher described (in his *Musurgia universalis* of 1650) a 'stylus phantasticus' that gradually became associated directly with freer instrumental music. Such music draws upon the mind's fantasy and thus embodies the essence of what it is to be a creative, even inspired, musical artist. According to a Platonic model, fantasy is placed above both reason and the senses, coming close to the poetic *furor* that allows those who have climbed the ladder of self-awareness and know-ledge to enter a supra-rational state where one can touch upon the Divine.[37] By this reading, Biber's meditations on the rosary allow a more, not less, direct apprehension of divine mystery than, say, a set of motets on rosary-based texts precisely because we can feel the import of these mysteries without the inter-ference of rational thought.

Such a mystical view also had the benefit of being self-serving propaganda, and certainly, had Frescobaldi articulated it, it would have put Doni in his place. Yet the problem remained of granting some kind of structure to these fantas-tic musical visions. Again, rhetoric offered a solution. The standard modes of organising a speech (in one scheme: *exordium, narratio, propositio, confirmatio, confutatio, peroratio*) could reasonably be transferred to non-verbal orations, where one or more musical ideas are proposed and affirmed, then rebutted (e.g., by contrasting musical ideas), and finally confirmed. The analogies may be metaphorical, but they do seem to have some bearing particularly on the multi-section movements that are quite characteristic of this period. For example, in

---

37 For the broader context, see Butler, 'The Fantasia as Musical Image'.

Table 7.3 *The six parts of Ciceronian rhetoric applied to the first movement of*
Arcangelo Corelli's Concerto grosso, *op. 6 no. 2 (1714)*

Exordium (introduction)	*Vivace*: a call to attention.
Narratio (statement of facts)	*Allegro*: imitative opening leads to passagework; pauses abruptly.
Propositio (forecast of main points in speaker's favour)	*Adagio*: intensely chromatic and dissonant; moves far flatwards.
Confirmatio (affirmative proof)	*Vivace*: reprise of opening in the dominant.
Confutatio (refutation or rebuttal)	*Allegro*: as first Allegro, but in the dominant and changes towards end.
Peroratio (conclusion)	*Adagio–Largo andante*: slow and expressive; two sequences each leading to a firm cadence in the tonic.

the case of the first movement of Arcangelo Corelli's *Concerto grosso* in F major, op. 6 no. 2 (published posthumously in 1714; see Table 7.3), there seems to be a set of musical 'arguments' within and between disparate musical elements distinguished by tempo, texture and chromatic complexity that is somehow resolved by the final peroration. One can quite easily perform a similar exercise on a Buxtehude prelude,[38] a Purcell sonata or a Couperin suite. The subject-matter of this discourse is chiefly musical, with little if any extra-musical reference. That does not make it any less interesting.

Text and performance

Biber's *Mystery Sonatas* remained in manuscript, and Schütz's setting of the Christmas story was only half published: the recitatives for the Evangelist were printed in 1664 but the *intermedia* remained in manuscript parts available from the composer's agents because they 'would not attain their proper effect except in princely chapels'. In part this may have been for reasons of economy – such music was unlikely to sell in great quantities – and we have already seen in chapter 4 the problems facing music printing in the seventeenth century. Yet there is also a strong sense in the period of some composers being reluctant to publish music that would thus become devalued by wide circulation. Composer-performers setting a high price on virtuosity could also appear ambivalent about committing themselves to print: they sought the kudos to be gained through

38 As John Butt treats the *praeludium* in F sharp minor, BuxWV 146, in his 'Germany and the Netherlands', pp. 196–9.

the press, but did not always want to give away the secrets of their art. A volume such as Giulio Caccini's *Le nuove musiche* (1602) may seem to provide a great deal of advice on the 'new' styles of solo singing of the late sixteenth and early seventeenth centuries by way of its long preface and its careful musical notation, but even then, significant information is lacking for the ideal performance of this music.

Even in less obviously problematic cases, these musical texts are designed to be somehow brought to life in performance, and thus, as we have seen (in chapter 2), they are by definition incomplete of and for themselves. This is inevitable, and of course, it provides one chief problem for any musicologist (of any period), who must decide whether to study texts or realisations of those texts. Baroque notation is often more specific than that of the Renaissance – in terms of embellishment, articulation, dynamics, tempo and instrumentation – in part as composers sought to maintain control over their music against the threat of attenuation posed by widespread dissemination. Yet significant gaps remain, most obviously in the shorthand 'figured bass' needing to be filled out by the continuo player(s). It is also clear that notated melodic lines in this period usually required some kind of further embellishment to a degree determined by tempo, style and performance environment, and by the skills and taste of the performer: Corelli may initially have published his violin sonatas in relatively 'simple' versions, but other near-contemporary editions reveal the extent of ornamentation that could be applied (tastefully or not) to, say, the slower movements. Furthermore, this music draws significantly upon the non-musical – the facial expressions, gestures, and location of the performers – to achieve signification and also significance. The problem for modern performers is to gain the knowledge (from treatises and similar sources), technique, sensitivity and even courage to deliver these works effectively.

If notated composition, organised in the manner of persuasive oratory, belongs to the rhetorical category of *dispositio* (the arrangement of one or more ideas into the parts of an oration), this is only one of the tasks of the musician. Prior to *dispositio* is the creative impulse of *inventio* (the 'finding' of an idea, from whatever source), and following it are *elocutio* (also called *decoratio* and *elaboratio*; the elaboration or decoration of the idea) and *pronuntiatio* (the delivery or performance of the oration). But while musical *inventio* and *dispositio* are primarily matters for the composer – save in the case of improvisation – and *pronuntiatio* an issue for performers, *elocutio* sits somewhere between the two: a composer will certainly elaborate a musical idea, and yet elaboration will further occur in the act of *pronuntiatio* to an extent inversely proportional to the performer's adherence to a fixed musical text. It follows that while such a text may contain meaning within itself, this meaning will primarily be conveyed by performance, and may even be located chiefly within performance depending on the distribution of the responsibilities for *elocutio*. Or to put the point another way, the composer's task is not so much to create meaning as to determine a space in which meaning might be created, by the performer on the one hand, and for that matter, by the listener on the other, each engaging (not necessarily consistently) with a wide range of elaborative possibilities on which limits may or may not be set by the individuals involved, or by contextual presuppositions.

The immanence (or not) of meaning within the text has an obvious impact on the concept of the 'work', which in this period, if not others, is not so much an autonomous, free-standing object as a set of activities. These activities (on the part of the composer, performer and listener) can each be construed as essentially performative: the composer performs, say, a reading of the verbal text being set to music; the performer performs a reading of the music; the listener performs a reading of the performance and of the music together. All these performances contribute to the construction of meaning. Each such activity may also constitute meaning of and for itself, such as when the prime aim of the performance is to demonstrate the technical and expressive virtuosity of the performer. But more often, we are required to engage with a nested sequence of performative acts. Such multi-tasking is not untypical of aesthetic responses in general – we can appreciate a work's form while at the same time being moved by its content – but the issue comes to the musical fore perhaps for the first time in the seventeenth century. It is one reason why this music can be so slippery; it is also why it embodies a physical, almost erotic pleasure in the promiscuous play of signs.

The *stile rappresentativo*

It is no coincidence that the discussion thus far, and the musical works chosen to illustrate it, has largely focussed on the earlier rather than the later part of the seventeenth century. This is not to say that things do not change in the period: we shall see plenty of examples in the chapters below. But in the last decade of the sixteenth century and the first third or so of the seventeenth, stylistic and semiotic principles, and dilemmas, took shape in ways that seem to have animated the period as a whole: Monteverdi's *concertato Gloria* in the *Selva morale e spirituale* (1640–41) is much closer in form and content to, say, Vivaldi's well-known *Gloria* (RV 589), written over eighty years later, than it is to the Gloria movement of a late sixteenth-century Mass, or even of Monteverdi's own Masses in the *stile antico*, one of which he also published in 1640–41. For all the differences in scale, their music speaks some kind of common language, using consistent codes and similar modes of representation.

A number of the issues of meaning discussed in this chapter were in the seventeenth century viewed in terms of representation. The Florentine theorist Giovanni Battista Doni, resident in Rome and active within the artistic circles of the Barberini family, cast a critical eye over modern music from a Humanist perspective. In his various treatises – the *Compendio del trattato de' generi e de' modi della musica* (1635), the *Annotazioni sopra Il compendio de' generi e de' modi della musica* (1640) and *De praestantia musicae veteris libri tres* (1647)[39] – he treads the well-worn path of comparing the music of Classical Antiquity with modern endeavour. Given the Barberini's interest in opera, and doubtless Doni's pride in his native city, he devotes considerable attention to that Florentine invention, the *stile recitativo* (or 'stile monodico'), and to its use in the theatre as the *stile rappresentativo* ('representative style'), which is classified in various ways.

According to the theorists of early opera and monody, music gained its power by being a heightened, yet still verisimilar, representation of oratorical delivery: early recitative was a form of musical speech (*recitar cantando*). In contrast to polyphony, one voice could represent one speaker, using all the new-found musical–rhetorical means to teach, move and delight the listener. Pietro de' Bardi (1634) said that 'il canto in istile rappresentativo' had been developed by Vincenzo Galilei in Giovanni de' Bardi's Camerata;[40] the term also first appeared in print on the title-page of a work associated with the Camerata, Giulio Caccini's *Euridice* (1600; 'composta in stile rappresentativo'). Other composers linking it with the theatre include Girolamo Giacobbi (his *Aurora ingannata* of 1608 includes 'canti rappresentativi') and Monteverdi in his *Madrigali guerrieri, et amorosi* (1638). But like the term *stile recitativo*, it was not restricted to stage music. 'Stile rappresentativo', 'musica rappresentativa', 'genere rappresentativo', etc., are used for solo songs or dialogues (in the preface to Caccini's *Le nuove musiche* of 1602; the 'lettera amorosa' and 'partenza amorosa' in Monteverdi's Seventh Book of madrigals of 1619; Francesco Rasi's *Dialoghi rappresentativi* of 1620), for sacred *concerti* (Bernardino Borlasca in 1609), and even, somewhat paradoxically, for polyphonic *seconda pratica* madrigals (Aquilino Coppini describing Monteverdi's Fifth Book in 1608). Thus it denotes music for the theatre, music in a recitative style, or music that (re)presents a text in a particularly dramatic or emotional way. More important,

---

39 Others were published much later in the collection *Lyra barberina amphichordos: accedunt eiusdem opera* (Florence, 1747).

40 Pietro de' Bardi's letter to Giovanni Battista Doni describing his father's Camerata and early opera in Florence is translated in Strunk, *Source Readings in Music History, Revised Edition*, iv: *The Baroque Era*, pp. 15–17.

the *stile rappresentativo* chiefly involves music that somehow manages to address the listener through the first person rather than by way of some kind of third-person mediation. It enacts, rather than tells, a story.

Sixteenth-century polyphonic madrigals and motets had used the poetic 'I', and had even represented the speech of a single character, but it was an implausible, if powerful, fiction.[41] Polyphony in essence fostered a narrative mode where the story (not its actors) is the subject. Several voices might speak for one in a liturgical or devotional context, where the 'I' is the heart and mind of each individual member of the congregation whose address to God is mediated and amplified by a choir just as by a priest. But the inverisimilitude of a single 'I' speaking to, rather than for, an audience by way of five voices requires the acceptance of conventions that, in turn, seem (to the modern reader, at least) to prompt contemplation more than involvement:[42] one can certainly reflect upon the actions of a lamenting nymph expressed within a five-voice madrigal, but on the face of it, it seems harder to identify with her. Yet when Virginia Andreini played out the lament of Arianna in Monteverdi's eponymous opera performed in Mantua in 1608, the fact that 'there was not one lady who failed to shed a tear' suggests that catharsis had been achieved by association rather than by contemplation.

This is not to say that opera is verisimilar: it patently is not, even if it pretended to be so in its early stages (hence the subjects dealing with the great musicians of classical myth, Apollo and Orpheus). Rather, it is to argue that notions of representation and its consequences are somewhat differently configured in the seventeenth century than they were previously. The modern style was particularly well suited to (if not founded upon) some kind of equation between the poetic and the musical 'I', be that 'I' represented within an operatic role, or for that matter, within the first-person 'songs' of David (the psalms) and of Solomon (the Canticum Canticorum). However, the fact that the version of the *Lamento d'Arianna* first published by Monteverdi was a five-voice arrangement (in his Sixth Book of madrigals of 1614) gives some pause for thought. Doni thought it a mistake forced upon the composer by one of his Venetian patrons, arguing that the solo version was (and must inevitably be) more effective in rhetorical and expressive terms.[43] Yet the new recitative did bring with it a sense of loss: it was 'boring' and 'tedious', according to some

41 This is probably true, on stylistic grounds, even if such polyphonic madrigals were performed by solo voice and some kind of instrumental accompaniment: in such cases, the vocal line still remains rhythmically and melodically constrained by its contrapuntal frame.
42 I am aware of Tomlinson's argument (*Music in Renaissance Magic*, p. 244) for acknowledging, even if we cannot cultivate, a different, 'Renaissance' mode of listening. For the broader issues, see also Pesce (ed.), *Hearing the Motet*; Wegman, 'Music as Heard'.
43 Fabbri, *Monteverdi*, trans. Carter, p. 140.

contemporary comments,[44] and it must have been hard for a composer such as Monteverdi to deny the gains of the second half of the sixteenth century in terms of expressive counterpoint and dissonance treatment: this is one reason, perhaps, why he and a number of other composers (Schütz, for example) seem to have preferred the duet to the solo song as a way of keeping some of the best of both worlds.

Herein lies the paradox: polyphony might be inverisimilar and might confuse a text, but it certainly offered a more inherently musical means of text expression. Monteverdi includes in his Fourth Book of five-voice madrigals (1603) a setting that illustrates the point:[45]

> Sfogava con le stelle
> un infermo d'Amore
> sotto notturno Cielo il suo dolore;
> e dicea fisso in loro:
> O imagini belle
> dell'idol mio, ch'adoro,
>   . . .

[Under the stars in the night sky, a lovesick man proclaimed his grief. And he said, fixed on them: 'O beautiful images of my idol whom I adore . . .']

The poem, perhaps by Ottavio Rinuccini, mixes narrative (the first four lines) with direct speech (by the 'I' of the lover). Monteverdi distinguishes between the two by musical means, playing off a chordal, recitational style (derived from *falsobordone*) against contrapuntal elaboration. But somewhat counterintuitively, it might seem, it is the latter that is used for the lover's expostulation: at 'O . . .' the setting suddenly flowers into glorious double counterpoint, expanding outwards to cover the full range of the five-voice texture in a moment of intensely musical expression.

Monteverdi included a setting of another 'stars' text in his Seventh Book (1619), in this case dealing with the conventional metaphor equating the stars in the heavens with the eyes of the beloved. The duet (for two tenors) 'Non vedrò mai le stelle' adopts a tactic similar to 'Sfogava con le stelle', with an opening statement ('Non vedrò mai le stelle / de' bei celesti giri . . .'; 'Will I never see the stars / of those beautiful, heavenly motions') leading to an invocation to the beloved's beautiful eyes ('o luci belle'). The opening statement involves both voices moving in the contrapuntally enlivened homophony typical of Monteverdi's emerging duet style. The invocation is initially set for solo voice

44 Gianturco, 'Nuove considerazioni su *il tedio del recitativo* delle prime opere romane'; Carter, *Monteverdi's Musical Theatre*, p. 45.

45 Carter, '"Sfogava con le stelle" Reconsidered'; compare also Tomlinson, *Music in Renaissance Magic*, pp. 234–46.

to a melody bearing some similarity to the soprano line in 'Sfogava con le stelle', but for all its lyricism it lacks force when deprived of the rich counterpoint. It is significant that Monteverdi soon shifts to something very different, the two voices intertwining in an extended lyrical episode in triple time.

Dance-like triple times (and similarly derived structured duple times) had long been associated with canzonettas and other 'lighter' forms in the sixteenth century, and with their equivalents in the early monody repertory, the 'arias' (in the technical sense of a setting of strophic poetry) often in the new poetic metres cultivated by Gabriello Chiabrera (for example, four-, five- and eight-syllable lines). Their evident mutation into something more forceful in the first third of the seventeenth century – in both secular and sacred music – is one of the more striking features of the period, and it has yet to be fully charted or explained:[46] it is no less significant a feature of Monteverdi's *Lamento della ninfa* or Purcell's lamenting Dido than their use of the descending tetrachord ground bass. These 'aria' styles and structures become typical of formal musical and rhetorical articulation by the middle of the century, and develop still further in the later Baroque period. Sometimes their impulse is mimetic, whether for word-painting (images expressing physical movement or change; explicit or implicit references to the Holy Trinity) or simply to represent 'singing' or 'song' (so I construed the triple-time 'Glorificamus te' in Monteverdi's *Gloria*, above). Sometimes they respond to a new metrical pattern in a text (raising the question of how aware librettists were of the musical implications of their verse). Sometimes they reflect instead (or in addition) some kind of syntactic and/or rhetorical shift, as with the vocative construction at Monteverdi's 'o luci belle'.[47] In short, they need not always involve affective expression: to assume that they do is to project back into the earlier seventeenth century the presumed aesthetic of High Baroque *opera seria* (and even here, that aesthetic is open to question). But whatever the case, they involve a new type of musical utterance that would seem to have nothing to do with the representation of heightened speech, or even with clarity of text presentation given that in such arias, the words tend to get displaced by virtue of the musical repetitions.

Some might deplore the loss of the declamatory innocence that had been captured so briefly at the beginning of our period; others might breathe a sigh of relief at the return to music as music rather than as a spurious form of speech. But these duple- and triple-time melodies do more than just tickle the ear's

46 Carter, 'Resemblance and Representation'; Whenham, '"Aria" in the Madrigals of Giovanni Rovetta'.
47 Calcagno (see his '"Imitar col canto chi parla"') would place such constructions (vocatives, imperatives, pronouns, prepositions of time or place, etc.) under the broad category of 'deictics'; his observation
of the fact that many 'aria' settings focus on deictic words permits a different (but not mutually exclusive)
explanation of their purpose than the conventional claim that arias are expressive.

fancy, or offer the singer (or instrumentalist) the chance to display her ability to perform *cantabile*. Their potential association with the mechanistic theory of emotional arousal developed by Descartes (in his *Des passions de l'âme* of 1649) – achieved by the physical motions of the bodily humours – is enhanced by their origins in the dance: they embody a physicality of gesture and movement inspiring sympathetic motion in the listener's body that can itself quite literally 'move' the humours, or (if one prefers) the heart and soul. This (e)motion has a power of its own, but it may also be a motion to something else, including the transcendental stasis of the sublime.[48] The sheer joy of song for song's sake in the seventeenth century is perhaps the period's most lasting contribution to the Western art tradition.

Bibliography

Allaire, G. G., *The Theories of Hexachords, Solmization and the Modal System*, 'Musicological Studies and Documents', 24. American Institute of Musicology, 1972

Baker, N. K., and Hanning, B. R. (eds), *Musical Humanism and its Legacy: Essays in Honor of Claude V. Palisca*. Stuyvesant, NY, 1992

Bartel, D., *Musica poetica: Musical-Rhetorical Figures in German Baroque Music*. Lincoln, NE, 1997

Berger, K., review-essay on Tomlinson, *Music in Renaissance Magic*. *Journal of Musicology*, 13 (1995), 404–23

Besutti, P., Gialdroni, T. M., and Baroncini, R. (eds), *Claudio Monteverdi: studi e prospettive; atti del convegno, Mantova, 21–24 ottobre 1993*, 'Accademia Nazionale Virgiliana di Scienze, Lettere e Arti: Miscellanea', 5. Florence, 1998

Buelow, G. J., 'Rhetoric and Music'. In S. Sadie (ed.), *The New Grove Dictionary of Music and Musicians*. 20 vols, London, 1980, xv: 793–803

Butler, G. G., 'The Fantasia as Musical Image'. *Musical Quarterly*, 60 (1974), 602–15

Butt, J., 'Germany and the Netherlands'. In A. Silbiger (ed.), *Keyboard Music Before 1700*. 2nd edn, New York, 2003, pp. 147–234

Calcagno, M., '"Imitar col canto chi parla": Monteverdi and the Creation of a Language for Musical Theater'. *Journal of the American Musicological Society*, 55 (2002), 383–431

Carter, T., *Music in Late Renaissance and Early Baroque Italy*. London, 1992

  'Artusi, Monteverdi, and the Poetics of Modern Music'. In Baker and Hanning (eds), *Musical Humanism and its Legacy*, pp. 171–94

  '"An air new and grateful to the ear": the Concept of *Aria* in Late Renaissance and Early Baroque Italy'. *Music Analysis*, 12 (1993), 127–45

  'Resemblance and Representation: Towards a New Aesthetic in the Music of Monteverdi'. In Fenlon and Carter (eds), *'Con che soavità'*, pp. 118–34

  '"Sfogava con le stelle" Reconsidered: Some Thoughts on the Analysis of Monteverdi's Mantuan Madrigals'. In Besutti, Gialdroni and Baroncini (eds), *Claudio Monteverdi*, pp. 147–70

---

48 Compare Murata, '"Quia amore langueo" or Interpreting "Affetti sacri e spirituali"' and '"Singing", "Acting", and "Dancing" in Vocal Chamber Music of the Early Seicento'.

Monteverdi's Musical Theatre. New Haven and London, 2002

Chafe, E. T., *Monteverdi's Tonal Language*. New York, 1992

Chew, G., 'The Perfections of Modern Music: Consecutive Fifths and Tonal Coherence in Monteverdi'. *Music Analysis*, 8 (1989), 247–73

Collins Judd, C., 'Modal Types and *Ut, re, mi* Tonalities: Tonal Coherence in Sacred Vocal Polyphony from about 1500'. *Journal of the American Musicological Society*, 45 (1992), 428–67

Dahlhaus, C., *Untersuchungen über die Entstehung der harmonischen Tonalität*. Kassel, 1968; trans. R. O. Gjerdingen as *Studies on the Origin of Harmonic Tonality* (Princeton, 1990)

Fabbri, P., *Monteverdi*, trans. T. Carter. Cambridge, 1994

Fenlon, I., and Carter, T. (eds), *'Con che soavità': Essays in Italian Baroque Opera, Song and Dance, 1580–1740*. Oxford, 1995

Freitas, R., 'Singing and Playing: the Italian Cantata and the Rage for Wit'. *Music and Letters*, 82 (2001), 509–42

Gianturco, C., 'Nuove considerazioni su *il tedio del recitativo* delle prime opere romane'. *Rivista italiana di musicologia*, 17 (1982), 212–39

Haar, J., 'A Sixteenth-Century Attempt at Music Criticism'. *Journal of the American Musicological Society*, 36 (1983), 191–209

Hammond, F., *Girolamo Frescobaldi*. Cambridge, MA, 1983

Hanning, B. R., 'Monteverdi's Three *Genera*: a Study in Terminology'. In Baker and Hanning (eds), *Musical Humanism and its Legacy*, pp. 145–70

Harper, J., 'Frescobaldi's Early *Inganni* and Their Background'. *Proceedings of the Royal Musical Association*, 105 (1978–9), 1–12

Jackson, R., 'The *Inganni* and the Keyboard Music of Trabaci'. *Journal of the American Musicological Society*, 21 (1968), 204–8

Kurtzman, J., and Koldau, L., '*Trombe, Trombe d'argento, Trombe squarciate, Tromboni*, and *Pifferi* in Venetian Processions and Ceremonies of the Sixteenth and Seventeenth Centuries'. *Journal of Seventeenth-Century Music*, 8 (2002) <http://www.sscm-jscm.org/jscm/v8/no1/Kurtzman_V.html>

McClary, S. K., 'The Transition from Modal to Tonal Organization in the Works of Monteverdi'. Ph.D. thesis, Harvard University (1976)

Meier, B., *Die Tonarten der klassischen Vokalpolyphonie*. Utrecht, 1974; trans. E. S. Beebe as *The Modes of Classical Vocal Polyphony* (New York, 1988)

Moore, J. H., '*Venezia favorita da Maria*: Music for the Madonna Nicopeia and Santa Maria della Salute'. *Journal of the American Musicological Society*, 37 (1984), 299–355

Murata, M., 'Scylla and Charybdis, or Steering between Form and Social Context in the Seventeenth Century'. In E. Narmour and R. A. Solie (eds), *Explorations in Music, the Arts, and Ideas: Essays in Honor of Leonard B. Meyer*. Stuyvesant, NY, 1988, pp. 67–85

'"Quia amore langueo" or Interpreting "Affetti sacri e spirituali"'. In Besutti, Gialdroni and Baroncini (eds), *Claudio Monteverdi*, pp. 79–96

'"Singing", "Acting", and "Dancing" in Vocal Chamber Music of the Early Seicento'. *Journal of Seventeenth-Century Music*, 9 (2003) <http://www.sscm-jscm.org/jscm/v9/no1/Murata.html>

Owens, J. A., 'Music Historiography and the Definition of "Renaissance"'. *MLA Notes*, 67 (1990), 305–30

'How Josquin Became Josquin: Reflections on Historiography and Reception'. In J. A. Owens and A. M. Cummings (eds), *Music in Renaissance Cities and Courts: Studies in Honor of Lewis Lockwood*, 'Detroit Studies in Musicology', 18. Warren, MI, 1997, pp. 271–80

Palisca, C. V., '*Ut oratoria musica*: the Rhetorical Basis of Musical Mannerism'. In F. W. Robinson and S. G. Nichols Jr (eds), *The Meaning of Mannerism*. Hanover, NH, 1972, pp. 37–65: reprinted in Palisca, *Studies in the History of Italian Music and Music Theory*, pp. 282–311

 'Marco Scacchi's Defense of Modern Music (1649)'. In L. Berman (ed.), *Words and Music – the Scholar's View: a Medley of Problems and Solutions Compiled in Honor of A. Tillman Merritt by Sundry Hands*. Cambridge, MA, 1972, pp. 189–235; reprinted in Palisca, *Studies in the History of Italian Music and Music Theory*, pp. 88–145

 Humanism in Italian Renaissance Musical Thought. New Haven and London, 1985

 Baroque Music. 3rd edn, Englewood Cliffs, NJ, 1991

 Studies in the History of Italian Music and Music Theory. Oxford, 1994

Pesce, D. (ed.), *Hearing the Motet: Essays on the Motet of the Middle Ages and Renaissance*. New York and Oxford, 1997

Pirrotta, N., *Music and Theatre from Poliziano to Monteverdi*, trans. K. Eales. Cambridge, 1982

Porter, W. V., '*Lamenti recitativi da camera*'. In Fenlon and Carter (eds), '*Con che soavità*', pp. 73–110

Powers, H. S., 'Tonal Types and Modal Categories in Renaissance Polyphony'. *Journal of the American Musicological Society*, 34 (1981), 428–70

Rosand, E., 'The Descending Tetrachord: an Emblem of Lament'. *Musical Quarterly*, 55 (1979), 346–59

 Opera in Seventeenth-Century Venice: the Creation of a Genre. Berkeley, Los Angeles and Oxford, 1991

Smither, H. E., *A History of the Oratorio*, i: *The Oratorio in the Baroque Era: Italy, Vienna, Paris*. Chapel Hill, NC, 1977

Steblin, R., *A History of Key Characteristics in the Eighteenth and Early Nineteenth Centuries*. 2nd edn, Rochester, NY, 2002

Stein, B. A., 'Between Key and Mode: Tonal Practice in the Music of Giacomo Carissimi'. Ph. D. thesis, Brandeis University (1994)

Strunk, O., *Source Readings in Music History, Revised Edition*, iii: *The Renaissance*, ed. G. Tomlinson. New York and London, 1998

 Source Readings in Music History, Revised Edition, iv: *The Baroque Era*, ed. M. Murata. New York and London, 1998

Tomlinson, G., *Monteverdi and the End of the Renaissance*. Oxford, 1987

 Music in Renaissance Magic: Toward a Historiography of Others. Chicago and London, 1993

Wegman, R. (ed.), 'Music as Heard' (proceedings of the symposium 'Music as Heard: Listeners and Listening in Late-Medieval and Early Modern Europe (1300–1600)', Princeton University, 27–8 September 1997). *Musical Quarterly*, 82/3–4 (1998)

Whenham, J., '"Aria" in the Madrigals of Giovanni Rovetta'. In Fenlon and Carter (eds), '*Con che soavità*', pp. 135–53

8

Power and display: music in court theatre

LOIS ROSOW

The seventeenth century inherited a well-established tradition of magnificent courtly spectacle. For centuries, European rulers had celebrated special occasions with feasts, tournaments and jousts, and parade-like entries into their domains, all involving spectacular decoration, costume and pageantry. By the latter part of the sixteenth century, particularly under the influence of the Medici court in Florence, such events had developed a vocabulary and set of values that reflected both the Humanist spirit of the age and the growing notion of the prince as the repository of absolute power.[1] From these elements came important new theatrical genres in which music played a central part.

The Medici, and those who emulated them, regarded magnificence as a princely virtue. Lavish spending on building projects and artworks served the state by displaying the monarch's power and prestige. Moreover, the arts had a special ability to express the court's values and confirm the importance of politically significant events. Theatrical spectacles brought the arts together. According to the Neoplatonic ideals of the era, poetry, music, dance, painting and architecture, working in harmony, were thought to reflect in microcosm the orderly harmony of the universe, recreated here on earth under the wise and virtuous rule of the prince. Theatrical entertainments were thus an important part of major dynastic celebrations. Though ephemeral, such entertainments were often recorded in lavish detail in commemorative volumes sponsored by the court; the music, too, might sometimes be published. Those who were not privileged to attend could thus experience the event vicariously, in all its magnificence. Only unofficial or private descriptions were likely to mention the imperfections of the occasion – for instance, the stage machinery that refused to work properly or the discomfort of the hall – thus underscoring the propagandistic nature of the official record.

Essential to the theatrical experience at these events was a sense of wonder, exalted by theorists of the time (following Aristotle) for its ability to arouse the emotions.[2] Theatres and theatrical spaces had developed accordingly. To

---

1 Strong, *Art and Power.*   2 Ibid., p. 39; Ossi, '*Dalle machine . . . la maraviglia*', pp. 15–17.

the Italian courts of the Renaissance we owe the modern theatre with raked stage, wings and proscenium arch; movable scenery in single-point perspective; and machinery allowing mythological gods to descend and scenery to change instantaneously and spectacularly, in full view of the audience.[3] (According to the conventions of the time, the curtain, once open, did not close until the end of the play.) While theatrical spaces varied according to locale and genre, they normally featured the central placement of the monarch as the principal member of the audience, directly opposite the focal point of the scenery, and thus a focal point himself (or herself). From this privileged position the ruler experienced a drama that allegorically or metaphorically celebrated the strength of the state.

Yet not all of the productions held at palace venues were official state occasions promoted by the ruler. Some were sponsored by learned academies or individual aristocrats, and these – if they were documented at all – were clearly sometimes modest in presentation. Still, the economics of these productions, generally involving artists connected to the court and a private, non-paying audience, resembled those of official court celebrations more than those of the public theatre. Moreover, aristocratic sponsorship of such events reflected the high value placed on intellectual accomplishment and artistic connoisseurship, as advocated since the time of Baldassare Castiglione's influential *Book of the Courtier* (*Il libro del cortigiano*, 1528). These were the same cultural values that drove the patricians who organised and directed official state-sponsored theatrical events at the Medici court and elsewhere.

While theatrical entertainments occurred at courts throughout seventeenth-century Europe, the following discussion is limited to several important topics that are linked by ethos if not always by direct historical connections: two seminal events of the 1580s, the *Ballet comique de la reine* and the *intermedi* for *La pellegrina*; the invention of opera around the turn of the century and the first operatic masterpiece, Monteverdi's *Orfeo*; dynastic festivals in northern Italy in the early decades of the century; the Stuart court masque; the Barberini operas in Rome; Italian influences in mid-century Paris and Madrid; and ballet and opera at the French court under Louis XIV.

Setting the stage (1): the *Ballet comique de la reine*

The significance of court spectacle is well exemplified by two celebrated, and also seminal, theatrical events in the 1580s, one at the royal court of France

---

3 Povoledo, 'Origins and Aspects of Italian Scenography'; Nagler, *A Source Book in Theatrical History*, pp. 15–35, 297–305; Ossi, '*Dalle machine . . . la maraviglia*', pp. 15–35.

(where the queen mother was a Medici), and the other at the grand-ducal court of Florence. In 1581 Henri III of France arranged the marriage of the queen's sister, Marguerite of Lorraine, to one of his favourite courtiers, the Duc de Joyeuse. Among the high points of the two weeks of festivities was a theatrical production known simply as the *Ballet comique de la reine* ('The queen's comic ballet'). This was devised principally by a violinist and choreographer at court, Balthazar de Beaujoyeux, a transplanted Italian. Working with him was a court poet named La Chesnaye, the court composer Lambert de Beaulieu, and the court painter Jacques Patin. (It is interesting that the more celebrated court artists, the poets Pierre Ronsard and Jean-Antoine de Baïf and the composer Claude Lejeune, were allocated the tournament, carousel, banquet and the like, leaving the theatre piece to their less important colleagues.) The following year Beaujoyeux published an elegant commemorative volume giving a detailed account of the event, along with the complete text of the work. It included numerous illustrations by Patin and music for the songs and dances. Thus although this work was performed only once, we have a good deal of evidence on which to build an assessment of it.

Beaujoyeux explained his use of the word 'comique': 'I called [the story] comic more for its beautiful, calm and happy conclusion than for the quality of the characters, who are nearly all gods and goddesses or other heroic persons'.[4] The plot, derived from Greek mythology, pits the evil power of the enchantress Circé against the virtuous power of the King of France. Though this was a politically and financially difficult time at the French court, the work presents Henri's reign as a golden age, equivalent to that of ancient myth, and Henri himself as the sole power capable of vanquishing Circé. The performance took place in the Great Hall of the Louvre, the king enthroned at the centre, the queen mother beside him, and the other spectators in two-tiered balconies on either side. Directly opposite the king at the far end of the hall was Circé's beautiful enchanted garden. Though there was no raised stage, her castle and a town receded in the distance behind the garden according to the rules of perspective. Lovely trellises framed the garden, artfully hiding the entrances for performers on either side. Under the spectators' balconies to the king's left was a 'gilded vault' hiding a large number of instrumentalists and singers. Under the balconies to the right were a forest inhabited by the god Pan and a grotto with more musicians. A cloud machine attached to the ceiling enabled two of the gods to descend to earth.

---

4 B. de Beaujoyeux, *Balet comique de la royne* (Paris, 1582), facs. ed. M. McGowan, 'Medieval and Renaissance Text and Studies', 6 (Binghamton, NY, 1982), 'Au lecteur'. McGowan's introduction here is particularly useful. For a modern edition with English translation, see MacClintock and MacClintock (eds), *Le ballet comique de la royne*, at p. 33.

The story unfolds in an almost seamless intermingling of long solo speeches in alexandrines (the standard twelve-syllable lines of spoken French plays), strophic songs for soloists and ensembles, and two important and lengthy dance episodes, one of them at the very end. For five and a half hours the spectators saw a succession of entrances by mortals, gods and minor deities such as nymphs and satyrs, all in elaborate costume and some on richly decorated floats. In addition to speaking or singing, each character or group 'passed before the king', then 'made its tour around the hall'. Some interacted with others in pantomime as part of the drama (apparently without accompanying music, or at least, without any that was notated). Many of these roles were taken by courtiers; others, involving singing or the playing of instruments, were taken by professional court musicians.

Queen Louise herself and eleven of her ladies (including the bride), dressed as bejewelled naiads, were the principal performers in both sets of dances. The elaborate, complex choreography was deceptively simple in conception: a seemingly endless set of geometrical figures (triangles and the like) continuously evolving out of each other – forming, breaking apart and re-forming. The inspiration for this style had come from Baïf's Académie de Poésie et de Musique, which a decade earlier had set out to rediscover the union of poetry and music in antiquity, and had ultimately encompassed dance in its programme as well. According to the academy's Neoplatonic cosmology, geometrical forms were thought to contain hidden meanings and eternal truths. By 'writing' these shapes on the dance floor for the monarch to read, and in the process subordinating their personal individuality to patterns intelligible only as a harmonious whole, the ladies enacted the ideal of a courtly community, itself a reflection of the orderly harmony of the universe. The dance movements themselves were probably more dynamic than serene, with brusque transitions and an exhilarating sense of controlled chaos between figures; the nymphs did not simply glide from one shape to another.[5] Viewed from the balconies above, this precise patterning by the queen and her ladies must have been very impressive.

The songs involved a different kind of patterning, with choral refrains between stanzas often provided by characters other than those singing the stanzas, or by the ensemble of singers hidden in the vault. They too were inspired by the theories of Baïf's academy, in particular the subservience of musical rhythms to speech rhythms. Many songs in the *Ballet comique* are essentially syllabic settings, in the rhythmic style known as *musique mesurée à l'antique*, emphasising note-values in a 2 : 1 ratio (for 'long' and 'short' syllables) in a metrically flexible musical context. In ensemble pieces, chordal textures are

---

5 Franko, *Dance as Text*, pp. 21–5.

emphasised; the solos include a filigree of melodic ornamentation. In the commemorative volume, Beaujoyeux often mentions the music with admiration. Thus, for instance, the organ music from Pan's grotto was 'sweet, pleasant and harmonious'; and the resonant sound of the ensembles inside the gilded vault was, 'according to those learned in Platonic philosophy, the true harmony of the heavens'.[6]

An unusual item, which prefigures the dialogue *airs* of seventeenth-century French ballet and opera, is the dialogue of Glaucus and Tethys. It unfolds in eight-line stanzas, each comprising four alexandrines for Glaucus and four lines in *vers libres* (mixed line-lengths) for Tethys – with polyphonic interjections by a chorus of Tritons echoing Tethys's words after each exchange – and then reaches a climax in the last stanza with a burst of florid melismas and an accelerated rate of alternation by the soloists, masking the unchanged pattern of line-lengths. Here Tethys confesses that her powers have been transferred to 'the nymph' Louise, who then dances with her ladies.

At the end, with a clap of thunder, Jupiter descended, accompanied in six-part harmony by 40 voices and instruments hidden in the gilded vault, singing the praises of the kings of France for banishing war and promoting virtue. Circé was defeated, and her wand presented to Henri. After general praise for the king and queen mother, the performance concluded with the grand ballet by the queen and her ladies (the twelve naiads now interacting with four dryads), its ever-changing geometrical figures celebrating peace and order. Then the spectators were invited to join the richly costumed performers in a ball, thus affirming the symbolic inseparability of the ideal world of the ballet and the real world of the court.

Beyond courtly circles, there was considerable grumbling in Paris about the enormous expense of the wedding festivities. Yet the actual precariousness of his court must have been precisely the reason why Henri celebrated this wedding in such a lavish fashion. However, the intended demonstration of strength was a futile gesture. Nothing so grand happened again, political troubles grew, and with the assassination of Henri III in July 1589, the Valois dynasty came to an end.

The *Ballet comique de la reine* was not the first Valois entertainment to integrate music and dance with drama and political allegory, or to focus on geometrical dancing of this type (itself an outgrowth of Italian choreography), but it transcended its predecessors in variety and splendour. Moreover, none had hitherto been documented so thoroughly or so publicly. Beaujoyeux himself presented his creation as a novelty, explaining in his prefatory note to the reader that

6 Beaujoyeux, *Balet comique de la royne*, ff. 39r, 5v.

in order to create something 'magnificent and triumphant', he had decided to mix dance and drama together, and 'to diversify music with poetry and interlace poetry with music'. He further clarified that he had 'at all times given the highest honour to dance, and the second to the plot . . . Thus I have brought the ballet to life and made it speak, and made the comedy sing and resound.'

This celebrated entertainment is generally credited with giving rise to the *ballet de cour* (court ballet) tradition that flourished in France for about a century. Ironically, Beaujoyeux's 'comedy' as a whole, with its lengthy speeches and well-developed plot, is atypical of the genre. Spoken text was rare in seventeenth-century ballets, and a unified dramatic structure was the norm only around the second decade of the seventeenth century.[7] Yet the *Ballet comique* contains the genre's essential elements: choreographed dances for courtiers, richly costumed and masked to represent allegorical, mythological, chivalric or burlesque characters; interpolated vocal *airs*; a theatrical setting. The *ballet de cour* quickly established itself as the dominant form of music theatre at the French court, and one that strongly influenced courtly entertainments in other parts of Europe as well.

Setting the stage (2): the *intermedi* for *La pellegrina*

In May 1589, eight years after the performance of the *Ballet comique*, a politically more important wedding occurred at the Medici court in Florence, then at the height of its power and prestige. The new Grand Duke of Tuscany, Ferdinando I, married Christine of Lorraine, niece of Henri III; Ferdinando thus allied himself with the court of France and distanced himself from his predecessor's pro-Habsburg policies. Thanks to the Medici propaganda machine, all the events of the three-week wedding celebration were painstakingly documented.[8]

The festivities reached a grand climax in the *intermedi* for the comedy *La pellegrina* by Girolamo Bargagli. *Intermedi*, musical interludes framing the acts of spoken plays, had developed in the northern Italian courts over the course of the preceding century. By the late sixteenth century, those at the Medici court were spectacular mythological tableaux, grandiose spectacles that overshadowed the play itself in importance. The Uffizi Theatre, built three years earlier and remodelled for this occasion, permitted the most impressive scenic illusions ever seen.

While the acts of *La pellegrina* all took place in the same setting, a realistic view in perspective of the Tuscan city of Pisa, the scenery of the *intermedi* underwent

7 Prunières, *Le ballet de cour en France avant Benserade et Lulli*, pp. 110–23, 249–65.

8 Saslow, *The Medici Wedding of 1589*. For the music, see D. P. Walker (ed.), *Les fêtes du mariage de Ferdinand de Médicis et de Christine de Lorraine: Florence 1589*, i: *Musique des intermèdes de 'La pellegrina': édition critique* (Paris, 1963; repr. 1986).

a series of spectacular metamorphoses in full view of the audience. As was customary at the time, the official description (by the Humanist scholar Bastiano de' Rossi) refers repeatedly to the astonishment of the audience over the various scenic effects – for instance, Apollo descended 'from the skies, to the utter stupefaction of all who saw it: a ray of light could not have descended more quickly, as he appeared miraculously (for, whatever the mechanism that held him up, it was not visible)'.[9] The nominal stage-director and creative overseer of the *intermedi* was the courtier Giovanni de' Bardi (1534–1612), working in concert with the architect–engineer Bernardo Buontalenti. (We now know Bardi's name primarily in connection with the so-called 'Camerata' that had gathered at his palace during the 1570s and early 1580s to discuss the arts and music according to ancient principles.) In actuality, the Roman composer Emilio de' Cavalieri (*c.* 1550–1602), whom the grand duke had recently brought to Florence, seems to have had substantial authority, and there was apparently considerable friction between him and Bardi. Several additional composers and poets contributed to the *intermedi*, principally the musicians Luca Marenzio and Cristofano Malvezzi and the poet Ottavio Rinuccini (1562–1621). The composer–singers Jacopo Peri (1561–1633) and Giulio Caccini (1551–1618) made smaller contributions; they (along with Rinuccini) would soon play important roles in the development of opera. Several of these artists had been involved in the Camerata's recent discussions on musical reform.

The six *intermedi*, forming a prologue, entr'actes and an epilogue to the play, celebrated the power of music. The first dealt with the Platonic 'music of the spheres': Dorian Harmony, represented allegorically by the famous soprano Vittoria Archilei, appeared on a cloud, singing a highly ornamental line to the accompaniment of lutes: 'From the highest spheres . . . I am Harmony who comes to you, o mortals . . .' Then the backdrop opened to reveal the starry heavens and an orderly Platonic cosmos, populated by heavenly bodies and mythological figures, all sitting on clouds and singing nuptial blessings for Ferdinando and Christine. The central four *intermedi* represented mythological tales: the triumph of the Muses in a singing contest; Apollo's victory over the Python; the apparition of celestial and infernal spirits; and Arion rescued from the sea by dolphins. Their settings included pastoral scenes, the heavens, the Underworld as described in Dante's *Inferno*, and an ocean populated by gods and mythological sea creatures – thus, the four elements: earth, air, fire and water. Each tableau included flattering references to the nuptial couple and their hoped-for progeny. Moreover, the god Apollo in the third *intermedio* was understood to represent the grand duke. (Local courtiers, at least, would have

9 Weiss, *Opera*, p. 6.

been familiar with such Medici symbolism, made ubiquitous through numerous visual and poetic images.[10]) Finally, at the conclusion of *La pellegrina*, the gods descended to earth and taught the mortals to dance. Here deities joined a large chorus of nymphs and shepherds in a final choral *ballo* (ballet), in which Ferdinando's rule was represented as a golden age.

Each *intermedio* comprised a series of independent musical numbers, without any spoken words. The music includes virtuosic accompanied solo songs, ensemble madrigals in elaborate counterpoint, accompanied choruses for a choir located in a balcony at the back of the hall, and sinfonias (instrumental movements). A wide variety of bowed, plucked and wind instruments were used, and these had symbolic connotations: for instance, harps, citterns and viols for the celestial spirits gave way to viols, a *lira* and trombones for the infernal ones. While a number of singers carried instruments and accompanied themselves, most accompanying instruments were placed behind the scenes. Only one madrigal setting, by Bardi himself, reflects the intellectual preoccupations of the musical reformers by being chordal in texture and sensitive to poetic declamation.

Florentine *intermedi*, and this set in particular, served as an important precursor both to opera and to seventeenth-century ballet and masque. Elements widely imitated throughout Europe include the stagecraft and supernatural spectacle, the stock pastoral and Underworld settings, and the use of allegorical figures. More narrowly, the *intermedi* perpetuated longstanding poetic forms and musical traditions in Italy, such as, for instance, the 'echo lament'.[11] The 1589 *intermedi*, moreover, were also influential because of their conclusion. While sets of *intermedi* conventionally ended with a dance, the *ballo* by Cavalieri that concluded the final *intermedio* in 1589, celebrating the union of gods and mortals, was unusually complex in construction, perhaps in emulation of French ballet. Detailed choreography, for seven principal dancers and twenty others surrounding the principals in a semicircle, was published along with the music in 1591. (The official description of the festival gives a somewhat different version of the *ballo* from the one found in this after-the-fact publication. The former presumably reflects Bardi's original conception rather than Cavalieri's final product.) While the steps were those of social dance, the frequent leaps and intricacy of the floor patterns transcended the normal behaviours of the ballroom, suggesting that heavenly perfection could be attained in Ferdinando's realm.[12]

The music involves an alternation of segments for five-part chorus with accompanying instruments, and sections for a trio of dancing soprano soloists,

10 Hanning, 'Glorious Apollo', pp. 500–501.   11 Sternfeld, *The Birth of Opera*, pp. 197–226.
12 Mamone, 'La danza di scena negli intermedi fiorentini', pp. 18–19.

accompanying themselves on guitars and a *cembalino*. (The three ladies, who had descended to the stage on a cloud, were apparently Florence's answer to the famous *concerto di donne* at the rival court of Ferrara.) An associate of Cavalieri's later wrote that the 1589 *ballo* had been 'sung by the same as those who danced'.[13] This statement clearly refers to the trio of sopranos. It presumably also indicates that the twenty figurants, whose steps were much simpler than those of the seven principal dancers, doubled the choir in the balcony. By emulating the choruses of antiquity, which were thought to have danced while singing,[14] Cavalieri took quite a different approach to the relationship of song and dance from that evident in Valois court ballet, where dances were untexted.

After initial statements of the basic material in the two textures, the music continues with an orderly series of fragmentary references to that material. An intricate pattern of metres, comprising duple, slow triple and fast triple, complements the pattern of segmentation.[15] The published description of the *ballo* specifies that the words – by Laura Lucchesini de' Guidiccioni, 'prominent gentlewoman from the city of Lucca' – were written 'following' Cavalieri's choreography and music. Thus the metrical changes and repetitive patterns within the music controlled the poetry, not the other way around.

This particular *ballo* turned out to be enormously influential, and not only on the stage. The catchy bass pattern, identified as either the *Aria di Fiorenza* or the *Ballo del Granduca*, took on a life of its own: it was the basis for numerous sets of instrumental variations in the ensuing decades.[16] Direct imitations of the *ballo* itself appeared in a number of theatrical entertainments in Florence and beyond during the early seventeenth century. Moreover, these general principles for structuring theatrical dance music – from interlocking variations of basic material, and with musical structure controlling poetic structure – would resonate in French opera a century later.

The beginnings of opera

Shortly after the 1589 wedding, several members of the creative team for the *intermedi* became involved with the nobleman and amateur musician Jacopo Corsi, whose Florentine home served as a gathering place for poets, musicians and scholars. They developed an interest in the rich possibilities of the pastoral,

13 E. de Cavalieri, *Rappresentatione di Anima, et di Corpo* (Rome, 1600; repr. Bologna, 1977), preface (by Alessandro Guidotti), trans. in Carter and Szweykowski (eds), *Composing Opera*, pp. 78–9.

14 Fenlon, 'The Origins of the Seventeenth-Century Staged *Ballo*', pp. 28–9.

15 There is a helpful table in Sternfeld, *The Birth of Opera*, p. 95.

16 Bianconi, *Music in the Seventeenth Century*, p. 99; Kirkendale, '*L'Aria di Fiorenza*' id est '*Il Ballo del Granduca*'.

a dramatic genre laden with opportunities for songs, dances and choruses. Recent inspiration came from pastorals by the Ferrarese court poets Torquato Tasso and Battista Guarini; an older model, Angelo Poliziano's *La favola d'Orfeo* of *c.* 1480, provided additional stimulus. Cavalieri was the first in this group to collaborate on such productions; unfortunately, his music for *Il satiro* and *La disperatione di Fileno* (1590), and *Il giuoco della cieca* (1595, based on an episode in Guarini's *Il pastor fido*), is now lost. A decisive step in a new direction, towards what Cavalieri would later call *recitar cantando* ('to declaim in song'),[17] was taken by Rinuccini, Peri and Corsi in the mid 1590s. Inspired by the 'belief of many' that ancient tragedy might have been sung throughout (a much-discussed topic in the late sixteenth century), and looking for new means of expression in their own music,[18] they experimented by preparing an entirely sung pastoral play entitled *Dafne*. Only fragments of the score are known today, though Rinuccini's poetry survives intact. *Dafne*, first performed at Corsi's palace for Carnival in 1598, was repeated as a Carnival entertainment in successive years.

An opportunity to build on *Dafne*'s success came in October 1600, in the celebrations honouring the wedding of Maria de' Medici and King Henri IV of France. Caccini, whose experiments in new modes of musical expression had thus far concentrated on songs for the chamber, was invited to compose the music for the major theatrical entertainment of the festivities: a pastoral by Gabriello Chiabrera entitled *Il rapimento di Cefalo*.[19] The score is now lost except for fragments, but the words were apparently sung throughout. The performance took place in the Uffizi Theatre, with spectacular staging and machinery, and before an enormous audience: 3,000 gentlemen and 800 ladies, according to the official report. At the other end of the spectrum was the modest production sponsored by Corsi and held in a relatively small room in the Pitti Palace for no more than 200 guests: the sung pastoral *Euridice*, with poetry by Rinuccini and music by Peri.

Apart from its lavish scenic effects, *Il rapimento di Cefalo* made a poor impression. The music was tedious, 'like the chanting of the Passion' according to one audience member. As for *Euridice*, the scenery was incomplete, and petty personal squabbles marred the presentation. The Florentines' jealousy of the Roman Cavalieri was exceeded only by the rivalry between Caccini and Peri. Caccini had made his own setting of Rinuccini's text for *Euridice* and insisted that singers in his stable should perform his music instead of Peri's. Thus the audience was treated to a Euridice singing Caccini's music, performing alongside Peri in the role of Orfeo, singing his own music. While court

17 The phrase appears on the title-page of Cavalieri's *Rappresentatione di Anima, et di Corpo.*
18 Carter, 'Jacopo Peri's *Euridice* (1600)', p. 87 and n. 18 (quoting Rinuccini's preface to *Euridice*).
19 Carter, 'Rediscovering *Il rapimento di Cefalo*'.

entertainments of the time often involved contributions by more than one composer, in this case Peri had composed a complete score, and Caccini's intrusions probably distorted its character.[20]

Cavalieri, who had supervised the festivities, returned to Rome in disgust. His own experiment with 'declaiming in song', a spiritual work entitled *Rappresentatione di Anima, et di Corpo* ('Drama of the Soul and the Body'), now regarded as his masterpiece, had been produced in a Roman oratory the previous winter. In view of the atmosphere of competition, it is hardly surprising that the three composers had their scores published in quick succession in autumn 1600 and early winter 1601: first Cavalieri's *Rappresentatione*, then Caccini's *Euridice* (rushed into print to precede Peri's though no performance had yet occurred), and finally Peri's *Euridice*. The extravagant claims made in the prefaces to these publications make clear the importance these artists placed on finding new musical means to move the emotions.[21] In the end it was Peri's approach to musical recitation that caught the imagination of the musicians and literati who studied the scores and read the prefaces. Rinuccini and Peri's *Euridice* thus provided the stylistic foundation for the genre that eventually came to be called 'opera'.

Euridice tells the mythological tale of Orpheus and Eurydice.[22] Though not divided explicitly into acts, it is presented in a Classical five episodes, separated by choruses in strophic verse. The opening and closing scenes of general rejoicing provide a frame. Each episode is dominated by an expansive monologue: Orfeo expressing his happiness in a hymn to nature; the nymph Dafne recounting Euridice's tragic death; the shepherd Arcetro describing the rescue of Orfeo by Venere (Venus) in a golden chariot; Orfeo, having been brought to the gates of Hell by Venere, lamenting Euridice's death so movingly that the gates open; and, back in the pastoral world, the shepherd Aminta sharing the good news that Plutone (Pluto) has returned Euridice to Orfeo. The chorus is used flexibly: as participants in the action during the episodes, and as a 'Greek chorus', offering commentary at the ends of episodes. The final scene of rejoicing concludes with an intricately patterned *ballo*. Rinuccini eliminated any requirement that Orfeo not look back while leading Euridice out of Hades: as he explained in his prefatory letter dedicating the printed libretto to the new queen, 'Some perhaps may think it excessively bold in me to have altered the ending of the fable of Orpheus; but I thought it more seemly to do so on so festive

20 Harness, '*Le tre Euridice*'.

21 See the material translated in Carter and Szweykowski (eds), *Composing Opera*, pp. 21–42, 69–88; Weiss, *Opera*, pp. 11–23.

22 J. Peri, *Le musiche . . . sopra Euridice* (Florence, 1600; repr. Bologna, 1969), ed. H. M. Brown, 'Recent Researches in the Music of the Baroque Era', 36–7 (Madison, WI, 1981).

an occasion, having as my justification the example of Greek poets in other fables'.[23]

In keeping with the conventions of the time, a prologue in strophic poetry introduces the work. It is sung by La Tragedia (Tragedy), represented allegorically by a soprano. She explains that in honour of the royal wedding, she will banish her usual topics and 'tune her song to happier strings'. Thus Rinuccini invokes ancient tragedy, the avowed inspiration for presenting drama in song, but declares that this play will evoke 'sweet pleasure' rather than the pity and terror that preceded Aristotelian catharsis.[24]

Contemporary theorists of the stage cited the relatively new genre of the pastoral play as an appropriate literary type for opera because of its mythological setting: while ordinary people converse in prose, the shepherds and deities of ancient Arcadia could reasonably be presumed to have communicated in poetry and music.[25] Thus a play could be sung throughout without violating the expectations of verisimilitude. In this particular case, moreover, the myth provided a special opportunity for the use of music to advance the plot: Orpheus was known for his musical abilities and used them to overcome the power of Hades. In general, the versions of mythological stories favoured for opera were those of the ancient Roman poet Ovid, as told in his *Metamorphoses*, tales of magical transformation. The interventions by gods and goddesses, along with the transformations they might cause, provided opportunities for spectacle. Even a simple theatre without machinery could manage an effective scenic transformation by sliding new sidepieces in from the wings and simultaneously changing the backdrop. Michelangelo Buonarroti 'il giovane' described the first of the two scenic transformations in *Euridice* thus:

> [There] appeared the most beautiful woods, both painted and in relief, arranged with good design and, through the clever disposition of the lighting, seeming to be full of daylight. But when it became necessary that the Inferno should be seen, everything changed, and we saw fearful and horrible rocks which seemed real; and above them appeared leafless stumps and ashen grass. And yonder, through a crack in a large rock, we perceived that the city of Dis burned, pulsating tongues of flame [visible] through the openings of its towers, the air around blazing with a colour like that of copper.[26]

Of course, Rinuccini's inspiration came as much from the treatment of mythology and the supernatural in Florentine *intermedi* as from the recent pastoral

---

23 Weiss, *Opera*, p. 13.   24 Hanning, *Of Poetry and Music's Power*, pp. 4–5.

25 Battista Guarini, in Pirrotta, *Music and Theatre from Poliziano to Monteverdi*, pp. 264–5; Anon., *Il corago*, in Bianconi, *Music in the Seventeenth Century*, p. 175; Giovanni Battista Doni, in Hanning, *Of Poetry and Music's Power*, p. 46.

26 Whenham (ed.), *Claudio Monteverdi: 'Orfeo'*, p. 47.

plays he had encountered in Corsi's salon. Indeed, the plot of *Dafne* expands the third *intermedio* from the production of 1589, for which Rinuccini himself had been the poet.

Peri's novel contribution was his musical version of dramatic declamation – what later came to be called 'recitative'. Apart from a few closed forms, most of Rinuccini's poetry for the dialogues and monologues in *Euridice* consists of *versi sciolti*: rhymed, freely alternating seven- and eleven-syllable lines, with the final accent most often on the penultimate syllable. This was standard madrigal poetry, but unlike madrigals, Peri's recitative abandons a consistent contrapuntal relationship between melody and bass line. Instead, the bass moves very slowly, with harmonic changes limited to major stressed syllables, selected to mimic the natural cadences of speech. 'I realised', Peri wrote in his preface to the published score, 'that in our speech some words are intoned in such a manner that harmony can be founded upon them, and that while speaking we pass through many others which are not intoned, until we return to another capable of movement to a new consonance'.[27] Coupled with this harmonic procedure was a supple handling of melodic rhythm and pitch accent, imitating the ebb and flow of an actor's declamation.[28] Instruments placed backstage provided a basso continuo accompaniment: a harpsichord, a large *lira* (a bowed instrument), a large lute and a *chitarrone*.[29] Eight years later, in the preface to his own setting of Rinuccini's *Dafne*, the composer Marco da Gagliano (1582–1643) would refer to Peri's 'discovery' as 'that artful manner of sung speech that all Italy admires'.[30]

Monteverdi's *Orfeo*

The central role of Florence in the development of theatrical spectacle involving music was not lost on Duke Vincenzo Gonzaga of Mantua. In a spirit of emulation and competition, he determined to increase the importance of his own court as a centre for theatre. Starting in 1592, he worked for several years to arrange the first full-scale staging of Guarini's important play *Il pastor fido*, finally succeeding in 1598. The long delay resulted mainly from technical problems with the 'Giuoco della cieca' (blind-man's buff) scene in Act II, where music had to be fitted to pre-existing choreography, and words then fitted to the music (a compositional order of events we have already encountered in Cavalieri's *ballo* of 1589), after which three speeches had to be gracefully inserted among the four sung and danced madrigals.[31]

27 Carter, *Monteverdi's Musical Theatre*, p. 25.   28 Brown, 'How Opera Began', pp. 432–42.
29 Carter and Szweykowski (eds), *Composing Opera*, pp. 30–31; Weiss, *Opera*, p. 16.
30 Carter, *Monteverdi's Musical Theatre*, p. 17.
31 Fenlon, *Music and Patronage in Sixteenth-Century Mantua*, i: 146–52.

It is ironic that the work we now regard as the earliest operatic master-piece, which had its premiere at the Mantuan court on 24 February 1607, came into being with little public fanfare and left behind little formal record other than its libretto and score. The opera is *Orfeo* by Claudio Monteverdi (1567–1643), *maestro* of the duke's *musica di camera*. Information about the premiere comes mainly from private correspondence.[32] The plans for staging the story of Orpheus and Eurydice during Carnival, as a 'fable in music' (*favola in musica*), originated with Prince Francesco Gonzaga, Duke Vincenzo's heir. While the musical resources of the court were available for the occasion, the performance was intended not for a general courtly audience but for the membership of a learned academy to which Francesco Gonzaga belonged (the Accademia degli Invaghiti), and it occurred in a relatively intimate room in the palace, not a large theatre. The important tenor Francesco Rasi, a court singer, took the role of Orfeo. Other male court singers constituted a tiny chorus and took the other male roles. Female performers were excluded: Francesco Gonzaga obtained from the Medici court the loan of a castrato who joined others to sing the female roles. The libretto, by the court poet and secretary Alessandro Striggio (d. 1630; also a member of the academy), was printed and made avail-able to members of the audience so they could follow along. The novelty of the event is clear from a letter written by a court official, Carlo Magno: 'Tomorrow evening the Most Serene Lord the Prince [Francesco Gonzaga] is to sponsor a performance . . . It should be most unusual, as all the actors are to sing their parts.'[33] In addition to the premiere – attended by the duke and duchess as well as the gentlemen of the academy – a court-sponsored performance was given for the ladies of the city. Though the court produced no official record of any performance, a commemorative score was printed in 1609, with a dedication by Monteverdi to Francesco Gonzaga; it must have sold well, for the same publisher brought out a second edition (without dedication) in 1615.[34]

Orfeo is divided into five 'acts' – not separate acts in the modern sense but episodes that were performed without break (as in Peri's *Euridice*, which clearly served as a model).[35] As expected, the chorus participates in the action, and then marks the ends of episodes by offering some commentary or moral. The general shape of the work is much like that of *Euridice*, with outer portions in the pastoral world (Acts I–II and V) framing a central section in the Underworld (Acts III–IV). Unlike Rinuccini, however, Striggio retained Euridice's double death as in the myth: Orfeo looks back as he leads her away from the Inferno

32 Fenlon, 'The Mantuan *Orfeo*'.   33 Ibid., p. 1.
34 C. Monteverdi, *L'Orfeo: favola in musica* (Venice, 1609; repr. Kassel, 1998), 2nd edn (Venice, 1615; repr. Farnborough, 1972).
35 Whenham (ed.), *Claudio Monteverdi: 'Orfeo'*, pp. 42–7.

and thus loses her again. Act v is dominated by Orfeo's extended lament over this second loss.

From that point forward the libretto and score differ. Striggio's libretto follows the myth (though without its explicit violence): Orfeo flees an angry chorus of Bacchantes. Monteverdi's score, published two years after the libretto, omits the Bacchantes and substitutes a *deus ex machina* to effect a happy ending: Apollo descends, takes pity on his son Orfeo and transports him to the heavens where he will see Euridice in the sun and stars for eternity. The date of the revision is unknown, but the style of the poetry suggests that Monteverdi turned to someone other than Striggio as his collaborator, perhaps to Rinuccini.[36] A possible motive for preparing a happier ending might have been a performance planned for spring 1607 (which never actually took place), intended to honour the Duke of Savoy as Prince Francesco's future father-in-law.[37]

Orfeo begins with an instrumental fanfare (called 'toccata'). Then, as one would expect, an allegorical figure presents a prologue in strophic verse (quatrains of eleven-syllable lines, as was the norm). It is La Musica (Music), who addresses her audience as 'heroes' of noble blood. This deferential gesture, intended here for the Gonzaga family, was emerging as a convention of the genre. In identifying herself ('I am Music'), she extols her power to move the passions and to 'enfold souls' in the 'harmony of heaven', and she makes clear the reason for her interest in Orpheus, whose music tamed the Inferno. As was customary for such prologues, Monteverdi sets the text as strophic variations, the harmonies of the basso continuo remaining constant from one stanza to another, but each stanza having its own expressive vocal declamation. (Peri presumably intended the same effect in his prologue to *Euridice*, though he wrote out the music for only one stanza and left the rest to the singer.[38]) Framing and separating the stanzas is an instrumental ritornello, during which La Musica might have walked about the stage.[39]

Thus Striggio and Monteverdi announce in the prologue that their 'favola in musica' will use music to celebrate music. The building blocks are drawn from the standard musical fare of late Renaissance Italy, along with such forward-looking elements as vocal virtuosity, duet textures for two treble voices or instruments with bass, ritornello structures and recitative. There are strophic songs (representing actual songs sung by the characters in the drama), both in traditional verse forms and in the light canzonetta poetry that had recently become popular; five-part madrigals sung by the chorus; a *balletto* in a succession

36 Hanning, 'The Ending of *L'Orfeo*'.
37 Fenlon, 'The Mantuan *Orfeo*', p. 18; compare other theories summarised in Kelly, *First Nights*, pp. 351–2.
38 Hansen, 'From Invention to Interpretation'.
39 Savage and Sansone, '*Il corago* and the Staging of Early Opera', p. 500.

of metres (sung as well as danced); and sinfonias, ritornellos and accompaniments provided by a large and colourful array of instruments. Complementing these elements are introductory and linking statements in recitative, expressive recitative monologues that reflect Monteverdi's longstanding techniques as a composer of madrigals, and occasional moments of passionate recitative dialogue.

The musical and dramatic centre-piece of the work is Orfeo's prayer to Caronte (Charon) in Act III, 'Possente spirto e formidabil nume', a set of strophic variations over a slow-moving bass. In this aria Orfeo pleads to be allowed into the Underworld, modelled again on the Hell of Dante's *Inferno*. Dante's famous inscription, 'Abandon all hope, ye who enter', appears over the gates, and as in the Florentine *intermedi*, the solemn sound of trombones marks the Underworld setting. (The poetic form of Orfeo's stanzas, *terza rima*, is another reference to Dante.) The audience of 1607 would have known that Dante's Charon is a 'demon . . . with eyes of burning coal'. Monteverdi gave Caronte a bass voice, a sign of his advanced age and authority, and designated a strident reed organ to accompany him. It is this frightful figure that Orfeo addresses: 'Powerful spirit and formidable god'.

Orfeo attempts to persuade Caronte with the power of his singing. Monteverdi presented the vocal music in two parallel versions: one quite plain, indicating the basic melodic line, and the other with elaborate, virtuosic ornamentation of the sort a singer of the time would have added. (Might the ornamental version reflect Monteverdi's recollection of Rasi's performance?) Taking turns punctuating the vocal line and playing ritornellos between the stanzas are two violins, two cornetts, and a double harp; these instruments make echo effects that evoke the cavernous setting. After four stanzas of virtuosic display, during which Orfeo addresses Caronte, the text and music abruptly shift in style. As he addresses the absent Euridice ('O serene light of my eyes'), the bass line changes and Orfeo has just a simple melody; as he turns back to make one last plea to Caronte, the strophic bass returns for a final statement, but Orfeo continues to sing simply, now accompanied by an ensemble of bowed strings. The strings surely represent Orpheus's lyre, often depicted in the Renaissance as a *lira da braccio*;[40] Monteverdi maintains this musical association even though Striggio's libretto sometimes refers to the singer's instrument as a 'cetra' (cittern).

Caronte professes to be flattered but unmoved. Having failed to persuade him with splendour and virtuosity, Orfeo cries out in frustration and then tries another tack. Playing his lyre, he lulls Caronte to sleep and is thus able to cross the River Styx into the Underworld. Monteverdi directed the strings

40 Pirrotta, *Music and Theatre from Poliziano to Monteverdi*, illus. 5–6.

and organ to play this sinfonia 'very quietly'. Instructions by the composer Marco da Gagliano for a different opera (his own setting of Rinuccini's *Dafne*, performed in Mantua in 1608, with Rasi now in the role of Apollo) suggest a way in which the final stanza of the aria and the sinfonia might have been staged if Rasi held a bowed rather than plucked instrument:

> Since Apollo . . . must place the *lira* to his breast (which he must do with good attitude), it is necessary to make it appear to the auditorium that from Apollo's *lira* appears a more than ordinary melody. So let there be placed four string players (*da braccio* or *da gamba* matters little) in one of the exits close by, in a position where, unseen by the audience, they see Apollo, and as he places his bow on the *lira* they should play the three notes written, taking care to draw equal bow-strokes so that it appears one stroke only. This trick cannot be recognised except by the imagination of someone who knows about these things, and it brings no little delight.[41]

While La Musica's prologue refers only to the ability of music to move and to exalt, *Orfeo* also reveals inventive uses of music as an organising device, to control the pace and flow of a dramatic work. Act II, for instance, begins with eleven quatrains of light *canzonetta* poetry for Orfeo and various combinations of shepherds and nymphs. Monteverdi groups the six stanzas for the shepherds into three contrasting pairs, each pair having its own key and metre, as well as its own ritornello marked by distinctive instrumentation. He also elides all sections metrically, thus ensuring that the entire passage will be performed without a break, with stanzas and ritornellos in regular alternation. In this way, he creates the illusion of a series of strophic pieces, each cut short when interrupted by the ritornello for the next.[42] Only the climactic piece, the four-stanza 'Vi ricorda, o boschi ombrosi', where Orfeo contrasts the painful past with the joyful present in exuberant hemiola rhythms, is apparently heard in its entirety. Its final cadence thus makes a strong punctuation mark, clearly setting off the celebration just ended from the ensuing encounter between Orfeo and the Messenger. In that encounter it is the repetitions of the Messenger's initial cry of pain, and the eventual expansion of that cry into a moralising madrigal for the chorus, that provide internal punctuation. On a much larger scale, the recurrence of the ritornello from the Prologue at the end of Act II and again at the beginning of Act V, as a musical bridge between the pastoral world and the Underworld (and as an accompaniment to the changes of scenery), suggests a spatial as well as temporal linking and layering of segments. Like the patterned imagery of geometrical ballet, the refrain patterns in *Orfeo* combine balance and symmetry with dynamic motion.

---

41 Carter, *Monteverdi's Musical Theatre*, p. 90.
42 Ossi, 'Claudio Monteverdi's *Ordine novo, bello e gustevole*', pp. 283, 287–8.

This opera has another message besides the power of music, the one found in the succession of moralistic statements concluding the acts. These reveal *Orfeo* to be a human drama, the story of a young man unable to control his emotions. At the end of Act IV, the chorus summarises: 'Orfeo conquered the Inferno and was conquered by his own passions. Only he who is victorious over himself shall be worthy of eternal glory.' The revised ending of Act V contains a thinly veiled Christian message: Orfeo surrenders to the counsel of his 'heavenly father' Apollo and is rewarded with 'grace in heaven'.

Northern Italian festivals in the early decades of the century

Orfeo stood alone as a courtly entertainment: the Humanist project of a learned academy, it was a self-contained event. By contrast, a courtly entertainment celebrating a politically significant occasion belonged to a larger whole: a festival comprising a series of events. With the Medici in Florence as their model, the ruling families of Mantua, Modena and Ferrara, Parma, and Savoy strove to impress their guests with festivals of enormous magnificence and complexity.[43]

At major dynastic festivals nearly every activity was 'theatrical', in the broad sense of the word. For instance, at a wedding banquet in Turin in 1608, the goddess Ceres and her nymphs served the bread 'and made a beautiful ballet *entrée* around the table'.[44] Festivals at the Italian courts typically included plays and *intermedi* presented by professional actors and musicians, and sometimes operas as well. Otherwise, most entertainments were enacted in dance or pantomime by the courtiers themselves, with the help of professional singers and instrumentalists. Genres included staged military actions on mythological or chivalric themes – such as naval battles, tournaments and equestrian ballets – as well as masquerades and other genres focussed on dance. In addition to ancient mythology and other Classical sources, poets and choreographers borrowed material from the sixteenth century's two great epic romances of medieval chivalry: *Orlando furioso* (1516) by Lodovico Ariosto, and *Gerusalemme liberata* (1581) by Torquato Tasso.

Thanks both to the model provided by Cavalieri in 1589 and to Italian experiences at the French court – the poet Rinuccini in particular made frequent trips to France between 1600 and 1604 as a courtier of Maria de' Medici – theatrical genres featuring choreographed dance grew in importance, as did

43 Strong, *Art and Power*; Nagler, *Theatre Festivals of the Medici*; Molinari, *Le nozze degli dèi*; Southorn, *Power and Display in the Seventeenth Century*; Carter, 'The North Italian Courts'; Hill, 'Florence'.
44 Rizzi (ed.), *Repertorio di feste alla corte di Savoia (1346–1669) raccolto dai trattati di C. F. Menestrier*, p. 10, also given in J. Gordon, 'Entertainments for the Marriages of the Princesses of Savoy in 1608', p. 132.

choreographed dance episodes within *intermedi*. Sometimes dance pieces were texted, in which case they were sung chorally as well as danced (though not necessarily by the same performers). Important genres include the *ballo* or *balletto*, generally a short operatic work that culminated in choreographed ballet, and the *veglia*, a long evening entertainment that alternated scenes presented in song with choreographed ballet episodes. As in France, courtiers now did the dancing.

A much reproduced etching by Jacques Callot shows the first *intermedio* from a *veglia* entitled *La liberazione di Tirreno e d'Arnea, autori del sangue toscano*, performed in the Uffizi Theatre during a Florentine wedding festival in 1617.[45] The plot concerns the liberation of the mythical founders of Tuscany, Tirreno and Arnea, from the seductions of Circe, permitting their eventual union – an obvious reference to Florentine prestige and to the political importance of dynastic marriage. Though the libretto includes no singing roles for the title pair, this *intermedio* featured them in dance. The picture shows two graceful flights of steps at the front of the stage, allowing performers to descend into the auditorium, where the main floor area is open and free of seats. Some audience members occupy the raised seating on either side of the hall; others stand, forming a horseshoe around the perimeter of the open area. The rulers do not occupy their usual place of honour in the audience, for they are the principal dancers. Grand Duke Cosimo II and his wife Archduchess Maria Magdalena represent Tirreno and his beloved Arnea; other dancers act as his companions and her handmaidens. The etching conflates a series of actions: an Olympian chorus descends on a cloud machine over the scenery-filled stage; 22 dancers, in pairs, move from the stage to the floor; and once there they form concentric circles, with the grand duke and archduchess in the centre.[46] The artist captures well the graceful poses of the dancers, though not, of course, their movement. The engraving provides an excellent illustration of dance as an enactment of courtly power, and also of the way in which the typical early Baroque court theatre accommodated dance. This manner of organising a performance space clearly lent itself well to a pervading element of such events: the blurring of boundaries between heaven and earth, actor and audience, ideal and real.

The festivals for the wedding joining the ruling families of Mantua and Savoy in 1608 provide a useful illustration of the unified messages that might be presented with a series of entertainments. For Duke Carlo Emanuele I of Savoy,

45 Hill, 'Florence', illus. 27; Nagler, *Theatre Festivals of the Medici*, frontispiece; Ossi, '*Dalle machine . . . la maraviglia*', fig. 1.1; Pirrotta, *Music and Theatre from Poliziano to Monteverdi*, illus. 33; Strong, *Art and Power*, illus. 47.

46 Strong, *Art and Power*, pp. 57–8; Nagler, *Theatre Festivals of the Medici*, pp. 131–3; Solerti, *Musica, ballo e drammatica alla corte medicea dal 1600 al 1637*, pp. 121–4.

who strengthened his relationship with the other northern Italian duchies by simultaneously marrying his daughter Margherita to Francesco Gonzaga of Mantua and her sister Isabella to Alfonso d'Este of Modena, the central message of the festival in Turin was the internal stability and military strength of Savoy. He hoped for the eventual unification of the Italian states. Aside from the many chivalric events, the principal entertainment was a lengthy 'Balletto alla Savoiarda'. This comprised seven successive ballets celebrating the provinces and peoples of Savoy: fishermen of Nice, peasants of Val-d'Aoste, and so forth. Several days later, the festivities concluded with *Le trasformazioni di Millefonti*, an aquatic entertainment devised by the duke in collaboration with Ludovico d'Aglié. The play was presented 'in music and speeches' at the edge of a small lake, on a fanciful stage constructed of rocks, shells and mirrors, and decorated with waterfalls and statues of maritime deities. In the first of the aquatic *intermedi*, Arion arrived on the back of a dolphin via a canal, then he sang and accompanied himself on a harp; he was represented by 'the extremely famous Rasi', lent by the Duke of Mantua for the occasion. Rasi's performance was followed by a ballet of aquatic deities, dancing in the water. Then Amore (Cupid), dressed as a fisherman, recited the prologue (in *versi sciolti*): having changed his bow into a fishing-rod, he has gone fishing with golden hooks for the hearts and souls of lovers, in town and at court. Savoy, nestled in the Alps and blessed with a multitude of rivers, lakes and waterfalls, took particular delight in such aquatic imagery. Thus Duke Carlo Emanuele's festival combined images of love, appropriate to a wedding, with images of a prosperous and well-ordered domain.[47]

At the ensuing festivities in Mantua, Venus and Cupid certainly made appearances, as did local images that blurred the boundary between reality and myth: at the opening of the first *intermedio* for Guarini's play *L'idropica*, 'one saw . . . many palaces and towers standing out, partitioned by loggias and porticos done with such realism that everyone quickly recognised the scene for the city of Mantua'.[48] Nevertheless, a different thematic thread ran through the Mantuan festival, one that might alarm our 21st-century sensibilities. It is most starkly evident in Rinuccini and Monteverdi's *Ballo delle ingrate*, a relatively short work in which eight ladies and eight gentlemen, including Prince Francesco and Duke Vincenzo, represented the spirits of 'ungrateful ladies' consigned to eternal pain in the afterlife for refusing to fulfil the demands of Amore, despite their lovers' sighing and pleading. Wearing grotesque masks and ashen

47 J. Gordon, 'Entertainments for the Marriages of the Princesses of Savoy in 1608'; Bouquet-Boyer, 'Les éléments marins dans les spectacles à la cour de Savoie', pp. 58–9, 63; C.-F. Menestrier, *Traité des tournois, joustes, carrousels et autres spectacles publics* (Lyons, 1669), pp. 356–8.

48 Carter, 'The North Italian Courts', p. 37 (quoting Follino).

garments bejewelled with tears, they emerged in pairs from the mouth of Hades, led by Plutone (Pluto), and made their descent from the stage:

> Having reached the floor of the theatre, they did a *balletto* so beautiful and delightful, with steps, movements and actions now of grief and now of desperation, and now with gestures of pity and now of scorn, sometimes embracing each other as if they had tears of tenderness in their eyes, now striking each other swollen with rage and fury . . . There was no one in that theatre who did not feel his heart move and be disturbed in a thousand ways at the changing of their passions.[49]

Monteverdi's dance music follows Cavalieri's model: it comprises a series of sections based on two musical ideas, varied melodically and metrically. At the heart of the work, between its two dance episodes, Plutone (a singing role) delivered a series of moralising quatrains, addressed directly to the bride and the other ladies in the audience. (An extended dialogue of Venere and Amore that introduced the work and a sung lament that closed it were late additions, made to give the piece greater lustre in the face of competition from a rival creative team.[50]) Federico Follino's official description of the festivities, quoted above, suggests not geometrical dance but 'imitative' dance, in which the dancers' movements imitated the characters' passions. Theorists of the time described dance as 'a type of mute rhetoric, by which the orator can, with his movements, without speaking a single word, make himself heard and persuade the audience'.[51] In short, this *balletto* was a danced lament, the 'ungrateful ladies' expressing themselves eloquently without the aid of words.[52]

Among Chiabrera's sumptuous *intermedi* for *L'idropica* was one devoted to the story of the rape of Europa. Riding on the back of a magnificent bull, a regal Europa lamented her fate. The opera *Arianna* by Rinuccini and Monteverdi, the other principal entertainment of the festivities, tells the story of Ariadne, who betrayed her father to save her lover, Theseus, and was subsequently abandoned by him. In the celebrated lament, Arianna alternates between sorrow and love, rage and remorse. Finally, among the smaller entertainments was a *balletto* by Gagliano and Striggio featuring a poignant lament for Iphigenia, about to be sacrificed at the altar by her father Agamemnon. We might guess that this set of entertainments was all about female grief, especially that arising from poor decisions, and thus was designed to frighten the young bride into submission.

---

49 Carter, *Monteverdi's Musical Theatre*, p. 155 (quoting Follino). Follino's account of the *Ballo delle ingrate* and the libretto are given in Solerti, *Gli albori del melodramma*, ii: 247–59. The music survives only in a revised version in Monteverdi's *Madrigali guerrieri, et amorosi . . . Libro ottavo* (Venice, 1638).
50 Carter, *Monteverdi's Musical Theatre*, pp. 152–4.
51 T. Arbeau, *Orchésographie* (Langres, 1588), p. 5, in McGowan, *L'art du ballet de cour en France*, p. 31.
52 Compare B. Gordon, 'Talking Back'.

Yet a repeated formula in Follino's description suggests otherwise. As Europa delivered her lament, 'tears of pity arose in the audience'. As Arianna lamented, 'there was not one lady who failed to shed some little tear'. Iphigenia and the ungrateful ladies were likewise said to have brought tears to the audience's eyes. Whether or not the audience actually wept, their tears are clearly part of Follino's rhetoric, the indication of an appropriate emotional catharsis. In fact, recent research has placed Renaissance wedding celebrations in a broader cultural context. As in many traditional societies around the world, a wedding was first and foremost a rite of passage, in which the bride ritualistically mourned the loss of her childhood and virginity, and experienced a metaphorical abduction and abandonment, even a death, as she made the important transition from her father's protection to that of her husband. For an early seventeenth-century courtly audience (male as well as female), the entertainments in Mantua used traditional metaphors to welcome Margherita of Savoy into the Gonzaga family and to initiate both bride and groom into their new responsibilities and roles.[53] Moreover, each entertainment represented their new state as a happy one: Arianna and Iphigenia are each saved by a *deus ex machina*, Europa becomes the beloved bride of the king of the gods, and at the conclusion of the *Ballo delle ingrate*, the mouth of Hell is transformed into a lovely flower garden, where nymphs and shepherds happily sing and dance.[54]

Arianna's recitative lament made such an impression that copies immediately began to circulate as chamber music. As a result, this is the one piece that survives from the complete opera. Years later, Monteverdi declared that in composing this lament, he had discovered 'the natural way' to imitate the passions. Scholars have attempted to infer his meaning by studying the score: melodic gestures mirror poetic rhetoric in a way not evident in *Orfeo*, and pitch and motivic material are subtly manipulated to reflect Arianna's psychological development.[55] An intriguing hypothesis concerns the performer who eventually took the role in 1608, not a court singer but the accomplished professional actress Virginia Andreini: was it exposure to her style of delivery that led Monteverdi to his 'natural way of imitation'?[56] Whatever the case, the *Lamento d'Arianna* inaugurated a genre of chamber music and had a powerful influence on later musical monologues for the stage as well.

In light of the theme of the Mantuan wedding festivities of 1608, it is interesting to consider the Florentine regency of Archduchess Maria Magdalena and Grand Duchess Christine, mother and grandmother of Grand Duke

---

53 MacNeil, 'Weeping at the Water's Edge'.
54 Carter, *Monteverdi's Musical Theatre*, p. 158 n. 25 (citing Federico Zuccari).
55 Tomlinson, 'Madrigal, Monody, and Monteverdi's "via naturale alla immitatione"'; Cusick, "'There Was Not One Lady Who Failed to Shed a Tear"'.
56 Carter, 'Lamenting Ariadne?'.

Ferdinando II, who together ruled Tuscany on his behalf from 1621 to 1628. For seven years, operatic works, tournaments and sacred dramas all dwelt on topics concerning heroic women. The pair even commissioned a *balletto* from a woman composer, Francesca Caccini (Giulio's daughter). Her *La liberazione di Ruggiero dall'isola d'Alcina* (1625) tells a familiar story from *Orlando furioso* in an unfamiliar way, by using pitch-centres to contrast the male perception of the sorceress Alcina with a more sympathetic female viewpoint.[57] In Marco da Gagliano's pastoral opera *La Flora*, performed for the wedding of Ferdinando's sister Margherita to Duke Odoardo Farnese of Parma in October 1628, three months after Ferdinando had taken the throne, a strong Venere resolves the plot by conceding power to her son Amore. The opera thus allegorically reenacts the transfer of power in Florence from female to male rule.[58]

The Stuart court masque

By the early years of the seventeenth century, the symbolic vocabulary and visual narrative strategies of Italian court festivities had been adopted by many courts across Europe, thanks to the widespread dissemination of published descriptions and illustrations, as well as informal reports from individual travellers. Ballet spread rapidly, too, often carried by French dancing-masters who willingly relocated to foreign courts. (Opera did not travel well initially. Outside a small group of Italian courts, it remained an occasional curiosity until redefined as a 'public' genre in Venice from 1637.) A particularly felicitous mingling of Italian scenography and French ballet with an indigenous dramatic genre occurred in the English court masque, which flourished at the courts of the Stuarts, King James I (*reg.* 1603–25) and Charles I (*reg.* 1625–49).[59]

While several poets and playwrights wrote masques, the prevailing design was largely the invention of Ben Jonson (b. 1572 or 1573, d. 1637), working with the architect Inigo Jones. A typical Jonsonian masque, performed during the Christmas revels or at Shrovetide, began with the ceremonial entrance of King James into the Whitehall Banqueting House, where he ascended to his raised seat of honour facing a temporary stage. His entrance was accompanied by a wind band ('loud music'). A large aristocratic audience occupied tiered seating on three sides of the hall. The stage – decorated with perspective scenery, an idea newly imported from Italy – served as an elaborate entryway from which

57 Cusick, 'Of Women, Music, and Power'; F. Caccini, *La liberazione di Ruggiero dall'isola di Alcina* (Florence, 1625; repr. 1998), ed. D. Silbert, 'Smith College Music Archives', 7 (Northampton, MA, 1945).
58 Harness, '*La Flora* and the End of Female Rule in Tuscany'.
59 Holman, 'Music for the Stage, i'; Holman, *Four and Twenty Fiddlers*, pp. 179–93, 359–73; Walls, *Music in the English Courtly Masque*.

the performers descended to the main floor area. Ensembles of instruments occupied various places around the hall: strings to accompany most of the dances, winds for transitions and to cover the noise of the machinery, lutes to accompany singers.

The entertainment began with what Jonson called the 'antimasque': a grotesque or comic enactment of a vulgar, graceless society by professional actors speaking in verse. (The term 'antimasque' is a pun: *anti-*, opposed to appropriate courtly behaviour; *ante-*, before the main masque; *antic*, eccentric in appearance or movement.) More 'loud music' accompanied a spectacular scenic transformation, during which the world of the antimasque vanished, and the elegant, graceful world of the main masque took its place. The transformation was often heralded by a song, marking the articulation of the entertainment. Now entered the masquers – elaborately costumed courtiers who represented mythological or fanciful characters that reflected the individuals' actual roles in court society. They performed several figure-dances, choreographed in the manner of French ballet. Spoken verses intervened, as did songs. The masquers then invited members of the audience to join them in an extended period of social dancing, called 'the revels'. A final song or dance (or both) brought the entertainment to a close.

While the principal attention was focussed on the dancing courtiers, many professionals participated as well. Court musicians, dancing-masters and professional actors (nearly always male, even when representing female characters) performed the speeches, songs, instrumental music and antimasque dances. A variety of composers supplied vocal music: Alfonso Ferrabosco the younger (*c.* 1575–1628), John Coprario, Thomas Campion (1567–1620) and Nicholas Lanier (1588–1666) in the Jacobean years, and William Lawes (1602–45) and others in the Caroline period. Dancing-masters, who were generally violinists, composed the dance tunes (and presumably the bass lines) as well as the choreography; court musicians later filled in the harmonies. Jonson himself wrote the commemorative texts associated with his masques, and these were printed. These texts function as detailed descriptions of ephemeral events, as literary works in their own right (the complete poetry is included), and also as learned disquisitions on the Classical allusions and (largely Neoplatonic) symbolism. In a well-known comment, Jonson made a distinction between 'present occasions', by which he meant the surface of the event as entertainment, and 'more removed mysteries', the hidden meanings available to the erudite.[60]

Much of the music for Jacobean masques is lost or survives only in collections of lute songs and dances intended for the amateur market. Even less survives

---

60 Strong, *Art and Power*, pp. 20, 28–30.

for Caroline masques, although for three of them, the vocal music and staging can be substantially reconstructed,[61] and John Playford eventually printed two collections of dance tunes. Nonetheless, enough music survives from both periods to provide a general sense of the sounds that were heard.[62] Masque dances are usually sectional, mostly in duple metre and sometimes concluding with a section in triple metre. Their tunes rely on a repertory of recurring motives and formulas – 'music composed as much by the [dancing-master's] fingers as in the head'[63] – and were presumably designed to suit the intended choreography rather than the other way around. The songs for the Jacobean masque came out of the lute-song tradition of the time; some are in dance rhythms, but many are in a sophisticated 'declamatory' style that avoids simple tunefulness. Some were sung by groups, to the accompaniment of massed lutes, and others by a soloist. The Caroline masques had the benefit of much larger musical forces, with choruses on stage supporting solo singers on cloud machines, all accompanied by ensembles of bowed and plucked instruments. Lawes provided partsongs in polyphonic textures, and also pieces with complex scoring patterns, involving the alternation of instrumental ensemble, solo singers and chorus.

While there is considerable variety among masques, the general model might be illustrated by an early masque of Jonson's, the *Masque of Queens* (1609), one of several sponsored by Anne of Denmark, Queen Consort of James I.[64] Jonson's description makes frequent references to music and includes several attributions, naming a tenor and two choreographers, and identifying Ferrabosco as a composer. The opening scene represented 'an ugly hell'. A troupe of grotesquely attired witches, representing Ignorance, Suspicion, Credulity and the like, entered to 'a kind of hollow and infernal music'. Playing rattles and other noisy instruments, they performed a ritual in spoken verse and dancing, made up of odious words and bizarre gestures: 'With a strange and sudden music they fell into a magical dance full of preposterous change and gesticulation . . . [doing] all things contrary to the custom of men, dancing back to back and hip to hip . . . with strange fantastic motions of their heads and bodies'. The music for this dance survives; it is marked by bizarre syncopation and metric changes within the strain.[65] Their spells were ineffective: 'In the heat of their dance on the sudden was heard a sound of loud music, as if many instruments

61 M. Lefkowitz (ed.), *Trois masques à la cour de Charles I d'Angleterre* (Paris, 1970).

62 P. Walls and B. Thomas (eds), *Twenty-one Masque Dances of the Early Seventeenth Century*, 'English Instrumental Music of the Late Renaissance', 2 (London, 1974); A. J. Sabol (ed.), *Four Hundred Songs and Dances from the Stuart Masque* (Providence, RI, 1978).

63 Ward, 'Newly Devis'd Measures for Jacobean Masques', p. 130.

64 S. Orgel (ed.), *Ben Jonson: The Complete Masques* (New Haven and London, 1969), pp. 122–41.

65 Walls and Thomas (eds), *Twenty-one Masque Dances of the Early Seventeenth Century*, no. 3 (compare also no. 2).

had made one blast; with which not only the hags themselves but the hell into which they ran quite vanished'.

That scene was instantly replaced by a 'glorious and magnificent building', the house of Fame. (Jones copied this set-design from one by Giulio Parigi for the spectacular *intermedi* produced in Florence the preceding autumn.[66]) The masquers could be seen within, sitting on a throne in the shape of a pyramid, bathed in light. They were Queen Anne and eleven of her ladies, representing famous queens of mythology and antiquity. An allegory of Heroic Virtue, dressed as Perseus, then descended to the floor and introduced the queens in a lengthy speech, which culminated in references to the real queen and king. Fame appeared, holding her trumpet in one hand and an olive branch in the other – thus juxtaposing symbols of war and peace – and announced a triumphal procession. The queens descended and 'rode in state' in three chariots, each preceded by several of the witches bound as captives. Their procession was accompanied by a song celebrating the 'birth of Fame from Virtue', sung by 'a full triumphant music'. (Those who sang, while undoubtedly costumed, did not represent particular characters.) Alighting from the chariots, the queens performed a pair of dances 'full of subtle and excellent changes', the first accompanied by cornetts and the second by violins.[67] They then invited men from the audience to 'dance the measures' for an hour. A solo song praising Queen Anne led to the third choreographed dance.[68] Rather than abstract geometrical shapes, its ever-changing figures formed letters of the alphabet (a practice borrowed from French *ballet de cour*), spelling the name of Anne's young second son, Prince Charles, Duke of York. 'After this, they danced galliards and corantos'. The queens then returned via their chariots to the house of Fame, and a final song concluded the entertainment; it praised 'good Fame', which endures forever even after political power perishes.

As in contemporary *ballets de cour*, a disorderly world (that of the antimasque) was replaced by an orderly one: a monarchical European culture. Theatrical dances in symmetrical figures then enacted the triumph of courtly culture, while lively and festive social dances such as galliards and corantos mimed the universal dissemination of that culture.[69] In constructing the literary text of each masque, the poet worked in collaboration with the patron, negotiating a path between that individual's chosen manner of self-presentation and the need to affirm the authority of the king. In the *Masque of Queens*, Queen Anne

---

66 Peacock, 'Italian Libretti and the English Court Masque', p. 99.

67 Sabol (ed.), *Four Hundred Songs and Dances from the Stuart Masque*, nos 225, 226, 239, 315; Holman, *Four and Twenty Fiddlers*, pp. 189–92.

68 The song was 'If all the ages of the earth' in A. Ferrabosco, *Ayres (1609)*, ed. E. H. Fellowes, 'The English School of Lutenist Song Writers', 2/16 (London, 1927), pp. 41–2.

69 Howard, *The Politics of Courtly Dancing in Early Modern England*, pp. 110–32.

chose to demonstrate the worth and dignity of women by representing herself and her selected group of ladies as warrior-queens. Jonson, in turn, used that discourse of war to celebrate King James's commitment to peace. This approach is evident in details of language as well as the image of Fame holding the olive branch. Moreover, the masculine image of Heroic Virtue affirmed the monarch's ultimate authority and role in preserving an orderly and just society.[70]

Like the French ballet and the Italian *ballo*, masque blurred the boundary between fiction and reality, ideal and real. Charles I (unlike James I) regularly danced the leading parts in numerous masques produced at his court. In a commentary on the masque *Tempe Restored* (1632), Inigo Jones wrote, 'In Heroic Virtue is figured the king's majesty . . . he being the only prototype to all the kingdoms under his monarchy of religion, justice, and all the virtues joined together'.[71] Thus did Charles think of himself: as the representative of God on earth and the embodiment of all virtues.

The Barberini operas in Rome

In 1623 Cardinal Maffeo Barberini was elected Pope Urban VIII. As such he was both an ecclesiastical and a secular ruler, and in this double capacity he enjoyed enormous wealth and power, which he shared with his family in blatant acts of nepotism. He and his three nephews – Cardinal Francesco Barberini, Don Taddeo Barberini and Cardinal Antonio Barberini – engaged in extensive building projects and lavish artistic patronage in and around Rome. From 1631 until Urban's death in 1644, the nephews, especially Francesco, regularly sponsored the composition and production of operas that were highlights of the Carnival season.[72] These operas reflect a dual purpose: the religious desire to teach while entertaining, and the worldly need to demonstrate princely magnificence. Their success led the nephews to construct a permanent theatre, capable of holding three to four thousand people.

Rome was well acquainted with opera. The grand households of various cardinals and statesmen (including the Barberini) had sponsored occasional pastorals in the Florentine manner, and Jesuit colleges and other religious institutions produced sacred music-dramas. Nonetheless, this group of Barberini operas represented a new departure: a regular series of court productions for successive Carnival seasons, independent of dynastic celebration. The

70 Holbrook, 'Jacobean Masques and the Jacobean Peace', pp. 78–82; Barroll, 'Inventing the Stuart Masque', pp. 135–6; Orgel, 'Marginal Jonson', pp. 151–3, 164.

71 Strong, *Art and Power*, p. 159.

72 Murata, *Operas for the Papal Court*; Hammond, *Music and Spectacle in Baroque Rome*.

composers included Stefano Landi (1587–1639), Michelangelo Rossi (1601/2–1656), Virgilio Mazzocchi (1597–1646), Marco Marazzoli (d. 1662) and Luigi Rossi (d. 1653). All the librettos came from the same pen, that of the ecclesiastical administrator Giulio Rospigliosi (later Pope Clement IX), who also performed the duties of a director and theatre manager.

These were sumptuous and expensive productions. Invited guests included high officials of the Church as well as aristocracy from Rome and beyond. Others who could make themselves suitably presentable simply turned up and the hosts squeezed them in, apparently in large numbers. The printed *argomento* (plot summary), distributed to the whole audience, was elegantly bound for the highest-ranking guests. Several productions used machinery designed by the brilliant Ferrarese engineer Francesco Guitti. Each opera required several changes of elaborate scenery, designed by the greatest artists in Rome.[73]

Presumably at the request of Cardinal Francesco, who understood his uncle's distaste for pagan mythology in a papal setting,[74] Rospigliosi adopted unconventional and varied plot-types: stories from the lives of the saints, episodes from the epics of Ariosto and Tasso, and even a sentimental tragicomedy drawn from Boccaccio's *Decameron*. The genre name 'fable' (e.g., *favola in musica*) does not appear; it is replaced by 'comedy' in one instance, but more usually by 'drama' (e.g., *dramma musicale*). Despite their variety, the Rospigliosi operas had a unifying subtext. The *argomenti* encouraged the audience to interpret each plot as a metaphorical morality tale, an exploration of the role of virtue in a complex world. Thus the 'comedy' *Chi soffre speri*, by Mazzocchi and Marazzoli, was intended to 'instruct while pleasing', according to the *argomento* for the first version (1637), for it demonstrated the power of virtuous love.[75] The plot, taken from Boccaccio, concerns an impoverished nobleman who makes material sacrifices in order to persuade the widow he loves of his good intentions. Each sacrifice leads first to suffering but then to an unexpected positive consequence.

Thanks to the influence of Guarini's tragicomedy *Il pastor fido*, the new literary fashion favoured plays with intricate reversals, intrigues and multiple plot-lines. Rospigliosi's librettos, though having only three acts, are correspondingly long and complex. (Each performance of the 1639 version of *Chi soffre speri* lasted five hours, approximately twice the length of Monteverdi's *Orfeo*.) Even the most serious plots are broken up by passages of comic relief by, for example, impudent pages or clownish characters derived from the *commedia*

---

73 Bianconi and Walker, 'Production, Consumption, and Political Function of Seventeenth-Century Opera', pp. 215–21.
74 Murata, *Operas for the Papal Court*, pp. 5–6, 17.
75 Osthoff, 'Dokumente zur italienischen Oper von 1600 bis 1706', pp. 38–9.

dell'arte. Tuneful arias and duets for these secondary characters are purely diver-
sionary, and not part of the main story-line. Choruses might end the acts, but
dances are just as likely, or even *intermedi* only loosely connected to the main
plot. The most celebrated example of the last is the splendid *intermedio* for the
1639 version of *Chi soffre speri*, depicting merchants selling their goods at a
town fair.[76] That episode ended with a spectacular depiction of the sun setting
over the sea, designed by Gianlorenzo Bernini.

Each act of a libretto was now divided into several explicit 'scenes' (defined
by the entrance and exit of characters), and composers treated each as a closed
musical unit. While recitative dialogue dominates, some of the most moving
scenes are soliloquies, portraying a character's shifting emotions and inner
arguments; they are set almost entirely in recitative and are given dramatic
shape by tonal contrast, harmonic expansion and thematic recall.[77] Other scenes
might include occasional short arias (usually strophic), duets or trios. An aria
for a principal character might introduce his thoughts before other characters
enter and dialogue commences, or it might sum up preceding action. Frequently
in triple metre, the arias have lilting melodies over moving bass lines; they
erupt in decorative melismas from time to time. In addition, composers placed
occasional brief arioso passages (aria fragments) and florid cadences in the
recitative itself, to make a rhetorical point, to emphasise an emotion, or to give
shape to a passage.

Since women were forbidden to perform publicly in Rome, the casts were
entirely male. Castratos, falsettists and boys took the female roles. Boys who
served as pages in Don Taddeo's household regularly made up the dance troupe.
The records of the Cappella Pontificia show that the Pope and his nephews
routinely commandeered the best singers for their personal use, including the
production of operas. Sometimes the Cappella simply cancelled sung performances during Carnival for want of enough sopranos.[78] Thus some of the finest
voices of the era sang these operas – the great castratos, tenors and basses of
the Cappella Pontificia, supplemented by boys from the choir at St Peter's
for the youthful roles. Meanwhile, the instrumental ensemble was quite limited in scope: just two to four violins to play sinfonias, ritornellos, dances
and occasional accompaniments, in addition to a large continuo group. The
latter typically included lutes, theorbos, harpsichords, harps and low strings.
(Presumably this ensemble sat in a floor-level enclosure at the front of the
stage, the newly preferred arrangement at other theatres.[79]) When varied

---

76 Second *intermedio*, 'La fiera di Farfa', in V. Mazzocchi and M. Marazzoli, *Egisto, overo Chi soffre speri*,
'Italian Opera, 1640-1770', 61 (New York and London, 1982).
77 Murata, 'The Recitative Soliloquy'.
78 Hammond, *Music and Spectacle in Baroque Rome*, pp. 170-76.
79 Pirrotta, 'Orchestra and Stage in Renaissance *Intermedi* and Early Opera', pp. 214-15.

instrumental timbres were desired, in scenes of magical enchantment or military pomp, the Barberini paid for extra players. For the most part, though, symbolic 'colour' now belonged to voices.

The success of the first opera in the series set the tone for the entire venture. This was Landi's *Il Sant'Alessio* (composed 1631, performed 1632, revised 1634), which tells the bittersweet tale of St Alexis, a fifth-century Roman who abandoned his grieving family to dedicate himself to prayer.[80] For the first time, a castrato represented the protagonist of an opera. In setting that role for a soprano, Landi perhaps meant to emphasise the otherworldly nature of this saintly man.[81] (At all events, the heroes of the remaining Barberini operas are tenors in some cases, and male sopranos in others.) The centre-piece of the work is a moving recitative soliloquy for Alessio, who is torn between duty to God and love for his family. Vying for his allegiance are the Devil, whose powerful bass voice spans two and a half octaves, and an angel (who flew on and off by machine). The comic element is provided mainly by a pair of pages, whose youthful treble voices, tuneful melodies, consonant harmonies and recitative patter reflect their carefree attitude. The saint's grief-stricken family sings moving chromatic madrigals. An observer in 1632 said of the final set, a 'glory of Paradise' populated by a chorus of angels, that 'The clouds parted and there appeared a place so resplendent and luminous that one could hardly bear to look at it'.[82]

It is surely no coincidence that the plots treating the lives of saints are all set in Rome. In the prologue to *Il Sant'Alessio*, an allegorical figure of Rome (La Roma) repudiates the warlike imagery of ancient times in favour of the gentle and loving rule of modern Rome. Her message might have seemed ironic in 1634: the pope had recently been forced by his political enemies to denounce his old friend, the scientist Galileo, for publishing a supposedly heretical monograph in support of Copernican theory. Whatever the case, the score of the 1634 version of the opera was immediately printed in an elegant edition (one of only two printed scores for the entire series of operas), and La Roma's prologue was among the engraved illustrations.

Urban VIII's death in 1644 left the Barberini in a precarious political state, and they fled into temporary exile in France. As for Rospigliosi, he lived in Spain for several years, serving the new papal family. By 1653 Cardinal Francesco, Cardinal Antonio, and Rospigliosi had all returned to Rome. Reunited, they produced additional operas, still concerned with the human struggle to lead a virtuous life, but with librettos highly influenced by Spanish dramatic conventions. The final Barberini production, *La vita humana* with music by Marazzoli,

80 S. Landi, *Il S. Alessio: dramma musicale* (Rome, 1634; repr. Bologna, 1970).
81 Leopold, 'Rome', p. 62.   82 J.-J. Bouchard, in Weiss, *Opera*, p. 33.

occurred in 1656 and was a great success. After that, under the patronage of Queen Christina of Sweden (living in Rome as an expatriate), operatic taste began to change, reflecting a new reality. Throughout Italy travelling troupes from Venice – including women as well as men – presented entirely secular works to an expanded public. Ironically, the seeds of Venetian public opera had been planted in 1637 by a group of performers from Barberini-dominated Rome.[83]

Mid-century Italian influence in Paris and Madrid

An important footnote to the subject of Barberini patronage concerns the interventions of Italians in musical theatre at the royal courts of France in the 1640s and Spain in the 1650s. Cardinal Giulio Mazzarini, a diplomat in the service of the Barberini, travelled between Rome and France in the 1630s, settled permanently in France in 1639, and in 1643 was appointed prime minister to Queen Regent Anne of Austria (Louis XIII's widow). Well aware of the political power of patronage and the ideological role of Barberini opera, Mazarin (as he was called in France) began a single-minded effort to bring Roman opera to Paris, starting as early as 1640. Despite the efforts of his agents in Italy, practical problems repeatedly intervened. In 1644 he succeeded in bringing several star singers from Rome and Florence, and their chamber concerts in the Palais-Royal turned the queen into an avid fan of Italian music (and incidentally introduced her to the idea of the female professional singer); but after a few months the singers returned to Italy. In the end it was the great scenographer Giacomo Torelli (1608–78) and the choreographer G. B. Balbi, called to France to work with a *commedia dell'arte* troupe, who in 1645, and with the financial backing of a French diplomat in Rome, succeeded in organising a large-scale operatic production at the French court: a version of Francesco Sacrati's *La finta pazza*, first performed in Venice in 1641.[84]

This was the first of six Italian operas performed at the French court during a seventeen-year period, the last of them a newly commissioned work by the great Venetian composer Francesco Cavalli (1602–76), his *Ercole amante* (commissioned for 1660 but performed only in 1662). The first to have been newly written for Paris – *Orfeo* (1647), by the Roman Luigi Rossi to a libretto by Francesco Buti – had its run of performances on the brink of the nobles' rebellion known as the Fronde (1648–53). Ironically, instead of cementing Mazarin's power, as he had earlier envisaged, this expensive display of magnificence only

83 Bianconi, *Music in the Seventeenth Century*, p. 181; Hammond, *Music and Spectacle in Baroque Rome*, p. 82.
84 Murata, 'Why the First Opera in Paris Wasn't Roman'.

increased the antagonism against him.[85] After the Fronde was defeated (by which time Louis XIV had reached his majority), Mazarin astutely combined political triumph with artistic compromise: he encouraged the enactment of courtly culture in frequent *ballets de cour*, and he saw to it that Italian operas would henceforth be interwoven with elaborate ballet episodes in the French manner, in which the courtiers could dance.

Mazarin failed to instal a permanent Italian opera troupe at the French court: after each opera the Italian cast dispersed. Moreover, French courtiers were ambivalent about works in an unfamiliar language and an equally foreign musical style. They reserved most of their admiration for the dazzling stage effects and the inserted ballets. Mazarin's death in 1661 brought an end to Italian opera in France. Yet the influence of his project on the long-range development of French music and theatre was enormous. In the short term, it led to French experiments with pastoral dialogues in music, and with spoken plays containing spectacular scene-changes. In the longer term, Mazarin's 'attempt at politico-cultural colonisation constituted nothing less than the introduction of the Baroque style to France'.[86]

Like France, Spain had its own strong theatrical and musical traditions. In addition to masques, pageants, mock tournaments and the like, court entertainments featured spoken plays that incorporated songs and dances in traditional styles. The Italian intrusion of the 1650s (while slight compared with Mazarin's activities in France) was not the first. King Philip IV's earlier court scenographer, the Florentine Cosimo Lotti, had twice attempted to impose Italian taste on the Spanish court, in 1627 by arranging for the composition and production of an opera in Spanish (*La selva sin amor*) that mimicked Italian versification and recitative, and in 1635 by proposing *intermedi* in the Florentine manner for the *comedia* (play) *El mayor encanto amor* by Pedro Calderón de la Barca. The opera, planned in cooperation with Florentine diplomats as a way to curry political favour, turned out to be a solitary curiosity. As for the *intermedi*, Calderón rejected them in favour of realistic stage-music within the play – ballads and other traditional song types – according to Spanish custom. Nevertheless, a few of Lotti's suggested insertions, such as a danced tournament, did appeal to him because they suited the established conventions of the *comedia*.

In 1652 the court's new Florentine scenographer, Baccio di Bianco, together with Giulio Rospigliosi (in his final year as papal nuncio in Madrid), persuaded Calderón to include passages of recitative in a play, again by writing Italianate verses in Spanish. This modest experiment led Calderón to try another tack, one

85 Isherwood, *Music in the Service of the King*, pp. 123–5.
86 Zaslaw, 'The First Opera in Paris', p. 7.

with longer-lasting success: the invention of a new Spanish style of recitative, using the octosyllables of the Spanish *romance* (ballad). Starting with *Fortunas de Andrómeda y Perseo* (1653), he and composer Juan Hidalgo made use of this style in several 'semi-operas': plays on mythological subjects, mingling speech and song. These were performed at the Buen Retiro palace with spectacular machinery and staging. The pair ultimately wrote two operas, *La púrpura de la rosa* and *Celos aun del aire matan*, performed in 1660 in honour, respectively, of the signing of the Peace of the Pyrenees with France, and of the wedding of the Infanta to the French king, Louis XIV. Hidalgo's recitative is metrically regular and marked by word-painting devices; it is expressive, but clearly distinct from the Italian style. In the semi-operas, the type of text setting is symbolic: mortals converse in spoken dialogue and sing well-known traditional songs; gods communicate directly with mortals in newly composed solo songs; gods communicate indirectly and mysteriously with mortals in ensemble songs; and finally, gods communicate with each other in recitative.[87]

Ballet and opera at the French court under Louis XIV

A well-known costume sketch depicts Louis XIV at the age of fourteen, richly adorned as the 'rising Sun' for his sixth and final role in the *Ballet de la Nuit* (1653).[88] The attractive young king stands in an elegant pose, his headdress a radiating golden sunburst. Isaac de Benserade's verses in the printed programme booklet allude metaphorically to Louis's youth and to the power of the throne:

> At the top of the mountains, beginning to glow,
> I already receive such admiring regards
> Though I've barely begun my long course through the sky.
> I give colour and shape to all things in my path,
> And whoever wants not to acknowledge my light
> Will soon suffer my heat.

The *air* for L'Aurore (Dawn) that precedes the king's entrance alludes to the defeat of the Fronde: 'The noble stars of the night, which triumphed in [the Sun's] absence, dare not bear his presence'.[89] With the Fronde undone, parliament and the rebellious nobles were forced to accept the unprecedented degree

87 Stein, *Songs of Mortals, Dialogues of the Gods*, pp. 104–12, 126–68, 191–257; Stein, 'The Origins and Character of *Recitado*'.

88 Christout, *Le ballet de cour au XVIIᵉ siècle*, illus. 23 (in colour); Anthony, *French Baroque Music*, plate 1; Massip, 'Paris', illus. 50.

89 *Ballet royal de la Nuict, divisé en quatre parties ou quatres veilles, et dansé par sa Majesté le 23 février 1653* (Paris, 1653), pp. 65–6.

of monarchical power that had been established by Louis XIII's prime minister, Cardinal Richelieu, and maintained by Mazarin. Thus began the era of the Sun King.

Louis's reign entered a remarkable new phase with the death of Mazarin in 1661. The king appointed no replacement, having resolved to rule personally, without a prime minister. Shortly thereafter, he imprisoned his finance minister, Nicolas Fouquet, and appropriated Fouquet's wealth and cultural projects for the royal court. Fouquet had made the mistake of flaunting the opulence of his château at Vaux-le-Vicomte, and thus his personal ambitions, in a magnificent festival. To replace him, the king appointed Jean-Baptiste Colbert, who established a series of royal academies, all engaged in ensuring that the arts served the state by glorifying the king. Louis then focussed his attention on one of his several royal residences, Versailles, beginning the long process of turning a modest country lodge into a splendid château. (Eventually, in 1682, he would move the entire court into apartments at Versailles, thus cementing his control over the activities of the nobility.) In 1664, 1668 and 1674, while remodelling was in progress, the king bedazzled the aristocracy with grandiose festivals at Versailles, modelled on Fouquet's ill-fated event, the décor allegorizing royal power.[90]

Throughout the 1650s and 1660s many ballets and *mascarades* occurred at the various royal residences, often for Carnival but during other seasons as well. These entertainments were rich in political allegory, *galanterie*, fantasy and sometimes satire. Since the life of the court revolved incessantly around the person of the king, and the monarch was young and virile, important topics for ballet included the pleasures of love. Especially in the early years, Louis played all sorts of roles, not only those of gods, heroes and heroic lovers, and his skill as a dancer was itself a *topos*. If his costume suggested a less-than-kingly character – say, a madman or a demon – his splendid body, agility and grace, along with the mitigating verses in the programme booklet, left no doubt of the king underneath. Nor did he always dance as a soloist. Part of the conventional rhetoric had to do with the audience's supposed ability to identify the king among several dancers similarly costumed and masked.[91]

At this time, a *ballet de cour* consisted of an extended series of *entrées* ('entrances') for different characters or groups, each *entrée* comprising one or more dances. Interspersed here and there were a small number of vocal pieces, usually *récits* (solo *airs*) or dialogues but sometimes choruses. The presence of Italian virtuosos at court provided opportunities for occasional variety, as in the

90 Isherwood, *Music in the Service of the King*, pp. 116–17, 150–69, 265–80; Benoit, 'Paris', pp. 240–46; Apostolidès, 'From *Roi soleil* to Louis le Grand'; Aercke, *Gods of Play*, pp. 184–200.

91 Pruiksma, '"Dansé par le roi"', pp. 92, 105–10.

splendid Italian lament sung by Anna Bergerotti in the *Ballet des Amours déguisés* of 1664.[92] Large consorts of court musicians provided the instrumental music, starting with an overture. The instrumentalists were typically costumed and an integral part of the choreographed spectacle.[93] A climactic 'grand ballet' brought the entertainment to a close. Ballets were now performed on stages, facing the audience. The symmetrical figures of the choreography were thus meant to be appreciated from the front rather than from above.

Ballets rarely had plots but always had themes; for instance, the *Ballet de la Nuit* represented a succession of unrelated events starting at dusk and ending at daybreak. Its *entrées* ranged from the mythological to the exotic and burlesque, its characters from allegorical figures and gods to merchants and bandits. In addition to the texts to be set to music, the poet wrote clever verses for the spectators to read, metaphorically merging the courtly behaviour of each noble dancer with the character he or she portrayed. Some, such as those from the *Ballet de la Nuit* given above, were political and deferential; others alluded obliquely to courtiers' personalities. A ballet thus served as a mirror, representing the court to itself and to foreign dignitaries by cleverly interweaving veiled gossip with magnificent spectacle.[94]

As part of his consolidation of authority in 1661, Louis chose a favourite musician. Among several professional artists who had danced alongside the courtiers in the *Ballet de la Nuit* in 1653 was a young Italian whose French-styled name was Jean-Baptiste Lully (1632–87). Lully had begun his career in the household of the king's cousin; this ballet was his first opportunity to dance at the royal court. A month later he received the first of his appointments to the *Musique de la chambre du roi*, as a composer of instrumental music. In 1661 he was appointed *surintendant* of the *Musique de la chambre* and was granted French citizenship by the king. Thanks to his talent as violinist, composer and dancer, and also to his skill at self-promotion, Lully virtually monopolised the role of composer of theatre music at court for a period of about three decades. He wrote music for some thirty *ballets de cour* and *mascarades*, at first as part of a team of composers but soon alone. From 1664 to 1670 he also collaborated with the great comic playwright Molière on *comédies-ballets*, plays ranging from pastoral to burlesque in character, incorporating extended passages of song and dance. (These were performed both at court and at Molière's public theatre in Paris.) The last fifteen years of Lully's life would be devoted mainly to opera.

---

92 J.-B. Lully, *Les Amours déguisés*, ed. J. R. Anthony and R. Harris-Warrick, in Lully, *Œuvres complètes*, 1/6 (Hildesheim, 2001), pp. 127–32.

93 Harris-Warrick, 'Magnificence in Motion', pp. 195–203.

94 Ibid.; Couvreur, *Jean-Baptiste Lully*, pp. 111–15.

In 1670 the king was scheduled to dance in a new *comédie-ballet*, but his health did not permit it.[95] He never returned to the stage. Louis's withdrawal, coupled with the poet Benserade's decision to retire, effectively brought an end to the continuous stream of *ballets de cour*. Lully's brilliant *Ballet de Flore* (1669), in which Louis had again danced as the Sun, turned out to be the last of the long series. (Isolated court ballets, featuring a younger generation of dancers, would occur in the 1680s.) As for Molière's *comédies-ballets*, after falling out with Lully the playwright continued the series in Paris with the composer Marc-Antoine Charpentier (1643–1704) until his death in 1673. The most successful *comédies-ballets*, such as *Le bourgeois gentilhomme* (1670; Lully) and *Le malade imaginaire* (1672–3; Charpentier), were sometimes revived at court in subsequent years.

It was in the transitional atmosphere of the early 1670s that French opera took hold, initially through the efforts of the poet Pierre Perrin but ultimately through the inspired partnership of Lully and the poet Philippe Quinault (1635–88). In 1672 the king and Colbert granted Lully a monopoly on the establishment of an Académie Royale de Musique in Paris. The official document specified that the charge of the academy was to produce operas before the king, but that to defray expenses, Lully was permitted to produce them before a paying public as well. In actuality, the academy was principally a public opera theatre. A year after its formation, Louis gave Lully the theatre in the Palais-Royal in Paris (which had been Molière's) for his public productions.[96]

New operas appeared almost on an annual basis. They were enormously successful, and Lully eventually began publishing the scores. The king took a direct interest in these works, often selecting the subject-matter for the librettos and sometimes even attending rehearsals at court. Separate librettos were printed for court and public audiences, the former by royal command and the latter (to be sold at the door of the theatre) at Lully's expense. The presence of court musicians on Lully's payroll, officially not permitted, was, at least initially, a simple necessity: the best-qualified musicians were those he had trained at court.[97] In short, here the distinction between 'court opera' and 'public opera' becomes blurred.

In 1673 Lully and Quinault created a new genre, the *tragédie en musique*, which occupied them for the remainder of their careers. The librettos, written entirely in *vers libres*, are drawn from ancient myth (e.g., *Alceste*, *Atys*, *Phaéton*) and chivalric romance (*Amadis*, *Roland*, *Armide*). Laden with supernatural spectacle, they mingle heroic tragicomedy, pastoral and ballet. For dialogues and monologues

---

95 La Gorce, *Jean-Baptiste Lully*, pp. 156–7.

96 Weiss, *Opera*, pp. 39–44; Wood and Sadler, *French Baroque Opera*, pp. 1–3, 6–9; Coeyman, 'Walking through Lully's Opera Theatre in the Palais-Royal'.

97 Ducrot, 'Lully créateur de troupe', pp. 95–8; La Gorce, *Jean-Baptiste Lully*, pp. 190–92.

Lully invented a melodious sort of recitative over an active bass line. In using pitch and rhythm to match the shifting accentuation of the poetry, he is said to have imitated the declamation of the great tragedienne La Champmeslé.[98] The musical style as a whole is short-breathed and characterised by the artful arrangement of linked and nested segments, much like the organisation of plantings in a formal French garden. Miniature *airs* (each crystallising a thought or emotion), cadential refrains for solo singers, brief ensembles and occasional instrumental ritornellos mingle with passages of recitative to create large-scale, patterned scene structures. The scenes within a given act, in turn, are elided; modulatory gestures in the continuo mark the entrance and exit of characters. Finally, at the highest organisational level, the five acts – performed without pause and marked by spectacular changes of scenery during the entr'actes – form a symmetrical structure, with keys and dramatic settings often pivoting around a weighty action in Act III.[99]

Each act includes a *divertissement*, a group action central to the plot, such as a celebration or ritual, in which musical speech gives way to dance and song as the means of communication. It typically comprises dances, choruses with danced interludes, brief *airs*, and reprises of these items, all in a loosely symmetrical arrangement. Some dances have names denoting particular rhythmic and expressive types ('sarabande', 'gavotte' and the like); others are labelled vaguely 'entrée' or 'air'. In all cases, choreography ranged from regular step patterns and figures to the use of gesture and pantomime to paint character and action. Lully's chorus and dance troupe represented the voices and bodies of the same collective characters – e.g., 'shepherds who sing and shepherds who dance'. Choral singers, dance troupe and soloists performed in seamless alternation: the audience was invited to focus now on dance, now on song, each elucidating the meaning of the other.[100] In the case of a song based on dance rhythms (and juxtaposed with the related dance), Lully wrote the dance music first, and Quinault later added words.[101]

A principal element of the music is Lully's distinctive orchestral style, exploiting the contrasting sonorities of the violin band and the oboe band, as well as contrast between trio and tutti textures.[102] The style is evident in the stately French overtures, the introductory *ritournelles* and *préludes* that set the mood for

98 Rosow, 'French Baroque Recitative as an Expression of Tragic Declamation'.

99 Couvreur, *Jean-Baptiste Lully*, pp. 339–42; Legrand, '*Persée* de Lully et Quinault'; Rosow, 'The Articulation of Lully's Dramatic Dialogue'; Rosow, 'Making Connections'; Wood, *Music and Drama in the 'Tragédie en musique'*.

100 Harris-Warrick, 'Recovering the Lullian *Divertissement*'; Pierce and Thorp, 'The Dances in Lully's *Persée*'.

101 J.-L. Lecerf de La Viéville, *Comparaison de la musique italienne, et de la musique françoise*, 2nd edn (Brussels, 1705–6; repr. Geneva, 1972), part 2, pp. 218–19.

102 Spitzer and Zaslaw, *The Birth of the Orchestra*, pp. 70–104.

entering characters, the dance music, and accompaniments of all sorts. Much of Lully's conventional imagery involves the orchestra – for instance, the oboe band in rustic settings, murmuring recorders and strings in *sommeils* ('sleep scenes'), or fast orchestral runs and dotted rhythms in depictions of monsters and Furies.

The plots are allegories of courtly society. Audiences were moved because they could identify with the situations and emotions they saw portrayed on stage.[103] A characteristic example is *Persée* (1682), derived from the myth of Perseus and Andromeda.[104] It is founded on two intertwined themes. The first is political: a succession of terrors brought upon a population whose queen has angered a powerful goddess, coupled with deliverance from those terrors by a courageous young demigod, with the help of other powerful deities. France was at war in 1682; and whether or not the libretto is an 'opera *à clef*', representing particular real campaigns and battles,[105] it certainly concerns heroic victory over a series of enemies. The second theme is a complex love entanglement involving four people, three of them racked by guilt, fury and pain. The pair who love unwisely are a tragic woman and a villainous man (bass); the latter serves as a foil for the young hero (*haute-contre*), triumphant in love as well as in battle. A chorus and a dance troupe take a variety of collective roles, some supernatural (e.g., the 'infernal divinities' who bring Pluto's assistance to Persée) and others human. Their most important role is that of the populace, who participate in the action as it unfolds. The pivotal third act focusses on Méduse (Medusa; a tenor role, since men normally portrayed grotesque females). She presents herself not just as a snake-headed monster but also as a wronged and defiant woman.[106] The *passacaille* danced by joyful courtiers in the presence of Vénus near the end of the opera unites the two themes.[107] Its lush variations over the descending minor-tetrachord ostinato represent the restoration of monarchical social order,[108] and also the triumph of love.

While Louis was often apotheosized as Apollo or Hercules in his youth, the propaganda machine of the 1660s had gradually transformed the king himself into a demigod.[109] In several *tragédies en musique*, youthful heroes reflect Louis (forever frozen in his youthful prime), not the other way around. 'In

103 Norman, *Touched by the Graces*, pp. 33–8.
104 *Journal of Seventeenth-Century Music*, 10/1 (2004) <http://sscm-jscm.org/jscm/v10/no1.html>, is devoted entirely to studies of Lully's *Persée*. For the music, see J. B. Lully, *Persée: tragédie en musique* (Paris, 1682; repr. New York, 1998).
105 Couvreur, *Jean-Baptiste Lully*, pp. 344, 364–5.
106 Bolduc, 'From Marvel to Camp'.
107 Pierce and Thorp, 'The Dances in Lully's *Persée*', para. 3.24, section 4, and video 2.
108 Burgess, 'The Chaconne and the Representation of Sovereign Power in Lully's *Amadis* (1684) and Charpentier's *Medée* (1693)', pp. 84–6.
109 Néraudau, *L'Olympe du Roi-Soleil*, chaps 2–4; Apostolidès, 'From *Roi soleil* to Louis le Grand'.

Perseus', wrote Lully, 'I discovered the image of Your Majesty . . . In describing the wonderful gifts that Perseus received from the gods, and the astonishing undertakings that he achieved so gloriously, I trace a portrait of the heroic qualities and prodigious actions of Your Majesty.'[110]

The extended prologue of *Persée* is a conventional panegyric to Louis, performed by the allegorical figures of La Vertu (Virtue) and La Fortune and their followers. La Vertu's followers, a high-voiced chorus and female dance troupe, inhabit a pastoral setting. La Fortune's followers, a mixed choir and male dance troupe, enter to a powerful march, the scene having been transformed into a formal garden, with symmetrically arranged statues, flowers and fountains. The two troupes agree that their unnamed 'Hero' (understood to be the king) tempers his quest for fortune with virtue, and is a gift of the gods for the benefit of humankind. La Fortune's formal garden evidently represented the civilised ambience of French courtly culture, carried far and wide 'for the benefit of humankind' – in part, ironically, by Louis's wars of aggression.

For a variety of reasons – in particular Louis's increasing preoccupation with religion and morality, along with Lully's personal disgrace over a sex scandal – the king distanced himself from opera starting in the mid 1680s. Lully's academy passed to his heirs at his death as a simple public theatre. Moreover, in all the arts the powerful state mythology waned in significance. By presenting himself as the equal of the gods, Louis had irrevocably weakened them. The gods became (in the words of one art historian) 'convenient instruments of pleasure'.[111] As the seventeenth century gave way to the eighteenth, French opera turned away from heroism and increasingly towards charming tales of human and divine love, much influenced by the visual imagery of the *commedia dell'arte* and the lush music of the Italian cantata. Only Venus and Cupid maintained their dominion.

Bibliography

Aercke, K. P., *Gods of Play: Baroque Festive Performances as Rhetorical Discourse*. Albany, NY, 1994

Anthony, J. R., *French Baroque Music: from Beaujoyeulx to Rameau*. Rev. edn, Portland, OR, 1997

Apostolidès, J.-M., 'From *Roi soleil* to Louis le Grand'. In D. Hollier (ed.), *A New History of French Literature*. Cambridge, MA, 1989, pp. 314–20

Barroll, L., 'Inventing the Stuart Masque'. In Bevington and Holbrook (eds), *The Politics of the Stuart Court Masque*, pp. 121–43

---

110 Lully, *Persée* (1682), 'Au Roi', also given in Schneider, 'Dokumente zur französischen Oper von 1659 bis 1699', pp. 149–51; Norman, *Touched by the Graces*, pp. 244–5; Couvreur, *Jean-Baptiste Lully*, pp. 342–5.
111 Le Leyzour, 'Myth and Enlightenment', p. 22.

Becker, H. (ed.), *Quellentexte zur Konzeption der europäischen Oper im 17. Jahrhundert.* Kassel, 1981

Benoit, M., 'Paris, 1661–87: the Age of Lully'. In Price (ed.), *The Early Baroque Era,* pp. 239–69

Bevington, D., and Holbrook, P. (eds), *The Politics of the Stuart Court Masque.* Cambridge, 1998

Bianconi, L., *Music in the Seventeenth Century,* trans. D. Bryant. Cambridge, 1987

Bianconi, L., and Walker, T., 'Production, Consumption, and Political Function of Seventeenth-Century Opera'. *Early Music History,* 4 (1984), 209–96

Bolduc, B., 'From Marvel to Camp: Medusa for the Twenty-First Century'. *Journal of Seventeenth-Century Music,* 10 (2004) <http://sscm-jscm.org/jscm/v10/no1/bolduc.html>

Bouquet-Boyer, M.-T., 'Les éléments marins dans les spectacles à la cour de Savoie 1585–1628'. In Canova-Green and Chiarelli (eds), *The Influence of Italian Entertainments on Sixteenth- and Seventeenth-Century Music Theatre in France, Savoy and England,* pp. 53–67

Brown, H. M., 'How Opera Began: an Introduction to Peri's *Euridice* (1600)'. In E. Cochrane (ed.), *The Late Italian Renaissance, 1525–1630.* London, 1970, pp. 401–43; reprinted in E. Rosand (ed.), *Garland Library of the History of Western Music,* v. New York, 1985

Burgess, G., 'The Chaconne and the Representation of Sovereign Power in Lully's *Amadis* (1684) and Charpentier's *Medée* (1693)'. In McCleave (ed.), *Dance and Music in French Baroque Theatre,* pp. 81–104

Canova-Green, M.-C., and Chiarelli, F. (eds), *The Influence of Italian Entertainments on Sixteenth- and Seventeenth-Century Music Theatre in France, Savoy and England,* 'Studies in History and Interpretation of Music', 68. Lewiston, 2000

Carter, T., 'Jacopo Peri's *Euridice* (1600): a Contextual Study'. *Music Review,* 43 (1982), 83–103; reprinted in Carter, *Music, Patronage and Printing in Late Renaissance Florence,* Aldershot, 2000

'The North Italian Courts'. In Price (ed.), *The Early Baroque Era,* pp. 23–48

'Lamenting Ariadne?' *Early Music,* 27 (1999), 395–405

Monteverdi's Musical Theatre. New Haven and London, 2002

'Rediscovering *Il rapimento di Cefalo*'. *Journal of Seventeenth-Century Music,* 9 (2003) <http://sscm-jscm.org/jscm/v9/no1/Carter.html>

Carter, T., and Szweykowski, Z. M. (eds), *Composing Opera: from 'Dafne' to 'Ulisse errante',* 'Practica musica', 2. Kraków, 1994

Christout, M.-F., *Le ballet de cour au XVIIᵉ siècle / The Ballet de Cour in the 17th Century,* 'Iconographie musicale', 8. Geneva, 1987

Coeyman, B., 'Walking through Lully's Opera Theatre in the Palais-Royal'. In Heyer (ed.), *Lully Studies,* pp. 216–42

Couvreur, M., *Jean-Baptiste Lully: musique et dramaturgie au service du prince.* Brussels, 1992

Cusick, S. G., 'Of Women, Music, and Power: a Model from Seicento Florence'. In R. Solie (ed.), *Musicology and Difference: Gender and Sexuality in Music Scholarship.* Berkeley, Los Angeles and London, 1993, pp. 281–304

'"There Was Not One Lady Who Failed to Shed a Tear": Arianna's Lament and the Construction of Modern Womanhood'. *Early Music,* 22 (1994), 21–41

Ducrot, A., 'Lully créateur de troupe'. *XVIIe siècle*, 98–99 (1973), 91–107

Fenlon, I., *Music and Patronage in Sixteenth-Century Mantua*. 2 vols, Cambridge, 1980, 1982

'The Mantuan *Orfeo*'. In Whenham (ed.), *Claudio Monteverdi: 'Orfeo'*, pp. 1–19

'The Origins of the Seventeenth-Century Staged *Ballo*'. In I. Fenlon and T. Carter (eds), *Con che soavità: Studies in Italian Opera, Song, and Dance, 1580–1740*. Oxford, 1995, pp. 13–40

Franko, M., *Dance as Text: Ideologies of the Baroque Body*. Cambridge, 1993

Gordon, B., 'Talking Back: the Female Voice in *Il ballo delle ingrate*'. *Cambridge Opera Journal*, 11 (1999), 1–30

Gordon, J., 'Entertainments for the Marriages of the Princesses of Savoy in 1608'. In J. R. Mulryne and M. Shewring (eds), *Italian Renaissance Festivals and Their European Influence*. Lewiston, 1992, pp. 119–40

Hammond, F., *Music and Spectacle in Baroque Rome: Barberini Patronage under Urban VIII*. New Haven and London, 1994

Hanning, B. R., 'Glorious Apollo: Poetic and Political Themes in the First Opera'. *Renaissance Quarterly*, 32 (1979), 485–513

Of Poetry and Music's Power: Humanism and the Creation of Opera. Ann Arbor, 1980

'The Ending of *L'Orfeo*: Father, Son, and Rinuccini'. *Journal of Seventeenth-Century Music*, 9 (2003) <http://sscm-jscm.org/jscm/v9/no1/Hanning.html>

Hansen, J. B., 'From Invention to Interpretation: the Prologues of the First Court Operas; Where Oral and Written Cultures Meet'. *Journal of Musicology*, 20 (2003), 556–96

Harness, K., '*La Flora* and the End of Female Rule in Tuscany'. *Journal of the American Musicological Society*, 51 (1998), 437–76

'*Le tre Euridice*: Characterization and Allegory in the *Euridici* of Peri and Caccini'. *Journal of Seventeenth-Century Music*, 9 (2003) <http://sscm-jscm.org/jscm/v9/no1/Harness.html>

Harris-Warrick, R., 'Magnificence in Motion: Stage Musicians in Lully's Ballets and Operas'. *Cambridge Opera Journal*, 6 (1994), 189–203

'Recovering the Lullian *Divertissement*'. In McCleave (ed.), *Dance and Music in French Baroque Theatre*, pp. 55–80

Heyer, J. H. (ed.), *Lully Studies*. Cambridge, 2000

Hill, J. W., 'Florence: Musical Spectacle and Drama, 1570–1650'. In Price (ed.), *The Early Baroque Era*, pp. 121–45

Holbrook, P., 'Jacobean Masques and the Jacobean Peace'. In Bevington and Holbrook (eds), *The Politics of the Stuart Court Masque*, pp. 67–87

Holman, P., 'Music for the Stage, i: Before the Civil War'. In I. Spink (ed.), *The Blackwell History of Music in Britain*, iii: *The Seventeenth Century*. Oxford, 1988, pp. 282–395

Four and Twenty Fiddlers: the Violin at the English Court, 1540–1690, Oxford, 1993

Howard, S., *The Politics of Courtly Dancing in Early Modern England*. Amherst, MA, 1998

Isherwood, R., *Music in the Service of the King: France in the Seventeenth Century*. Ithaca, 1973

Kelly, T. F., *First Nights: Five Musical Premieres*. New Haven and London, 2000

Kirkendale, W., '*L'Aria di Fiorenza' id est 'Il Ballo del Granduca'*. Florence, 1982

La Gorce, J. de, *Jean-Baptiste Lully*. Paris, 2002

Legrand, R., '*Persée* de Lully et Quinault: orientations pour l'analyse dramaturgique d'une tragédie en musique'. *Analyse musicale*, 27 (April 1992), 9–14

Le Leyzour, P., 'Myth and Enlightenment: on Mythology in the Eighteenth Century'. In C. B. Bailey (ed.), *The Loves of the Gods: Mythological Painting from Watteau to David*. New York, 1992, pp. 20–31

Leopold, S., 'Rome: Sacred and Secular'. In Price (ed.), *The Early Baroque Era*, pp. 49–74

McCleave, S. (ed.), *Dance and Music in French Baroque Theatre: Sources and Interpretations*, 'Study Texts', 3. London, 1998

MacClintock, C., and MacClintock, L., *Le ballet comique de la royne, 1581*, 'Musicological Studies and Documents', 25. American Institute of Musicology, 1971

McGowan, M., *L'art du ballet de cour en France, 1581–1643*. Paris, 1963

MacNeil, A., 'Weeping at the Water's Edge'. *Early Music*, 27 (1999), 406–17

Mamone, S., 'La danza di scena negli intermedi fiorentini: 1589–1637'. In Canova-Green and Chiarelli (eds), *The Influence of Italian Entertainments on Sixteenth- and Seventeenth-Century Music Theatre in France, Savoy and England*, pp. 13–27

Massip, C., 'Paris, 1600–61'. In Price (ed.), *The Early Baroque Era*, pp. 218–37

Molinari, C., *Le nozze degli dèi: un saggio sul grande spettacolo italiano nel Seicento*. Rome, 1968

Murata, M., 'The Recitative Soliloquy'. *Journal of the American Musicological Society*, 32 (1979), 45–73

    Operas for the Papal Court, 1631–1668, 'Studies in Musicology', 39. Ann Arbor, 1981

    'Why the First Opera in Paris Wasn't Roman'. *Cambridge Opera Journal*, 7 (1995), 87–105

Nagler, A. M., *A Source Book in Theatrical History*. New York, 1952

    Theatre Festivals of the Medici, 1539–1637. New Haven, 1964; repr. New York, 1976

Néraudau, J.-P., *L'Olympe du Roi-Soleil: mythologie et idéologie royale au Grand Siècle*. Paris, 1986

Norman, B., *Touched by the Graces: the Libretti of Philippe Quinault in the Context of French Classicism*. Birmingham, AL, 2001

Orgel, S., 'Marginal Jonson'. In Bevington and Holbrook (eds), *The Politics of the Stuart Court Masque*, pp. 144–75

Ossi, M., 'Claudio Monteverdi's *Ordine novo, bello e gustevole*: the Canzonetta as Dramatic Module and Formal Archetype'. *Journal of the American Musicological Society*, 45 (1992), 261–304

    '*Dalle machine . . . la maraviglia*: Bernardo Buontalenti's *Il rapimento di Cefalo* at the Medici Theater in 1600'. In M. A. Radice (ed.), *Opera in Context: Essays on Historical Staging from the Late Renaissance to the Time of Puccini*. Portland, OR, 1998, pp. 15–35

Osthoff, W., 'Dokumente zur italienischen Oper von 1600 bis 1706'. In Becker (ed.), *Quellentexte zur Konzeption der europäischen Oper im 17. Jahrhundert*, pp. 11–67

Peacock, J., 'Italian Libretti and the English Court Masque'. In Canova-Green and Chiarelli (eds), *The Influence of Italian Entertainments on Sixteenth- and Seventeenth-Century Music Theatre in France, Savoy and England*, pp. 93–110

Pierce, K., and Thorp, J., 'The Dances in Lully's *Persée*'. *Journal of Seventeenth-Century Music*, 10 (2004) <http://sscm-jscm.org/jscm/v10/no1/pierce.html>

Pirrotta, N., *Music and Theatre from Poliziano to Monteverdi*, trans. K. Eales. Cambridge, 1975

'Orchestra and Stage in Renaissance *Intermedi* and Early Opera'. In Pirrotta, *Music and Culture in Italy from the Middle Ages to the Baroque: a Collection of Essays*. Cambridge, MA, 1984, pp. 210–16

Povoledo, E., 'Origins and Aspects of Italian Scenography'. In Pirrotta, *Music and Theatre from Poliziano to Monteverdi*, pp. 281–383

Price, C. (ed.), *The Early Baroque Era: from the Late Sixteenth Century to the 1660s*, 'Man and Music', 3. London, 1993

Pruiksma, R., '"Dansé par le roi": Constructions of French Identity in the Court Ballets of Louis XIV'. Ph.D. thesis, University of Michigan (1999)

Prunières, H., *Le ballet de cour en France avant Benserade et Lulli*. Paris, 1913

Rizzi, G. (ed.), *Repertorio di feste alla corte di Savoia (1346–1669) raccolto dai trattati di C. F. Menestrier*. Turin, 1973

Rosow, L., 'French Baroque Recitative as an Expression of Tragic Declamation'. *Early Music*, 11 (1983), 468–79

'Making Connections: Some Thoughts on Lully's Entr'actes'. *Early Music*, 21 (1993), 231–8

'The Articulation of Lully's Dramatic Dialogue'. In Heyer (ed.), *Lully Studies*, pp. 72–99

Saslow, J. M., *The Medici Wedding of 1589: Florentine Festival as 'Theatrum mundi'*. New Haven and London, 1996

Savage, R., and Sansone, M., '*Il corago* and the Staging of Early Opera: Four Chapters from an Anonymous Treatise circa 1630'. *Early Music*, 17 (1989), 495–511

Schneider, H., 'Dokumente zur französischen Oper von 1659 bis 1699'. In Becker (ed.), *Quellentexte zur Konzeption der europäischen Oper im 17. Jahrhundert*, pp. 103–60

Solerti, A., *Gli albori del melodramma*. 3 vols, Milan, 1904; repr. Hildesheim, 1969

Musica, ballo e drammatica alla corte medicea dal 1600 al 1637. Florence, 1905; repr. Hildesheim, 1969

Southorn, J., *Power and Display in the Seventeenth Century: the Arts and Their Patrons in Modena and Ferrara*. Cambridge, 1988

Spitzer, J., and Zaslaw, N., *The Birth of the Orchestra: History of an Institution, 1650–1815*. Oxford, 2004

Stein, L. K., *Songs of Mortals, Dialogues of the Gods: Music and Theatre in Seventeenth-Century Spain*. Oxford, 1993

'The Origins and Character of *Recitado*'. *Journal of Seventeenth-Century Music*, 9 (2003) <http://sscm-jscm.org/jscm/v9/no1/Stein.html>

Sternfeld, F. W., *The Birth of Opera*. Oxford, 1993

Strong, R., *Art and Power: Renaissance Festivals, 1450–1650*. Woodbridge, Suffolk, 1984

Tomlinson, G., 'Madrigal, Monody, and Monteverdi's "via naturale alla immitatione"'. *Journal of the American Musicological Society*, 34 (1981), 60–108

Walls, P., *Music in the English Courtly Masque, 1604–1640*. Oxford, 1996

Ward, J. M., 'Newly Devis'd Measures for Jacobean Masques'. *Acta musicologica*, 60 (1988), 111–42

Weiss, P. (ed.), *Opera: a History in Documents*. Oxford, 2002

Whenham, J. (ed.), *Claudio Monteverdi: 'Orfeo'*, 'Cambridge Opera Handbooks'. Cambridge, 1986

Wood, C., *Music and Drama in the 'Tragédie en musique', 1673–1715: Jean-Baptiste Lully and his Successors*. New York, 1996

Wood, C., and Sadler, G., *French Baroque Opera: a Reader*. Aldershot, 2000

Zaslaw, N., 'The First Opera in Paris: a Study in the Politics of Art'. In J. H. Heyer (ed.), *Jean-Baptiste Lully and the Music of the French Baroque: Essays in Honor of James R. Anthony*. Cambridge, 1989, pp. 7–23

9

Mask and illusion: Italian opera after 1637

TIM CARTER

There are several different histories of seventeenth-century opera that might be written. One would take as its starting-point Jacopo Peri's *Euridice* (libretto by Ottavio Rinuccini), staged in Florence on 6 October 1600 during the festivities for the wedding of Maria de' Medici and Henri IV of France. *Euridice* has obvious roots in sixteenth-century theatrical traditions, including the *intermedi*, and also immediate precedents in various Florentine entertainments staged during the 1590s. Yet it remains totemic because it is the first example of the genre to survive complete. Locating the 'beginning' of opera in 1600 is obviously convenient: the new century coincides with what many have subsequently viewed as a new artistic era, the Baroque, and indeed, opera is often viewed as the Baroque genre *par excellence*. This history would also have other merits, not least because seventeenth-century (and, indeed, later) opera could not have been conceived without Peri's invention of musical recitative, and no less important, without Rinuccini's precedent for what quickly became standard poetic techniques for librettos.

But we could tell another, different history. The operas performed in the north Italian courts and in Rome in the first third or so of the seventeenth century formed just part of a broader gamut of princely entertainment that also embraced plays with *intermedi*, *balli*, *mascherate*, and various kinds of tournaments (on foot, horseback or water).[1] Court operas were not necessarily identified as belonging to a distinct genre – given that the parameters of such works remained in flux – and indeed few courts appreciated them specifically as music-dramas. Early comments that the recitative-style was 'tedious' square with the notion that princes and their courtiers were reluctant merely to sit and watch a drama played out in music, preferring instead to be amazed by spectacular scenic display, and also to participate actively in the spectacle, for example by way of dance. Thus the history of court opera comprises only isolated, one-off works, each of which were *sui generis*, and each beholden to the changing demands for court entertainment in specific times and places.

---

1 Carter, 'The North Italian Courts'.

By this reading, the 'real' history of opera might begin only in 1637, when the Teatro San Cassiano in Venice opened its doors to a paying public and began to perform operas on a regular basis, soon to be joined by other commercial theatres in Venice and, eventually, elsewhere in Italy. The year 1637 may not be so convenient as 1600, but the geographical location of this new start in operatic history has distinct advantages. Venice was a republic, not a duchy, and was governed at least in principle (although not in fact) on near-democratic lines. The Venetian state was also (in appearance, but again, not in fact) resolutely secular: its famous resistance to ecclesiastical interference was made concrete in the Interdict of 1606, when Venetians as a body were threatened with excommunication by the Pope. As a secular republic – the last surviving such state in Italy except for Genoa – Venice has obvious attractions for those modern historians who prefer to regard both the Church and the court as the last bastions of repressive orthodoxy and thus unable to promote or even countenance political, economic, social or cultural innovation. In the context of this Whig (rather than Tory) view of history, it is almost inevitable that opera, a genre of such significance for the Western art tradition, should seem to have found its ideal home in a republican environment.

Venice already had 'public' and other theatres that staged dramatic performances, often with considerable amounts of music.[2] But there is no doubt that opera underwent a new start in 1637. The Teatro S. Cassiano was quickly followed by the Teatro SS. Giovanni e Paolo (1639), the Teatro S. Moisè (1640) and the Teatro Novissimo (1641). Five new operas were performed in Venice in the three seasons following the opening of the Teatro S. Cassiano: some 50 had been performed there by 1650. Here, then, we tend to find established the production mechanisms that dominate opera for at least the next two centuries: opera-houses offering regular seasons mixing new operas with revivals to a ticket- (or subscription-) buying audience and managed by an owner or impresario; star singers commanding sizeable fees; and large production teams ranging from poets, scene-designers, composers and choreographers through the rank and file of the chorus and orchestra to the lowly sellers of tickets, printed literature and refreshments. Similarly, the steady stream of new works for which contemporary audiences clamoured – coupled with the growth of fixed conventions that make many of them variations on a basic theme – also gave opera a permanence and a tradition that had been so sorely lacking before. Venetian theatres and their impresarios had found a recipe for success that, if not without risk, could generate profit. Indeed, one can speak of a veritable opera factory, with librettists, singers, stage and costume designers, and – not necessarily towards

---

2 Shiff, 'Are the Grimani Banquet Plays "Rappresentazioni musicali"?'; MacNeil, *Music and Women of the Commedia dell'Arte in the Late Sixteenth Century*.

the top of the pecking order – composers all earning something of a living from what was clearly a growth industry.

In economic and other terms, the contrast with court opera could not be more marked: court entertainments may have been important for prestige, and may also have served other symbolic purposes, but they inevitably resulted in financial loss rather than gain: profit, at least in modern capitalist terms, did not even figure in the equation. However, the conventional view of Venetian (re)public(an) opera is somewhat simplistic: it was by no means as 'public' (or for that matter, as republican) as Whiggish commentators have wished to assume. Indeed, it often relied on the support of noble patrons and academies in ways not so different from its court counterpart, and it tended, at least in its early stages, to follow earlier examples of the genre in thematic and stylistic terms. Venetian opera, like its courtly counterpart, could also serve political purposes, whether to glorify the state and its government or to fix a social agenda. Moreover, to make a clear-cut distinction between court and public opera is also to ignore the mixed modes of production and consumption that in fact tended to dominate the period.[3] Jean-Baptiste Lully's *tragédies en musique*, while certainly courtly in orientation and function, were also performed in a reasonably public theatre in an urban environment (the Palais-Royal in Paris) frequented by the lesser French nobility and gentry. Conversely, even when operas were performed at court, they were scarcely the opposite of 'public', i.e., private, with all that implies in terms of location, function and consumption. Even if we must treat with a grain of salt the claim that Monteverdi's *Arianna*, for the festivities celebrating the wedding of Prince Francesco Gonzaga and Margherita of Savoy in Mantua in 1608, was presented before an audience of 6,000,[4] it is clear that courtly entertainment also had its public face. Later in the century, leading members of the ruling Medici family in Florence worked closely with Venetian theatre-owners to recruit, nurture and exploit talented singers, and acted as impresarios to arrange performances in a number of different theatrical spaces within their state, some courtly, some public, and some linked to academies.[5] Similarly, Duke Francesco II d'Este of Modena was quite happy, it seems, to stage operas imported from Venice with singers from his *cappella*, from other nearby courts, and even professionals recruited on the 'open' market, in a theatre that was seemingly independent from the court (and run by an impresario, Marchese Decio Fontanelli) and yet strongly supported by the ducal treasury.

---

3 Bianconi and Walker, 'Production, Consumption and Political Function of Seventeenth-Century Opera'.

4 Another contemporary estimate was 4,000, which also seems too high; see Carter, *Monteverdi's Musical Theatre*, p. 79.

5 Mamone, 'Most Serene Brothers–Princes–Impresarios'.

It is clear that operas written for, and first performed in, Venice could quite easily be transplanted into court theatres with or without adjustment, and composers could move quite easily from one type of theatre to the other. The rather chequered career of Antonio Cesti (1623–69) is a good example, taking him from his native Arezzo through Volterra, Florence, Venice, Innsbruck, Rome, Vienna and back to Florence, where he met an untimely death (he may have been poisoned by his rivals) at the age of 46. He was a tenor, an organist and above all a composer of cantatas and of operas for the theatres of Venice, Innsbruck and Vienna. His works include the sumptuous court opera *Il pomo d'oro*, with 24 different stage sets and a large-scale orchestra, staged in Vienna in 1668 (it was originally intended to celebrate the marriage of Emperor Leopold I in 1666). But he also wrote operas on the Venetian model, including *Alessandro vincitor di se stesso* (1651), *L'Argia* (1655), *Orontea* (1656) and *La Dori* (1657). To judge by its number of performances, *Orontea* (to a libretto by Giacinto Andrea Cicognini) was one of the most successful operas of its time: it was performed in Genoa (1660, 1661), Rome and Florence (1661), Turin (1662), Ferrara (1663), Milan (1664), Macerata (1665) and Bologna (1665, 1669), Venice (1666), Bergamo, Brescia and Palermo (1667), Lucca (1668), Portomaggiore (1670), Naples (1674), Reggio Emilia (1674), Hanover (1678) and Venice (1683).

This spread of performances was not unusual. The relatively short seasons for opera in Venice (the main one was Carnival, traditionally from 26 December, St Stephen's Day, to just before Lent) left considerable time for touring, and by the mid 1640s a group known as the Febiarmonici ('Musicians of Apollo') was performing operas across northern Italy (for example, Sacrati's *La finta pazza* in Piacenza in 1644) and in Paris in early 1645.[6] The company was modelled on the touring *commedia dell'arte* troupes that had been a part of the Italian theatrical scene long before the development of opera. Performances by the Febiarmonici – there may have been several companies with the name – are recorded in Genoa (1644), Florence and Lucca (1645), Genoa and Florence (1646), Genoa, Bologna and Milan (1647), Bologna, Turin, Reggio Emilia, Ferrara and Rimini (1648), Milan (1649) and Lucca (1650), with operas such as *La finta pazza* and Cavalli's *Egisto* and *Giasone*. In early 1650, the company was brought to Naples by the Viceroy, Count d'Oñate, who was anxious to exploit theatrical entertainments as a means of restoring normality after the Masaniello uprising of 1647–8. Cavalli's *Didone* was staged in October, and in 1651, the Febiarmonici performed *Egisto* and *Giasone*, and also Monteverdi's *L'incoronazione di Poppea* (as *Il Nerone*). They also gave the premiere of Cavalli's *Veremonda* to celebrate the Spanish victory in Catalonia (and also the Queen

---

6 Bianconi and Walker, 'Dalla *Finta pazza* alla *Veremonda*'; Murata, 'Why the First Opera Given in Paris Wasn't Roman'.

of Spain's birthday) in December 1652. With the departure of Count d'Oñate in late 1653, the company transferred to the Teatro San Bartolomeo (from April 1654). Their precarious financial position was exacerbated by the plague of 1656, but performances resumed the following year until 1668, largely of revised Venetian operas.

Of course, taking a work from one city to another might prompt changes and revisions to suit the new context – substitute prologues could be particularly useful in this light – and different audience expectations. For example, when Jacopo Melani's *Ercole in Tebe*, staged by the Accademia degli Immobili in Florence to celebrate the wedding of Grand Duke Cosimo III and Marguerite Louise of Orléans in 1661, was revived in Venice a decade later, the plot was reworked, the *intermedi* removed, the spectacular stage effects cut down, recitatives shortened or omitted, and the whole compressed from five to three acts. However, the mere possibility of such changes is witness to the increasingly fixed and formulaic nature of the genre: the codification of literary and musical conventions, and the stabilising of fixed textual and musical forms, permitted the easy and effective interpolation or substitution of discrete units within the whole without necessarily affecting its integrity.

Part of the problem of definition, and at the root of many other difficulties in creating a convincing history of seventeenth-century opera, is the sheer scale of the repertory, which is hard to conceive and impossible to rationalise. To judge by Claudio Sartori's catalogue of printed opera librettos to 1800, the number of seventeenth-century operas stretches into four figures even accepting that not every surviving libretto represents a different opera. In effect, composers operated on a production line. There are 30 operas securely attributed to Francesco Cavalli (1602–76), and perhaps another 10. Giovanni Legrenzi (1626–90) wrote 18, Cesti and Alessandro Melani (1639–1703) 12 each, and Melani's elder brother, Jacopo (1623–76), 10. Pietro Andrea Ziani (1616–84) produced 28 operas, mostly for Venice, and the list of theatrical works by his nephew, Marc'Antonio (*c.* 1653–1715), has 47 items, 24 of which are new operas (the rest are adaptations and other theatrical genres), produced at a rate (at his peak) of 2 or 3 new works per year. Antonio Sartorio (1630–80) wrote 15 operas mostly for Venice; Agostino Steffani (1654–1728) wrote 17 for Munich, Hanover and Düsseldorf; and Alessandro Scarlatti (1660–1725) wrote some 35 operas before 1700, and another 30 or so after. Even relatively minor figures could produce works in significant numbers: Giovanni Antonio Boretti (*c.* 1640–1672), 8 operas, 1666–72; Domenico Freschi (*c.* 1630–1710), 13, 1677–85; Carlo Grossi (*c.* 1634–1688), 4; Francesco Lucio (*c.* 1628–1658), 5; Francesco Sacrati (1605–50), 6. These numbers are not unusual for opera composers in later generations: Handel wrote 46, Cimarosa almost 60, Paisiello 80 or so, Rossini 39, Donizetti some 65, and Verdi 28. But for the seventeenth century (and also the eighteenth), a huge amount of the surviving repertory – itself only a proportion of what was staged – lies unperformed, unedited, unstudied and therefore unknown.

It is usually the case in music-historical inquiry that we are aware only of the tip of the iceberg: much the same applies to, say, the symphony in the second half of the eighteenth century, or the piano sonata in the nineteenth. Yet in the case of these later repertories, the works that percolate to the surface and therefore come to our attention normally do so by way of canon-forming processes, and thus by some measure of aesthetic value, however much we might deplore the blind prejudices that this entails. A canon is, of course, highly exclusive, and will rarely operate fairly, so it must be some part of the job of the musicologist to expose canonic chauvinism and to discover new musical worlds. But this is not to say that works already elevated by the canon should consequently be ignored. For seventeenth-century opera, however, a canon is hardly yet in place, and therefore it is very hard to know even where to start in producing an account of the repertory. Even assuming that one can get some kind of grip on so large a corpus, the question remains of how to identify works of value, or even to decide how value might be determined in the first place.

One might, of course, rely on some contemporary measure of popularity (e.g., number of performances or revivals) or indeed on what seventeenth-century audiences and critics had to say about these operas. However, popularity is fickle, and there is little opera criticism as such from this period. More problematic, if by no means untypically so, is just what audiences might have valued anyway. John Evelyn, for example, was mightily impressed by Giovanni Rovetta's *Ercole in Lidia*, which he saw during his visit to Venice in June 1645:

> This night . . . we went to the Opera, which are Comedies & other plays represented in Recitative Music by the most excellent Musitians vocal & Instrumental, together with variety of Seeanes [*sic*] painted & contrived with no lesse art of Perspective, and Machines, for flying in the aire, & other wonderfull motions. So taken together it is doubtlesse one of the most magnificent & expensfull diversions the Wit of Men can invent: The historie was *Hercules* in Lydia, the Seanes chang'd 13 times, The famous Voices, *Anna Rencia* a Roman, & reputed the best treble of Women; but there was an *Eunuch*, that in my opinion surpass'd her, and a *Genoveze* that sung an incomparable Base: This held us by the Eyes and Eares til two in the Morning . . .[7]

Evelyn was delighted by the experience, he admired the lavish scenery and the machines, and he enjoyed the singers, including the famous Anna Renzi, a

7 E. S. de Beer (ed.), *The Diary of John Evelyn* (London, 1959), pp. 228–9.

castrato and a bass from Genoa. He seems to have cared little about the story, and he says nothing about the musical score (which is now lost).

A further difficulty for the scholar is the status of those scores that do survive – almost all in manuscript – and of the 'works' that they contain. Seventeenth-century opera manuscripts range from rough copies bearing all the signs of (repeated) use in the theatre – performance annotations, instructions for trans-position, pages added and removed (by inserts, paste-overs, excisions), and material revised or deleted – to 'clean' copies with little or no trace of direct use and probably serving as an object to be presented to a patron, treasured by a connoisseur, or lodged in a library. The closer the copy to some performance environment, the more scrappy it usually becomes: gaps are left (e.g., in the inner instrumental parts) to be filled out on demand, and successive layers of alterations (in rehearsal and through performance) make it ever harder to con-struct an 'original' text, or to determine which of several possible texts is the 'finished' work. The most famous example of the period is also quite typical: the two surviving scores of Monteverdi's *L'incoronazione di Poppea* (both probably from the early 1650s) differ quite widely on numerous levels of detail ranging from the large scale (scenes and their order, the extent and nature of the music within them) to the small (different instrumental ritornellos, a host of varia-tions at the level of the phrase or even bar). It is now widely accepted that not all the music in the surviving versions of *Poppea* is by Monteverdi (whether some earlier version of the opera ever was entirely by him is a different question), and that it is presently impossible to recover the musical text as it was first performed in 1643.[8]

One might reasonably treat the *Poppea*(s) we have as works in and of them-selves, independent of the problematic issues of their attribution or whether they were actually used on the stage. Thus we may or may not be able to per-form and study a given composer's *Poppea* (Monteverdi's), but we can do so for either version of the opera that survives. This position would trouble only those fiercely (if unreasonably, for the seventeenth century) committed to notions of the composer's authoritative 'voice' and/or of a definitive *Urtext*. But even this 'work' is only partial. Our sources certainly preserve traces of something called *L'incoronazione di Poppea* (or *La coronatione di Poppea*, or *Il Nerone*), but as Evelyn's comments suggest, what we see on the page provides only the barest starting point for what we actually experience in the theatre, given that the overall theatrical context (sets, staging, movement and dancing, and the grain of the voices) is an integral part of the operatic exercise. The musical manuscript is as close to the staged work as an architect's drawings to a finished building.

---

8 Curtis, '*La Poppea impasticciata*'.

This is not to say that these scores necessarily, or even somehow, need fleshing out in terms of musical notes, as has often been assumed.[9] The claim that the musical sources for *Poppea*, and for most Cavalli operas, are in the manner of sketches (or 'skeletons', as they have been called) has regularly been used as an excuse for all manner of additions, only sporadically tasteful, ranging from lavish orchestral accompaniments to more modest ritornellos and sinfonias. This has been done on the somewhat dubious grounds that it gets us closer either to what the composer 'intended' (even if he did not necessarily get what he wanted) or to what regularly happened in the seventeenth-century opera-house (even if it was not what the composer wished). 'Intention' is, of course, famously problematic, particularly in a period, and in a genre, where the compositional act was not granted quasi-scriptural significance. A claim for common practice might seem more reasonable (although it would still exclude the notion that the Teatro SS. Giovanni e Paolo in Venice had a modern symphony orchestra in its pit). It was a fact of operatic life that should a singer need an aria adjusted to suit the voice, or should a change of set or movement from A to B require some extra instrumental music, then it would be done without question or fuss. In this sense, 'authenticity' would permit taking any liberties with a seventeenth-century operatic score that might be needed for performance's sake, within the bounds of contemporary practice.

For the historian, however, the problems are of a different order. The perils of looking at operatic music (in the sense of the score) divorced from everything else that goes to make an opera (the libretto, staging, performance) are obvious. But failures to understand the intricacies of Seicento Italian poetry and its musical (or not) implications, to realise just how many sets are needed to stage a given Venetian opera and how they might be changed in view of the audience, or even to consider the casting of singers, have led to some famously inadequate readings, and at times drastic misreadings, of works in the seventeenth-century repertory. Our rather Romantic belief that opera is, in the end, an inherently musical art-form is in part conditioned by the historical roots of our discipline, and in part (if more perniciously) by an attempt to rescue opera from the messy and contingent world of the theatre to place it on the pedestal of absolute music. It also, one must admit, reflects the common experience of seeing an opera in a terrible production with fourth-rate singers still managing to make some musical and dramatic effect. Operas can be very resilient from that point of view, and one might assume that they were equally so in the seventeenth century: the more interesting question is just what gave them this resilience in the first place.

---

9 For the various positions adopted by Alan Curtis, Nikolaus Harnoncourt, René Jacobs and Raymond Leppard, see Carter, *Monteverdi's Musical Theatre*, pp. 11–12.

The problems of handling this massive repertory in terms of its sheer numbers, and of defining the seventeenth-century operatic 'work', have produced some rather odd distortions in the literature. Aside from Monteverdi, Cavalli, Steffani, Stradella and Alessandro Scarlatti,[10] there are few Italian opera composers who seem significant or colourful enough to warrant a standard life-and-works treatment. The relative lack of a canon of 'great' seventeenth-century operas within the regular operatic repertory also means that there are very few single operas that will gain a monograph all of their own: the well-known series of Cambridge Opera Handbooks included just Monteverdi's *Orfeo*, and not even Purcell's *Dido and Aeneas* (or a single Handel opera). Accordingly, the tendency has been to try to make sense of this broad canvas by way of generic narratives focussing in large part on typologies or specific themes.[11] Useful though these narratives are, they often fail to treat individual works as a whole, and the central sections of the present chapter mark a conscious attempt to redress the imbalances that ensue. I have chosen three Italian operas from the period that have scant canonic status (save that they are available in facsimile or modern edition), that are rarely performed, and indeed that tend to be dismissed in studies of this repertory. I place each in its various historical and other contexts. But most important, I try to show how and why we might care about them as objects in and of themselves. Much of this music has been silent for centuries, and it is impossible to bring it to life in printed prose. Yet it is worth giving it some kind of voice.

Francesco Cavalli (1602–76), *Gli amori di Apollo e di Dafne* (1640)

If one seeks a connection between court opera of the first third of the seventeenth century and Venetian 'public' opera from 1637 onwards, it is probably to be found in Rome. The new theatrical genres involving music took root there in both spiritual and secular contexts.[12] Emilio de' Cavalieri's *Rappresentatione di Anima, et di Corpo* (1600), the first fully sung music-drama to survive complete (although it is not very dramatic), was in the mould of a *sacra rappresentazione* linked to Oratorian traditions; other 'sacred' operas were closer to

---

10 Glover, *Cavalli*; Timms, *Polymath of the Baroque*; Gianturco, *Alessandro Stradella*; Grout, *Alessandro Scarlatti*.

11 The obvious example is Ellen Rosand's very fine *Opera in Seventeenth-Century Venice*, to which the present chapter might appear to be a countertext, although in fact it is an intertext. My specific remarks on the operas, below, are best anchored within the broader contexts and typologies established by Rosand. For important examples of other thematic approaches, see Heller, *Emblems of Eloquence*; Schulze, *Odysseus in Venedig*.

12 A convenient overview is provided in Hammond, *Music and Spectacle in Baroque Rome*, pp. 183–254. See also Murata, *Operas for the Papal Court*.

Jesuit school-dramas, as in the case of Agostino Agazzari's *Eumelio* (Seminario Romano, 1606) and Ottavio Catalani's *Davidus musicus* (Collegio Germanico, 1613). However, the confluence of prelates and princes in Rome also prompted secular entertainments in the manner of (and on similar mythological subjects to) operas typical of the north Italian courts: Stefano Landi's *La morte d'Orfeo* (1619), Filippo Vitali's *Aretusa* (1620), and Domenico Mazzocchi's *La catena d'Adone* (1626; libretto by Ottavio Tronsarelli). When Maffeo Barberini (a Florentine) was elected Pope Urban VIII in 1624, he and his family initiated a long-term programme of cultural renewal wherein the arts might serve both political and religious propaganda. This mixing of secular and sacred concerns should not come as a surprise, and although Roman operas might be divided into one or the other categories by way of subject-matter, it is probably inappropriate to do so: Greek myths and Ovidian metamorphoses had long been moralised during the Renaissance to produce a suitably 'Christian' message, while the lives of saints usually provided enough material for spectacular stage effects. The Barberini did not sell tickets for their operas, but in almost every other sense they were 'public', if by invitation, with repeat performances for the Roman aristocracy (cardinals and prelates, noblemen, noblewomen), foreign dignitaries, and visitors to the city.

It is now clear that musicians somehow associated with Rome had a significant influence on the emergence of opera in Venice. For example, the composer and singer Francesco Manelli and his wife Maddalena, herself a virtuoso singer, lodged in the house of Stefano Landi around 1630: Maddalena was later involved in the tournament *Ermiona* performed (with music by Giovanni Felice Sances) in Padua in 1636 that has been viewed as a precursor of Venetian opera. Similarly, Francesco Manelli's later collaborator, the poet, composer and lutenist Benedetto Ferrari (1603 or 1604–1681), was trained in Rome, even if he later found employment (from 1619 to 1623, at least) in Parma. Manelli, as composer, and Ferrari, as librettist, provided the first operas staged at the Teatro S. Cassiano in Venice, *Andromeda* (1637) and *La maga fulminata* (1638). Only then did composers already resident in Venice, notably Francesco Cavalli, Claudio Monteverdi and Francesco Sacrati, take to the operatic stage.

The history of Venetian theatrical entertainments before 1637 is hazy, although it is clear that visiting *commedia dell'arte* troupes appeared there before paying audiences, and included music in their performances.[13] Venetian noblemen also commissioned staged entertainments in spite of their traditional reluctance to engage in ostentatious display dictated in part by Venetian sumptuary legislation. Thus Monteverdi provided the opera *Proserpina rapita* for the

---

13 MacNeil, *Music and Women of the Commedia dell'Arte in the Late Sixteenth Century.*

wedding of Giustiniana Mocenigo and Lorenzo Giustiniani on 16 April 1630 (the music is almost entirely lost). Venice was by no means the virgin territory for musical theatre it is often assumed to have been: it had the spaces, the patrons and the performers necessary to sustain the genre. But none of this explains the huge popularity of the genre; nor, one suspects, could Manelli and Ferrari have foreseen its explosion.

Opera soon became firmly entrenched within the so-called 'myth of Venice', the tropes by which the city projected its self-image as a republican paradise. Maiolino Bisaccioni made the point in his account of the spectacular stagings achieved by the scene-designer Giacomo Torelli (1608–78) in the Teatro Novissimo:

> Venice, always and on every occasion extraordinary, and never tired of displaying her greatness, has discovered the remarkable also in virtuoso entertainment, having introduced a few years ago the presentation in music of grand drama with such sets and stage-machines that they surpass all belief; and what the richest treasuries can produce only with difficulty (and only rarely) in royal halls here we see easily achieved with private resources, not only in one, but in three theatres at once; and competing with each other for the greatest perfections, they each draw spectators from the most remote parts of Italy.[14]

The reality was more hard-headed. Venice was the pleasure-garden of Europe, an essential stopping point on the 'grand tour' and a common winter resort for Italian and northern princes and prelates who, travelling incognito, could enjoy the licence of Carnival in apparent anonymity. The collapse of trade and industry during difficult economic times, and in the face of increasing competition, forced the city to reconfigure its economy towards what might broadly be defined as tourism, with all manner of licit and illicit pleasures available on tap. Selling sex came high on the agenda, and for all the noble claims of seventeenth-century Venetians and modern scholars, the opera consumed in Venice presented the perfect combination of wine, women and song.

The subjects of early Venetian opera were chosen accordingly, offering a voyeuristic titillation rendered all the more enticing by the relative freedom with which women singers could appear on the stage (they were disbarred from so doing in the Papal States). Myth, epic (Homer and Virgil, or Ariosto and Tasso) and history were all fair game for operatic subject-matter. Ostensibly 'sacred' subjects were necessarily taboo – they were neither appropriate to Carnival nor fitting for a republican agenda that argued fiercely for the separation of (Roman) church and (Venetian) state – although the ecclesiastical

---

14 Rosand, *Opera in Seventeenth-Century Venice*, p. 104. Rosand places Venetian opera and its subjects squarely in these broader political contexts; see also her 'Music in the Myth of Venice'.

censors could be appeased (at least for the purposes of obtaining a licence to print a libretto) by some kind of moral framed in a prefatory 'argomento' and/or by a standard disclaimer that references to 'love' or to the heavens were to be read metaphorically and thus were not contrary to the Faith. As for the erotic play of the gods, the magical spells of chivalric romance, or the (mis)deeds of a pagan past, the prudish mind could always glean stern lessons from such topics, if only by negative example; most readers had long been trained to do just that. Indeed, it was probably the sheer diversity of possible interpretations of these operas that helped secure their success: their polyvalency meant that one could read into them whatever one wished. But one wonders just how much people cared.

Cavalli's first three operas for S. Cassiano – *Le nozze di Teti e di Peleo* (1639), *Gli amori di Apollo e di Dafne* (1640) and *Didone* (1641) – fit the mould. While *Didone* has gained some favour for its powerful heroine and its place as a precursor of other seventeenth-century 'Dido' operas,[15] the first two have tended to be ignored, chiefly, one suspects, because their mythological subjects would seem to make them too close to court opera for the historian's comfort.[16] Something similar has happened to Monteverdi's first new opera for Venice, *Il ritorno d'Ulisse in patria* (1640), which lies in the shadow of his much more provocative (and it would seem, more modern) *L'incoronazione di Poppea*.

Cavalli's *Gli amori di Apollo e di Dafne* conflates (probably unknowingly) the subjects of two of the very first Florentine operas, Jacopo Peri's *Dafne* (1598; libretto by Ottavio Rinuccini) and *Il rapimento di Cefalo* (1600; libretto by Gabriello Chiabrera, and music by Giulio Caccini and others).[17] It does so in the manner of a series of static tableaux that scarcely constitute a 'drama' in any conventional sense of the term. This is doubly surprising not just because of the presumed dramatic force of Venetian opera, but also because the opera's librettist, Giovanni Francesco Busenello (1598–1659), is usually regarded as a principal model for the new breed of theatre poets, influenced by Spanish drama and willing to fuse a gritty realism with the sort of libertine political scepticism that is customarily identified with Venice's brand of republicanism. This is the reading normally applied to texts by Busenello and his colleagues in the Venetian Accademia degli Incogniti, a literary group which had an undoubted

---

15 Heller, "'O castità bugiarda'".

16 Strictly speaking, *Le nozze di Teti e di Peleo* is drawn from Homer (Peleus and Thetis were the parents of Achilles) and thus forms the first in a sequence of 'Trojan War' operas that Ellen Rosand (*Opera in Seventeenth-Century Venice*, pp. 59–60) notes was typical of Venetian opera (in one version of the myth of Venice, the city saw itself as a new Troy). However, the handling of the subject is very close to myth, with not much political capital made of the outcome. The subject was not unusual in court operas; see Carter, *Monteverdi's Musical Theatre*, pp. 198–9.

17 For the latter, see Carter, 'Rediscovering *Il rapimento di Cefalo*'.

influence (as poets, impresarios and patrons) on opera in Venice in the 1640s: the *ne plus ultra* is, of course, Monteverdi's *Poppea*. However, none of this seems to apply to Busenello's very first libretto.

Gli amori di Apollo e di Dafne is in the now standard three acts.[18] Aurora (Dawn), wife of Titone (Tithonus) is enamoured of Cefalo (Cephalus), who loves her in return, much to the chagrin of his wife, Procri (Procris); thus there is no need for Aurora to kidnap Cefalo as told by Ovid in Book 7 of his *Metamorphoses* (and as represented by Chiabrera). A second strand comes from Book 1 of the *Metamorphoses*. Apollo vaunts his power over Cupid, who gains revenge by making the sun-god fall in love with the chaste nymph Dafne, devoted to the cult of Diana and preferring the delights of hunting to the pleasures of men. She flees Apollo and seeks help from her father Peneo (Peneus) who turns her into a laurel; Apollo rues his rashness and wears the laurel branch as a crown, consecrating himself to art. Ovid's explanation for Cupid's animosity towards Apollo is the latter's bragging of his skills as an archer on having slain the Python. Busenello, however, has it prompted by Venere (Venus; Cupid's mother), who seeks Giove's (Jove's) permission to take her revenge on Apollo for having exposed her naked with Mars to the gaze of her husband, Vulcan. Busenello also gives Dafne one last chance (just as her metamorphosis nears completion) to regret her choice of chastity and to proclaim her eternal love for Apollo, and for the finale he brings in the god Pane (Pan, whose love for Syrinx had resulted in another metamorphosis) to provide an apotheotic conclusion, with the transformed lovers lauded in the heavens. Finally, he adds an elderly nymph, Cirilla (an alto, probably male in a transvestite role), who dreams of the Apollo/Dafne story and seeks out its meaning from the soothsayer Alfesibeo, and another nymph, Filena, who tries to dissuade Dafne from virtuous chastity. All this is set in context by the Prologue, delivered by Sonno (the god of sleep) and his helpmates (Morfeo, Itaton and Panto), who promise to conjure up 'pleasant images and strange forms' ('immagini gioconde e strane forme') so that frail mankind might learn to read supernatural signs ('l'huomo frale a indovinar s'insegni'). We never really discover what the 'signs' here might mean: the closest we get to a 'message' in *Gli amori di Apollo e di Dafne* is Alfesibeo's interpretation (II.2) of Cirilla's dream, and therefore of the opera's main story, as a warning against ignoring the wishes of the gods. But the 'dream' scenario is a conventional gambit to permit the representation of magical events on the stage; it also provides a tenuous connection between the Aurora/Cefalo story

---

18 I have used the facsimile of the score (Venice, Biblioteca Nazionale Marciana, MS It. IV.404) published as F. Cavalli, *Gli Amori d'Apollo e di Dafne*, ed. H. M. Brown, 'Italian Opera, 1640–1770', 1 (New York and London, 1978). For the libretto in a later edition in Busenello's collected works, *Delle hore ociose* (1656), see H. M. Brown (ed.), *Italian Opera Librettos, 1640–1770*, ii (New York and London, 1979), no. 1.

on the one hand, and the Dafne/Apollo one on the other, given that (so the Prologue says) such dreams occur just before dawn.

Initiating the plot at dawn is a conventional bow to at least one of the so-called Aristotelian unities that governed the proper construction of a drama, the unity of time (that the action should take place within the 12 or 24 hours of a single day). The double story-line here is more problematic in that it violates the unities of action, and also, it would seem, of place (although we have few clear details of the staging of the opera). Such violation of the rules may, in the end, just be inevitable, as Vincenzo Nolfi admitted in the preface to his libretto *Bellerofonte* (1642):

> You waste your time, O reader, if, with the *Poetics* of the Stagirite [Aristotle] in hand you go tracking down the errors in this work, because I freely confess that in composing it I did not aim to observe any precepts other than the desires of the scene designer.[19]

But Busenello was a little more sensitive to convention, at least on transplanting his text from the stage into a more literary context: when he included *Gli amori di Apollo e di Dafne* in his collected works (*Delle hore ociose*, published in 1656), he provided it with a preface claiming justification for its multiple strands in the famous late Renaissance pastoral play, Battista Guarini's *Il pastor fido*.[20]

It was not a strong defence – *Il pastor fido* had also been condemned for its violation of the unity of action – and there are other consequences. Aside from the three roles in the prologue, there are fifteen named characters in the opera, plus parts for three Muses (accompanying Apollo in what seems to be a descent of Parnassus at the start of Act II), two choruses, and dancers for a 'ballo de fantasmi' at the end of the prologue, and a dance of nymphs and shepherds in Act I scene 4.[21] However, six of these characters appear in only one scene each – Cirilla (1.2), Giove and Venere (1.3), Procri (an extended lament in 1.8), Peneo and Pan (III.2) – which means that they do not develop as characters through the opera. This may respond at least in part to pragmatic requirements. With some fast costume-changing, the opera can be done by nine singers doubling up roles, comprising four sopranos, one alto, two tenors, one baritone, one bass. This is a standard number for operas of the period.[22]

Gli amori di Apollo e di Dafne is economical in other ways, too. The sets are not specified in the score but were presumably drawn from the standard stock in the Teatro S. Cassiano, with a woodland scene to represent Thessaly, some

---

19 Rosand, *Opera in Seventeenth-Century Venice*, p. 100.   20 Ibid., pp. 51, 411–12.
21 The choreography was presumably by Giuseppe (Schioppi) Alabardi, who regularly produced dances for S. Cassiano. For the broader issues, see Alm, 'Theatrical Dance in Seventeenth-Century Venetian Opera'.
22 Carter, *Monteverdi's Musical Theatre*, pp. 99–108.

kind of cloud machine for the scenes for the gods, and perhaps the 'macchina con l'Olimpo' seen in the Manelli–Ferrari *Andromeda* for Apollo and the Muses in Act II scene 1.[23] In terms of instruments, the sinfonias at the start of the opera and at the end of Act I to cover the descent of Apollo for the beginning of Act II (suggesting that the opera played without intervals), and the ritornello concluding Act II, are in five parts (SSATB), presumably for strings, whereas the ritornellos punctuating the aria strophes are normally in three (SSB). Thus one could perform the opera quite cheaply. Its tableau-like organisation also suggests that it was primarily a showcase for particular singers, including what must have been a virtuoso soprano as Dafne and a fine male alto (C3 clef) as Apollo.

Busenello's libretto adopts the now normal poetic structures that had been formulated by Ottavio Rinuccini some 40 years earlier. Texts for recitative are in free-rhymed verse with seven- and eleven-syllable lines (*versi sciolti*); texts for what are called 'aria' in the score are strophic, with two to five stanzas, either in seven- and eleven-syllable lines (ababCC is one popular format),[24] or in eight- or five-syllable ones.[25] These arias are set by Cavalli in some form of structured musical style, normally in triple time but sometimes in duple, with strong-phrased melodies and active bass lines that drive to cadences; they almost all have instrumental ritornellos between the stanzas which normally develop a melodic idea first presented by the voice, although the 'ornamental' instruments (i.e., those save the continuo, the 'fundamental' instruments) never play along with the singer. The arias are, quite literally, songs, that contrast with the musical 'speech' of the recitative; they are also often given an explicit or implicit diegetic function for the sake of verisimilitude (i.e., they are played out as 'real-life' music-making). Arias can come at the beginning, middle or end of a scene, i.e., as an entrance song to set the character, a moment of reflection, or an exit song; they can include internal sections in recitative or arioso if the character pauses to take thought; they can also serve for word-painting or just to emphasise a shift in the syntax (a vocative, imperative etc.) or in the rhetoric, say for a maxim or an invocation. They are not affective or emotional in any strong sense of the term.

For example, in 1.4 Dafne enters (with nymphs and shepherds) singing a three-stanza 'aria' ('O più d'ogni ricchezza') that extols a life free of amorous

---

23 For the sets used in S. Cassiano and other Venetian opera-houses, see Mancini, Muraro and Povoledo, *I teatri del Veneto*, i/1.

24 Lower-case stands for seven-syllable lines (save where another line-length is indicated by a superscript number), and upper-case for eleven-syllable ones. Superscript letters 't' and 's' are used to indicate *versi tronchi* (accent on the final syllable) and *versi sdruccioli* (accent on the antepenultimate syllable).

25 For an easy introduction to Italian verse types, see Sadie (ed.), *The New Grove Dictionary of Opera*, iv: 964–6. The best history of the seventeenth-century libretto is Fabbri, *Il secolo cantante*.

attachments; then she has a recitative in which she vows never to succumb to love and invokes the delights of nature, moving briefly to triple time to praise the 'sunny hill, shady wood and green field' ('Colle aprico, / bosc'ombroso, / verde prato', a shift in poetic metre) and also at the end to paint the word 'liberty' ('libertà'). A three-part 'sinfonia' introduces another aria, 'Libertade gradita' (again, three stanzas), which Dafne 'plays and sings on the lyre' ('suona e canta nella cetra', presumably a fake instrument, if one with impeccable Classical credentials). She then has a brief recitative prompting the nymphs and shepherds to sing and dance in honour of being free from love, which they do to an SATB chorus ('Danzat'o ninfe, pastorelli, e siano'), a sung and danced *ballo* with a refrain set over a repeating *ciaccona* bass pattern. After two stanzas of the chorus, Dafne has a set of strophic variations to a text lauding music ('Musica, dolce Musica, tu sei'; two stanzas) in duple-time arioso with elaborate vocal embellishments written into the score. The *ballo* then returns for two more stanzas to end the scene, although Dafne stays on stage for her subsequent dialogue with Filena (who enters with an aria to begin 1.5). The scene is handled by Cavalli to perfection as a glorious musical display of Dafne's voice; it does almost nothing to project any drama, save allowing a character to state her position several times over.

Dafne's brief shift to triple time within a recitative (at 'Colle aprico . . .') is not called an 'aria' in the score: the text is not strophic, even though the verse shifts very briefly to four-syllable lines. Here, then, Cavalli is responding to a metrical cue in the text, and also perhaps to word-painting (or perhaps better, Busenello perceived an opportunity for musical word-painting and therefore made the metrical shift). This is by no means unusual for contemporary librettos, where some kind of metrical, registral or rhetorical shift within recitative verse may prompt the composer to move from declamatory recitative to more structured arioso in triple or duple time. Act 1 scene 1, for Aurora and Titone, reveals the technique. At the scene's opening, Titone asks his wife why she is so eager to leave the marriage bed to start the day. He receives a churlish reply:

Aurora

E che voi ch'io consumi	7	And why would you have me eat away
in siapite dimore	7	in tasteless dalliance
la vita mia con otioso Amante,	11	my life with a lazy lover,
ch'in pigra volontà le forze tiene,	11	who suppresses his strength by indolent desire,
e gode in fredda immagine il suo bene?	11	and takes his pleasure as a cold reflection?
Abbraccia queste piume,	7	Embrace these feathers,
baccia questi guanciali,	7	kiss these cushions,

| con essi puoi sfogar in dolci errori | 11 | with them you can unfold in sweet delusions |
| tuoi disarmati et impotenti amori. | 11 | your unarmed, impotent love. |

Titone

La mia fede così	7^t	My faith thus
tra scherni e sprezzi va.	7^t	goes amid scorn and disdain.
Sdegnosa meco sta	7^t	Contemptuous of me is
colei che mi ferì.	7^t	she who wounded me.
Infelice Titon,	7^t	Unhappy Titone,
mal veduto amator,	7^t	ill-starred lover,
quella che t'arde il cor	7^t	she who set your heart alight
non vuol udir ragion.	7^t	does not want to hear reason.
Ma, lasso, ad ogni ingiuria, ad ogni oltraggio	11	But, alas, to every injury, to every outrage
si fa scopo et oggetto,	7	is he the aim and target
chi col peso degl'anni aggrava il letto.	11	who burdens the bed with the weight of years.

Aurora

Giovanetta che tiene	7	A young girl who holds
il senso pien dell'amoroso affetto,	11	her feelings full of amorous desire,
tra mortire et isviene	7	only with pain and suffering
s'è forzat'a tenersi un vecchio al petto,	11	does she force herself to hold an old codger to her breast,
che solo sa tra stenti e tra rumori	11	who knows only amid snores and grunts
tossir i baci, e borbotar gl'amori.	11	to cough out kisses and mumble of love.

[Ritornello]

| La possanza che manca | 7 | Failing strength |
| empie di sdegno il garulo canuto, | 11 | fills with anger the talkative greybeard, |

etc.

Aurora's aria 'Giovanetta che tiene' has four stanzas, each rhyming aBaBCC (the quotation above stops at the end of line 2 of the second stanza). Prior to this aria, the text is in *versi sciolti*, although Titone's response begins in *versi tronchi* (with the accent on the final syllable rather than the more normal penultimate one) and therefore is set by Cavalli in triple time, moving back to 'recitative' at the return of the *versi piani* ('Ma, lasso, ad ogni ingiuria, ad ogni oltraggio'). Again, Titone's 'La mia fede così' is not, strictly speaking, an aria – it is not strophic – although the presence of the *versi tronchi* permits stronger cadential articulations given that the weak–strong ending of the line (as distinct from the strong–weak ending of a normal *verso piano*) matches the weak–strong position of musical cadences. Aurora's 'Giovanetta che tiene', on the other hand, is indeed an aria text: Cavalli sets the first three stanzas strophically, and then the fourth differently so as to point up Aurora's scornful accusation of Titone's love being merely the 'folly' of age. Her insults continue to the end of the scene: it is small wonder that we never see poor old Titone again.

Cavalli's choice of musical styles is quite strongly determined by Busenello's poetic structure, as is typical of all operas with librettos in verse, i.e., up to the end of the nineteenth century. Yet he does have choices. *Gli amori di Apollo e di Dafne* has two scenes each containing what is labelled (in the score) a 'lamento'. Act I scene 8 is for Procri, who bemoans the loss of Cefalo to the wiles of Aurora in a powerful recitative ('Volgi, deh volgi il piede') that adopts the usual textual and musical tropes of a recitative lament. The model is Monteverdi's well-known *Lamento d'Arianna* from his opera *Arianna* (1608), which was revived in Venice at the Teatro S. Moisè in the same season as *Gli amori di Apollo e di Dafne* (one assumes that Busenello and Cavalli were aware of the competition). Busenello unifies the scene with a plangent refrain, 'Lassa, io m'inganno, e non son quella più' ('Alas, I deceive myself, and I am no longer she'), a one-line *verso tronco* (although Cavalli stays in recitative). Procri need appear just once in the opera because she represents a standard type, the abandoned woman who laments: her tropes recur in the countless Penelopes, Didos, Ottavias and others of the same who regularly appear in the repertory.[26]

The second lament is intriguing for different reasons. As Apollo sees Dafne's metamorphosis into a laurel in III.2, he initiates a long sequence of self-recrimination, 'Ohimè, che miro, ohimè, dunque in alloro'. Busenello casts this in nine four-line stanzas in eleven-syllable lines (ABBA): such formalism harks back (again probably unknowingly, although one starts to wonder) to Rinuccini's handling of the same scene in his *Dafne*, where Apollo began in recitative but then lamented in *terza rima* ('Non curi la mia pianta, o fiamm'o gelo'). Cavalli sets Apollo's first two stanzas in recitative, the next three in triple time, then two more in recitative, then the final two in a duple-time aria style (but not strophically), with the last stanza repeated. The 'lamento' labelled in the score is the triple-time section (stanzas 3–5), where each stanza is set strophically over a bass line that begins with four iterations of a descending minor tetrachord in A minor (a–g–f–e) before moving to cadences in C major, E minor, C major and then back to A minor. Thus the piece is in the mould of Monteverdi's well-known *Lamento della ninfa* (which has the same bass line, if more strictly repeated as a ground) and other triple-time laments of the period. It is not clear whether Apollo's lament is more structured, and more carefully

---

26 The broader issues are discussed in Heller, 'Chastity, Heroism, and Allure' and *Emblems of Eloquence*.

crafted, than Procri's because of his gender, or because he is a god consecrated to the art of heroic song. Or perhaps Cavalli just wanted to delight his audience with the gamut of musical styles of his time.

Gli amori di Apollo e di Dafne is saturated with references to music, as if the conventional association of the pastoral environment with the power of music were not in itself sufficient to secure verisimilitude for song. In addition to Dafne's eloquent (and musically virtuosic) praise of music in I.4, Apollo extols the music of nature on his appearance in II.1, and the final duet of the opera is prompted by his agreeing to 'sing' with Pane in praise of Dafne and Syrinx's 'beautiful, welcome metamorphoses', with 'joyous symphonies' on pan-pipes and lyre ('Cantiam di Dafne e di Siringa insieme / con sinfonie gioconde / le belle metamorfosi gradite').[27] It helps, of course, that here the characters are gods and nymphs living in an Age of Gold: this had been the justification for music in the very first operas, not least those based on the Orpheus myth. Apollo's comments in II.1 on just how musical the world he has come to visit might be are also a pointed, presumably witty, reference to the musicality of Venice's own opera-houses. What was to happen when more 'normal' character-types appeared on the stage, however, is a matter for further discussion.

Yet in one sense these characters are already 'normal'. We have already seen that Procri conforms to type. So, too, do Aurora and Cefalo, who take on the textual and musical manners of the maidservant and page dallying in love (Damigella and Valletto in Monteverdi's *L'incoronazione di Poppea* are a case in point), while the old nymph Cirilla verges on being a nurse-figure (as Arnalta and Nutrice in *Poppea*, both roles also written in the C3 clef and probably also transvestite roles). No less typical is the type of language found here. Aurora's invective against Titone, quoted above, is surprisingly frank in its sexual innuendo; the erotic titillation and none too subtle word-play continue in her subsequent scenes with Cefalo. This is certainly not the genteel recounting of myth of earlier court operas. The only slight oddity is casting the ageing Titone as a tenor rather than a bass, but if Cavalli had only one bass available, he was needed for Giove and Peneo. In general, however, we are not so far from the characters and situations occupying the operas by Cavalli that would sweep the operatic stage in Venice and across Italy in the coming decades.

Antonio Sartorio (1630–80), *Giulio Cesare in Egitto* (1676)

Cavalli and his collaborators, notably the librettists Giovanni Faustini (*c.* 1619–1651) and Niccolò Minato (*c.* 1630–1698), established a template for Venetian

---

27 But oddly, there are no instrumental ritornellos here. Busenello's 1656 libretto concludes with two additional scenes, a *ballo* in which Dafne's name is spelt out in flowers, and then Filena and Cirilla discussing the action that has just taken place.

opera based on standard plot-types: an exotic location, two entangled pairs of lovers, comic servants, conventional stage business (disguises, letters, sleeping potions) to knot, and at the very last moment unknot, the action. No less a part of that template was glorious music. For much of his career, Cavalli was able to produce one opera per year, and sometimes two. The number of theatres in Venice, however, also left space for other composers who vied with Cavalli and eventually supplanted him. One was Antonio Sartorio, whose reputation has not been enhanced by Ellen Rosand's accusation that his *Orfeo* marked the decline of the 'classic' phase of Venetian opera.[28] He composed some fifteen operas between 1661 and his death, mostly for the Teatro S. Salvatore (popularly known as the Teatro S. Luca), while also holding down the position of *Kapellmeister* to Duke Johann Friedrich of Brunswick-Lüneburg in Hanover; the duke gave Sartorio regular leave to spend winter (and Carnival) in Venice to work in the theatre (it probably helped that the duke, too, often wintered in Venice and was an avid patron of opera there). Sartorio famously clashed with Cavalli over the latter's commission of *Massenzio* (libretto by Giacomo Francesco Bussani) for the Teatro S. Salvatore in Carnival 1672–3. Sartorio's *Orfeo* (which had its première on 14 December 1672) was the theatre's other opera for the season, and when Cavalli's *Massenzio* went into rehearsal, it was thought to be a failure because of the lack of 'spirited ariettas', so the project was turned over to Sartorio, whose own setting of Bussani's libretto, composed in thirteen days, was performed on 25 January 1673.[29] It had some 78 arias and duets: the world of opera was changing fast, and the ageing Cavalli was unable to keep up.

Bussani was then the librettist for Sartorio's *Giulio Cesare in Egitto*, premièred at S. Salvatore on 17 December 1676, and for three subsequent operas by the composer. His *Giulio Cesare* libretto is also noteworthy for having been a source for Nicola Haym's *Giulio Cesare in Egitto* set by Handel (London, 1724).[30] Sartorio's setting was revived in Naples in 1680; other revivals of the libretto in Messina (1681), Milan (1685) and Bergamo (1689) most probably had music by different composers. Only the Naples 1680 version of *Giulio Cesare* survives complete (Naples, Conservatorio di Musica San Pietro a Majella, MS 33.6.29), although the first, Venice, version can mostly be reconstructed by reference to a manuscript (Venice, Fondazione Querini-Stampalia, MS Cl. VIII Cod. IV) belonging to a series containing arias (some transposed) from Venetian operas year by year.

28 Rosand, *Opera in Seventeenth-Century Venice*, pp. 387–91.
29 Sadie (ed.), *The New Grove Dictionary of Opera*, iv: 186–7.
30 A. Sartorio, *Giulio Cesare in Egitto*, ed. C. Monson, 'Collegium Musicum: Yale University', ii/12 (Madison, WI, 1991). Monson's important preface provides much of the factual information presented here, although the interpretation is my own.

The majority of Sartorio's operas take subjects drawn from ancient (normally Roman) history, including his *Seleuco* (1666), *La prosperità di Elio Seiano* and *La caduta di Elio Seiano* (1667), and *Ermengarda, regina de' Longobardi* (1669). Much has been made by modern scholars of opera's apparent turn away from myth towards history, which is presumed to have begun with Monteverdi's *L'incoronazione di Poppea* (1643), often called the first 'historical' opera, although where this leaves the saints' lives portrayed in Roman operas of the early 1630s is a matter for debate. Here the scholarly agenda is fairly clear: mythical subjects might suit the political, spectacular and functional purposes of court opera, but 'public' opera should be made of sterner stuff, offering the moral and ethical lessons that only 'real' history can provide. It is also convenient that the Venetian republic should seemingly have favoured historical subjects (it did not, in fact), allowing the past to serve the political needs of an anti-imperial present by the example of 'good' ancient Roman republicans or 'bad' ancient Roman emperors.[31]

But alas, Venetian operatic histories are not like Shakespeare's history plays, and fidelity to some kind of historical truth does not always come high on the agenda. Busenello admits as much in the preface to *L'incoronazione di Poppea*, where he outlines historical events according to Tacitus' *Annals* (a common source for historical subject matter) but then admits that 'here we represent these actions differently'. Contemporary spoken plays and *commedia dell'arte* scenarios also reveal that the 'theatergrams' of modern drama – i.e., the conventional plot-types and thematic tropes – operated equally well under the guise of myth, legend, epic or history (the last invented or somehow 'real').[32] The same is true of a relatively unexplored source of subjects for Baroque opera, namely contemporary novellas and related 'popular' literature. It probably mattered little whether the conventional love-triangle was between a Nero, Poppaea and Otho, or a Mars, Venus and Vulcan, so long as the audience had sufficient familiarity with the characters and their (hi)stories to avoid a librettist having to spend too long introducing them. And even if characters were unfamiliar, usually they were soon shown to conform to some kind of type. But the common factor in all this is probably the need also for some kind of distance – putting 'contemporary' comedies on the operatic stage was more an eighteenth-century phenomenon – that, in turn, enhanced notions of exotic Others separate from any manner of day-to-day reality. This contributed to a sense of alienation that allowed theatrical works to work their different magic; it also, of course, provided a convenient excuse for spectacle. At that point, imperial Rome was

31 See, for example, the reading in Heller, 'Tacitus Incognito'.
32 The term comes from Clubb, *Italian Drama in Shakespeare's Time*, pp. 1–26.

probably no more or less exotic than ancient Abyssinia, Armida's magic island, or the pastoral playground of the gods.

This is not to say that Venetian opera, or any other, could not serve some kind of moral or ethical purpose, whether by way of the action or, if more problematically, by presumed knowledge of events preceding or succeeding what is represented on the stage. This has often been treated as one way of excusing the supposed immorality of *L'incoronazione di Poppea*, which concludes with Nerone and Poppea celebrating their passionate, if illicit (we assume), love: we all know our Roman history, so the argument goes, and therefore are fully aware of the fact that Poppaea will soon be murdered by Nero, who will himself come to a fiery end. Such a reading has obvious problems – do any dramatic characters have a life beyond the start and end of their theatrical representation? – and it has also served to obscure the 'messages' of *Poppea*, if such there be. Venetian operas will certainly concern themselves with the nature of 'good' and 'bad' love (and its counterpart, lust), with conflicts between love and duty, with honour and dishonour, and with political necessity versus individual need. They have their heroes and villains, and their women virtuous and loose, and we normally know who is who save when some reversal occurs to tie the dramatic knot. Problems only occur when we start to take the 'wrong' side, but then, music always has the power to generate some kind of emotional empathy, if not sympathy, even when it is not deserved by the culprits at hand. At the end of Sartorio's *Giulio Cesare in Egitto*, it is hard not to feel sorry for the wicked Tolomeo in his chains, with his recitative lament 'Fortuna, che m'atterri' and his aria 'O voi datemi la morte', even though Bussani and Sartorio tried to avoid the danger (if it is) of identifying too closely with him by having the comic nurse Rodisbe pour scorn on the former King of Egypt for his hubris.

Thus although *Giulio Cesare in Egitto* might derive its story-line from histories of Julius Caesar by Dio Cassius, Plutarch, Suetonius, Lucan and Appianus,[33] it is chiefly a pretext for playing out much broader, more universal issues. As usual in Venetian opera, love (often invoked as Amor) is the driving force. Cesare, supported by the tribune Curio, has defeated Pompey the Great on the battlefields of Egypt, but thanks to the persuasion (it does not take much) of Pompey's wife, Cornelia, and son, Sesto (Sextus), he is willing to deal magnanimously with his enemy. Tolomeo (Ptolemy), King of Egypt, however, seeks to ingratiate himself with the Roman emperor by presenting him with Pompey's head, which causes universal revulsion. Tolomeo's sister, Cleopatra, meanwhile seeks an alliance with Cesare to wrest the throne from her brother. She enters his camp disguised as Lidia, and inevitably, Cesare falls in love with her. Tolomeo,

---

33 Sartorio, *Giulio Cesare in Egitto*, ed. Monson, p. xi.

on the other hand, falls for Cornelia and imprisons her in his seraglio so that he can have his wicked way. Sesto decides to disguise himself as a eunuch (which the original singer would have been) and then as his mother so as to get close to Tolomeo and kill him, while Cornelia disguises herself first as a eunuch (which, this time, the singer was not), and then as a knight. Cleopatra and Tolomeo fight a naval battle for the throne of Egypt, and Cleopatra is vanquished, only to be rescued by Cesare who, though feared dead in an earlier skirmish, has in fact been saved from the waves. Tolomeo ends up imprisoned; Cornelia, having seen her husband avenged, agrees to marry Curio; and Cleopatra and Cesare are joyfully united.

The opera has nine characters: five sopranos – the women Cleopatra and Cornelia, and the castratos Cesare, Sesto and Nireno (the last a page and Cleopatra's confidant) – and an alto castrato (Tolomeo), two tenors (Curio and Cleopatra's nurse, Rodisbe, in the traditional comic transvestite role) and a bass (Achilla, Tolomeo's general). The instrumental parts are for two violins and continuo (and occasional trumpets); the violins play in a good number of the arias, but tend not to do so at the same time as the voice, presumably for fear of problems of balance. The high voices (soprano, tenor) are the 'good' characters, whereas the lower voices (alto, bass) are the 'bad' ones. Looked at another way, the cast is made up of four Romans who are 'good' by definition, and five Egyptians, two of whom are definitely evil (Tolomeo, Achilla), two of whom act for good (Nireno and Rodisbe, in typical servant roles), and one of whom is worthy of marriage to a Caesar. All this is conventional enough, even if Bussani and Sartorio have to work quite hard to negotiate a position for Cleopatra somewhere between a dangerous exotic seductress (singing in 'foreign' keys and with flirtatious dotted rhythms and luxuriant embellishments) and a moral exemplar, although it helps that she is a wronged queen, fights her brother with the Romans on her side, and aids Cornelia in resisting Tolomeo's advances. No less conventional are the other (fairly modest) scenic and similar devices used in the opera alongside stage-sets that were probably not as grand as the libretto implies: an eclipse of the sun in I.1, Cornelia's attempted suicide by jumping into a menagerie in II.13, a sleep scene in II.17 (Cleopatra, as Lidia, pretends to be asleep so as to gauge Cesare's feelings for her), stage battles in III.1, and various disguises (Cleopatra, Cornelia, Sesto), not to mention the transvestite nurse.

One question, of course, is what these characters might plausibly sing, rather than just 'speak' in music. Court opera, at least in its early stages, had been concerned with the ever-problematic question of the verisimilitude of singing on stage. This explains the preference for mythological and pastoral subject matter, given that the gods and the shepherds and shepherdesses of the Age of

Gold might reasonably be expected to use some kind of heightened language beyond the ken of mere mortals: in this, at least, Cavalli's *Gli amori di Apollo e di Dafne* is entirely typical. The issues had already been played out in the Renaissance to justify poetry rather than prose in the spoken theatre, and the argument was extended easily enough (and on rather similar terms) to music. More human, 'historical' characters, however, raised a different set of issues. Lower-class individuals (servants, nurses etc.) might sing with reason – their social status is clear, and important precedents had been established within the *commedia dell'arte* – while noble characters could sing when in disguise (indeed, singing enhances the disguise).[34] Librettists could also provide convenient excuses for plausible diegetic songs (lullabies, drinking songs, battle pieces and the like) and for conventional moments of formal invocation or expostulation (e.g., appeals to the gods, laments etc.), or could just rely on the association of singing with love.

For the most part, librettists bowed to the inevitable. Giacomo Badoaro admitted in the preface to his *L'Ulisse errante*, set by Francesco Sacrati in 1644, that

> Today, no one worries, to increase the delight of the spectators, about giving way to something not lifelike, which does not damage the action. Thus we see that to give more time for the changes of scene, we have introduced music, in which we cannot avoid something not lifelike – that men should carry out their most important business in song. Moreover, so as to enjoy all kinds of music in the theatre, we are accustomed to hearing pieces for two, three and more voices: this produces something else not lifelike – that talking together men should without thinking happen to say the same things. Therefore it is no wonder that, devoting ourselves to pleasing modern taste, we have rightly moved away from the ancient rules.

Similarly, Francesco Sbarra claimed in the preface to his *Alessandro vincitor di se stesso* (1651):

> I know that the *ariette* sung by Alexander and Aristotle will be judged as contrary to the decorum of such great personages; but I also know that musical recitation is improper altogether ... and yet this defect is not only tolerated by the current century but received with applause.

He adds that 'if the recitative style were not mingled with such *scherzi*, it would give more annoyance than delight'.[35] However, as we shall see, the problems

---

34 Rosand, *Opera in Seventeenth-Century Venice*, pp. 120–21.
35 These two passages are given in ibid., pp. 410 (Badoaro), 421 (Sbarra). For the Sbarra, I have used in part Rosand's translation on p. 45.

continued to be troublesome even as the pressures in favour of aria, and of fine singing, became overwhelming. Bussani and Sartorio remain surprisingly sensitive to the issue.

In *Giulio Cesare in Egitto* there are almost 60 arias (more were added for Naples) – many of which are quite short – plus six duets (plus two for Naples), and one brief (offstage) chorus; there is also a 'Ballo de guerrieri' ('Dance of warriors') at the end of Act II for which no music survives. These arias are distributed according to the 'rank' of the character: in the Venice version, Cleopatra and Cesare have the most (13 and 9, respectively, by one method of counting), then Cornelia (7), Tolomeo (7) and Curio (6), then Achilla (5), Nireno (4), Sesto (4) and Rodisbe (3). Most of the arias were determined by Bussani who, like Busenello, uses free-rhyming seven- and eleven-syllable *versi sciolti* for the recitative, and strophic, regular rhymed verse in other line-lengths (most often in Chiabrera-like eight- or five-syllable lines) for the arias. The arias tend to crystallise some manner of response to a dramatic situation, state an epigram, or otherwise make one or other kind of rhetorical point (often by way of a vocative or an imperative). However, some, especially by the comic characters, are (not unusually) directed across the footlights to the audience, as with Rodisbe in 1.22 as the concluding gesture of the act:

Voi scherzate, o giovinette,	a^8	You make a game, o maidens,
per l'acquisto d'un'amante,	b^8	of gaining a lover,
ma in tal guisa, o semplicette,	a^8	but in this manner, o simpletons,
v'incatena un crin vagante.	b^8	you enchain a wandering brow.
V'adornate il crin, e il petto,	c^8	You adorn your hair and your breasts,
v'abbigliate nel sembiante,	b^8	you make your face beautiful,
ma in tal moda il vostro affetto	c^8	but in this way is your affection
vi rapisce il dio volante.	b^8	stolen by the flying god [of Love].

Nireno also has comic duple-time patter songs (in what would become a characteristic G major) making witty points to the audience that would not be out of place in an eighteenth-century comic opera (as with his 'Con le donne s'ha fortuna' in 1.15 in the Venice version; in Naples, perhaps significantly, this was changed to a more elegant triple-time aria).

Sartorio usually follows the implications of the verse quite closely, writing in sophisticated triple or duple times. Therefore he sets Rodisbe's aria strophically. Other of Bussani's texts prompt a rondo-type structure with returns to a refrain. Cleopatra's 'Non voglio amar, o voglio amar per sempre' (1.21), is a typical example, with the refrain (line 1) an eleven-syllable line and two interior stanzas in eight-syllable lines (most *tronchi*):

Non voglio amar, o voglio amar per sempre.	A	I do not want to love, unless I love for ever.
Se mi pongo in servitù,	b^{8t}	If I place myself in servitude,
più non torno in libertà,	c^{8t}	I will never be free again,
e se giuro fedeltà,	c^{8t}	and if I swear fidelity,
questo cor non frange più	b^{8t}	this heart will never again break
d'una chioma l'auree tempre.	a^8	the golden tempers of a hair.
Non voglio amar, o voglio amar per sempre.	A	I do not want to love, unless I love for ever.
Se mi pongo intra Amor,	d^{8t}	If Cupid places himself within me,
più non m'esce fuor dal sen,	e^{8t}	he will never leave my breast,
e se volto si seren	e^{8t}	and if so serene a face
m'incatena questo cor,	d^{8t}	enchains my heart,
mai più sciolgo l'auree tempre.	a^8	never again will I loosen the golden tempers.
Non voglio amar, o voglio amar per sempre.	A	I do not want to love, unless I love for ever.

Sartorio sets the first line as a separate section (which therefore returns with the refrain), and the two interior stanzas to the same music. It is tempting to argue that these kinds of *ABAB'A* structures (other versions include *ABAA'B'A'* and *ABAA'B'A*) might eventually be reduced to a typical da-capo structure (*ABA*), and indeed in the opera there are some single-refrain arias that are, in effect, in a da-capo (or sometimes dal-segno) form. However, Bussani is probably relying instead on repetition patterns typical of earlier seventeenth-century verse, and he does not usually exploit the balanced structures and closing *versi tronchi* generally found in later da-capo aria texts (we shall see an exception below). Nevertheless, the urge for repetition is so strong that when it does not occur it is very striking, as in Cornelia's poignant lament in 1.14, 'Nel tuo seno, amico sasso' (the text is in a rather odd $a^8b^8a^8b^8CC$).

Clearly all this is a far cry from the flexible shifting between aria, arioso and recitative typical of some earlier Venetian opera (as in the case of Monteverdi's *Poppea* and Cavalli's operas of the later 1640s and 1650s), and accordingly, Sartorio has less freedom of choice in what to do with the verse. Sometimes, however, he seems to work on his own initiative. In 1.11, Cesare mourns the death of Pompey with a text in *versi sciolti* that Bussani therefore designed as some kind of recitative (abcdD), although Sartorio sets it as a powerful arioso over a ground bass elaborating a descending chromatic tetrachord (signifying lament, one assumes) and with string parts (two violins) that accompany the voice rather than just alternate with it (as otherwise is the norm in the opera). However, Sartorio clearly was worried about there being too much of a good thing: he cut the rest of Cesare's speech (an additional nine lines) musing on the frailty of life.

A similar sense of initiative may also have determined Sartorio's handling of II.4. Cesare enters declaring that he is a prisoner of love, Nireno (at first hidden) observes the scene, and Cleopatra is heard singing a love-song from offstage:

Cesare		
Son prigioniero	5	I am a prisoner
del nudo arciero	5	of the blind archer
in laccio d'or.	5^t	in a golden trap.
Ma non so come	5	But I do not know how
m'hanno due chiome	5	two locks of hairs
legato il cor	5^t	have bound my heart.
Vaga Lidia, ove sei? Se un sol tuo sguardo	11	Beautiful Lidia, where are you? If just a single glance
trasse quest'alma ad abitarti in fronte,	11	led this soul to fix upon your brow,
fu in si bel ciel d'amore aquila un occhio,	11	then under such a beautiful sky of love, an eagle's was the eye,
e Ganimede un core . . .	7	and Ganymede's the heart.
Nireno (hidden)		
(Ora è il tempo opportuno.)	7	(Now the time is right.)
Cleopatra (offstage, singing)		
V'adoro, pupille,	6	I adore you, o eyes,
saette d'amore . . .	6	arrows of love
Cesare		
Qual voce ascolto mai?		What voice do I hear?
Nireno (to himself)		
Questa è Cleopatra.	11	This is Cleopatra.
Intendo, del suo amor son arti e frodi.	11	I understand, these are the arts and deceits of her love.
Femina inamorata	7	A woman enamoured
per discoprirsi amante ha mille modi.	11	has a thousand ways of revealing herself as a lover.
Cleopatra		
le vostre faville	6	your sparks
son faci del core.	6	are torches of the heart.
Nireno		
Signor.		My lord.
Cesare		
Nireno, udisti	7	Nireno, have you heard
questa angelica voce?	7	this angelic voice?

Cesare's aria (two stanzas of five-syllable lines) is set in *ABA'* form (Sartorio repeats the first stanza after the second), and the music then moves to recitative. Cleopatra's offstage song (in a glorious triple time in C major) may originally have been written by Bussani as a single four-line stanza ($a^6b^6a^6b^6$), but Sartorio allows Cesare to interrupt after the first two lines, while Nireno makes his typically comic aside about feminine wiles. Cleopatra's offstage song then resumes (moving to a wonderfully exotic E minor) before Cesare comes in again. In the continuation of this scene, Cleopatra is once more heard offstage singing a reprise of the first two lines (so, producing a spaced-out *ABA* structure). Handel was to do something very different with Haym's version of this text (in his II.1, with the last line of the stanza altered to a *verso tronco* and another stanza added to produce a da-capo format).[36] But Sartorio's stylish treatment is not without effect.

The idea of having Cleopatra sing offstage was established at the beginning of Act II, which opens with her 'sitting pensively at a spinet' singing a love-song ('Nudo arcier, se non sospendi', again in E minor) and then interrupting its second line to muse (in recitative) on how much in love she is; she then repeats the opening of the song and takes it (through B minor back to E minor via a colourful Neapolitan sixth) to the end of its first stanza, and starts the second stanza ('Dio de' cori . . .') before breaking off at the entrance of Nireno to start the action. The use here and elsewhere of diegetic song does not seem so much to reflect a fear of inverisimilitude as to signify a typically reflexive moment where opera acknowledges itself to be opera. The game is not unusual by this period – it is often played by secondary characters for some kind of comic effect – and it even implicates the characters themselves. No longer do 'noble' characters in fact have to adopt some kind of disguise or deception in order to be able to sing arias. Indeed, Cleopatra has some glorious arias in this opera, but never when she is presenting herself to another character as Lidia (save in the offstage 'V'adoro, pupille' noted above, and in her asides during the sleep scene): as a result, part of Lidia's disguise is, precisely, the absence of singing. Indeed, when Cesare hears 'V'adoro, pupille' and is told (by Nireno) that the singer is Lidia, he registers his surprise that a mere maid should have such vocal prowess and feels all the more attracted to her. He is as much seduced by her singing as we in the audience are meant to be.

Nevertheless, some surprising canons of verisimilitude remain. When analysing Baroque opera, it is worth asking not just who is singing what, but

---

36 The famous 'Parnassus' scene in Handel's *Giulio Cesare in Egitto* seems to come from the Milan 1685 version of Bussani's libretto, which may have been Haym's chief source (see Sartorio, *Giulio Cesare in Egitto*, ed. Monson, p. xi), although Monson suggests that in general Handel may even have known Sartorio's music.

also who is singing to whom. Almost half of the arias in *Giulio Cesare in Egitto* are real or virtual soliloquies, with characters alone on stage or observed only from a distance singing to themselves (or directly to the audience): such soliloquies can happen at the beginning of scenes, with a character musing on a situation before the action continues with the entrance of another character (as in the extract from 11.4 given above), or at the end, whereupon an exit is made (although the exit convention is by no means as well established here as in later *opera seria*). Otherwise, characters tend to sing arias only to their familiars, such as Cleopatra in the presence of Tolomeo, Nireno and Rodisbe, or Cornelia to her son Sesto (they also have two duets); the chief exceptions are when characters need to put on a heroic display (Cesare to Tolomeo in battle) or to declare ignoble love (Tolomeo and Achilla to Cornelia). The relative absence of aria-based interactions between the principal lovers (Cesare and Cleopatra) is surprising by later standards, although it makes their love-duet in the final scene all the more powerful. It remains significant, however, that the opera ends, rather, with a da-capo aria (the da capo is written out) for Cleopatra singing just in the first person ('Ho un'alma che brilla').

Cleopatra's final aria has a trumpet obbligato, matching Cesare's opening aria in Act I ('Su, trombe guerriere'); the trumpet also appears in the battle scene between Cleopatra and Tolomeo in III.1, and elsewhere at appropriately 'regal' points in the opera (functioning in part as diegetic music). Sartorio was fond of trumpet arias, it seems, using them often in his operas; so, too, was Naples, given that for the 1680 performance another trumpet aria (again on a battle theme) was added for Cornelia towards the end of Act II. Other changes for Naples include the addition of two more arias for Cesare (to come closer to the total for Cleopatra?), reducing the role of Achilla (did they have a problem with the bass?), fleshing out the interaction of Cesare and Tolomeo, and strengthening the roles of Cornelia and Curio. The most striking addition, however, was a revised finale to the end of Act I (1.22). As we have seen, the Venice version ends with the ageing nurse Rodisbe warning the young ladies of the audience of the amorous dangers of flirtation ('Voi scherzate, o giovinette'). In Naples, this led to a new sequence for Rodisbe and Nireno, where the nurse proclaims her wish to counter the effects of age with cosmetics so that she, too, can attract men, at which point Nireno proceeds to woo her before exposing her true ugliness. The scene could have come straight from the *commedia dell'arte*; it is also very funny.

These changes between the Venice and Naples versions of *Giulio Cesare in Egitto* are not dissimilar in nature and scope to the Venice and Naples versions of Monteverdi's *L'incoronazione di Poppea* of some thirty years before, where scenes were expanded or contracted to alter the pacing, characters were strengthened

drama on a society rendered corrupt by monstrous theatrical fantasies.[38] Even Venetian opera's great apologist and chronicler Cristoforo Ivanovich used his historical account, *Minerva al tavolino* (1681), to lament the decline of the genre at the hands of unscrupulous librettists and composers, and of impresarios (not, he hastens to add, his patrons the Grimani) happy to lower their ticket prices and thereby open opera to the lower classes.

But Crescimbeni's more damning literary criticisms are normally associated with the Arcadian Academy, founded in Rome in 1690 for the reform and 'purification' of Italian poetry. It emerged like many such Roman gatherings from the circles of specific patrons, in this case Cardinal Pietro Ottoboni (1667–1740), whose vast wealth and artistic interests protected and nurtured poets and musicians admitted to the group: indeed, Ottoboni employed Arcangelo Corelli among his household musicians. Although the Arcadians assumed fanciful academic names (Ottoboni's was 'Crateo Pradelini', an anagram), one perhaps should not refer to them as a formally constituted academy. However, their influence spread widely through Italy and abroad for several decades, in part by way of letters and treatises but also by virtue of the general commerce in opera in this period. Many cities had gatherings of literati variously allied to the Arcadian cause, and numerous librettists were to lay claim to its ideals, including Ottoboni himself, Apostolo Zeno, Gian Vincenzo Gravina, Silvio Stampiglia and Pietro Metastasio (Ottoboni's godson and Gravina's pupil), all of whom sought to restore order to the genre by regularizing its structures, themes and affective content.

The founding of the Arcadian movement coincided with the reopening of the Teatro Tordinona in Rome following its closure during the pontificate of Innocent XI (d. 1689). An older Pietro Ottoboni became Pope Alexander VIII (reg. 1689–91), and his great-nephew Pietro was made cardinal. Cardinal Pietro seems to have decided early on to celebrate his elevation, and the new support for the arts in Rome, with an opera to his own libretto, the music commissioned from Alessandro Scarlatti. Scarlatti was already well enough known on the operatic stage, having written some seven operas for private theatres in Rome, and another six for Naples. The performance of *La Statira* at the Tordinona on 5 January 1690 was clearly designed with propaganda in mind.[39] Ottoboni originally conceived a finale with the descent of Fame to sing the praises of the Ottoboni family. However, this was removed on the

---

38 Freeman, *Opera without Drama*, p. 3.

39 A. Scarlatti, *La Statira*, ed. W. C. Holmes, 'The Operas of Alessandro Scarlatti', 9 (Cambridge, MA, and London, 1985); see also Holmes, '*La Statira' by Pietro Ottoboni and Alessandro Scarlatti*. The main musical source is Munich, Staatsbibliothek, Mus. MS 144 (from the Ottoboni collection), although there are three other contemporary copies, plus manuscripts with collections of arias, a printed libretto, and an autograph libretto.

order, it seems, of Cardinal Pietro's father, Don Antonio, presumably because it smacked of hubris; it was replaced by the descent of Diana to bless the unions of the opera's lovers (for which the music may have been written by Flavio Carlo Lanciani, another of Ottoboni's household musicians). *La Statira* was not a particularly successful opera: it had only six other performances that year (some unstaged as an 'oratorio') and it does not seem to have toured. Nevertheless, it reveals both the strengths and the weaknesses of opera towards the end of the seventeenth century.

The story of Statira would suit Crescimbeni's search for moral probity. Cavalli had set Busenello's version in 1655 or 1656, and the Persian princess appeared in later operas by Francesco Gasparini (1705; libretto by Apostolo Zeno and Pietro Pariati), Tommaso Albinoni (1726; Ottoboni), Pietro Chiarini (1741; Carlo Goldoni), and Nicola Porpora (1742; Francesco Silvani). Ottoboni's three-act libretto draws on the standard source, Plutarch's *Moralia* (iv) and *Lives* (viii), to tell how Statira, daughter of the Persian King Darius, falls prisoner to Alexander the Great on his defeat of the Persians in battle. According to Plutarch, Alexander's subsequent marriage to Statira was a political gesture to unite the Macedonians and Persians, although that would not have sufficed for a seventeenth-century opera. Nor can we have Statira murdered and buried in a well (so Plutarch recounts) by Alexander's mistress, Roxanne, although Ottoboni does have an attempt on her life by Alessandro Magno's betrothed, Campaspe. Ottoboni devises a lover for Statira, Oronte (who was played by the Modenese castrato Antonio Borosini), and adds the story of the painter Apelles from Pliny's *Natural History* (xxxv), where Apelles, painting a portrait of another of Alexander's mistresses, Pancaspe, falls in love with her and is generously given her as a bride. Although (in Ottoboni's libretto), Apelle loves Campaspe (standing for Pancaspe), she scorns him, at least until Oronte and Apelle manage to rescue her from a lion that pursues her onstage. Oronte is less fortunate: although Alessandro is in the end willing to yield to him both Statira and his crown, Oronte and Statira decide that this is too great a sacrifice, so he withdraws and she gives Alessandro her hand in marriage. The 'message' is presumably the one of the prologue that Ottoboni included in his autograph libretto but not, it seems, in the opera: Tempo (Time) and Fortuna (Fortune) argue over their respective powers until Pallade (Pallas Athene) enters to settle the dispute once and for all: virtue reigns supreme. This is a striking, if not untypical, reversal from, say, the prologue to Monteverdi's *L'incoronazione di Poppea*, where Fortune and Virtue must bow to Love, but then, we are now in a very different moral and political world. Alessandro, Statira and Oronte are all supremely virtuous, and even Campaspe comes round in the end. However, she is a much more interesting character before that point than after.

Added to the mix are a Macedonian general, Demetrio, and a typical comic servant, Perinto, who spends the opera claiming that he will have nothing to do either with love or with the honour of battle. The result is a compact cast of seven characters – three sopranos (Alessandro, Campaspe, Perinto), an alto (Statira), two tenors (Apelle, Oronte) and a bass (Demetrio) – plus Diana (soprano) as the *dea ex machina*. Five are Macedonians and two are Persians (Statira and Oronte). However, the ethnic lines are not so clearly drawn as between Romans and Egyptians in Sartorio's *Giulio Cesare in Egitto*, and casting Statira as an alto means that she cannot play the exotic sex-kitten, even if it were appropriate for her role. Nor, however, can Campaspe, even though she is in the right range, given that the entire opera was given (as was the Roman practice) by an all-male cast. Sartorio may have been able to end his opera with Cleopatra flaunting her charms now that her love has been fulfilled. Scarlatti, however, can end only with a double aria for the male lovers, the first stanza (with a da capo) for Alessandro, and the second (also with a da capo) for Apelle.

The sets required of the opera are reasonably spectacular, and presumably were newly built for the refurbished Teatro Tordinona: (Act I) a wide field by moonlight, a pavilion, a royal room with statues, and a prison; (Act II) a portrait gallery, the royal room with statues again, a mountain scene with Statira's hut (where she has exiled herself) and King Darius' mausoleum; (Act III) an underground cavern, a wood descending to Statira's hut in a valley, a city square with triumphal arches and a royal palace, and Diana's temple, with sacrificial victims and 'four musical choirs' in its roof (although there is no music for them). In terms of machines and the like, II.7 has Campaspe arrive on a huge float decorated with flowers and drawn by two white chargers (she is playing Flora so as to seduce Alessandro; the scene has echoes of the Parnassus episode inserted in later versions of Bussani's *Giulio Cesare in Egitto*), and III.16 has Diana on a cloud. Nor should we forget the lion in III.4. The battle scenes in Act I prompt diegetic trumpets leading to a trumpet aria for Alessandro (I.2, 'Invitti guerrieri / al suon della tromba') and a *sinfonia di trombe* to mark his victory. The great disappointment, however, is the music for the end of Act II, when Demetrio enters to murder Statira (conveniently asleep on a rock) but is frightened off by thunder, lightning and earthquakes. Ottoboni's original libretto went still further: it gives stage directions for the rock turning into a dragon and carrying Statira into the air, the earth opening up to reveal the river Lethe, with Charon ferrying souls across the waters, and some of these souls rising on a cloud to console Statira.[40] He may have been too ambitious: Scarlatti provides just a brief recitative that led, according to the printed libretto, to a

---

40 Holmes, '*La Statira' by Pietro Ottoboni and Alessandro Scarlatti*, p. 55.

ballo of nymphs in the forest (we never discover what they are doing there). This plus the *ballo* for Persian soldiers at the end of Act 1 are the only dances in the opera: the music does not survive for either. There must also be other instrumental music missing from the surviving scores. Most of what is there, including an opening two-part *sinfonia* (Largo leading to a gigue-like Allegro) and various ritornellos, is scored for two violins, viola, and bass (contemporary records suggest that the Teatro Tordinona had four violins, two violas, one 'cello, one double bass and continuo), although as we have seen, there are sporadic parts for trumpets.

La Statira has 53 arias, fewer than in Sartorio's *Giulio Cesare in Egitto* although in musical terms they are longer; they also tend to make greater use of the instruments, either in final ritornellos or playing throughout, if not always at the same time as the voice. The final double aria for Alessandro and Apelle noted above produces an *ABAA′B′A′* pattern found in nine of these arias; it may also include a ritornello either between the stanzas or at the end, or both (*ABARA′B′A′R*). This is not dissimilar to the strophic refrain forms used by Bussani. The bulk of Scarlatti's arias, however, are in some kind of da-capo (or dal-segno) format, i.e., with two stanzas of text set to two musical sections, the first of which returns at the end. The pattern is clear in II.8 where Campaspe angrily rejects Apelle and the painter responds:

Campaspe

Ma tu, per cui mi è forza	7	But you, by whom I am forced
soffrir scherno si fiero,	7	to suffer such haughty scorn,
vanne, va tanto lungi	7	leave, go far away
del mio furor baccante,	7	from my Bacchic fury,
che mai più ti rivegga.	7	so that I might never see you again.

Apelle

| Alle tue piante . . . | | At your complaints . . . |

Campaspe

| Ancor! . . . | | Still more! . . . |

Apelle

| Morir risolvo. | 11 | I resolve to die. |

Campaspe

Sarà troppo la morte	7	Death would be too
pigra in rapire l'odiata vita,	11	slothful to take your hated life,
nè soffrirti più voglio.	7	nor do I wish to suffer you any longer.
Parti.		Go.

Apelle

| Vado a morir, core di scoglio. | 11 | I go to die, O heart of stone. |

Questo è il premio che si deve,	8	This is the reward due
all'amor, alla mia fè.	8^t	to love, to my faith.
Sì, tiranna, morirò,	8^t	Yes, tyrant, I will die,
e darò	4^t	and I will yield
l'alma in preda ad aura lieve	8	my soul to be borne by a light breeze
perchè giri intorno a te.	8^t	so that it might flutter around you.

The scene begins in recitative (as dictated by Ottoboni's seven- and eleven-syllable *versi sciolti*), with five short lines for Campaspe's invective, a divided eleven-syllable line for the two characters, and four more lines concluding with a rhyming couplet. Apelle then reflects on his situation, still addressing Campaspe, in his aria 'Questo è il premio che si deve'. The aria text is predominantly in eight-syllable lines, although there is a rather odd four-syllable line in the middle. The text here consists of two 'stanzas', one of two lines and one of four, each ending with a *verso tronco* that rhymes (there are also internal *versi tronchi*). The music is in a somewhat relentless G minor marked 'a tempo giusto', with the voice moving largely in quavers. The continuo anticipates the melody of the vocal line and then continues as a 'walking bass' through the A section (ten bars) and the B section (eight bars), leading to a dal-segno repeat of the A section (omitting the continuo's introduction) followed by the instrumental ritornello (four bars echoing the opening melody and leading to a cadence). All this is standard: in fact, the only slightly odd thing about his setting of this scene is that for Apelle's final line of recitative ('Vado a morir, core di scoglio'), Scarlatti moves to a poignant triple time, marked 'Largo'. Presumably, the shift to a lyrical arioso was encouraged by the rhetorical and emotional force of the moment; it is also prompted by the fact that Apelle's nine syllables (the other two of the eleven-syllable line have been given by Campaspe) break down into 5^t + 5. But this arioso in the context of recitative seems strikingly old fashioned.

The fact that Apelle sings to Campaspe (who remains on stage for the next scene) suggests that characters (and composers) are no longer as reticent about aria as in the case of Sartorio. *La Statira* has its soliloquies, including one at the opening for Oronte starting with an eloquent accompanied recitative (invoking night), and other powerful ones for Statira. But they are fewer than in the case of *Giulio Cesare in Egitto*, and in general, characters seem to have no qualms about singing to other characters: Statira even sings to Alessandro. In terms of their position, we find arias fairly indiscriminately at the beginning of scenes, in the middle, and at the end. However, exit conventions start to become established: for example, the last four scenes of Act i (1.11–14, a single scene-complex on the prison set) start with four main characters on stage (Statira, Alessandro, Demetrio and Perinto) who are then reduced successively by one, each leaving at the end of an aria. Perinto is the last to go, ending with an aria addressed to the Persian soldiers on the theme that days are too fleeting to be spent weeping, which is presumably what prompts the soldiers' dance that concludes the act. This conveniently winds down the action to the end of the act, although it is not yet the consistent design principle it would be in later Baroque *opera seria*: Alessandro still has an additional aria in the middle of I.11, well before his exit in I.12.

Not that Alessandro has much to sing about. Once he has been painted as heroic in battle, and clement in defeat, all that is left is his drawn-out indecision over whether he loves Campaspe or Statira. Apelle, Oronte and Statira are also monochromatic characters who do not so much engage in action as respond to it, however affectingly, and nothing much changes in their situations. Scarlatti seems somewhat troubled over what to do with them: he takes their music into distant tonal regions (Statira in F minor in II.11; Apelle in C sharp minor in III.2) but appears to find it hard to give them a strong musical focus save when on conventional heroic or lamenting ground. It also seems that he was constrained by his singers or by other circumstances: a Neapolitan source preserves more virtuosic settings of an aria for Alessandro and one for Oronte that were probably early versions. Campaspe must have been easier to handle. She stands out, not just because of her 'bad woman' role (even if she turns to good at the end) but also because she is presented in a wider range of dramatic situations: in love with Alessandro, spurning Apelle, allying herself deceitfully with Statira, then, in a jealous fury, persuading Demetrio to kill her rival. Scarlatti jumps at the chances, and his music for her is consistently more interesting and more varied, his trademark Neapolitan sixths adding exotic colour to the cadences. Even her shift to loving Apelle in III.5 is handled nicely: a recitative for the two characters, a C major da-capo aria marked 'Andante et amoroso' for Campaspe ('Sì, sì caro, tua sarò'), a further exchange (including a brief 'arietta' for Apelle), the C major aria for Apelle (so, the *A'B'A'* to Statira's *ABA*), another exchange in recitative, and a duet (one of two in the opera) for both of them ('Pace, pace mio core piagato') singing in blissful thirds, with a written out da capo.

Elsewhere, however, Scarlatti struggles. At the beginning of Act III, Alessandro is still in some doubt about whom he loves and where his responsibilities might lie. His opening invective is against the 'tyrant' Love:

Tiranno, e che pretendi	7	Tyrant, and do you pretend	
domar quest'alma ancor?	7t	to tame my soul as well?	
No, no, non vincerai,	7	No, no, you will not win,	
chè fulmini non hai	7	for you do not have the thunderbolts	
d'abbattere il mio cor.	7t	to conquer my heart.	
Solo otterrà la palma	7	The palm will be won	
la gloria di quest'alma;	7	only by the glory of my soul;	

tutti i vezzi d'amor mi prendo in ira.	11	I rage at all the charms of love.
Ah Campaspe, ah Statira,	7	Ah Campaspe, ah Statira,
in qual per voi mi trovo	7	because of you, in what
confuso laberinto?	7	confused labyrinth do I find myself?
Il vincitor del mondo avete vinto.	11	You have conquered the conqueror of the world.
Vinto sono, e del nume bendato	10	I am beaten, and of the blindfolded god
bacio l'arco ed adoro gli strali	10	do I kiss the bow, and adore the arrows
che temprati nel volto adorato	10	which tempered by the adored face
di Statira fan piaghe mortali.	10	of Statira produce mortal wounds.

This soliloquy scene opens with an aria ('Tiranno, che pretendi') in two stanzas defined by cadential *versi tronchi*. Scarlatti sets this in an *ABA* form, with the *A* section in the manner of an accompanied recitative (C, Andante), and the *B* section in a contrasting 3/4 Allegro. The seven *versi sciolti* are set to recitative, and then we have a concluding aria ('Vinto sono, e del nume bendato') in a rather languid 3/8 (Grazioso) in F sharp minor, with long roulades for the 'arrows' of love.

The librettist's use of ten-syllable lines here is not unusual: Ottoboni broadens considerably the range of line-lengths available for aria verse, presumably not just for the sake of variety or to show off his poetic abilities, but also to provide for greater emotional contrasts. However, he can also seem too clever by half. Although 'Vinto sono, e del nume bendato' is an exit-aria (the next scene is a soliloquy for Apelle) and seems designed for setting in *ABA* form (Scarlatti writes a dal-segno aria), the enjambment between the second and third lines, and treating lines 3–4 as a subordinate relative clause to lines 1–2 ('which . . .'), mean that the return to the first two lines and ending the aria at the end of line 2 create syntactical problems. Also, the absence of concluding *versi tronchi* here makes it hard for the music to achieve cadential closure. As an Arcadian, Ottoboni may have wished for greater clarity, naturalness and variety in contemporary theatrical poetry, but there are distinct advantages to having stereotypical formal and metrical conventions, not least so that the composer might know where he stands. The common complaint made of later *opera seria* librettos – precisely that they are formulaic, conventionalised and, indeed, of limited poetic interest – somewhat misses the point: this is precisely what the music needed.

The fact that the focus of this chapter thus far has unashamedly been on Italy simply reflects the realities of a genre which was to remain dominated by Italians (both composers and performers) through the eighteenth and nineteenth centuries. Opera could, of course, be exported to other countries, where it might, in turn, vie with more indigenous forms of entertainment. But it would be dangerous to view such exports as essentially being something 'foreign' impacting deleteriously on native trade. For example, German princes often appropriated Italian culture (and language) not as something 'other' but, rather, as part of noble discourse and as a sign of education, social standing and even good breeding. We have already seen Cesti move fairly effortlessly between north and south of the Alps, and likewise Antonio Sartorio and his patron, Duke Johann Friedrich of Brunswick-Lüneburg. The arm of Italian opera stretched widely through Germany, and even east to Poland (at least from 1635 to 1648 under the influence of the secretary to the royal court, Virgilio Puccitelli). True, in Germany native composers did have a part to play. Heinrich Schütz (1585–1672) provided the first German opera, *Dafne* (to a translation of Rinuccini's libretto by Martin Opitz), performed in Torgau in 1627 for the marriage of Landgrave Georg II of Hesse-Darmstadt and Princess Sophia Eleonora of Saxony. Sigmund Theophil Staden's *Seelewig* (1644) was a Singspiel modelled on contemporary school-dramas: as such it is more a moral allegory than an opera. And after the horrors of the Thirty Years War, the grand opera-house in Munich was inaugurated in 1657 with *L'Oronte* by Johann Caspar Kerll (1627–93). But both Schütz and Kerll had studied in Italy, and typically, the first opera performed in Munich was Giovanni Battista Maccioni's brief allegorical *L'arpa festante* in 1653. Benedetto Ferrari had preceded Cesti to the imperial court, arranging tournaments and ballets, and providing the libretto for *L'inganno d'amore* (Regensburg, 1653; music by Antonio Bertali, court *Kapellmeister*). Agostino Steffani (1654–1728), Kammermusikdirektor of the Bavarian court from 1681 to 1688, composed five operas for Munich – including *Servio Tullio* to celebrate the wedding of Elector Maximilian II Emanuel to Maria Antonia, Archduchess of Austria, in 1686 – before moving to Hanover (from 1688 to 1703), where he produced some eight operas to librettos by Ortensio Mauro for the permanent Italian opera company there founded by Duke Ernst August. Similarly, opera in Dresden was in the hands of Giovanni Andrea Bontempi (*c*. 1624–1705) – whose grand *Il Paride* was staged for the wedding of Christian Ernst, Margrave of Brandenburg, and Erdmuthe Sophia, Princess of Saxony, in 1662 – and later, Carlo Pallavicino (d. 1688), who as musical director of the Ospedale degli Incurabili in Venice from 1674 to 1685 had made a name for himself as a leading composer of Venetian operas. The only consolidated moves towards a native opera were made in Hamburg, where the important 'public' Theater am Gänsemarkt was founded on the Venetian model, presenting year-round performances of opera in German. The theatre opened with Johann Theile's *Der erschaffene, gefallene und auffgerichtete Mensch*, based on the

Adam and Eve story, in 1678, inaugurating a rich tradition that was to extend through the operas of Reinhard Keiser (1674–1739), Handel and Telemann.

The fact that England, France and Spain were better able to cultivate national operatic traditions was in part due to their different political circumstances, and also, one suspects, to language. The story of French court opera rightly belongs elsewhere in this book (see chapter 8), although the repeated failures of Italian opera in Paris and Versailles – most notably (at least, so scholars argue) with Francesco Cavalli's *Ercole amante*, commissioned for the wedding of Louis XIV and Maria Theresa of Spain (1660) but staged only in 1662 – show that Italian fashions could be resisted by a strongly centralised monarchy and no less strong cultural traditions. Spain also maintained its own linguistic boundaries, and had important native drama (not least by way of the great playwrights of the Golden Age, including Félix Lope de Vega and Pedro Calderón de la Barca), although the Neapolitan connection encouraged cultural transfers (Naples was governed by a Spanish viceroy and the predominant language was Spanish). Thus the first wholly sung drama performed in Spain, *La selva sin amor* (1627) had a text by Lope de Vega, music by the Bolognese musician Filippo Piccinini and Bernardo Monanni, and sets by the Florentine Cosimo Lotti. Similarly, *La púrpura della rosa*, to a libretto by Calderón and with music perhaps by Juan Hidalgo, and Calderón and Hidalgo's *Celos aun del aire matan* (both staged at the royal palace in Madrid in 1660) have strong Italian influences, if adapted to local traditions and to the stresses of Spanish poetry.[41]

England is probably, for present purposes, the special case.[42] After the Restoration of the monarchy in 1660, French influence was particularly strong at court, not least because Charles II had himself spent much of the Commonwealth in exile in Paris. Thus French models provided the most immediate influence on early English opera. However, London was also a cosmopolitan city, and English musicians were well aware of Italian styles in vocal and instrumental music: for example, Cavalli's *Erismena* (1655–6) seems to have been known there. Henry Purcell (1659–95) claimed in the preface to the score of *The Prophetess, or The History of Dioclesian* (pub. 1691) that English music is 'now learning Italian which is its best master, and studying a little of the French ayre, to give it somewhat more of gayety and fashion'. We in England, 'being farther from the Sun', are 'of later growth' and so must 'shake off our barbarity by degrees'. Nevertheless, 'The present age seemes already dispos'd to be refin'd, and to distinguish betwixt wild fancy, and a just, numerous

---

41 For *La púrpura della rosa* in a later version for performance in the Americas, see T. de Torrejón y Velasco and J. Hidalgo, *La púrpura de la rosa*, ed. L. K. Stein (Madrid, 1999); Stein, 'De la contera del mundo'. Stein is also preparing an edition of *Celos aun del aire matan*.

42 See Price, *Music in the Restoration Theatre* and *Henry Purcell and the London Stage*.

composition'. As a result, in English opera and related genres both French and Italian traits merge with native traditions in intriguing ways.

The king's power was significantly devolved, and also came under periodic threat, such that London's theatrical life again relied on mixed modes of production – in part commercial, in part relying on noble patronage – and also tended to prefer plays with incidental music (which could often be extensive) rather than operas *per se*. Fully sung dramas might appear in court contexts: Pierre Perrin and Robert Cambert's *Ariane, ou L'amour de Bacchus* (sung in French) in 1674 for the wedding of the Duke of York (later James II) and Mary of Modena; John Blow's 'Masque for y[e] Entertainment of the King', *Venus and Adonis* (*c.* 1683); and, by one reading at least, Purcell's *Dido and Aeneas* (to a libretto by Nahum Tate), which may have been performed at court before it was staged in 1689 at a girls' school in Chelsea run by Josias Priest (also a professional dancer involved with the London theatres). But if one went to, say, the Dorset Gardens Theatre, one would most often see a play with songs, as with Thomas Betterton and Henry Harris's revival of Shakespeare's *The Tempest* (1674) and Shadwell's tragedy *Psyche* (1675, with music by Locke and Giovanni Battista Draghi, perhaps modelled on Lully and Molière's *tragédie-ballet* of 1671). The poet John Dryden (1631–1700) spoke eloquently in the preface to his *Albion and Albanius* (1685) – set by Louis Grabu as the first full-length opera in English – of the problems of opera for English tastes, and indeed for the English language. Purcell rose to the challenge by producing a splendid series of semi-operas for the London stage, including Betterton's *Dioclesian* (1690; after Fletcher and Massinger), Dryden's *King Arthur, or The British Worthy* (1691) and *The Indian Queen* (1695), and *The Fairy Queen* (1692; after Shakespeare's *A Midsummer Night's Dream*). Even *Dido and Aeneas* succumbed: in 1700 (five years after Purcell's death) it was revised and inserted into an adaptation of *Measure for Measure*, and in 1704 it was attached both to Edward Ravenscroft's three-act farce *The Anatomist* and to George Etherege's *The Man of Mode*. The semi-opera may have its roots in earlier forms of English and Continental courtly entertainment, and its apparent generic mixtures make more sense in that light. But as Handel was to prove, the types of Italian opera discussed in this chapter would soon gain their revenge.

Bibliography

Alm, I., 'Theatrical Dance in Seventeenth-Century Venetian Opera'. Ph.D. thesis, University of California, Los Angeles (1993)

Bianconi, L., and Walker, T., 'Production, Consumption and Political Function of Seventeenth-Century Opera'. *Early Music History*, 4 (1984), 209–96

'Dalla *Finta pazza* alla *Veremonda*: storie di Febiarmonici'. *Rivista italiana di musicologia*, 10 (1975), 379–454

Carter, T., 'The North Italian Courts'. In C. Price (ed.), *The Early Baroque Era: from the Late 16th Century to the 1660s*, 'Man and Music', 3. Basingstoke and London, 1993, pp. 23–48

Monteverdi's Musical Theatre. New Haven and London, 2002

'Rediscovering *Il rapimento di Cefalo*'. *Journal of Seventeenth-Century Music*, 9/1 (2003) <http://www.sscm-jscm.org/jscm/v9/no1/Carter.html>

Clubb, L. G., *Italian Drama in Shakespeare's Time*. New Haven and London, 1989

Curtis, A., '*La Poppea impasticciata* or, Who Wrote the Music to *L'incoronazione* (1643)?'. *Journal of the American Musicological Society*, 42 (1989), 23–54

Fabbri, P., *Il secolo cantante: per una storia del libretto d'opera nel Seicento*. Bologna, 1990

Freeman, R. S., *Opera without Drama: Currents of Change in Italian Opera, 1675–1725*. Ann Arbor, 1981

Gianturco, C., *Alessandro Stradella (1639–1682): his Life and Music*. Oxford, 1994.

Glover, J., *Cavalli*. London, 1978

Grout, D. J., *Alessandro Scarlatti: an Introduction to his Operas*. Berkeley, 1979

Hammond, F., *Music and Spectacle in Baroque Rome: Barberini Patronage under Urban VIII*. New Haven and London, 1994

Heller, W., 'Chastity, Heroism, and Allure: Women in the Opera of Seventeenth-Century Venice'. Ph.D. thesis, Brandeis University (1995)

'"O castità bugiarda": Cavalli's *Didone* and the Question of Chastity'. In M. Burden (ed.), *A Woman Scorn'd: Responses to the Dido Myth*. London, 1998, pp. 169–225

'Tacitus Incognito: Opera as History in *L'incoronazione di Poppea*'. *Journal of the American Musicological Society*, 52 (1999), 39–96

Emblems of Eloquence: Opera and Women's Voices in Seventeenth-Century Venice. Berkeley, Los Angeles and London, 2003

Holmes, W. C., '*La Statira' by Pietro Ottoboni and Alessandro Scarlatti: the Textual Sources, with a Documentary Postscript*, 'Monographs in Musicology', 2. New York, 1983

MacNeil, A., *Music and Women of the Commedia dell'Arte in the Late Sixteenth Century*. Oxford, 2003

Mamone, S., 'Most Serene Brothers–Princes–Impresarios: Theater in Florence under the Management and Protection of Mattias, Giovancarlo, and Leopoldo de' Medici'. *Journal of Seventeenth-Century Music*, 9/1 (2003) <http://www.sscm-jscm. org/jscm/v9/no1/Mamone.html>

Mancini, F., Muraro, M. T., and Povoledo, E., *I teatri del Veneto*, i/1: *Venezia: teatri effimeri e nobili imprenditori*. Venice, 1995

Murata, M., *Operas for the Papal Court, 1631–1668*. Ann Arbor, 1981

'Why the First Opera Given in Paris Wasn't Roman', *Cambridge Opera Journal*, 7 (1995), 87–105

Price, C. A., *Music in the Restoration Theatre, with a Catalogue of Instrumental Music in the Plays 1665–1713*. Ann Arbor, 1979

Henry Purcell and the London Stage. Cambridge, 1984

Rosand, E., 'Music in the Myth of Venice'. *Renaissance Quarterly*, 30 (1977) 511–37

Opera in Seventeenth-Century Venice: the Creation of a Genre. Berkeley, Los Angeles and Oxford, 1991

Sadie, S. (ed.), *The New Grove Dictionary of Opera*. 4 vols, London, 1992

Sartori, C. (ed.), *I libretti italiani a stampa dalle origini al 1800: catalogo analitico con 16 indici*. 7 vols, Cuneo, 1990–

Schulze, H., *Odysseus in Venedig: Sujetwahl und Rollenkonzeption in der venezianischen Oper des 17. Jahrhunderts*, 'Perspektiven der Opernforschung', 11. Frankfurt am Main, 2004

Shiff, J., 'Are the Grimani Banquet Plays "Rappresentazioni musicali"? A Reappraisal'. *Studi musicali*, 19 (1990) 71–89

Stein, L. K., 'De la contera del mundo: las navegaciones de la ópera entre dos mundos y varias culturas'. In E. Casares and A. Torrente (eds), *La ópera en España e Hispanoamérica*. Madrid, 2001, pp. 79–94

Timms, C., *Polymath of the Baroque: Agostino Steffani and his Music*. Oxford and New York, 2003

10

The Church Triumphant: music in the liturgy

NOEL O'REGAN

During the seventeenth century, religious observance played an essential part in people's lives, both as the consequence of a pervasive system of belief that was seldom questioned, and as the crucial declaration of a confessional allegiance that might also have strong political overtones. Music had an important part to play in the articulation of this allegiance, whether by an aggressive presence, as in a Catholic festal Vespers in southern Europe, or a conspicuous absence, as in Calvinist-inspired preaching services north of the Alps. In most denominations, music was recognised as a powerful if somewhat dangerous weapon, able to attract and sway men's souls, and thus subject to sometimes considerable ecclesiastical control. As a rhetorical art, it was akin to preaching – indeed it was at times deliberately linked to it:[1] composers were expected not only to 'read' sacred texts through their music but also to interpret them for their listeners. On the Catholic side, the new orders, especially the Jesuits and the Oratorians, made explicit use of music for evangelisation. Already in the 1580s, Annibale Stabile, *maestro di cappella* of the Jesuit-run German College in Rome, could state that he had learnt more about the setting of words from its Jesuit rector, Michele Lauretano, than he had in years of previous musical study (which had included a spell under Palestrina).[2] The German College remained hugely influential, sending priests to all parts of Germany and as far afield as Hungary. Jesuit missionaries were also sent all over Europe and to the New World, bringing with them the advocacy of music, not least in the education of the young and in their targeting of the aristocracy; their preference was for Italian, especially Roman musical styles. It was the teaching aspect, too, which particularly encouraged liturgical music among the followers of Martin Luther. One of the more remarkable features of seventeenth-century Lutheran music

---

1 The connection between music and preaching has long been recognised in the Lutheran tradition, but this was also evident in the Catholic Church; for Bonifazio Graziani's (1604/5-1664) direct comparison between sacred oratory and solo singing, see Miller, 'Music for the Mass in Seventeenth-Century Rome', i: 478.

2 Culley, *Jesuits and Music*, i: 78. The trope is not uncommon: Giulio Caccini said something similar (in the preface to his *Le nuove musiche* of 1602) of the influence on him of the Camerata, from which he had learnt more than from 30 years of studying counterpoint.

was the speed and extent to which it opened itself to new Italian (and therefore Catholic) influences. Only the Calvinists held back, their Augustine-inspired suspicion of elaborate music largely overruling its potential role in education and in attracting and uplifting worshippers. Even here there was some polyphonic elaboration of basic metrical psalm-singing, especially outside of the formal liturgy, while in the Calvinist Netherlands, the organ developed a distinctive role as a recital instrument in the newly secularised churches which was to influence its more directly liturgical use in Lutheran Germany.

Places and forms of service

For seventeenth-century town-dwellers, whatever their confessional allegiance, religious observance was built into the fabric of the day, season and year. The sound of bells, the chanting of offices, the celebration of Mass or other services, and the annual round of temporal and sanctoral feast-days and processions all divided up urban time and space. While the focus of this chapter will be largely on the formal liturgical music composed for major services of various denominations, it is important to emphasise that polyphonic art music formed only a part of any church service in the seventeenth century: it was composed for, and experienced as part of, a broader liturgical context, knowledge of which is essential if we are to understand its function and meaning. Plainchant intonations, plainchant or organ *alternatim* verses, chanted prayers and readings, are only the most obvious ways in which polyphony was spaced and framed. For Catholics, ritual gestures and movements, the perfume of incense, the relative locations of clergy and choir(s), vestments, paintings, tapestries and platforms, all had a role to play in the overall experience. On the Protestant side, the much barer ritual spaces and comparative lack of gestures could be equally important in focussing attention more directly on the music and its text, while in the Lutheran context, complex polyphony was framed by simpler congregational chorale singing (which was often unison and unaccompanied).

Catholic churches retained the high altar as their major focus, though also making provision for preaching to large crowds; the new wide-naved Baroque design facilitated this, while including a large number of side-chapels for the individual celebration of Mass. The decision by Pope Paul V in 1605 to replace the surviving half-nave of the Constantinian St Peter's basilica not with the fourth arm of Michelangelo's symmetrical Greek cross, but with a long nave in order to accommodate Tridentine liturgical demands, was a key one.[3] It gave

---

3 The views of the papal Master of Ceremonies, Paolo Mucanzio, were significant in reaching this decision; see Pastor, *The History of the Popes*, xix: 386.

papal approbation to the new type of church pioneered at the Jesuit Chiesa del Gesù and the Oratorian Chiesa Nuova which were taken as models by their orders all over Catholic Europe. As the century progressed, Catholic churches abandoned the Oratorian founder Philip Neri's ideal of simple decoration in favour of ever more elaborate ceiling- and wall-paintings and a profusion of marble, paintings and statues. Churches such as the Jesuit San Ignazio in Rome were given three-dimensional ceiling-paintings whose clouds and saints gave the illusion of continuing up into the heavens. This illusion was mirrored in the music for multiple choirs of voices and instruments on platforms or in balconies, even positioned in the dome, as at patronal feast-day celebrations in St Peter's: such music was designed to give the sensation of listening to heavenly choirs. Unless part of princely palaces, churches were open to everyone and provided the only readily available experience of art music for many. While some seventeenth-century church music was composed for the select ears of aristocratic connoisseurs, the majority was intended for a very wide public, and was designed accordingly, in a style which Stephen Miller has called *musica comune*, following Palestrina's use of that term.[4]

Protestant churches had their main focus on the pulpit rather than on the communion table; many were adapted from existing Medieval churches, but newly built ones – particularly Calvinist – were designed as preaching auditoria.[5] The precentor or cantor took a prominent role, leading the congregation in the hymn- and psalm-singing which marked one of the main distinctions between Protestant and Catholic liturgies; in Catholic Mass and Office celebrations, such participation was not normal, but paraliturgical and other devotional services, particularly those organised by lay confraternities, could indeed provide opportunities for congregational singing. Another clear distinction between the various confessions was language, with the Catholic liturgy retaining Latin exclusively (although vernacular pieces such as the Spanish *villancico* could find a place alongside official texts); Lutherans used both Latin and the vernacular, and Calvinists eschewed Latin altogether. Another significant difference was the Protestant lack of any cult of saints, so important for Catholic devotion and liturgy.

There were differences, but also many similarities, in the forms of the major services in the different confessional traditions. For Catholics, the Mass remained the central act of worship, with settings of the five movements of the Ordinary (Kyrie, Gloria, Credo, Sanctus–Benedictus, Agnus Dei) continuing to

4 Miller, 'Music for the Mass in Seventeenth-Century Rome', i: 29ff. In a letter to Duke Guglielmo Gonzaga of 1570, Palestrina contrasted 'musica comune' with the terms 'artificio' and 'fughe' applied to music for connoisseurs.

5 See, for example, the Zuyderkerk in Amsterdam, built in the early 1600s as the first Protestant church in the city.

be written throughout the century, often in a retrospective style. In northern Italy, the Sanctus and Agnus Dei could be downplayed musically or replaced with motets, a procedure with some analogies to Lutheran practice.[6] From the *Libro di punti* of Carlo Vanni for 1616 we know that in the Cappella Pontificia, motets were invariably sung during the Offertory at High Mass, and at Low Mass during the Offertory, Elevation, and distribution of Communion.[7] These three key loci for Eucharistic devotion could similarly be accompanied by motets or instrumental music throughout the Catholic world. A large measure of flexibility in the choice of motet texts, even when substituting for liturgical items such as the Gradual or Offertory, seems to have been common up to 1657 when a bull of Pope Alexander VII, reiterated in 1665, tried to curtail it by legislating that only the texts appointed in the Missal and Breviary should be sung.[8] Motets could also be used in semi-liturgical or non-liturgical contexts, as for example during processions, state ceremonial occasions, papal consistories, or meals on major feasts.

From the late sixteenth century, Vespers, celebrated in the fashionable late afternoon, became an equally important focus for musical elaboration on major Catholic feast-days, with first Vespers on the vigil and second Vespers on the feast itself. The items set to polyphony included some or all of the five psalms and antiphons, the hymn and the Magnificat; the prescribed psalms for major feast-days were fortunately limited in number, allowing composers and publishers to cover many in a single publication. The most elaborate (usually polychoral) settings were used for the opening psalm, always 'Dixit Dominus' on Sundays and feast-days, and the Magnificat; other psalms might be set on a smaller scale or simply harmonised in *falsobordone* (chordal singing, usually around a plainchant). The antiphons could be sung in improvised *contrappunto alla mente* over the plainchant, or could be substituted by small-scale motets.[9] A motet was often sung at the end 'in loco *Deo gratias*' (i.e., substituting for the final response); it was common to follow this with the Marian antiphon appropriate to the season ('Alma redemptoris mater' in Advent, 'Ave Regina coelorum' in Lent, 'Regina coeli' in Paschaltide, and 'Salve Regina' for the rest of the year). In contrast to the Mass, Vespers was almost entirely static liturgically speaking, the only activity being the incensation of the altar during the Magnificat; attention was thus almost completely focussed on words and music. The other Offices were normally confined to plainsong, though Terce could be celebrated with some solemnity immediately before High Mass on

6 Schnoebelen, 'Bologna, 1580–1700', p. 114.

7 Frey, 'Die Gesänge der sixtinischen Kapelle an den Sonntagen und hohen Kirchenfesten des Jahres 1616'; Cummings, 'Toward an Interpretation of the Sixteenth-Century Motet'.

8 Bianconi, *Music in the Seventeenth Century*, pp. 107–10; Lionnet, 'Una svolta nella storia del Collegio dei Cantori Pontifici'.

9 Kurtzman, *The Monteverdi Vespers of 1610*.

feast-days, and Matins was celebrated with polyphony at Christmas and dur-ing the last three days of Holy Week. Solemn Compline could follow on a festal Vespers or could be sung during Lent.[10] The *Breviarium romanum* (1568) and *Missale romanum* (1570), issued in the aftermath of the Council of Trent, brought a high degree of conformity within the Roman Catholic Church. This was cemented in terms of ritual by the issue of the *Caeremoniale episcoporum* in 1600. While the adoption of these books might have been slower in some places than in others, an ever greater level of centralisation ensued during the century. Apart from the Roman rite, only the Ambrosian and Mozarabic rites survived the Council of Trent, and these held on to a relatively precarious existence in Milan and Toledo Cathedrals respectively. However, some older religious orders, particularly the Dominicans, also retained their distinctive usages.

The reform of plainchant had been a troubling issue from the 1570s, with a Humanist-inspired desire to cleanse what were seen as the accretions of the late-Medieval period (mainly melismas). This reform was eventually brought to a conclusion with the publication of the *Graduale mediceo* in Rome in 1614.[11] Its adoption, however, was somewhat piecemeal even in Rome, where the older large manuscript chant books continued in use. In the France of Louis XIV, there were increasing tendencies towards a national Gallican church in only limited contact with Rome. In parallel with this was the development, in Paris in particular, of a series of alternative missals and breviaries and of distinctive variations of chant known as *plainchant musical* and *chant figuré*.[12] French bishops issued their own revised *Ceremoniale parisiense* in 1662. Under Pope Urban VIII, a revised set of texts for the Office hymns was issued in 1632 in an attempt to replace what was seen as corrupt Latin with more literary texts. In many cases, existing collections of hymns, such as those of Palestrina, were adapted to fit new texts which kept the same metrical form.[13] In France, new hymns replaced many of the Roman ones, while Henry Du Mont's *Cinq messes en plain-chant* in 1669 achieved an extraordinary popularity that continued until the 1960s.[14]

Lutheran services mirrored Catholic ones, but without such a centralised governing structure, practice could vary considerably. The *Hauptgottesdienst* and *Vespergottesdienst* corresponded to Mass and Vespers and retained many

10 Roche, '*Musica diversa di Compietà*'; Dixon, 'Lenten Devotions in Baroque Rome'.

11 A modern edition is available in two volumes: see Giacomo Baroffi and Manlio Sodi (eds), *Graduale de Tempore iuxta ritum sacrosanctae Romanae ecclesiae. Editio princeps (1614)*; *Graduale de Sanctis iuxta ritum sacrosanctae Romanae ecclesiae. Editio princeps (1614–1615)* (Rome, 2001).

12 Launay, *La musique religieuse en France*; S. Sadie and J. Tyrrell (eds), *The Revised New Grove Dictionary of Music and Musicians* (London, 2000), s.v. 'Plainchant: Neo-Gallican Reforms'.

13 Gregorio Allegri was chosen to adapt the revised texts to Palestrina's hymn-settings for use in the Cappella Pontificia; see Hammond, *Music and Spectacle in Baroque Rome*, pp. 177–8.

14 Anthony, *French Baroque Music*, p. 214.

of the same items;[15] moreover, early in the century many cities and towns continued to use Latin plainchant and polyphony. Mass settings were gradually reduced to just the Kyrie and Gloria, while the German chorale assumed an ever greater role in worship; composers also found more elaborate ways of treating the chorale in both vocal and organ settings. A Vespers service held in Dresden on 31 October 1617 (with music by Heinrich Schütz) to mark the centenary of the Reformation included the opening versicle and response, an antiphon and Ps. 100 ('Jubilate Deo') for five choirs; this was followed by a single choir singing part of Ps. 118 (the verses beginning 'This is the day which the Lord has made') and by the Creed, sung with the congregation in German ('Wir glauben all an einen Gott'). The sermon was followed by the Magnificat in Latin, sung by six choirs including instruments, but sandwiched between its verses was Luther's German hymn 'Erhalt uns Herr bey deinem Wort' sung by the congregation. Two further Congregational hymns followed before the final 'Benedicamus Domino'.[16] This was typical of many festal celebrations before the devastating effect of the Thirty Years War (1618–48) on German musical establishments (noted by Schütz in the preface to his 1636 *Kleine geistliche Concerte*) hastened the adoption of smaller-scale forms. In Lutheran churches, motets could also be sung on festive occasions such as victory celebrations or weddings.[17]

In England the Anglican church spent much of the seventeenth century bouncing from one liturgical extreme to the other as the Stuart monarchs and their bishops, on the one side, tried to impose more 'high church' liturgy with candles, vestments, ritual gestures and concomitant music, and the more Calvinist clergy and middle classes resisted. Service settings bore some resemblance to Mass Ordinaries, though normally only the Kyrie (to a modified English text) and Creed were set; they also contained the major canticles and hymns from Morning and Evening Prayer, adapted by Thomas Cranmer from the monastic Offices, including the *Venite, Benedicite, Te Deum*, Magnificat and *Nunc dimittis*, all sung in English. Many composers also wrote settings of the so-called Festal Psalms, those prescribed for major feast-days such as Christmas, Easter or Pentecost. While Service settings could be seen as routine, composers often poured their strongest efforts into the composition of anthems which were sung at the end of major services. Like the Catholic Latin motet, these did not have to set specifically liturgical texts but were loosely related to the themes of the liturgy on the particular day. The period of the English Civil War marked the supremacy of the Puritan party, with severe consequences for

15 Webber, *North German Church Music in the Age of Buxtehude*, chap. 2.
16 Leaver, 'Lutheran Vespers as a Context for Music'.
17 For example, Frederick Gable has edited a series of polychoral wedding motets composed by Jacob Praetorius in Hamburg in the early 1600s; see *The Motets of Jacob Praetorius II*, 'Recent Researches in the Music of the Baroque Era', 73 (Madison, WI, 1994).

polyphony; this fifteen-or-so-year break marked a watershed in English sacred music even more severe than that which the Thirty Years War did for church music on the Continent.

In Scotland, the Protestant Netherlands, and parts of France, Switzerland and other areas under Calvinist influence, public worship remained extremely spartan from a musical point of view, largely confined to the harmonised singing of metrical psalms with or without organ. On the other hand, private devotional music was encouraged, and it would appear that the bulk of published polyphonic music was composed for this market, such as, for example, the Latin *Cantiones sacrae* of Jan Pieterszoon Sweelinck (Antwerp, 1619). In France, where an official tolerance allowed Catholics and Huguenots to co-exist before the Edict of Nantes in 1685, there was a porosity between the confessions in their use of such music, and this was true in Germany, too. In general, the boundaries between formal liturgical and private devotional use of music in this period were not always tightly drawn, particularly in genres such as the motet, the anthem, and the Spanish and New World *villancico*.

Another porous boundary was the one between formal services and paraliturgical celebrations such as processions or the Catholic Forty Hours' Devotion. Processional activity was ubiquitous in Catholic Europe, ranging from the quasi-liturgical processions held on Rogation Days or on Corpus Christi, through those held by the multitudes of lay confraternities and guilds, to large state-organised processions held, for example, to welcome visiting dignitaries or to intercede against plague. In Rome and Venice especially, but in all Catholic cities, confraternities or *scuole* organised charity and welfare services under the watchful eye of both Church and state.[18] Their patronal feast-days were occasions for huge displays by their members, parading themselves, the attributes of the particular company, and very often young girls to whom dowries were to be given. These processions involved a number of musical groups singing polyphony, *falsobordone* or plainsong, and performing on instruments. Psalms, litanies and motets were regularly sung, either while processing or at stopping places along the route. Two sets of five partbooks from the holdings of the Arciconfraternita del Santo Spirito in Sassia in Rome were first copied around 1600 and subsequently augmented: they contain motets by various Rome-based composers for major processional occasions such as the patronal feast of Pentecost, Palm Sunday and Easter, as well as for Eucharistic processions.[19] For Milan, Robert Kendrick has detailed numerous processions which he has described as 'sonic expressions of urban identity': these were organised, for

18 O'Regan, *Institutional Patronage in Post-Tridentine Rome*; Glixon, *Honoring God and the City*.
19 O'Regan, 'Processions and their Music in Post-Tridentine Rome'.

example, to pray for relief from the plague of 1630–31, and to welcome Margaret of Austria on her way to marry Philip III of Spain in 1598, or Maria Anna of Austria taking the same route to marry Philip IV in 1649. For this last occasion, the *maestro di cappella* of the Duomo, Antonio Maria Turati, composed two motets, 'Ingredere, augusta proles' and 'Cantemus hilares' sung respectively as the queen-to-be entered the Duomo and kissed the cross. Processional psalms and a *Te Deum* were also sung.[20] Throughout Catholic Europe, the Eucharistic processions held during the octave of Corpus Christi (the Thursday after the octave of Pentecost) were usually the largest and most devotional of the Church year; these were occasions for the singing of Eucharistic motets such as 'O salutaris hostia' and 'O sacrum convivium', or the hymn 'Pange lingua . . . corporis'.

The forces involved in performing liturgical music could vary widely depending on the resources of the institution putting it on, and on the relative importance of the occasion. Only the richest of establishments could afford to keep on their payroll the numbers of singers and instrumentalists necessary for large-scale ceremonial music; for most, a big splash once or twice a year – generally for the patronal feast-day – was as much as could be done. Religious orders, male and female, had the advantage of the free services of singers and instrumentalists from their ranks; as a consequence these performers often do not appear in archival records of such occasions. Female convents regularly supplied their own liturgical music; some, such as those in Milan, were renowned for the quality of their music. Most hired in male musicians and instrumentalists to play in the outer, public church for large-scale feast-day celebrations.[21]

In Rome the Cappella Pontificia contained around 32 singers in the early 1600s and this number stayed more or less constant throughout the century. It is clear, however, that not all singers sang on every occasion or even for every polyphonic item on any particular day. The choir was divided into two halves for weekday work, each taking alternate weeks. There was always a number of *giubilati*, singers with 25 or more years' service, for whom attendance was optional, and there were absences through illness, permitted visits to families away from Rome etc. Cardinal-nephews and other important figures could also borrow singers for diplomatic missions, private performances, operas or patronal feast-day celebrations at institutions of which they were Cardinal-Protectors. So the average working strength of the choir was much less than its full complement, and there is a convincing body of evidence that much of the repertory, with the possible exception of Mass Ordinaries, was performed with

---

20 Kendrick, *The Sounds of Milan*, pp. 366–7.
21 Kendrick, *Celestial Sirens*; Monson, *Disembodied Voices*; Reardon, *Holy Concord within Sacred Walls*.

one singer per part.[22] The Cappella Giulia in St Peter's had twelve adult singers and up to six boys. The other major Roman basilicas and some churches of foreign nations had two adult singers per part (ATB) and up to four boys, while another dozen or so churches struggled to support four adults and two boys, enough for small-scale music with organ accompaniment.[23] Many churches had only an organist and one or two priests to sing plainchant. The picture was the same in other Italian cities. In Bologna, for instance, the large civic basilica of S. Petronio had 36 singers and about 10 instrumentalists at the start of the century, and this remained fairly constant; here as elsewhere, the types of instruments used changed in the course of the century, the predominance moving from wind to strings.

In France, the Chapelle Royale in 1645 consisted of two *sous-maîtres*, six boys, two falsettists, eight *haute-contres*, eight tenors and eight basses, plus eight chaplains, four chapel clerks and two grammar instructors for the children. There were also two cornettists and an organist. From the 1660s the number of instrumentalists was increased, and by 1708 there were six violins and violas, three bass violins, one *grosse basse de violon*, one theorbo, two flutes, two oboes, one bass crumhorn, two serpents and one bassoon, as well as four organists.[24] Other establishments in Paris and elsewhere, however, made do with many fewer singers and musicians. In Protestant Dresden, Heinrich Schütz had sixteen singers and a similar number of instrumentalists in 1616, although the total then fluctuated considerably owing to the vicissitudes of the Thirty Years War. In Protestant Hamburg, where singers and instrumentalists were supported by the city rather than by individual churches, there were eight town singers in 1607 as well as a further eight teachers from the Johanneum Latin school who also sang, all under the direction of the cantor, Erasmus Sartorius. There were four organists in the city and eight *Ratsmusikanten* who played cornett, viol or violin, and sackbut.[25]

In England the Chapel Royal had a complement of around 32 men and 12 boys up to the death of Charles I (1649). As in Rome, the whole choir sang only on the biggest occasions; otherwise, half or fewer of the men attended on a rota system. After the Restoration (1660), the choir was brought back to strength and some members of the newly established group of 'four-and-twenty fiddlers' regularly

22 Lionnet, 'Performance Practice in the Papal Chapel during the Seventeenth Century'; Sherr, 'Performance Practice in the Papal Chapel during the Sixteenth Century'; O'Regan, 'Evidence for Vocal Scoring in the Late Sixteenth- and Early Seventeenth-Century Polyphony from Cappella Sistina Musical and Non-Musical Documents'.
23 O'Regan, 'Sacred Polychoral Music in Rome', chap. 1.
24 Anthony, *French Baroque Music*, pp. 24, 26.
25 F. K. Gable (ed.), *Dedication Service for St. Gertrude's Chapel, Hamburg 1607*, 'Recent Researches in the Music of the Baroque Era', 91 (Madison, WI, 1998), pp. xxiv–xxvi.

took part in services. The Chapel's most impressive occasion of the century
was probably the coronation of James II in 1685, when all the singers and
the instrumentalists performed nine anthems at the ceremony in Westminster
Abbey, partly to cover the fact that James refused to take communion according
to the Anglican rite. The Catholic James all but ignored the Protestant Chapel
Royal during the rest of his short reign, and his successors, William and Mary,
did little to revive its splendour. Although the Restoration led directly to the
re-establishment of church music, not all English cathedrals and colleges fared
as well as the Chapel Royal, and they suffered decline under William and Mary,
often struggling to support twelve singing men and a similar number of boys.
Parish churches were lucky if they had an organ and organist, and they relied
largely on a precentor to 'line out' successive lines of metrical psalms which
were then repeated by the congregation.

Taxonomies of style

Traditionally, scholarly discussion of seventeenth-century sacred music has
tended to focus on style, particularly on a perceived polarity between the *stile
antico* and the *stile moderno*, the former viewed as conservative, looking backwards to the music of Palestrina in particular, and the latter seen as forward-
looking, breaking established rules in order better to express the words. Historians have privileged the *stile moderno* at the expense of the *stile antico*, and have
also tended to label centres as predominantly leaning one way or the other
(Rome, Milan and Vienna as conservative; Venice, Florence and Dresden as
forward-looking). The *seconda pratica* was seen as exciting and challenging; the
prima pratica as dull and conventional.

Inevitably the reality was more complicated. Various different approaches
to the writing of liturgical music were adopted in every European state and
confession, from the beginning of the century to its end, and they existed side
by side. This diversity had much to do with liturgical function on the one hand,
and with institutional factors such as the availability of musicians and type of
acoustic on the other. Four such approaches can be identified and will form
the basis for the following discussion. It might seem remarkable that these can
broadly be found in every centre and in all religious confessions, but all sought
to solve the same problems: the audibility and rhetorical demands of the text;
the filling of big sonic spaces; the need to write for very large forces on major
feast-days, and for much leaner groups at routine liturgical celebrations; and
the desire both to impress with sizeable forces and to seduce with solo voices.
These different approaches could happily coexist within the same service or
group of services, producing what Robert Kendrick has labelled 'polystylism'

and Steven Saunders 'multilingualism'.[26] Indeed it is this stylistic cohabitation which is perhaps the most characteristic feature of seventeenth-century sacred music when compared with anything that went before. The most emblematic publication of the early seventeenth century, Monteverdi's Mass and Vespers for the Blessed Virgin of 1610, is perhaps the clearest example of combining them in a single volume.

The first approach might best be identified as one of continuity with the past or pasts. This could frequently involve imitation, in both senses in which that term is commonly used: music modelled on an existing composition or compositional format (*imitatio*); music which made use of the pervasive imitative counterpoint characteristic of much sixteenth-century church music. Under this heading can be included musics as diverse as Monteverdi's *Missa 'In illo tempore'* (1610), Thomas Tomkins's Fifth Service (based on William Byrd's Second Service), Eustache Du Caurroy's *Requiem* used for King Henri IV of France (1610) and for French royal funerals regularly thereafter until the early eighteenth century, antiphons sung in improvised counterpoint by three or four of the highly trained singers in the Cappella Pontificia in Rome, the motet-style settings of Lutheran chorales in Johann Hermann Schein's *Cymbalum sionium, sive Cantiones sacrae*, 5, 6, 8, 10, 12 vv. (Leipzig, 1615), and a Mass Ordinary or motet by Alessandro Scarlatti. Such continuity with the past was seen as particularly appropriate for certain core parts of the liturgy: Mass Ordinaries and Vesper hymns for Catholics, Service settings for Anglicans, psalm settings 'in reports' (i.e., with limited imitation) for English and Scottish Calvinists. This retrospective *stylus ecclesiasticus* came to act as a signifier for religious orthodoxy and continuity in various religious traditions, with much sixteenth-century sacred music continuing to be performed well into the seventeenth and beyond.[27]

The second approach involved an extension of the first by expanding forces, leading to large-scale music for two or more choirs, sometimes referred to as *coro pleno* (or *coro pieno*), generally used for impressive purposes or to fill large buildings. Into this category comes one of the century's best known labels for sacred music, the 'colossal Baroque' as represented, for example, by the polychoral Masses of the Roman Orazio Benevoli and many other Italian composers.[28] Other examples might be some of the *symphoniae sacrae* of Giovanni

---

26 Kendrick, *The Sounds of Milan*, p. 256; Saunders, *Cross, Sword and Lyre*, p. 159.

27 Witness, for example, the continued use of the music of Palestrina in the Cappella Pontificia, or of Lassus in many German centres. In his *Osservazioni per ben regolare il coro dei cantori della Cappella pontificia* (Rome, 1711), Andrea Adami goes to great lengths to establish a historical pedigree for the Cappella Pontificia's practice of *falsobordone*, going back to Guido of Arezzo.

28 Dixon, 'The Origins of the Roman "Colossal Baroque"'; Luisi, Curti and Gozzi (eds), *La scuola policorale romana del Sei-Settecento*, pp. 20–41, 65–90.

Gabrieli or the psalm 'Nisi Dominus' and the hymn 'Ave maris stella' from
Monteverdi's 1610 Vespers, Tomkins's 'Great' Service, the large-scale German
polychoral music of composers such as Hieronymus and Jacob Praetorius at
Hamburg, Heinrich Schütz's *Psalmen Davids* (Dresden, 1619), or the four-choir
Masses written for Emperor Ferdinand II in Graz and Vienna. This music was
invariably accompanied by organ(s) and frequently by other instruments. What
distinguishes it from the fourth approach, described below, is that the organ
and instruments either accompanied or substituted for lines in what was essentially conceived as a vocal piece. The organ part was normally a *basso seguente*
rather than a basso continuo, thus reproducing the lowest sounding part rather
than presenting an independent line. Occasionally, single voices from across the
choirs would be grouped together, but however the voices might be ordered,
they maintained a consistent musical flow in contrast to the more fragmented
textures typical of music for voices and basso continuo, and indeed enabled by
such a continuo. Theorists such as Marco Scacchi saw this as part of the *stylus
ecclesiasticus*,[29] but the increased forces required a different, significantly less
contrapuntal style compared with four-, five- or six-voice writing.

The third approach represented a paring-down of resources, reducing the
number of singers and relying on an accompanying instrument or instruments
to fill out the harmony implied by a basso continuo. Developed in parallel with
new directions in secular music, the small-scale *concerto ecclesiastico* variously
filled the need for clear declamation of the text, the expectations of increasingly
virtuosic singers, and the requirements of those institutions without the means
to employ large performing groups. The small-scale concerto also increasingly
found a place in larger churches, particularly for settings of antiphons or of
the motets which substituted for them, and also for Vesper psalms and for
motets sung during Mass, especially at the Elevation. Under this heading can
be included the *concerti ecclesiastici* of Lodovico da Viadana, the four *concerti*
of Monteverdi's 1610 Vespers, the strongly Italianate concertos of Schein and
Schütz, and the somewhat independent traditions of the English verse-anthem
and the French *petit motet*. While this approach overlapped to an extent with
both monody and the tenets of the *seconda pratica*, they are by no means coterminous. Both the *concerto ecclesiastico* and the verse-anthem were rooted in
traditional counterpoint, and indeed in sixteenth-century genres and performance practices, and they continued this vein even when they expanded to
include instruments.

The fourth approach can be seen as a fusion of the second and third, combining the small-scale *concertato* motet for soloists with music for one or more choirs

29 For a translation of Scacchi's *Breve discorso sopra la musica moderna* (Warsaw, 1649), see Palisca, 'Marco
Scacchi's Defense of Modern Music (1649)'.

of voices and instruments. Applied especially to extended texts in verse structures, such as psalms and the Magnificat, this approach combined all the available forces on large-scale feasts in a kaleidoscope of varying textures. Individual verses could run into each other in what Jerome Roche labelled 'mixed concertato' or could be separated off by pauses and bar-lines in print and manuscript in the style known as 'concertato alla romana'.[30] Into this category comes much of the later output of Giovanni Gabrieli and the larger-scale Schütz, psalm settings such as the 'Dixit Dominus' from Monteverdi's 1610 Vespers, the French *grand motet*, the symphony-anthems of John Blow and Henry Purcell, and the *Missa salisburgensis* for eight 'choirs' of voices and instruments once attributed to Orazio Benevoli but now recognised as having been composed by Heinrich von Biber to celebrate the 1100th anniversary of the founding of the bishopric of Salzburg in 1682.[31] Much of this music was composed for exceptional celebrations of coronations, battles won, births of royal heirs etc.; it can thus have all the brashness and pomposity of state music, but combined with the subtlety and responsiveness to the text of the small-scale *concertato* setting.

One advantage of discussing 'approaches' in this way is to emphasise that they are more strongly linked to particular performance practices than to musical styles *per se*. For example, a small-scale *concerto ecclesiastico* by Viadana (approach 3) can be quite contrapuntally conceived and thus can come close to the *stile antico* (approach 1); Viadana made the connection explicit when claiming that his *concerti* were intended for institutions wishing but unable to perform larger-scale polyphony. In turn, a piece in the *stile antico* may be made to sound more 'modern' depending on the performance resources used and the elements added to the musical framework (embellishments, instrumentation), while the apparent differences between a polychoral setting and a mixed *concertato* setting (approaches 2 and 4) are in part contingent upon performance practices (e.g., identifying one 'choir' as one or more solo voices and continuo, another as a group of instruments, etc.). As we shall see, there are indeed important stylistic distinctions to be made in seventeenth-century liturgical music, but their operation, and their impact on musical sonority, is not quite as straightforward as might at first appear.

Continuity: the *stylus ecclesiasticus*

The institution which, more than any, came to be identified with conservative musical practices in the seventeenth century was the papal Cappella Pontificia.

30 Roche, *North Italian Church Music in the Age of Monteverdi*; Dixon, '*Concertata alla romana* and Polychoral Music in Rome'.
31 Hintermaier, '"Missa salisburgensis"'.

Increasingly isolated from their fellow Roman singers in the Compagnia dei Musici and constricted by the lack of an organ or other instruments, the papal singers formed an elite which saw itself, and was seen, as first and foremost the guardians of a tradition.[32] Early in the century this tradition was already associated with the name of Giovanni Pierluigi da Palestrina (1525/6–1594), who had served as composer to the Cappella for much of his life. The myth (for which there is no real evidence) that Palestrina had somehow 'saved' polyphonic music at the time of the Council of Trent (1545–63) was first propounded by Agostino Agazzari in 1607, in a context which saw Palestrina as a moderniser, simplifying polyphony for the sake of clarity of the words. For Agazzari, the largely homophonic style with variegated textures of the *Missa Papae Marcelli*, or of Palestrina's considerable number of double- and triple-choir settings, had shown the way forward. As the century progressed, however, the composer's name became more identified with the imitative counterpoint and cantus-firmus techniques he had used in his earlier music; this went together with a conscious re-creation of a Palestrina-derived *stile antico* that was still very much part of the musical present.

Even the papal singers, however, did not confine themselves to singing unaccompanied music in their increasingly traditional idiom. They regularly took part in patronal feast-day celebrations throughout the city, while jealously guarding their privileged position; they also took part in opera productions. And on four occasions during the year, they brought the latest musical styles into the Vatican by singing the *Vespro segreto*, not in the Cappella Sistina or its equivalent in the Quirinale, the Cappella Paolina, but in a private palace chapel for the Pope and his household only.[33] Here organ accompaniment was used, and music in the *concertato* style frequently sung. At the start of the century the Cappella included a number of highly competent composers: Giovanni Maria Nanino, Ruggiero Giovannelli, Archangelo Crivelli, Vincenzo de Grandis. Although not a singing member, the highly prolific Felice Anerio (*c*. 1560–1614) held the title of Composer to the Cappella, a position he owed largely to the powerful patronage of Cardinal Aldobrandini.[34] After his death, the position was never subsequently filled. Singers continued to compose, most famously Gregorio Allegri (1582–1652), but less and less new music entered the Cappella's repertory. For example, the 1616 *Libro di punti*, the Cappella's record of its activities (including fines for non-attendance), gives all the titles

32 Claudio Annibaldi is currently working on a history of the Cappella Pontificia in the seventeenth century. See also the many essays of Jean Lionnet, particularly 'Performance Practice in the Papal Chapel during the Seventeenth Century' and 'L'évolution du répertoire de la Chapelle Pontificale au cours du 17ᵉᵐᵉ siècle'.

33 Lionnet, 'Le répertoire des vêpres papales'.

34 Couchman, 'Felice Anerio's Music for the Church and for the Altemps *Cappella*'.

and composers of pieces sung; it is the only one to do so in a systematic way. Comparing it with Andrea Adami's *Osservazioni per ben regolare il coro dei cantori della Cappella pontificia* of 1711 is instructive. In 1616, there was a good mix of old and new; by the end of the century the repertory had in effect become fossilised. The most famous piece of music to come from the Cappella in the seventeenth century was Allegri's 'Miserere'. In its earliest notated form this was little more than a standard *falsobordone* setting for two contrasting choirs (four and five voices respectively), alternating with each other and with plainchant recitation; what made it famous was not Allegri's prescribed framework but the *abbellimenti* or ornaments applied by the singers in the four-voice verses.

Other Roman basilicas and churches balanced tradition with innovation. At the Cappella Giulia in St Peter's, Francesco Soriano (1548/9–1621) re-worked Palestrina's six-voice *Missa Papae Marcelli* for double choir and published it in a collection of largely retrospective Masses in score format in 1609. His successor, Vincenzo Ugolini, introduced some modernising changes from 1621; these seem to have been unwelcome to a section of the chapter, and when, in 1626, Paolo Agostini challenged Ugolini to a contest based on their respective abilities in what Stephen Miller has labelled *artificio*, again following Palestrina's terminology[35] – a challenge which Ugolini refused – the chapter appointed Agostini in his place. Agostini responded by issuing a series of publications containing Masses and motets in a learned style and in score. On the other hand, on Agostini's untimely death in 1629, the canons appointed Virgilio Mazzocchi (1597–1646) and later Orazio Benevoli (1605–72), both experienced in the city's other institutions and both champions of large-scale music. At the less-well-endowed S. Maria ai Monti, Giovanni Francesco Anerio (*c.* 1567–1630) also reworked the *Missa Papae Marcelli* but reduced to four voices (published in 1619). Anerio, unlike his older brother Felice, had no ties to papal institutions but, rather, worked in the milieu of Philip Neri's Oratorians and the Jesuits. These bold adaptations of the *Missa Papae Marcelli* to both the large- and small-scale idioms are a mark of an active and vibrant traditionalism which was the reality in early seventeenth-century Rome, not the backward-looking stuffiness too often portrayed by historians of the past.

In Rome, as throughout Catholic Europe, it was the Mass Ordinary which remained most closely bound up with stylistic continuity. This may have been because the documents of the Council of Trent that called for reform had specifically mentioned the Mass but not Vespers or other services. Stephen Miller has identified over 400 Ordinary settings composed in the city, singling out three composers working in mid-century: Gregorio Allegri, Bonifazio

---

35 Miller, 'Music for the Mass in Seventeenth-Century Rome', i: 29ff.

Graziani (1604/5–1664) and Francesco Foggia (1604–88). A singer in the Cappella Pontificia from 1629 to 1652, Allegri was seen as the standard-bearer for traditional values and it was he who was chosen by his fellow singers to rework Palestrina's hymns after the revision of their texts by Urban VIII.[36] His six-voice Missa 'Vidi turbam magnam' and Missa 'Salvatorem expectamus' are based on motets by Palestrina; the former updates Palestrina's darker SAATTB scoring to SSATTB. Allegri uses a profusion of motivic elements in a contrapuntal format reminiscent of the model, but the emphasis is more on control of sonorities than on the text. He seems preoccupied with bass lines and with their motivic and harmonic potential, so that an impression of undifferentiated, imitation-free counterpoint marks out his Masses from other seventeenth-century music as having been written for connoisseurs at the papal court. By contrast the mid-century Masses of Graziani and Foggia, while grounded in contrapuntal technique, pay a great deal of attention to the words, using finely chiselled motives, great rhythmic variety including frequent changes to triple metre, and significant contrasts of textures. By the end of the century composers such as Giuseppe Ottavio Pitoni (1667–1743) and the theorist Antimo Liberati (1617–92) were self-consciously writing both stile antico masses in long note-values and concertato masses in sectionalised form. According to Miller and other commentators,[37] it was this generation, separated by nearly a century from Palestrina, who reinvented the stile antico in order to mark off church music from secular.

There was more flexibility in approach in the case of Mass Ordinary settings in northern Italy, but here too continuity and tradition played an important part. Monteverdi's Missa 'In illo tempore', included in his Missa . . . ac Vespere of 1610, took a six-voice motet by Nicolas Gombert (first published in 1547) as its model and seems to have been a deliberate attempt both at historicism and at demonstrating Monteverdi's abilities in sixteenth-century techniques. His two later four-voice Mass settings also appear deliberately archaic in approach. In the case of Milan, Robert Kendrick has described the contrapuntal ingenuities of Vincenzo Pellegrini's Missa 'Ecce sacerdos magnus' as reflecting a 'Romanizing' of the liturgy and a consequent cultural emulation after 1610.[38] The label 'da cappella' was used to distinguish such Masses from those needing basso continuo and marked 'in concerto', as in the 1622 Messe of the prolific Lombard

---

36 The moving announcement of Allegri's death in an entry of 18 February 1652 in the Libro di punti of the Cappella Pontificia speaks of his having 'become so advanced in the excellence of counterpoint and composition that he had almost equalled his teacher [Giovanni Maria Nanino] in the subtleties of music, and future generations will find evidence of this in the works he composed with the highest exquisiteness for our chapel' (Biblioteca Apostolica Vaticana, Fondo Cappella Sistina, Diarii, 1652).

37 For example, Silke Leopold in Sadie and Tyrrell (eds), The Revised New Grove Dictionary of Music and Musicians, s.v. 'Liberati, Antimo'.

38 Kendrick, The Sounds of Milan, p. 279.

composer Ignazio Donati (*c.* 1570–1638). Like those of his Roman contemporaries, Donati's Masses show an adaptation of the older idiom to give greater emphasis to sonority.

In Spain and Portugal, the use of imitative polyphony for Mass Ordinary settings continued through the seventeenth century and beyond. The publication of Tomás Luis de Victoria's (1548–1611) six-voice *Officium defunctorum* (Madrid, 1605) provided a foundation on which Iberian composers would continue to build. Among these the Requiems of the Portuguese composers Duarte Lobo and Manuel Cardoso stand out. As well as Victoria's Roman influence, the long-standing Flemish hold on the Spanish Royal Chapel continued well into the century through its director Matthieu Rosmarin (also styled Mateo Romero and Maestro Capitán). The annexation of Portugal by Philip II of Spain in 1580 led to a flowering of polyphony inspired by the Roman and Spanish styles which continued after independence in 1640 under King João IV. The latter's obsessive interest in music was reflected in two polemic publications, one in defence of the music of Palestrina and his generation, and the other on the modal purity of Palestrina's *Missa 'Panis quem ego dabo'*; he also amassed an enormous musical library which was destroyed in the Lisbon earthquake of 1755. João IV supported the composer João Lourenço Rebelo (1610–61) by having his music published; the king also dedicated his first treatise to the composer, a unique reversal of the normal situation. Rebelo's music reflected his sovereign's traditionalist tastes; his seven-voice Eucharistic motet 'Panis angelicus' is a sonorous *tour de force*, with close imitative writing punctuated by quasi-homophonic cries of 'O res mirabilis' ('O thing of wonder'). Spanish conquest of the New World was thorough to the extent that Spanish liturgical and musical practices were exported complete to Bolivia, Mexico, Peru and the Philippines. Spanish-born composers who emigrated, such as Gutierre Fernández Hidalgo (Lima, Cuzco and La Plata) or Juan Gutiérrez de Padilla (Puebla), continued to write in traditional idioms, while also composing *villancicos* incorporating local dance rhythms for the native population.

It was a Requiem that was most emblematic of continuity within the French tradition: the setting by Eustache Du Caurroy (1549–1609), published in 1606, was sung at the funeral of Henry IV in 1610 and subsequently for every French king and prince up to 1725. Du Caurroy's music reflected that of Orlande de Lassus (d. 1594), which was dominant in the early years of the century in France. The Requiem by Etienne Moulinié, printed by Robert Ballard in 1636, followed the same retrospective style, as did the many Masses by lesser-known composers which survive.[39] Steven Saunders has also pointed out that

---

39 Anthony, *French Baroque Music*, pp. 203–4.

writing in a retrospective style was a *sine qua non* for court composers at the aggressively Catholic Habsburg court in the early seventeenth century. One of those composers, Giovanni Priuli (*c.* 1575–1626), dedicated his *Missae . . . quatuor, sex, et octo vocibus* (Venice, 1624) to the newly elected Pope Urban VIII, expressing the hope that the style used in the Imperial Chapel might also find favour at the throne of St Peter. In the same year, Priuli dedicated a follow-up volume of eight- and nine-voice Masses in *concertato* style to Sigismund III of Poland, a ruler noted for his up-to-date Italianate tastes.[40]

The sense of continuity is perhaps strongest of all in early seventeenth-century English church music.[41] On his accession in 1603, James I saw a continuation of the religious policies of his predecessor, Elizabeth I, as the best guarantee of a successful transition from the Tudor to the Stuart dynasty. This was reflected in an Anglican church music under James and his son, Charles I, which is often seen as a seamless flow from the Elizabethan. The established division of the choir into two equal blocks which sang facing each other (*decani* and *cantoris*) but doubled on the same music in tutti sections encouraged a resilience against the Italian polychoral style of quick antiphonal exchanges and separate music for all parts. The Elizabethan compromise between traditional Catholic music and the demands of the Anglican rite, worked out in practice by Thomas Tallis (*c.* 1505–1585) and William Byrd (*c.* 1540–1623) in particular, provided a model for liturgical music in English which also proved resistant to change given that it served its purpose well. In many ways the English Chapel Royal can be compared to the Cappella Pontificia in using an increasingly retrospective musical style as a badge of orthodoxy, exclusivity and even cultural and political absolutism. The most significant figures up to the Civil War were Orlando Gibbons (1583–1625) and Thomas Tomkins (1572–1656), both of whom composed elaborate 'Full' Service settings modelled on those of Tallis and Byrd, and 'Short' Services which are masterly lessons in compactness. Both also wrote some extremely fine anthems in the styles established under Elizabeth: full, short, and verse anthems. Full anthems such as Gibbons's 'Hosanna to the Son of David' or Tomkins's 'When David heard' display a control of texture, as well as of setting English texts, which place them among the finest music written anywhere in the early seventeenth century. Byrd's *Gradualia* of 1605 and 1607 contain a complete set of Mass Propers composed for liturgical performance in recusant Catholic communities; they presented a challenge which was not subsequently taken up, although Catholic music was composed for use in the chapels of the Catholic consorts of both Charles I and Charles II.

---

40 Saunders, *Cross, Sword and Lyre*, pp. 159–77.
41 Surveys of English liturgical music are given in Caldwell, *The Oxford History of English Music*, i; Spink (ed.), *The Blackwell History of Music in Britain*, iii; Spink, *Restoration Cathedral Music*.

Large-scale non-*concertato* writing

The polychoral idiom had been gaining ground throughout the second half of the sixteenth century, particularly in Italy where it grew from antiphonal beginnings within Vespers in the Veneto to the preferred medium throughout Italy for Vespers psalms, Magnificats, Marian antiphons, litanies and many motets by the early 1600s. Southern Germany, too, saw it flourish under Lassus in Munich and at the Habsburg courts under composers such as Alexander Utendal, Philippe de Monte (1521–1603) and Jacobus Handl (1550–91). Anthologies such as the three volumes of Erhard Bodenschatz's *Florilegium* series published in Leipzig (1603, 1618, 1621), or the four volumes of *Promptuarii musici* published by Abraham Schadeus in Strasbourg from 1611 to 1627, ensured a constant flow northwards of Italian models, in particular by Roman and Venetian composers. These anthologies were used by Catholic and Protestant churches alike, both sides of the religious divide finding in the polychoral style the ideal combination of sumptuous sonority and clarity of text-setting.

In Rome, members of the post-Palestrina generation all wrote music for two, three and four choirs as a matter of course. Churches, convents and lay confraternities multiplied and created a competitive market for musicians to help celebrate patronal and other major feasts. The Church's increasing control of lay confraternities enrolled them as key players in the propagation of the faith and thus encouraged them in this competitive environment. National churches, particularly S. Luigi dei Francesi, S. Giacomo degli Spagnoli and S. Maria dell'Anima (respectively, French, Spanish and German) – all situated close to the Piazza Navona – strove to outdo each other in the magnificence of their processions and festal Masses and Vespers. It was the same in other major centres. The printed market catered largely to the need for double-choir settings; those for three or more choirs remain available only in manuscript sources, with a few exceptions such as Francesco Soriano's *Psalmi et mottecta* for eight, twelve and sixteen voices and continuo (Venice, 1616); this gives the festal repertory composed by him for use at St Peter's, the building of which had been completed in 1615. For the early part of the century the most significant sources for this music in Rome are the two sets of partbooks copied, probably by Felice Anerio, for the private chapel of Duke Giovanni Angelo Altemps, an unusual example of a non-clerical patron with an obsessive interest in sacred music.[42] A large manuscript collection formerly belonging to the basilica of S. Maria in Trastevere gives further evidence of a substantial repertory of polychoral music covering the remainder of the century, especially of parts for extra *ripieno* choirs (see below). Much has not survived, especially where the Mass Ordinary

---

42 Couchman, 'Musica nella cappella di Palazzo Altemps a Roma'.

was concerned: archival sources would imply that three and four choirs of musicians regularly attended Roman festal Masses, but comparatively few such settings survive. Essentially, this was ephemeral music, composed for the day and retained only by the *maestro* for his own use. However, another composer who did publish two triple-choir Masses was Soriano's successor at St Peter's, Vincenzo Ugolini (*c.* 1580–1638). His *Missa 'Quae est ista'* (1622) parodies his own motet, and the movements are scored as separate sections, tutti scoring alternating with reduced-voice groupings taken across the three choirs:[43]

Kyrie eleison	12 vv.
Christe Eleison	SSSAAA
Kyrie Eleison	12 vv.
Gloria	
Et in terra pax	12 vv.
Domine fili	SSSA
Qui tollis peccata	12 vv.
Credo	
Patrem omnipotentem	12 vv.
Crucifixus	TTTBBB
Et resurrexit	12 vv.
Et iterum	SSSAAA
Et unam sanctam	12 vv.
Sanctus	12 vv.
Hosanna	12 vv. (in canon)
Benedictus	SSSAAA
Hosanna II	12 vv.
Agnus Dei	12 vv.

Performance practice in Rome and elsewhere involved the construction of platforms on opposite sides of the nave, each with at least one group of singers (and sometimes two) and with a portable organ; the Italian word *coro* applied as much to the platform as to the singers on it. Instrumentalists could also form part of these choirs. In addition, *coretti* built over arches could be used when permitted by the architecture of the church.[44] The practice of adding *ripieno* choirs, already in use in the late sixteenth century, was to expand considerably in the seventeenth.[45] These doubled the music of other choirs so that a

---

43 Dixon, 'Liturgical Music in Rome', i: 154.

44 As, for instance, at Giovanni Francesco Anerio's first Mass in the Gesù in 1616, when the use of the newly constructed *coretti* was not an unqualified success; see the report of the ambassador from Urbino in the *Avvisi di Roma*, 10 August 1616, quoted in G. Gigli, *Diario romano (1607–1670)*, ed. G. Ricciotti (Rome, 1958), p. 37.

45 O'Regan, 'Roman Polychoral Music'.

piece written for, say, six real choirs could be performed by twelve; this was most likely the case, for instance, at St Peter's in the late 1620s when Paolo Agostini was reputed to have had twelve choirs representing the twelve apostles (including one in the balcony of the dome).[46] Music was conceived for four/five or eight/nine basic parts and then, depending on the size of building and availability of musicians, tutti sections could be reinforced by the addition of further choirs doubling the existing parts, perhaps with some rewriting or transposition. Charlotte Leonard has recently reported on a large cache of *ripieno* vocal and instrumental parts written in mid-century Breslau to supplement two of Andreas Hammerschmidt's publications.[47] Jean Lionnet has insightfully explored what he called 'hidden polychorality': a shorthand practice of publishing or recording in manuscript pieces for five voices (SSATB) which were, in fact, meant to contrast two solo sopranos in one choir with a *ripieno* SATB choir, the second soprano part in the five-voice scoring including both solo and simpler tutti writing.[48]

By mid century, Roman composers such as Benevoli, Mazzocchi, Foggia and Graziani had developed the Roman polychoral idiom into an impressive but flexible medium for settings of Vespers psalms, Magnificats, Marian antiphons and festal psalm-motets such as 'Jubilate Deo'. On the whole, Roman composers preferred to write for choirs with the same clef-combination in contrast to northern Italian composers, who exploited the contrasts available from mixing high and low clefs (e.g., *chiavette* and *chiavi naturali*). Later in the century, Roman composers such as Francesco Berretta, Ercole Bernabei and Paolo Petti continued to provide large-scale music for patronal feast-day celebrations.

In Venice, the posthumously published *Symphoniae sacrae . . . liber secundus* (1615) of Giovanni Gabrieli (d. 1612) contain pieces both with *concertato* elements and without. This trend was also sometimes found in Rome, most notably in Paolo Tarditi's eight-voice *Psalmi, Magnificat cum quatuor antiphonis ad vesperas* (Rome, 1620). Gabrieli's use of formal designs in a number of these pieces – ABB or ABAC schemes, for example – showed the way for later composers, as did his exploitation of what Jerome Roche has called 'tertial harmonic juxtapositions';[49] both can be found in his extremely affective 'O Jesu mi dulcissime'.[50] Viadana gave detailed performance instructions for his own four-choir settings in the foreword of his *Salmi a quattro chori*, op. 27

46 Dixon, 'The Origins of the Roman "Colossal Baroque"'. No music for twelve choirs survives in the musical holdings of the Cappella Giulia, but there are a number of settings for six.
47 Leonard, 'Hammerschmidt's Representation in the Bohn Collection'.
48 Lionnet, 'Les musiques polychorales romaines'.
49 Roche, *North Italian Church Music in the Age of Monteverdi*, p. 115.
50 The 1615 setting is published in D. Arnold (ed.), *Giovanni Gabrieli: opera omnia*, iii, 'Corpus mensurabilis musicae', 12 (American Institute of Musicology, 1962).

(Venice, 1612); these match similar recommendations by Michael Praetorius, also based on north Italian practice.[51] Viadana's four groups consisted of a choir of five solo voices, a *cappella* choir of at least sixteen singers with instrumental doubling, a high choir with violins and cornetts and three voices on the lowest three parts, and a low choir with cornetts, trombones and bassoons, and violins doubling its top part (normally in an alto range) an octave higher. Choir I should sing with the main organ and be directed by the *maestro*, with Choirs III and IV accompanied by separate organs playing in high and low registers. Viadana states further that Choirs III and IV are optional: the music will work as well with Choirs I and II only, or extra choirs can be added to bring the four up to eight. His writing contains many parallel octaves which he excuses on the grounds that these are more graceful than the rests, imitations and syncopations which other composers employ to avoid them. This flexibility of performance practice is entirely characteristic of the entire polychoral repertory, though Roman composers on the whole managed to avoid consecutives.

Protestant composers made use of similar resources. In Dresden, Schütz directed the largest Protestant musical establishment, that of the Elector of Saxony, Johann Georg I, from 1618 to 1657; a number of detailed musical service-lists survive. His *Psalmen Davids* of 1619 contain psalm-motets written largely for two choirs, one of solo *favoriti* and the other *a cappella* on the north Italian model. Like Viadana, Schütz also included parts for two or three further optional choirs. We are also fortunate in having a detailed description of the Lutheran Communion service celebrated at the dedication in 1607 of the octagonal St Gertrude's Chapel in Hamburg, recently reconstructed by Frederick Gable. The music, under the direction of Hieronymus Praetorius (1560–1629), who together with his son Jacob (1586–1651) contributed much to the German polychoral repertory, included items for two, three and four choirs. This highly important account, which appeared as part of a now-lost sermon by the Hamburg pastor Lucas van Cöllen, is worth quoting extensively in Gable's translation:

> A little before seven our school cantor began to sing the [hymn] 'Veni Sancte Spiritus' in chant. After that was sung the Introit 'In nomine Jesu' in eight parts by Bandovius [Pierre Bonhomme]. Next followed the *Missa super 'Deus misereatur nostri'*, also in eight parts, by the excellent composer Orlando [Lassus; the Mass was in fact by Arnold Grothusius based on Lassus's motet]. Instead of the sequence, *Alleluia* ['Cantate Domino'] by [Jacobus] Handl was sung, composed for twelve parts, but in three choirs. The first choir was sung by the boys

51 Roche, *North Italian Church Music in the Age of Monteverdi*, pp. 118–19; L. Grossi da Viadana, *Salmi a quattro chori*, ed. G. Wielakker, 'Recent Researches in the Music of the Baroque Era', 86 (Madison, WI, 1998); M. Praetorius, *Syntagma musicum*, 3 vols (Wolfenbüttel, 1619; repr. Kassel, 1958).

and musicians in the chancel, the second by cornetts and sackbuts, the third by the organ. Both these choirs were placed on special platforms, in the corners of the octagonal chapel... After the sermon, 'O Gott, wir dancken deiner Güt' was begun from the pulpit. After a short prelude played by the organist, by which the pitch was given, the whole congregation sang the chorale in unison. The other parts were played polyphonically by the organs, cornetts and sackbuts, and so it was completed. Then the usual blessing was spoken from the pulpit. After that was sung 'Herr Gott, dich loben wir' which Hieronymus Praetorius, our church organist, composed for sixteen parts in four choirs. The first choir was sung, the second was played by cornetts and sackbuts from a special platform, the third by string instruments and regals from another place, the fourth by the organ. In this way the boys intoned the usual melody and the Sanctus was repeated three times. Following was sung the 'Cantate [Domino]' in eight parts, by the same Hieronymus Praetorius, by the choir, organs, cornetts and sackbuts all together. To conclude, 'Sey lob und Ehr mit hohem preiss' was sung by the congregation, choir, organ and instruments.[52]

Apart from the congregational singing of the two German chorales, this report could almost be describing a Catholic service in southern Germany, or indeed a festal mass in Rome or Venice (though only the Kyrie and Gloria of the Mass were sung, in accordance with current Lutheran practice in some areas). As in these centres, large numbers of singers and players were brought together for major festal celebrations. The climax of the service, aurally and visually, was the four-choir setting of the German *Te Deum*, 'Herr Gott, dich loben wir', a compositional *tour de force* with spatial separation of the four highly contrasted groups. The polyphony briefly breaks off early in the setting for the boys' triple plainchant intonation of 'Heilig ist unser Gott'.

The accession of the Holy Roman Emperor Ferdinand II in 1619 brought to Vienna a ruler and court which were already steeped in music while Ferdinand was Archduke in Graz. Educated by the Jesuits, Ferdinand was fired with Catholic Reformation zeal while in Italy as a young man, which led to his vigorous prosecution of the Thirty Years War. He favoured Italian composers for his propagandistic music, especially the Venetians Giovanni Priuli and Giovanni Valentini (d. 1649). A manuscript compiled at Graz in about 1610 (Vienna, Österreichische Nationalbibliothek, Musiksammlung, Cod. 16702) contains twelve Masses for 16, 17 and 26 voices in multiple choirs by Priuli and other composers associated in one way or another with Venice. In his 1621 *Missae quatuor* for eight and twelve voices, Valentini included a twelve-voice *Missa 'Diligam te Domine'* based on Giovanni Gabrieli's eight-voice motet. Steven Saunders's recent work has underlined the importance of both composers for

52 Gable (ed.), *Dedication Service for St. Gertrude's Chapel*, p. viii.

the transmission to Vienna of contemporary Italian styles. This was continued by Valentini's successor as *Kapellmeister*, the Veronese Antonio Bertali (1605–69). Ferdinand II's son and grandson, Ferdinand III and Leopold I, both composed sacred music for use in the court, seeing it as part of their total commitment to the Catholic cause.

In France, two volumes of *Preces ecclesiasticae* by Du Caurroy were issued just after his death in 1609. Written for up to seven voices, many are polychoral pieces with three voice-parts in one of the choirs. Influenced more by Lassus than by Italian models, French composers such as Valérien Gonnet, Jean and Valentin de Bournonville and Charles d'Ambleville wrote Masses and motets for equal choirs until Nicolas Formé, Du Caurroy's successor at the Chapelle Royale, established the contrast of a *petit chœur* of four voices and a *grand chœur* of five. In Spain the re-publication by Victoria of a compendious collection of his polychoral music in Madrid in 1600 provided a model which matched the new, lighter religious atmosphere under Philip III after the austerity of Philip II. Because of Victoria's long association with Rome, he was influential in transmitting the Roman dialect of the polychoral idiom to Spain. It was taken up by composers such as Juan Bautista Comes (*c.* 1582–1643) in Valencia who left five Mass Ordinaries for two and three choirs, as well as a very large number of successful psalms, Magnificats and motets in the same idiom.[53] Joan Cererols, who spent his life at the monastery of Montserrat, wrote polychoral settings in all the major liturgical genres: Masses, psalms, Magnificats, Marian antiphons and hymns. His twelve-voice *Missa de batalla*, loosely based on Clément Janequin's chanson, continued a Spanish tradition from Francisco Guerrero and Victoria. Comes and Cererols are but two of a large number of Iberian composers working in the non-*concertato* polychoral idiom in the seventeenth century. Miguel Querol has listed at least 67 composers of polychoral liturgical music and vernacular *villancicos* working in Spain, almost all of them little researched up to the present.[54] In Spanish colonies such as Puebla, Mexico, composers such as Padilla also produced a considerable body of double-choir liturgical settings and *villancicos*.

The English *decani/cantoris* tradition had some features in common with the Continental polychoral idiom, but the alternations between the two sides remained quite spaced out, and, most significantly, when they sang together they either doubled with the same music or combined into an undifferentiated polyphonic texture. The scoring of each side – in five or six parts usually with two countertenor parts per side – could, however, lead to considerable

---

53 J. B. Comes, *Masses*, ed. G. Olson, 2 vols, 'Recent Researches in the Music of the Baroque Era', 96, 99 (Madison, WI, 1995).

54 M. Querol Gavaldà (ed.), *Música barroca española*, ii: *Polifonía litúrgica* (Barcelona, 1982), pp. ix–x.

variety in sub-groupings, as in the most ambitiously conceived Service setting of the century, Thomas Tomkins's 'Great' Service for ten parts, or the same composer's full anthem for twelve, 'O praise the Lord'. Under Charles I and his Archbishop of Canterbury, William Laud, a crusader for elaborate liturgy and ritual, cathedral worship became more devotional. At Durham, for instance, John Cosin's appointment as chaplain to the bishop in 1624 proved a catalyst for greater musical elaboration and provided an opportunity for William Smith to produce large-scale anthems such as 'O God which has taught' for nine voices in various combinations plus a five-voice tutti.[55] Under Charles II, Chapel Royal composers developed the symphony-anthem (see below); the Catholic James II ignored the Anglican Chapel after his accession, bringing Innocenzo Fede from Rome in 1686 to direct the choir of his separate Catholic chapel at Whitehall.[56] Of Fede's sacred music, only a double-choir setting of the psalm 'Laudate pueri' survives.

Italian influence reached Poland and, by way of the Ukraine, as far as Moscow. The accession to the Polish throne of Sigismund III Vasa in 1587 accelerated a process of Romanisation of the Polish church and its liturgical music. A stream of Roman-trained composers including Annibale Stabile, Luca Marenzio, Vincenzo Lilius, Asprilio Pacelli, Giovanni Francesco Anerio and Marco Scacchi transplanted both large- and small-scale compositional styles to the East. Pacelli (1570–1623) moved from St Peter's in Rome to Warsaw in 1603 and remained until his death. He published his *Sacrae cantiones*, 5–10, 12, 16, 20 vv. (Venice, 1608), and polychoral Masses for eight, ten, twelve, sixteen and eighteen voices were issued posthumously in Venice in 1629. Lilius edited an important collection of polychoral motets by members of the Polish Royal Chapel, *Melodiae sacrae*, in 1604. Among native Polish composers of polychoral music were Mikolaj Zieleński who may have studied in Italy, and whose *Offertoria . . . cum Magnificat*, 7, 8, 12 vv. (Venice, 1611) follows Venetian practice in using high and low choirs. Later composers such as Marcin Mielczewski (d. 1651) and Bartłomiej Pękiel introduced *concertato* elements into their polychoral music. The idiom reached Moscow via Ukrainian musicians in the reign of Tsar Alexei Mikhailovich (1645–76) and led to a unique fusion with older Russian church music traditions in the polychoral service music and sacred concertos of Vasilii Titov.[57] Titov also published a three-voice setting of the complete versified Russian psalter in 1680.

55 W. Smith, *Preces, Festal Psalms, and Verse Anthems*, ed. J. Cannell, 'Recent Researches in the Music of the Baroque Era', 135 (Middleton, WI, 2003). Technically this and similar pieces could also be seen as verse-anthems with solo verses for a variety of voice combinations alternating with tuttis.

56 Corp, 'The Exiled Court of James II and James III'.

57 Dolskaya-Ackerly, 'Vasilii Titov and the "Moscow" Baroque'.

Small-scale writing: the *concerto ecclesiastico*

Traditionally the origins of the *concerto ecclesiastico* have been ascribed to Lodovico da Viadana (*c.* 1560–1627), whose *Cento concerti ecclesiastici*, op. 12 (Venice, 1602) certainly played a crucial role.[58] Viadana claimed in his foreword to that publication that the main drive behind his innovation was a desire to provide music tailor-made for institutions with only limited numbers of singers who had been in the habit (particularly in Rome) of just leaving out parts of existing polyphonic pieces. There is evidence, however, that smaller-scale settings were in fact favoured by Roman *cappelle* in the late sixteenth century, especially at the German College, where Asprilio Pacelli issued his four-voice *Chorici psalmi, et motecta* in 1599–1600; these are small-scale *concerti* in all but name.[59] Viadana's north Italian contemporary Gabriele Fattorini had preceded Viadana by two years with his *I sacri concerti* for one and two voices and organ in 1600.[60]

Whatever the priorities of origin, the technique of writing for small groups of voices quickly became a major compositional tool which spread throughout Europe. In Rome, the chief early exponents were Agostino Agazzari (*c.* 1580–1642), the highly prolific Anerio brothers, Felice and Giovanni Francesco, Antonio Cifra and Giovanni Bernardino Nanino. Their earliest examples effectively reduced the number of lines in music still conceived contrapuntally, and used the organ to complete the harmony. Indeed the *bassus ad organum* part functioned generally as a *basso seguente*, doubling the lowest-sounding voice except in those motets written for solo voice. In these last, there is an independent organ bass, but this still tends to function like an untexted vocal part. The same was true in northern Italy: Robert Kendrick has counted 29 prints of small-scale *concerti* there in the first decade of the century;[61] 13 were issued by the printer Filippo Lomazzo in Milan, including an anthology of *Concerti di diversi eccellentissimi autori*, 2–4 vv. (1608) compiled by Francesco Lucino and containing works by Giovanni Paolo Cima and Giulio Cesare Gabussi, among others. These *concerti*, too, stuck largely to the sixteenth-century contrapuntal tradition, as did the Vicenza-based Leone Leoni's *Sacri fiori: motetti a due, tre et a quattro voci* (Venice, 1606) or the Benedictine nun Caterina Assandra's *Motetti a due et tre voci* (Milan, 1609), dedicated to the Bishop of Pavia, where she had been born.

---

58 Roche, *North Italian Church Music in the Age of Monteverdi*, pp. 51ff.

59 O'Regan, 'Asprilio Pacelli, Ludovico da Viadana and the Origins of the Roman *Concerto ecclesiastico*'.

60 G. Fattorini, *I sacri concerti a due voci*, ed. M. C. Bradshaw, 'Early Sacred Monody', 2 (American Institute of Musicology, 1986).

61 Kendrick, *The Sounds of Milan*, p. 234.

The publication of Monteverdi's 1610 Vespers marked something of a sea-change, its four *concerti*, or antiphon-substitutes, showing the range of possibilities available. 'Nigra sum' is a monody, as is the first part of 'Audi coelum', the latter punctuated by echoes and rounded off by a dance-like six-voice section, presumably in response to the text which begins 'omnes hanc ergo sequamur' ('So let us all follow her'); 'Pulchra es' is a strictly structured duet in AABB form; 'Duo Seraphim' displays some uniquely virtuosic written-out ornamentation. At a stroke, Monteverdi pushed forward the boundaries, and the challenge was taken up particularly by Alessandro Grandi (1586–1630), who was Monteverdi's assistant at St Mark's, Venice, from 1620 to 1627 before leaving to take charge of the important S. Maria Maggiore in Bergamo. Grandi was a prolific publisher of his music, and his small-scale motets cover the whole range of voices and voice-combinations. Jerome Roche has charted Grandi's adaptation of more formalised structures and his development of extended melody over increasingly independent and varied bass lines.[62] As the idiom was adopted for more extended psalm-settings, refrain structures and ground basses became popular ways of providing unity. The competing demands of vocal virtuosity and the expression of the text were addressed in Ignazio Donati's didactic *Il secondo libro de motetti a voce sola*, op. 14 (Venice, 1636).

In 1620s Rome, the most significant composer of small-scale settings was Giuseppe Giamberti, whose comprehensive series of Vespers antiphons show a varied and imaginative approach to the text.[63] Here as elsewhere by mid century, the small-scale motet, especially that for solo voice, became more extended and moved closer to the secular cantata in structure. Bonifazio Graziani, *maestro* at the Jesuit Chiesa del Gesù (1648–58), was the genre's chief exponent, publishing a steady stream of *Sacrae cantiones, Motetti* and *Antifone* which had an influence well beyond the city due to northern reprints and manuscript copies. As Susanne Shigihara has pointed out, the solo motets show a move from strophic structures, with a regular repetition of arioso and aria elements, to a less predictable alternation of recitative, arioso and aria, relying on motivic relationships for unity.[64] Triple-time aria sections became more prevalent, too, with an emphasis on extended and lilting melodic lines. Duets increased in popularity and followed the same trends.

The best-known Roman composer at mid century, Giacomo Carissimi (1605–74), also made widespread use of unifying structural devices in his considerable number of motets for the full range of voice combinations. Working at the Jesuit German College, he, too, made use of extended texts compiled

62 Roche, *North Italian Church Music in the Age of Monteverdi*, pp. 63–4.
63 Dixon, 'Liturgical Music in Rome', i: 250ff.   64 Shigihara, 'Bonifazio Graziani'.

from a variety of sources; excerpts from scripture are combined with newly written texts of a highly affective nature. Typical is 'O vulnera doloris' for solo bass and continuo: the opening words and music, referring to Christ's wounds, are added as a refrain to the end of each line of text. Such Passion – and passionate – texts were an important concomitant of Eucharistic devotion. The same growing structural coherence is found throughout northern Italy: Robert Kendrick's recent pioneering work on Milan, for instance, has drawn attention to the small-scale works of such mid-century composers as Antonio Maria Turati, Gasparo Casati and Francesco dalla Porta. As for Pope Alexander VII's attempts to curtail the solo motet in 1657, favouring the polychoral idiom instead, there is sufficient surviving music to suggest that they were honoured as much in the breach as in the observance.

The small-scale label can be extended to cover sacred music for four to six voices with or without obbligato instrumental parts. Here the emphasis was on textural contrast in an ever-changing landscape of vocal groupings, as in the psalm 'Laetatus sum' from Monteverdi's 1610 Vespers. The extended psalm texts, often without so much scope for word-painting or affective rhetorical devices, provided a challenge which was more easily met with the large-scale *concertato* approach discussed below. However, not all institutions had such resources, and composers who did rise to the challenge included Ignazio Donati, who added some psalms to his *Motetti concertati a cinque e sei voci* (Milan, 1618), and the Venetian Giovanni Rovetta in his *Salmi concertati a cinque et sei voci* of 1626. One of the most successful was another Venetian, Giovanni Antonio Rigatti, whose *Messa e salmi parte concertati* of 1640, for three and five to eight voices and two violins (dedicated to Emperor Ferdinand III), and *Salmi diversi di Compieta in diversi generi di canti* of 1646 (for one to four voices, partly with instruments and partly without) have been described by Jerome Roche as moving towards coherent musical structures involving refrains, ritornellos and ground basses.[65] Roche has drawn particular attention to a setting of the psalm 'Nisi Dominus' which is written over a ground bass consisting of the descending (major) tetrachord; Rigatti specifies a high number of tempo changes within this regular format, in response to the words. In a rubric to the piece, he also emphasised flexibility of tempo: 'the opening of this work should be grave, with alterations of tempo in appropriate places as I have advised in the singers' and players' parts, so that the text is matched by as much feeling as possible'. The words are further underlined by imaginative harmonic touches.

Apart from psalms, the few-voiced *concertato* style with textural contrast was particularly appropriate for dialogue texts which came with an inherent

---

65 Roche, *North Italian Church Music in the Age of Monteverdi*, p. 104.

structure; much of this music was not strictly liturgical, although it could find a place as an antiphon-substitute at Vespers or as a final motet. In Rome, dialogues were particularly associated with confraternity oratories, and with composers active at the German College such as Ottavio Catalani, Annibale Orgas and Carissimi; as they became more extended, such dialogue-motets were effectively indistinguishable from mini-oratorios.[66] Dialogue elements are underlined by contrasting solo and groups of voices in Virgilio Mazzocchi's four-voice (ATTB) 'Filiae Jerusalem' from his *Sacri flores*, 2–4 vv., op. 1 (Rome, 1640), which is set in what is effectively a series of recitative- and aria-like sections.[67] The choice of texture (in particular, the solo sections) is also determined by the use of the first person or by shifts of register in the text:

Filiae Jerusalem . . .	Alto solo
Quo abiit . . .	Tenor duet (triple time, with prominent parallel thirds)
Quaesivi illum . . .	Alto solo
Formosam vidimus . . .	ATTB
Adjuro vos . . .	Bass solo
Vox dilecti mei . . .	Alto solo
Surge propera . . .	ATTB

Early in the century, instruments simply substituted for the lower voices, playing lines that were vocally, rather than instrumentally, conceived. This is the case, for example, in Viadana's 'Repleatur os meum' for alto, tenor and two trombones found in his *Il terzo libro de' concerti ecclesiastici*, op. 24 (Venice, 1609), or Schütz's 'Fili mi, Absalon' (*Symphoniae sacrae*, Venice, 1629) for solo bass and four trombones. Instruments were also used in dialogue with voices, or to accompany voices in dialogue. Again, Monteverdi may have kick-started the use of idiomatic writing for high instruments in the 1610 Magnificat for seven voices and six instruments, featuring pairs of violins, cornetts and recorders, as well as low instruments. Thereafter the most common scoring was for a pair of violins, with composers such as Alessandro Grandi and Orazio Tarditi leading the way. The violins provided ritornellos or *sinfonie*, as in Monteverdi's well-known setting of 'Beatus vir' of 1641 for six voices and two violins (and optional trombones), which also relies on both a ground bass and a textual refrain, 'Beatus, beatus vir . . .' ('Blessed, blessed [is] the man who fears the Lord'), to achieve maximum coherence.

In Lutheran Germany the small-scale sacred *concerto*, whether in Latin or in the vernacular, provided an ideal medium for taking the chorale away both

---

66 O'Regan, 'Sacred Polychoral Music in Rome', pp. 26off.; Whenham, *Duet and Dialogue in the Age of Monteverdi*.

67 Dixon, 'Liturgical Music in Rome', i: 279.

from its monodic roots and from its strongly imitative presentation in the chorale-motet. Johann Hermann Schein (1586–1630) was one of the first to look to Italian models (the *concerti* of Pacelli and Viadana were often reprinted in Germany in the first decade of the century and had a very great influence) in his *Opella nova: Geistlicher Concerten . . . auf italiänische Invention componirt*, 3–5 vv. (Leipzig, 1618; a second edition appeared in 1627). Samuel Scheidt (1587–1654) at Halle had studied with both Michael Praetorius and Sweelinck and produced his own fusion of traditional German and newer Italian *concerti*. The composer who did most to establish the Italian styles in Germany, however, was Heinrich Schütz (1585–1672), who had studied with Giovanni Gabrieli from 1609 to 1612 or 1613, and who paid a further visit to Venice in 1629 while searching for Italian singers for the Dresden court chapel. His two volumes of *Kleine geistliche Concerte* (Dresden, 1636, 1639) set predominantly Old Testament texts in German to be sung at the Gradual of the Mass. For voices and continuo only, these certainly reflect the straitened circumstances of court chapels during the Thirty Years War, but the pared-down medium also allowed a flexible response to the text. On his second visit to Italy, Schütz got to know the music of Monteverdi and Grandi, and while there, he published his Latin-texted *Symphoniae sacrae* (Venice, 1629) for one and two voices accompanied by various combinations of instruments. Back in Germany, Schütz published two further volumes of instrumentally accompanied *Symphoniae sacrae* in 1647 and 1650, this time with German texts. It was in adapting Italianate styles to the German language that Schütz perhaps made his most significant contribution, allowing the Lutheran Church to exploit the full range of contemporary vocal and instrumental idioms in its liturgy.

Schütz became increasingly frustrated at the Elector Johann Georg I's indifference to his *Kapelle* while refusing to allow the composer to retire. Waiting in the wings was the Elector's son who succeeded as Johann Georg II in 1657. Unusually interested and gifted in music, Johann Georg II cultivated Italian musicians and composers, both as prince and as elector. On succeeding his father, he appointed the castrato Giovanni Andrea Bontempi (1625–1705) and Vincenzo Albrici (b. 1631) as joint *maestri di cappella* with Schütz; thereafter it was the music of Albrici and of his successor, Marco Giuseppe Peranda (c. 1625–1675) which dominated at Dresden.[68] Schooled in the Rome of Carissimi and Graziani, the Italians brought the extended small-scale motet, with its compilation texts centred heavily on what Mary Frandsen has called an often almost erotic Christocentricism, its use of unifying structural devices and its tonally directed harmony. This they combined with a typically German use of

---

68 Frandsen, 'The Sacred Concerto in Dresden'.

instrumental sinfonias. The resulting 'concertos with aria' in which a strophic aria was framed by two concerted movements can be seen to have laid much of the groundwork for the later German cantata. Typical is Albrici's Christmas *concerto* 'Benedicite Domine Jesu Christe' (*c.* 1661) for two sopranos and bass, accompanied by two cornetts and a bassoon. Three verses of the hymn 'O Jesu nostra redemptio' are sung by each of the soloists in turn, sandwiched between instrumental ritornellos. This is preceded and followed by a tutti rendering of the text 'Benedicite, Domine Jesu Christe, benedicite virginis fructus, benedicite fili aeterni Patris unigeniti' ('Blessed be the Lord Jesus Christ . . .') and the whole is prefaced by an instrumental sinfonia.

In England, the development of the verse-anthem supplied the needs filled on the Continent by the small-scale *concerto*. Growing out of the consort song, the small-scale verse-anthem alternated contrapuntal sections for one, two or three solo voices accompanied by organ or viols, with more declamatory homophonic sections for the tutti. In tutti sections the soloists either were silent or merged into the full choir. In Orlando Gibbons's 'This is the record of John', the largely homophonic tutti repeats the second half of each of the three verses for the solo countertenor, who is accompanied by imitative contrapuntal lines for four viols or organ. Verse-anthems were also a staple of English liturgical and paraliturgical repertories after the Restoration, where they were often expanded into the symphony-anthem (see below).

Music to Latin texts had all but died out in the Anglican church after 1600, but the Catholic chapels of Queens Henrietta Maria and Catherine of Braganza had some need for it, often reflecting strong Italian influence. Richard Dering (*c.* 1580–1630), a Catholic who had studied in Italy and then worked in Brussels, was appointed organist to Henrietta Maria in 1625, for whom he wrote two- and three-voice *concerti* which proved very popular even, it is said, with Oliver Cromwell. Matthew Locke, also a Catholic, combined a number of positions at court including that of organist to Queen Catherine, for whom he may have written his Latin motets for two to five voices with two violins in the most up-to-date Italian style; these might also have been composed for private use by Catholic families or in Oxford colleges. The most extended of these, 'Audi, Domine, clamantes ad te' for five solo voices and two violins (or viols) and bass viol alternates largely homophonic SSATB sections with short aria-like solos and duets (plus sinfonias and a ritornello), all composed very much in an Italianate style.[69]

French composers were slow to adopt the small-scale *concertato* idiom until the Belgian-born Henry Du Mont (*c.* 1610–1684) published his *Cantica sacra*,

---

69 M. Locke, *Anthems and Motets*, ed. P. Le Huray, 'Musica britannica', 38 (London, 1976), pp. 7–21.

2–4 vv., in Paris in 1652, the first French book to have a figured basso continuo part. Composed for two to four voices and dedicated to *dames religieuses*, they provide great freedom of choice, with alternative vocal tessituras and *ad libitum* instrumental parts. These were close in style to the immediate post-Palestrina Italian model. Du Mont's later *petits motets*, as the genre came to be called, are more extended, in line with mid-century Italian developments, and they include a number of dialogues. Under Louis XIV, the main liturgical position of the *petit motet* was during the Elevation at the Low Mass which Louis preferred. Texts such as 'O salutaris hostia' or 'O sacrum convivium' dominate the small-scale compositions of later seventeenth-century composers such as Lully, Robert and even Charpentier, who did not hold an official position at the Chapelle Royale. Small-scale motets by Italian composers were also regularly performed in France: a manuscript collection of *Petits motets et Elévations de MM. Carissimi, de Lully, de Robert, de Daniélis et Foggia à 2, 3, 4 voix et quelques unes avec des violons* was copied in 1688.[70] Out of 72 motets, 32 are by Carissimi and 7 by Francesco Foggia, with only 10 each by Lully and Robert. Outside the Chapelle Royale, the *petit motet* enjoyed great popularity, particularly at convents and institutions with only a handful of singers available. Charpentier left nearly 50 elevation motets for small forces, composed mainly for the Jesuit church of Saint-Louis in Paris. At the royal convent-school of Saint-Cyr, near Versailles, founded by Madame de Maintenon in 1686 for daughters of the impoverished nobility, Guillaume Gabriel Nivers wrote and compiled a large manuscript collection, particularly of *petits motets* for the *Salut du Saint Sacrement*, a devotion which combined homage to both the Blessed Sacrament and the Blessed Virgin.

Large-scale *concertato* settings

The incorporation of small-scale *concertato* elements into the polychoral idiom opened up a bonanza of compositional possibilities for the seventeenth-century composer: it is no coincidence that as the century progressed, the non-*concertato* polychoral motet receded in importance in favour of large-scale *concertato* pieces. The best-known early example is Giovanni Gabrieli's 'In ecclesiis' published posthumously in his *Symphoniae sacrae . . . liber secundus* (Venice, 1615). Four soloists (SATB) alternate and combine with a *cappella* SATB choir and two three-part instrumental groups. What is most significant is that each of the solo parts (including the bass) singly and in small groups sings lines which need basso continuo support, while the instruments play an independent

---

70 Paris, Bibliothèque Nationale, Rés Vmb MS 6; see Anthony, *French Baroque Music*, p. 225.

sinfonia in the middle of the piece. An *alleluia* refrain recurs five times to provide formal unity, and by varying the vocal and instrumental texture, it articulates the structure, building up to a glowing climax.

In Rome an isolated early example, the Magnificat *Tertii toni* by Giovanni Maria Nanino (1543/4–1607), was copied posthumously into a set of partbooks in the Cappella Giulia. The distribution of the verses is as follows:

1	Anima mea . . .	Choir I (SATB)
2	Et exultavit . . .	Choir I (SATB), Choir II (SATB)
3	Quia respexit . . .	SSA
4	Quia fecit . . .	Choir II (*falsobordone*)
5	Et misericordia . . .	B, violin
6	Fecit potentiam . . .	Choirs I, II
7	Deposuit . . .	Choirs I, II
8	Esurientes . . .	BB, violin, cornett
9	Suscepit . . .	SSAT (organ *tacet*)
10	Sicut locutus . . .	AA
11	Gloria Patri	SSATB (organ *tacet*)
12	Sicut erat	Choirs I, II

The soloists are drawn from across the two choirs. The verses are marked off from each other by barlines (except the first and second, and sixth and seventh), producing a sectional style of composition that came to be described as 'concertato alla romana' when used by north Italian composers, in contrast to their more continuous *concertato* procedures. Having a break between verses was particularly suited to sectional texts, and to performing situations with considerable spatial separation, as in Rome where such large-scale writing remained more strongly tied to liturgical needs, particularly for Vespers. In Venice, the needs of the state often took precedence, with the production of dazzling motets for major state feast-days a priority. In other respects, too, Rome and Venice differed. Rome-based composers preferred to write for equal choirs, while their north Italian counterparts combined both high- and low-cleffed groups. Nanino's Magnificat is a rare Roman example of a piece with surviving instrumental parts: unlike Venetian composers, Romans seem not to have written out such parts, though archival sources testify that instrumentalists commonly performed. Players most likely improvised from the vocal parts. This has the effect of making Roman music look dull on paper in comparison.[71] However, even without instruments the result could be a sonic extravaganza, as André Maugars suggests when describing (in 1639) a Roman Vespers in the Dominican church of S. Maria sopra Minerva:

---

71 Dixon, '*Concertata alla romana* and Polychoral Music in Rome', p. 133.

The church is very long and spacious and there are two organs placed high up, one on the left and the other on the right of the high altar; alongside these two choirs were placed. Along the nave there were another eight choirs, four on one side and four on the other, raised on platforms eight to nine feet high, equidistant one from the other and opposite each other in such a way that everyone could see everybody else. With each choir there was a portative organ, as was customary, and this should surprise no one, since one can find more than 200 of these in Rome, whereas in Paris one can hardly find two in tune with each other. The *maestro*-composer gave the beat to the first choir, which contained the most beautiful voices. With all of the other choirs there was someone who did nothing else but watch the main beat of the first choir and relay it to his own group, so that all of the choirs sang to the same beat without delay. The music was polyphonic, full of beautiful melodies and a large number of pleasing solos. At one time a soprano from the first choir sang a solo, to which those of the third, fourth and tenth choirs responded, at another two, three, four or five voices from different choirs sang together, yet again, all the singers from the different choirs sang in turn, one after the other. Occasionally two choirs sang together and then another two responded; at other times three, four or five choirs would sing together, followed by one, two, three, four or five solo voices. At the *Gloria patri* all ten choirs sang together.[72]

This quotation mirrors similar descriptions in other places, especially that by the English traveller Thomas Coryat, who visited Venice in 1608. Similarly, the birth of the future Louis XIV in 1638 was the occasion of a major celebration by the French community in Venice at the church of S. Giorgio, with music for Mass and Vespers by the *maestro di cappella* of St Mark's, Giovanni Rovetta (d. 1668). In the following year Rovetta published his *Messa e salmi concertati*, op. 4, for five to eight voices and the two violins which, by mid century, had effectively replaced cornetts and trombones in church music.[73] Like Monteverdi's 1610 print, Rovetta's contains a Mass Ordinary setting, though here in *concertato* style and without the Sanctus and Agnus in accordance with some north Italian practice; Rovetta also provides twelve Vesper psalm settings, including most of those needed for major feast-days, and a Magnificat. He was not alone in writing *concertato* Mass settings: Grandi's *Messa concertata* was published posthumously in 1630, also without Sanctus and Agnus, with varying solo, full choir and instrumental groupings. Francesco Cavalli (1602–76), organist at St Mark's, also published a *Messa concertata* in 1656 which is conceived on a grand scale for one choir of four soloists and a second choir of soloists and ripieni, with instrumental ensemble. The Gloria begins as follows:

72 I translate the text in Lionnet, 'André Maugars'.
73 G. Rovetta, *Messa, e salmi concertati, op. 4 (1639)*, ed. L. M. Koldau, 2 vols, 'Recent Researches in the Music of the Baroque Era', 109–10 (Middleton, WI, 2001).

Gloria in excelsis Deo,	AT solo (Choir I)
Gloria,	Tutti
Gloria in excelsis Deo,	SAT solo (Choir I)
Gloria	Tutti
in excelsis Deo,	ATB solo (Choir II)
Gloria in excelsis Deo et in terra pax	Tutti
hominibus bonae voluntatis.	
	Sinfonia
Laudamus te. Benedicimus te.	SAT solo (Choir I) and ATB solo
Adoramus te. Glorificamus te.	(Choir II); tutti
Gratias agimus tibi propter magnam	Tutti
gloriam tuam. Domine,	
Domine Deus, Rex coelestis, Deus	ATB solo (Choir II)
pater omnipotens	
etc.	

Key phrases are repeated by different vocal groups. The major sections are divided off by instrumental sinfonias, while other sinfonias and ritornellos also divide the parallel phrases of text which occur in the second half of the movement. Here, as usual in *concertato* settings, vocal textures are carefully orchestrated to match the text.

Robert Kendrick has described the changes which took place on the appointment of Ignazio Donati as *maestro di cappella* at the Duomo in post-plague Milan in 1631.[74] Donati already had a considerable reputation for *concertato* writing, which he brought to setting the Ambrosian liturgy on the Duomo's three major feast-days,[75] introducing large-scale *concertato* psalm-settings with a pair of trombones to double the alto and tenor lines. His Ambrosian Vespers psalm-complex 'Deus misereatur nobis' pits a six-voice Choir I (SSATTB) against a five-voice Choir II (SSATB) and two further four-voice choirs (each SATB), i.e., nineteen parts in all. All four choirs have the same clef-combination, as in Roman practice; also typically Roman is the opening for four solo sopranos, taken from Choirs I and II. Untypical of Rome is the considerable doubling of parts between the choirs in tuttis in the manner of Viadana, so that there is, for instance, only one actual bass line. A composer who generally avoided such doubling by using contrary motion in bass lines was the Milanese nun Chiara Margarita Cozzolani. Robert Kendrick has noted how the psalms in her *Salmi a otto . . . motetti, et dialoghi* (Venice, 1650) are imbued with the *concertato* style, giving all the voices florid solos and duets while using largely homophonic tuttis containing close antiphonal exchanges between the choirs. Cozzolani

74 Kendrick, *The Sounds of Milan*, chap. 9.
75 3 May (Finding of the Holy Cross), 8 September (Nativity of the BVM), 4 November (S. Carlo Borromeo).

brought a wholly individual approach to her psalms which has prompted Kendrick to label them *salmi bizarri*, in the sense of 'fashionable'.[76] Most have refrain or da-capo structures, achieved either by inserting repetitions of the opening verse into later sections or by anticipating the doxology, as in her 'Dixit Dominus'.[77] She set the Vespers psalms most commonly used for feast-days in the Roman rite, presumably for liturgical performance at S. Radegonda, one of Milan's convents famous for the quality of its music in this period. More mundane settings, meanwhile, were being composed for use at the Duomo in Milan by Giovanni Antonio Maria Turati (1608–50) and his successor Michel'Angelo Grancini (1605–69); a considerable number of their works survive in manuscript in the cathedral's archive.

Italian sacred music in the second half of the century has received relatively less attention from historians than that of the first half. Opera, oratorio and cantata composition undoubtedly occupied an increasing amount of composers' time, as it has the attention of historians, but sacred music in all the main styles continued to be written, adopting much from the lyricism of these other forms. At St Mark's, Venice, for example, Giovanni Legrenzi (1626–90) presided as vice-*maestro* (1681–5) and *maestro* (1685–90) over a very large ensemble of 36 voices and 43 instrumentalists. He had had a distinguished career in centres such as Bergamo and Ferrara, and he wrote in all four styles described here, publishing small-scale *concerti* and psalms as well as large-scale *concertato* settings, including his *Sacri e festivi concenti: messa e salmi a due chori* (Venice, 1667); his non-*concertato* polychoral works remain in manuscript. One of Legrenzi's violinists at St Mark's was Giovanni Battista Vivaldi, father of Antonio whose compositions for the Pio Ospedale della Pietà continued to develop these styles in the early eighteenth century. At S. Petronio in Bologna, Maurizio Cazzati (1616–78), the *maestro di cappella* from 1657 to 1671 and most famous for developing instrumental music, published an enormous amount of liturgical music in all of the current styles, much of it on his own printing press. His time in Bologna was dogged by one of the century's numerous polemics over correctness in *stile antico* writing: one of the Kyrie movements from his *Messa e salmi a cinque voci*, op. 17 (Venice, 1655) was attacked by two colleagues in S. Petronio, Lorenzo Perti and Giulio Cesare Arresti, on the grounds of its misuse of mode, but Cazzati vigorously defended himself in later publications.[78] In Naples, composers such as Pietro Andrea Ziani (1616–84) and Francesco Provenzale (d. 1704) wrote sacred music in a variety of styles for use in the royal chapel and other institutions; the arrival of the young Alessandro Scarlatti (1660–1725)

---

76 Kendrick, *Celestial Sirens*, p. 339.   77 Ibid., pp. 339–40.
78 Schnoebelen, 'Cazzati *vs.* Bologna'.

in 1683 brought to Naples a major composer with considerable experience in Roman churches, whose sacred music was to run the gamut of styles, including a revitalised *stile antico*.

In France Jean Veillot, active in the 1640s and 1650s, was the first to establish the role of instrumental *symphonies* in polychoral music, the instruments also doubling the voices in tuttis. This helped lay the ground for the *grand motet*, the major form of large-scale church music during the reign of Louis XIV; the performance of a *grand motet* began at the start of a Low Mass (which Louis preferred and in which none of the liturgical text was sung) and continued until the Elevation, when one or two *petits motets* were sung. Towards the end of the Mass, a setting of 'Domine, salvum fac regem', a prayer for the king, was sung in a restrained and often contrapuntal style. Starting with Henry Du Mont (*c.* 1610–1684), every French composer wrote *grands motets*, the generic title covering not just motets but also Vesper psalms, litanies and settings of the *Te Deum* and of the *Miserere*.[79] Perhaps the best-known example is Jean-Baptiste Lully's *Miserere* of 1664 set for a *petit chœur* of five soloists (SSATB), a *grand chœur* of five parts (SATBarB), and a mainly five-part string ensemble (at times the top violin line divides). Much of the *grand motet* repertory is rather pompous state music, in which the King of Heaven is equated with the King of France, but in the hands of a non-court composer such as Marc-Antoine Charpentier (1643–1704) it could display a keen sensitivity to the text, as in his 'Salve Regina' for three choirs and instruments composed for the Jesuit church in Paris. Apart from Lully, the most important composer of *grands motets* was Michel-Richard de Lalande (1657–1726), who continued to develop and expand the genre up to his death. But Du Mont's 'Dum esset Rex' is one of the finest and most complex examples in terms of scoring. Copied into a Chapelle Royale manuscript for use in 1677, it is thought to have been composed earlier. It is set for a solo *petit chœur* (SATBarB), a *grand chœur* (SATBarB), and a four-part instrumental ensemble. The text is largely compiled from the Song of Songs and the scoring is carefully chosen to reflect it, particularly its dialogue elements.[80]

On his return to London in 1660 from exile in the French court, Charles II encouraged French musical styles. This led to the creation of the 'symphony-anthem'[81] based on both the *grand motet* and the verse-anthem, in which soloists, full choirs and instrumental groups take their turn. John Evelyn was unimpressed, claiming that the genre was 'better suiting a tavern or playhouse

79 Anthony, *French Baroque Music*, p. 218.
80 H. Du Mont, *Grands motets*, ii, ed. N. Berton (Versailles, 1995), pp. 57–95.
81 This is the usual term. Caldwell, *The Oxford History of English Music*, i, chap. 10, prefers 'orchestral anthem'.

than a church'.[82] Samuel Pepys, on the other hand, found Matthew Locke's 'Be thou exalted, Lord' to be 'a special good anthem'. Performed in the Chapel Royal on 14 August 1666 to celebrate a naval victory over the Dutch, the piece opens and closes with a tutti setting of the last verse of Ps. 21 for triple choir and string band; this frames the rest of Ps. 21 ('The King shall rejoice') set for various combinations of voices and punctuated by instrumental sinfonias. In the works of Pelham Humfrey, John Blow and Henry Purcell the symphony-anthem reached new heights, particularly in the music composed for the coronation of James II in 1685. John Caldwell has drawn attention to Blow's 'God spake sometimes in visions' composed for this occasion, in which Blow builds up a coherent structure by carefully controlling the length and weight of contrasting sections. On the other hand, Caldwell finds Purcell's 'My heart is inditing', written for the same occasion, rather overblown and long.[83] That, however, may have been precisely the point: pomp and circumstance was the main purpose of much of the grandest music composed throughout Europe in the seventeenth century. Like the lavishly constructed platforms, the elaborate decorations, the costumes and wigs, this music was ephemeral and not made to last, except perhaps as a memorial of the occasion. Purcell's other symphony-anthems are less brash: they include a number written to exploit the extraordinarily wide range of the bass John Gostling, particularly 'Those that go down to the sea in ships'.[84]

The approaches to setting sacred texts that emerged in Italy around 1600 proved durable throughout the century, particularly by way of their fusion into the large-scale *concertato* idiom with instrumental participation. By the end of the century the *stile antico*, now a genuinely retrospective contrapuntal style, could also form part of that fusion, applied to particular sections of text such as the 'Crucifixus' of the Credo or certain verses of psalms. The increasing sectionalisation of such settings, beginning with the *concertato alla romana* style of psalm-setting, prepared the way for the large-scale motets, Masses and psalms of the eighteenth century with their separate movements. Italian dominance also proved very long-lasting, though interaction with local dialects and traditions could modify it considerably, as in France, England and Lutheran Germany.[85] Just as Italian, and particularly Roman, Baroque church design was copied over and over again in Europe and beyond, so the large-scale music written for these churches was also widely imitated, proving especially

82 Caldwell, *The Oxford History of English Music*, i: 515.
83 Others take a kinder view of this piece; see Spink, *Restoration Cathedral Music*, p. 161.
84 Holman, *Henry Purcell*, pp. 134–5.
85 Webber, *North German Church Music in the Age of Buxtehude*, stresses the continuation of Italian influence on north German sacred music through to the end of the century.

useful in reinforcing the century's absolutist tendencies in both Church and state.

Only a fraction of the liturgical music written in the seventeenth century has been reviewed here; rather, a series of snapshots has endeavoured to give the flavour of the variety and flexibility which composers brought to bear on sacred texts. All over Europe the production rate was phenomenal, and much of this music was never published, particularly after the relative decline in music printing in the 1630s. Outside of the major centres there was an equally active liturgical musical life in cities and towns, in convents and in monasteries, much of which has gone unrecorded or unresearched up to the present. While this music might not have reached the artistic heights or the monumental quality of that written for princes and popes, it nevertheless uplifted, educated and brightened the lives of millions in a century where these lives were often blighted by religious and political strife. We are still overly reliant on studies of a limited number of major institutions and of composers judged to be canonic; much work needs to be done in libraries and church archives throughout Europe and the New World before we might have anything approaching a comprehensive knowledge of seventeenth-century liturgical music.

Bibliography

Anthony, J. R., *French Baroque Music: from Beaujoyeulx to Rameau*. Rev. edn, Portland, OR, 1997

Bianconi, L., *Music in the Seventeenth Century*, trans. D. Bryant. Cambridge, 1987

Caldwell, J., *The Oxford History of English Music*, i. Oxford, 1991

Corp, E., 'The Exiled Court of James II and James III: a Centre of Italian Music in France, 1689–1712'. *Journal of the Royal Musical Association*, 120 (1995), 216–31

Couchman, J. [P.], 'Musica nella cappella di Palazzo Altemps a Roma'. In R. Lefevre and A. Morelli (eds), *Musica e musicisti nel Lazio*, 'Lunario Romano 1986'. Rome, 1985, pp. 167–83

'Felice Anerio's Music for the Church and for the Altemps *Cappella*'. Ph.D. thesis, University of California, Los Angeles (1989)

Culley, T., *Jesuits and Music, i: A Study of the Musicians Connected with the German College in Rome during the 17th Century and of their Activities in Northern Europe*. Rome, 1970

Cummings, A. M., 'Toward an Interpretation of the Sixteenth-Century Motet'. *Journal of the American Musicological Society*, 34 (1981) 43–59

Dixon, G., 'The Origins of the Roman "Colossal Baroque"'. *Proceedings of the Royal Musical Association*, 106 (1979–80), 115–28

'Liturgical Music in Rome, 1605–45'. 2 vols, Ph.D. thesis, University of Durham (1982)

'Lenten Devotions in Baroque Rome'. *Musical Times*, 124 (1983), 157–61

'*Concertata alla romana* and Polychoral Music in Rome'. In Luisi, Curti and Gozzi (eds), *La scuola policorale romana del Sei-Settecento*, pp. 129–34

Dolskaya-Ackerly, O., 'Vasilii Titov and the "Moscow" Baroque'. *Journal of the Royal Musical Association*, 118 (1993), 203–22

Frandsen, M., 'The Sacred Concerto in Dresden ca. 1660–1680'. Ph. D. thesis, University of Rochester (1996)

Frey, H. W., 'Die Gesänge der sixtinischen Kapella an den Sonntagen und hohen Kirchenfesten des Jahres 1616'. In *Mélanges Eugène Tisserant*, 'Studi e testi della Biblioteca Apostolica Vaticana', 231–7. 7 vols, Vatican City, 1964, vi: 395–437

Glixon, J., *Honoring God and the City: Music at the Venetian Confraternities, 1260–1807*. Oxford, 2003

Hammond, F., *Music and Spectacle in Baroque Rome: Barberini Patronage under Urban VIII*. New Haven and London, 1994

Hintermaier, E., '"Missa salisburgensis": Neue Erkenntnisse über Entstehung, Autor und Zweckbestimmung'. *Musicologica austriaca*, 1 (1977), 154–96

Holman, P., *Henry Purcell*. Oxford and New York, 1994

Kendrick, R. L., *Celestial Sirens: Nuns and their Music in Early Modern Milan*. Oxford, 1996
   The Sounds of Milan, 1585–1650. Oxford, 2002

Kurtzman, J. G., *The Monteverdi Vespers of 1610: Music, Context, Performance*. Oxford, 1999

Launay, D., *La musique religieuse en France: du Concile de Trente à 1804*. Paris, 1993

Leaver, R. A., 'Lutheran Vespers as a Context for Music'. In P. Walker (ed.), *Church, Stage, and Studio: Music and its Contexts in Seventeenth-Century Germany*. Ann Arbor, 1990, pp. 143–61

Leonard, C. A., 'Hammerschmidt's Representation in the Bohn Collection: the *Capella* Tradition in Practice'. Paper presented at the international conference 'Early Music: Context and Ideas', Kraków, September 2003

Lionnet, J., 'Una svolta nella storia del Collegio dei Cantori Pontifici: il decreto del 22 Giugno 1665 contra Orazio Benevoli; origine e conseguenze'. *Nuova rivista musicale italiana*, 17 (1983), 72–97
   'André Maugars: "Risposta data a un curioso sul sentimento della musica d'Italia"'. *Nuova rivista musicale italiana*, 19 (1985), 681–707
   'Performance Practice in the Papal Chapel during the Seventeenth Century'. *Early Music*, 15 (1987), 3–15
   'L'évolution du répertoire de la Chapelle Pontificale au cours du 17ᵉᵐᵉ siècle'. In A. Pompilio, D. Restani, L. Bianconi and F. A. Gallo (eds), *Atti del XIV congresso della Società Internazionale di Musicologia: trasmissione e recezione delle forme di cultura musicale (Bologna, 27 Agosto–1 Settembre 1987; Ferrara–Parma, 30 agosto 1987)*. 2 vols, Turin, 1991, ii: 272–7
   'Le répertoire des vêpres papales'. *Collectanea II: Studien zur Geschichte der päpstlichen Kapelle; Tagungsbericht Heidelberg 1989*, 'Capellae Apostolicae Sixtinaeque collectanea acta monumenta', 4. Vatican City, 1994, pp. 225–48
   'Les musiques polychorales romaines: problèmes d'interprétation'. In Luisi, Curti and Gozzi (eds), *La scuola policorale romana del Sei–Settecento*, pp. 103–18

Luisi, F., Curti, D., and Gozzi, M. (eds), *La scuola policorale romana del Sei–Settecento*. Trento, 1997

Miller, S., 'Music for the Mass in Seventeenth-Century Rome: *Messe piene*, the Palestrina Tradition, and the *Stile antico*'. 2 vols, Ph. D. thesis, University of Chicago (1998)

Monson, C., *Disembodied Voices: Music and Culture in an Early Modern Italian Convent*. Berkeley, 1995

O'Regan, N., 'Sacred Polychoral Music in Rome, 1575–1621'. D. Phil. thesis, University of Oxford (1988)

'Processions and their Music in Post-Tridentine Rome'. *Recercare*, 4 (1992), 45–80

Institutional Patronage in Post-Tridentine Rome: Music at Santissima Trinità dei Pellegrini, 1550–1650, 'Royal Musical Association Monographs', 7. London, 1995

'Asprilio Pacelli, Ludovico da Viadana and the Origins of the Roman *Concerto ecclesiastico*'. *Journal of Seventeenth-Century Music*, 6 (2000), <http://sscm-jscm.org./jscm/v6/no1.html>

'Evidence for Vocal Scoring in the Late Sixteenth- and Early Seventeenth-Century Polyphony from Cappella Sistina Musical and Non-Musical Documents'. In A. Roth and T. Schmidt-Beste (eds), *Der Fondo Cappella Sistina als musikgeschichtliche Quelle: Tagungsbericht Heidelberg 1993*, 'Capellae Apostolicae Sixtinaeque collectanea acta monumenta', 6. Turnhout, 2001, pp. 97–107

'Roman Polychoral Music: Origins and Distinctiveness'. In Luisi, Curti and Gozzi (eds), *La scuola policorale romana del Sei–Settecento*, pp. 43–64

Palisca, C. V., 'Marco Scacchi's Defense of Modern Music (1649)'. In L. Berman (ed.), *Words and Music – the Scholar's View: a Medley of Problems and Solutions Compiled in Honor of A. Tillman Merritt by Sundry Hands*. Cambridge, MA, 1972, pp. 189–235; reprinted in Palisca, *Studies in the History of Italian Music and Music Theory* (Oxford, 1994), pp. 88–145

Pastor, L., *The History of the Popes*, trans. R. F. Kerr *et al*. 40 vols, London, 1930

Reardon, C., *Holy Concord within Sacred Walls: Nuns and Music in Siena, 1575–1700*. New York, 2002

Roche, J., '*Musica diversa di Compietà*: Compline and its Music in Seventeenth-Century Italy'. *Proceedings of the Royal Musical Association*, 109 (1982–3), 60–79

North Italian Church Music in the Age of Monteverdi. Oxford, 1984

Saunders, S., *Cross, Sword and Lyre: Sacred Music at the Imperial Court of Ferdinand II of Habsburg (1619–1637)*. Oxford, 1995

Schnoebelen, A., 'Cazzati *vs*. Bologna: 1657–1671'. *Musical Quarterly*, 57 (1971), 26–39

'Bologna, 1580–1700'. In C. Price (ed.), *The Early Baroque Era: from the Late 16th Century to the 1660s*, 'Man and Music', 3. Basingstoke and London, 1993, pp. 103–20

Sherr, R., 'Performance Practice in the Papal Chapel during the Sixteenth Century'. *Early Music*, 15 (1987), 453–62

Shigihara, S., 'Bonifazio Graziani (1604/5–1664): Biographie, Werkverzeichnis und Untersuchungen zu den Solomotetten'. Ph. D. thesis, University of Bonn (1984)

Spink, I., *Restoration Cathedral Music 1660–1714*. Oxford, 1995

Spink, I. (ed.), *The Blackwell History of Music in Britain*, iii: *The Seventeenth Century*. Oxford, 1992

Webber, G., *North German Church Music in the Age of Buxtehude*. Oxford, 1996

Whenham, J., *Duet and Dialogue in the Age of Monteverdi*. 2 vols, Ann Arbor, 1982

11

Devotion, piety and commemoration:
sacred songs and oratorios

ROBERT L. KENDRICK

To study the vast amount of sacred and spiritual music outside the liturgy as a part of the great efflorescence of religious expression in seventeenth-century Europe (not to mention its outposts in the Americas and in Asia) is to encounter a fascinating repertory in a little-known context. From a 'top down' perspective, historians have marked the century as one wherein structures became increasingly formalised, the distinctions between Christian churches became more marked, and belief systems were rigidified, all in a process called (for northern Europe) 'confessionalisation'.[1] Whether or not one adheres to the historiographical truism of the 'crisis of the seventeenth century', it is clear that the destruction wrought in central Europe by the last major conflict to be waged, at least nominally, on confessional grounds – the Thirty Years War (1618–48) – as well as the increasing difficulty in reconciling religious and empirical knowledge (a problem provisionally bridged, if not solved, by Descartes) had a real effect on sacred music, whether directly or indirectly.[2]

Yet crisis and separation were not the whole story. In all the traditions – Calvinist, magisterial Protestant (Lutheran and Anglican), Roman Catholic – the century was characterised by one or another form of a turn towards interiority: the believer's personal relationship with Christ, his or her internal illumination, the reality of sin, the vanity of the world, and the possibility for redemption. The best-known manifestation of this trend was Franco-Spanish

---

I wish to thank Benjamin Brand, Tim Carter, Alexander Fisher, Kasia Grochowska, Metoda Kokole, Arnaldo Morelli, Piotr Poźniak, Anne Robertson, Louise Stein, Stanislav Tuksar and Michael Zell for their help. Abbreviations used below include: *DKL* = K. Ameln, M. Jenny, and W. Lipphardt, *Das deutsche Kirchenlied: Kritische Gesamtausgabe der Melodien*, vol. i, pt. 1, *Verzeichnis der Drucke*, 'Répertoire international des sources musicales', B/VIII/1 (Kassel etc., 1975; index ed. M. Jenny, Kassel etc., 1980]); *RRMBE* = 'Recent Researches in the Music of the Baroque Era' (Madison, later Middleton, WI).

1 The idea of linking the phenomenon to state formation in early modern Europe, developed by Wolfgang Reinhard and Heinz Schilling, has generated an enormous literature; for one summary, see Schilling, 'Die Konfessionalisierung von Kirche, Staat und Gesellschaft'.

2 For one view of the effect of the 'crisis' on the chorale repertory as a turn away from Luther's practice, see Kemper, 'Das lutherische Kirchenlied in der Krisen-Zeit des frühen 17. Jahrhunderts'.

Quietism, finally condemned but not entirely cowed by Pope Innocent XI's decree *Caelestis pastor* (1687). Similarly, 'pre-Pietist' streams in German Lutheranism, and even the 'metaphysical' bent of English religious poetry, bear witness to the lasting effect of this piety, in part as a last flowering of the *devotio moderna*, and in part as a reaction to the new epistemologies and political strife.[3] The difficulties in religious knowledge, and the century's conflicts, also led to the creative resurgence of mystical (i.e., non-scholastic) theology adhering to orthodoxy to greater or lesser degrees, and many texts set to music (notably dialogues) partake of these forms and methods of devotional thought.

For all that the confessions were drawing apart (and the religious and territorial map of Europe was stabilised by the Peace of Westphalia in 1648), men and women still did not define themselves completely in terms of one church's identity. It is precisely 'high-culture' music that provides some of the best examples of how the common heritage of the Latin Bible (especially such key books as the Song of Solomon) and the personalised spirituality mentioned above were able to circulate, especially in domestic settings, across the confessions. The best-known case is that of Heinrich Schütz's 1625 *Cantiones sacrae*, which contains texts of pseudo-Patristic and Protestant heritage, and is dedicated to an Imperial counsellor who had converted from Lutheranism to Catholicism. But no less telling are the ways in which the *collegia musica* of Dutch burghers sang Latin works written by both Catholic and Lutheran composers along with Genevan psalm settings.[4] In the 1640s, amateurs in the heartland of Swiss Calvinism, Zurich, wasted no time in acquiring the recent motet editions of the Milanese cathedral organist Michelangelo Grancini.[5] In so doing, they rewrote the original Marian or sanctoral texts, unacceptable in their confession, into a personalised Christological language (similar to the literary style being set by the leading Italian motet composers, Gasparo Casati, Giovanni Rovetta, Orazio Tarditi and Francesco della Porta). Such contrafacting was also carried out by Matthias Weckmann when transcribing Italian and German pieces into a manuscript perhaps for his own use in Dresden, finished in Hamburg in 1647.[6]

---

3 The presence of the Rhineland mystics in two Protestant figures is traced in Ingen, 'Die Wiederaufnahme der Devotio Moderna bei Johann Arndt und Philipp von Zesen'.

4 For individuals' ownership of musical editions, and the *collegia musica* in the northern Netherlands, see Noske, *Music Bridging Divided Religions*, i: 22–7.

5 The copy of Grancini's *Il sesto libro de sacri concerti a due, tre, e quattro voci*, op. 12 (Milan, 1646) now in Zurich, Zentralbibliothek, shows such rewritten texts clearly.

6 For the case of Lüneburg, Ratsbücherei, Musikabteilung, Mus. ant. pract. KN 206, see Silbiger, 'The Autographs of Matthias Weckmann'.

This flexibility of the musical expression of belief involves the anthropological category of religious behaviour and experience, an idea not simply reducible to a 'devotion' separable from the rest of life.[7] Sacred music was made across a range of ritual or habitual activities outside the prescribed liturgy, and the space – corporate or personal – in which the art was to have its effect was also variable. The domestic context was central to much of the repertory, but other locations included monasteries, convents and the residences of single extended families in addition to the more familiar burghers' houses of Protestant northern Europe.[8] Music structured time sacrally, as in the case of the (sometimes complex) continuo songs in J. H. Calisius's domestic Lutheran breviary, *Andächtige Haus-Kirche oder Aufmunterung zur Gottseligkeit* (Nuremberg, 1676; *DKL* 1676[09]), the contents of which were assigned to different days and hours of the week. To judge from the number of printed editions, the demand for such music was high in seventeenth-century Europe, whether for personal (domestic and/or recreational) use or for corporate (processional or festal).

The repertory took various forms. At one end of the scale were motets to Latin texts which circulated from Italy northwards and were also set by Protestant composers; at the other were the vernacular traditions (devotional monodies, *canzonette spirituali* or *laude, airs spirituels, geistliche Lieder, villancicos*). But another characteristic of the century's music was the possibility for aspects of 'low' culture to appear in a fairly stylised context. This is evident in the motets on the *piva*, or bagpipe drone, written in the later Seicento by composers as diverse as Francesco Provenzale in Naples and Isabella Leonarda in Novara. The combination of sacred and secular texts could also be found in composers' 'secular' song publications: half of Francesca Caccini's *Primo libro delle musiche* (Florence, 1618) is made up of settings of devotional texts, and Tarquinio Merula's lullaby of the Madonna to the Christ-Child, 'Hor ch'è tempo di dormire' (printed in his secular *Curtio precipitato et altri capricci . . . a voce sola*, Venice, 1638), is another setting that underscores the cohabitation of 'high' and 'low' elements in the repertory. It sets Mary's presentiment of Christ's Passion as a set of strophic variations over a simple two-note bass figure (A–B♭):[9]

7 For the role of personal experience in seventeenth-century German Catholic devotion, see Holzem, 'Bedingungen und Formen religiöser Erfahrung im Katholizismus zwischen Konfessionalisierung und Aufklärung'.

8 Perhaps most useful for musical practice is Veit, 'Die Hausandacht im deutschen Luthertum', which considers how such devotion served corporate ends (e.g., by structuring the year) and also personal ones (e.g., in individual song 'treasuries'). For wider (but not musical) perspectives, comparative studies are found in Sarti, *Europe at Home* (see esp. pp. 125–6 on instruments in the home); Kertzer and Barbagli (eds), *Family Life in Early Modern Times*.

9 The metrical variety of its declamation is discussed in Leopold, '*Al modo d'Orfeo*', pp. 265–7.

Hor ch'è tempo di dormire,
dormi, figlio, e non vagire,
perche tempo ancor verrà
che vagir bisognerà.
Deh, ben mio, deh, cor mio,
fa la ninna ninna na ...

[Now that it is time to sleep, / sleep, my Son, and don't cry, / for a time will come / when crying will be necessary. / Oh, my love, oh, my heart, / sing 'Ninna ninna na' . . .]

But no matter what its literary register, the devotional music of all the confessions was characterised by the century's passionate concern with the overriding themes of spirituality: the sense of sin and the transitoriness of life; penitence and conversion; the quest for Divine illumination and the personal union with Christ the Redeemer. The interiority of European spirituality found one of its best expressions in music.[10]

Amidst the variety of Christian genres, it should also be remembered that this era also witnessed the first surviving printed polyphony for Jewish use, probably both liturgical and domestic: Salamone Rossi's *Songs of Solomon* (Venice, 1622). Rossi's edition came at the same time as polemics among Italian Jews concerning the suitability of polyphony for devotional music.[11] His volume was only one visible sign of the flourishing musical life of such communities, at least where they were tolerated (in Holland, Provence, Poland, and some Italian and German states).[12]

Rhetorics and texts

It has rightly been observed that in no epoch have texts been so implicated in generating musical structures as in the seventeenth century.[13] Part of the search for personalised devotion and for a resolution to the epistemological crises was a marked change in the forms and vocabulary of sacred art and literature as a whole,[14] and the texts for music 'high' and 'low' showed the

10 The best overview of Catholic music is in Bianconi, *Music in the Seventeenth Century*, pp. 119-33; see also Braun, *Die Musik des 17. Jahrhunderts*, pp. 228-37. The stimulating reflections on the ideology and aesthetics of the Italian repertory in Stefani, *Musica e religione nell'Italia barocca*, pp. 187-231, remain invaluable, despite the author's binary structuralist approach.

11 For a sense of the polemics, see Harrán, *Salomone Rossi*, pp. 201-19.

12 The evidence is assembled in Adler, *La pratique musicale savante dans quelques communautés juives en Europe aux XVIIe et XVIIIe siècles*. Adler also provides scores of Carlo Grossi's *Cantata ebraica* (possibly written for a Jewish confraternity in Modena) and Louis Saladin's *Canticum* (for a circumcision rite in southern France).

13 Chafe, *Monteverdi's Tonal Language*, p. 6.

14 For the use of emblematics and iconicity in Seicento still-lifes, see Pozzi, 'Rose e gigli per Maria'; for the centrality of Jesuit rhetoric in the French Golden Age, see Fumaroli, *L'âge de l'éloquence*, pp. 343-91.

change. The new principles of text construction – the emblem ('concetto' in Italian), constructivism, parataxis – and the sheer intensity of the vocabulary and the themes (sin, redemption, Marian intercession, the suffering of martyrs) led to the creation of some remarkable settings.

Gradations of all kinds are to be found in both Latin and vernacular texts for music. That both languages were sung as part of domestic or personal devotion is evident from those (largely Italian) musical editions that mix the two, a kind studied insightfully by Jerome Roche.[15] The clearest case is the even mixture in a print based on the poems of the abbot Angelo Grillo (Livio Celiano), the codifier of a new aesthetic in Italian sacred poetry:[16] *Motetti et madrigali cavati da le poese sacre del reverend.mo padre D. Angelo Grillo* (Venice, 1614), with monodic settings by Grillo's fellow Benedictine monk Serafino Patta, working in Emilia. Patta's vernacular pieces are glosses on the preceding Latin motets, and they give a sense of the meaning of these standard items for men and women of the time.

As in other musical genres, Italy led the way, and motet texts from the peninsula began to change dramatically around 1625, with a move away from biblical or liturgical passages towards a freer centonisation (again notable in texts derived from the Song of Solomon) and the use of first-person pronouns. The shift is evident in the motet books of composers (Merula, Rovetta) working in the wake of the establishment of the genre's norms by Alessandro Grandi (1586–1630) and Ignazio Donati (*c.* 1567–1638) in the previous decade. One of Merula's duets from his *Libro secondo de' concerti spirituali*, 2–5 vv. (Venice, 1628) shows the new Christological fervour, ending with an unanswered question:

O bone Jesu, et dulcis spes animae meae, aperi cor meum ad vulnera tua, ut quantum me diligis cognosciam. O Jesu, o amantissime Jesu, amator mei, desidero te millies. Mi Jesu, quando venies, quando me laetum facies?

[O good Jesus, and sweet hope of my soul, open my heart to Your wounds, so that I may know how much You love me. O Jesus, O most beloved Jesus, my lover, I desire You greatly. My Jesus, when will You come, when will You make me happy?]

The goals of such settings related to the famous triad of rhetorical goals, *docere-delectare-movere*, of which obviously the last was most suited to music's powers. Indeed, the classic passages of Athanasius Kircher (in his *Musurgia universalis* of 1650) on the force of Carissimi's music refer directly to the moving of the emotions. Rhetoric, however, also influenced the music and words of motets

---

15 Roche, 'On the Border Between Motet and Spiritual Madrigal'.
16 For Grillo's centrality, if not absolute priority, in the formation of the new aesthetic, see Föcking, *'Rime sacre' und die Genese des barocken Stils*, pp. 155–61.

on a structural level (by way of *dispositio*, *inventio* and parataxis), as well as on the more immediate level of 'rhetorical figures' codified by German theoretician-composers and discussed elsewhere in the present book.

Rhetoric had no meaning without a public. In semi-public venues (oratories, processions), music functioned as a parallel to sacred oratory; in private devotion, it was connected with prayer. From the Viennese Abraham a Sancta Clara to the Portuguese Antonio Vieira, the century was filled with virtuoso preachers. The 'moderate' conceptualist Paolo Aresi, a leading practitioner and theoretician of such oratory in northern Italy, compared music to the word of God, sweetened and made perceptible so as to steer the will of the individual to divine command.[17] For the Catholic world, the affinity between music and prayer was debated and discussed in Part V of Grazioso Uberti's dialogue *Contrasto musico* (Rome, 1630).[18] Uberti resolved the objections to the use of music in personal prayer by pointing to the use of the voice as an external expression and stimulant of internal devotion, and of song as one of the most perfect and regulated forms of vocal communication. Taking Boethius's tripartite division of *musica* as a guide, the dialogue suggested that *musica instrumentalis* (i.e., that of voices and instruments) was not only useful in prayer, but served also to raise the soul to God, and to rouse the mind and the heart.

Commentators from the magisterial Protestant traditions expressed similar sentiments, albeit shorn of the scholastic terminology. In the preface to the fourth volume of the *Himlische Lieder* (Lüneburg, 1642; *DKL* 1642[07]) by Johann Rist (1607–67) – the first collection of texts meant for musical setting by this central figure in seventeenth-century sacred German poetry – the author linked the simplicity that he (together with his musical collaborator, Johann Schop) had sought in the songs directly to a sense of the inner self:

> As for the melodies, once again in this volume I have preferred the plain; and I asked my esteemed friend Johann Schop to set them simply and intelligibly, especially those whose difficult tunes are not pleasant to learn . . . I have consciously and industriously desired to give them such simplicity (underneath which, as wise people know, there hides a high and almost unbelievable art), as I have wished to seek and encourage the pleasure of not the outer but the inner person.[19]

If there was one biblical source whose vocabulary and themes (in Latin or the vernacular) united all the confessions, it was the Song of Solomon (the

---

17 P. Aresi, *Della tribolazione e dei suoi rimedi* (Tortona, 1624), pp. 15–16, discussed in Ardissino, *Il Barocco e il sacro*, p. 334.

18 G. Uberti, *Contrasto musico, opera dilettevole* (Rome, 1630; repr. Lucca, 1991), p. 109.

19 J. Rist (and J. Schop), *Himlische Lieder* (Lüneburg, 1642; repr. Hildesheim, 1976), 'Vorrede an den christlichen Leser', sig. A8.

Canticum Canticorum or the Canticles), with its allegorical text capable of different kinds of meaning depending upon the exegetical tradition adopted by an author.[20] For Protestants, for example, the interpretation of the passionate love between the Canticles' male and female spouses (Sponsus/Sponsa) tended towards the personal relationship between Christ and the believer, or between Christ and the Church. In Germany, Martin Opitz's paraphrase of the Song of Solomon (*Salomon des hebreischen Königes hohes Lied*, Breslau, 1627) mixed metres and genres, employing a more exotic vocabulary than the one that the poet had used in his hymn cycle on the annual Epistles and in his psalm paraphrases.[21] This remarkably variegated text inspired several composers, among them Schütz (the three settings preserved in manuscript, SWV 441, 451 and 452) and Johann Erasmus Kindermann (*Concentus Salomonis*, a collection of duets published in Nuremberg in 1642). The last major appearance of such a Protestant collection was in Philipp von Zesen's paraphrase *Salomons des ebreischen Königes geistliche Wohl-lust oder Hohes Lied* (Amsterdam, 1657; *DKL* 1657[20]), with melodies by Schop. Lutheran Canticles settings could also serve wedding ceremonies.[22] One of the longest such pieces produced, the nuptial dialogue 'Meine Freundin, du bist schön' by Johann Christoph Bach (1642–1703; organist in Eisenach and an older cousin to J. S. Bach), seems to have borne hidden personal meaning for its composer.[23]

The use of the Song of Solomon in Catholic motet texts also blurs the boundary between the 'liturgical' and the 'non-liturgical'.[24] In many cases, the love of the two Spouses referred directly to the relationship of Mary and her Son, and thus the music functioned as part of Marian devotion. But in so far as such pieces were sung at the Elevation of the Mass, they were also a musical personalisation of a ritual moment, meant to prepare the believer for union with Christ in the reception of the Eucharist. On the other hand, the same goal of fusion with the Redeemer was an integral part of individual devotion, and thus it supported the private performance of such pieces. One of Orazio Tarditi's solo motets, 'Descende, dilecte mi, in hortum meum' (in his *Motetti a voce sola, il quarto libro*, Venice, 1648) is an excellent example: its text (which opens 'Come, my [male] beloved, into my garden') is a collage of slightly altered Canticles verses referring to such union, all in the literary voice of the Sponsa.

---

20 For some ideas on exegesis and musical reflection, see Kendrick, '*Sonet vox tua in auribus meis*'.

21 The fundamental study of the German devotional song repertory is Scheitler, *Das geistliche Lied im deutschen Barock*; see pp. 180–91 for the innovativeness of Opitz's paraphrase of the Song of Solomon and for details of its musical settings.

22 As in the case of Melchior Franck's nineteen settings for five, six and eight voices published in his *Geistliche Gesäng und Melodeyen* (Coburg, 1608), ed. W. Weinert in *RRMBE* 70 (1993). Von Zesen's verse was set again in 1674 by the Bern cornetto player Johann Ulrich Sulzberger.

23 Wollny, 'Johann Christoph Bachs Hochzeitsdialog *Meine Freundin, du bist schön*'.

24 Dahlenburg, 'The Motet *c.* 1550–1630'.

Thus it could function both as an *oratio ante communionem* and as a more general mark of personal Christological devotion. Such ambiguity was typical, as Serafino Patta's *Sacra cantica*, 1–3 vv. (Venice, 1611) showed; set out as a cycle, its verses were capable of Marian, personal or monastic (male and female) interpretation.

A similar flexibility characterised Marc-Antoine Charpentier's (d. 1704) two major works based on the Canticles, the dramatic motet 'Nuptiae sacrae' (H. 412; 1683–5) and the motet-cycle *Quatuor anni tempestates* (H. 335–8; 1685). The former, a large-scale piece for soloists, chorus and instruments (written for the singers of the composer's patroness Mlle de Guise, among them Charpentier himself), replicates the Song of Solomon's characters and divides its chorus into two; the latter's small-scale Italianate motets assign favourite Canticles passages to each season of the year, in a pattern possibly inspired by the Benedictine breviary, which apportioned selections from the book to various months; if the composer was writing for Benedictines male or female, there was a logic to these textual choices.

Although vernacular Canticles settings were often linked to Protestants, and Vulgate verses to Catholics, the spectacularly beautiful Song of Solomon motets in Schütz's first book of *Symphoniae sacrae* of 1629 show the flexibility of the Latin text, here seemingly related to the individual soul's search for its Redeemer. Similarly, the 21 Italian-language paraphrases written and set by the Olivetan monk Pietro Orafi (*La Cantica*, 2–5 vv., Venice, 1652) recall both his order's musical traditions and the special place of the Canticles for cloistered men and women.

Just as the tradition of Song of Solomon settings dated back to the sixteenth century, another long-standing genre that witnessed its final flowering in the early part of the seventeenth was the spiritual madrigal. In Italy, its rhetoric was conditioned by the innovations of Angelo Grillo: the anti-Petrarchan mixing of rhetorical levels, the personalisation of devotional focus, and the frequent use of surprise conceits or similes. For the young Philip III of Spain, the expatriate Milanese violinist Stefano Limido composed a cycle of settings to texts by Grillo published as *Regii concenti spirituali*, 5–6 vv. (Milan, 1605; the edition also contains Castilian devotional settings). In a more traditional scoring for domestic use, Oliviero Ballis's *Canzonette amorose spirituali a tre voci* (Venice, 1607) is made up almost entirely of settings of *capitoli* and passages from Petrarch's *Trionfi*.[25] More modern texts are instead found in Marcantonio Tornioli's *Canzonette spirituali a tre voci* (Venice, 1607), which sets a cycle of Christological meditations from Grillo's *Pietosi affetti*, the favourite collection of the new sacred rhetoric.

25 Ed. R. Tibaldi (Crema, 2001).

In those centres which witnessed a retrospective turn in the early Seicento (Rome and Milan), the spiritual madrigal and sacred contrafacta continued to hold strong sway. But at the beginning of the century, the three-voice reper-tory was one of the first formats for settings of the new poetics of Grillo and Giambattista Marino: Agostino Agazzari's First and Second Books of *madri-galetti a tre voci* (Venice, 1607), and a Marino cycle in Francesco Bianciardi's *Canzonette spirituali a tre voci* (Venice, 1606), in addition to the Tornioli vol-ume mentioned above. This scoring shared a common public with the popular Latin *tricinia* for sanctoral or Christological devotion, notably those of Antonio Mortaro: pieces from his three-voice *Sacrae cantiones* (Venice, 1598) were often reprinted in German anthologies by Protestant and Catholic editors, together with three-voice works (conceived with basso continuo) by Lodovico Viadana and the Roman Antonio Cifra.

The most extensive settings of sacred vernacular texts in Rome are found in the three volumes by Giovanni Francesco Anerio (*c.* 1567–1630), the *Selva armonica*, 1–4 vv. (1617), the massive *Teatro armonico spirituale di madrigali a cinque, sei, sette, et otto voci* (1619), and the *Rime sacre concertate a doi, tre, et quat-tro voci* (1620).[26] With this series, Anerio set an astounding number of pieces of Oratorian inspiration, identifiable both by the devotional focus and by the popular (not 'high') tone of the poetry: the *Selva armonica* contains three set-tings, two multipartite, of words by the leading Oratorian Agostino Manni, and its five Latin-texted duets are almost all Marian in address. The pieces range from strophic songs through *concertato* madrigals to dramatic dialogues. Anerio's achievement was remarkable in its sheer scope, but was further removed from the new Grillo-inspired poetry which was the catalyst for new musical procedures in central and northern Italy.

The last printed examples of *concertato* spiritual madrigals were produced by the Roman-influenced Giovanni Pietro Biandrà – his *Il primo libro de madrigaletti a una, doi e tre voci* (Venice, 1626), with settings of Rinuccini and Marino among others – and by the Neapolitan Oratorian priest Scipione Dentice, a member of the religious order most central to sacred vernacular music. Dentice's remark-able Second Book (1640) of four-voice spiritual madrigals 'in stile recitativo' (a late appearance of the designation) includes *concertato* pieces for saints, Mary, and Passion devotion, a sign of the sophisticated practice of the Oratory in Naples.[27] Outside Italy, the form had a few late examples, the most obvi-ous being Johann Hermann Schein's *Israelis Brünlein* (Leipzig, 1623). This

---

26 Hobbs, 'Giovanni Francesco Anerio's *Teatro armonico spirituale di madrigali*'; Smither, *A History of the Oratorio*, i: 118–26. Filippi, '*Selva armonica*' and 'Spiritualità, poesia, musica'. An edition of Anerio's *Selva armonica* (ed. D. V. Filippi) is forthcoming in *RRMBE*. For Anerio's dialogues, see below.

27 Martin, 'Scipione Dentice'.

collection of settings based on Old Testament texts displays some of Schein's most innovative techniques, simultaneously a worthy tribute to the traditions of the spiritual madrigal and a harbinger of the future.

The influence of sacred rhetoric was evident in the newly published (if not new in practice) scorings of songs for solo voice and duet with continuo. One of the first volumes of Florentine monody in this genre was Severo Bonini's *Madrigali, e canzoni spirituali . . . a una voce sola* (Florence, 1607), containing virtuosic and highly affective settings of devotional texts (to saints) by Marino and by Crisostomo Talenti, thus linking these musical innovations to the new rhetoric perhaps even more directly than was the case for secular song. Indeed, Marino's own display and defence of his conception of sacred literary creation, his pseudo-sermons published as the *Dicerie sacre* of 1614, took music (after painting) as a symbol of Christ's suffering on the Cross.[28] Such texts of the new religious poetics were also set in the small-scale madrigal and aria repertory: Antonio Cifra produced two sacred volumes after the success of his secular *scherzi* (*Scherzi sacri*, 1–4 vv., opp. 22 and 25, Rome, 1616 and 1618); while Pietro Pace used stock basses in his two books of *Scherzi et arie spirituali* (Venice, 1615, 1617).[29] The practice of casting sacred texts in common formats for secular song can be found in the works of the important Turin-based composer Enrico Radesca di Foggia, whose *Il quinto libro delle canzonette, madrigali et arie a tre, a una, et a due voci* (Venice, 1617) was exclusively devoted to religious poetry.

Later in the century, a special kind of vernacular text in northern Italy was the moral sonnet or (later) moral cantata. Its best-known examples are the five pieces which introduce Monteverdi's *Selva morale e spirituale* (Venice, 1640–41). Such pieces first appeared individually, then were gathered into volumes of *cantate spirituali e morali* from the 1650s onwards. Perhaps the most innovative edition of this type was the first, Domenico Mazzocchi's *Musiche sacre e morali, a una, due e tre voci* (Rome, 1640), containing monodic multipartite settings of sonnets and *ottave rime*. Its sacred poetry, including verses by Marini and Claudio Achillini, also featured Giulio Rospigliosi's brilliant Christmas parody of Tancredi's lament in Tasso's *Gerusalemme liberata*, 'Giunto alla cuna' ('Having arrived at the crib' for 'Giunto alla tomba', i.e., 'tomb'). The solo cantata tradition extends through Maurizio Cazzati's *Cantate morali, e spirituali a voce sola*, op. 20 (Bologna, 1659; dedicated to a Milanese nun) to Giacomo Antonio Perti's *Cantate morali, e spirituali a una, et a due voci*, op. 1 (Bologna, 1688). Extended three-voice pieces were published in Mario Savioni's *Concerti morali, e spirituali, a tre voci differenti* (Rome, 1660), and Savioni also contributed

---

28 G. B. Marino, *'Dicerie sacre' e 'La strage de gl'innocenti'*, ed. G. Pozzi (Turin, 1960).

29 Rorke, 'The Spiritual Madrigals of Paolo Quagliati and Antonio Cifra'. Even Pace's secular book of 1613 contains a dialogue between a sinner and Death.

to a closely related subgenre with his *Madrigali morali, e spirituali a cinque voci concertati* (Rome, 1668). A mixed volume of moral and spiritual madrigals with other songs was also published by the young Maria Francesca Nascimbeni (soon to become a nun) as *Canzoni e madrigali morali e spirituali a una, due, e tre voci* (Ancona, 1675). One of the distinguishing features of these *morale* texts, whether classic (Petrarch) or newly written, was the studious avoidance of any mention of God (or even the supernatural). Instead, the pieces concentrated on a familiar trinity of themes: transience, vanity and the deceitfulness of appearances. In contrast, the *spirituale* texts often made explicit reference to Catholic doctrine.

That such works were not confined to Italy is evident in one of the young Henry Purcell's most striking devotional pieces, 'O, I'm sick of life' (Z. 140, from about 1677), to words by the early seventeenth-century sacred poet George Sandys. Sandys paraphrased verses from another key text for seventeenth-century interiority, the Book of Job (chap. 10), and Purcell scored his setting for a vocal sonority (TTB) which seems to have connoted *gravitas* for the composer. The piece's grinding dissonances and passionate solos render it one of the best examples of its kind, a late-century *cantata morale* in all but name.

Yet the most innovative endeavours of the century occurred not in received poetic or musical forms, but in new ones: Italian canzonettas, French airs, and the most recent German chorales (with their newly emerging metrical structures). National traditions had different forms: in Italy, *arie spirituali*; in France, contrafacta of the *air de cour* or *air de luth*; in Protestant Germany, the new kinds of devotional (and normally extra-liturgical) poetry spawned by Opitz's formal and metrical experiments. This new poetry had a much harder time penetrating the congregational hymn repertory in various German cities, but it inspired several composers, among them Schütz.[30]

Occasions

A sociology of seventeenth-century devotional music has yet to be written. One important principle is that musical genres cannot simply be reduced to social class, and thus some of the vernacular sacred pieces discussed in this chapter

30 One should keep in mind the essential difference between collections of sacred songs (*geistliche Lieder*) for domestic or informal use, and church (and city-specific) hymnbooks, even though repertory may be shared therein. The standard edition of German Lutheran hymn texts is Fischer and Tümpel, *Das deutsche evangelische Kirchenlied des 17. Jahrhunderts*; for earlier collections, see Wackernagel, *Das deutsche Kirchenlied von der ältesten Zeit bis zu Anfang des XVII. Jahrhunderts*. Catholic songbooks (including polyphonic editions) are discussed and listed in Bäumker, *Das katholische deutsche Kirchenlied in seinen Singweisen von den frühesten Zeiten bis gegen Ende des siebzehnten Jahrhunderts*, which also includes the tunes for many hymns. According to Scheitler, *Das geistliche Lied*, pp. 172–80, Opitz found no reception in congregational hymnals, and the texts of Simon Dach (ibid., pp. 206–7) gained only slow entry thereto.

ranged from the top to the bottom of society. The tradition of royal piety continued from before: the Marian/Cross devotion of Emperor Ferdinand II, a direct outgrowth of the traditional Habsburg themes of the *pietas austriaca*, had remarkably direct expression in the motet production of his Italian *Kapellmeister* Giovanni Valentini (1582/3–1649).[31] For the Spanish branch of the family, Limido's spiritual madrigals mentioned above would have been joined by *villancicos* and motets. At the end of the century, the great dramatist Jean Racine had his *Cantiques spirituels* (1694) set to music and performed in the presence of Louis XIV by the female pupils (*demoiselles*) of the royal convent-school of Saint-Cyr; the music heard here was probably by Jean-Baptiste Moreau (1656–1733).[32] Another kind of private sacred music for royalty was the Christmas carol practised at the London and Oxford courts of Charles I before and during the Civil War.[33] In 1648, Henry Lawes compiled a collection that both commemorated his brother William and was further geared towards the beleaguered sovereign's private taste: the *Choice Psalmes* consisted largely of settings by the two siblings (30 each) of Sandys's psalm paraphrases.[34] Even during the Commonwealth, John Wilson's *Psalterium carolinum* (London, 1657) represented a posthumous musical tribute to the king's devotions.

Sacred music in noble or ecclesiastical households was performed, like secular music, especially 'at the hour of recreation' (*all'hora di ricreazione*), as Fabio Costantini put it in the dedication to Cardinal Pier Paolo Crescenzi (1572–1645), Bishop of Orvieto, of his secular anthology *L'aurata cintia armonica* (Orvieto, 1622).[35] In the case of Giovanni Angelo Altemps, Duke of Gallese, patron of the important Roman composer Felice Anerio (*c.* 1560–1614) and himself an amateur composer, the music books kept at the ducal villa in Frascati and presumably used for informal music-making included motets by Anerio, madrigals by Ruggiero Giovannelli, Marenzio and Orazio Vecchi, and the 1618 edition of Cifra's *Scherzi sacri*.[36] In 1602, the Milanese composer Orfeo Vecchi (*c.* 1553–1603) linked the domestic prudence of the noblewoman Ippolita Borromeo to her practice of music, as noted in his dedication to her of his collection of Marian madrigal settings, *La donna vestita di sole, coronata di stelle, calcante la luna* (Milan, 1602).[37] A special case of domestic musical piety is found in those

---

31 The classic study of Habsburg piety and sacred music is Saunders, *Cross, Sword, and Lyre*.

32 For the repertory, see Favier, 'Les cantiques spirituels savants', which supersedes Boulay, 'Les cantiques spirituels de Racine mis en musique au XVIIᵉ siècle'; Bert, 'La musique à la Maison Royale Saint-Louis de Saint-Cyr'.

33 Pinto, 'The True Christmas'.   34 A. Robertson, '"Choice Psalms"'.

35 The anthology includes works by Giovanni Francesco Anerio, Fabio Costantini and Frescobaldi; see Paquette-Abt, 'A Professional Musician in Early Modern Rome', ii: 603–5.

36 According to an inventory (*c.* 1620) now in Chicago, Newberry Library, see Couchman, 'Felice Anerio's Music for the Church and for the Altemps *Cappella*', pp. 438–48.

37 Kendrick, *The Sounds of Milan*, p. 185.

patrician institutions of the Catholic world dedicated to contemplation, the male and female monasteries. The inscription of Aquilino Coppini's second volume (Milan, 1608) of contrafacta of Monteverdi's (and others') madrigals to Sister Bianca Lodovica Taverna at the Augustinian house of S. Marta in Milan is well known, while in the same city the Benedictine organist Serafino Cantone (*c.* 1565–*c.* 1630) attempted to preserve a standard form of the previous century, the madrigal comedy, in his *Academia festevole concertata a sei voci* (Milan, 1627). Designed specifically for recreation, this cycle uses the genre's standard procedures (quodlibet citations of classic pieces, imitations of animals and instruments, solmization puns) in a musical narration of the physical and spiritual journey of five monastic characters up and down Mount Etna in Sicily.

At the other end of the social scale, the average French or German peasant would have learned, by ear, the hymns sung in an oratory or in church; it should also be remembered that the 'downward' transmission of Roman *falsibordoni* to the confraternity members of Sardinian villages also seems to have begun in this period.[38] In between there lay the great market for devotional music: patrician and middle-class households, but also (in the Catholic world) confraternities, schools of Christian doctrine, oratories, and educational institutions run by religious orders. Thus in early seventeenth-century Augsburg, Eucharistic and Marian confraternities sponsored music on major feasts.[39]

For much of Catholic Europe, religious orders were central to vernacular music; in Italy the most obvious case is the Oratorians, the institutional patrons and transmitters of the *lauda* repertory old and new.[40] The editions by Anerio and Dentice mentioned above highlight music's vital role, using more or less complex forms, in the propagation of the order's message of the joyous renunciation of the world. One motet by Cristoforo Caresana (*c.* 1640–1709), preserved in the order's Neapolitan library, typifies this well, beginning with the famed biblical quotation 'Vanitas vanitatum . . .' (Ecclesiastes 1: 2): 'Vanity of vanities, all is vanity; neither is the eye satisfied with what it sees, nor the ear with what it hears, for all is vanity . . . Despise riches, and you will be rich; abandon glory, and you will be glorious; neglect rest, and you will find it.'[41] Caresana sets this as an extrovertly happy duet, with repeated notes over a four-note ostinato bass which serves simultaneously as emblem (the endless cyclicity of

38 The interaction between written and orally transmitted polyphonic recitation formulas is brilliantly discussed in Macchiarella, *Il falsobordone fra tradizione orale e tradizione scritta*, pp. 243–87.

39 Fisher, *Music and Religious Identity in Counter-Reformation Augsburg*, pp. 163–9.

40 Arnaldo Morelli's now-classic study, '*Il tempio armonico*', esp. pp. 67–73, shows how a largely late Cinquecento repertory was preserved in manuscripts associated with the Vallicella.

41 Caresana's motet is preserved in Naples, Biblioteca Oratoriana dei Gerolamini (Filippini); there is a recording in F. Provenzale, *Vespro*, Opus 111, OPS 30–210 (1998).

worldly desires) and structure, and concluding with a repeat of the opening section in a manner which recalls the norms of the instrumental canzona. The openness of the Oratorians to such diverse aesthetic impulses was of central import in the creation of new vernacular repertory. In a far less urban setting, the manuscript written by a Pauline priest in northern Croatia in 1644 (now in Zagreb, National and University Library, R 3629) contains Gregorian chants and Croatian and Latin songs for the major feasts of the church year and of the order, as well as for Passion and Marian devotion.[42] Thus informal musical devotion ran through all the classes and castes of European society, serving to link them into a community of belief.

Similarly, occasion and environment were not coterminous with form. The major genres of the century – solo motet, chorale, dialogue, *villancico* (and the parallel if not related *cantio natalitia* in the Southern Netherlands), psalms or their paraphrases, noëls – all had uses in and out of the liturgy. Published pieces could be heard even in the most intimate settings, those for a single singer-lutenist or two musicians, an ensemble that the Dutch polymath and amateur composer Constantijn Huygens used for the pieces included in his *Pathodia sacra et profana* (Paris, 1647). Huygens's settings of psalm verses were performed by the composer and his favourite pupil, Utricia Ogle Swann. When Huygens sent the English musician Nicholas Lanier a copy of his edition on 20 January 1654, he also invited him 'if you will bee so good to us one day, as to come where you may heare My Lady Swann and me make a reasonable *beau bruict* about some lessons of this Booke. The Psalms she most loveth and doth use to sing are named here in the margent, as allso some of the Songs' (nine settings are listed in the margin).[43] Huygens's simple binary or da-capo structures use the standard gestures of *anaphora* (sequential repetition) and local chromaticism to reflect their personalised texts. The combination of songs and psalms reflects how, for men and women across the confessions, the psalter was the literary compendium of the human experience of the sacred. To sing its texts was to express both the personal and the universal.

Especially in northern Europe, domestic situations constituted the major part of the market for printed editions of *geistliche Lieder*. Lutheran Germany, relatively literate, provides the best case of such prints, mixing sacred songs, chorales in monophony or *Kantionalsatz* (i.e., four-voice homophonic settings), and more complicated pieces. In Lutheranism, the spaces used for domestic devotion (reading or singing) were clearly designated, in contrast to the more numerous ritual loci of Catholicism, and the sense of making residential

---

42 *Pavlinski zbornik 1644*, ed. K. Kos *et al.* (Zagreb, 1991).

43 Huygens's *Pathodia sacra et profana* has been edited by F. Noske (Amsterdam, 1958; 2/1976); for the letter, see Worp, 'Nog eens Utricia Ogle en de muzikale correspondentie van Huygens'.

domains sacred is evident in the presentation of musical editions formulated for use in *Hausmusik*.[44] A number of titles referred to such space, ranging through the century from Bartholomaeus Gesius's *Christliche Hauß- und Tisch-Musica* (Wittenberg, 1605/*DKL* 1605[04]) to Tobias Zeutschner's *Musicalischer Hauss-Andacht erstes Zehen* (Breslau, 1667/*DKL* 1667[01]). The first large-scale collection of this kind was the four volumes of Johann Staden's *HaussMusic: Geistlicher Gesäng* (Nuremberg, 1623, 1628; *DKL* 1623[08], 1628[16]), and the daily practice of house music was reflected in another collaboration between Rist and Schop, *Frommer und gottseliger Christen alltägliche Haußmusik* (Lüneburg, 1654/*DKL* 1654[04]). The clearest link between domestic and psychological intimacy was made in the title of Johann Heermann's *Devoti musica cordis: Haus- und Herzens-Musica* (Leipzig, 1630/*DKL* 1630[05]; a collection of texts only). In the Catholic centres of southern Germany, several editions mixed a domestic destination with the more common occasions of procession and pilgrimage, as in the 203 texts and 135 melodies of the *Alt und newe Geistliche, außerlesene Gesäng* (Würzburg, 1628/*DKL* 1628[08]), the publication of which was supported by Bishop Philipp Adolf von Ehrenberg.[45] Much household devotion in northern Europe seems to have taken place on Sunday, the one day of the week devoted to rest and recreation. The psalms and sacred songs of Lutheranism both reinforced the themes of the biblical readings of the day's liturgy and provided opportunities for personalised choices of devotional themes. The day after Christmas in 1669, the German Lutheran poet Sigmund von Birken noted in his diary that he celebrated the liturgy at home, singing Christmas songs and his own version of Psalm 103.[46]

The domestic locus also raises the central issue of gender in these non-public venues. One of the more striking aspects of informal sacred music in almost all Europe is the role of women. From the dedicatees of French Catholic editions of contrafacta, to the involvement of German princesses in poetic-musical academies, to the cloistered processions of Italian nuns, female participation in the repertory was central and cannot be overlooked. The 'feminisation of piety' typical of the century had one of its best reflections in music. On a personal level, the testimony of Sister Maria Francesca Piccolomini in Siena, miraculously cured of her afflictions just before playing the theorbo on a Marian feast, reveals the ways in which informal sacred music could show personal devotion and advance a woman's own standing inside the cloister; the dual use both of

---

44 Greyerz, 'Religiöse Erfahrungsräume im Reformiertentum'.

45 This edition (formerly in Dresden, Sächsische Landesbibliothek – Staats- und Universitäts-Bibliothek, Musikabteilung) is probably lost; it is cited in Bäumker, *Das katholische deutsche Kirchenlied*, i: 271, ii: 72.

46 Scheitler, *Das geistliche Lied*, p. 404; see also Kroll (ed.), *Die Tagebücher des Sigmund von Birken*, i: 520–21. For the general practice, see Scheitler, *Das geistliche Lied*, pp. 90–99.

sentiment common to nuns and of personal expression is evident as well in the choice of texts set by Lucrezia Vizzana (1590–1662) in her *Componimenti musicali de motetti concertati a una e piu voci* (Venice, 1623).[47] In France, the first volume of simple two-voice vernacular settings of Christmas and Marian texts, *Noëls et cantiques spirituels sur les mystéres de la naissance de Nostre Seigneur* (Paris, 1644), was dedicated to the abbess of Saint-Anthoine des Champs in Paris. The piety of such Protestant noblewomen as Sophie Elisabeth of Brunswick-Lüneburg, an occasional pupil of Schütz, resulted in the 60 or so sacred songs and motets that she composed in the middle decades of the century.[48] In the course of her career, Sophie made progress as a composer, setting many of her texts (including a few by her stepson, the important poet Anton Ulrich of Brunswick) for her private devotion; some of the texts reflect her own Calvinist convictions.

One of the most personal effects of music was rapture, and it also seemed often linked to gender. Musical ecstasy was more evident in the Catholic world, especially among those contemplative women and men engaged in personal music-making, although the sounds of Milanese nuns or Roman motets seem also to have induced sentiments of a similar kind in northern Protestants. Perhaps the most famous Italian visionary was the monasticized former courtesan Caterina Vannini of Siena (1562–1606), whose mystical abduction while singing (presumably *laude* or *canzonette spirituali*) fascinated Cardinal Federigo Borromeo and made its way into the prelate's writings on 'true' and 'false' female ecstasy.[49] Less famous nuns, such as Vizzana, Piccolomini, or the Milanese Angela Confaloniera, echoed some of the issues present in Vannini's case: the lack of a connection between rapture and specific musical genres, the suspension of physical fatigue and the presence of 'automatic' behaviour during musical trance, and the occurrence of the phenomenon during personal spiritual recreation.

Yet these roles included more than just performers. In the Catholic world, the important role of female sanctoral intercession (not confined to Mary) generated a wave of Marian music, as seen in such books as Johannes Khuen's *Marianum epithalamium* (Munich, 1638/*DKL* 1638⁰²), which contains sacred songs in German dedicated to the Virgin and other female saints. In the first half of the century, the positing of Mary Magdalene as a model for all penitents

---

47 For Piccolomini, see Reardon, *Holy Concord Within Sacred Walls*, pp. 98–122; for Vizzana's textual choices and musical settings as responses to her personal and social situation, see Monson, *Disembodied Voices*, pp. 92–130. An important collection of vernacular monody, Paolo Quagliati's *Affetti amorosi spirituali* (Rome, 1617), was dedicated to Sister Anna Maria Cesis in S. Lucia in Selci.
48 Geck, *Sophie Elisabeth Herzogin zu Braunschweig und Lüneburg (1613–1676) als Musikerin*.
49 Her case is discussed in Kendrick, *Celestial Sirens*, and more extensively in Reardon, *Holy Concord Within Sacred Walls*, pp. 104–8.

(i.e., all Christians) resulted in some striking laments and dialogues in which she was given voice, including Luigi Rossi's extended and passionate 'Pender non prima vide' (in Oxford, Christ Church, Mus. MS 998, ff. 79–92v), Kapsberger's 'Dolcissimo signore' (from his *Libro secondo d'arie passeggiate* (Rome, 1623), Frescobaldi's *Maddalena alla croce* (from his *Primo libro d'arie musicali*, Florence, 1630) and Domenico Mazzocchi's double-choir *Dialogo della Maddalena* (published in his *Sacrae concertationes* of 1664, but probably written much earlier).[50] In this last piece, probably composed for a Roman oratorio or confraternity, the Magdalene who searches for Christ (using language derived from the Song of Solomon) is used as a metaphor for the quest of all Christians. An analogous procedure is found in a dialogue by the Milanese Benedictine nun Chiara Margarita Cozzolani (in her *Salmi a otto voci concertati . . . motetti et dialoghi*, op. 3, Venice, 1650), reflecting her own foundation of S. Radegonda and also its urban musical public.[51]

Images that clearly depict informal sacred music are often hard to identify, all the more so given that the archetypal patroness of music, St Cecilia, was shifted early in the century from being the protectress of exclusively sacred works to being that of all music. One of the most striking representations of professional musicians, however, is a depiction of the saint with music-making companions commissioned by the Neapolitan *Congregazione dei musici della Reale Cappella di Santa Cecilia* (and its organist, Giovanni Maria Trabaci). Trabaci and his colleagues entrusted the work to the painter Carlo Sellitto, and it was placed in 1613 on the saint's altar in the now destroyed church of Santa Maria della Solitaria (it is now in the Museo di Capodimonte in Naples).[52] Although the music being performed is not identifiable, the organ-playing saint looks up to heaven in a standard pose, while her colleagues (obviously representatives of the musicians' guild) sing, play chitarrone or theorbo and violin, and look variously at the music, at the audience, and upwards. Not only the chiaroscuro but also the relative humility of the figures mark the work as one of the century's best corporate representations of musicians involved in the sacred.

Other depictions run the range from the individual to the familial. The *Lute Player* engraved by Ludolph Büsnick in Calvinist Münden (1630) sings from a Latin-texted motet book, while the epigraph underneath mixes two different

50 G. Frescobaldi, *Arie musicali, libri primo e secondo*, ed. C. Gallico and S. Patuzzi, 'Girolamo Frescobaldi: opere complete', 7 (Milan, 1998), pp. 12–13; Mazzocchi, *Sacrae concertationes*, ed. W. Witzenmann, 'Concentus musicus', 3 (Cologne, 1974). Dentice's 1640 collection featured two Magdalene pieces.

51 See the 'Dialogo fra la Maddalena, e gli Angeli, nella Resurettione di N. S.' in C. M. Cozzolani, *Motets*, ed. R. L. Kendrick, *RRMBE* 87 (1998), pp. 227–36.

52 The most accessible reproduction is in F. Petrelli's entry on the painter in Whitfield and Martineau (eds), *Painting in Naples from Caravaggio to Giordano*, p. 245.

psalm verses.[53] The theological eclecticism and the varied sources of the text are entirely typical of solo motets throughout Europe. Different kinds of families and different confessions were also represented. Girolamo Martinelli's portrait of *A Concert in Casa Lazzari* (Carpi, Museo Civico) shows five members of a family in their future vestments – two of the three women are depicted as nuns (one the conductor) – collaborating in performance.[54]

A middle-class Dutch Mennonite family, that of David Leeuw (1631/2–1703), was portrayed at music-making in one of the last paintings of the Amsterdam painter Abraham van den Tempel (1671). Remarkably, the music can be read: a *balletto* ('Lo Spensierato', or 'The Thoughtless Man') from Giovanni Giacomo Gastoldi's *Balletti a tre voci* (Venice, 1594), in the form of a double-texted Dutch sacred contrafactum ('Wat is van 's mensen leven') published in an Amsterdam edition of *c.* 1657.[55] Two of the family's daughters, the eight-year-old Cornelia and the eighteen-year-old Maria, sing parts, while the twelve-year-old Weyntje plays harpsichord, and the only son, Pieter, plays bass viol. The portrait obviously displays the qualities of family harmony enacted through music, with the simple verse on Christian life intended as a kind of motto, sung in consort so as to unite and identify the group: 'What is there in human existence / (Which God has given to each person) / beyond that which is driven by His spirit / and raised so as to strive / for eternal life?' The scene is a remarkable tribute to the staying power of a sixteenth-century Italian repertory in a very different time and place. The use of a simple *tricinium* as the musical emblem of this ideology again resonates with the other domestic sacred music produced in this format in Italy and Germany, as discussed above.

Domestic settings did not exhaust the venues for vernacular or extra-liturgical (Latin-texted) settings. The majority of ritual occasions for polyphony outside the formal feasts prescribed by liturgical books was to be found in Catholic, and not Protestant, traditions: celebrations of Marian or sanctoral feasts (city protectors), Eucharistic or Passion commemorations, local penitential or annual processions often involving the more or less musically elaborate projection of a litany text.[56] Here, Marian litanies provided a frequent occasion

---

53 Reproduced in Braun, *Die Musik des 17. Jahrhunderts*, p. 232, which also comments on the image and its textual content.

54 <http://www2.comune.carpi.mo.it/musei/sito/civico/3frame.html>.

55 The melody was identified by A. Teensma, and the painting is discussed and reproduced in P. Fischer, 'Music in Paintings of the Low Countries in the 16th and 17th Centuries', pp. 105–9, also at <http://www.rijksmuseum.nl/collectie/zoeken/asset.jsp?id=SK-A-1972&lang=en>. See also Thiel *et al.*, *All the Paintings of the Rijksmuseum in Amsterdam*, pp. 534–5. The edition of contrafacta in question is Gastoldi's *Balletten, lustigh om te zingen en spelen* ... (Amsterdam, *c.* 1657); an earlier edition (1628) contained a different contrafactum.

56 On music for one Eucharistic practice, see Smither, 'The Function of Music in the Forty Hours' Devotion of 17th- and 18th-Century Italy'.

for the performance of polyphony. The century saw a diffusion of a single standard text associated with the major Italian shrine of the Santa Casa di Loreto (itself the site of an important musical *cappella*, closely linked to Rome, as was the whole pilgrimage site). After the Vatican mandated its use, it became popular in all of Europe, normally linked to Saturday Marian devotions. In Paris, Charpentier wrote his nine settings (*Litanies de la vierge*) for varied ensembles, in one case (H. 83) for the private chapel of Mlle de Guise, and in others possibly for the Jesuit church of St-Louis, with a few (linked to settings of the *De profundis*) also for funerals.[57]

Litanies also functioned in more public venues. Major civic processions to the Bolognese shrine of S. Luca were accompanied by the singing of the formulaic petitions, both in chant and in figured music.[58] In Germany, Catholic devotion to the Blessed Virgin included the performance of the litany in Munich and Augsburg. A. H. Brunner in Bamberg composed a group of vernacular glosses on Mary's appellations found in the litany, presumably for use in extra-liturgical contexts.[59] Brunner followed it with 64 German songs for Eucharistic adoration (*Eucharistiae divino-humanae epulae ... oder Seraphische Tafel-Music*, Frankfurt am Main, 1692; *DKL* 1692[01]). In all of Catholic Europe, litanies were used to ward off the plague and other disasters, to invoke the Virgin's protection of individual and corporate bodies, and to mark sonically the routes of sacred geography.

The function of music in the delineation of sacral space also included other kinds of petition formulas, such as the sanctoral texts sung on the Greater and Lesser Litany days (25 April and Ascensiontide). In Rome, the sixteenth-century traditions of these processions continued, providing employment for many city musicians.[60] Local saints, protectors or symbols of a given city were also musically commemorated, ranging from St Januarius in Naples to the massive cult of St Charles Borromeo in Milan.[61] One case of vernacular sacred song generated by devotion to Borromeo can serve to represent a far wider Catholic practice of celebrating specific occasions. On 11 November 1610, the confraternity of Lombards living in Rome organised a massive procession to move (from St Peter's to their national church of S. Ambrogio, now

---

57 Cessac, *Marc-Antoine Charpentier*, p. 124; M. A. Charpentier, *Nine Settings of the 'Litanies de la Vierge'*, ed. D. C. Rayl, *RRMBE* 72 (1994).

58 The basic study on the Marian and sanctoral litany is Blazey, 'The Litany in Seventeenth-Century Italy'; see pp. 97–110 for Rogationtide and other litany processions to S. Luca.

59 Brunner's collection is *Teutsch-Marianische Lieder, über jeden Titul der Lauretanischen Lytaney*, 2–4 vv. (Bamberg, 1670; *DKL* 1670[16]).

60 O'Regan, 'Processions and their Music in Post-Tridentine Rome'.

61 For a musical procession in the war-torn autumn of 1638 which exhumed Borromeo's body and paraded it through the streets of his city so as to implore peace among Christian princes, see Kendrick, *The Sounds of Milan*, pp. 142–5.

SS. Ambrogio e Carlo al Corso) the ten banners representing the saint's life that had been used in his canonisation ceremonies on 1 November.[62] The parade's participants ranged from cardinals through members of most male religious orders in Rome to young boys dressed as angels, and it took the *strada papale* from St Peter's to the Jesuit Chiesa del Gesù and then up the Corso. It was punctuated by some seven different musical ensembles, of which the third (between the monks and the confraternity members) sang 'various motets, hymns, and *laude spirituali* with great tunefulness and sweetness'.

Such marking of space, however, took on a special edge in the bi-confessional cities of the Holy Roman Empire. In early seventeenth-century Augsburg, and as part of a larger self-assertion of the city's Catholic minority, the Good Friday and Corpus Christi processions were extended to Protestant neighbourhoods, accompanied by motets and German Catholic songs.[63] Under Jesuit influence, the vernacular songs taught and transmitted among the city's Catholic population reflected the great intensity of Eucharistic and Passion devotion, and they began to serve some of the same function that they always had for Protestant communities: confessional identity.

Similar issues are evident in the songs taught to children and students, especially in northern Europe. A now-lost Catholic hymnal, the *Ausserlesene, catholische, geistliche Kirchgesäng* (Cologne, 1623/DKL 1623⁰⁴) described part of its purpose thus: 'This small book is meant also to draw small children, with their innate desire to sing (like a small bird with a little pipe), to Christian children's doctrine; thus they, like young nightingales, can learn heavenly songs, and have something good to ponder and to say and sing at their daily work, and to chew on heavenly matters like sugar or honey in their mouths, and thereby not bring the plague-like poison of secular songs over their tongues'.[64] Not for nothing was music an essential part of education in northern European schools.[65]

That the century was a golden age for hymnals and vernacular songbooks is evident also in the lesser-known European traditions. In Denmark, the voice and continuo settings of Thomas Kingo's two-volume *Aandelige siunge-koor* (Copenhagen, 1674, 1681) form the first canonical group of Danish vernacular hymns after the Reformation. The Transylvanian convert from Orthodoxy, Ioan Căianu (1629–87), a Franciscan, provided a massive collection of Hungarian and Latin Catholic songs, the *Cantionale catholicum* (1676), with

62 'Relatione sommaria della solenne processione fatta nella traslazione de i stendardi doppo la canon-izazzione di S. Carlo Borromeo . . . da la Chiesa di San Pietro a quella di Sant'Ambrogio giovedì alli 11 di Novembre . . . 1610' (Pesaro, Biblioteca Oliveriana, MS 1644, ff. 21–32).

63 Fisher, *Music and Religious Identity in Counter-Reformation Augsburg*, pp. 232–4, 258–61.

64 Bäumker, *Das deutsche katholische Kirchenlied*, ii: 62.

65 Butt, *Music Education and the Art of Performance in the German Baroque*, pp. 12–51.

Marian, sanctoral and penitential texts.[66] The different confessional traditions in Bohemia are represented on one hand by the three Catholic publications of Adam Michna z Otradovic (*c.* 1600–1676), and on the other by the retrospective hymn compilation and collection of the last bishop of the Bohemian Brethren, Jan Amos Komenský (Comenius), the *Kancionál*, published in Dutch exile (Amsterdam, 1659).[67] Michna's 1647 collection of simple four-part Marian hymns in Czech was aimed at both sophisticated and provincial musicians; it was followed by a book of two-voice spiritual songs in 1653, and in 1661 by another hymn collection for saints' days.[68] The first edition of Croatian devotional songs for Catholic feasts, both texts and music, was Athanasius Georgiceus's (Atanazije Grgičević) *Pisni za naypoglavitiye, naysvetye i nayveselye dni svega godischia sloxene: i kako se u organe s'yednim glasom mogu spivati* ('Songs for the most important, most holy and most joyous feasts of the whole year, which can be sung with the organ and one voice'; Vienna, 1635); the first Slovenian hymns (also Catholic) with music were printed in Matija Kastelec's *Bratovske buquice* (Graz, 1678). Genres and generations mixed as well: a seventeenth-century Slovakian manuscript (now in Lipany, Lutheran Church, no shelfmark) contains monophonic Latin hymns, *Kantional* settings, and contrapuntal pieces on Latin, German, Slovak and macaronic texts.[69] In far-off Riga, Carolus Pictorius published the first Finnish-language hymns in his *Suloista ja lohdullista kijtos* (1622).[70]

In the case of Poland, despite (or perhaps because of) the massive re-Catholicisation of the country, the production of vernacular songs and hymns for Calvinists and Lutherans was conservative, with many reprints of the standard editions; the Lutheran hymnal of Piotr Artomius (published in Torun, with multiple editions between 1596 and 1646) matched the popularity of the Calvinist *Kancyonal* issued in Danzig (Gdańsk), similarly reprinted from 1633 to 1706.[71] The Catholic repertory was small, with simple hymn-settings by the court musicians Diomedes Cato and Franciszkus Lilius appearing in the first half of the century, and a few sacred songs in miscellanies.[72] Most polyphony seems to have been focussed on Latin liturgical settings for court. Thus it

---

66 '. . . *édes Hazámnak akartam szolgálni* . . .': Kájoni János 'Cantionale Catholicum', ed. P. P. Domokos (Budapest, 1979).

67 There is a partial edition in J. A. Comenius, *Kancionál*, ed. O. Settari (Prague, 1992).

68 For the Marian volume, see A. Michna z Otradovic, *Česká mariánská muzika*, ed. J. Sehnal, 'Compositiones', 1 (Prague, 1989); Michna's two-voice songbook, *Loutna česká* (Prague, 1653), has been edited by J. Hůlek and M. Horyna (Prague, 1984).

69 Rybarič, 'Zur Frage des sogenannten "slowakischen" Bestandteils in dem mehrstimmigen Gesangbuch aus Lubica'.

70 Haapalainen, *Carolus Pictoriuksen suomenkieliset virret vuodelta 1622*.

71 See the lists in Poźniak, *Musica antiqua polonica: Renasans*, iii: *Piésni/Songs*; Poźniak, *Repertuar polskiej muzyki wokalnej w epoce Renesansu*.

72 Kraków, Biblioteka Jagiellońska, MS 127/56 is an anthology, ed. J. Golos and J. Stszewski as *Muzyczne silva rerum z XVII wieku* (Warsaw, 1970). Cato's hymns appeared in *Rytmy lacińskie dziwnie sztuczne* (Kraków, 1606).

remains unclear whether Polish song was the catalyst for a new polyphonic, partly domestic, genre of Russian sacred pieces, the *kant*, which began to appear in the seventeenth century.[73]

National traditions and innovations

The existence of a ritual language (Latin) for the Catholic liturgy provides a clearer demarcation for extra-liturgical repertories in modern languages. All the various genres, and their linguistic sub-types, had their roots in the previous century (or earlier), but the stylistic range of music subsumed under a single generic label was broad.

Italy

Not surprisingly, the chief centres of production were Rome and Florence. The generic and often traditional labels applied to Italian collections – *laude*, *canzoni spirituali*, *arie spirituali* – mask subtle differences in style, occasion and audience.[74] The *Scelta di laude spirituali* published in 1657 by the Florentine Noferi Monti and dedicated to the confraternity of S. Benedetto il Bianco, contained some 300 pages of texts; the compiler noted that he had included ancient *laude* fallen into disuse. But the collection's second part contains far more modern pieces in canzonetta and aria forms, sometimes with the traditional 'cantasi come . . .' rubric ('to be sung to the tune of . . .') for contrafacta. Some of these were written for the confraternity's pilgrimage to Rome in the Holy Year of 1650, and to Loreto in the following year. One of the four pieces for which music is included is another text on the harmful vanities of the world ('le nocive vanità del mondo'), dedicated to St Philip Neri, 'Dove ne fuggi errante, incauto piè?' Its message of renouncing the world shows how even the newer layer of the *laude* repertory continued to transmit Neri's philosophy of Christian optimism, and its penitential message is underscored by the shifts to flat pitch regions, especially in the B section:

> Dove ne fuggi errante, incauto piè,
> per ritrovar il ben ove non è?
> Riedi, non seguir più gloria mentita
> sempre seco alle pene il mondo invita.

[Where do you flee, lost, o heedless foot, / seeking good where it does not exist? / Return, and do not follow false glory, / for the world always invites to sufferings.]

---

73 One early source is in O. Dolskay (ed.), *Spiritual Songs in Seventeenth-Century Russia* (Cologne, Weimar and Vienna, 1996).

74 Mischiati, 'Per una bibliografia delle fonti stampate della lauda (1563–1746)', has now been updated and expanded in Rostirolla, *La lauda spirituale fra Cinque e Seicento*.

One edition which is set entirely to polyphony is the *Canzonette spirituali, e morali*, 1–3 vv. (Milan, 1657) for the oratory of Chiavenna, in the Italian-speaking part of the Swiss Confederacy, with texts of an explicitly religious and generally moralising stamp. As recent research has shown, it was probably compiled by an Italian Oratorian as part of a project to introduce the order into the city, another mark of Oratorian influence.[75] It reworked secular canzonettas, stock basses and traditional tunes, and its range of performance possibilities is underscored by the note that the three-voice pieces could be performed as solos or duets as necessary. The collection's musical eclecticism, and its openness to 'secular' originals, were also entirely in keeping with Neri's 'optimistic' use of the most popular materials in the service of the order's message. Its dialogues between various characters (such as angels and souls) are of special importance: there is even one between an angel and a musician shown the path to 'good' music-making by divine inspiration.

Simplicity was not only an aesthetic goal but also a pedagogical necessity in the case of one of the largest European cities, Naples, with a massive plebeian population: the printer (Tarquinio Longo) of the *Lodi, e canzonette spirituali*, 3 vv. (Naples, 1608) noted in its 'Avvertimento primo' that one of his desires was that 'the *laude* should not be so beautiful, elaborate, and far from common speech [*non fussero tanto vaghe, artificiose, & dal dir commune lontane*] that they could not be both sung and understood, not only by common people but also by children and women'. For this reason, he used *villanelle* and other tunes, sorting the 400 pages of texts by verse-type and providing some 26 model *arie*, thus avoiding the 'cantasi come . . .' rubric. A series of *laude* glosses on the Pater Noster explicated the text memorised by every Christian, literate or not, while *toni* for the articles of the catechism ('per la prosa della Dottrina') gave both teachers and students a musical way to learn the items by heart. There is no better example of the function of song in teaching, transmitting and propagating the basic elements of belief to an urban public.

While sharing a similar title, the *Laude spirituali*, 1–6 vv., produced twenty years later by Giuseppe Giamberti and published in his place of employment, Orvieto, highlights the stylistic diversity of the *lauda* repertory. It consists of *arie*, nominally compiled for the Saturday Marian services in the provincial cathedral, but probably originating at least partly in Roman Oratorian circles. The duet entitled 'Anima inamorata di Cristo' ('The Soul in love with Christ') shows the style:

---

75 Moretti, 'L'Oratorio filippino di Chiavenna e la pratica del "contrafactum" nelle "Canzonette spirituali e morali" (1657)'. In an excellent study, Moretti discusses the sources of the melodies and basses used for the strongly Neri-like texts of the collection.

S'acceso ha del suo foco
Christo Giesù 'l mio core,
come v[u]oi ch'altro ardore
in me, senso crudel, ritrovi loco?

. . .

Se d'amor saggio e forte
io son legato e vinto,
in altri lacci avvinto
non sarò mai, ne sciormi può la morte.
Dunque, mia vita, lieta sempre sarai,
mentre unita starai
con vivo affetto alla bontà infinita.

[If enflamed with his fire / Jesus Christ has made my heart, / how can you desire
that another flame, / o cruel sense, should find a place in me / . . . / If by a
wise and strong love / I am bound and vanquished, / in other snares never / will
I be trapped, nor can death frighten me. / Thus you, my life, will always be
happy, / while you stand joined / with warm emotion to Eternal Goodness.]

Like any good aria, Giamberti's works by building to a simple climax. The
second strophe is a variation of the first, and the closing duet uses suspensions
and contrast to match its verbal ideas.

France

Vernacular religious music in France has been magisterially described by Denise
Launay.[76] One striking feature of the repertory is the contest between confessions in the widely diffused metrical psalter. The Calvinist texts by Clément
Marot dating back to the 1540s continued to represent a pole of attraction for
the whole century. The settings of these texts by Claude Le Jeune (d. 1600),
distributed among the four-voice cantus-firmus settings from 1601 (*Les cent
cinquante pseaumes de David*, 4 vv.), the *Pseaumes en vers mesurez*, 2–8 vv. (Paris,
1606) and the almost complete set of imitative *tricinia* (three books of psalms
published in 1602, 1608 and 1610), remained popular.[77] The metric flexibility
of Le Jeune's settings had great influence on contemporary audiences, and the
European durability of the 1601 volume is revealed by the Dutch-language
edition of 1664.

In imitation of the success of Marot's work, the various 'Catholic' versions
of the psalms – the early paraphrases by Philippe Desportes, and the more
popular texts by Bishop Antoine Godeau (1605–72) – received a number of

76 Launay, *La musique religieuse en France*.
77 C. Le Jeune, *Les cent cinquante pseaumes de David (1601)*, ed. A. H. Heider, 'Recent Researches in
the Music of the Renaissance', 74–6 (Madison, WI, 1995). Editions of the other two publications are
forthcoming from the Centre de Musique Ancienne of Tours. See also His, *Claude Le Jeune*, pp. 89–94.

musical settings. Godeau's verses were set by various figures in mid century.[78] At the simplest level, there were the easily sung tunes (again plagiarising the Genevan psalter) of Artus Aux-Cousteaux (Paris, 1656) and Antoine Lardenois (Paris, 1655). At the other extreme, Henry Du Mont's settings of the bishop's paraphrases – found in his *Meslanges*, 2–5 vv. (Paris, 1657) and *Airs à quatre parties* (Paris, 1663) – are far more serious and contrapuntal.

In a typically French way, the politics of confessionalism had an impact on this repertory. Godeau had himself been inspired to write these texts by the practice of the Protestant community of Antibes, in his provincial diocese of Grasse: 'Those whose separation from the [Catholic] Church we deplore have made the version [of the psalms] which they use famous for the sweet melodies, to which learned musicians adhere when they compose them. To know them [the tunes] by heart is for them a mark of their communion.'[79] Ironically enough, Godeau's own Catholic psalm texts had to be withdrawn in 1686 when their use by Protestants forcibly converted after the revocation of the Edict of Nantes became an embarrassment to the French Church.

Thus the French repertory developed within a more or less politically and linguistically unified nation (in contrast with Germany), with a clearly hegemonic Catholic majority whose musical activity, however, had to catch up with that of its opponents. For this reason, and also because of the traditional independence of Gallican Catholicism, religious orders took on a leading role, not least the Capuchins. The attractions of the Huguenot song repertory also meant that the Catholic production of vernacular music was more overtly polemical in its anti-Protestantism than was the case in Italy or even Germany.

The other factor which tended to channel sacred music into a predictable direction was the popularity of the *air de cour*. The bulk of vernacular Catholic editions was comprised of polyphonic or monophonic contrafacta of the lute-song repertory, of greater or lesser fidelity to the originals' verbal or affective content. The Jesuits led the way in sponsoring the rather different editions of contrafacta early in the century. *Les rossignols spirituels* (Valenciennes, 1616) featured dialogues and had a clear pedagogical bent; its two-voice musical settings by Peter Philips boasted clear and singable simple counterpoint. The monophonic *La pieuse allouette* (Valenciennes, 1619) and *La despouille d'Aegipte* (Paris, 1629) targeted 'libertine' secular airs as well as Protestant opponents, and the more ambitious *Odes chrestiennes* (Paris, 1625) included a wider range of devotional subjects in its four- and five-voice settings.[80]

---

78 This discussion relies heavily on Launay, *La musique religieuse en France*, pp. 324–45.
79 Ibid., p. 325.   80 Again, I summarise ibid., pp. 180–274.

Later in the century, greater aesthetic pretensions became evident in the Catholic repertory, seen first in the vernacular settings of Etienne Moulinié and Du Mont. The former's treatment of two Biblical paraphrases by Godeau, the Canticles of Moses and of the Three Boys in the Flaming Furnace, appeared in his *Meslanges de sujets chrestiens*, 2–5 vv. (Paris, 1658).[81] The latter motet is a close-woven three-voice contrapuntal work, while the former is a massive eighteen-section setting for five voices, varying strictly contrapuntal approaches with more modern ones. It is one of the largest and most striking pieces in the French vernacular repertory; whether Moulinié wrote it for his employer, the cathedral of Saint-Just in Narbonne, or for another (possibly purely aesthetic) purpose is not clear. Marin Mersenne singled out these two texts in his *Harmonie universelle* (Paris, 1636–7) as particular challenges to compositional ingenuity.

In the preface to the first book of his *Les airs spirituels* (Paris, 1672), Bénigne de Bacilly set himself the task of rescuing the genre of the sacred air from the disdain and suspicion in which the repertory, chiefly comprising contrafacta, was held. In the hands of Bacilly and François-Nicolas Fleury (*Airs spirituels à deux parties*, Paris, 1678), the form became a text-sensitive analogue to the *air de luth* at its moment of closing glory, a final step in the process of 'aestheticising' this originally unpretentious genre. At the end of the century, a similar raising of the level of vernacular sacred music is evident in the settings of Racine's *Cantiques spirituels*, the only text by the dramatist written explicitly for musical treatment. The four poems were crafted so as to be capable both of orthodox and of Jansenist interpretations (the latter in line with Racine's own education and leanings): the praise of charity (a standard Catholic theme, but also a defence against attacks on Quietism), the happiness of the just individual, the Christian's complaints about conflicts in the inner self, and the vanity of the world. In addition to Moreau's settings, the texts were also put to music by Jean-Noel Marchand and by Pascal Collasse, whose approaches compensated for the evident monotony of Moreau's. Collasse used a quasi-operatic variety of textures and declamatory styles, while the contrapuntal intensity of Marchand's treatment sets him apart from the others.[82] Another important publication in the same genre (but on different texts) was Claude Oudot's *Stances chrestiennes*, 2–4 vv. (Paris, 1692), whose popularity extended into the eighteenth century.

---

81 Ibid., pp. 363–5; E. Moulinié: *Meslanges de sujets chrétiens (1658)*, ed. J. Duron (Versailles, 1996), pp. xxix–xxx.

82 Favier, 'Les cantiques spirituels savants', pp. 195–205 (Moreau), 206–19 (Collasse), 251–64 (Marchand).

The Southern Netherlands

In the Dutch-speaking but Catholic Spanish Netherlands, volumes of contrafacta were also produced, among them the 51 pieces in Salomon Theodotus's *Het Paradys der geestelijcke en kerckelijcke Lof-Sangen* ('s-Hertogenbosch, 1621; with reprints up to 1638). In order to serve Catholics in the Calvinist United Provinces, the missionary Christiaan de Placker (1613–91) produced the simple 'cantasi come . . .'-like texts of his *Evangelisch-leeuwerck . . . op de evangelien der Sondagen* (Antwerp, 1667; the second edition of 1682 includes melodies borrowed and original), another testimony to Catholic musical devotion on Sundays. But the most important indigenous genre was the *cantio natalitia*, a piece sung within or outside the liturgy at Christmas or Epiphany.[83] It first appeared linked to yet another late medieval tradition, the *lof* (Marian praise service) on Saturday, which was essentially like the Italian or Spanish 'Salve' service. Some of its first texts were therefore in Latin, but the form increasingly employed vernacular (Dutch) texts, stanzaic and simply written in their praise of the Christ-Child or of the mystery of the Incarnation. Its form also gradually increased in complexity, with couplets or half-refrains added to its refrain structure, while its musical style seems to have moved from a more polyphonic texture to one emphasising the priority of the outer voices. In one of the few cases of influence between national vernacular genres, the *cantio* also seems to have paralleled some of the structural features of the *villancico*, at least in the couplet structure of Pedro Rimonte's (1565–1627) *El Parnaso español de madrigales y villancicos*, 4–6 vv. (Antwerp, 1614).[84]

Germany and the Northern Netherlands

The first striking feature of the vernacular German repertory, Lutheran or Catholic, is its extent. The authoritative modern catalogue (*DKL*) lists more than 2,000 printed editions between 1601 and 1700 (more must be lost). There must have been a large musically literate public, and a continuous market. As noted above, domestic settings (especially in Lutheran Germany) must have played a major role. The interplay of simple monophony, *Kantionalsatz* and more ambitious settings is also evident, as some editions contained all three.

The Lutheran repertory was conditioned by the unquestioned presence, central to the confession's entire self-expression, of a 'classic' repertory: the chorale melodies and tunes crafted by Luther and Johann Walther in the sixteenth century. This repertory was small and resistant to change or addition. Under the

---

83 Rasch, *De 'cantiones natalitiae' en het kerkelijke muziekleven in de zuidelijke Nederlanden gedurende de zeventiende eeuw*. This also provides a host of information on other paraliturgical music and on church music as a whole in the Spanish Netherlands.

84 Ibid., p. 136.

pressure of the calamity of war, and of the general uncertainty of the mid century, however, the technically conservative but affectively audacious textual style of Paul Gerhardt made its mark in the German hymn repertory, albeit not without opposition.[85] Gerhardt's highly personalised chorale texts were systematically disseminated by way of the musical settings of Johann Crüger (1598–1662). The latter's tunes achieved popularity through their relatively diatonic and conjunct lines, in combination with Gerhardt's affective imagery.

Not all hymnodic innovations were accepted universally, and the issue of which chorale would be adopted in a given town clearly depended on local circumstances. Johann Rudolf Ahle's tunes, for instance, were not always widely adopted in the cities of his native Thuringia.[86] Overall, there is a strong sense of the struggle between tradition and innovation in the chorale repertory, and of several different poetic and musical projects to intervene in it, such as Rist's *Himlische Lieder* set by Schop, and the various melodies for Gerhardt's *Geistliche Andachten* by Crüger and others.

Rist and his collaborators hold a central position in German devotional song viewed on the broadest scale.[87] Between 1643 and 1664, the poet published no fewer than eleven song collections, canonising a 'moderate' Baroque style of syntactic complexity but restrained imagery. These texts moved their composers to a variety of solutions, ranging from Schop's simplicity to the rhythmically ornamented, melodically irregular, and sometimes harmonically adventurous settings of Christian Flor in the two volumes of the *Neues musikalisches Seelenparadis* (Lüneburg, 1660, 1662; *DKL* 1660[07], 1662[08]).[88] Flor actually had to defend his practice in a letter to the poet printed in the preface to the second volume, also furnishing a group of skeletal versions of his melodies. The complexity of domestic sacred song is quite evident.

Beyond the chorales, the repertory of devotional song was marked by well-known names such as Heinrich Albert (1604–51), whose settings of poems by Simon Dach and others in his *Erster Theil der Arien oder Melodeyen* (Königsberg [Kaliningrad], 1638) mixed the secular and sacred. Lesser-known figures such as Christoph Werner (*c*. 1619–1650) and Georg Weber (*c*. 1615–after 1652) worked in and around the Baltic cities. One of Weber's publications, *Sieben Theile wohlriechender Lebens-Früchte eines recht Gott-ergebenen Herzen* – issued serially (Königsberg, 1648–9) and then collectively (Danzig, 1649) – gives a

---

85 The contested acceptance of Gerhardt (along with the melodic appeal of Crüger's tunes) is detailed in Jenny, 'Paul Gerhardt in der Musikgeschichte'.

86 See H. J. Moser's preface to the revised edition of Ahle's *Ausgewählte Gesangswerke*, 'Denkmäler der Deutscher Tonkunst', i/5 (Wiesbaden, 1957).

87 For Rist, a poet with a keen musical ear (he was himself an amateur performer), see Scheitler, *Das geistliche Lied*, pp. 230–71.

88 Kremer, 'Der "kunstbemühte Meister"'.

sense of the stylistic range of German sacred song in the middle of the century. Its 82 items are divided into seven volumes, of which the first three contain simple four- and five-voice hymns for daily devotion (awakening, work, meal-times), annual events (church feasts, the Passion) and hourly piety. The fourth combines motets and solo songs, and the higher aims of this and later volumes are evident in the figural poetry that introduces them (for example, a 'staircase of devotion' is a text shaped like a flight of stairs). The fifth includes Eucharistic hymns ('The soul's hunger and thirst for Christ'), the sixth ('On Love's time, or on spiritual love') adumbrates the Song of Solomon's idea of Christ as the soul's Bridegroom in cantatas for solo voice with strings, while the last volume contains music for a good Christian death. Weber noted that instruments could be used to substitute for lower vocal parts, and indirectly suggests that hymns must have been sung quickly, given that, he says, the motets need a slower beat.[89]

An example of the sophistication of this motet style is the second piece in the fourth volume, a five-voice setting (with continuo) of a typical text (with the heading 'Seelen-Seufzer nach Jesu Christo'; 'Soul-sighing for Jesus Christ'):

> Bist nicht du, du theurer Schatz,
> Mier verlassnen müden Seelen
> Noch ein sanfter Ruhe-platz,
> Wenn mich Kreuz und Trübsal quelen?
> Du bist ja mein starker Thurm
> Für der Feinde Trutz und Sturm.

[Are you not always, o precious treasure, / for me (a lost and tired soul), / a sweet resting-place / when cross and sorrow afflict me? / Yes, you are my strong tower / against the attack and storm of my enemies.]

The Catholic repertory, the uses of which have been noted above, obviously laboured under the pressure to respond to the popularity of Lutheran chorales. Its liturgical use also fluctuated, given that synods in different parts of Germany decreed widely different purposes for these sacred songs. The Mainz *Cantual* of 1605 allowed for vernacular settings at seven places during Mass, and the Münster orders of 1677 even permitted the substitution of Ordinary items by German songs.[90] But an earlier order from Münster in 1655 gave only the Elevation as a permissible location for vernacular music, a policy rather more

---

89 G. Weber, *Sieben Theile wohlriechender Lebens-Früchte eines recht Gott-ergebenen Herzen* (Danzig, 1649), iv: 243: 'Diese 5. Stimmigen [as opposed to the chorale-like pieces in the first three parts of the collection] bedürffen nun eine langsamere Mensur'. See also ibid., iv: 280: 'Auch in Mangel der Singe[-stimmen] kann man hier wie in den anderen 5-Stimmigen den Cantum allein singen lassen / die anderen Parteyen aber mit Instrumenten als Viol. di Bracien oder Viol. di Gamben'.

90 The Münster orders are given in Bäumker, *Das katholische deutsche Kirchenlied*, ii: 14–19.

characteristic of most diocesan decrees in the century. Issues similar to that of local Protestant usage were evident in an edition aimed at the Catholic enclaves in northern Germany, the *Nord-Sterns Führer zur Seeligkeit . . . Psalterbuch zum Gebrauch der teutschen Nation und in sonderheit der Nordländerer* (Amsterdam, 1671; *DKL* 1671⁰⁷). The seventeenth century also witnessed a rise in the quality of Catholic song collections. The *Catholisch Gesang-Buch* of Nicolaus Beuttner (Graz, 1602/*DKL* 1602⁰³; with eleven editions until 1718) incorporated the compiler's own notation of orally transmitted tunes, as well as his reworking of some earlier melodies in the interest of metric clarity.[91] It also drew on the Lutheran heritage of song, despite its appearance in the midst of the fierce re-Catholicisation of Styria led by Beuttner's Jesuit patrons.

Spain, Portugal and the Americas

The sheer size of the *villancico* repertory, the major (if not the only) form of vernacular sacred song in Spain and its American empire, renders the genre one of the largest (if least studied) of any in Europe.[92] It is also one of the most interesting. Many of the occasions with which the *villancico* was associated had to do with the corporality of Christ – Christmas, Epiphany and Corpus Christi – and this sense of the Saviour's humanity seems to have carried over into the texts and even the musical settings in yet another mixture of 'high' and 'low' styles. Other venues for its performance included the professing of nuns (an occasion for much music also in Italy, although it was sometimes banned), and other major Marian feasts (the Immaculate Conception, Visitation, Assumption).

The theatrical and literary nature of the texts rendered the form one of the most thematically and structurally 'open' in European literature. *Villancicos* could feature dialect (Asturian or Galician) or indigenous languages (in the *villancico negro*), providing an obvious way of incorporating native peoples in the colonial sacred repertory.[93] They could also use unusual or striking poetic conceits, and employ a wide range of musical styles. Their various structural elements – *tonada*, *responsión*, *coplas* (respectively, the 'tuneful' A section, the contrasting B section and the successive stanzas) – were also open to manipulation and recombination. Thus some of the earliest seventeenth-century examples, those of Juan Bautista Comes (1582–1643) for Valencia, feature simple responsory (ABCB) form, while later composers such as Diego Durón

91 See the postface to N. Beuttner, *'Catholisch Gesang-Buch' (1602)*, ed. W. Lipphardt (Graz, 1968).
92 Laird, *Towards a History of the Spanish Villancico*.
93 For examples by Gaspar Fernandes and Juan Gutiérrez de Padilla, see Stevenson, 'Ethnological Impulses in the Baroque Villancico'.

(1653–1731) combined the sections in freer ways. The genre even saw such structures as strophic variation.[94]

The inventiveness and fertility of *villancico* texts are evident, as well, in the poetic output of the major authors of the latter part of the century. The focus on specific occasions, and the immense popularity of the genre, meant that intertextuality was a constant in the words, as poets recalled, re-used, and re-circulated parts or wholes of other *villancicos*, even across continents.[95] The ways in which a single poetic conceit normally governed a given text is evident in Matías Ruiz's (*fl.* 1670) 'En la cárcel de Belén', in which sinful humanity is compared to the population of a prison all released by the Nativity, with the remainder of the text working out the opening image.[96] Furthermore, the innate theatricality of the Christmas and Epiphany scenes was clearly evident; the genre thus became a way both to enact Catholic belief and to forge a community, often (as in the Americas) for audiences of heterogeneous social and racial backgrounds. The sheer range of human experience included here, which is unparalleled in any other genre of vernacular sacred music, can be seen in the allegorical figures and personalised references found in the works of Manuel de León Marchante (1631–80).

The major Spanish composers also employed a wide variety of forms. Most *villancicos* are set in triple time, and the shorter sections employ a kind of arioso that has nothing to do with Italianate styles and structures. Like much other Iberian music, *villancicos* also employed modal/tonal types from early in the century. Comes's settings are still largely sixteenth-century in their pitch structure, but they range from unaccompanied solo song to polychoral settings.[97] The links between earlier settings and madrigals are evident in the works of Mateo Romero and Cristóbal de San Jerónimo, and continued in the works of Ruiz and Cristóbal Galán.

The popularity of the *villancico* also crossed the political divide between Spain and Portugal after 1640, as the Portuguese repertory included almost exclusively Spanish-language pieces. The melomane Portuguese King João IV collected some 2,300 of them, while the Coimbra sources studied by Manuel Carlos de Brito include largely Castilian-texted *villancicos*, albeit with some

94 As in the anonymous 'Con el sayal que se viste' for St Clare, found in the *villancico* sources from the Portuguese monastery of Santa Cruz in Coimbra; see M. C. de Brito (ed.), *Vilancicos do século XVII do mosteiro de Santa Cruz de Coimbra*, 'Portugaliae musica', 43 (Lisbon, 1983), pp. 1–11.

95 Some texts by the Zaragoza poet Vicente Sánchez (1643–80) find echoes in the Mexican Sor Juana Inés de la Cruz (1651–95), as noted in Laird, *Towards a History of the Spanish Villancico*, pp. 156–7. On Sor Juana's production of, and relation to, *villancicos*, see also Stevenson, 'Sor Juana Inés de la Cruz's Musical Rapports'.

96 Laird, *Towards a History of the Spanish Villancico*, pp. 92–6.

97 J. B. Comes, *Obras en lengua romance*, ed. J. Climent Barber, 4 vols (Valencia, 1977). For an overview, see Laird, *Towards a History of the Spanish Villancico*, pp. 69–97.

'patriotic' Portuguese pieces, as well.[98] *Villancicos* travelled quickly to Spanish America. Of the widespread examples in Guatemala, Mexico and Peru, perhaps the most obviously interesting are the some 50 surviving settings of the Spanish-born Juan Gutiérrez de Padilla (*c.* 1590–1664), *maestro de capilla* of Puebla cathedral from 1622 until his death. His works combine the typical local and ethnic forms and references ('gallegos', 'negrillas', 'jacaras'). Even such a piece as the six-voice Christmas *romance* 'De carámbano el día viste', starting with a series of straightforward strophes, bursts out into florid polyphony for its final praise of Mary: 'At seeing her the benevolent heavens celebrated her with tender songs, distichs like pearls for a bridal chamber that Bethlehem dedicated to her, honouring a magnanimous God'.[99]

England

As in other countries, domestic sacred song had a long tradition in England, even if the canonical consort-song repertory seems to have come to an end by the 1630s.[100] Hymns and metrical psalms (or paraphrases) were written throughout the century. But the devotional song, a rough counterpart to some of the Italian and German genres mentioned above, found its major expression across a divide of some three generations: the work of Henry Lawes (1596–1662) at mid century, and the chamber works of Henry Purcell (1659–95), circulating in manuscript and in John Playford's two-volume *Harmonia sacra, or Divine Hymns and Dialogues* (London, 1687, 1693).[101] John Wilson's *Psalterium carolinum*, for three voices, was inscribed by its composer, an Oxford professor, to God, to the memory of King Charles I and to the Anglican clergy. Its dedicatory poem by Henry Lawes provided a clear link to royal musical practice. The volume's texts, written in the king's voice, refer directly to his downfall and must have been arranged after 1649. The opening piece begins by characterising Charles's death as castigation (possibly also referring to the actual act of beheading): 'Thou, Lord, hast made us see that pious thoughts / Of future reformation for past faults, / Nor satisfy thy justice nor prevent / Always the strokes of just punishment'. The remaining 27 songs use the language of psalm paraphrases in delivering their penitential message.

98 For João IV's collection, see the *Primeira parte do index da livraria de musica . . .* (Lisbon, 1649), cited in R. Stevenson, *Vilancicos portugueses*, 'Portugaliae musica', 29 (Lisbon, 1976). For Coimbra, see de Brito (ed.), *Vilancicos do século XVII do mosteiro de Santa Cruz de Coimbra*, p. xvii.

99 R. Stevenson (ed.), *Christmas Music from Baroque Mexico* (Berkeley, 1974), pp. 80, 124–8. Stevenson also edits other examples, and provides contextual information.

100 For the sixteenth-century origin and use of the practice, see Milsom, 'Sacred Songs in the Chamber'.

101 For Purcell, see Fortune, 'The Domestic Sacred Music', esp. pp. 72–4 on 'O, I'm sick of life' mentioned above. For the roots of Purcell's early sacred songs in the vernacular tradition, see Holman, *Henry Purcell*, pp. 47–58.

The relatively limited compass of domestic sacred music (Lawes, Wilson, Richard Dering's Latin motets for Queen Henrietta Maria's devotion and chapel) prior to the Restoration has often been discussed by scholars. It is therefore all the more surprising that the young Henry Purcell would turn to these forms (in some 35 pieces) at several points in his career, and at times when he was experimenting with tradition and innovation. A first attempt just before 1680 seems to have been sparked by the psalm paraphrases of John Patrick, and Purcell responded with a series of three- and four-voice works which exploit a single affect and frame soloistic verses with imitative ensembles. These interesting but somewhat monochromatic works were followed a few years later by experiments in solo song, normally on freer texts by Cowley, Nahum Tate and others; some of these appeared in the first volume of Playford's *Harmonia sacra*, and possibly compensate for the decline in the composer's Anglican liturgical production under James II. These pieces are characterised by local effects (which are sometimes striking), and normally respond to the increased affective contrast in the texts by way of levels of dissonance or modal contrast. A third group of three pieces appeared in the second volume (1693) of the Playford anthology; these are the most obviously theatrical. They are also the ones in which moralising intent is most clouded: Nahum Tate's *The Blessed Virgin's Expostulation* and Purcell's setting focus on Mary's grief at her Child lost in the Temple, while 'In guilty night' devotes most of its energy to the Witch of Endor. Some of this music was written for personal or familial use, but the existence of a wider market is clear in the two volumes of the Playford series. Their content is also different, as the autochthonous pieces (Humfrey, Blow) in the first give way to greater international variety (Bonifazio Graziani, Carissimi) in the second.

Outside Europe

Far from the middle-to-high culture of Europe, devotional music played an important role in the spread of Western ideologies. Much of it was linked to Catholic missions in Asia, Africa and the Americas. But the ways in which remote parts of Europe could seem just as alien were evident in the production of hymn-tunes and songs for missions in Brittany. Here again, an otherwise 'unmusical' order, the Capuchins, was centrally involved. One missionary manual from 1702, studied by Launay, gave detailed instructions for the use of vernacular music – litanies and *cantiques spirituels* – in dramatic ceremonies such as the 'Address to the Cross' as well as in the catechism.[102] Simpler and easily memorisable melodies were obviously essential in this context.

---

102 Launay, *La musique religieuse en France*, pp. 345–9. For the ways in which missionaries in rural Europe operated under similar hostile conditions as on other continents, see Chatillon, *The Religion of the Poor*.

Music in the overseas missions was also part of the efforts of the religious orders, first and foremost the Jesuits, Franciscans and Dominicans. Sometimes polyphony was linked to feast-days and major celebrations, such as the pieces performed in the Philippines for the beatification of Ignatius Loyola and Francis Xavier in June 1611.[103] These included motets, *villancicos* and liturgical items, but also native genres ('Indian' dance and song). Similar syncretism followed in Manila for the ceremony of the 'defence' (a very Spanish idea) of the Immaculate Conception in 1620. Thus mission music also could involve the synthesis of local culture with Catholic devotion, a phenomenon most evident in the Jesuit missions in Paraguay, Bolivia and Brazil. Jesuits and Franciscans working in Brazil produced Portuguese contrafacta and new songs in the Tupí and Cariri languages, largely for didactic purposes as native peoples were evangelised. At the Mughal court, the playing of organs, wind instruments, and vocal music for feast-days, was part of an unsuccessful mission to the North Indian empire.

Domestic motets and vernacular dialogues

The devotional, ideological and pedagogical use of vernacular sacred music across Europe is clear, at least in general outline. The question remains, however, of whether and how Latin-texted pieces might have functioned in the same sorts of ways. Two rather different pieces, by composers born in the sixteenth century, may serve to illustrate the point. Schütz's five-section setting of a text compiled largely from the *Meditations* of pseudo-Augustine, 'Quid commisisti, o dulcissime puer?', occupies a prominent place in the 1625 *Cantiones sacrae* for four voices (nos. 4–8).[104] As with some of Grillo's poetry set by Tornioli, the words contemplate the innocence of the Christ-Child, and the text is carefully structured as a passage from meditation to conversion. The first part asks the question, addressing Christ, of the Infant's lack of guilt; the second provides the answer, moving to personal reflection; the third works around the binary contrast of human sin and Christ's unmerited suffering; the fourth is a catalogue of Christ's virtues, leading to the first direct Scriptural quotation; and the final part limns the Christian's resolve to suffer and be saved ('Calicem salutaris accipiam') in imitation of the Saviour.

Schütz cast the piece in a tonal type reminiscent of the penitential connotations of E-final pieces. All but the fourth section begin on E, and all but the last move elsewhere, setting the various psychological progressions of the text

---

103 These examples are taken from O'Malley *et al.* (eds), *The Jesuits*. This collection contains the following useful essays: Bailey, '*The Truth-Showing Mirror*'; Castagna, 'The Use of Music by the Jesuits in the Conversion of the Indigenous Peoples of Brazil'; Summers, 'The Jesuits in Manila'.

104 The new edition by H. Volckmar-Waschk, *Neue-Schütz-Ausgabe*, 8/9 (Kassel etc., 2004) provides a reliable text at the original pitch; for this motet, see pp. 17–45.

by shifting modal centres. The norms of the *concertato* motet – short phrases repeated (*anabasis*) and developed, alternating with declamatory sections – are combined with clear rhetorical sectioning. The climax of the first section is the combined motives for the double question 'Quae causa mortis / quae occasio tuae damnationis?' ('What is the cause of death, / what of your damnation?'). The introduction of first-person subjectivity in the second section leads to faster motion and to melodic reminiscences of the opening ('Quid commisisti, o dulcissime puer' echoed by 'Ego tuae mortis meritum'; 'What have You done, o sweetest young boy . . . I have earned Your death'). With its fundamental contrast, the third section is clearly the fulcrum and conceptual heart of the piece, and so its recall of 'ego' and its double counterpointing of subjects make perfect sense; after two sections that have concluded on A and C, the third's move to the furthest reaches of *cantus durus* on B is also no surprise. The first self-question of the text's speaker in the fourth section ('Quid tibi retribuam pro omnibus quae retribuisti mihi?'; 'What shall I give back to You for all that You have given to me?') is a direct scriptural quotation (Ps. 115: 12), and the sudden arresting of the musical pace and the temporary return to the modal world of E marks the beginning of the conversion experience. As might be expected for resolve, the final section remains firmly anchored in the world of E-cadences, also recalling the melodic subjects of the first and second sections ('vota mea reddam tibi Domine'; 'I will render my prayer to You, o Lord'). The piece ends with a reference to the personal song of eternal life ('et misericordias tuas in aeternum cantabo'; 'and I will sing of Your mercies in eternity'), set to another double subject, repeated in the longest anaphora of the motet and recalling the initial motion of the first part towards A.

If Schütz's piece displays a larger-scale kind of personalisation, a motet from perhaps a decade later by Ignazio Donati involves the direct speech between a Christian and the soul. The seemingly discontinuous text of 'O anima mea, narra mihi' stands in a long tradition of late medieval spirituality (for example, as articulated by Henry Suso) while evoking the 'fragmented' vocabulary of a contemporary saint, Maria Maddalena de' Pazzi.[105] The piece is found in Donati's *Il secondo libro de motetti a voce sola*, op. 14 (Venice, 1636), a collection of solo motets explicitly designed for the training of 'figlioli' and 'figliole' (older children or young teenagers), or nuns, and it appears in a kind of appendix, after the standard texts set and ordered by voice-type at the beginning of the book. Other texts set in this same section use literary conceits: an echo dialogue

---

105 For examples of such mystical speech, see M. M. de' Pazzi, *Selected Revelations*, trans. A. Maggi (New York and Mahwah, 2000), for example at pp. 240 or 246 (from Pazzi's *Dialogues*). Suso's mystical language was also evident in the tenors of Guillaume de Machaut's motets; see A. W. Robertson, *Guillaume de Machaut and Reims*, pp. 96–102.

for solo voice between the soul and God ('Quid agit, Domine?'), and a Christological piece based solely on vocal assonance ('Pete, pete et agam'). That this text should appear in a collection aimed partially at young nuns (and in one composed by Donati, who owed his appointment in Milan at least in part to Federigo Borromeo, the great supporter of female religious, their music and their mysticism) seems no accident.

> O anima mea, narra mihi, obsecro, dulcidinem contemplationis tuae. Quibus affluent delitiis non audis, non loqueris, rapta esne a dilecto tuo[?] O felix anima, quo abiisti, nuntia mihi.

> [O my soul, tell me, I beg you, the sweetness of your contemplation. To those who abound in delights you do not listen nor speak; have you been enraptured by your Beloved? O happy soul, let me know where you have gone.]

The piece, in three clear sections, employs vocal melismas as structural markers, together with the exploration of registers and modal octaves in the voice part, and a sense of progression away from its final in order to make its effect (the setting is in the transposed Hypodorian mode in *cantus mollis*, i.e., plagal, with a final on G). Each of the statements is rounded off by a long roulade ('contemplationis', '[es]ne a', 'nuntia'), of which the first two are repeated and extended at higher pitch levels (*anaphora*), while the final one is the longest (two bars) and thus provides climax. The exordium explores the higher pentachord of the modal octave ($g''-d''$) plus its extension (up to f''), while the question descends to the lower limit (d') of the octave at the mention of Christ who has abducted the soul ('dilecto tuo'). The opening also cadences on the final, G, while the question goes first to D and then (to reflect the soul's ultimate remove) B♭; the brief third part functions as a return. The essentially balanced structure of the piece finds its climax in this last section, where the melisma simultaneously serves pedagogical and rhetorical ends.

The importance of dialogues is clear from their irruption into even the solo motet repertory, as in the case of Donati's book and others early in the century. As a genre, dialogues had a history in the sixteenth century, although most pieces so designated were either secular or liturgical.[106] Of all the new century's modes of mystical understanding, however, the dialogue as a heuristic means (for turning away from sin, resolving crisis and conflict, or achieving understanding) had an unparalleled weight in spiritual thought.[107] Quite apart

---

106 The Latin repertory has been studied in Noske, *Saints and Sinners*; Smither, 'The Latin Dramatic Dialogue and the Nascent Oratorio'; Smither, *A History of the Oratorio*, i. Smither has also edited vernacular dialogues in *Oratorios of the Italian Baroque*, i: *Antecedents of the Oratorio: Sacred Dramatic Dialogues, 1600–1630*, 'Concentus Musicus', 7 (Laaber, 1985), pp. 235–501.

107 Certeau, *La fable mystique*, pp. 216–25, underlines the centrality of the genre to mystic discourse and its contribution to the waning distinction between divine and human *oratio*.

from any teleological perspective on the genre as the precursor of the oratorio, this special quality seems to have generated composers' choices. Dialogues set the most varied kinds of discourse, from Biblical (or Apocryphal) stories to colloquies of the soul with Christ (or, in some Catholic versions, with guardian angels). Because of their stress on psychological change, they were attractive to both Protestants and Catholics, and Latin dialogues were set throughout Europe for almost the whole century, only tailing off towards the end in the wake of turns away from the medium in devotional literature. Here as well, the mystically charged interchanges of the Song of Solomon provided a language ready to be employed in Marian, Christological and sanctoral pieces.

The influence of the dialogue was also manifest in vernacular settings. Their message of resolved conflict or conversion had a special relevance to oratories, schools (Protestant and Catholic) and domestic venues. Besides the numerous dialogues in the Italian *canzonetta spirituale* and *laude* editions mentioned above, and even in the cantata repertory, they also appear in Anton Ulrich of Braunschweig's *Himlische Lieder* (1655; the Christian Soul and its Spouse, a paraphrase of Song of Solomon 7), Michna's *Loutna česká* (Adam and the angel after the Fall), and other sources too numerous to mention here. In a conjunction of the new German poetics, the dialogue, the Song of Solomon, and music, the Zittau organist Andreas Hammerschmidt (1611/12–1675) included twelve selections from Opitz's version of the Canticles in his *Geistlicher Dialogen ander Theil*, 1–2 vv. (Dresden, 1645); this followed quickly upon the first volume, *Dialogi, oder Gespräch zwischen Gott und einer gläubigen Seelen*, 2–4 vv. (Dresden, 1645).

The major Roman venue for the form was the Oratorio della Vallicella, but although the dialogue thus shared an institutional context with the later Latin or vernacular oratorio, it should not be viewed merely as its precursor. The dialogue repertory is evident in Giovanni Francesco Anerio's *Selva armonica* (1617) and most spectacularly in his *Teatro armonico spirituale di madrigali* (1619); several other vernacular dialogues were published by Cifra and Quagliati, among others. In best Oratorian fashion, the twelve extremely elaborate dialogues in Anerio's 1619 volume concentrate on moments of individual conversion, obedience or decision, taken largely from the Old and New Testaments. The Old Testament stories range from Adam and Eve to David and Goliath, while the final piece in the volume, 'Eccone al gran Damasco', expands on the story of St Paul's conversion.[108] Its militarisation of Saul's character (by way of the *concitato genere*, in an instrumental *combattimento*) immediately links the setting

---

108 Smither (ed.), *Oratorios of the Italian Baroque*, i: 422–69.

to the topic of martyrdom, an important theme in contemporary devotional life. And the addition of an entire Christian side of the dialogue (by way of Ananias, represented by a double choir to match the scoring for Saul's fellow persecutors earlier in the setting) provides a series of musically marked characters with whom the listener could identify. In its length and resources, 'Eccone al gran Damasco' is theatre indeed, not so much in prefiguring the oratorio as in providing a staging-place for the real battle, that of Christ for Saul's soul.

There was nothing of quite this weight in the Protestant repertory, but the themes of dialogues remained similar. One of Georg Weber's portrays the encounter between the Christian soul, sick from sin, and its Bridegroom in a setting for soprano (Soul), bass (Jesus), two violins and continuo:[109]

> [*Soul:*] Du ewiger Lebens-Held,
> Mein Breutgam und mein Seelen-Schatz,
> Willkommen, willkommen sey deine Liebte
> Daß du nicht verschmähest, mich hoch Vertrübte
> Besuchst das Herz, den Sünden-Platz!
> Aus lauter Gnad als dier's gefällt
> Erlaubst du so was Angst zerschöllt.
> . . .
> [*Jesus:*] Du arme Seele, du
> Geliebte Braut von Ewigkeit,
> Ich hörte dein Schreyen – dein Weh' ohn' maßen
> Da wallte mein Herze – nicht kont' ichs laßen
> Ich mußte sehn dein grosses Leid,
> Dich trosten, dier helffen schaffen Ruh'
> Und eilend so dier sprechen zu.
> . . .

[(*Soul:*) You, eternal hero of life, / my bridegroom and soul's treasure, / let Your love be welcome, / since You do not disdain me, the troubled one, / but visit my heart, that place of sin, / out of grace, since it pleases You, / You permit that which destroys fear . . .

(*Jesus:*) You poor soul, you / beloved bride for all eternity, / I heard your cries, your pain beyond measure, / and my heart trembled, I could not avoid it, / but I had to see your great suffering, / comfort you, help you find peace, / and speak while rushing towards you . . .]

Weber structures this emotive text as declamatory strophic variation.

109 'Der seltene Flug und kurze Verzug, oder das Gespräch bey der unbeschreiblichen freuden-reichen Erscheinung Jesus, des allerliebsten Himels-Breutgams, in der Sünden-kranken Seele', no. 3 in pt 6 of Weber's *Sieben Theile wohlriechender Lebens-Früchte eines recht Gott-ergebenen Herzen* (1649).

Oratories and oratorios

Unlike other sacred genres arising in the seventeenth century, the oratorio has always enjoyed serious study, if only on the basis of the later examples of the genre: given the centrality of Handel's works to both German and English musical cultures of the nineteenth century, it is no surprise that early scholars would look back for precedents. Here, again, the broad trends of the music have been magisterially outlined.[110] In the wake of the revival of seventeenth-century opera, oratorios (largely Roman and Neapolitan) have also recently found their way into the early-music performing repertory. In that sense, the genre needs little emphasis as to its importance. Rather, the task for future research is that of detailing the specific circumstances of oratorio production and patronage, examining its music analytically (beyond simple formal taxonomy), and in the broadest view, obtaining a sense of its importance in the religious, aristocratic and civic ideologies which it seems to have served. The most insightful scholarship has focussed on its place of origin, Rome,[111] and on some northern Italian centres as well as Naples.[112]

Although there is much discussion about the parameters of the term, the early oratorio can be described, if not defined, as an extended sacred composition with characters (sometimes also with narrator and chorus), to be sung in an oratory or similar location chiefly during Lent as an exemplification of a moral point. The centrality to the genre of Passion meditation and sermonising is clear, with the music driving home the point of repentance by means of positive or negative example.[113] Most texts involve at least three characters (with female

---

110 See Smither, *A History of the Oratorio*. For an up-to-date overview, see the entry by G. Massenkeil and J. Riepe in the new *MGG: Sachteil*, vii (Kassel, 1997), cols 741–58. Speck, *Das italienische Oratorium*, is a new account of the repertory from the viewpoint of the interaction of poetry and music. The latest bibliography is Smither, 'A Survey of Writings since 1980 on Italian Oratorio of the Seventeenth and Eighteenth Centuries'.

111 André Maugars (*Response faite à un Curieux, sur le sentiment de la musique d'Italie* (1639) trans. H. W. Hitchcock (Geneva, 1993), pp. 9–12) describes performances of 'une histoire du vieil Testament, en forme d'une Comedie spirituelle', clearly some kind of oratorio, at the Oratorio del Crocefisso in Rome in the late 1630s. For Roman oratorio, see the following texts by Arnaldo Morelli: *'Il tempio armonico'*; 'Alessandro Scarlatti maestro di cappella in Roma ed alcuni suoi oratori'; *'Il Theatro spirituale* e altre raccolte di testi per oratori romani del Seicento'; 'La circolazione dell'oratorio italiano nel Seicento'. On Roman style, see Witzenmann, 'Zum Oratorienstil bei Domenico Mazzocchi und Marco Marazzoli'. The study of the genre has recently been advanced significantly by the essays in Franchi (ed.), *Percorsi dell'oratorio romano*. For a catalogue of the entire repertory, see Franchi, *Drammaturgia romana*. Some of the earliest oratorios (by Pietro della Valle, Francesco Foggia, Bonifazio Graziani and Marco Marazzoli) are reproduced in H. E. Smither (ed.), *The Italian Oratorio, 1650–1800*, i (New York, 1986).

112 Arnold and Arnold, *The Oratorio in Venice*; Besutti, 'Oratori in corte a Mantova: tra Bologna, Modena e Venezia'; Cafiero and Marino, 'Materiali per una definizione di "oratorio" a Napoli nel Seicento'; Crowther, *The Oratorio in Modena* and *The Oratorio in Bologna*; Hill, 'Oratory Music in Florence'. One recent study has shown the patterns of patronage by one Bolognese confraternity in the last decade of the century, linking its sponsorship of Good Friday performances to Lenten devotional themes; see Riepe, *Die Arciconfraternita di S. Maria della Morte in Bologna*.

113 Botti Caselli, 'Parafrasi e meditazioni sulla Passione nell'oratorio romano del Seicento'.

roles normally played by men or boys) and consist of roughly 500 lines. Typical of the mid-century style, much of the writing is in declamatory recitative, with space for ensembles and choruses; as the century went on, and again as in opera, there was a growing division into recitative and aria, with a closing chorus. Although some of the early (and Latin) examples are in one part, the majority of the repertory is constructed in two parts, which were normally separated by a sermon.

Oratorios came in different languages and had different associations in different geographical areas. The situation is clouded by problems of genre and of attribution. There are essentially two different views of the oratorio's roots, one which stresses its links with the long tradition of musical dialogue and *sacre rappresentazioni*, and one which emphasises the differences between dialogue and oratorio.[114] Depending on this view, some of the sacred dialogues discussed above may or may not be viewed as (proto-)oratorios; similarly, the work sometimes described as the 'first' oratorio, Emilio de' Cavalieri's *Rappresentazione di Anima, et di Corpo*, staged in the oratory linked to S. Maria in Vallicella in Rome in February 1600, might better be seen as a *sacra rappresentazione*, or a particularly Oratorian kind of counter-Carnival sacred opera. In terms of attribution, the number of Latin oratorios credited to Giacomo Carissimi (1605–74) ranges from eleven to fourteen, although contemporary sources apply the term 'oratorium' to only five such works (none by Carissimi).[115]

Even when the genre was treated by theorists, problems are apparent. The veteran librettist Arcangelo Spagna (*c.* 1632–1726) prefaced his collection of thirteen *Oratorii, overo Melodrammi sacri* (Rome, 1706) with a 'Discorso intorno a gl'Oratorii' codifying his own practice, dating back to 1656: the abolition of the *testo* (narrator), the use of exclusively real (not allegorical) characters, and the adherence to the Aristotelian unities.[116] These trends were far from universal in oratorio texts, however, and no musical settings of Spagna's texts survive. No less troublesome is the other issue normally used to distinguish oratorios from other dramatic genres, that oratorios were unstaged. While most oratorios clearly were performed without sets, costume and acting, some variously combined all three in different degrees,[117] and the obvious question

114 To oversimplify, these views are represented respectively by Smither (*A History of the Oratorio*) and by Noske (*Saints and Sinners*); see also Dixon, 'Oratorio o motetto?'. In Sicily, the term 'dialogo' was used until the end of the century; see Buono, 'Forme oratoriali in Sicilia nel secondo Seicento'.

115 For contemporary manuscripts (in Bologna, Civico Museo Bibliografico Musicale) using the term, see Jones, *The Motets of Carissimi*, i: 112. For attributions to Carissimi, see ibid., i: 118 (11); Dixon, *Carissimi*, p. 33 (12); G. Massenkeil, *MGG: Personenteil*, iv (Kassel, 2000), col. 207 (13 or 14).

116 A. Spagna, *Oratorii overo melodrammi sacri* (Rome, 1706; repr. Lucca, 1993). On Spagna's aesthetics, see Sarnelli, 'Percorsi dell'oratorio per musica come genere letterario fra Sei e Settecento'.

117 For an early eighteenth-century example, see Smither, *A History of the Oratorio*, i: 269.

of when a 'staging' might or might not be a staging is rendered complex by the use of some kind of scenic apparatus even in oratory halls and the like (a backdrop, a cloud machine etc.). It is a moot point whether it is worth trying to make distinctions within this broad field (for example, among dramatic motets, oratorios and sacred operas) on the basis of content, function, location and mode of presentation.

Many oratorios in Latin were associated with the renowned Oratorio del Santissimo Crocefisso in central Rome (the confraternity associated with this institution would sponsor such performances into the eighteenth century). The Italian-text variety was almost contemporaneous in its origin; among other works with claims to precedence, the two librettos written by Francesco Balducci (1579–1642) towards the end of his highly chequered life, *La fede* and *Il trionfo* (published in his *Rime*, Rome, 1645), deal respectively with the Abraham and Isaac story and with the Coronation of the Blessed Virgin (a version of *Il trionfo* was set to music by Carissimi, the only surviving musical record of these two librettos). The theme of Marian praise is also present in the first musical piece referred to as an 'oratorio' by its author, the traveller, polymath and amateur composer Pietro della Valle (1586–1652): his *Per la festa della santissima purificatione*, a 'dialogo in musica' written for Rome in 1640.[118] The vernacular form would have far greater diffusion and cultural impact over the course of the century. The connection to the Chiesa Nuova (S. Maria in Valicella) and its oratory (constructed by Francesco Borromini) was important but by no means exclusive. Outside these two sites, important Roman venues (all for vernacular oratorios) included S. Girolamo della Carità, S. Maria dell'Orazione e Morte, and S. Maria della Rotonda.

The association of oratorios with Lent (therefore countering the excesses of Carnival) and with a penitential message remained constant, at least in mid century. Even if their performance did not induce a definitive change of life (*metanoia*) in their audiences (as opposed to the sixteenth-century idea of a single conversion evident, for instance, in the biography of Ignatius Loyola), the conclusions to be drawn from them could be drastic. Carissimi's *Jephte*, for instance, may have elicited Kircher's enthusiasm not only for its moving music but also for its lesson (taken from Judges 11: 29–40). This story of filial murder (Jephte vows to sacrifice to God the first being he sees should he be granted victory in battle, who turns out to be his daughter) was shaped by the anonymous librettist into a narrative with added (non-Biblical) affective dialogue between Jephte and his daughter, and a long closing lament with the youth of Israel ('Plorate, filii Israel, plorate, omnes virgines . . . lamentamini';

118 Ibid., i: 174–85.

'Weep, children of Israel, weep, all ye virgins . . . lament') with a memorable setting for the daughter solo and then for the whole ensemble.

Although this may seem an odd story for Lent, it resonated with a particularly Roman search for extreme (*magis*) sanctity found in sacred oratory and represented also in the Barberini sacred operas of the 1630s, with their heroes and heroines (St Alexis, St Eustachius) brilliantly characterised by the librettist Giulio Rospigliosi and set to music by Stefano Landi and Virgilio Mazzocchi. A closer look at Kircher's – and Carissimi's – world both complicates and clarifies the meaning. The foremost Catholic Biblical exegete of the century, the Southern Netherlandish Jesuit Cornelius a Lapide (1567–1637), was teaching at the Collegio Romano, one of the two Jesuit seminaries in Rome (the other was the Collegio Germanico, where Carissimi was based). In his commentary on this passage in Judges, and in a way proper to his order, Lapide duly weighed the divided Patristic opinion on the holiness or sinfulness of Jephte's vow, finally deeming it 'imperfect' because of its good intent but wrong means, and hence typical of the Old Testament, a stage of salvational history that the Passion had overcome (which explains the suitability of this oratorio's theme for Lent).[119] Lapide gave the killing of the daughter (omitted in Carissimi's *Jephte*) a 'tropological' (spiritual) meaning as equalling the individual's mortifying his or her soul for God. He then listed eight ways in which Jephte was a forerunner of Christ, ending with the daughter's sacrifice prefiguring Christ's sacrifice of His flesh and humanity. As for the 'many years' that the daughters of Israel would mourn the daughter after her death, Lapide paralleled their long-lasting weeping to the collective grieving of the Church, expressed by singing the Lamentations of Jeremiah during Holy Week to mourn the sins of the faithful. Thus the text and music of Carissimi's *Jephte* united the idea of penance, the imperfection of humanity, the perfect sacrifice of Christ prefigured by His forerunners, and the collective grief of the Church to be expressed later in the Lenten season. In Seicento Rome, Holy Week witnessed the full panoply of musical expression, from chant through polyphony to monody. The long anaphoric calls of 'lamentamini' with which the oratorio ends linked a historical past to a ritual future by way of a performative present.

The topos of sacrifice runs through the repertory, both Latin and Italian, with the Abraham and Isaac story particularly prominent (Balducci's *La fede*, Carissimi's *Abraham et Isaac*, and a host of dialogues). Like penance, sacrifice restored the natural order of the universe, and its musical enactment became increasingly central to the representation of religious and social ideologies. By the last decade of the century, however, Italian oratorios covered the whole range

---

119 C. a Lapide, *Commentarius in Iosue, Iudicum, Ruth . . .* (Antwerp, 1653), pp. 153–6.

of salvational history, from Adam (Carlo Donato Cossoni's *L'Adamo*, Bologna, 1663; the music is lost), the first sin after the Fall (Cain and Abel, the subject of oratorios by Carissimi, Bernardo Pasquini, Alessandro Melani and Alessandro Scarlatti), through various Old Testament figures, a restricted number of New Testament personages, early Christian martyrs, medieval urban saints, all the way to the Last Judgement (Carissimi's *Judicium extremum*; Giuseppe Cavallo's *Il giudizio universale*, Naples 1681; Bernardo Sandrinelli's oratorio with the same title, Venice, 1684; and Charpentier's *Extremum Dei judicium* for Paris, H. 401). Often performed during Holy Week, the oratorio enacted some of the fundamental values of a community just at the moment in the ritual calendar when its salvational act was commemorated.

In their range of themes, oratorios could also embody civic and dynastic pride. Thus an early Modenese oratorio, Antonio Ferrari's *San Contardo d'Este* (1677), commemorated a sainted forebear of the ducal house. This piece survives in manuscript placed at the head of a series of oratorios collected by, and performed for, Duke Francesco II d'Este, and with such pieces as Alessandro Stradella's *La Susanna* (1681), the Modenese court became the most innovative centre for oratorios in Italy. Other oratorios could praise a patron (in)directly: a recent study of Prince Livio Odescalchi (1658–1713) – the nephew of Pope Innocent XI and a major supporter of the arts – lists some 41 works with direct or hidden political references produced in and around Rome during the second half of the century.[120] There could also be other contemporary resonances: the victory of the Christian forces over the Turks near Vienna in 1683 was lauded in oratorios such as Alessandro Melani's *Golia abbattuto* (Rome, 1684; based on the story of David and Goliath)[121] and Giovanni Battista Bassani's *La morte delusa dal pietoso suffragio* (Ferrara, 1686).

Because of its centrality to articulations of spiritual identity, and also its adaptability, the vernacular oratorio seems to have enjoyed a flourishing growth in Italy in the last quarter of the century. Regular performances of oratorios in Bologna and Lucca date from around 1660, while Ferrara and Brescia witnessed annual performances from the early 1670s onwards. The Venetian Oratorians' experiments in that same decade, with works by Giovanni Legrenzi (1626–90), failed for lack of funds, and the genre moved to the Ospedale dei Mendicanti and Ospedale della Pietà in the 1690s.[122] To be sure, some cities did not host regular oratorios until the new century (for example, Genoa and Turin), but many others up and down the peninsula – and whether or not the seats of

---

120 Franchi, 'Il principe Livio Odescalchi e l'oratorio "politico"'.
121 Broom, 'Political Allegory in Alessandro Melani's Oratorio *Golia abbattuto*'.
122 The continuity with Oratorian practice elsewhere is underlined in Steffan, 'L'oratorio veneziano tra Sei e Settecento'.

ducal courts – began annual series of oratorios in the last two decades of the century (Palermo, Cremona and Ancona in 1678; Milan, Mantua and Siena from about 1680; Parma and Naples from 1685). Choices of plot and character could be geared to serve as models for specific audiences (e.g., in academies or educational institutions).[123] The oratorio also extended its reach into non-penitential contexts, with performances during the Christmas season,[124] and also for Marian feasts.

As we have already seen in the case of Carissimi's *Jephte*, the continuing growth of the genre raises questions of its location within the theological debates of the time. Perhaps it is too much to read subtle Quietism into the patient suffering of the title-characters in Alessandro Scarlatti's (1660–1725) first vernacular oratorio, *Agar ed Ismaele esiliati* (Rome, 1683; libretto by Giuseppe Domenico de Totis). Yet Scarlatti's two settings of the story of Judith and Holofernes, *La Giuditta* (Rome, 1693, 1697) – the first in heroic mode and the second far more introverted and focussing on psychological issues – show how the same Biblical episode could generate completely different emphases.[125] A generation earlier, Queen Christina of Sweden's commissioning of *Sant'Alessio* (Rome, 1675; music by Bernardo Pasquini, and libretto by Pietro Filippo Bernini, the son of the sculptor) inevitably evokes the parallels between the queen and St Alexis, both offspring of noble lineages who abandoned everything for religious convictions (at least nominally, in the case of the queen) and who lived in marginalised conditions. Similarly, the choice of martydom as a subject for oratorios had obvious resonances for contemporary notions of Christian heroism,[126] while representations of gender performed important roles in identifying the different kinds of virtues and agency allotted to male and female protagonists.

Some of the most striking oratorios are to be found among the examples of the genre by Alessandro Stradella (1639–82).[127] His six oratorios demonstrate a wide variety of literary approaches and musical styles, ranging from the introspection of the three on early Christian and medieval figures (*S. Giovanni Chrisostomo, S. Editta, S. Pelagia*) to the more extrovert Biblical pieces (*Ester, S. Giovanni Battista, La Susanna*). *S. Giovanni Battista* (Rome, 1675), dealing with the patron saint of Florence and written for the church of S. Giovanni dei Fiorentini in Rome, and *La Susanna* (Modena, 1681) are both examples of the genre in which sexuality (and not simply gender, or simply female sexuality)

---

123 An excellent example is provided by the Collegio de' Tolomei in Siena; see Lorenzetti, 'Natura e funzioni nell'oratorio di collegio'.
124 Marx, '". . . da cantarsi nel Palazzo Apostolico"'; Gianturco, '*Cantate spirituali e morali*'.
125 Dubowy, 'Le due "Giuditte" di Alessandro Scarlatti'.
126 Kendrick, 'Martyrdom in Seventeenth-Century Italian Music'.
127 Gianturco, *Alessandro Stradella*, pp. 187–206.

was an important part of the plot and the characterisation.[128] In all these works, however, the mixture of contrapuntal sections ('madrigali'), duets and trios, and solo writing imparts a richness and diversity not always to be found in other contemporary examples.

The oratorio spread from Italy. Charpentier, who studied in Rome, took the Latin-texted model back to Paris, and his works written for various venues there take as their point of departure (if not arrival) Roman practices of the mid century.[129] His longest oratorio is also the one closest to its Biblical source: *Judith, sive Bethulia liberata* (H. 391) again accentuates interior psychological characterisation (notable in the rondeau setting of the heroine's prayer), a characteristic shared by the large-scale martyrological drama *Caecilia virgo et martyr* (H. 397).

A subgenre of the oratorio intimately bound to royal devotion and to the place of its performance was the Passion *sepolcro* of the Habsburg court in Vienna.[130] These were particular emblems of the *pietas austriaca*; they were performed during Holy Week, either on Thursday in the dowager Empress Eleonora Gonzaga's chapel, or on Friday in the Hofkapelle. For both, there were scenic elements: the Thursday performance took place around a simulacrum of Christ's tomb (hence the generic label), and for the Friday one, the court architect and designer Ludovico Buracini provided a painted backdrop related to the oratorio's theme. More important, their librettos by court poets (Francesco Sbarra and Nicolò Minato), and sometimes by the composer Antonio Draghi (1634/5–1700) and even by Emperor Leopold I (ruled 1658–1705), provide complex allusions to, and allegories on, the Habsburg devotion to the Cross. Their music, normally provided by Draghi, who was court *Kapellmeister*, mixed recitative, arioso and full-fledged arias.[131] The pious and musical Leopold I's support for the *sepolcro* – he sometimes composed them himself – was crucial to a genre which would last into the new century, even after Draghi's death. However, the prestige of the *sepolcro* did not impede the production of Lenten

---

128 See the analysis of Susanna's opening aria, focussing on tonal markers of eroticism and attraction, in McClary, *Conventional Wisdom*, pp. 9–21.

129 The chief study remains H. W. Hitchcock's pioneering 'The Latin Oratorios of Marc-Antoine Charpentier'.

130 For its origins at mid century, see Saunders, 'The Antecedents of the Viennese *Sepolcro*'; for a somewhat different account, see Seifert, 'The Beginnings of Sacred Dramatic Musical Works at the Imperial Court of Vienna'. The documentable performances are listed in Seifert, *Die Oper am Wiener Kaiserhof im 17. Jahrhundert*, while Bletschacher, *Rappresentazione sacra*, provides an introduction to the genre and also some librettos. For the overlap of the *sepolcro* themes with contemporary Italian poetry, and for the use of Passion images, see respectively Girardi, 'Al sepolcro di Cristo', and Zane, 'Oratorii al SS. Sepolcro e immaginario barocco'. Sadly, M. Gouloubeva's otherwise excellent *The Glorification of Emperor Leopold I in Image, Spectacle, and Text* omits discussion of the *sepolcri* and oratorios altogether.

131 Schnitzler, 'The Sacred Dramatic Music of Antonio Draghi'. It is symptomatic of the state of research on this genre that only two of the essays in Sala and Daolmi (eds), '*Quel novo Cario, quel divino Orfeo*', consider Draghi's sacred works, and neither from a musical standpoint.

and Advent oratorios for Vienna and Prague: Draghi wrote 16 (compared with his 26 *sepolcri*).

In Germany, Schütz's *historiae* for Easter (1623; SWV 50) and for Christmas (*c.* 1660, published in part in 1664; SWV 435) take their point of departure from Renaissance models (unaccompanied recitative in the former; *intermedi*-like sections in both). But both are set apart from other works in the Protestant tradition by virtue of their musical complexity in the concerted sections. Late in the century, the one partially extant work by Dieterich Buxtehude (*c.* 1637–1707) in Lübeck that bears some similarity to the oratorio, his *Die Hochzeit des Lammes* (we have the text but not the music), would seem from its libretto to have been very interesting in musical terms. This draws on the parable of the wise and foolish virgins (also with quotations from the Song of Solomon) and was performed as the *Abendmusik* on two Advent Sundays in 1678.[132] Other examples in Protestant Germany, in Latin or in the vernacular, seem to have more to do with the dialogue tradition, and the oratorio's impact in Germany would be delayed until Reinhard Keiser's (1674–1739) working of the newly codified genres of opera and oratorio for the Hamburg public around 1700.

Part of that codification was due to the oratorios of Alessandro Scarlatti, and although he was less prolific here than in operas, the range of his works in the genre, and also the new approaches to the subject-matter, suggest that a new era was at hand.[133] Among his oratorios written before 1700, two of several Latin-texted ones for the Roman Oratorio del Santissimo Crocefisso survive (*Samson vindicatus*, 1695; *Davidis pugna et victoria*, 1700). The vernacular pieces were written on commission variously for Rome, Naples and Modena. They engage with Old Testament heroines (Hagar, Judith), again St Mary Magdalene (*Il trionfo della gratia*, Rome, 1685), virgin martyrs (St Theodosia and St Ursula), and the Passion viewed via the Addolorata (*I dolori di Maria sempre vergine*, Naples, 1693). These topics include a wide range of dramatic situations, including the patient suffering of Hagar, the decision for martyrdom of Theodosia, the penance of Mary Magdalene, and the strikingly different but hardly passive heroism seen in the two settings of the Judith story. The stress on female agency is not entirely new, but it is now much in the foreground.

Scarlatti brought to the oratorio a greater homogeneity in terms of aria forms – the da-capo aria dominates, though not exclusively – plus a new sense of instrumental virtuosity reflecting the affect of the textual moment, and a limiting of contrapuntal sections to the conclusions of the now-standard two parts or to moments of high dramatic tension. The two settings of *La Giuditta*

132 Snyder, *Dieterich Buxtehude*, pp. 60–62.

133 Poultney, 'The Oratorios of Alessandro Scarlatti'; Morelli, 'Alessandro Scarlatti maestro di cappella in Roma ed alcuni suoi oratori'.

(the 1693 one to a libretto by Cardinal Pietro Ottoboni and the 1697 setting to one by Pietro's father, Antonio) provide some of the best examples.[134] Despite, as we have seen, their different focus, they are linked by subtle intertextual references, they each have cantata-like features such as the interruptions of the lullaby meant to put Holofernes to sleep, and they also contain difficult instrumental obbligato parts used for purposes ranging from deception to divine invocation (as with 'Non ti curo, o libertà' and 'Tu che desti' in the 1697 setting). The closing ensemble of the 1693 setting, 'Alle palme, alle gioie', is also particularly striking as it promises heavenly rewards after the tribulation of earthly life.

The end of the century

For vernacular sacred and spiritual music, as in many other fields, the final decades of the seventeenth century marked a codification of past styles and a decisive turn in aesthetics. In the case of the Italian repertory, the three editions of the Florentine priest Matteo Coferati's collection *Corona di sacre canzoni, o laude spirituali* (1675, 1689, 1710) represented the end of the great anthologising tradition. Coferati's first edition contains some 283 texts, some ancient (i.e., from the fifteenth century on) and more new, about a third of which were given monophonic tunes (tenor clef) while the rest had 'cantasi come...' indications. The second edition dropped some older texts and added dialogues and even an 'Alarm-bell for sinners' (a simple pentachord up and down). Coferati also transposed pitch levels and 'regularised' metres, another example of the standardisation of vernacular repertories typical of all Europe in an age of increasing rationalism. The mixture of ancient and modern in Coferati's collection, however, represents the last innovation in a repertory whose social base was currently being undermined by mercantilism, and whose propagation through the religious orders was irretrievably damaged by their decline.

The other decisive change at the end of the century was the revocation of the Edict of Nantes and the consequent dispersal of the French Huguenot community. The vernacular traditions of *grand-siècle* France were profoundly changed by this event. In Germany, Gerhardt's innovations were accepted in part, often on a local level, but the major codifications of Pietism would not arrive until the new century. The profile of vernacular sacred music began to be altered significantly. In Catholic Europe, and except for the *villancico*, it was

---

134 Dubowy, 'Le due "Giuditte" di Alessandro Scarlatti'. I also draw on two unpublished papers: Tcharos, 'Alessandro Scarlatti's Two *Judiths*', and my own 'Intertextuality in Scarlatti's Cambridge [1697] *Giuditta*'.

marginalized and channelled into the hymn repertory, only to be revived at the end of the eighteenth century in Emperor Joseph II's church reforms as a vehicle for liturgy. In Protestant lands, the new century saw a canonisation of the standard hymns, and a shift in creative energy towards the new currents, among them Pietism and English Methodism. The Lutheran chorale had already undergone a process of 'de-modalisation' and rhythmic 'levelling'.[135] An age of individualised creativity in vernacular repertories was over.

But the great flowering of devotional song in the seventeenth century suggests some wider implications for cultural history. The sheer size of the output reveals the spread of musical ability both geographically and socially, including artisans, city-dwellers, and other 'middle-level' social layers. The range of musical expression of devotion went far outside the ritual prescriptions of liturgy, underscoring the centrality of religious thought to personal and corporate identity. For example, the real battles, on a local and national level, in the Lutheran tradition might lead us to question the monolithic nature of the chorale repertory and to re-emphasise local practice. In addition, the enormous number of solo and ensemble devotional songbooks suggests that for all the symbolic weight of the hymns and their role in articulating confessional identity, the actual musical experience of ordinary Lutherans was far wider than scholarship has realised (a point that van den Tempel's family portrait, discussed above, could underscore for the Mennonites). Similarly, the diversity and activity of Catholic song might call into question the traditional anthropological explanation of Catholic Baroque art as an attempt to overwhelm the senses of an essentially passive audience; rather, the *laude*, hymns, chaconnes and song-settings underscore the initial point of this chapter, namely the remarkable similarities in musical activity, at least on a personal level, across different confessions in seventeenth-century Europe.

Bibliography

Adler, I., *La pratique musicale savante dans quelques communautés juives en Europe aux XVIIe et XVIIIe siècles*. Paris and The Hague, 1966

Ameln, K., 'Kirchenliedmelodien der Reformation im Gemeindegesang des 16. und 17. Jahrhunderts'. In Dürr and Killy (eds), *Das protestantische Kirchenlied*, pp. 61–71

Ardissino, E., *Il Barocco e il sacro: la predicazione del teatino Paolo Aresi tra letteratura, immagini e scienza*. Vatican City, 2001

Arnold, D., and Arnold, E., *The Oratorio in Venice*. London, 1986

Ashbee, A. (ed.), *William Lawes (1602–1645): Essays on His Life, Times and Work*. Aldershot, 1998

---

[135] The point is underscored by the three synoptic examples in sources from 1500 to 1666 given in Ameln, 'Kirchenliedmelodien der Reformation im Gemeindegesang des 16. und 17. Jahrhunderts'.

Bailey, G. A., '*The Truth-Showing Mirror*: Jesuit Catechism and the Arts in Mughal India'. In O'Malley *et al.* (eds), *The Jesuits*, pp. 380–401

Bäumker, W., *Das katholische deutsche Kirchenlied in seinen Singweisen von den frühesten Zeiten bis gegen Ende des siebzehnten Jahrhunderts*. 4 vols, Freiburg im Breisgau, 1883–1911; repr. Hildesheim, 1962

Bert, M., 'La musique à la Maison Royale Saint-Louis de Saint-Cyr'. *Recherches sur la musique française classique*, 5 (1956), 91–127

Besutti, P., 'Oratori in corte a Mantova: tra Bologna, Modena e Venezia'. In Besutti (ed.), *L'oratorio musicale italiano e i suoi contesti*, pp. 365–421

Besutti, P. (ed.), *L'oratorio musicale italiano e i suoi contesti (secc. XVII–XVIII)*. Florence, 2002

Bianconi, L., *Music in the Seventeenth Century*, trans. D. Bryant. Cambridge, 1987

Blazey, D., 'The Litany in Seventeenth-Century Italy'. Ph.D. thesis, University of Durham (1990)

Bletschacher, R., *Rappresentazione sacra: Geistliches Musikdrama am Kaiserhof*. Vienna, 1985

Botti Caselli, A., 'Parafrasi e meditazioni sulla Passione nell'oratorio romano del Seicento'. In Franchi (ed.), *Percorsi dell'oratorio romano*, pp. 1–53

Boulay, L., 'Les cantiques spirituels de Racine mis en musique au XVIIe siècle'. *XVIIe siècle*, 14 (1957), 79–92

Braun, W., *Die Musik des 17. Jahrhunderts*, 'Neues Handbuch der Musikwissenschaft', 4. Wiesbaden and Laaber, 1981

Broom, W. A., 'Political Allegory in Alessandro Melani's Oratorio *Golia abbattuto*'. *Journal of Musicological Research*, 3 (1981), 383–97

Buono, L., 'Forme oratoriali in Sicilia nel secondo Seicento: il dialogo'. In Besutti (ed.), *L'oratorio musicale italiano e i suoi contesti*, pp. 115–39

Butt, J., *Music Education and the Art of Performance in the German Baroque*. Cambridge, 1994

Cafiero R., and Marino, M., 'Materiali per una definizione di "oratorio" a Napoli nel Seicento: primi accertamenti'. In D. A. D'Alessandro and A. Ziino (eds), *La musica a Napoli durante il Seicento*. Rome, 1987, pp. 465–510

Castagna, P., 'The Use of Music by the Jesuits in the Conversion of the Indigenous Peoples of Brazil'. In O'Malley *et al.* (eds), *The Jesuits*, pp. 641–58

Certeau, M. de, *La fable mystique, XVIe–XVIIe siècles*. Paris, 1982

Cessac, C., *Marc-Antoine Charpentier*. Paris, 1988

Chafe, E. T., *Monteverdi's Tonal Language*. New York, 1992

Chatillon, L., *The Religion of the Poor*. Cambridge, 1997

Couchman, J. P., 'Felice Anerio's Music for the Church and for the Altemps *Cappella*'. Ph.D. thesis, University of California, Los Angeles (1989)

Crowther, V., *The Oratorio in Modena*. Oxford, 1992

The Oratorio in Bologna, 1650–1730. Oxford, 1999

Dahlenburg, J., 'The Motet *c.* 1550–1630: Sacred Music Based on the Song of Songs'. Ph.D. thesis, University of North Carolina at Chapel Hill (2001)

Dixon, G., 'Oratorio o motetto? Alcune riflessioni sulla classificazione della musica sacra del Seicento'. *Nuova rivista musicale italiana*, 17 (1983), 203–22

Carissimi. Oxford, 1986

Dubowy, N., 'Le due "Giuditte" di Alessandro Scarlatti: due diverse concezioni dell'oratorio'. In Besutti (ed.), *L'oratorio musicale italiano e i suoi contesti*, pp. 259–88

Dürr, A., and Killy, W., (eds), *Das protestantische Kirchenlied im 16. und 17. Jahrhundert*, 'Wolfenbüttler Forschungen', 31. Wiesbaden, 1986

Favier, T., 'Les cantiques spirituels savants (1685–1715): contribution à l'histoire du sentiment religieux à la fin du Grand Siècle'. Ph.D. thesis, University of Paris 4 (1997)

Le chant des muses chrétiennes: cantiques spirituels et dévotion (1685–1715). Paris, 2005

Filippi, D. V., '*Selva armonica*: Giovanni Francesco Anerio e la musica spirituale a Roma nel primo Seicento'. Ph.D. thesis, University of Pavia (2003)

'Spiritualità, poesia, musica: per ricomprendere le esperienze oratoriane del Cinque–Seicento'. *Annales oratorii*, 3 (2004), 91–137

Fischer, A., and Tümpel, W., *Das deutsche evangelische Kirchenlied des 17. Jahrhunderts*, 6 vols, Gütersloh, 1904–16

Fischer, P., 'Music in Paintings of the Low Countries in the 16th and 17th Centuries'. *Sonorum speculum*, 50–51 (1972), 1–128

Fisher, A. J., *Music and Religious Identity in Counter-Reformation Augsburg, 1580–1630*. Aldershot, 2004

Föcking, M., '*Rime sacre*' und die Genese des barocken Stils: Untersuchungen zur Stilgeschichte geistlicher Lyrik in Italien, 1536–1614*. Stuttgart, 1994

Fortune, N., '[Purcell:] The Domestic Sacred Music'. In F. W. Sternfeld *et al.* (eds), *Essays on Opera and English Music in Honour of Sir Jack Westrup*. Oxford, 1975, pp. 62–78

Franchi, S., *Drammaturgia romana: repertorio bibliografico cronologico dei testi drammatici pubblicati a Roma e nel Lazio, secolo XVII*. Rome, 1988

'Il principe Livio Odescalchi e l'oratorio "politico"'. In Besutti (ed.), *L'oratorio musicale italiano e i suoi contesti*, pp. 141–258

Franchi, S. (ed.), *Percorsi dell'oratorio romano: da 'historia sacra' a melodramma spirituale*. Rome, 2002

Fumaroli, M., *L'âge de l'éloquence: rhétorique et 'res literaria' de la Renaissance au seuil de l'époque classique*. Geneva, 1980

Geck, K. W., *Sophie Elisabeth Herzogin zu Braunschweig und Lüneburg (1613–1676) als Musikerin*. Saarbrücken, 1992

Gianturco, C., '*Cantate spirituali e morali*, with a Description of the Papal Sacred Cantata Tradition for Christmas 1676–1740'. *Music & Letters*, 73 (1992), 1–31

Alessandro Stradella (1639–1682): his Life and Music. Oxford, 1994

Girardi, M., 'Al sepolcro di Cristo: una poetica consuetudinaria; *religio*, prassi, devozione, rappresentazione nei riti oratoriali del Venerdì Santo, a Vienna e a Venezia'. In '*Il tranquillo seren del secol d'oro*': musica e spettacolo musicale a Venezia e a Vienna fra Seicento e Settecento*. Milan, 1984, pp. 127–96

Gouloubeva, M., *The Glorification of Emperor Leopold I in Image, Spectacle, and Text*. Mainz, 2000

Greyerz, K. von, 'Religiöse Erfahrungsräume im Reformiertentum'. In Münch (ed.), '*Erfahrung*' als Kategorie der Frühneuzeitgeschichte*, pp. 307–16

Haapalainen, T. I., *Carolus Pictoriuksen suomenkieliset virret vuodelta 1622*. Helsinki, 1975

Harrán, D., *Salomone Rossi: Jewish Musician in Late Renaissance Mantua*. Oxford and New York, 1999

Hill, J. W., 'Oratory Music in Florence, i: *Recitar cantando*', 'ii: At San Firenze in the Seventeenth and Eighteenth Centuries', 'iii: The Confraternities from 1655 to 1785'. *Acta musicologica*, 51 (1979), 108–36, 246–67; 58 (1986), 129–79

His, I., *Claude Le Jeune (v. 1530–1600): un compositeur entre Renaissance et Baroque*. N. p., 2000

Hitchcock, H. W., 'The Latin Oratorios of Marc-Antoine Charpentier'. Ph. D. thesis, University of Michigan (1954)

Hobbs, W. C., 'Giovanni Francesco Anerio's *Teatro armonico spirituale di madrigali*: a Contribution to the History of the Oratorio'. Ph. D. thesis, Tulane University (1971)

Holman, P., *Henry Purcell*. Oxford and New York, 1994

Holzem, A., 'Bedingungen und Formen religiöser Erfahrung im Katholizismus zwischen Konfessionalisierung und Aufklärung'. In Münch (ed.), *'Erfahrung' als Kategorie der Frühneuzeitgeschichte*, pp. 317–32

Ingen, F. van, 'Die Wiederaufnahme der Devotio Moderna bei Johann Arndt und Philipp von Zesen'. In D. Breuer *et al.* (eds), *Religion und Religiosität im Zeitalter des Barock*, 'Wolfenbüttler Arbeiten zur Barockforschung', 25. Wiesbaden, 1995, pp. 467–76

Jenny, M., 'Paul Gerhardt in der Musikgeschichte'. In B. Hangartner and U. Fischer (eds), *Max Lütolf zum 60. Geburtstag: Festschrift*. Basle, 1994, pp. 177–204

Jones, A. M., *The Motets of Carissimi*. 2 vols, Ann Arbor, 1982

Kemper, H. G., 'Das lutherische Kirchenlied in der Krisen-Zeit des frühen 17. Jahrhunderts'. In Dürr and Killy (eds), *Das protestantische Kirchenlied im 16. und 17. Jahrhundert*, pp. 87–107

Kendrick, R. L., '*Sonet vox tua in auribus meis*: Song of Songs Exegesis and the Seventeenth-Century Motet'. *Schütz-Jahrbuch*, 16 (1994), 99–118

Celestial Sirens: Nuns and their Music in Early Modern Milan. Oxford, 1996

'Intertextuality in Scarlatti's Cambridge *Giuditta*'. Unpublished paper presented at a symposium on the oratorio at Northwestern University (Evanston, IL), May 2001

'Martyrdom in Seventeenth-Century Italian Music'. In P. Jones and T. Worcester (eds), *From Rome to Eternity: Catholicism and the Arts in Italy, ca. 1550–1650*. Leiden, 2002, pp. 121–41

The Sounds of Milan, 1585–1650. New York, 2002

Kertzer, D. I., and Barbagli M. (eds), *Family Life in Early Modern Times, 1500–1789*. New Haven and London, 2001

Kremer, J., 'Der "kunstbemühte Meister": Christian Flor als Liedkomponist Johann Rists'. In F. Jekutsch, J. Kremer and A. Schnoor (eds), *Christian Flor (1626–1697) – Johann Abraham Peter Schulz (1747–1800): Texte und Dokumente zur Musikgeschichte Lüneburgs*. Hamburg, 1997, pp. 52–85

Kroll, J. (ed.), *Die Tagebücher des Sigmund von Birken*, i. Würzburg, 1971

Laird, P. R., *Towards a History of the Spanish Villancico*. Warren, MI, 1997

Launay, D., *La musique religieuse en France du Concile de Trente à 1804*, 'Publications de la Société Française de Musicologie', 3/5. Paris, 1993

Leopold, S., *'Al modo d'Orfeo': Dichtung und Musik im italienischen Sologesang des frühen 17. Jahrhunderts*, 'Analecta musicologica', 29. Laaber, 1995

Lorenzetti, S., 'Natura e funzioni nell'oratorio di collegio: il caso del "S. Ermenegildo", da tragedia Latina a "sacra tragedia musicale"'. In Besutti (ed.), *L'oratorio musicale italiano e i suoi contesti*, pp. 289–308

Macchiarella, I., *Il falsobordone fra tradizione orale e tradizione scritta*. Lucca, 1995

Martin, L. W., 'Scipione Dentice: a Neapolitan Contemporary of Gesualdo'. *Studi musicali*, 10 (1981), 217–40

Marx, H. J., "". . . da cantarsi nel Palazzo Apostolico": Römische Weihnachtsoratorien des 17. Jahrhunderts'. In P. Petersen (ed.), *Musikkulturgeschichte: Festschrift für Constantin Floros zum 60. Geburtstag*. Wiesbaden, 1990, pp. 415–24

McClary, S., *Conventional Wisdom: the Content of Musical Form*. Berkeley and Los Angeles, 2000

Milsom, J., 'Sacred Songs in the Chamber'. In J. Morehen (ed.), *English Choral Practice*. Cambridge, 1995, pp. 161–79

Mischiati, O., 'Per una bibliografia delle fonti stampate della lauda (1563–1746)'. *Note d'archivio per la storia musicale*, n.s. 4 (1986), 203–25

Monson, C. A., *Disembodied Voices: Music and Culture in an Early Modern Italian Convent*. Berkeley, 1995

Morelli, A., 'Alessandro Scarlatti maestro di cappella in Roma ed alcuni suoi oratori: nuovi documenti'. *Note d'archivio per la storia musicale*, n.s. 2 (1984), 114–44

'Il *Theatro spirituale* e altre raccolte di testi per oratori romani del Seicento'. *Rivista italiana di musicologia*, 21 (1986), 61–143

'*Il tempio armonico*': musica nell'Oratorio dei Filippini in Roma (1575–1705)', 'Analecta musicologica', 27. Laaber, 1991

'La circolazione dell'oratorio italiano nel Seicento'. *Studi musicali*, 26 (1997), 105–86

Moretti, M. R., 'L'Oratorio filippino di Chiavenna e la pratica del "contrafactum" nelle "Canzonette spirituali e morali" (1657)'. In M. Caraci Vela and R. Tibaldi (eds), *Intorno a Monteverdi*. Lucca, 1999, pp. 367–420

Münch, P. (ed.), '*Erfahrung' als Kategorie der Frühneuzeitgeschichte*, 'Historische Zeitschrift, Beihefte', n.s. 31. Munich, 2001

Noske, F., *Music Bridging Divided Religions*. 2 vols, Wilhelmshaven, 1989

Saints and Sinners: the Latin Musical Dialogue in the Seventeenth Century. Oxford, 1992

O'Malley, J. W., et al. (eds), *The Jesuits: Cultures, Sciences, and the Arts 1540–1773*. Toronto, 1999

O'Regan, N., 'Processions and their Music in Post-Tridentine Rome'. *Recercare*, 4 (1992), 45–80

Paquette-Abt, M., 'A Professional Musician in Early Modern Rome: the Life and Print Program of Fabio Costantini, c. 1579–c. 1644'. 2 vols, Ph.D. thesis, University of Chicago (2003)

Pinto, D., 'The True Christmas: Carols at the Court of Charles I'. In Ashbee (ed.), *William Lawes*, pp. 97–120

Poultney, D. J., 'The Oratorios of Alessandro Scarlatti: their Lineage, Milieu, and Style'. Ph.D. thesis, University of Michigan (1968)

Poźniak, P., *Musica antiqua polonica: Renasans*, iii: *Pieśni/Songs*. Kraków, 1994

Repertuar polskiej muzyki wokalnej w epoce Renesansu. Kraków, 1999

Pozzi, G., 'Rose e gigli per Maria: un'antifona dipinta'. In Pozzi, *Sull'orlo del visibile parlare*. Milan, 1993, pp. 185–214

Rasch, R. A., *De 'cantiones natalitiae' en het kerkelijke muziekleven in de zuidelijke Nederlanden gedurende de zeventiende eeuw*. Utrecht, 1985

Reardon, C., *Holy Concord Within Sacred Walls: Nuns and Music in Siena, 1575–1700*. New York and Oxford, 2002

Riepe, J., *Die Arciconfraternita di S. Maria della Morte in Bologna: Beiträge zur Geschichte des italienischen Oratoriums im 17. und 18. Jahrhundert*. Paderborn, 1998

Robertson, A., '"Choice Psalms": a Brother's Memorial'. In Ashbee (ed.), *William Lawes*, pp. 175–95

Robertson, A. W., *Guillaume de Machaut and Reims*. Cambridge, 2002

Roche, J., 'On the Border Between Motet and Spiritual Madrigal: Early 17th-Century Books that Mix Motets and Vernacular Settings'. In A. Colzani *et al.* (eds), *Seicento inesplorato: l'evento musicale tra prassi e stile, un modello di interdipendenza*. Como, 1993, pp. 305–17

Rorke, M. A., 'The Spiritual Madrigals of Paolo Quagliati and Antonio Cifra'. Ph.D. thesis, University of Michigan (1980)

Rostirolla G. (with contributions by D. Zardin and O. Mischiati), *La lauda spirituale fra Cinque e Seicento: poesie e canti devozionali nell'Italia della Controriforma*. Rome, 2001

Rybarič, R., 'Zur Frage des sogenannten "slowakischen" Bestandteils in dem mehrstimmigen Gesangbuch aus Lubica'. *Musicologica slovaca*, 7 (1978), 213–24

Sala, E., and Daolmi, D. (eds), *'Quel novo Cario, quel divino Orfeo': Antonio Draghi da Rimini a Vienna*. Lucca, 2000

Sarnelli, M., 'Percorsi dell'oratorio per musica come genere letterario fra Sei e Settecento'. In Franchi (ed.), *Percorsi dell'oratorio romano*, pp. 137–97

Sarti, R., *Europe at Home: Family and Material Culture, 1500–1800*. New Haven and London, 2002

Saunders, S., *Cross, Sword, and Lyre: Sacred Music at the Imperial Court of Ferdinand II of Habsburg (1619–1637)*. Oxford, 1995

'The Antecedents of the Viennese *Sepolcro*'. In A. Colzani *et al.* (eds), *Relazioni musicali tra l'Italia e Germania nell'età barocca*. Como, 1997, pp. 61–84

Scheitler, I., *Das geistliche Lied im deutschen Barock*. Berlin, 1982

Schilling, H., 'Die Konfessionalisierung von Kirche, Staat und Gesellschaft: Profil, Leistung, Defizite und Perspektiven eines geschichtswissenschaftlichen Paradigmas'. In W. Reinhard and H. Schilling (eds), *Die katholische Konfessionalisierung*. Gütersloh, 1995, pp. 1–49

Schnitzler, R., 'The Sacred Dramatic Music of Antonio Draghi'. Ph.D. thesis, University of North Carolina at Chapel Hill (1971)

Seifert, H., *Die Oper am Wiener Kaiserhof im 17. Jahrhundert*. Tutzing, 1985

'The Beginnings of Sacred Dramatic Musical Works at the Imperial Court of Vienna: Sacred and Moral Opera, Oratorio and *Sepolcro*'. In Besutti (ed.), *L'oratorio musicale italiano e i suoi contesti*, pp. 489–511

Silbiger, A., 'The Autographs of Matthias Weckmann: a Re-evaluation'. In A. Ø. Jensen and O. Kongsted (eds), *Heinrich Schütz und die Musik in Dänemark zur Zeit Christians IV*. Copenhagen, 1989, pp. 117–43

Smither, H. E., 'The Latin Dramatic Dialogue and the Nascent Oratorio'. *Journal of the American Musicological Society*, 20 (1967), 403–33

A History of the Oratorio, 4 vols. Chapel Hill, NC, 1977–2000

'The Function of Music in the Forty Hours' Devotion of 17th- and 18th-Century Italy'. In C. P. Comberiati and M. C. Steel (eds), *Music from the Middle Ages through the Twentieth Century: Essays in Honor of Gwynn McPeek*. New York, 1988, pp. 149–74

'A Survey of Writings since 1980 on Italian Oratorio of the Seventeenth and Eighteenth Centuries'. In Besutti (ed.), *L'oratorio musicale italiano e i suoi contesti*, pp. 3–19

Snyder, K. J., *Dieterich Buxtehude: Organist in Lübeck*. New York, 1987

Speck, C., *Das italienische Oratorium 1625–1665: Musik und Dichtung*, 'Speculum Musicae', 9. Turnhout, 2003

Stefani, G., *Musica e religione nell'Italia barocca*. Palermo, 1975

Steffan, C., 'L'oratorio veneziano tra Sei e Settecento'. In Besutti (ed.), *L'oratorio musicale italiano e i suoi contesti*, pp. 423–52

Stevenson, R., 'Ethnological Impulses in the Baroque Villancico'. *Inter-American Music Review*, 14 (1994), 67–106

'Sor Juana Inés de la Cruz's Musical Rapports: a Tercentenary Remembrance'. *Inter-American Music Review*, 15 (1996), 1–21

Summers, W. J., 'The Jesuits in Manila, 1581–1621: the Role of Music in Rite, Ritual, and Spectacle'. In O'Malley *et al.* (eds), *The Jesuits*, pp. 659–79

Tcharos, S., 'Alessandro Scarlatti's Two *Judiths*'. Unpublished paper presented at a symposium on the oratorio at Northwestern University (Evanston, IL), May 2001

Thiel, P. J. J. van, *et al.*, *All the Paintings of the Rijksmuseum in Amsterdam*. Amsterdam, 1976

Veit, P., 'Die Hausandacht im deutschen Luthertum: Anweisungen und Praktiken'. In F. van Ingen and C. N. Moore (eds), *Gebetsliteratur der frühen Neuzeit als Hausfrömmigkeit: Funktionen und Formen in Deutschland und den Niederlanden*, 'Wolfenbüttler Forschungen', 92. Wiesbaden, 2001, pp. 193–206

Volckmar-Waschk, H., *Die 'Cantiones sacrae' von Heinrich Schütz: Entstehung, Texte, Analysen*. Kassel etc., 2001

Wackernagel, P., *Das deutsche Kirchenlied von der ältesten Zeit bis zu Anfang des XVII. Jahrhunderts*. 5 vols, Leipzig, 1864–77

Whitfield, C., and Martineau, J. (eds), *Painting in Naples from Caravaggio to Giordano*. London, 1982

Witzenmann, W., 'Zum Oratorienstil bei Domenico Mazzocchi und Marco Marazzoli'. *Analecta musicologica*, 19 (1979), 52–93

Wollny, P., 'Johann Christoph Bachs Hochzeitsdialog *Meine Freundin, du bist schön*'. In M. Märker and L. Schmidt (eds), *Musikästhetik und Analyse: Festschrift Wilhelm Seidel zum 65. Geburtstag*. Laaber, 2002, pp. 83–98

Worp, J. A., 'Nog eens Utricia Ogle en de muzikale correspondentie van Huygens'. *Tijdschrift der Vereeniging voor Nord-nederlands Muziekgeschiedenis*, 5 (1897), 133–4

Zane, M., 'Oratorii al SS. Sepolcro e immaginario barocco: aspetti dell'espressionismo fastoso delle devozioni musicali leopoldine'. In *'Il tranquillo seren del secol d'oro': musica e spettacolo musicale a Venezia e a Vienna fra Seicento e Settecento*. Milan, 1984, pp. 197–224

12

Image and eloquence: secular song

MARGARET MURATA

In ceremonies such as a Mass of thanksgiving or the performance of a royal birthday ode, the music embraces the aims of the event as a whole, whether trumpets are playing simple tattoos or the best soprano warbles the verse of the court poet. Such public displays could proclaim and reinforce political and social hierarchies in many ways, at the very least by confirming the prestige of the employer–patrons of those who made the music. Yet even in the largest cities of Europe, such public performances would have been fairly rare occasions. What of more ordinary and personal music-making: the servant singing as she washes linens, or the Dutch merchant's wife at her keyboard? Samuel Pepys singing Carissimi to his guitar, or castratos singing love-duets in a palatial but private performance? What we call secular vocal music comes from all social classes and includes traditional songs, popular songs, and music to the newest poetry; music written down as well as music learnt only by ear; tunes sung to oneself, sung with friends or accompanied by a professional instrumental ensemble.

General surveys have tended not to explore such diversity in seventeenth-century music-making and have typically been content to open the new century by calling attention to a shift from singing in parts to accompanied solo song. For the period roughly between 1580 and 1620 one finds comparisons drawn between the 'old' unaccompanied polyphonic madrigal (and its presumed emphasis on counterpoint) on the one hand, and on the other, the solo madrigal with continuo accompaniment (and its presumed homophony). But both belong to the same fairly refined repertory for the literati and musically literate. For many composers in these years, having to choose between counterpoint and homophony, or between polyphony and monody, was neither self-evident nor necessary. These decades witness the peak production of the Italian canzonetta in three and four parts, the major manuscript collections of Spanish *romances* (predominantly in three parts), and nearly two-thirds of the prints of *airs de cour*, whose predominantly homophonic textures appeared in various scorings from five or six voices to lute airs or monophonic melodies. In England, airs were sung in four parts, to written-out lute accompaniments, or even in duet with just a bass viol.[1] Giovanni Girolamo Kapsberger (*c.* 1580–1651), an Austrian noble and theorbist in Rome, published one volume of five-voice madrigals with continuo in 1609, seven of villanellas for one to four voices between 1610 and 1640, and only two of solo arias, in 1612 and 1623 (the latter also contains five duets). The non-madrigalian genres, furthermore, were not uniformly 'light' in tone (nor, for that matter, were madrigals uniformly serious). Orazio Vecchi (1550–1605), in particular, extended the subjects and expressive range of the canzonetta, and composers set strophic canzonetta verse as musical madrigals, just as madrigal texts could be treated as strophic canzonettas.[2] Equally, solo aria styles of the 1640s show up in the latest polyphonic madrigals.[3] Such diversity, from individual composers, within print anthologies, and even in individual works, was far more common than we might think. Monteverdi's Seventh Book of madrigals of 1619, given the title *Concerto*, contains continuo madrigals and other varied types of compositions (such as a variation-duet over a Romanesca bass) for one, two, three, four and six voices. Although nothing is in the old-fashioned five-voice texture, only 4 of its 29 pieces are solo songs. This volume especially influenced the composition of few-voiced secular music with continuo in Germany. The French appear to have become acquainted with continuo practice only in the 1630s; the first Ballard publication, however, in which all the compositions required continuo bass was a 1647 print by the Italian-trained Dutchman Constantijn Huygens (1596–1687), containing Italianate settings of Latin, Italian and French texts.[4]

Surviving scores, moreover, hardly give a complete picture of seventeenth-century singing. In most compositions with or without continuo, any line or lines could be made more or less prominent than the others by instrumentation, and any line could be rendered more audibly soloistic by a singer's embellishments. Instrumental accompaniments, whether notated, improvised, or both notated *and* improvised upon in performance, could be variously contrapuntal or chordal depending on the rhetorical or expressive needs of the moment. Melodies in themselves, of course, have always passed from singer to singer, without need of notation. In short, musical styles, textures and modes of performance did not conform to tidy or stable categories, despite their apparent uniformity in the sources. This is also true of sixteenth-century secular repertories. But given the greater variety of seventeenth-century song, it is useful to keep in mind that alternative *genres of performance* may have had more significance than different genres of song *per se*, or than any one version of a work.

1 As in W. Corkine's *Second Book of Ayres* (London, 1612; repr. 1977).
2 Assenza, *La canzonetta dal 1570 al 1615*, pp. 172–3, 227–57.
3 Whenham, ' "Aria" in the Madrigals of Giovanni Rovetta'.
4 C. Huygens, *Pathodia sacra et profana* (Paris, 1647), ed. F. Noske (Amsterdam, 1957; repr. 1976).

At any time, 'domestic' singing – whether in a farmhouse, country manor or urban apartment – is perhaps the most widespread kind of music and also the kind most subject to simplification as well as elaboration. Thus we are concerned with performance practices that depend as much on social context as on musical genre.

Social contexts of secular singing

Historical evidence

Because singing 'in private' does not require expenditure each time it happens, the historical evidence for it is scattered and of necessity incomplete. The main sources comprise documents, wordbooks, scores, visual depictions and verbal descriptions. Evidence such as household account books or notarial records tends to provide information about the well-to-do. We can know the number and names of chamber singers retained by the King of France, for example (five to eight at mid century), but this does not tell us what they sang in his chambers, such as Latin prayers at meals. The household of one Roman cardinal (Cardinal Montalto) numbered around 170 individuals *circa* 1613. It included a soprano (wife of a composer-in-residence), a castrato and two basses. Research in this case has matched up scores with musicians, yielding some idea of what they may have sung for their patron, although not when or under what circumstances.[5] Notarial documents in Paris reveal the kinds of people who privately studied lute, organ and singing, including a printer's son, a parliamentary lawyer, a priest and a lord.[6] Instruments that accompanied singing, such as spinets, lutes or guitars, appear in the inventories of women's dowries and in the wills of the bourgeoisie – notaries, doctors, grocers, a tax collector, a master pewterer. Collections of scores are also sometimes noted in inventories of the estates of the civic elite. These were the kinds of individuals with the income and time to enjoy music as a leisure activity.

The lives of classes lower in society are not often reflected in contracts regarding property and services. Printed wordbooks and broadsheets that offer only words to melodies that people already knew, as well as manuscript copies of song texts, provide evidence of more popular repertories and of a much vaster oral culture. Devotional and secular poems are often side by side, both equally part of 'popular' music. Printed and manuscript wordbooks may also include chord-symbols for guitar accompaniment. Several volumes of the words to over 400 Italian 'canzonette musicali' were published by Remigio Romano

---

5 Hill, *Roman Monody, Cantata, and Opera from the Circles around Cardinal Montalto*, i: chap. 5.
6 Jurgens (ed.), *Documents du Minutier Central concernant l'histoire de la musique*, ii: 70–71.

between 1618 and 1625. By comparing those texts provided with guitar chords by Romano with the musical scores published elsewhere, Silke Leopold has concluded that 'singing to the Spanish guitar at this time seems to have taken place on what was the most low-brow level of musical practice . . . in which the only important part of the musical composition to survive was the tune'.[7] In the *rasgueado* style of guitar accompaniment (strumming across all strings), chord formations are limited by available fret-positions and so are often 'inverted' or reconstituted with respect to prevailing norms. But amateur hands from all social classes propagated a large repertory of such tunes that were heard accompanied by rhythmic strumming. This strong characteristic of performance would have overridden lapses in harmonisation, as indeed it still does.

Manuscripts that served as personal commonplace books can reveal the repertories of amateur performers, especially of women. The 'Songbook of Lady Ann Blount' (dated *c.* 1650–60) with songs in English, French and Italian, or the 'Virginal Book' (dated 1656) that belonged to Elizabeth Rogers, preserve rare examples of domestic repertories.[8] Such anthologies often include songs with religious texts, just as one finds in contemporary wordbooks and collections of poetry. Many volumes of Italian canzonettas and cantatas likewise include 'spiritual' or penitential pieces without distinguishing them from surrounding love-songs. Fifteen of the solo songs in Elizabeth Rogers's manuscript are marked 'vocall lessons'. Songs also appear in lesson books for guitar and lute pupils.

Some manuscripts belonged to professional singers; others are anthologies made by or for music-lovers. The castrato Marc'Antonio Pasqualini (1614–91), for example, left a large number of his autograph volumes of cantatas to the family of his patron, Cardinal Antonio Barberini the younger (who died before him). Some of the scores owned by Andrea Adami (1663–1742), another papal singer and a member of the Arcadian Academy, have sumptuous bindings embossed with an Adami device, indicating his high economic status. A thick but visually far less impressive manuscript is the densely copied anthology owned in 1703 by 'The Right Honorable' Henry Roper, Baron of Teynham.[9] It contains nearly 90 Italian cantatas and opera arias from *c.* 1640–80, some copied from published music. The bulk of sources surviving in manuscript, however, are professional copies which may have been for the use of specialist singers or made for interested collectors. Most Italian chamber cantatas were

7 Leopold, 'Remigio Romano's Collection of Lyrics', p. 57.

8 London, Lambeth Palace MS 1041 (Blount); facs. in E. B. Jorgens (ed.), *English Song, 1600–1675* (New York and London, 1986–7), xi; in G. J. Callon (ed.), *Songs with Theorbo (ca. 1650–1663)*, 'Recent Researches in Music of the Baroque Era', 105 (Madison, WI, 2000). London, British Library, Add. MS 10037 (Rogers); facs. in Jorgens (ed.), *English Song, 1600–1675*, ii; ed. C. J. F. Cofone (New York, 1975).

9 Now Paris, Bibliothèque Nationale de France, Rés. Vmc MS 77; it was once owned by Henry Prunières.

disseminated only in manuscript and never saw publication. This may be an indication of the exclusivity of the repertory or a recognition that few were qualified to perform them well.

Printed music was largely destined for a commercial market of educated amateur performers. Between 1600 and 1664, nearly one hundred imprints of French *airs de cour* appeared. These volumes were certainly not destined for the royal court, which commanded performances, not scores. In London, John Playford began a series of popular anthologies and tutors in 1651 that were revised and reprinted into the eighteenth century. Scores could also be produced as 'luxury' books that sought in their dedications the favours of old or new patrons. Fortunately, such prints sometimes became collectors' items, to which we owe their survival as library copies. On a modest scale, occasional compositions could be printed singly, as commemorative souvenirs: Heinrich Albert's 'Alle die ihr freyen wolt' ('All who wish to celebrate'), a short strophic song in homophony for five voices in celebration of a wedding, has a title-page, a page and a half of music, and the words for eight strophes, with a final page bearing dedicatory poems.[10] More chamber cantatas did begin to appear in print in the latter part of the century, largely by composers with relatively independent careers who did not owe exclusive service, or their compositions, to their patrons. In 1682, the Bolognese music publisher Giacomo Monti indexed the 112 volumes he had published, of which a little over half were sacred.[11] The category 'canzonette' listed fifteen items, including cantatas by Maurizio Cazzati (1616–78), Giovanni Maria Bononcini (i; 1642–78), Giovanni Legrenzi (1626–90) and his pupil Giovanni Battista Bassani (*c*. 1650–1716). By comparison, only a handful of the more than 600 cantatas by Alessandro Scarlatti (1660–1725) ever appeared in print, four of them in Bassani's volumes of 1680 and 1682.

Paintings often render quite accurate images of musical instruments. Singing, however, is typically shown in 'genre scenes', that is, realistic depictions that were subject to allegorical interpretation. Although particularly cultivated in Dutch painting, genre scenes drew upon a common European knowledge of emblems and parables.[12] One subject shows well-dressed youths and shabbier folk in taverns, inns and brothels, with music and drink. Bare-breasted women singing with fancily dressed men playing lutes, gambas or fiddles not only connoted excess and licentiousness, but together were understood as a scene from the Biblical parable of the prodigal son (then a common subject of school plays). Two paintings of peasant weddings from the 1660s by the Dutch

---

10 H. Albert, *Rechte Heyrats-Kunst bey hochzeitlichen Ehren-Frewden des . . . Herrn Christoff Pohlen . . . und . . . Ursulen [Stangenwald]* (Königsberg, 1650); facs. in *Sämtliche Gelegenheitskompositionen* (Stuttgart, 2001).
11 Mischiati, *Indici, cataloghi e avvisi degli editori e librai musicali italiani*, pp. 264–70, items 66–80.
12 Austern, ' "For Love's a good musician" '.

painter Jan Molenaer have been shown to be related to a popular song printed in 1622 that disapprovingly describes their riotously drunk celebrations with singing, gambling and dancing. The song 'Boeren-Gezelschap' ('The company of peasants') warns pious gentlemen and burghers to keep away.[13] The caption-poem to a French engraving of a sad-faced, well-dressed lutenist explains that he sings from lovesickness. As an emblem, the portrayal of a man with a similar expression and clothing adds to the message of a painting such as Hendrik Terbrugghen's *Lute Player and Singer* (1628), in which the man with the lute turns his eyes upward and away from the singing woman of easy virtue who stands at his shoulder. As in the case of the French lovesick lutenist, he may be thinking not of the singer, but of the one he truly loves. The painting thus warns women who are inclined to say 'no' not to drive men to more than playing on their lutes.

Written descriptions of singing may be eye- or ear-witness accounts, such as entries in diaries, although these can tend to be uninformative. After hearing the king's mistress at a concert given at the home of the Master of the Mint in December 1674, John Evelyn simply noted in his diary that Mrs (Mary) Knight, a former pupil of Henry Lawes, 'sung incomparably, and doubtless has the greatest reach of any English woman; she had been lately roaming in Italy, and was much improved in that quality'. Scenes in plays, fiction and poems often offer more vivid portrayals. *Jack of Newberie* by Thomas Deloney (who in real life was a silk weaver and wrote broadside ballads) has a scene in a cloth factory where the women who are carding and spinning sing a known folk ballad.[14] But imaginative writing often presents exaggerated stereotypes and, as in paintings, concisely drawn emblems. In English drama the balladmonger could be a comic figure or one feared and despised.[15] In a magical moment in Cervantes's *Don Quixote* (part 1, chap. 43), the guests at an inn, who have retired to their rooms, listen enraptured by a muleteer's song, not knowing that the singer is really an Aragonese *caballero*. A popular *romancillo* by Juan de Salinas, published in 1605, capitalises on the common association of music with seduction and on word-plays between making music and making love. It must be read from an erudite perspective (Salinas was university-trained) rather than a populist one. 'La moza gallega' ('The girl from Galicia') has been taken advantage of by a *mocito* 'que canta bonito y tañe guitarra' (a young fellow who 'sings well and plays the guitar'), who had stopped at the inn where she works. Weeping bitterly because he is about to leave without her, she appears to be a

---

13 On Molenaer's 'Peasant Wedding' (Museum of Fine Arts, Boston), see Weller, *Jan Miense Molenaer, Painter of the Dutch Golden Age*, pp. 171–76.

14 Smith, *The Acoustic World of Early Modern England*, pp. 170–73.

15 Würzbach, *The Rise of the English Street Ballad*, p. 242.

stereotypical warning to women not to believe the words of love-songs.[16] Her lament repeats the refrain line '¡Mal haya quien fía de gente que pasa!' ('Woe to those who trust passers-by!'); and just before he leaves, the traveller sings a different song refrain to her, 'Isabel, no llores; no llores, amores' ('Isabel, don't cry; don't cry, my love'), to which he adds, 'If now in your eyes I seem tarnished, there are others who are worse'.[17] During her lament, the girl describes her first sexual experience in a text full of erotic double meanings. Seduced by singing, as it were, she is trying to use the same means to retain the man's attentions. She does not succeed with respect to him, but perhaps she has affected others who have heard her song. As a self-satisfied recitation of a stereotyped male behaviour, the *romancillo* warns against its own kind of song duplicitously, for it, too, is intent on conquest.

General discussions of singing also tend to have little practical application to performance. They can, however, reveal the social attitudes and anxieties that were associated with both popular and literary music. It is not surprising that then, as now, popular singing – by Molenaer's peasants or the Galician girl – was often seen as dangerous, providing an impetus for moralistic discourse. Writing in 1630, the Italian essayist Grazioso Uberti describes street serenades as the cause of many evils 'that do not yield much good harmony', especially when they cause jealous husbands to become angry:

> Behold, all of a sudden, a relative comes out, or the husband; and even some-times the rival. Whoever it is makes a huge fuss and interrupts the concert. It gets noisy, it comes to arms. Sometimes rocks get thrown at the musicians, the instruments get dropped, with people running this way and that. Oh, what kind of beautiful effect do these serenades make?[18]

To this Uberti contrasts a 'bella serenata' that soothes the cares of a poor, worried father. His examples represent two commonly encountered views of secular music-making. In one, it is primarily a behaviour which either can be socially disruptive and harmful, or can cement social harmony and keep those who are performing out of trouble. The other view judges the effects of music as sound, with its ability either to rouse or to soothe listeners and performers, as when a child falls asleep to the nurse's song and the regular creak of its cradle.[19] Like Uberti, the Englishman Henry Peacham prefers to value music for its potential beneficial effects.

---

16 'Pensé que el amor – y fe que cantaba, / supiera rezado – tenerlo y guardarla' (ll. 25–8); J. de Salinas, *Poesías humanas*, ed. H. Bonneville (Madrid, 1987), pp. 109–13.

17 From ll. 91–7: 'y si me desdoras, – otros hay peores'.

18 G. Uberti, *Contrasto musico, opera dilettevole* (Rome, 1630; repr. Lucca, 1991), pp. 136, 140.

19 Steinheuer, 'Fare la ninnananna'.

> If all arts hold their esteem and value according to their effects, account this goodly science [of music] not among the number of those which Lucian placeth without the gates of hell as vain and unprofitable . . . it gives delight and ease to our travails, it expelleth sadness and heaviness of spirit, preserveth people in concord and amity, allayeth fierceness and anger, and lastly, is the best physic for many melancholy diseases.[20]

Like Peacham, Uberti also expresses the worry that an interest in music may be 'vain and unprofitable'. He considers whether music is a serious enough pastime for professional men of distinction and *gravitas*. After citing a host of examples from antiquity, he concludes that music is *civilitatis magistra*, a teacher of what it means to be civilised. He also discusses whether, correspondingly, women should sing and make music. A doctor devoted to music might seem merely neglectful of his profession; for a woman, however, music-making reflects on her honesty and chastity.[21] Singing can expose a woman to admiring gazes and the desires of others, but Uberti concludes that within the home it is honest recreation.

A number of seventeenth-century prints and paintings show a young man with a lute and a (literate) woman of his class either singing or peering intently at her music. As an allegory of hearing, such a scene represents music-making as a form of communication and agreement, in addition to representing the pleasure of 'true' harmony. For Uberti, making music in itself does not make a woman wanton, but wanton women – courtesans, for instance – can use singing and playing to charm and deceive men. Thus when women are portrayed playing the lute, the instrument can often be read as an emblem of lust unless there is other evidence to suggest an alternative reading.[22] As with the emblematic depictions of popular music-making, moralising images do more than suggest; they also assume an essentialist view of character in relation to social class that makes what the singer sings more or less immaterial. This 'code' of musical communication is relatively simple. We need not know the melody of the entrancing song heard at the inn in *Don Quixote*. Its effect on the noble guests upholds the social order, because it is sung by a *caballero* and not by the muleteer the listeners think they are hearing. It is the transparency of these assumptions that makes it difficult to bridge the gap between seventeenth-century discourse about music and the music itself. We need not hear the song of the Galician girl. She is now wanton, and so her melody will seduce. A trained voice, moreover, can add the deception of artifice to singing. For a moralist like the Dutchman

20 In *The Complete Gentleman*, chap. 11 ('Of Music'); see H. Peacham, *The Complete Gentleman, The Truth of our Times, and The Art of Living in London*, ed. V. B. Heltzel (Ithaca, NY, 1962), p. 116.
21 Uberti, *Contrasto musico*, pp. 67–73. For an English translation of this section, see Strunk, *Source Readings in Music History, Revised Edition*, iv: *The Baroque Era*, pp. 85–7.
22 Craig-Mcfeely, 'The Signifying Serpent'.

Jacob Cats (1577–1660) songs were even more 'wicked' if they were well sung, something he thought worse than reading bad books.[23] Fear of music's ability to seduce or corrupt its listeners was (indeed, is) not based just on aspects inherent in specific compositions themselves, but was inseparable from the context of a performance, the social value of what was being sung, the sex and abilities of the singer or singers, and the 'essential' nature of the performing voice. It is Salinas's clever, learned conceit that keeps 'La moza gallega' from being a 'wicked song': erotic, yes, but base, no. The greater the technique, the less the message is to be trusted; professional performance belongs to the illusionistic (or deceiving) realm of the artful.

'The Nightingale', an English ballad published as a broadside in 1633, puts social class and singing in a simple perspective.[24] The city 'gallants' of Hyde Park and Tottenham Court are invited to leave their usual haunts and to come and listen to the nightingale (stanza 1). Courtiers walking in the woods (stanza 2) 'fancy best / the nightingale's sweet breast' as the bird strives to make 'music fit for a king'. While the nightingale sings 'jug, jug', the 'prentices, in contrast, simply carry on, taking their pleasures in the same woods (stanza 4). The nightingale's song, performed as a refrain after each stanza, does not itself ever change, but each social class has a different relation to it. The upper class attune their refined ears, and the gallants are to emulate them. For the lower orders, birdsong is as much a part of nature as their own mating instincts. Between the stanzas of the courtiers and the apprentices, however,

> The Citizens would fain
> hear Philomel's sweet strain,
> but that they fear
> when they come there,
> the curious constant Note to hear;
> and therefore they refuse
> and will not use
> the woods if they can choose.

The social analysis in this ballad is more than folk wisdom. We shall see in the next part of this chapter that the moral issues attached to music apply exactly to the increasingly cultured 'citizens' of the upper bourgeoisie, even to those who had risen to high ranks within the Roman Church or to families with newly purchased titles of nobility. For them, high culture was a matter of making choices. Discussions of music-making as honest or dishonest recreation are aimed at them, not at 'prentices. Such discussions also sought the definitions

---

23 Kyrova, 'Music in Seventeenth-Century Dutch Painting', p. 35.
24 Simpson, *The British Broadside Ballad and its Music*, pp. 511–13; recorded by the Camerata Trajectina in *Jacob van Eyck and Dutch Songs of the Golden Age*, Philips Classics, CD 442 624-2 (1994). There is also a setting of the same tune in Elizabeth Rogers's Virginal Book.

and limits of gentility – that is, the extent to which their social betters could or should be emulated – with different arenas and boundaries for 'honest' men and for virtuous women. Peacham warns against excessive addiction to trivial pursuits. With regard to music-making, he restricts a gentleman to 'no more . . . than to sing your part sure and at the first sight withal to play the same upon your viol or the exercise of the lute, privately, to yourself'.[25] In so doing, one might develop the assured ear of a courtier, or at least protect oneself from behaving in public like a prodigal son.

Education, poetry and song

Men of letters such as Uberti and Evelyn, and the proliferation of learned academies and salons, were the crest of a wave of increasing literacy that had begun in the previous century. By the middle of the sixteenth century, the teaching of Latin grammar, dialectics and rhetoric had been adapted to instruction in modern languages in new petty and grammar schools, colleges and charity-endowed institutions. Although education differed from country to country, the aims of the new establishments had much in common. 'Founded, endowed, administered, and staffed by the notable bourgeoisie', these schools, concludes George Huppert, 'were to accomplish what wealth alone could not: they were to teach the bourgeois to live nobly'.[26]

Accompanying the new literacy was a movement to transform poetry in modern languages through emulation of Classical literature. In France, the debates of a literary group called the Pléiade produced Joachim Du Bellay's *Deffence et illustration de la langue françoyse* ('Defence and illustration of the French language') in 1549. It argued that French could become a vehicle for serious, expressive poetry by following ancient models – as Italian Renaissance poets had already done – and by becoming 'illustrated' (that is, adorned) with Classical figures of speech. A similarly inspired movement influenced poetry in every modern language, which directly affected secular song. In France, the *voix de ville* transformed into the *air de cour*. In Italy, the already-achieved Latinate style was deemed 'classic', or worse, 'pedantic', so modern poets experimented with increasing knowledge of ancient Greek. The Pléiade and Greek varieties of forms and mixed metres led Gabriello Chiabrera (1552–1638) to new, gracefully deft Italian lyrics. Musical settings of his verses would determine the break between sixteenth-century canzonettas in music and those of the seventeenth century.[27] In Spain, Classical erudition led to difficult and hermetic poetry by writers such as Luis de Góngora y Argote (1561–1627) and the

25 Peacham, *The Complete Gentleman*, ed. Heltzel, p. 112.
26 Huppert, *Les bourgeois gentilshommes*, p. 60.
27 Assenza, *La canzonetta dal 1570 al 1615*, pp. 67–8.

literary sect of the *culteranos*,[28] whose poems did not lend themselves well to musical enhancement. The ideas of the Pléiade influenced Martin Opitz, who modernised German poetry with his *Buch von der Deutschen Poeterey* ('Book on German poetry', 1624). Heinrich Albert, Andreas Hammerschmidt, and composers at the court of Dresden from Caspar Kittel (1603–39) to Constantin Dedekind (1628–1715) all set his poems to music.

Subjects such as eloquence (*elocutio*) and elocution (*pronuntiatio*), furthermore, which were not new to Humanistic education, were also now brought to bear on the vernacular. Eloquence derived from the use of rhetorical figures of speech. Highly 'eloquent' texts, such as Elizabethan and Jacobean poems, needed effective elocution, or delivery, in order for listeners to grasp their figures and make sense of them. To this same end, a 1993 book by Robert Toft tries to teach modern singers to deliver the poetic tropes and figures that 'educated people in early seventeenth-century England, including singers, would have studied'.[29] When the early Italian monodists so strongly emphasised how the 'new music' should deliver words, they were talking about musical *pronuntiatio* for the new Italian poetry.

But just as some poems in Italian, French, and English were set with scrupulous attention to their musical delivery, there were also quantities of poems written to fit pre-existing music. These contrafacta existed within single genres, such as the *air de cour*, the broadside ballad or the German strophic *Lied*, or across genres (e.g., Caccini's solo song 'Amarilli, mia bella' rendered in four parts to a Dutch text).[30] Writing poetry to already existing music also crossed language barriers, high and low genres of song, and the secular and religious spheres. A courtly aria became a popular *lauda*; a French popular song a German chorale; a Spanish tune a French *air de cour*.[31] The ability to compose contrafacta was a useful talent in the salons of Paris, where the enjoyment of airs was a highly social form of entertainment. As Lisa Perella notes:

> Creating words for music was a 'divertissement' similar to many games ('jeux') in the salon. Writing *couplets* for *airs* (additional verses for pre-existing melodies) was apparently a popular pastime, one often depicted in contemporary fictionalized portrayals . . . Indeed, the composition of these song texts provided a vehicle for social mobility.[32]

---

28 Its manifesto was the *Liber unus de eruditione poetica* (1611) by Luis Carrillo y Sotomayor (1583–1610).

29 Toft, '*Tune thy musicke to thy hart*', p. 10. Toft's approach needs to be balanced by Fischlin, 'The Performance Context of the English Lute Song', pp. 49–55.

30 See Rasch, 'The Editors of the *Livre septième*'. For the broader fortunes of Caccini's song, see also Carter, 'Giulio Caccini's *Amarilli, mia bella*'.

31 The last case is documented in Durosoir, *L'air de cour en France*, p. 80, with respect to Pierre Guédron's 'Le premier jour que je vei' from his second book of *Airs de cour* (1612).

32 Perella, 'Bénigne de Bacilly and the *Recueil des plus beaux vers, qui on esté mis on chant* of 1661', pp. 247–50.

Other kinds of 'borrowing' between song repertories included translations of song texts from one language to another, or the use of a metric model to create an unrelated text (e.g., Dutch to German, or German to Danish). Some of these song translations have become classics of poetry in their own languages. Textual contrafacta, however, could also be sung to melodies different from the tunes of their models.

In short, everyone in the seventeenth century with a pretence to culture versified in his or her native tongue. Many were prolific, many facile. For some, their sheaves of poems represented pastimes to be shared with like-minded friends; others sought with them noble patronage and entry to higher social levels.[33] Poetising was also seen as a waste of time. Jonathan Dewald notes 'the appearance of a new social type in seventeenth-century Paris, the young man of good family whose love of poetry had drawn him out of respectability and into a literary career'.[34] Few sought publication, which was to expose oneself to public scrutiny or, worse, to accusations of intent to gain. Thus many collections of poetry and, similarly, of poetry for music were printed posthumously or, as a common phrase put it, 'at the insistence of others'. Peter Walls has observed that 'the vast majority of poetry set in the [English] lute-song volumes is anonymous, and it seems that lyrics may have been given to composers by people whose social status meant that they would have been embarrassed by any publicity their literary efforts might have brought'.[35] Yet there was some kind of market for, and even respect for, poetry to be set to music: texts for *airs de cour*, for instance, appeared in Bénigne de Bacilly's 'collection of the most beautiful poems set to music' of 1661, and those for Italian cantatas appeared in posthumous publications of their authors' collected verse. Poems were produced in a wealth of genres: heroic and satirical epics; pithy distichs and epigrams; freer lyric verse such as the Italian madrigal and canzonetta; German poems with numerous strophes. The Englishman Thomas Campion, who was both poet and composer, took the trouble to note that one of his songs was in the form of a Sapphic ode, and defended his short airs by comparing them to the poetic genre of the epigram (of which he published a whole book). 'Light' poems, satiric poems, classic forms such as the sonnet, and experimental verse all resulted in different sorts of musical settings. The intense production of poetry during the entire seventeenth century is the necessary

---

33 In *The Truth of our Times* (1638), however, Henry Peacham declared, 'I have never gained one halfpenny by any dedication [of a book] I have ever made . . . So that I would wish no friend of mine in these days to make further use of English poesy than in epitaphs, emblems, or encomiastics for friends.' See Peacham, *The Complete Gentleman*, ed. Heltzel, p. 192.

34 *Aristocratic Experience and the Origins of Modern Culture*, p. 177.

35 Walls, 'London, 1603–49', p. 289. Dewald, *Aristocratic Experience and the Origins of Modern Culture*, pp. 182–5, also cites evidence of the importance in France of the distinction between writing and publication.

context for much of the diversity and quantity of secular vocal music of the time.

Education also brought like-minded men together. I have already mentioned Heinrich Albert (1604–51), a man from a family of civic officials who read law and was a soldier before he chose to be a musician. In 1645 he published twelve short vocal trios with basso continuo under the title *Musicalische Kürbs-Hütte* ('A musical pumpkin-arbour'), which referred to a sort of pumpkin pergola under which he and his friends in Königsberg wrote short poems (*Sprüche*) on the fleetingness of life as they watched the vegetation change with the seasons.[36] That Albert's partsongs were not intended for popular consumption is apparent in external aspects of his publications. Each piece in his first four volumes of *Arien oder Melodeyen* (1638–41) bears a Latin title. Albert set the first stanza of 'Mein Urtheil widerräth es mir' ('My judgement disagrees with me') in just eleven bars.[37] It takes all of its eleven strophes, however, for the poem to bear out its Latin caption 'Illicitum frustra Venus improba vexat amorem' ('Wanton Venus stirs up illicit love in vain'). In Parisian salons and in Italian and German-language academies, the titled mixed with educated commoners of high social standing. This was particularly the case in those major European centres, such as the Republic of Venice or the free city of Hamburg, that had no court in the technical sense, but where academies or similar gatherings of the cultured could provide the 'society' in which chamber singing of a literary nature could be enjoyed. One example is the Venetian Accademia degli Unisoni of Giulio Strozzi, at which some of the performances by Barbara Strozzi (1619–77) would have taken place.

Against this rising tide of educated commoners, old noble families sought to distinguish themselves from their social inferiors. Despite the increasingly literate population, in France one mark of distinction remained the language itself, with the best French usage determined not only by the vocabulary but also by the manner of speaking heard at court. It was inculcated in aristocratic households, in the bosom of the family, along with proper gender roles and the distinctive skills such as etiquette and foreign languages that were essential for social interaction among peers. The very wealthy placed their sons as pages in the households of their social superiors with this kind of acculturation in mind.[38] Noble youths who boarded at colleges and academies were attended

36 *Musicalische Kürbs-Hütte* (Königsberg, 1645; repr. Stuttgart, 2001); ed. J. M. Müller-Blattau, 'Bärenreiter Editions', 609 (Kassel and Basle, 1932). Selections have been recorded by Cantus Cölln on Deutsche Harmonia Mundi HM/IOM 906-2 (1988).

37 Ed. E. Bernoulli in 'Denkmäler der Deutscher Tonkunst' i/12 (Wiesbaden, 1958), no. 16A (no. 16B is a version for two sopranos and continuo).

38 In France, pages appear to have been maintained by their own families, not by their patrons. Louis XIV had 76 royal pages in 1669, and 91 in 1680.

by private tutors who could teach skills not offered in institutional curricula, including writing in the vernacular, dancing, musical performance, fencing and drawing. During the course of the century, instruction in these subjects became increasingly available in colleges themselves.

At the end of the sixteenth century, the social and linguistic divide between the nobility of the sword and the educated classes became a matter of public polemics and was well entrenched by the mid seventeenth century.[39] This divide was reinforced by the founding of separate academies for noble sons that emphasised military curricula and which were intended to counterbalance the increasing roles of the so-called 'nobility of the robe' in governing the state. Riding, fencing and dancing formed the 'trivium' of studies in most French academies, well fortified with the kind of geometry useful in siege warfare. The first in France was founded in 1594.[40] In 1636, a year after Cardinal Richelieu created the Académie Française, he established the Académie Royale for 'the young nobility'. Its programme included history and biography alongside the usual subjects with military applications. The proliferation of such academies in France was centralised under the *grand écuyer* in 1680. In Germany, the earliest Collegium Illustre in Tübingen was quickly followed in 1598 by the Mauritianum in Kassel, founded by the Landgrave Moritz of Hessen, patron of Heinrich Schütz (from the beginning, it taught noble pages and the boys of the *cappella* together). For nobles attempting to maintain their class, then, learning for its own sake was not especially encouraged, except for sons who would pursue ecclesiastical careers.

It is easy to see that the musical tastes of these nobles might differ from the obsessions of those immersed in rhetorical invention and modern poetry. An early example of music for the military caste comes from two musical prints of 1605 and 1607 by the professional soldier, 'gentleman' and amateur viol player, Tobias Hume. 'I doe not study Eloquence', he wrote to his readers in both volumes, 'or professe Musicke, although I doe love Sence, and affect Harmony. My Profession being, as my Education hath beene, Armes, the onely effeminate part of mee, hath beene Musicke; which in me hath beene alwaies Generous, because neuer Mercenarie.' In addition to a 'Souldiers Song' and an ode to tobacco ('Tobacco, tobacco, / sing sweetly for tobacco, / Tobacco is like love'), he wrote a programmatic and descriptive 'Hunting Song to be sung to the Bass-Viol' which 'was sung before two Kings, to the admiring

---

39 Dewald, *Aristocratic Experience and the Origins of Modern Culture*, pp. 192–8, also sees this divide as the divergence of personal writing (on the part of nobles) from formal (by the educated).
40 Motley, *On Becoming a French Aristocrat*, chap. 3.

of all brave Huntsmen'.[41] The Italian poet Giovanni Filippo Apolloni was a widely posted professional soldier before he was seriously wounded and had to change careers. He became a courtier and court librettist who nonetheless hated court politics, which he expressed in several satirical texts for cantatas. As for dancing, it is well known that social dancing in the noble style became increasingly important during the century, reaching its height at the French royal court and spreading to major and minor courts across Europe. Although around 1600 there were singers of noble birth who performed professionally – Francesco Rasi in Florence and Mantua comes to mind – in the course of the century, the figure of the nobleman as poet–singer gave way to the more achievable ideal of the excellent dancer.

Patronage

Nobles brought up more to lead cavalry and dance than to write poetry could with ample resources still cultivate the arts in a distinctive manner, that is, through patronage. High-ranking nobles with private chapels could call upon their singers for secular entertainments. Castratos closely associated with the Baroque cantata in Rome, such as Marc'Antonio Pasqualini or Andrea Adami (both mentioned earlier), were in the first place singers in the pope's private chapel. As the best church and chamber singers alike increasingly began to appear in theatrical entertainments, the situation reversed. When the alto-castrato Siface (Giovanni Francesco Grossi) was taken on by the Duke of Modena in 1679 for his operatic and chamber singing, he was given a nominal appointment in the Duke's private chapel.

A well-endowed household without a private chapel could still include musically able servants or retainers. The amateur model is provided by the third Lord North, who employed a professional organist in his household in Cambridgeshire. His grandson Roger North recalled that the 'old Lord' had the '[music] masters' set his poetry, 'and then his grandchildren, my sisters, must sing them'. The household made music together three or more times a week, with the sisters accompanied by 'the servants of parade, as gentleman ushers, and the steward, and the clerk of the kitchen'. Consort songs with viols as well as keyboard and instrumental music were specifically composed for these occasions, especially for performance in an outdoor pavilion the lord had constructed.[42] Roger North recollected how, in the course of the seventeenth

---

41 T. Hume, *The First Part of Ayres: French, Pollish, and Others* (London, 1605; repr. 1969), and *Captaine Humes Poeticall Musicke* (London, 1607; repr. 1977); ed. S. Jones, 'Prattica musicale', 2 (Winterthur, 1980). The preface and song texts are given in Doughtie (ed.), *Lyrics from English Airs*, pp. 197-9, 284-5, 287-9.

42 See Roger North's 'Notes of me' in Wilson (ed.), *Roger North on Music*, pp. 9-12; see also Strunk, *Source Readings in Music History, Revised Edition*, iv: *The Baroque Era*, pp. 89-92.

century, there came to be less and less music-making at home, as his peers and their children gravitated to London and became accustomed to hearing professional concerts and music of a difficulty amateurs could not master. Households with many professional musicians in service usually had them as retainers or tutors, who lived separately. The English composer Henry Lawes, for example, taught the children of the Earl of Bridgewater, to whom he later dedicated several volumes of music. The most active patrons of vocal chamber music usually also had regular channels to poets, composers and even music copyists. Beyond this, one can also find expenses for the long-term training of singers as well as payments for such minor but necessary items as music paper and replacement strings.

From the sixteenth century on, then, despite the courtly ideal of a noble singer–poet, the history of secular song in the hands of nobles becomes a history more of patronage than of practice, involving the cultivation and maintenance of professional singers, male and female. Coupled with the tendency of court records to predominate in the surviving documentary sources, and with the prominence of court composers, this phenomenon has led to a lopsided vision of secular music in the seventeenth century, making this music seem almost co-extensive with aristocratic culture, even though an academy education and court culture in itself did not particularly encourage vocal chamber performance. In courts, furthermore, it is difficult to discern performers' duties *in camera* as opposed to their singing in various kinds of court spectacle, such as plays, masques and ballet. We usually do not know how much *chamber* music was actually commanded by individuals such as the Duke of Savoy, the Duke of Saxe-Weimar, or the Princess of Rossano. In this regard, it is also difficult to match surviving scores to documented or hypothetical chamber performances at court, or even to place them within the extended libraries of music copied for certain patrons. Gordon Callon reports an excerpt from a letter of 1619 that describes three stages of one post-prandial entertainment for a gathering of nobles and diplomats (all men). First, the musicians of the Queen of England offered 'french singinge' (music not specified). In another space, the men heard an 'Irish harpp, a violl, and mr. Lanyer, excellently singing & playinge on the lute'. This was followed by a play presented in a third chamber.[43] A comic depiction of entertainment in royal chambers is Marc-Antoine Charpentier's *Les plaisirs de Versailles* (H. 480) from the early 1680s.[44] The figures of La Musique and La Conversation argue with each other, because Conversation

---

43 Sir Gerrard Herbert to Sir Dudley Carleton, 24 May 1619, quoted in N. Lanier, *The Complete Works*, ed. G. J. Callon, 'Boethius Editions', 11 (Hereford, 1994), p. x.

44 Ed. R. Blanchard (Paris, 1974); recorded on *Charpentier: Les plaisirs de Versailles*, Les Arts Florissants, Erato 063014774-2 (1996).

cannot stop talking, much to Musique's exasperation. Comus tries to soothe things with chocolate and wine, jams and pastries. Le Jeu (Gaming) tries to divert them with cards, dice, backgammon and chess, but Musique demands silence and Conversation chocolate, which shuts her up, but only for a short while.

Noblewomen could retain female singers in their households. The mores of the time also looked the other way when noblemen courted and kept women singers – but not on their palace rolls. Now, as then, we are reliant on rumour and the occasional lawsuit to know about 'illicit' relationships, and we can only speculate on whether the most famous women chamber singers of the age were honestly supported, had an affair or two that it would have been foolish to refuse, or were in fact courtesans. At court and in the larger noble households, it was common to provide women singers with suitable husbands. Some women continued to perform after marrying; others appear to have retired. In the first third of the century, singers of renown such as Adriana Basile and Leonora Baroni were, like their sixteenth-century counterparts, typically heard only in private performances, of which there are few reports. After the 1630s, opera provided more public opportunities for women singers to be heard and seen (and also gossiped about).

The patronage of chamber singing was thus an aristocratic activity with multiple motivations – the conspicuous consumption expected of the class, the expectation of having the means for domestic music-making, concerts or lovers on command, and, in some cases, the desire to foster specific kinds of rare or modern music. In most instances, the music that was sung on command was newly written or at least recent. In this, patronage varied little in the seventeenth century from the practices of the sixteenth.

Repertories

The enormous variety of secular music in the seventeenth century drew on the even wider range of contemporary verse forms and poetic styles. In each linguistic region, however, repertories were on the whole quite local. Repertories coming under cross influences were also local phenomena, such as the English and French tunes in German and Dutch popular song, or the interest of Oxford–London composers in French and Italian art music. Within vocal repertories, it was the character of pieces that was generally recognised, rather than technical aspects of musical composition. Designations like *canzonetta* and *cantata*, or even *ayre*, were loose. Furthermore, while the Florentine *stile rappresentativo* remained one of the defining styles of the period, emphasis on it by modern historians has obscured popular music, the continuation and transformation of songs accompanied by lute and guitar, the cultivation of duets, trios and larger ensembles with varying kinds of instrumental participation, and also social partsongs. Little falls readily into genres, a word that implies distinctions of taxonomy that did not worry those who sang or heard glees and serenatas.[45] The word 'repertories', moreover, implies sets of individual compositions shared by definable populations of performers and listeners; but except for a patron trying to keep his private music as exclusive as possible, evidence to match specific repertories to classes of singers, or even to individuals, is hard to come by and is largely anecdotal. This chapter on non-theatrical secular vocal music can of necessity discuss only a few principal categories of music for singing, rather than complete repertories, and does not venture into unsettled questions of typology.

Popular song

> With elegies, sad songs, and mourning lays,
> While Craig his Kala would to pity move,
> Poor brainsick man! he spends his dearest days;
> Such silly rhyme cannot make women love.
> Morice, who sight of never saw a book,
> With a rude stanza this fair virgin took.
> (William Drummond of Hawthornden)

Perhaps the wickedest of 'wicked songs', to use Jacob Cats's phrase, were popular songs, although those who objected to them were more concerned with their subjects – love, lovesickness and good thighs – and the situations in which they were sung, than with particular musical attributes. Singers and singing may be seductive, but no melody more so than any other. Moreover, it is difficult to know much about most of the tunes that were in the oral repertory at a given moment. Modern research can sometimes match formulas or tunes in surviving 'folk' music to historical song texts, as has been the case with several Elizabethan ballads. Sometimes popular tunes were incorporated into notated polyphonic pieces and thus preserved. Conversely, a melody from composed polyphony could become popular and take on an existence independent of its original setting. An air that Marc-Antoine Charpentier wrote for a Molière play became a French noël, known in English as the Christmas carol 'Bring a torch,

---

45 A catalogue of 1662 for the Venetian music publisher Alessandro Vincenti (Mischiati, *Indici, cataloghi e avvisi degli editori e librai musicali italiani*, pp. 213–41) lists the following 'genres' among the title-pages of published vocal music with chitarrone, theorbo, harpsichord, Spanish guitar 'or other similar instrument': *arie, canzonette, concerti, dialoghi recitativi, madrigali, scherzi, scherzi recitativi*. Unaccompanied polyphonic madrigals are listed in a separate section. Some titles, however, are clearly old stock.

Jeanette Isabelle'.[46] Tunes re-used with new texts could change function, go from the street to the stage, from profane to religious sentiment. Some of the most re-used melodies were not unique tunes at all, but melodic formulas to standard harmonic patterns. As in any other period, we also find popular songs with music of a kind associated with dancing, or actual dance-songs. The puritanically minded could doubly fault these.

Seventeenth-century Spanish *romances* illustrate the elusiveness of popular singing. In the sixteenth century, *romances* and *villancicos* had diversified from the expressive range and styles of their earlier courtly existence. The sung, narrative *romances* retained a tradition of chivalric love stories, but also came to incorporate more popular language and characters. The new *romance*, as characterised by Louise Stein, 'developed its broad appeal through reference to the everyday and the true-to-life. The popular borrowed element may be an entire pre-existent tune, a refrain, or simply a popular saying, rustic expression, or topic from popular lore.'[47] Such elements moved across generic and social barriers. A court composer could work a commonly known tune into a polyphonic arrangement; the arrangement might then be inserted into a play – perhaps with altered text – and given a new, oral diffusion. Stein notes that 'the best songs of this repertory' that have survived are mostly in manuscript collections from the first half of the seventeenth century and are by, or arranged by, court composers. Numerous prints and reprints of their texts prove their popularity. Jack Sage reports that 'thousands of so-called *romances* for three to six voices and accompaniment are extant' and makes the observation that ballad texts sometimes appear with symbols for guitar chords over the words.[48] Strummed guitars could have accompanied solo performances or reinforced the harmony of a vocal ensemble, whether that harmony was generated 'by ear' or from notated parts. The many *romances* sung in plays staged in the public *corrales* of Madrid would have been heard accompanied by a group of guitars, presumably with a number of stanzas that would make them more like lyric songs than narrative ballads. In the typical manner of popular music, both 'traditional' and newly composed tunes persisted and were disseminated in the same way, becoming one and the same repertory, whether they were performed as tunes only or with improvised or written-out parts.

---

46 Hitchcock, 'Marc-Antoine Charpentier's Vocal Chamber Music', p. 58.

47 Stein, *Songs of Mortals, Dialogues of the Gods*, pp. 46–9. Fifty sources of Spanish secular music are catalogued in her Appendix I (pp. 354–60), including nine *cancioneros*. See also J. Etzion (ed.), *The 'Cancionero de la Sablonara' (Critical Edition)* (London, 1996).

48 'Romance, i: Spain', in S. Sadie and J. Tyrrell (eds), *The New Grove Dictionary of Music and Musicians: Revised Edition*, 29 vols (London, 2000), xxi: 571–3. For other discussion and music examples, see Hill, *Roman Monody, Cantata, and Opera in the Circles around Cardinal Montalto*, i: 69–75 (and Exx. 3-3, 3-4).

Like the Spanish *romances* disseminated in *pliegos sueltos*, the words to English street ballads have been preserved in printed broadsides and broadsheets. Balladmongers sold their sheets in the open air, singing newly written texts to a repertory of common tunes. The balladmonger in Brathwait's *Whimzies* (1631) has 'one tune in store that will indifferently serve for any ditty . . . His workes are lasting-pasted monuments upon the insides of Country Alehouses . . . He stands much upon Stanza's, which halt and hobble as lamely as that one legg'd Cantor that sings them.'[49] In their heyday, these ephemeral ballads were much disparaged, but by around the middle of the seventeenth century, ballads if not balladeers were received with greater acceptance.[50] Indeed it appears that in the course of the period, the street-ballad went from being primarily a living practice to becoming a subgenre of written verse, to be collected and anthologised. (Samuel Pepys's continuation of John Selden's collection forms one of the great legacies; it is now in Magdalene College, Cambridge.) The banning of public ballad-singing during the Commonwealth (from 1649) no doubt hastened this secondary development. New tunes, however, continued to be added to the repertory, so that a theatrical song by Purcell might quickly be reborn as a political parody.[51] Ballads made up about two-fifths of the songs in the 1728 *Beggar's Opera*, sung alongside more modern music by composers such as Purcell, Handel and Giovanni Bononcini. Musical broadsheets also existed in other countries. In many German-speaking areas, *Flugblätter* with songs are as often devotional or moralistic as satirical or newsworthy and thus are not predominantly secular. Obviously secular broadsheets, however, appear in Dutch genre paintings set in inns or with peasants. They can be seen, for example, in six paintings by Adriaen van Ostade (1610–85).[52]

The singing of Italian *ottave rime* is one improvised genre of popular music for which there exist both historical and modern traces. Rhymed, eight-line *ottava rima* stanzas with eleven syllables in each line are 'made up' on the spot. The stanzas are sung freely to recitation formulas rather than to distinct tunes of fixed melodic or metric character. The literary and oral traditions of sung *ottave rime* are consistently if obscurely intertwined from the fourteenth century up to Giambattista Marino's lengthy *Adone* (1623), the last major literary epic to provide material for the *improvvisatori*. Other poetic epics that were and continued to be sources of stories and characters were Ariosto's *Orlando furioso* (1516) and Torquato Tasso's *Gerusalemme liberata* (1581). Giovanni Kezich

49 A. H. Lanner (ed.), *A Critical Edition of Richard Brathwait's 'Whimzies'* (New York and London, 1991), pp. 151–2. For later collections, including Pepys's, see <http://emc.english.ucsb.edu/ballad_project/index.asp>.
50 Würzbach, *The Rise of the English Street Ballad*, p. 250.
51 Spink (ed.), *The Blackwell History of Music in Britain*, iii: *The Seventeenth Century*, pp. 3–13.
52 Brednich, *Die Liedpublizistik im Flugblatt des 15. bis 17. Jahrhunderts*, i: chap. 8, and see p. 321.

argues that the popular practice that we know of from historical evidence developed along with increasing literacy in rural Italy in the sixteenth century, but it divided from – or was denied – new sources by the climate of the Counter-Reformation. Improvising poets from the countryside or the mountains, however, were brought to court during the seventeenth century, and the following century saw 'an explosion of the art of improvised poetry' among commoners and educated academicians alike.[53] Singing narratives in *ottava rima* continued well into the twentieth century and has its echoes in Italy even today.

The 700 years of a continuous practice of sung poetic improvisation in Italy is of particular interest for seventeenth-century music because of the non-metric, recitational nature of singing *ottave* and the question of its relationship to the rise of Florentine monody. Furthermore, notated models for singing *ottave* appear in late sixteenth- and early seventeenth-century sources of solo vocal music. (These present a freely declamatory style, but one more fixed in its rhythmic notation than one hears from modern-day improvisers.) New compositions with several *ottave* written out in variation also appear in vocal anthologies of the first half of the Seicento. In 1965 Paul Collaer suggested that folk traditions had served as a ready inspiration for the 'inventors' of *recitar cantando*.[54] John Walter Hill has more recently summarised the attempts to connect the rise of early Baroque Florentine and Roman solo singing to late sixteenth-century musical formulas (*arie*) for reciting poetry, albeit to the urban music of Naples and Rome, not to the music of peasants.[55] Kezich's overview of improvised *ottave rime* supports Hill's line of investigation, since we cannot presume that oral tradition in the sixteenth and seventeenth centuries constituted a purely 'folk' practice, much less imagine that such practice would have been adopted directly by scholars searching for models of ancient Greek monody.[56] Rather, by the later sixteenth century, the 'oral tradition' was probably already a set of diversified practices that permeated Italian society so that whatever was heard

53 Kezich, *I poeti contadini*, pp. 115–18. In his chap. 4, Kezich also offers a useful social history of the *ottava rima*.

54 Collaer, 'Lyrisme baroque et tradition populaire'; Agamennone, 'Cantar l'ottava', pp. 187–8. Musical transcriptions of performances recorded between 1964 and 1984 are in Kezich, *I poeti contadini*, pp. 201–18. Agamennone's musical model for each quatrain consists of two line pairs. The first line descends from a recitation tone to the tonic followed by a second line ending on the step above the tonic. The third line ends on the fifth scale degree or a similar open tone, followed by the last line, which closes to the tonic. In each quatrain, the first line is typically the longest, the second shorter, the third the shortest; the final line approximates the second in duration. Melismatic line closures appear to be the norm.

55 Hill, *Roman Monody, Cantata, and Opera from the Circles around Cardinal Montalto*, pp. 60–65.

56 Kezich's view (*I poeti contadini*, pp. 35, 107–9) is that *cantar ottave* was adopted by street entertainers and wandering minstrels towards the end of the Middle Ages and became a courtly and classicised genre in the urban centres of the early Renaissance. Ivano Cavallini explores in his 'Sugli improvvisatori del Cinque–Seicento' the context out of which 'the new improvisers' emerged towards the end of the sixteenth century, tying their strophic performances to ostinato bass patterns.

in Neapolitan villas sounded different from *ottave* in public hostelries of the Tuscan Maremma.

There is also the question of accompaniment. None of Kezich's historical witnesses from the seventeenth century on mentions the presence of instruments or singing in parts; nor is this apparent in photographic evidence of more recent performing practices. The social aspect of *cantar ottave* in the countryside, in fact, lies in contests of unaccompanied solo improvisation, with poets inventing and answering stanzas in alternation. In the eighteenth century, Goethe heard two Venetian boatmen loudly singing 'Tasso' and 'Ariosto' to each other from opposite ends of the gondola in which he sat. At one point they were answered by a gondolier in another boat. In modern Italy, singing *ottave* seems to have remained strictly solo and monophonic. Professional ballad-singers in medieval and Renaissance times may have sung to a lute, but we do not know whether the instrument doubled the singer, played heterophonically, or executed some kind of independent accompaniment. Seventeenth-century notated models and compositions are harmonised, whether they are in the form of polyphonic art settings executed with lute or in rougher renditions with chordal accompaniment on instruments such as the guitar. This suggests performance options parallel to those for Spanish *romances*: chordal harmonisation, if courtly or urban, and otherwise, monophony. From at least the sixteenth and early seventeenth centuries, sung *ottave rime* demonstrate the remarkable extent to which elements of 'high culture' in Italy were – and remained – common across social classes, but with differing musical manifestations. Anyone could improvise text and music for *ottave* within the oral tradition. Any written-out poem in *ottave* could be performed by singing one of the 'arie per cantar ottave rime' included in countless printed and manuscript collections of the period (along with similar models for sonnets and *terza rima*). In a stylised vein, a composer such as Kapsberger could set a newly written, single *ottava* stanza as refined chamber music, to be sung while he realised a continuo part on theorbo. Domenico Mazzocchi's dialogue for four voices on the Olindo and Sofronia episode from *Gerusalemme liberata*, however, suggests a different context: an academic, unstaged, dramatic adaptation of court practice of at least 50 years past.[57] A tenor embodies the role of the poet Tasso (as narrator) and sings Tasso's original *ottave* over an 'aria de' sonetti'. (For many of the *ottave*, the continuo line is omitted in the 1638 print, probably because the bass formula simply repeats. However, there is a more florid, less narrative section where the continuo shifts to the Romanesca bass.) The parts of the other characters are freer, in different modal areas, but with a similar harmonic flavour. Chamber

---

57 In Mazzocchi's *Dialoghi, e sonetti posti in musica* (Rome, 1638; repr. Bologna, 1969).

works like Mazzocchi's and Kapsberger's, however, did not preclude rustics from being invited to court. Kezich places the Tuscan shepherd and popular poet Giovanni Dionisio Peri (1564–1639) at the Florentine court of Grand Duke Cosimo II, and Benedetto di Virgilio (1602–67) improvising *ottave* on saints' lives at the papal court.[58] It seems impossible to say, however, whether the Mazzocchi performance would have resembled the shepherd's in any way, or whether Di Virgilio sounded more like Mazzocchi pretending to be Tasso or like a present-day *contadino* improvising.

Social music

We have already seen family members and the domestic staff of Lord North's household making music at home. In paintings and engravings, scenes of domestic music are typically portrayals of upper-middle-class families that emphasise wealth, leisure and harmony. One easily imagines consort songs, the socialised counterpart to the lute ayre, being performed early in the century in England. In his compendious *Musurgia universalis* of 1650, the Jesuit Athanasius Kircher named 'arias and villanellas' as private 'house' and 'country' music, describing strophic music in two, three, or four parts with repeating poetic lines. He may have been thinking, for example, of Johann Nauwach's *Teutsche Villanellen* ('German villanellas', 1627) that included settings of poems by Martin Opitz; the three-part 'villanellas' in Johann Schein's volumes of *Musica boscareccia* (1621, 1626, 1628); or the villanellas of Kapsberger, mentioned earlier and published in Rome. Although Werner Braun has called Heinrich Albert's partsongs from 'a pumpkin arbour', mentioned earlier, a 'gloomy emblem of Königsberg camaraderie', Albert's largely syllabic settings, simple imitative writing and diatonic harmonies recall the earlier English canzonet, with occasional rhythmic touches of the Italian *scherzo*. In an engraving on the title-page of Albert's 1650 *Arien*, three men wearing hats sit at a round table in a grove. They sing from scores, and there is a wine carafe on the ground and at least one drinking glass.[59]

Peacham's admonition to 'sing your part sure' reminds us that, at least in northern Europe, amateur part-singing remained an aspect of male sociability well into the middle of the century. A French priest and his nephews in Paris were to be taught to sing 'all kinds of *airs de cour*, from printed books as well as not printed, to beat the measure . . . to know how to sing their parts from

---

58 Kezich, *I poeti contadini*, pp. 44–5.

59 Braun, '*Concordia discors*', p. 100. The entire title-page of the 1650 print is reproduced in H. Albert, *Arien*, vol. 2, ed. E. Bernoulli, rev. H. J. Moser, 'Denkmäler der Deutscher Tonkunst', i/13 (Wiesbaden, 1958), p. 241. A fourth man sits apart. Braun ('*Concordia discors*', pp. 101–2) interprets the groups of human figures in the engraving as emblems of Albert's social music: music for weddings, camaraderie and burials.

open books' and also to make lute intabulations and compose similar pieces in three and four parts.[60] English catches and partsongs are well known, with a constant tradition of publication from the sixteenth century into the 1670s. Ian Spink has sensibly sorted out the generic differences among these kinds of social music, which are more differences of character than of form:

> A catch tended to be humorous or bawdy, a canon moral and sober, while a round might have a folk or traditional origin . . . The terms glee, ballad and ayre . . . are applied to freely composed partsongs in from two to four voices. But again one detects a difference in character. Most glees (so called) are light-hearted and 'gleeful', ayres are usually more serious and ballads have a traditional 'folk flavour'.[61]

Composers of 'serious' music did not necessarily stay away from more ribald texts. William Lawes (1602–1645), who served the king, made a gift volume for one Richard Gibbon which contained lyric songs and pastoral dialogues as well as a good number of drinking-songs. Among them is 'The catts as other creatures doe', featuring a trio of street toms (who sing 'meow' in chromatic slides), and another trio wishing 'A health to the no[r]therne Lasse' with its recurring phrase 'she that has good eyes has good thighs' (based on Sir John Suckling).[62] Nicholas Lanier's trio 'Young and simple though I am / I have heard of Cupid's name' (in his *The Second Book of Ayres, containing pastoral dialogues*, London, 1652) has a suggestive text spoken from a girl's point of view. Yet one can imagine the humour of a performance by two 'falsettists' and a bass, who by the sixth stanza would all declare, 'Yet no churl or silken gull / Shall my virgin blossim pull'.[63]

Spink has observed that many English partsongs appear to be arrangements of solos. This indicates a need for polyphonic 'light' music for amateur performance that appears to have outlasted the vogue for original, more literary, music in parts. In fact, the contents of some seventeenth-century 'madrigal' prints by Henry Lichfild or Francis Pilkington are more like partsongs than the earlier, more challenging Elizabethan madrigals. (The amateur Lichfild appears to have composed his pieces, published in 1613, for the family of his employer, a Lady Cheyney of Toddington.) A similar demand may have sustained the three-voice

---

60 See the contract between Master Jean Delin and André Barral, priest, 9 October 1640, given in Jurgens (ed.), *Documents du Minutier Central concernant l'histoire de la musique*, ii: 36, 455–6.

61 Spink, *English Song from Dowland to Purcell*, pp. 135–6.

62 Both songs are in London, British Library, Add. MS 31432 (respectively, ff. 22v–23v and 21v–22); facs. in Jorgens (ed.), *English Song*, ii. They are edited in W. Lawes, *Collected Vocal Music*, ed. G. J. Callon, 'Recent Researches in Music of the Baroque Era', 121, 4 vols (Middleton, WI, 2002), ii: 8–9, 10–12 (for possible references to actual persons in 'The catts', see ibid., pp. xxi–xxii, note 8).

63 Lanier, *The Complete Works*, ed. Callon, pp. 110–11. See also ibid., pp. 183–4, where Callon notes that the literary source is Thomas Campion's Fourth Book of airs (1618).

'madrigaletto' in northern Italy. Melchior Franck incorporated older popular tunes in polyphonic arrangements in his *Opusculum etlicher und alter Reuter-liedlein* (Nuremberg, 1603) and *Newes teutsches musicalisches fröliches Convivium* (Coburg, 1621), and many other German partsongs are arrangements of foreign melodies. Chronological precedence among polyphonic and homophonic versions and putative monophonic oral repertories is tricky to establish and was undoubtedly of little concern to those who sang any of them. German student-songs also belong in this category; like the English partsong, they run through a similar range of popular flavours together with an emphasis on drink.[64] Schein, who wrote his own texts, published his *Venus-Kräntzlein* of trios (1609) while he was a law student in Leipzig; his *Studenten-Schmauss* of five-part music appeared in 1626 after he became cantor at the Thomasschule there.

The French *air de cour*, like Italian *ottave rime*, varied in modes of performance and in function. Georgie Durosoir classifies the polyphonic – usually original – versions of French airs as 'musique savante', the lute-accompanied versions as their means of diffusion, and the monophonic prints issued between 1608 and 1628 as destined for an even larger public for whom the airs may have already become a partly 'oral' repertory.[65] First written for the French royal court, *airs de cour* continued to be produced by court composers until mid century. Their prestige as court entertainment clearly encouraged their dissemination and imitation beyond royal chambers. Pierre Guédron was loath to have his airs in print, but the publisher Ballard flattered the king into backing their release. Outside the court, the airs were not just vehicles for listening enjoyment or amateur music-making. Inseparable from the mixed company of the Parisian salons, with their games and playful competitiveness, the airs were an element of a participatory sociability in that amateurs also wrote and discussed them in these gatherings. Those who could not write new music – Durosoir's 'unoc-cupied courtier, urbane abbot, the sentimental and idle ladies' man'[66] – wrote new texts for existing airs. Cleverness and wit counted, although technically the exercise was little different from the versifying of balladeers.

Indeed, given the French preoccupation with the language of the court, the poetic texts were the principal focus of the air. In his *L'art de bien chanter* ('Art of singing well', 1679), Bénigne de Bacilly, a composer and singing-teacher, gave scrupulous attention to *pronuntiatio*, with separate articles on single vow-els and certain consonants. He emphasised that French airs should conform to their lyric poetic forms, restricting the repetition of words and phrases, even

64 Harper, 'Gesellige Lieder, poetischer Status und Stereotypen'.

65 *L'air de cour en France*, pp. 200–201. Durosoir also points out that the 'repertory' was determined by what the publisher Pierre Ballard chose to print.

66 Durosoir, *La musique vocale profane au XVIIᵉ siècle*, p. 67.

if he himself felt that this restriction impeded French composers. With repetitions, he observed, the Italians could create a 'grand air' with only four short poetic lines. But grandness was not the goal of the French air. Bacilly discussed common criticisms of airs, beginning with 'it is too long':

> Those who wish to speak of an air with scorn . . . never fail to say 'that it is too long, and that it is an entire history; that it is bizarre, or that it is common; that it is made up of bits recalling or borrowed from a thousand other airs; that it sounds like plainchant, especially a Lamentation of Jeremiah. That its words are flat, and it has neither salt nor sauce, to use their terms; that the words sound rough, or else that it is *taillé en plein drap*, as one says – too fussy. And that if the words were made to fit the air, all the credit should be given to the one who wrote them and applied them to the air so well; in short, that the melody does not suit the words as well as the original ones did, and that it does not express the meaning of the words well; or, speaking on their terms, that the musician has not well understood the thought of the poet.' There it is, the usual language of these judges, whether their concerns come from ignorance or from malice . . .[67]

This list of critiques emphasises the strong forces of convention that made achieving a 'perfect' salon air quite difficult and that eventually ossified the form. But Bacilly's comments also indicate the general interest in airs in a milieu of lively, if narrowly focussed, social discourse outside of the court's private enjoyment of this music.

Other French airs are songs in the metres and binary forms of social dances. The singing of gavottes, sarabandes and menuets as 'very pretty and very entertaining little songs' (*petits Airs, fort jolis & fort divertissans*)[68] reinforced the common culture of French courtiers to which the men and women of the salon aspired or fancied themselves to belong. A separate French repertory of social music are *airs à boire* (drinking-songs), which are by no means to be thought of as only tavern music. The Duke of Orléans, brother of Louis XIII, favoured this type of air and was obliged by Etienne Moulinié, who served him from 1628 to 1660. Moulinié's Third Book of *airs de cour* (1629) includes eight, with tablature for lute. The male conviviality of the duke's milieu is also reflected in Moulinié's airs in Spanish and Italian that call for guitar accompaniment.

Songs on bass patterns

Improvising over various standard bass patterns was one of the most characteristic Baroque ways of making music. Many such patterns surfaced in the

---

67 B. de Bacilly, *L'art de bien chanter, augmenté d'un discours qui sert de réponse à la critique de ce traité* (Paris, 1679; repr. Geneva, 1993), pp. 99–100.
68 Ibid., p. 98.

sixteenth century, and the most distinctive were formulas with the symmetrical phrasing of dance music, such as the duple-time *passamezzo* (It.) and the triple-time *folía* and *chacona*, to use their original Spanish names. *Pasacalles* (Sp.) on guitar, in contrast, were associated with vocal music from the start. Serving as preludes, postludes or interludes, they were the least formulaic in progression, mode, and bass line. In the seventeenth century, they had migrated to supporting vocal lines and generating songs themselves. Other patterns associated with vocal improvisation, such as the Romanesca and *Ruggiero*, two Italian names for basses that frequently accompanied *ottave rime* (and other fixed poetic forms), were also not tied to dance phrasing. Rather than fixed reiterations of brief bass figures, as with the *ciaccona* (It.), or of two complementary phrases as in some folias, a series of related phrases (with or without repetition) would form the bass for a single vocal stanza. The whole would be repeated for subsequent stanzas, while the vocal line varied. (Such vocal pieces have sometimes been termed 'strophic-bass' compositions, but this modern designation also includes free basses not on standard patterns.) By the seventeenth century, this entire repertory of bass patterns was already in the hands and ears of both professional and amateur performers of the Spanish guitar, for which chord-symbol notation appeared in the 1590s.[69] Songs on common bass patterns appear in numerous Italian printed sources into the 1630s, and they are also found in early opera. Vocal music using such formulas thus ranged from tunes in the oral repertory to cleverly sectional *concerti*, elaborate sets of vocal variations, emblematic laments in cantatas, and Latin motets. Together they do not form any single repertory: some are tidily strophic, others require high vocal virtuosity as a cyclic variation form spins out. Developed and transformed, varieties of ostinato music became transnational, expressive musical emblems in their own right.

One patently popular example is the well-known English tune 'Greensleeves', whose strains were generated by the *passamezzo antico* and Romanesca basses. John Ward has traced its instrumental versions in the seventeenth century, as well as different contemporary texts for the tune, which was better known then as 'The Blacksmith'.[70] The Neapolitan lutenist Andrea

---

69 In 1596 Joan Carles Amat (d. 1642) used numbers to represent chords on the five-string guitar; Italians used letters (*alfabeto* notation) from about 1595. For the sources for and development of the *ciaccona*, *passacaglia* and *folía*, given in chronologically ordered complete pieces, see Hudson, *The Folia, the Saraband, the Passacaglia, and the Chaconne*. John Hill has also shown that the early monody repertory is included in text anthologies with chord symbols for guitar (*Roman Monody, Cantata, and Opera from the Circles around Cardinal Montalto*, i: 169–72). This phenomenon is to be interpreted as the 'higher' social level at which guitars are being played rather than as new-style, composed monodies entering the repertories of a 'lower' class of musician.

70 Ward, 'And Who but Ladie Greensleeves?', pp. 197–9, gives a classified chronological list of versions for the seventeenth century, including numerous 'substitute' song texts.

Falconieri provides a composed example of an 'aria sopra la ciaccona' in a popular vein with his 'O vezzosetta dalla chioma d'oro' (in his *Libro primo di villanelle a 1. 2. et 3 voci*, Rome, 1616);[71] it is a strophic villanella for tenor, bass and Spanish guitar. Such ostinato idioms, still with their popular flavours, were taken into the new music being composed for the Italian courts and patriciates. Stefano Landi's 'T'amai gran tempo e sospirai mercede', published in 1627 with symbols for guitar accompaniment, opens in a declamatory style, like an *ottava rima* performance over a *Ruggiero* bass.[72] Complaining that the woman he loves has turned to others, the singer then declares that he is now over her and shifts to a mocking *ciaccona* with a folk-like refrain alluding to his pecker: 'I don't want you, you know, for the blackbird has flown and passed over the Po. Hurry, hurry, and see him go!' At each repetition of the six stanzas, the *ciaccona* section intensifies the singer's wounded pride at the same time that its popular flavour makes his feelings a matter for amusement. One circumstantial irony must be noted: Landi likely wrote the song for his former pupil Angelo Ferrotti to sing at the Savoy court in Turin, and Ferrotti was a castrato.

Standard *passacagli* for guitar comprised four-bar harmonic cycles that closed each time on a tonic chord. One exceptional version, however, transformed into an ostinato bass that sinks to a dominant (e.g., Am–Em6–Dm6–EM, resolving to Am to begin the cycle anew). Frescobaldi's 'Così mi disprezzate?' appears to be the progenitor of this variant in vocal music (Florence, 1630). As a simple four-note pattern, the bass pervades the lover's complaint 'Usurpator tiranno', a 'cantada' by Giovanni Sances published in his *Cantade... Libro secondo, parte prima* (Venice, 1633).[73] Sances offers 51 repetitions of the ostinato, with a free, recitative interruption between statements 46 and 47. Like Landi's *ciaccona* refrain, the cantata by Sances is not far from its guitarist's milieu. The poem consists of eight quatrains. The triple-time melody is song-like and largely syllabic, but musically through-composed. As in Landi's aria, the singer is fighting jealousy and declaring his constancy to a generic 'Lilla', who has taken another lover. The singer is just a woebegone, guitar-strumming chap, not a bereft shepherd of the *seconda pratica*. His vocal line has

71 Hudson, *The Folia, the Saraband, the Passacaglia, and the Chaconne*, iv: 12; recorded on *Ciaccona: la gioia della musica nell'Italia del '600*, Ensemble Anthonello, Symphonia sy 01187 (2001).

72 S. Landi, *Il secondo libro d'arie musicali* (Rome, 1627; repr. Florence, 1980), pp. 14–15; for a modern edition, see Murata, '"Singing", "Acting" and "Dancing" in Vocal Chamber Music of the Early Seicento', ex. 9. It is recorded by L'Arpeggiata (dir. Christina Pluhar) on *Stefano Landi: 'Homo fugit velut umbra . . .'*, Alpha 020 (2003).

73 Hudson, *The Folia, the Saraband, the Passacaglia, and the Chaconne*, iii: 35–40; recorded on *Giovanni Sances*, Sarah Pillow (sop.) with Steven Player (guitar), Gaudeamus CD GAU 193 (2000). The word-form 'cantada' is likely a Venetian locution; see Cecchi, 'Le "cantade a voce sola" (1633) di Giovanni Felice Sances'; Leopold, '*Al modo d'Orfeo*', i: 260–82.

awkward moments, almost in parody of spontaneous improvisation; his insistent *rasgueado* strumming is a surrogate for love. Eleanor Caluori observed that in his cantatas Luigi Rossi used this sort of ostinato in 'verses emphasizing immutability, obsession, constancy, perseverance, endurance, or firm resolution'.[74] Constancy is also the emblem invoked in the 'major-mode' version of the descending, stepwise ostinato in Nicholas Lanier's 'No more shall meads be deck'd with flowers' (a sonnet by Thomas Carew).[75] But no ostinato figure in itself defines a work, and not all descending tetrachords are emblems of lament: rather, their emblematic significance needs to be 'read' as a component of, and in the context of, the musical portrait as a whole.

The transformation of guitar-style *pasacalles* into transcendental, lyric expressiveness is best known from theatrical music. A chamber twin to the 'Pur ti miro / Pur ti godo' love-duet that ended one version of the opera *L'incoronazione di Poppea* is Michel Lambert's *récit* 'Vos mespris chaque jour me causent mille allarmes' (first published in 1679).[76] With the same descending tetrachord in the same G-mode as the duet from the opera, the chamber solo takes pleasure in the tender sighs of love spurned. It is framed by a *ritournelle* of nine ostinato statements with two violins in gentle imitation above. They float the image of the singer's dreams, and the air itself seems more to emerge out of their music than to address the beloved. Another chamber solo tinged by the theatre is a 1681 setting of the lyric monologue that closes the first act of Pierre Corneille's play *Le Cid*. Marc-Antoine Charpentier set three of Corneille's six stanzas for the title character.[77] The declamatory first and third stanzas frame a triple-time, highly expressive *air sérieux* on a 'basse obligée'. Written out only once, the bass is an extension of the stepwise descending *passacaglia* bass, which repeats under a vocal line freely set in French 'chaconne' rhythms.[78]

Another Sances cantata from his 1633 volume addresses another fickle Lilla. In 'E così dunque, o Lilla' he uses even, descending octave scales as a ground-bass figure to set a five-stanza declaration of male constancy.[79] This compares nicely with Henry Purcell's setting of Katherine Philips's 'O solitude, my sweetest

---

74 Caluori, *The Cantatas of Luigi Rossi*, i: 83 (and ex. 72).

75 Lanier's melody survives with different basses, one called a 'ciacono'. The ground-bass version is from Playford's *Select Ayres and Dialogues . . . the Second Book* (London, 1669), where it is titled 'Loves Constancy'; see C. MacClintock (ed.), *The Solo Song, 1580–1730* (New York, 1973), pp. 146–8; Lanier, *The Complete Works*, ed. Callon, pp. 30–34, 169–70. It is recorded by Julianne Baird on *The English Lute Song*, Dorian DOR-90109 (1988); and by Paul Agnew on *Hero and Leander*, Metronome CDMET 1027 (1999).

76 From Lambert's *Airs à une, II, III, et IV parties* (Paris, 1689), pp. 186–8; it was also included in *XXII Livre d'airs de différents autheurs à deux parties* (Paris, 1679).

77 The three airs (H. 457–9), originally published in 1681 in the *Mercure galant* (January–March), have been recorded on *Charpentier: Les plaisirs de Versailles*, Les Arts Florissants, Erato 063014774-2 (1996). See also Hitchcock, 'Charpentier's Vocal Chamber Music'.

78 The pattern is G–F–Eb–D, extended by C–Bb, to which is added a cadential C–D–G.

79 In Leopold, *'Al modo d'Orfeo'*, ii: 105–11.

choice', dated 1684–5 (Z. 406).[80] Purcell fills out its *ciaccona* framework to create a similarly stepwise, though rising, ostinato bass (C–D–E♭–F–G–A♭ plus a cadential G–F–G–C). Compared to the equally stepwise and suave blandishments of Sances's singer – Silke Leopold calls the Italian vocal line an 'ostinato in an ostinato'[81] – Purcell's vocal line is eloquence itself in its irregular rhythms from French *récit* and the angular intervals of Italian soliloquy. The widely travelling line fully expresses the unspoken cares that have driven the singer to embrace her lonely state.

In these few examples of pieces built on standard bass patterns, the vocal lines maintain a consistent melodic style, despite some melismatic passages or interrupting declamatory sections. The vocal phrases are constantly varying, but neither they nor the stanzas they create are presented primarily as formal variations. In the first decades of the century, less simply repetitive basses underpinned vocal stanzas that were more systematically varied stanza by stanza, a genre parallel with instrumental sets of variations. Virtuoso examples abound. In Sigismondo d'India's *ottava rima* setting 'Dove potrò mai gir tanto lontano' (in his *Le musiche*, Milan, 1609),[82] the vocal cascades for two sopranos over a *Ruggiero* bass saturate the amorous text, investing every pair of lines with a material sensuousness only suggested by its conventional rhetoric. The accumulation of melismatic writing goes beyond *elocutio*, beyond the creation of a siren's song. Ippolito Macchiavelli (1568–1619) was a composer in the service of Cardinal Montalto in Rome. His 'Venuto è pur quel lagrimabil giorno' also sets pairs of poetic lines to a *Ruggiero* bass, for a total of eight *abb* stanzas, or *parti*, of equal length.[83] The first emphasises a narrative tone with slow, repeated declamatory tones. Subsequent *parti* focus on different types of figures and melismatic *passaggi*. The fifth, for example, shows off trills; in the last, continuous *passaggi* draw out each half line. In all this music performed by professionals and sung for their patrons, momentary sound becomes a palpable object of treasure, like a Baroque mirror framed with luxuriant curves of gilded, scrolling acanthus leaves.

One finds the export of this genre in Caspar Kittel's *Arien und Cantaten mit 1. 2. 3. und 4. Stimmen sambt beygefuegtem basso continuo*, op. 1 (Dresden, 1638).[84] Kittel was a theorbo player who had spent 1624 to 1629 in Venice, returning

---

80 *The Theater of Music, or A Choice Collection of the Newest and Best Songs Sung at the Court, and Public Theaters*, 4 vols (London, 1685–97), iv: 57–9; facs. in R. Macnutt (ed.), *Music for London Entertainment, 1660–1800*, A/1 (Tunbridge Wells, 1983).

81 Leopold, *'Al modo d'Orfeo'*, i: 270.

82 S. d'India, *Le musiche a una e due voci, libri I, II, III, IV e V* (1609–23), ed. J. Joyce, 'Musiche rinascimentali siciliane', 9/2 (Florence, 1989), pp. 99–106.

83 Venice, Conservatorio di Musica Benedetto Marcello, MS Torrefranca 250, ff. 17–21; in Hill, *Roman Monody, Cantata, and Opera from the Circles around Cardinal Montalto*, ii: 25–30.

84 Ed. W. Braun, 'Pratica musicale', 5 (Winterthur, 2000).

to Germany with Heinrich Schütz, with whom he then served in Dresden. He used a *Ruggiero* bass to set Opitz's 'Kombt, laßt uns ausspazieren' for bass soloist and continuo. (The bass pattern is identical to Macchiavelli's.) After a simple opening stanza in which the singer doubles the continuo, five more stanzas offer strings of dotted figures, fast repeated notes, and turning and scalar *passaggi* over a two-octave vocal range. These are justified by the poetic conceit. Birds are free, but even if the lover learned to sing like a bird, his love would not hear him. To be freed from his pain, he must be caught. Kittel's other 'cantatas' include another *Ruggiero* for two tenors, a 'Passeggiata' for solo tenor, and a Romanesca for two sopranos.

Although neither follows through as a consistently ostinato composition, the 'Rondeau sur le mouvement de la chacone' and a 'Passacagle' in the *Airs à deux parties* (1669) by Joseph Chabanceau de La Barre combine ostinato composition with the French practice of varying second strophes. Both present their bass patterns in instrumental introductions. 'Si c'est un bien que l'esperance' (the 'Rondeau . . .') has the tender 3/2 stateliness of the French noble style.[85] Its ostinato pattern is not the Italian *ciaccona* bass, but a descending stepwise scale in C major that sometimes turns at the F to move to the dominant, and sometimes extends down the whole octave. The short version appears in the instrumental *ritournelle* and, again unusually, in a second *ritournelle* that precedes the return of the second half of the air. This leads to the vocal refrain *en rondeau*, embellished, as is the entire second couplet. The long version of the ostinato bass supports the voice in both halves of the couplets, which adds an emblem of constancy beyond that of the refrains. Liberal 7–6 suspensions mark suffering sweetened by hope, or 'esperance' tinged with 'souffrance'. With a sarabande rhythmic figure marking the vocal line, the Spanish *chacona* and French *chaconne* are hardly recognisable as cousins.

Strophic forms and variation

Strophic settings form a major part of the early seventeenth-century vocal repertory, ranging from the popular to what might be defined as 'art'-song. In his *Le nuove musiche* of 1602, Giulio Caccini included both madrigals and arias, the latter being defined more by having poetry in several stanzas than by their musical style (e.g., as triple-time dance-songs). Also called canzonettas, the new strophic songs had variety in phrase lengths and an expressive grace that reflected the literary influence of the poet. The problem with any simple strophic setting, however, is that the music invented for the first stanza

85 J. Chabanceau de La Barre, *Airs a deux parties avec les seconds couplets en diminution* (Paris, 1669; repr. Paris, 1992), sig. B1v–B3r recorded by Jean-Paul Fourchécourt on *Airs de cour*, Glissando CD 779 013-2 (2000).

of a poem may not very well suit the content of the second and subsequent stanzas. In an Italian, French or Spanish poem, the word stresses in later stanzas might even be in different metric positions. Such mismatches between text and music might or might not be smoothed over in performance by means of inflection, adding judicious embellishment or even singing later stanzas as outright variations.

The vocal variations associated with pieces on formulaic basses remind us that the ability to ornament was the mark of a certain level of competence in singing. Johann Nauwach's 'Asterie mag bleiben wer sie will', from his *Teutsche Villanellen mit 1. 2. und 3. Stimmen* (Freiberg, 1627), is a bipartite *villanella* with clear, short phrases for two sopranos mostly in parallel thirds. He published its fourth and last stanza 'passeggiata', with both voices still largely in parallel thirds but with additional quick, decorative flourishes. Printed singing tutors explain the simplest embellishments but also admonish that not everyone has the throat to execute them well, much less the discernment to spout them tastefully. Giulio Caccini set the principles for the 'correct' use of embellishments in the preface to his *Le nuove musiche* (1602). These would serve as criteria for good improvisation or good composition for the rest of the century: use embellishments only where warranted by the text and at important cadences. The German Wolfgang Michael Mylius advocates the same in his 1685 treatise, although the style he had in mind was probably as much French as Italian.[86] In the refined environment of the *air de cour*, being able to embellish second strophes proved one's knowledge of its special musical language and, ideally, of one's ability in elocution, for properly placed embellishments could bring the 'air' of the first strophe into a closer relation to the words of the second. Few models exist for embellishing *airs de cour* proper before 1643,[87] although personal manuscript anthologies sometimes preserve samples of ornamentation practice. Three sources of mid-century English court song in Italian, French, and English have embellishments written out for their privileged users.[88] In the 1660s, composers already mentioned such as Lambert, Bacilly and Chabanceau de La Barre published their airs with ornamented second strophes. Bacilly's treatise on *L'art de bien chanter* (1679) also addressed the partisans and critics of embellishment in French singing. He pointed out that singers who embellish poorly were the ones who caused critics to say that diminutions ruin words. 'Variations are made more than ever', he tells us, as long as they suit the text.[89]

---

86 Butt, *Music Education and the Art of Performance in the German Baroque*, pp. 140–41. Here Butt also surveys instruction in ornamentation in German tutors across the century.

87 See the summary of the views on embellishment of Mersenne, Jean Millet and Bacilly in Durosoir, *L'air de cour en France*, pp. 311–25; for the later French repertory, see Massip, *L'art de bien chanter*, pp. 247–61.

88 In Callon (ed.), *Songs with Theorbo*.   89 Bacilly, *L'art de bien chanter*, pp. 205–27.

Except possibly for the French air, ornamentation in strophic vocal chamber music from the last third of the century probably resembled contemporary operatic practice, whether the sections to be ornamented were complete strophes, refrains or, at the end of century, da-capo sections in arias. Earlier practice and the advice of Mylius suggest that embellishments added in performance continued to retain the character of the melody, rather than transforming it in the excessive manner of the early eighteenth century.

Poems not in strophic form could be treated as if they were, in order to elicit (or compose) embellishments on the opening section. Certain fixed poetic forms were typically divided into *parti*: the eight lines of a stanza in *ottava rima* could be split into two- or four-line groupings, or a sonnet into two quatrains and two tercets. The second and subsequent *parti* would then be subject to variation, even though the separate musical sections might cover unequal numbers of poetic lines. (A three-line *parte* could simply repeat its last line to vary a fourth musical phrase.) Sometimes only the vocal lines would vary; sometimes changes also occurred in the basso continuo part. Musically, this procedure has been called 'strophic variation' whether the bass line is a standard ostinato pattern or a freely composed bass, whether the original poem itself is strophic or not, and whether the *parti* or strophes have quite similar musical shapes or veer off into fantasy. Up to about the middle of the century, embellishment on a more modest scale is frequently found, and was certainly expected, in the second and later stanzas of canzonettas or ariettas. The original melody may have a syllabic, 'walking' style and perhaps may even be lightly ornamented itself; it may also contain a declamatory passage with little melodic profile of its own. Melodic variants in the subsequent stanzas typically do not dramatically change the rhythmic or expressive character of the basic model. Caccini himself pointed out that he used *passaggi* more in 'those songs [that are] less expressive' (*quelle musiche meno affettuose*).[90] In this class are the hundreds of strophic Italian pieces for which prints usually give only the texts of subsequent stanzas.

Strophic pieces for which the composer writes out moderately varied stanzas often prove to be subtly nuanced musical readings of their poems. With stanzas that have subsections in different styles and metres, the whole with all its varied strophes can have the breadth of something both through-composed and coherent. A luminous example is Luigi Rossi's treatment of the four stanzas of the poem 'Precorrea del sol l'uscita' by Domenico Benigni.[91] A lover has spent a sleepless night alone, tossing and turning in Cupid's treacherous

---

90 G. Caccini, preface to *Le nuove musiche* (Florence, 1602; repr. New York, 1973), p. [iii].
91 Caluori, *The Cantatas of Luigi Rossi*, i, ex. 72; ii, no. 148.

seas. After a brief declamatory half-phrase, twelve passacaglia-like bars in a fluid triple time begin to capture in music the emotions suspended in that brief moment between sleeping and wakefulness. The aria-style shifts to a florid recitative conclusion that itself moves from dark to light. These stylistic contrasts remain in each stanza, as do the basic pitches of the continuo line. The vocal line, however, changes pitch, rhythm, contour and phrase lengths, while retaining a few distinct melodic and harmonic markers. In the course of the four stanzas the listener experiences an intimate view of a hopeful soul caught in the unpredictable undertows of love.

Strophic arias from theatrical works are often mixed with chamber compositions in manuscripts, where much of the chamber repertory after 1640 lies. They have yet to be separated out in many instances because their styles are similar, if not the same. A case in point are the 75 'moral and political' arias with instrumental ritornellos by Philipp Heinrich Erlebach, published in 1697 and 1710. Partly because of their highly strophic nature (many with up to five or six stanzas), they have been discussed as rare examples of German courtly chamber music as it 'developed' after Heinrich Albert. However, 60 of them, despite their multiple strophes, are now known to have come from stage works.[92]

Variety and voice in madrigal and cantata

At the beginning of this chapter, I noted that although the unaccompanied polyphonic madrigal and the solo madrigal differed in musical texture, in Italy the audiences for both were the same literary and musical elites. This was in part because both drew upon the same bodies of Italian poetry: classics such as the fourteenth-century poems of Petrarch and his later imitators, newer non-strophic lyric verse, and excerpts from, or imitations of, courtly pastoral plays (especially Tasso's *Aminta* and Guarini's *Il pastor fido*). Poetry for madrigals was consistently in freely rhymed lines of seven and eleven syllables. Composers even set more regular forms such as sonnets and *ottave rime* in through-composed madrigal style.

Whether in polyphony or in solo writing, by 1600 musical settings of such verse aimed both to express and deliver the words artfully and originally. The polyphonic madrigal could realise this through an ever-changing variety of styles, harmony, rhythm, and textures that included, by the 1620s, solo passages and duets. Solo continuo madrigals could employ changing speeds of declamation, varying senses of metre, plain as opposed to florid lines, and the strategic shaping of vocal registers and range. Instrumental passages could

---

92 B. Baselt, 'Erlebach, Philipp Heinrich', in S. Sadie (ed.), *The New Grove Dictionary of Opera*, 4 vols (London, 1992), ii: 68–9.

function as contrasting 'choral' textures in concerted works. An air by Dowland
or Boësset, in contrast, or an anonymous polyphonic *romance*, would tend to be
more uniform. This uniformity, in addition to the strophic repetitions, makes
airs and *romances* more like 'song' to us. By comparison, it is often extremes of
expressive means and not form or texture that mark a piece as 'madrigalian',
be it 'Cruda Amarilli, che col nome ancora' set for five voices by Marenzio in
1595, or by Monteverdi in 1605, or the same text set by Sigismondo d'India for
one voice and theorbo in 1609. Although formally it is a strophic *balletto*, we
hear Thomas Weelkes's 'O Care, thou wilt despatch me' (1600) as madrigalian,
not only because of the expressive dissonances it borrowed from the madrigal but also because its divergent moods exaggerate each other by reflection.
The same impulse to exploit expressive variety may juxtapose recitational and
song-like passages in many solo pieces of the first half century. We shall see that
in these solos, such variety often bears the extra responsibility of articulating
the progressive stages of the poetic discourse.

Not only did seventeenth-century polyphonic and solo madrigals set similar
poetry. Both also frequently set poems in the first person ('I') that directly
address another person or persons. Classicist Walter Johnson calls this principal
form of ancient Greek lyric the 'I–You' stance and distinguishes it from poems
in which the poet speaks to himself or addresses non-persons in a meditative
manner (such as breezes, birds, his own heart, etc.). 'I–You' poems were what the
Greeks termed 'monody'.[93] By the seventeenth century, this type was not new
in either French or Italian poetry but part of a chronologically broad genre of
lyric that also differs from narrative texts in ballad style, as well as from dialogues
and dramatic monologues; it could also be found in strophic poetry. 'Do you
think I live?' Guarini asks of his 'dear love' in Marenzio's five-voice setting of
'Credete voi ch'i' viva' in his *Nono libro de madrigali a cinque voci* (Venice, 1599).
'I will never let you free me from this tyranny' exclaims an ensemble by Antoine
de Boësset.[94] The accompanied vocal solo, it could be argued, adds an element
of the natural, or verisimilar, to the musical delivery of such poems. Although
neither sets an 'I–You' poem, John Dowland's lute-song 'Flow, my tears' (1600)
sung by one singer will seem more subjective than Weelkes's *balletto* 'O Care,
thou wilt despatch me' (1600) sung by five: we do not perceive Weelkes's singers
as five wretched individuals commiserating with each other. Not surprisingly,
Caccini's madrigals and arias in *Le nuove musiche* almost consistently adopt
'I–You' structures; they dominate the solos in Peri's *Le varie musiche* (1609).
(When Peri presents the second type of subjectivity, in which the poet talks to

93 Johnson, *The Idea of Lyric*, p. 3.
94 'Jamais n'auray je le pouvoir', from Boësset's 5me *Livre d'airs de cour à 4 & 5 parties* (Paris, 1626), in
Durosoir, *L'air de cour en France*, p. 395.

himself, it is through Petrarch sonnets, not contemporary poetry.) The monodic *Madrigali di diversi autori* of 1610 by Francesco Rasi, another member of the Florentine circle, have the same 'I–You' stance in solo madrigal, arietta and sonnet settings. The appeals, questions and complaints of these poems, though perennial to the human condition, were predominantly conditioned by the literary genre, irrespective of the musical forms in which they were set.

The diffusion of monody did not preclude two, three or five singers from continuing to speak as a singular 'I' in madrigals and canzonettas. 'I–You' poems dominate Monteverdi's Fourth Book of polyphonic madrigals (1603) as they do contemporary books of monody.[95] In his *Madrigali guerrieri, et amorosi* of 1638, Monteverdi calls for eight singers to sing the first-person text, 'Ardo, avvampo, mi struggo, ardo: accorrete' ('I burn, I catch fire, I'm consumed, I burn: run').[96] Its long opening section in the *concitato* style mimics the clamour and excitement of a fire, a fire brigade and onlookers, amplifying the heat of the poet's desire. Like an engraving, the music develops the madrigal as an emblematic illustration as well as if it were captioned 'The lover seeks to quench the fires of his passion', in the manner of Heinrich Albert's Latin tags or one of Menestrier's *emblemes passionez*.[97] The polyphonic, texturally diverse madrigal re-presents its poem by a series of musical extrusions, an 'ex-pressing' of its figures that in totality creates an objective rendering that can be scanned and read. Rhetorical figures are its components, which the composer has realised in a three-dimensional musical space. How could composers give up such a successful way to express this poetry, illustrating its illustrations?

Indeed the capacity of polyphonic settings to handle 'I–You' poetry is partly due to the rhetorical role of the 'I' in such poems. Johnson emphasises that we must suspend our post-Romantic expectations of lyric subjectivity when considering the Greek 'I', for Greek lyric 'is not mere *Gefühlspoesie* ("poetry of feeling") or *Erlebnislyrik* ("poetry of experience")'. Concerned with 'describing the reality of the inner passions and with deliberating on their nature and meaning', Greek lyric offers a 'criticism of human passion that will indicate which passions are to be embraced and which are to be shunned; the purpose of this demonstration is the education of the hearer'.[98] It is in such a

---

95 Of the twenty madrigals in Monteverdi's Fourth Book of madrigals (1603), four texts come from Guarini's play *Il pastor fido*; three mix narrative and direct speech; and one *ottava* from Tasso's *Gerusalemme liberata* is purely narrative. The others are 'I–You' addresses, of which in only two does the poet address himself. Monteverdi's Fifth Book (1605) sets many texts drawn from *Il pastor fido*.

96 Margaret Mabbett suggests that this scoring may be associated with performance for the Viennese court; see her 'Le connessioni stilistiche tra l'Ottavo Libro di Monteverdi ed il madrigale *avant-garde* a Vienna', p. 82.

97 C.-F. Menestrier, *L'art des emblemes ou s'enseigne la morale par les figures de la fable, de l'histoire & de la nature* (Paris, 1684; repr. Mittenwald, 1981), pp. 159–69.

98 Johnson, *The Idea of Lyric*, pp. 6, 35, 30, 31.

deliberative, even accusative, mode that many of the 'selves' of the sixteenth and seventeenth centuries speak. Johnson observes that not only do 'I–You' poems outweigh the other types of lyric at the outset of the seventeenth century, but also that the expression in them is closer to ancient lyric than to poetry of the eighteenth century or later. Such rhetorical comparisons help adjust our frame of reference with regard to the huge quantity of earlier Baroque music about lovesickness, flirtation and sexual desperation, whether it comes from the mouths of courtiers or of idealised shepherds. And who is the audience for an 'I–You' poem? For often in love poetry, it is the absence of the 'you' addressed that prompts the poem. Johnson clarifies:

> By focusing on what he has to say, on why he is saying it, and on the person *for* whom – not so much *to* whom – he is saying it, the speaker discovers the exact, the proper, form for his own character as speaker . . . By discoursing, describing, deliberating, he becomes himself.[99]

In polyphonic madrigals, that self is inventive, energetic, and as verbally adept as the composer can demonstrate. Whatever the specific moods expressed, in the madrigal the 'I' displays itself. The vocal solo, in contrast, may give the physical illusion that the inner self, rather than the self's eloquence, is shaping the utterances; but the emergence of that 'self' in a typical 'I–You' poem still depends on a dialectic of poetic discourse rather than transcendence or revelation. Self-expression in the solo presentation may thus seem more laboured, circuitous or coy, as the centripetal energy of the madrigal is, as it were, compressed and forced into delivery by a single melodic line. The audience for both, however, still consists of those viewing the 'I', rather than being the 'You.'

'The public representation of interiority', Daniel Fischlin perceptively observed of the English lute song, 'is rife with tensions between the conventions of external display and the hermetic dissimulation of private contemplation'.[100] In the modern style, the musical means for 'moving the passions' did not exist in the abstract, or just in the words, or just in *pronuntiatio*. They were always dependent on the poetic forms in which they could be expressed and on the social settings in which those expressions could be shared. Shifts in musical style within solos can signal the stages of the discourse; they also provide the means for playing with and against expectations of style and expression.[101] The tensions between 'social' and 'private' account for much of the archness and self-consciousness of vocal solos, which also developed various artful modes both to distance self-expression and to deliver it with deftness and surprise.

---

99 Ibid., p. 31.   100 Fischlin, 'The Performance Context of the English Lute Song', p. 61.
101 Freitas, 'Singing and Playing'.

These included in-jokes of exteriorizing wit and satire, and the use of theatrical impersonation to permit 'direct' emoting.

Many lyric texts establish just this dissimulation by beginning with a narrative section, naming, say, Fileno or Corydon, and placing him in the resonant hills or by a weeping stream, before the poem shifts into direct speech. This often sets up a performative frame with a return to third-person narrative at the end, in a closing that often functions like the moralising epigram at the foot of an emblematic engraving. A polyphonic or concerted madrigal can establish this audibly by means of textural change. Monteverdi provides numerous examples up to and including his *Lamento della ninfa* (1638), in which a men's trio sings a narrative frame for a woman's solo complaints to Cupid. Her solo, however, is a discontinuous madrigalian line sung over a bass ostinato; it is neither recitative nor air. Luigi Rossi's 'Al soave spirar d'aure serene' is a monologue of the shipwrecked Arion (the text is by Giulio Rospigliosi).[102] It is framed by a narrative introduction of twelve lines and a narrative closure of ten, both in the same key. When the monologue moves to Arion's direct discourse, the musical techniques of the mid-century lament come into play, as if this were a dramatic scene. Arion appeals in impassioned recitative to the heavens, to his own thoughts, to anyone who can hear him. 'Ahi, chi mi porge aita? / Chi da morte mi toglie?' ('Ah, who will help me? Who will snatch me from death?') After his legendary rescue by the dolphin, the cantata finishes with an aria. This aria, however, is not in Arion's voice but in that of the narrator. The singer asks his listeners directly, 'If music can do this', i.e., bring a beast to your rescue, 'is it any wonder that the song of a beautiful woman can soothe any soul?' The aria, then, is not any kind of emotional reaction or expression from the main character. Instead it snaps the listeners back from the powerful musical speech of the theatre to the 'real world' of the chamber performance itself.

In the 1640s, the *stile rappresentativo* is the language of theatrical illusion; this is how Rossi generates the image of Arion. Ordinary song, the aria, states the external, emblematic key to that image. The cantata 'Appena il sol con le sue chiome belle' by Barbara Strozzi (in her *Diporti di Euterpe*, op. 7, Venice, 1659) has a poetic form similar to Rossi's, if with a seemingly more conventional use of musical styles: (1) narrator in recitative (with an arioso close), (2) 'the character' in aria, (3) narrator in recitative also with an arioso close.[103] Here the opening narration is not in story-telling mode, but in a spacious lyricism (based on the melodic unfolding of triads) characteristic of setting pastoral scenes. Its closing arioso moves to *cheerful* music to announce the solo of a *grief-stricken* lover. This

---

102 Facs. in F. Luisi (ed.), *The Italian Cantata in the Seventeenth Century*, i (New York, 1986), no. 7.

103 Facs. in E. Rosand (ed.), *The Italian Cantata in the Seventeenth Century*, v (New York, 1985), no. 49.

unhappy Eurillo does not weep or gnash his teeth but, rather, sings a prayerful petition to Apollo in pastoral metres ('Aria adaggio' in 6/8 and 3) and in an entirely stable A major. This makes the narrator's closing all the more curious, when it remains persistently on major triads to describe Eurillo's 'shouting with grief' (*gridava . . . per soverchio dolore*) and then begins to fall into all kinds of patent madrigalisms: repeated quick quavers for 'passeggiando' (walking), sharp-to-flat chromatic slips for 'grief', turning figures for 'vacillating.' Finally, rushing descents in continuo and voice 'illustrate' the wretch slipping on the wet river bank and drowning. 'Thus', quips the closing arioso line, 'thus he quenched the flames of love'. The keyword 'quenched' (*amorzò*) is delayed to the last three notes, two semiquavers and, 'glug', a final quaver in voice and continuo – a stroke worthy of an animated cartoon. Pietro Dolfin's poem is a joke: the closing narrative section with its obvious word-painting is tongue-in-cheek, and Eurillo dies a victim of his sophisticated audience.

Similar shifts in musical styles easily signal changes in voice when a poem has only one speaker. Two text sources for Antonio Cesti's (1623–69) cantata 'Alpi nevose e dure' are captioned 'scherzo per musica' and 'capriccio per musica'.[104] In the poem by Giovanni Filippo Apolloni, a generic pastoral Fileno declares his desolation in recitative style to the snowy alps, to the echoing valleys and to hopeful memories. Cesti alternates musical styles to outline Fileno's 'dialectic', switching between an emotional recitative for his expostulations and a more balanced arioso for his reasoned responses.

> You, mountains, are hiding that sun from me which outshines the
>   sun . . . (recitative)
> *If I cannot enjoy the sun, at least I do not see it.* (arioso)
> And you, sweet thoughts . . . who disturb my peace and quiet,
>   (recitative)
> *cease! . . . Whoever asks for too much, does not really want it.* (arioso)

An interruption within the aria allows a third sententious triple-time arioso:

> Yes, yes! I want to die! . . . (aria)
> *And whoever does not know death does not deserve life.* (arioso)

This last aphorism lets Fileno sing *da capo* 'Yes, yes! I want to die' as a para-doxically positive claim to live. Does it all seem silly? Remember that Fileno, like Strozzi's swain Eurillo, is just a shepherd, and this is a *scherzo*. Fileno's reasoning consists of pastoral clichés cobbled together as argument. There is humour in its very clumsiness, and it is all due to the poet's wit. Cesti's

---

104 D. Burrows (ed.), *The Italian Cantata*, i: *Antonio Cesti (1623–1669)*, 'The Wellesley Edition', 5 (Wellesley, MA, 1963), no. 2; S. Fuller (ed.), *The European Musical Heritage, 800–1750* (New York, 1987), no. 67.

setting of emotional recitatives and 'resolute' passages in aria-style profiles and heightens its absurdities. Whether the aria-style passages are ariosos or arias is immaterial to understanding – and laughing at – poor Fileno's plight. Their use in such a satirical manner confirms their discursive rather than expressive function. Moreover, the convention of the sententious arioso remained valid even as the Italian cantata approached its more sedate, late Baroque shape with longer, more emotionally expressive full arias. In a seemingly more sincere vein is Alessandro Scarlatti's 'Piango, sospiro, e peno' ('I weep, I sigh, and I suffer'), one of his earlier pastoral cantatas for contralto, two violins and continuo (dated before 1693).[105] After three arias, which are now the scaffolding of the poetic discourse, the cantata closes with a recitative. It begins with the word 'Dunque' ('Therefore') and its closing line states the final judgement in a distinct arioso: 'To love you, Filli, is to not love oneself'.

The extension of these voice-shifting techniques through the century involved changes both in poetry and in music. The longest mid-century cantatas set texts that concoct inventive amalgams of conventional seven- and eleven-syllable lines for recitative coupled with texts in other poetic metres for arias in various styles, lengths and forms (not always strophic). Composers did and did not conform to the musical implications of the verse, and they were always free to turn a 'recitative' into an arioso. The resulting free sequences of narrative recitative, expressive recitative, florid recitative, syllabic arias in duple metre, lyric arias in triple metre, cheerful arias in compound metres, etc. – all bordered with ariosos – might be called 'patchwork', but that suggests a flat or abstract design. While their lack of narrative or dramatic structure classifies such cantatas as 'lyric', their deliberative discourse (to paraphrase Johnson) usually does aim at some emotional resolution, a point to the rhetorical exercise. While the discursive processes, however, may seem logical to the characters singing, most often they result in highly unstable wholes. They are sometimes exhausting in their changeability and held together only by the polished singing and committed delivery they require. Such fluid arguments persist in the cantatas by Pietro Simone Agostini (c. 1635–1680). In his *Observations on the Florid Song* (1723), Pierfrancesco Tosi judged Agostini and Alessandro Stradella (1639–82) the best of the last, lyric generation of Italian composers. Their cantatas offer the kind of indulgent musical inquiry into conflicting feelings – though often without the verbal wit of the earlier Seicento – that marks them as works for the chamber, rather than for the stage.

---

105 London, British Library, Add. MS 31506, ff. 121v–[126]; recorded by Brian Asawa on *Alessandro Scarlatti Cantatas*, iii, Deutsche Harmonia Mundi 75606 51325 2 (2000).

Genres of impersonation

Settings of lyric poetry in the madrigal and cantata repertory play with a characteristic set of ambiguities: the identity of the speaking 'voice' (which may be neither poet, nor composer, nor performer), the struggle between subjectivity and exteriority, and a pre-modern ambivalence between 'serious' expression and ironic deprecation tending to the parodic. These and other aspects of seventeenth-century 'wit' make this repertory both teasing and puzzling, and they help explain the difficulties encountered in most accounts of this music, whether on the part of scholars or of performers. We must remind ourselves that on the whole, seventeenth-century madrigals and chamber cantatas had exclusive audiences. One type of vocal chamber music from the period, however, would seem more straightforward, namely solo 'scenes' that brought the fiction of theatrical impersonation into the chamber. Such soliloquies were sung by 'named' figures – imaginary ones such as Ariadne from myth and Erminia from Tasso's epic, or historical personages such as General Albrecht von Wallenstein (d. 1634), who led Imperial troops in the Thirty Years War.[106]

For almost forty years, opera, like court ballets, was a private form of entertainment, heard only in courts and on occasion. The recitative soliloquies that so moved their audiences, however, quickly re-appeared as solo monologues heard in chamber performances (as well as in non-liturgical religious music). Expressive devices familiar then as now from Monteverdi's lament of the abandoned Ariadne from his 1608 opera *Arianna* were copied not just in free recitative compositions but also in older recitational forms such as the *ottava*. The corresponding French genre was the solo *récit*. The earliest, by Pierre Guédron, are from ballets written around 1610; but five by him that were published in 1620 in Antoine de Boësset's Ninth Book of lute airs appear to be independent of, and different from, his ballet music. In their unadorned declamatory style, says Georgie Durosoir, 'courtly lyricism reveals itself capable of a few tones of sincerity'.[107] Later, Bacilly observed that a 'grand Air, an *air de récit*, whose measure is slow' requires weight, steadfastness and force of expression other than the lightness suitable for an '*air de ballet*, a gavotte, a bacchic chanson'.[108] In Italy, the *stile rappresentativo* gave voice to mythological, historical or literary figures.[109] Sigismondo d'India set the dying Erminia's direct speech (an *ottava* from Tasso's *Gerusalemme liberata*) in 'Là tra 'l sangue e le morti egro giacente' (*Le musiche*, 1609).[110] Chromaticism, expanding and contracting

---

106 Dying and abandoned by his soldiers, he sings the anonymous cantata 'Ferma, ferma quel ferro.' A copy is in the Teynham MS (See note 9 above, p. 381).
107 Durosoir, *L'air de cour en France*, p. 106.   108 Bacilly, *L'art de bien chanter*, p. 89.
109 One subgenre of the solo monologue is discussed in Porter, '*Lamenti recitativi da camera*'.
110 D'India, *Le musiche a una e due voci*, ed. Joyce, pp. 62–3.

vocal intervals, poignant dissonance, and eerie harmonic shifts vivify the setting. Nicholas Lanier, an English court musician from a French musical family,
demonstrated his mastery of the Italian soliloquy style in 'Nor com'st thou yet,
my slothful love'.[111] Hero declaims for 191 bars before flinging herself into the
Hellespont after her drowned lover, Leander. Roger North dated this piece
to sometime in the later 1620s and reported a consort performance of it for
the king. Samuel Pepys later sang it to his guitar.[112] The dramatic recitative
styles of the tragic messenger and lamenting monody are joined in Domenico
Mazzocchi's Latin dialogue *Dido furens* (1638), most likely written for performance before the literary, antiquarian circles of his patron Cardinal Ippolito
Aldobrandini and his brother's patron, Cardinal Francesco Barberini.[113] The
poet Virgil narrates the departure of Aeneas from Carthage and Dido's suicide
in words from his own epic. Dido (soprano) and Aeneas (tenor) sing their own
roles. The continuo harmony throughout is broad and fundamentally simple,
in keeping with the notion of epic recitation; but in the vocal lines, ninths above
the bass, augmented intervals, chromatic shifts and rapid rhythmic changes,
as well as expression and tempo markings such as *arrabbiato, adagio, concitato*
and *presto*, all focus attention on the sheer emotional content of Virgil's noble
hexameters.

In 'Ferma, lascia ch'io parli', the poet Apolloni portrayed Mary Stuart, the
Catholic Queen of Scotland, staying the hand of her executioner to speak her last
words.[114] A century later in his *General History of Music*, Charles Burney singled
out Carissimi's cantata on this text with no fewer than five musical illustrations.
Not only is the declamation bold and forceful, the queen also rues her fate in an
embedded triple-time aria marked Adagio, in C minor. Its opening five bars set
only the words 'A morire' ('To die'). They serve as a ritornello and join the first
stanza to the second, which is varied; they also return at the end. In the closing
recitative the queen rails at London and the Jezebel who rules 'the Anglican
troops'. At the height of her defiance, which includes notated high Cs and B♭s,
she proudly repeats 'A morire, a morire' and gives her neck to the axe. Of the
same genre is Purcell's setting of Nahum Tate's *The Blessed Virgin's Expostulation*
('Tell me, some pitying angel', Z. 196), a monologue of a distraught mother
who cannot find her child.[115] It contains two sections in metric, song-like styles

111 Lanier, *The Complete Works*, ed. Callon, pp. 35–48; recorded by Richard Wistreich on *The Musical
Life of Samuel Pepys*, Saydisc CD-SDL 385 (1990); and by Paul Agnew on *Hero and Leander*, Metronome MET
CD 1027 (1999).

112 Lanier, *The Complete Works*, ed. Callon, pp. 170–71.

113 In Mazzocchi, *Dialoghi, e sonetti posti in musica* (Rome, 1638; repr. Bologna, 1969).

114 Facs. in G. Massenkeil (ed.), *The Italian Cantata in the Seventeenth Century*, ii (New York, 1986), no.
17; recorded by Jill Feldman on *Udite amanti: 17th-Century Italian Love Songs*, Linn Records CDK 005 (1991).

115 It was published in Henry Playford's anthology *Harmonia Sacra*, ii (London, 1693), f. 4v.

that have the same tonic as the whole and are strongly embedded in the flow of an otherwise declamatory air. The Virgin first calls upon Gabriel, resolving her first question, 'Tell me . . . where does my . . . darling stray?', with the answer 'The desert's safer than a tyrant's court'. Purcell sets this off with a cadential melisma. The Virgin's 'I–You' address then turns to four questions put to her lost son. The subsequent first song-like section, 'Me Judah's daughters once caress'd', represents a temporary shift in voice. An arioso in C major that sets two lines of a tercet, its thought resolves in the six bars of recitative that both complete the tercet and conclude the recitative portion of the soliloquy ('Now fatal change: [I am] of mothers most distress'd'). The next and final five lines of the poem could have formed a single closing aria. Purcell set the first three lines as a binary air in C minor – 'How shall my soul its motions guide? / How shall I stem the various tide? . . .' – but the composer chose to separate the closing couplet by returning to expressive recitative. By reversing the usual association of questions with recitative and of aria-style with conclusions, Purcell leaves the 'scene' unresolved, as is the Virgin herself.

Alessandro Stradella wrote a number of cantatas that display emblematic moments from the 'lives' of well-known ancient heroes. Some demand the verisimilitude of the tenor or bass voice or have survived in editions transposed for male voice. Belisarius after his downfall is scored for a tenor, while the emperor Nero watching Rome burn is a (rather imbecilic) bass. Other solo cantatas portray the deaths of Xerxes, Seneca and Germanicus. Stradella depicted only two women, Ariadne and Medea from Classical myth: these betrayed women rage, desire revenge, and rue lost love, and in the end, both are overcome by tenderness and constancy towards the men who abandoned them. Stradella's portrayal of Ariadne in 'Ferma il corso e torna al lido' evolves in six highly virtuoso aria sections and in forceful as well as florid recitative.[116] It takes nearly twenty minutes, far longer than the scene would be allowed in an opera. The arias are inventively bizarre. Moments of repeated ostinatos in the bass with bent and sliding chromaticism represent the conventional emblem of life on treacherous seas. Vigorous repeated chords invoke hell's creatures. An unaccompanied opening to an aria (imitated by the continuo) portrays Ariadne's vulnerability. There are walking and driving basses and a range of triple metres, including a fast 3/8. In short, there is so much variety that the expressiveness of the recitative passages is nearly obscured. The key of B minor anchors the dolorous first section and the end of the cantata. But the harmonic range in between is desperately wide. The third through sixth arias are in E minor ('I will conquer your pride'), C major ('In the embrace

---

116 Facs. in A. Stradella, *XII cantate a voce sola*, ed. P. Mioli (Florence, 1983), ff. 67–83; recorded by Christine Brandes on *Stradella Cantatas*, Harmonia Mundi USA HMU 907192 (1998).

of Erebus'), G minor ('In a sea of immense joy'), and D major ('Bleeding and unburied'). Stradella's Ariadne has none of the statuesque, sorrowful nobility of Monteverdi's heroine. She is as much a victim of her own passions as of Theseus' betrayal. Monteverdi's heroine is a martyr; Stradella's has no physical body to lose. She becomes whatever the artist paints of her gestures, whatever the sculptor moulds in the agonised folds of her gown, before she dissolves into the next passion. She is both Stradella's creature and his tortured victim. In the G minor aria, major and minor do not struggle against each other; rather Ariadne's vision of happiness is but a mist that cannot soothe her pain.

The conventions of late seventeenth-century opera, where emotion is open to public view, tamed such excess. The recitative/da-capo aria succession of the stage became more or less the parallel procedure in Italian cantatas by the end of the century. A case in point is Alessandro Scarlatti's cantata *Didone abbandonata* ('Alle troiane antenne', dated 1705), for voice and continuo only.[117] After a narrator's recitative opening, the sorrowful Dido speaks in three slow da-capo arias. In each one, a motivically rich basso continuo line sets a highly saturated mood and tone, as their keys progressively darken. In the first, she accuses Aeneas of betrayal in A minor. The second rues the depth of her love for him in D minor, in an Adagio 12/8. In the last, she labours to decide her own fate in a circular 6/4, in a chromatic F minor. Moments of contrast, or freedom, break through in the brief intervening recitatives. The last aria, 'A punir di quest'alma l'errore' ('To punish the sin of this heart'), is founded on a six-bar migrating ostinato figure that is a tonal variant of the earlier *passacaglio* line F–E♭–D♭–C plus the cadential A♭–B♭–C–F, but with an E♮ as the second bass note (Scarlatti's harmony is i–V–iv–V + i–iv–V–i). Throughout, the 'sharps' of secondary leading-tones penetrate the grimness of the flat harmonies, which extend to G♭ chords. Dido speaks of her shame in the B section of the aria, where the harmony dissolves and slides chromatically. But the ostinato returns in the *da capo*, inevitably, as Dido resolves that 'to punish the sin' of her heart, her only recourse is death. Yet the cantata is not an unstaged operatic suicide. Although the texture and harmonic language of the closing aria are modern, the cantata is related to its chamber antecedents in the educative logic of the series of recitatives and arias addressed 'to Aeneas', through the ostinato that leads Dido to realise her constancy, and by the moral purport (as self-punishment) of her decision to die.

Such cantatas are normally viewed as the epitome of the new styles and genres that emerged in secular vocal music in the seventeenth century, leaving the polyphonic madrigal far behind. Vincenzo Giustiniani ended his survey

117 Facs. in M. Boyd (ed.), *The Italian Cantata in the Seventeenth Century*, xiii (New York, 1986), no. 17.

(*c.* 1628) of music in his lifetime lamenting the decline of five-voice madrigals. In 1638, Domenico Mazzocchi dedicated a volume of such pieces to Cardinal Francesco Barberini (who encouraged their performance), observing, however, that 'today few compose them, and fewer sing them, seeing that they have been almost banished from academies, to their misfortune'.[118] Yet the madrigal, like the English consort song, did not entirely disappear, remaining music for *cognoscenti*. Composer Antonio Maria Abbatini in Rome headed an academy for musicians in the 1660s that met monthly and sang madrigals 'at table', and his star pupil Domenico dal Pane published at least two volumes of them (the second one in 1678). Giovanni Maria Bononcini's op. 11 madrigals, also of 1678, are written in each of the twelve *tuoni*, or modes. Printed books of madrigals from the first decades of the seventeenth century were still in stock in 1676 at the shop of Federico Franzini in Rome, as were also Caccini's *Le nuove musiche* of 1602 and Peri's *Le varie musiche* of 1609.[119] Five-voice madrigals 'per teorica e prattica' by Adrian Willaert sat on the shelf next to Domenico Mazzocchi's four- and five-voice madrigals of 1638, and the *Madrigali a 2. 3. e 4 voci* (1640) by a young Pietro Andrea Ziani, who would soon take up a post in Naples. Alessandro Scarlatti is credited with the composition of eight polyphonic madrigals, all preserved in manuscript.[120] That he set two poems by Marino and two other texts by Rinuccini and Torquato Tasso underscores the academic and antiquarian interest in the genre. Madrigals also acquired a new calling-card as representatives of the *stile antico*: a January 1733 concert of the London Academy of Ancient Music offered two madrigals by Marenzio and a 'Cruda Amarilli' attributed to Paolo Petti (d. 1678). Thus a genre that at one time was heard in the same venues as solo chamber singing, and that offered the most advanced forms of text expression, came to represent a minor genre of contrapuntal mastery attached to poetry of a past age, a fate that obscures the importance of the madrigal to Baroque musical expression.

Bibliography

Adam, W. (ed.), *Geselligkeit und Gesellschaft im Barockzeitalter*. 2 vols, Wiesbaden, 1997

Agamennone, M., 'Cantar l'ottava'. In Kezich, *I poeti contadini*, pp. 171–218

Assenza, C., *La canzonetta dal 1570 al 1615*. Lucca, 1997

Austern, L. P., '"For Love's a good musician": Performance, Audition, and Erotic Disorders in Early Modern Europe'. *Musical Quarterly*, 82 (1998), 614–53

Braun, W., '*Concordia discors*: Zur geselligen Musikkultur im 17. Jahrhundert'. In Adam (ed.), *Geselligkeit und Gesellschaft im Barockzeitalter*, i: 93–111

118 Mazzocchi, *Madrigali a cinque voci, et altri varii concerti* (Rome, 1638).
119 Mischiati, *Indici, cataloghi e avvisi degli editori e librai musicali italiani*, pp. 244–63.
120 A. Scarlatti, *Acht Madrigale*, ed. J. Jürgens (Frankfurt, 1980).

Brednich, R. W., *Die Liedpublizistik im Flugblatt des 15. bis 17. Jahrhunderts*. 2 vols, Baden-Baden, 1974–5

Buijsen, E., and Grijp, L. P. (eds), *Music and Painting in the Golden Age*. Zwolle, 1994

Butt, J., *Music Education and the Art of Performance in the German Baroque*. Cambridge, 1994

Caluori, E., *The Cantatas of Luigi Rossi: Analysis and Thematic Index*. 2 vols, Ann Arbor, 1981

Carter, T., 'Giulio Caccini's *Amarilli, mia bella*: Some Questions (and a Few Answers)'. *Journal of the Royal Musical Association*, 113 (1988), 250–73

    Music in Late Renaissance and Early Baroque Italy. London, 1992

Cavallini, I., 'Sugli improvvisatori del Cinque–Seicento: persistenze, nuovi repertori e qualche riconoscimento'. *Recercare*, 1 (1989), 23–40

Cecchi, P., 'Le "cantade a voce sola" (1633) di Giovanni Felice Sances'. *Rassegna veneta di studi musicali*, 5–6 (1989–90), 137–80

Collaer, P., 'Lyrisme baroque et tradition populaire'. *Studia musicologica Academiae Scientiarum Hungariae*, 7 (1965), 25–40

Craig-Mcfeely, J., 'The Signifying Serpent: Seduction by Cultural Stereotype in Seventeenth-Century England'. In L. P. Austern (ed.), *Music, Sensation, and Sensuality*. New York and London, 2002, pp. 299–317

Dewald, J., *Aristocratic Experience and the Origins of Modern Culture: France, 1570–1715*. Berkeley, Los Angeles and Oxford, 1993

Doughtie, E. (ed.), *Lyrics from English Airs, 1596–1622*. Cambridge, MA, 1970

Durosoir, G., *L'air de cour en France, 1571–1655*. Liège, 1991

    La musique vocale profane au XVIIe siècle. Paris, 1994

Fenlon, I., and Carter, T. (eds), *'Con che soavità': Studies in Italian Opera, Song, and Dance, 1580–1740*. Oxford, 1995

Fischlin, D., 'The Performance Context of the English Lute Song, 1596–1622'. In V. A. Coelho (ed.), *Performance on Lute, Guitar, and Vihuela*. Cambridge, 1997, pp. 47–71

Freitas, R., 'Singing and Playing: the Italian Cantata and the Rage for Wit'. *Music and Letters*, 82 (2001), 509–42

Harper, A. J., 'Gesellige Lieder, poetischer Status und Stereotypen im Barockzeitalter'. In Adam (ed.), *Geselligkeit und Gesellschaft im Barockzeitalter*, ii: 855–8

    'Everyday Life and Social Reality in the German Song of the Seventeenth Century'. In J. A. Parente, jr., and R. E. Schade (eds), *Studies in German and Scandinavian Literature after 1500: a Festschrift for George C. Schoolfield*. Columbia, SC, 1993, pp. 50–66

Hill, J. W., *Roman Monody, Cantata, and Opera from the Circles around Cardinal Montalto*. 2 vols, Oxford, 1997

Hitchcock, H. W., 'Marc-Antoine Charpentier's Vocal Chamber Music'. *Historical Performance*, 1 (1988), 55–61

Hudson, R., *The Folia, the Saraband, the Passacaglia, and the Chaconne: the Historical Evolution of Four Forms that Originated in Music for the Five-Course Spanish Guitar*. 4 vols, American Institute of Musicology, 1982

Huppert, G., *Les bourgeois gentilshommes*. Chicago and London, 1977

Johnson, W. R., *The Idea of Lyric: Lyric Modes in Ancient and Modern Poetry*. Berkeley, Los Angeles and London, 1982

Jurgens, M. (ed.), *Documents du Minutier Central concernant l'histoire de la musique (1600–1650)*. 2 vols, Paris, 1974

Kezich, G., *I poeti contadini*. Rome, 1986

Kross, S., *Geschichte des deutschen Liedes*. Darmstadt, 1989

Kyrova, M., 'Music in Seventeenth-Century Dutch Painting'. In Buijsen and Grijp (eds), *Music and Painting in the Golden Age*, pp. 30–62

Leopold, S., 'Remigio Romano's Collection of Lyrics'. *Proceedings of the Royal Musical Association*, 110 (1983-4), 45–61

'*Al modo d'Orfeo*': *Dichtung und Musik im italienischen Sologesang des frühen 17. Jahrhunderts*, 'Analecta musicologica', 29. 2 vols, Laaber, 1995

Mabbett, M., 'Le connessioni stilistiche tra l'Ottavo Libro di Monteverdi ed il madrigale *avant-garde* a Vienna'. In Alberto Colzani *et al.* (eds), *Il madrigale oltre il madrigale: dal Barocco al Novecento; destino di una forma e problemi di analisi*. Como, 1994, pp. 73–103

Massip, C., *L'art de bien chanter: Michel Lambert (1610-1696)*. Paris, 1999

Menestrier, C.-F., *L'art des emblemes ou s'enseigne la morale par les figures de la fable, de l'histoire & de la nature*. Paris, 1684; repr. Mittenwald, 1981

Mischiati, O., *Indici, cataloghi e avvisi degli editori e librai musicali italiani dal 1591 al 1798*, 'Studi e testi per la storia della musica', 2. Florence, 1984

Motley, M., *Becoming a French Aristocrat: the Education of the Court Nobility, 1580-1715*. Princeton, 1990

Murata, M., '"Singing", "Acting" and "Dancing" in Vocal Chamber Music of the Early Seicento'. *Journal of Seventeenth-Century Music*, 9/1 (2003) <http://www.sscm-jscm.org/jscm/v9/no1/Murata.html>

Perella, L., 'Bénigne de Bacilly and the *Recueil des plus beaux vers, qui on esté mis en chant* of 1661'. In K. van Orden (ed.), *Music and the Cultures of Print*. New York and London, 2000, pp. 239–70

Porter, W. V., '*Lamenti recitativi da camera*'. In Fenlon and Carter (eds), '*Con che soavità*', pp. 73–110

Rasch, R. A., 'The Editors of the *Livre septième*'. In E. Schreurs and H. Vanhulst (eds), *Music Printing in Antwerp and Europe in the 16th Century*, 'Yearbook of the Alamire Foundation', 2. Leuven, 1997, pp. 279–306

Simpson, C. M., *The British Broadside Ballad and its Music*. New Brunswick, NJ, 1966

Smith, B. R., *The Acoustic World of Early Modern England: Attending to the O-factor*. Chicago and London, 1999

Spink, I., *English Song from Dowland to Purcell*. London, 1974

Spink, I. (ed.), *The Blackwell History of Music in Britain*, iii: *The Seventeenth Century*. Oxford, 1992

Stein, L. K., *Songs of Mortals, Dialogues of the Gods: Music and Theatre in Seventeenth-Century Spain*. Oxford, 1993

Steinheuer, J., '*Fare la ninnananna*: Das Wiegenlied als volkstümlicher Topos in der italienischen Kunstmusik des 17. Jahrhunderts'. *Recercare*, 9 (1997), 49–96

Strunk, O., *Source Readings in Music History, Revised Edition*, iv: *The Baroque Era*, ed. M. Murata. New York and London, 1998

Toft, R., '*Tune thy musicke to thy hart*': the Art of Eloquent Singing in England, 1597-1622*. Toronto, Buffalo and London, 1993

Walls, P., 'London, 1603-49'. In C. Price (ed.), *The Early Baroque Era: from the Late Sixteenth Century to the 1660s*, 'Man and Music', 3. London, 1993, pp. 270–304

Ward, J. M., 'And Who but Ladie Greensleeves?'. In J. Caldwell, E. Olleson and S. Wollenberg (eds), *The Well-Enchanting Skill: Music, Poetry, and Drama in the Culture of the Renaissance; Essays in Honour of F. W. Sternfeld*. Oxford, 1990, pp. 181–211

Weller, D. P., *Jan Miense Molenaer, Painter of the Dutch Golden Age*. New York and
    Manchester, VT, 2002

Whenham, J., ' "Aria" in the Madrigals of Giovanni Rovetta'. In Fenlon and Carter (eds),
    'Con che soavità', pp. 135–53

Wilson, J. (ed.), *Roger North on Music, Being a Selection of his Essays Written during the Years
    c. 1695–1728*. London, 1959

Würzbach, N., *The Rise of the English Street Ballad, 1550–1650*, trans. G. Walls. Cambridge,
    1990

13

Fantasy and craft: the solo instrumentalist

ALEXANDER SILBIGER

You would hardly believe, sir, the high regard which the Italians have for those who excel on instruments, and how much more importance they attach to instrumental music than to vocal, saying that one man can produce by himself more beautiful inventions than four voices together, and that it has charms and liberties that vocal music does not have.

André Maugars, *Response faite à un curieux sur le sentiment de la musique d'Italie* (Rome, 1639)[1]

In Lorenzo Bianconi's *Music in the Seventeenth Century* (1987), arguably the most original and provocative recent study of the period, solo instrumental music is treated so marginally that it is not even given a chapter of its own: 'In "practical" and statistical terms, the role of seventeenth-century instrumental music is essentially modest and of minority significance – not at all what its relatively profuse cultivation on the part of modern "baroque" musicians would suggest'.[2] It is true that the percentage of purely instrumental volumes among surviving seventeenth-century musical editions is relatively small. Instrumental performances also left much less of a paper-trail than operas, oratorios or major civic or ecclesiastical celebrations. For a historian eager to embed music into larger political, social and cultural frameworks, they tend to remain below the horizon, in part because their functions and meanings are harder to assess.

Nevertheless, the wide popularity of Baroque instrumental music in modern times should be reason enough for giving it attention. In fact, interest in early instrumental repertories, particularly of solo music, is hardly a recent phenomenon. Pianists have been broadening their scope with anthologies of 'early keyboard music' since the later nineteenth century, if not before, and most young piano students have been exposed to the easier pieces of Byrd, Purcell and Pachelbel. Similarly, guitarists have been extending their repertory with adaptations of sixteenth- and seventeenth-century lute gems, while chorale settings and preludes from Sweelinck to Buxtehude have long

---

1 Bishop, 'Translation of Maugars' *Response faite a un curieux sur le sentiment de la musique d'Italie*', p. 11.
2 Bianconi, *Music in the Seventeenth Century*, p. viii.

been an important if not indispensable part of the church organist's working capital. Even leading twentieth-century composers did not escape the power and charms of this repertory: Béla Bartók eagerly studied the keyboard music of Frescobaldi, Michelangelo Rossi and others, and its impact on his compositional development has been viewed as significant.[3]

Do the modest statistics on surviving sources and references in public documents accurately reflect the extent of solo instrumental performance in the seventeenth century? Or might it be that solos by organists, harpsichordists, clavichordists, lutenists and guitarists, and for that matter, by players of the violin, recorder and viola da gamba, could be heard everywhere – in churches, chapels, monasteries, convents, palaces, taverns and modest homes – but because they were so much part of the fabric of musical life, they were taken for granted and left few traces in the recorded history of the period? Of course, plenty of evidence survives for an intensely active culture of solo playing throughout Europe. The extant repertory is large and diverse, if more so in manuscript than in print. We have countless witnesses to solo playing in the form of paintings and engravings, and observations in diaries, travel reports, tutors and other contemporary accounts. Lastly, the ceremony manuals of churches and similar documents provide generous testimony to the nearly universal presence of organ solos in the liturgy. This chapter seeks to do some justice to instruments and their repertories, to the functional and other contexts of solo instrumental performance, and to the music itself.

Instruments and their repertories

Most of the instruments used for solo performance have their own literature, with only sporadic overlap. By far the largest repertories are for instruments that ordinarily perform in a polyphonic or chordal manner, namely keyboards and lutes of various types. Solos for instruments that usually have a single voice were most often supported by continuo accompaniment. The literature for unaccompanied wind instruments is very small, but a not insignificant body of unaccompanied works does exist for bowed strings that often quite ingeniously exploits those instruments' limited capabilities of polyphonic performance. The repertory also divides along national or other geographical lines – even more so, surprisingly, than in the case of vocal music (where language makes a difference) – often encompassing distinct subtypes of genres, instruments and forms of notation. As a result, works from one region may

---

3 Gillies, 'A Conversation with Bartók: 1929', pp. 557, 558; Suchoff, 'The Impact of Italian Baroque Music on Bartók's Music'.

not always have been easily accessible to musicians from another.[4] Nevertheless, throughout the century both compositions and stylistic influences managed to make their way across political and notational boundaries, even if the agents of migration (and in some cases, their direction) often can no longer be determined.

Finally, the repertories of some instruments contain works written for a specific member of an instrument family that, because of differences in range or tuning, are not playable on another member without adaptation. This is especially common within the lute repertory. Owing to the increasing use of lute-family instruments for continuo accompaniment, and the resulting desire to strengthen and extend their bass register, a number of distinct instruments evolved that differed in construction, size, number of strings and/or tuning. Some of the larger, extended instruments were given special names, such as theorbo, chitarrone, archlute and *liuto attiorbato*, although not always consistently. New tunings were also introduced on ordinary lutes, especially in France, to facilitate the fingering of certain chords and to provide richer sonorities. Despite these variations, it remains possible to speak in general terms of a lute repertory, although a few lute-type instruments – including the so-called Spanish guitar and the cittern – were sufficiently different in construction and playing technique to have developed distinct types of music.

Although there are marked differences between the various kinds of keyboard instruments, and to some extent even between national types, all share essentially the same keyboard layout. Therefore the only limits to transferring music from one kind to another might relate to national and other characteristics of the designated instrument: German organ pieces often require pedals and multiple manuals, while Spanish ones frequently use single split manuals (which allowed the organist to set a different stop for the upper and lower halves of the keyboard), and most national organ schools (especially the French) require registrations that may not have been available elsewhere. On the whole, though, many keyboard works were not so instrument-specific save by way of function (e.g., liturgical music on the one hand, and dance music on the other).

Keyboards and lutes

Developments in the keyboard and lute repertories could both parallel one another and diverge notably, depending on the period and region.[5] When

---

4 Even when seemingly similar staff notation is used, as with English, French and Italian keyboard music, there may exist fundamentally different conceptions of how music should be notated; see Silbiger, 'Is the Italian Keyboard Intavolatura a Tablature?'.

5 For overviews, see Apel, *The History of Keyboard Music to 1700*; Ledbetter, *Harpsichord and Lute Music in 17th-Century France*; Spring, *The Lute in Britain*; Silbiger (ed.), *Keyboard Music Before 1700*.

comparing the scale and nature of these repertories, some differences in the social role of the instruments should be kept in mind. The use of the organ in church services gave rise to a large and distinguished body of music – perhaps more so during the seventeenth century than any other – to which there is no equivalent in the literature of other instruments. Nor was there an equivalent to the employment opportunities for organists in religious institutions. The lute, however, had a different kind of advantage. Although it shared with the keyboard the potential for producing sophisticated music along with pieces of a more popular nature, it took little space and was eminently portable. Thus it not only enjoyed great popularity with members of the educated classes, but often travelled with them. And along with the instruments and players – whether professionals or often highly accomplished dilettantes – went their repertory. Lute music circulated widely and was often at the forefront in spreading musical styles and fashions abroad, infiltrating not only local lute repertories but also keyboard ones. The most striking example is provided by the French lute styles which made their mark on the solo repertories of almost every region of Europe. The effect of this internationalisation can be seen in the often highly eclectic contents of manuscripts in which the players preserved their music. Some contain a staggering number of pieces, many more than are generally found in comparable keyboard collections.

Nevertheless (albeit a crude generalisation), the sixteenth century had been the lute's golden age; during the seventeenth, there was a gradual decline, paralleled by the relative ascendancy of the keyboard – a process that would reach its completion during the following century. (This 'decline' does not mean that people stopped playing the instrument altogether, but, rather, that the quantity of music preserved in the sources decreases substantially, and more important, that in its quality and interest it does not seem to compare with earlier repertories.) The process proceeded at a different pace in different areas, and did not prevent both instrumental families from enjoying some of their artistically most fruitful periods, as was the case in Italy as well as in England during the decades before and after 1600. To some extent, even keyboard instruments shared a decline in the period thereafter, although the one for the lute was much steeper in both countries. In Spain the change was, if anything, even more dramatic. The sixteenth-century players of the vihuela, the Spanish equivalent of the lute, had created a precocious solo repertory that introduced many sophisticated variation techniques into instrumental practice, but in the next century the instrument seems to have been nearly abandoned in favour of the five-course Spanish guitar. Spanish keyboard music, which had as its great early master Antonio de Cabezón (1510–66), managed to hold its own during the seventeenth century, but its flowering seems to have been mostly confined to the organ. In the Central European regions, the lute retained its popularity the longest, continuing through much of the eighteenth century, but its repertory appears to have been largely derivative of foreign, particularly French, models. On the other hand, the German keyboard tradition, while initially relying on stimuli from foreign sources – Dutch, English and Italian – entered a period of unprecedented accomplishment.

France departed most markedly from these general trends. The first half of the seventeenth century saw the tremendous blossoming of a lute culture that was to endure throughout most of the century and had a wide international impact. This was clearly associated with the transformation of the instrument and its tunings. Instrument developments also played a part in the ways in which keyboard repertories evolved. During the early years of the century, the main stringed keyboard instrument in France appears to have been the small spinet (*épinette*). Its repertory, of which very little is preserved, appears to have been closely tied to that of the lute, and may, in fact, have in part been identical with it.[6] Subsequently, with composers such as Jacques Champion, Sieur de Chambonnières (1601/2–73), there was a switch to the larger, wing-shaped harpsichord (*clavecin*), for which an extraordinary literature was created, fully paralleling that of the lute. At the same time, the music of the two instruments continued to be closely related.

The harp

The harp was cultivated especially in Spain and southern Italy. Its appearance in the central aria in Monteverdi's *Orfeo*, 'Possente spirto e formidabil nume', indicates the high level of artistry that must have existed among its best players. Because harp notation did not differ from that for keyboard, at least in Italy, it is difficult to identify a harp repertory, except when pieces are specifically designated for the instrument, as in a few works in keyboard publications by Neapolitan composers such as Ascanio Mayone (1565–1627), Giovanni Maria Trabaci (*c.* 1575–1647) and Gregorio Strozzi (1615–87). One possible tell-tale sign of further harp music within the Neapolitan repertory of the early 1600s is the presence of passages difficult to negotiate on a keyboard because of voice-crossings or large stretches.[7] In Spain, harp tablature continued to be used; examples are found in treatises, the most extensive collection appearing in Lucas Ruiz de Ribayaz's *Luz y norte musical* (1677).

---

6 It has in fact been suggested that spinet players were accustomed to reading lute tablatures, which might explain why no independent spinet literature had evolved. Some French keyboard tablatures exist that look much like lute tablatures, with letters representing pitches between the staff lines.

7 See, for example, the final partita in the *Partite sopra Ruggiero di Gio: Macque*, London, British Library, Add. MS 30491, f. 6v.

The Spanish guitar

Although the Spanish guitar is technically a type of lute, it differs sufficiently in tuning, playing technique and notation to have created a distinct literature of its own. This instrument ordinarily had five courses of which all but the top one were double strung (hence nine strings); it also used re-entrant tunings, in which the tuning order of the strings sometimes reversed direction (thus affecting the kinds of chordal sonorities that the instrument produced). The Spanish guitar gained enormous popularity during the seventeenth century, first in Spain, where it virtually supplanted the vihuela, and then in Italy, where far more collections were published for guitar than for lute. Later in the century its popularity spread to France and England, largely owing to the visits by the virtuoso Francesco Corbetta (1615–81), who taught both Louis XIV and Charles II. An important element of guitar technique was chord-strumming (*rasgueado* in Spanish; *battuto* in Italian), and in one form of tablature, a symbol (usually a letter of the alphabet, hence 'alphabet notation') indicated which chord was to be played, along with an indication of the direction of the strum. Some early seventeenth-century tablatures consisted entirely of such chord progressions, but later it became more common to combine chord-strumming with conventional string-plucking. The strumming and tunings make it difficult to represent these guitar tablatures in ordinary notation (in addition to the problem, shared with the lute, of there being no indication of how long a pitch is to be sustained). Compounding the problem is the fact that actual tunings are not always indicated in the sources.

Bowed strings and winds

Largest among the remaining repertories are those for various types of viols. The unaccompanied solo repertory for the violin is smaller, and that for wind instruments almost non-existent. These differences most likely reflect not so much how often the instruments were used for solos as the extent to which their players needed written music. Virtuoso solo literatures, both accompanied and unaccompanied, survive for several types of viols, including the *viola bastarda* and the lyra-viol. As with lutes, these labels seem to have been somewhat fluid, but most refer to some kind of bass instrument. The small but exceptionally brilliant body of Italian works for the *viola bastarda* was mostly performed with lute or harpsichord accompaniment, and does not employ multiple stopping.[8] On the other hand, the extensive and quite original English repertory for the unaccompanied lyra-viol makes the fullest use of the instrument's polyphonic

8 Paras, *The Music for the Viola Bastarda*.

capabilities, often further extended by the use of special tunings (*scordatura*). In addition to the rich accompanied solo literature from the later part of the century for the bass viola da gamba (at this stage, often with seven strings), a good number of unaccompanied solo works for that instrument survive from France, by Sieur De Machy and Dubuisson (1622–80), and from the Netherlands, by Johannes Schenck (1660–1710).

The violin was much used to accompany dances, and a large number of dance tunes scored for the instrument are found, for example, in Playford's popular *The English Dancing Master* (1651, with numerous later editions and reprints). A few collections of songs and dance tunes, some in violin tablature, also survive in manuscript.[9] More sophisticated unaccompanied solo music exploiting multiple stopping is rarer. The repertory includes some compositions by the German violinist Thomas Baltzar (1633–61), who in 1656 caused a stir among London musicians when he 'plaid on that single Instrument a full Consort, so as the rest, flung-downe their Instruments',[10] as well as the remarkable passacaglia with which Biber closed his 'Rosary Sonatas', and a few other German works from late in the century. A recently discovered early seventeenth-century manuscript (Wrocław, Biblioteka Uniwersytecka, MS 114) containing a large group of quite brilliant fantasias, toccatas and recercatas for violin solo with occasional double stops, suggests a much earlier tradition that was largely unnotated.[11]

Unaccompanied wind solos are even scarcer, but the huge collection of recorder pieces in Jacob van Eyck's (1589–1657) *Der fluyten lust-hof* (several volumes of which appeared between 1644 and *c.* 1655) gives a good idea of what solo playing on that instrument, and probably also on other monophonic instruments, might have been like.[12] Only five of its 143 pieces are not based on pre-existing melodies, including two preludes and three fantasias (one a 'Fantasia & Echo'). The others are settings of well-known tunes, generally followed by several divisions (variations), often of increasing virtuosity. The repertory is quite international, with songs and dances (in order of decreasing frequency) of French, English, Dutch, Italian and German origin. Also included are sixteen Psalm settings (not surprising in the Calvinist Netherlands) and a couple of other sacred melodies.

---

9 For example, a collection of unaccompanied violin solos, almost all anonymous settings of popular tunes, can be found in Bologna, Civico Museo Bibliografico Musicale, MS AA.360, along with solos for guitar, keyboard, lute and *tromba marina*; see Silbiger, *Italian Manuscript Sources of 17th-Century Keyboard Music*, pp. 94–6.

10 P. Holman, 'Thomas Baltzar', in S. Sadie and J. Tyrrell (eds), *The Revised New Grove Dictionary of Music and Musicians*, 29 vols (London, 2001), ii: 613–14.

11 Brooks, 'Etienne Nau, Breslau 114 and the Early Seventeenth-Century German Violin Fantasia'.

12 Baak Griffioen, *Jacob van Eyck's 'Der fluyten lust-hof'*.

The players

With the exception of some of the French court harpsichordists, virtually all those who contributed significantly to the seventeenth-century keyboard repertory held positions at Europe's major churches and court chapels. Obvious examples include Girolamo Frescobaldi (1583–1643) at St Peter's in Rome, Johann Jacob Froberger (1616–67) at the Imperial Chapel in Vienna, and Henry Purcell (1659–95) at Westminster Abbey. Some even served at more than one institution. Most appointments were, in fact, as organist rather than as music-director (*maestro di cappella, Cantor* etc.), which no doubt encouraged the writing of keyboard music. At the same time, almost all keyboard composers ventured to varying degrees into instrumental or vocal ensemble music, most often for use in churches but not infrequently also for the chamber. Such works probably owed their existence to these players moonlighting in other sacred and secular venues.[13]

Lutenists had to look elsewhere for their principal appointments. Fortunately, the leading players found plenty of opportunities at the major courts, especially during the earlier part of the century. In England, James I (*reg.* 1603–25) had five lutenists on his payroll throughout his reign, and additional players were employed by Queen Anne and Princes Henry and Charles.[14] Similarly, in France the best lutenists found positions in the various musical establishments at court. Their duties often included teaching members of the royal household as well as playing in various ensembles. The large number of lutenists, harpsichordists and string players employed as personal musicians to members of royal families suggests that music was a significant part of their lives.

Most of these composers and performers were born into families of professional musicians and probably received their early musical training at home. Many in fact belonged to notable musical dynasties, of which the Couperins are merely the best known. A large number of keyboard players – among them Jan Pieterszoon Sweelinck (1572–1621), Froberger, Matthias Weckmann (?1616–1674), Orlando Gibbons (1583–1625), Thomas Tomkins (1572–1656) and Purcell – had fathers, sons or brothers who also served professionally as organists. Like most church musicians, organists learned basic skills while serving as choirboys, but they usually went on to advanced study with a notable master, often travelling far from home. Sweelinck taught an entire generation of German organists, including Heinrich Scheidemann (1595–1663), Samuel

---

13 Silbiger, 'The Roman Frescobaldi Tradition', pp. 44–50. Those whose primary appointment was as organist rather than as *maestro* rarely contributed to theatre music. Francesco Cavalli is an obvious exception, as is Michelangelo Rossi, but he, despite holding an organ appointment, seems to have been primarily a violinist.

14 Spring, *The Lute in Britain*, pp. 210–11.

Scheidt (1587–1654) and Jacob Praetorius (1586–1651). Froberger was sent to Rome for studies with Frescobaldi and himself prompted a German interest in the Italian composer that extended through to J. S. Bach and beyond. Chambonnières, who never held an organ post himself, taught Louis Couperin (c. 1626–1661), Jean-Henri D'Anglebert (1629–91), Nicolas Lebègue (1631–92) and Guillaume Gabriel Nivers (c. 1632–1714). Often a tradition was passed on to a succeeding generation. Weckmann went to Hamburg to work with both Jacob Praetorius and Scheidemann, and the latter also taught Johann Adam Reincken (?1643–1722). Among lutenists, family relationships were just as common, as with Dowland father and son, the Gaultier cousins, and the several members of the Gallot clan.

Sweelinck's teaching is documented by his *Compositions-Regeln* ('Rules for composition') which survives in several copies, including those by Weckmann and Reincken.[15] These chiefly provide instruction in how to write increasingly complex counterpoint against a cantus firmus, an indispensable skill for those looking forward to a lifetime of crafting chorale settings. A different kind of evidence has survived of the training Frescobaldi provided for the circle of musicians working with him at St Peter's, in the form of manuscript workbooks of basic exercises, including crafting brief imitative ricercars, and variations on bass patterns such as the *Ruggiero*.[16]

The sources

The nature of musical sources strongly affects the meaning of what they transmit. We tend to assume that a piece of music in print is somehow fixed as a tangible object designed for an indefinite number of future performances, to be played more or less as given. Notating a piece in manuscript also defines its text for repetition over an indeterminate period, but often was prompted by more immediate needs: providing appropriate material for a student to practise; recording an attractive, possibly improvised performance that had just been heard; or establishing the idea for one to be given the following day. In other words, in the case of manuscript there may or may not have been any thought of a distant future rather than an immediate present.

There is another important difference between print and manuscript (even if one can always think of exceptions). Typically, there is a close connection between the person preparing a manuscript copy and its recipient. Often both are one and the same, or the copy may be given to a pupil, patron or colleague.

15 J. P. Sweelinck, *Werken*, ed. H. Gehrmann (Leipzig, 1901), x.
16 Annibaldi, 'La didattica del solco tracciato'.

Therefore the provider of the manuscript copy could easily transmit additional (if unrecorded) verbal instructions, and could assume a familiarity with the appropriate performance techniques and styles. After Froberger's death, Princess Sybilla of Württemberg, at whose court the composer had resided during his last years, refused to honour the request from the Dutch diplomat and music connoisseur Constantijn Huygens for copies of Froberger's pieces in the manuscripts in her possession because, she said, the composer had often complained of performers not knowing what to do with his music. She claimed that in the absence of Froberger teaching these pieces directly, it was impossible to perform them properly.[17] A composer had much less control over works in print, and over who performed them (and how). Such texts therefore tended to be prepared more carefully and accurately, and with greater detail. The differences are clear in the case of pieces preserved in both media (save where one was copied directly from the other). Some composers also provided explicit instructions to the prospective performer by way of prefaces or other illustrative material (e.g., the tables of ornaments not uncommon in later seventeenth-century prints). In publications prepared by composers themselves, much thought clearly went into the selection and arrangement of the contents. Often an effort was made to include samples of different genres and styles, sometimes in a full range of the commonly used modes or keys.

In manuscripts, pieces often seem to have been entered as they were needed or became available; of course, once copied, it was not possible to change their order without recopying the whole.[18] The resulting near-randomness is often apparent in what one might call 'practice-books', whether for students learning an instrument or composition – hence the frequent inclusion also of notes on musical 'fundamentals' (clefs, note-values, scales etc.) – or as a personal repository of favourite pieces. But it can also be found even in more formal collections of composers' works, as in the case of one that belonged to Bernardo Pasquini (1637–1710).[19] Some manuscripts, however, are much less *ad hoc*. We find fine, carefully notated and organised copies prepared for a patron or as exemplar for a printer; outstanding examples of this type are Froberger's autograph volumes dedicated to Emperor Ferdinand III.[20] These manuscripts in several respects resemble Frescobaldi's Roman publications, suggesting an

17 Rasch and Dirksen, 'The Huygens-Froberger-Sybylla Correspondence', p. 242.

18 If the pieces were copied into independent fascicles, these could, of course, be rebound in a different order, as sometimes happened. Thomas Tomkins left instructions for his son on how he wanted a manuscript of his brother's recopied, e.g., by placing pieces in the same key together; see T. Tomkins, *Keyboard Music*, ed. S. Tuttle, 'Musica britannica', 2 (London, 1955), p. 158.

19 Berlin, Deutsche Staatsbibliothek, MS L.215; facsimile in A. Silbiger *et al.* (eds), *17th-Century Keyboard Music: Sources Central to the Keyboard Art of the Baroque*, 24 vols (New York, 1987–8), vii.

20 Silbiger *et al.* (eds), *17th-Century Keyboard Music*, iii.

attempt to imitate an established format, even if printing was not a viable option in Vienna (or perhaps the composer or his patron wished to keep the music private). A more common type of carefully copied manuscript is the collector's anthology, assembled by, or perhaps more often for, an amateur. Their purpose may have been as much to possess as to perform their contents, which could have been valued more for their own sake than for any utilitarian reasons. The interest of non-professional musicians in 'possessing' such music is also evident in Huygens's request to Sybilla of Württemberg for pieces by Froberger, and in a similar one which Huygens had made to the composer himself many years earlier (when he also sent Froberger pieces by Chambonnières, whose works Froberger did not know).[21]

Collectors' anthologies are likely to contain a repertory of high quality, dominated by clean, complete copies of original works by well-known earlier and contemporary masters, including notable foreigners. As a rule, composers and titles are carefully indicated. Notable examples are the Fitzwilliam Virginal Book (Cambridge, Fitzwilliam Museum, 32.g.29) and the Bauyn and Babell Manuscripts (Paris, Bibliothèque Nationale, Vm[7] 674–5; London, British Library, Add. MS 39569). On the other hand, while practice-books may contain a few works by well-known composers (usually some of their most widely circulated ones), they often consist largely of rather casually notated, anonymous pieces. Many may well be the work of the copyist/owner of the book or a teacher, which would explain their often simple character and occasionally borderline competence. However, some practice-books come closer to anthologies, especially those of serious students interested in composition and needing a 'reference library' of works for study as much as for performance.[22]

Pieces surviving in different practice-books often do so in variant versions, be the differences slight or substantial. The once common assumption that these versions reflect compositional revisions is nowadays viewed with caution. More likely, when pieces were copied they were somehow 'edited' to suit particular needs or tastes, with difficult passages simplified or simple ones elaborated, perceived errors corrected, or the music adapted to suit a different time or place. Memorisation and aural transmission may also have played a part in destabilising the text, while repeated copying would also lead to variant readings.

---

21 Rasch, 'Johann Jakob Froberger and the Netherlands', p. 121.
22 A manuscript in Thomas Tomkins's hand (Paris, Bibliothèque Nationale de France, Conservatoire de Musique, Réserve MS 1122) started as an anthology of 'Lessons of worthe' by Byrd, Bull and himself, but after 70 pages turned into a depository for his own new or revised works; see Tomkins, *Keyboard Music*, pp. xiii, 155–62.

Even more polished, formal manuscripts can exhibit similar characteristics. For example, those containing French harpsichord repertory, which tend to be very carefully compiled, often reveal a startling range of differences between multiple versions of the same 'work'.[23] One need not be more 'corrupt' than any other; all may be viable in performance; and none can likely claim to be 'definitive'. Composers were not in the habit of playing their pieces always in exactly the same way; this was still true of, say, Chopin. But when faced with such textual differences, we are often hard-pressed to know their status, for example, in terms of chronology or of proximity to the composer. This argues against conflating sources to produce an 'ideal text' that may never have existed. It also suggests that save in the case of obvious errors, textual choices were, and remain, a matter of personal preference and/or performance circumstances.[24]

Whether in print or in manuscript, solo instrumental music was notated in various formats. Until the latter part of the seventeenth century, music for plucked strings was almost always notated in some form of tablature, where the notation relates directly to the finger placement and therefore cannot be 'read', or transferred to another instrument, in the manner of staff notation (which most players of plucked instruments probably could not read). Tablature was also often used for keyboard music in northern Germany and Spain, whereas Dutch, English, French and Italian keyboard music (and some from southern Germany and Austria) used some form of staff notation, normally on two staves, the upper one of five or six lines and the lower one of five to eight. Some collections of primarily contrapuntal keyboard music were notated in open score (one 'voice' per stave), whether for clarity of voice-leading and/or ease of printing, or to allow also for performance by an instrumental ensemble.

Performing environments

The two usual venues for solo playing, church and chamber, had quite different requirements. Churches (chapels etc.) were the domain of organists, trained professionals who often operated in a highly public arena on the largest instruments known to Christendom. Their professional work for the most part served the liturgy. In the chamber (be it in a palace, a salon or a private home), musicians performed on several different instruments, most relatively quiet, and the settings were intimate, with sometimes just a single musician playing for his own pleasure or for a few friends. Although other occasions

---

23 Examples are given in B. Gustafson and R. P. Wolf (eds), *Harpsichord Music Associated with the Name La Barre*, 'The Art of the Keyboard', 4 (New York, 1999).

24 Fuller, '"Sous le doits de Chambonniere"'; see also Silbiger (ed.), *Keyboard Music Before 1700*, pp. 16–19, 121–6.

were more formal, with a larger assembly of listeners, the purpose generally remained recreational and somewhat impromptu. Both types of solo performance nevertheless had something in common that distinguished them from many other kinds of music-making: they were conducive to improvisation, not least because they might entail circumstances which the performer could not anticipate.

Solo repertories for church and chamber tended to become distinct one from the other, with the differences becoming more marked as the century proceeded. Also important was the rise of instrument-specific writing that became increasingly idiomatic. Of course, a given performer might work in both environments and could bring from one to the other similar styles and techniques, if not the same music. Nevertheless, the differences are by and large sufficient to provide a convenient structure for the following survey.

Solo music in churches

Catholic liturgies: Italy, the Empire, France, Spain

Organists in Catholic churches were very busy during both Mass and Vespers. They needed to provide a huge amount of music, and before the liturgical reforms of the later sixteenth century many organists apparently were quite indiscriminate in terms of where they found it. They were often accused of introducing inappropriate material into services, including instrumental adaptations of songs whose texts had distinctly secular associations. Although such 'abuses' were not entirely eliminated, seventeenth-century organists mostly went out of their way to provide suitable music, as a result creating a large and dignified body of sacred organ works.

Information about the liturgical use of the organ comes from general regulations such as the *Caeremoniale episcoporum* (Rome, 1600) issued by Pope Clement VIII, and more specific 'ceremonials' for individual dioceses or churches, such as those for Paris and for St Mark's, Venice.[25] More details are provided by manuals for novice organists such as *L'organo suonarino* (Venice, 1605; regularly revised and expanded in subsequent editions up to 1638) by the Benedictine monk and organist Adriano Banchieri (1568–1634), and from collections of music designed expressly for liturgical use, such as Frescobaldi's *Fiori musicali* (Venice, 1635) for the Mass, and the more comprehensive *Annuale* (Venice, 1645) of Giovanni Battista Fasolo (1598–after 1664), which covers both Mass and Vespers. Banchieri's manual also includes sample pieces, whereas

---

25 For Paris, see Gustafson, 'France', pp. 97–104; for Venice, see Moore, 'The Liturgical Use of the Organ in Seventeenth-Century Italy'.

Frescobaldi's and Fasolo's collections include guidance for using their contents. Although the broad regulations issued from Rome supposedly applied across the Catholic communion, they left enough room for local practices. This in part explains the distinct natures of regional repertories, determined by local preferences, habits and musical traditions, as well as the marked regional differences in organ design.

The church organist's repertory divides broadly speaking into three categories: brief versets alternating with vocal chant or polyphony (so-called 'alternatim' practice); longer works (or improvisations) substituting for, played during, or somehow pacing particular liturgical elements (an antiphon substitute, a toccata for the Elevation etc.); and music for the beginning or end of the service that might or might not have direct liturgical associations. When instrumental music substituted for part of the liturgy, the appropriate text would usually still be recited by the celebrant. *Alternatim* performance was considered especially appropriate for the Ordinary of the Mass (the Kyrie, Gloria, Credo, Sanctus, Agnus Dei), and for the hymn and Magnificat at Vespers or their equivalents in other Offices. Sources contain numerous organ versets for these purposes going back as far as the early fifteenth century. When verses were sung polyphonically rather than as plainchant, the organ might intervene less often, perhaps only playing at the beginning and end. Instrumental substitutions for entire liturgical items were more common in the Mass Proper, and (in the Office) in antiphons for psalms and the Magnificat. Here, the character and/or genre of instrumental music was often specified: Italian sources indicate that the Gradual could be replaced by a short canzona and the Offertory by a ricercar, that during the Elevation something quiet and slow was required, that for the Communion a canzona or a *capriccio* would be appropriate, and that during the *Deo gratias* the organist could play another brief canzona or something else on the full organ.[26] Similarly, during Vespers a canzona could replace the antiphon following a Psalm, and a *capriccio* or another canzona the antiphon following the Magnificat. Before the Mass commenced, the organist could play a toccata; music could also be provided at the beginning of a Vespers service.

All this required a great deal of music. For example, Bruce Gustafson estimates that in France organists might be obliged to assist with as many as 400 different services per year, which could entail playing over 100 versets on a single day.[27] Each needed to fit smoothly with the alternating chants in terms of pitch and mode (or tone). The versets might or might not be based on the chant they were replacing, whether as a cantus firmus or used motivically. The

26 For other possibilities, see Bonta, 'The Uses of the *Sonata da chiesa*'.   27 Gustafson, 'France', p. 97.

Paris 1662 ceremonial stipulates that in specific versets, such as the first and last Kyrie, the chant melody had to be audible.[28] Considering that the choice of chants might depend not only on the particular feast but also on local practices, it would have been impossible for the organist to have a written collection of all the necessary music, and as today, organists clearly needed at least a modest level of skill in improvisation.

A large number of pieces do survive from the seventeenth century designed to meet specific liturgical needs. The sources from all the predominantly Catholic regions – Austria and southern Germany, France, Italy, Spain – include numerous versets as well as many canzonas, ricercars and *capricci* or similar pieces such as *fantasies* (France), *tientos* (Spain) or *tentos* (Portugal) suitable for antiphon substitutes. The length of some of these works suggests that they may not always have been performed complete. In the preface to his *Fiori musicali* (1635), Frescobaldi writes that 'My principal aim is to help organists . . . so that they will be able to respond at Mass and Vespers . . . in the canzonas as well as in the ricercars stopping at a cadence when they appear too long'. Often the mode is indicated in the title (e.g., *Canzona del primo tono*), which points to liturgical usage, and the publication of sets of, say, ricercars in all the modes offered a convenient resource for organists. Some of these pieces, particularly when they appeared in print, may also have served as models for aspiring improvisers, while the more modest examples in manuscripts may represent student exercises or examples prepared by organists for their own use. The magnitude of the repertory and the high quality of many of these pieces suggest that in the seventeenth century, skills in improvisation were not always particularly advanced, while the demands made upon organists for substantial and accomplished pieces were high, particularly in the case of preludes or antiphon substitutes.

In Italy, organists were well provided with systematic collections of service music, thanks to a thriving music-publishing industry: Frescobaldi's *Fiori musicali* is only the best-known example. The tradition went back far into the sixteenth century (Girolamo Cavazzoni, Andrea Gabrieli, Claudio Merulo), but diminished somewhat after 1650 or so, perhaps because of a growing preference at major churches for using instrumental ensembles. For *alternatim* practice, organists could also avail themselves of such large collections of *versetti* as the 96 (twelve for each of the eight modes) published in 1615 by Giovanni Maria Trabaci (1575-1647), or the two sets (1687, 1696), partly notated with figured bass, by Giovanni Battista degli Antoni (1639-1720). These versets are not based on specific chants and thus could be used anywhere in the Mass and

---

28 Ibid., pp. 100-104.

Office. For each mode they provide alternatives in different transpositions, further lightening the burden of the organist.

For other parts of the service, Italian organists could draw upon countless sets of canzonas, ricercars, toccatas and intonations ordered by mode. Their lucid counterpoint is ideally suited to the clear, balanced sound of Italian organs, which concentrate on a 'ripieno' of principals augmented by flute stops at the octave and higher harmonics, generally without a pedal section, and with little in the way of colourful solo stops.[29] The rare pieces with sustained pedal tones, such as the two in Frescobaldi's *Secondo libro di toccate* (Rome, 1627), would have to be managed with 'pull-downs', i.e., pedals that pulled down keys in the bass register by means of strings. Frescobaldi's two pedal toccatas were, in fact, ingeniously written so that they could be performed 'con pedale, o senza'. Some organs had a shimmering *vox humana* register (a set of pipes tuned slightly up or down to beat with the fundamental register, producing a tremulant effect), which organists today tend to associate with the Elevation toccatas discussed further, below.

Practices in the southern, Catholic portions of the Habsburg Empire were not very different, in part owing to the presence of many Italian musicians and to the Italian training of some prominent native ones such as Froberger, Johann Caspar Kerll (1627–93) and Georg Muffat (1653–1704). Froberger's only works with specific liturgical designations are two toccatas 'da sonarsi alla levatione' (for the Elevation; FbWV 105, 106), but Kerll published sets of versets for the Magnificat in all the tones (*Modulatio organica*, Vienna, 1686). All three composers wrote numerous toccatas and other works in the Italian manner well suited to the service. In addition, German and Austrian libraries, especially those of monasteries such as the Minoritenkonvent in Vienna, hold rich collections of seventeenth- and early eighteenth-century manuscripts containing countless versets. Some are manufactured from fragments of longer pieces such as toccatas by Frescobaldi and Froberger, suggesting that *alternatim* practice on the organ continued to thrive in those regions.[30]

Sources are scarce for French liturgical organ music from the earlier part of the seventeenth century, as with sources for any kind of French keyboard music from this period. However, they include two impressive volumes of almost 100 well-crafted, if conservative, hymn and Magnificats versets by Jehan Titelouze

---

29 Maugars (1639; trans. Bishop, p. 11) compared the Italian organs he heard in Rome with those in France: 'Their organs do not have as great a range and variety of stops as those we have today; it seems that most of their organs are intended to accompany voices and to put other instruments in advantageous settings'.

30 On the verset collections, see Riedel, *Quellenkundliche Beiträge zur Geschichte der Musik für Tasteninstrumente in der 2. Hälfte des 17. Jahrhunderts*, pp. 87–92; for a catalogue of the early manuscripts in the Minoritenkonvent, see Riedel, *Das Musikarchiv im Minoritenkonvent zu Wien*.

(*c.* 1562–1633) published in Paris in 1623 and 1626. The situation changes dramatically during the 'Golden Age' of Louis XIV, when one composer after another published a succession of impressive *Livres d'orgue*. Although the participation of the organ in the service continued to show few differences with Italy, the music took on an altogether different character, owing in part to the nature of the French instruments, and in part to the extraordinary inventiveness of the composers. The foundations were laid by Guillaume Gabriel Nivers, who in 1665 published a book 'containing 100 pieces in all the church tones', following it two years later with a second volume that included music specifically designated for the Mass. A third volume followed in 1675 with still more pieces grouped according to the modes. Nivers's pieces were not just generic versets, but fell into a number of distinct genres closely tied to the sumptuous polychromatic resources of French organs of the period. These instruments, despite individual variations, were sufficiently standardised to allow composers to specify certain registrations and voicings that, in turn, cemented certain generic and stylistic characteristics: an ensemble of loud snarling reeds (*Grand jeu*) or soft flutes (*Jeux doux*), an articulate solo set against a soft accompaniment (*Récit*), two-part counterpoint for contrasting voices (*Duo*), a *Dialogue* for two choirs, an *Echo*, and pieces named after the specific stop being featured, such as 'Basse de trompette' or 'Récit de cromorne'. All these reappeared in the *Livres d'orgue* of Nivers's followers. A fitting conclusion to the series, at least for the seventeenth century (the tradition continued into the next), was provided by the two organ Masses of the young François Couperin (1668–1733), which appeared in manuscript in 1690 with a printed title page, and the *Premier livre* by another brilliant young composer, Nicolas de Grigny (1672–1703).

Like France, Spain developed a distinct tradition as a result not so much of different liturgical practices as of differences in instruments and musical habits. In the sixteenth century, Antonio de Cabezón had contributed a few Kyries for the Mass and a much larger number of hymn, psalm and Magnificat versets for the Offices. It is believed that organ participation was in fact more favoured for the Offices, and hymn settings, especially of 'Ave maris stella' and 'Pange lingua', continued to be popular in Spain, becoming almost independent genres in their own right. Most of the major seventeenth-century composers, such as Francisco Correa de Arauxo (1584–1654) and Juan Bautista Cabanilles (1644–1712), concentrated, however, on the more substantial *tientos*, of which large quantities survive. Despite the uniform appellation and standard ricercar-like opening subjects, the *tientos* present an endless variety of forms and techniques which often are quite unorthodox if not occasionally bordering on the bizarre.

Lutheran (Evangelical) services

Music was central to the Lutheran service – Luther regarded polyphonic composition as God's gift to man – and early regulations urged congregations to appoint organists on the basis of their professional abilities and to pay them accordingly. Thus a tradition arose of seeking out musicians with outstanding accomplishments.[31] We learn from a vivid report of Matthias Weckmann's audition for the organ position at the Jacobikirche in Hamburg that the candidates were tested for a variety of skills, with the leading musicians of the town serving as jury.[32] Weckmann, who at the time was already serving as organist at the Dresden court chapel under Heinrich Schütz, was asked to improvise a fugue on a given subject, to create a fantasy on a chorale, to accompany a violinist from a figured bass, to play and vary on two manuals a six-part motet, and finally to play 'a lively fugue' on the full organ. He received the appointment.

In the *Hauptgottesdienst* (equivalent to the Mass), organ participation was especially important at the Introit and Gradual, and during Communion. At the Introit, the organist could play a prelude establishing the pitch for the choir, or even work in the melody of what the choir was about to sing, which could be a chant, a Latin hymn, or a German chorale. The Gradual also was often based on a chorale, in which the organist could either accompany the congregation or play solo versets in alternation with the choir. For Communion, Luther had recommended the singing of chorales, which customarily were introduced by organ preludes. Because of the time required for this ritual, it often provided the opportunity to improvise at greater length. *Vespergottesdienst* also offered opportunities for *alternatim* performance of hymns and Magnificat verses with either the choir or the congregation. At the conclusion of the service, after the Magnificat, the choir usually performed a motet, but sometimes the organist took over this role, playing either a motet intabulation (found in large number in German manuscripts) or an extended chorale setting, such as a fantasia or set of variations.

As in the Catholic service, there was much opportunity for shorter and longer pieces, with the difference that German chorale melodies were expected to play a central role. Thus we witness the gradual development of a repertory of chorale settings greatly varying in length and character, along with a sprinkling of Latin hymn and Magnificat settings, as well as free preludes or toccatas for the beginning of the service. This music takes advantage of the unparalleled resources of the large German organs, with the frequent requirement to

---

31 Edler, 'Organ Music within the Social Structure of North German Cities in the Seventeenth Century'.
32 Krüger, 'Johann Kortkamps Organistenchronik', pp. 205–6.

distribute voices over multiple manuals and pedals, although unlike the French repertory, it rarely indicates specific stops. Some German organ pieces, however, seem far too long to fit ordinary liturgical needs. Moreover, some of the big chorale-variation sets could not have been used for *alternatim* performance because, aside from questions of scale, they contain too few or too many verses, or have no break between successive sections.[33] As we shall see below, in some churches there existed other, non-liturgical occasions in which such works were welcomed.[34]

Anglican services

In England, a fine body of liturgical organ music had been created before the Reformation, but the new Church of England had only limited use for the instrument. In fact, the subsequent development of both organs and organ music experienced several stops and starts as the political and religious climate of the country went through successive upheavals. The instruments generally remained small and limited to one or two manuals without independent pedal divisions. The main opportunity for extended organ solos was the performance of a voluntary in the middle of Morning or Evening Prayer. In general, the early voluntaries were loosely constructed imitative pieces, essentially equivalent to fantasias; some later examples for 'Double Organ' take advantage of the contrast between different divisions. As is the case with similar but usually shorter pieces called 'Verse', none carries a specific liturgical designation. The large group of sometimes quite elaborate pieces based on Latin cantus firmi are believed to have been intended not for the service, but for performance on virginals, even if the genre probably originated in liturgical practice.

Reactions against organ music

There has always been tension between the beliefs that music can powerfully enhance the act of worship, and that it is more often a distraction. The debate flared up once again in mid seventeenth-century Germany, and some of the tirades afford us a rare glimpse of the congregational response to these large doses of organ music. A theology professor in Hamburg, Theophil Großbauer, complained: 'There sits the organist, playing and showing off his art. So that one man can show off his art, the entire congregation of Jesus Christ must sit and listen to the sound of the pipes. From this the congregation becomes drowsy and lazy: some sleep, some chat, and some look where they should not.'

33 Davidsson, *Matthias Weckmann*, pp. 6, 12–13. But as Davidsson suggests (p. 6), it is possible that sung verses were grouped together, with the organ playing between the groups.

34 Rampe, 'Abendmusik oder Gottesdienst?' is the first part of what promises to be an extremely detailed and comprehensive study of the intended purposes of the preserved organ repertory from seventeenth-century north Germany, including those problematic works of seemingly excessive length.

That 'one man' sitting at the organ apparently was none other than the celebrated Heinrich Scheidemann, organist of the Catharinenkirche. Before long, a response was published by the organist's brother-in-law, Hector Mithobius, who was a pastor in a nearby village: 'The organist sits there not to show off his art but to praise God in a skilful manner' and to move the congregation 'to ardent devotion, to spiritual thought, to joy in the Lord, and to awaken the spirit'. Apparently he does not always succeed, because, according to Mithobius, some members of the congregation leave the church during the organ playing to stroll and chat in the churchyard, while those who remain in the church 'sit there like stupid and unthinking cattle and do not consider that they owe thanks to God for this noble ecclesiastical grace'.[35]

Some Italians also seem to have had problems with organists who did not know when to stop. Pietro della Valle wrote in 1640: 'solo playing, no matter how well done, when it goes on for a long time becomes boring. It has often happened to different organists – and the best ones – that, when overly enamoured of their counterpoints, they made certain improvisations [*ricercate*] too long, the little bell had to be rung to make them stop'.[36] But André Maugars provided a more enthusiastic report of Italian organ playing, claiming no surprise at Frescobaldi's reputation across Europe: 'for although his printed works give sufficient evidence of his skill, to get a true idea of his profound knowledge, it is necessary that one hear him improvise toccatas full of admirable discoveries and inventions'.[37]

Performance outside the liturgy

The organ had no role to play in Reformed services because, following Calvinist doctrine, musical participation was limited to unaccompanied monophonic psalm singing. Thus there was no call for liturgical organ music, but in Amsterdam that ban resulted, paradoxically, in the creation of some of the finest organ works of the time.

The Amsterdam organs belonged to the city and were its pride and joy; the civic authorities employed the organists and charged them with playing for the community before or after services and on other special occasions. The idea was that such uplifting entertainment would keep citizens away from the taverns. The performances at the Oude Kerk by Sweelinck drew many listeners, including foreign visitors (given that Amsterdam was an important centre of international trade).[38] Sweelinck's daily, hour-long recitals, which continued

---

35 Edler, 'Organ Music within the Social Structure of North German Cities in the Seventeenth Century', pp. 28–9, 41–2.
36 Strunk, *Source Readings in Music History, Revised Edition*, iv: *The Baroque Era*, p. 38.
37 Bishop, 'Translation of Maugars' *Response* . . .', p. 10.
38 Noske, *Sweelinck*, pp. 3–4, 11.

for some 40 years (c. 1580–1621), were among the first public concerts in Europe. It is for these occasions that the composer must have developed not only his settings of melodies from the Genevan Psalter that his listeners might be singing in an ensuing service, but also grand fantasias, toccatas and variations. The popularity of these Dutch recitals spawned imitations even in some of the Lutheran churches of north German cities that had close commercial ties with Amsterdam. In the 1640s, Franz Tunder (1614–67) initiated organ recitals in Lübeck's Marienkirche to entertain merchants waiting for the opening of the stock exchange; these evolved into the celebrated *Abendmusiken*. Perhaps we should not picture these solid businessmen sitting in rapt attention throughout the long organ fantasias. In this period, churches also served as covered public meeting places in the hearts of the cities, in which children played, and dogs and cats ran to and fro. Even during the concerts, business was apparently transacted and lovers found their partners; indeed there is a report of citizens playing dice and drinking wine during an organ audition in Danzig (Gdansk).[39] One can well imagine that under these circumstances an organist might sometimes treat his listeners to a set of popular-song variations, which might explain their appearance in the works of Sweelinck alongside the chorale settings.

However, the Amsterdam custom does not explain the large numbers of pieces found among the keyboard works of organists from every part of Europe that are clearly unsuited to liturgical use. Furthermore, many of those works seem to have been intended for stringed keyboard instruments. This raises two related questions: how much of an organist's time went into playing for the services, and for what purposes might these 'secular' works have been written? From what we know about the professional life of some organists, it is evident that they could not have played for every service in a single church; a few even held simultaneous appointments at more than one institution – be it another church or at court – and also took on freelance engagements, often of a quite worldly nature, such as playing continuo for opera.[40] Frescobaldi earned only a fraction of his income from his position at St Peter's; in his later years he received a generous stipend for his services to his patron, Cardinal Francesco Barberini, while in addition, he took several prolonged leaves and not infrequently had someone else sign for his salary.[41] When the principal organist was not available,

---

39 Edler, 'Organ Music within the Social Structure of North German Cities in the Seventeenth Century', pp. 31–2.

40 In Rome, Frescobaldi served for some years at both St Peter's and S. Spirito in Sassia, and Bernardo Pasquini did likewise at S. Maria Maggiore and S. Maria in Aracoeli. We do not know whether such coterminous appointments meant that they alternated between the two, or whether one of the positions did not involve a regular playing commitment. See also Silbiger, 'The Roman Frescobaldi Tradition', p. 49.

41 However, on the title-pages of his publications, he generally only mentioned his position at St Peter's.

presumably an assistant or substitute took over. Some larger churches, such as St Mark's, Venice, had two or more organists on their payrolls, thus providing for a division of labour, although it also allowed for performances with multiple organs such as was common in polychoral works, and for occasional organ duets.[42] Why church organists wrote music so clearly oriented towards the harpsichord or clavichord becomes understandable, however, when one realises that the opportunities for using the organ outside the service, whether for practice, teaching or personal recreation, were severely limited. In the larger churches there was constant activity: aside from the regular daily services there were baptisms, weddings, funerals and other special services, and even when no service was in progress there may not have been much privacy owing to the public nature of the space. When not in use, churches tended to be cold and dark, and of course, the organs could not be played at all without the assistance of someone to pump the bellows. Thus the organist was likely to do most of his practising and teaching at home, and while a few wealthy homes might possess a chamber organ, the average musician had to manage with a harpsichord, virginal or clavichord.[43] Keyboard players were not necessarily unhappy about having to play on a harpsichord. In early seventeenth-century Rome, church performances of ensemble music often involved a battery of continuo instruments that included both organs and harpsichords (as well as lutes or theorbos), and payment records show that Frescobaldi usually played harpsichord rather than organ. This agrees with the report by Maugars of a performance in the Oratorio of S. Marcello: 'But most impressive of all was the great Frescobaldi displaying a thousand kinds of inventions on his harpsichord while the organ stuck to the main tune' (i.e., the harpsichord improvised variations against a ground-bass accompaniment by the organ).[44]

Solo music in the chamber

We are somewhat in the dark about the circumstances of solo performance outside the church, rarely knowing precisely who played what, where or when. There were no concert halls as such, and notwithstanding the north European organ concerts mentioned earlier, the solo recital as we know it was a later institution. There is no lack of documentary and pictorial evidence of music being played in palaces, coffeehouses and ordinary homes, but specific

42 Taminga, 'Music for Two Organs in Italy'.

43 Some organists possessed pedal clavichords or, less often, pedal harpsichords for this purpose; the popularity of two-manual harpsichords, rarely needed for seventeenth-century solo music, might also in part be connected with their use as a practice instrument for organists.

44 Bishop, 'Translation of Maugars' *Response . . .*', pp. 9–10; Silbiger, 'The Roman Frescobaldi Tradition', pp. 47–8.

information that survives, such as payment records for a special event, generally points to the participation of several musicians who may or may not have played solos. The little information we do possess is mostly anecdotal, but it affords us enough glimpses to place some of the surviving music in context.

Academies, collegia musica *and other organised gatherings*

In the dedication to his first publication of keyboard music, the *Primo libro delle fantasie a quattro* (Milan, 1608), Frescobaldi wrote that music 'today receives such esteem from the most noble taste your Excellency has for it as solace for your grave cares', the which cares were lessened by hearing him play many of the fantasies now published.[45] The dedicatee was Francesco Borghese, Captain-General of the Church and elder brother of Pope Paul V, who most likely heard Frescobaldi play these fantasies in early 1607 at an *accademia* in his palace, at which several musicians had been invited to perform. If Francesco indeed found solace by listening to these fantasies, he must have been an intelligent musical connoisseur with an exceptionally keen ear, for they are among the most dense and demanding music produced during the period.

Here we find a highly accomplished artist playing for a prominent and musically sophisticated patron and his guests. Two of Frescobaldi's later publications also refer to specific connoisseurs, their tone contrasting with the more *pro forma* rhetoric of most of his other dedications. To Cardinal-Duke Ferdinando Gonzaga of Mantua, dedicatee of the first edition of his *Toccate e partite* (Rome, 1615) and a well-known music patron and sometime composer, Frescobaldi declares: 'I dedicate [this volume] devotedly to Your Highness who in Rome deigned with frequent requests to stimulate me to the practice of these works, and to show that this style of mine was not unacceptable to you'. Since the volume contains no liturgical repertory and is specifically 'per il cembalo' (i.e., harpsichord), that occasion most likely also was at some kind of academy. A different relationship, perhaps that of teacher and pupil, is hinted at in the dedication of the *Secondo libro di toccate* (Rome, 1627) to Luigi Gallo, Bishop of Ancona: it refers to the dedicatee's harpsichord playing, which is praised even by professionals, and it expresses the hope that Gallo will employ these toccatas for his pleasure and do them honour 'when your serious duties will permit you to play them'.

During the course of the seventeenth century, an increasing amount of music was performed at academies, salons, *collegia musica* and other assemblies – some

---

45 Hammond, *Girolamo Frescobaldi: a Guide to Research*, pp. 184–5. See also Annibaldi, 'Frescobaldi's Early Stay in Rome', pp. 114–17.

beginning to approach later notions of public concerts – in a variety of venues including private homes, schools, coffeehouses and even church refectories. Generally the descriptions of what was heard are rather vague: for example, the *collegium musicum* in Hamburg, directed by Weckmann, performed 'the best things from Venice, Rome, Vienna, Munich and Dresden'.[46] One gets the impression that the repertory was quite diverse and involved a sizeable group of singers and instrumentalists (*c.* 25 singers and 25 instrumentalists in Hamburg); instrumental solo performances (or improvisations) more likely were the exception, although one cannot rule them out.[47] In 1641, Chambonnières inaugurated in Paris a series of musical assemblies that took place twice a week in a hall also used for weddings and equipped with benches. Some ten musicians were paid to take part; we can only guess whether Chambonnières performed any of his *Pièces de clavecin* at these occasions.[48] Beginning in 1683, Jacques Gallot (d. 1690) organised a series of Saturday-evening concerts in his home, and we have a more informative report regarding his participation in one of these, arranged in 1687 to honour a visiting Siamese ambassador. According to the *Mercure galant*, 'M. Galot played a lute solo and the ambassador said to him that, although he could think of nothing which would add to the beauty of the sound of the entire ensemble [that presumably had played earlier], there were delicacies when he played alone which ought not to be mixed with a great number of instruments since much would be lost'.[49]

Private music

Europe's monarchs usually had musicians on their personal staff, to divert them during dinner or when retiring to bed. Some even performed themselves. John Melville, Scottish ambassador to the court of Queen Elizabeth I, noted the queen's playing of the virginals: 'she used not to play before men, but when she was solitary', as she said, 'to shun melancholy'. According to a report from 1611, 'Louis XIII went to sleep to the spinet playing of Sieur de La Chapelle' (Chambonnières's father). Louis XIV seems to have taken a more active interest in the offerings of his private musicians: Le Gallois reports that he 'took special pleasure in hearing [Hardel's harpsichord pieces] played every week by Hardel himself in concert with the late lutenist, Porion'.[50]

---

46 Seiffert, 'Matthias Weckmann und das Collegium musicum in Hamburg', pp. 110–17.

47 Braun, *Die Musik des 17. Jahrhunderts*, p. 40.   48 Massip, 'Paris', p. 231.

49 Given in Ledbetter, *Harpsichord and Lute Music in 17th-Century France*, p. 13. See also Braun, *Die Musik des 17. Jahrhunderts*, p. 44.

50 For the reports cited in this paragraph, see respectively: Monson, 'Elizabethan London', pp. 331–2; Ledbetter, *Harpsichord and Lute Music in 17th-Century France*, p. 9; Fuller, 'French Harpsichord Playing in the 17th Century', p. 23. What Porion's role was in the performance of these harpsichord pieces (assuming that 'in concert' means they actually played together) is not clear; perhaps he supported their basses and harmonies.

A quite different type of private performance was reported by a member of Sweelinck's circle:

> I recall that once, with a few good friends, I went to visit my good friend Master Ian Petersz. Swelinck and yet other good friends, in the month of May, and after starting to play the harpsichord, he continued with this until about midnight, playing among other things *Den lustilicken Mey is nu in zijnen tijt* ['Jolly May is now in its time'], which he, if I remember this well, played in 25 different ways, now in this way, now in that way. When we got up to take our leave, he begged us we must still listen to this piece and then to that piece, not being able to stop, as he was in a very sweet mood, entertaining us, his friends, and also entertaining himself.[51]

Pepys provides us with a rather less enthusiastic description of a private harpsichord performance on 10 November 1666: 'Mr Temple's wife, after dinner, fell to play on the harpsicon, till she so tired everybody, that I left the house without taking leave, and no creature left by her standing to hear her'.[52] More touching, however, is the domestic scene reported by Thomas Mace (1612–?1706), when he played a 'lesson' composed before his marriage when he was suffering a painful separation from his wife-to-be:

> But after I was married and had brought my wife home to Cambridge, it so fell out that one rainy morning I stayed within; and in my chamber my wife and I were all alone, she intent on her needlework and I playing upon my lute at the table by her. She sat very still and quiet, listening to all I played without a word a long time, till at last I happened to play this lesson, which, so soon as I had once played, she earnestly desired me to play it again, for, said she, that shall be called 'My Lesson' . . . and [I] returned her this answer, viz. 'That it may very properly be called your lesson, for when I composed it, you were wholly in my fancy and the chief object and ruler of my thoughts', telling her how and when it was made. And therefore, ever after I called [the lesson] 'My Mistress'.[53]

Verbal descriptions of such domestic performances are rare, but visual portrayals are plentiful, especially from the Netherlands. One thinks of the various scenes by Vermeer, Ter Borch and their contemporaries of a lady playing a lute or virginal, either alone by herself, or with a gentleman (listener, teacher, suitor?) gazing at her intently, and absorbed by her music – as one imagines she is herself. Several such paintings with a single (usually female) performer and a (usually male) listener are today known under the title 'The Music Lesson'. Whether or not the description is accurate, lessons in music, as in dance, were

---

51 Tollefsen, 'Jan Pietersz. Sweelinck', p. 92.
52 Demuth (ed.), *An Anthology of Musical Criticism*, p. 37.
53 T. Mace, *Musick's Monument* (London, 1676; repr. Paris, 1958), i: 122–3 (spelling and punctuation modernised).

becoming common in the 'better' seventeenth-century homes. The practice of music was thought to promote family harmony and the development of a healthy body. Women were particular beneficiaries of domestic music education, because traditional forms of musical training such as choir schools or apprenticeship with a master were not open to them. And aside from conventional notions of musical ability adding to their marriage prospects, music no doubt provided a welcome outlet in their sheltered lives, both before and after marriage.

Not all music for teaching or practice need be simple: witness the four volumes of J. S. Bach's *Clavier-Übung* ('Keyboard Practice'). Pedagogical intent motivated several musicians to publish large collections of their own works – as is often made explicit in dedications (e.g., Samuel Scheidt's *Tabulatura nova*, Hamburg, 1624) or prefaces (Frescobaldi's *Fiori musicali*) – as well as anthologies of works of others (Matthew Locke's *Melothesia*, London, 1673). Furthermore, we have already seen that a large portion of the numerous manuscript keyboard books found throughout Europe can only be understood as personal collections of practice pieces, even when not explicitly indicated as such, or by extension, as pieces for personal recreation (given that a distinction between 'practice' and 'recreation' is not always clear, especially in the case of amateur performance). Contemporary accounts also explain the potential attraction of such performance:

> When a good player picks up his lute and fingers its strings, when from his end of the table, chords are heard seeking out a *fantasie*, and when he has plucked three chords and sent a tune into the air, then all eyes and ears are drawn to him. If he chooses to let the sound die away under his fingers, all are transported by a gay melancholy; one lets his chin fall on his chest, another sits head in hand . . . still another with mouth wide open and one with his mouth half opened as though all his attention were riveted on the strings.[54]

Solo music in theatres and out of doors

Seventeenth-century style classifications usually distinguish between music for churches, chambers and theatres. Although harpsichordists participated in operas and in other theatrical performances involving singing or dancing, they are not known to have played solos except for brief ritornellos, which would have been notated (if at all) as figured basses. The same applies to lutes and guitars; the latter instrument seems to have been especially popular in improvised theatre. The many collections of stock chord-strumming progressions

---

54 R. François, *Essais des merveilles de nature* (Paris, 1621), p. 474, given in Anthony, *French Baroque Music*, p. 233.

for guitar in alphabet tablature provided in a range of keys and rhythms were probably intended as models for strophic-song accompaniments and vamps, and thus could be regarded as theatre music; they include the well-known formulas of the period such as the *ciaccona*, *passacaglia* and *Romanesca*.

Despite their delicacy, and instability of pitch, various kinds of harpsichords, bowed and plucked strings and flutes occasionally show up in depictions of garden concerts, including depictions in verse. A poem by an obscure Dutch poet, Regnerus Opperveldt, published in 1640, describes an evening in the Janskerkhof, a large park in the centre of Utrecht which served as a favourite meeting and strolling ground, especially for young lovers. Opperveldt tells how after the sun sets, other suns begin to shine, those that burn in lovers' hearts as they slip through the dense trees. Suddenly a sweet, bright sound rings through the tender leaves. It is Eyckje (little Van Eyck – the diminutive being a form of endearment) starting to play his recorder. 'Oh! What a lovely tingle . . . am I in heaven! Oh! glorified boxwood holes, Oh! what superhuman measures flow from the artful round of a quick-breath mouth.'[55] Van Eyck was the city carillonneur, but one of his salary rises came with the stipulation 'that he occasionally in the evening entertain the people strolling through the *Kerckhof* with the sound of his little flute'.[56] Presumably he did so with the kind of variations on popular songs and dances that he published in *Der fluyten lust-hof*, where 'lust-hof' (pleasure garden) probably refers precisely to the Janskerkhof.

The outdoors is also the natural domain of carillons and trumpets. A couple of Belgian collections survive containing carillon pieces for automatic instruments. Most of the Netherlands carillon repertory, whether automatic or manual, apparently consisted of church hymns in up to three parts.[57] The north European outdoor trumpet repertory seems to have been similar: instructions for the trumpeters posted at Hamburg's main church towers stipulated that 'every night, after the church clock has struck nine, midnight and, in the morning, three and ten, he will honour God by playing a sacred psalm'.[58]

Varieties of solo music

The early seventeenth century saw an explosion of different musical styles and genres. This was true of music in general, but particularly so of solo music, where pieces were given a bewildering variety of genre titles. These might

---

55 Baak Griffioen, *Jacob van Eyck's 'Der fluyten lust-hof'*, pp. 44–6.   56 Ibid., p. 32.
57 L. Rombouts, 'Carillon', in Sadie and Tyrrell (eds), *The Revised New Grove Dictionary of Music and Musicians*, v: 133.
58 Buelow, 'Protestant North Germany', p. 196.

pertain to function, to compositional structure or procedure, and to character or other properties, and they also depended on national or regional practice. The terms were by no means used consistently, and all the shades of meaning cannot be explored within the confines of this chapter. Rather, I will look at a number of categories each of which highlights certain of solo music's special qualities and potentials.

Several writers of the time attempted to get a handle on this profusion of styles and genres by means of definitions and classification schemes. When used with awareness of the inherent limitations of all such attempts to force reality into a theoretical framework, they can prove helpful for understanding what contemporaries thought important about this music. In his *Plaine and Easie Introduction to Practicall Musicke* (London, 1597), Thomas Morley (1557–1602) presented a 'Division of music' that, like most of the period, was hierarchical, placing sacred music above secular, and vocal above instrumental.[59] The instrumental division begins with 'Fantasy', followed by dance types, ordered from 'grave' to 'light'. Although Morley's division, even when applied just to the English repertory of his time, omits a great deal (e.g., variations on popular songs, intabulations, cantus-firmus settings), it sets up for instrumental music a basic distinction between 'fantasy' pieces on the one hand, and dances on the other, which is followed, with elaborations, by later writers.

In the third volume of his *Syntagma musicum* (1619), Michael Praetorius (1571–1621) presents a much grander scheme that claims to incorporate Italian, French, English as well as German 'songs' (*Gesänge, cantilenae*), understood as any kind of piece, with or without text.[60] The multiple hierarchy is displayed as a 'genealogical' table, which is followed by discussions of individual genres and their interrelationships. Again, music without text is divided into two main branches: the second comprises dances, but the first is designated as 'praeludia' rather than as fantasies, with preludes being subdivided into works 'by themselves' – including fantasias (or *capricci*) and fugues (or ricercars) – and those introducing other pieces (toccatas, preludes, *praeambula*). Not much distinction is to be found between *praeludia* (in Praetorius's sense) that are preludial or not; nor should one worry about the apparent illogicality of the prelude being a subgenre of the prelude. Praetorius's main point is that all *praeludia* are pieces which, like Morley's fantasy, do not follow a set scheme, but which the player 'fantasises out of his head' (*aus seinen Kopff vorher fantasirt*). The

---

59 T. Morley, *A Plain and Easy Introduction to Practical Music*, ed. R. A. Harman (London, 1952), pp. 292–8.
60 M. Praetorius, *Syntagma musicum*, iii (Wolfenbüttel, 1619; repr. Kassel, 1958), p. 3.

presence or absence of such a scheme is evidently an important criterion for Praetorius; even the dances are subdivided into those that follow set patterns (e.g., pavans and galliards) and those that do not (e.g., courantes and allemandes).

Attempts to categorise genres often get mixed with style classifications, which, beginning with the Artusi–Monteverdi controversy, had become a charged issue. In 1643, Marco Scacchi (*c.* 1600–1662) supported a tripartite division of church, chamber and theatre styles, as well as a distinction between 'old' and 'modern' styles related to Monteverdi's *prima* and *seconda pratica*, and style classification was refined to a twelve-fold division by Athanasius Kircher (1601–80) in his *Musurgia universalis* (1650).[61] Two of Kircher's styles include instrumental solo genres: the *stylus phantasticus* and the *stylus hyporchematicus* or *choraicus* (dance style). This echoes Morley and Praetorius. The concept of fantasy or fantasia has shifted meanings several times in music history; to us the notion of a 'fantastic style' might suggest music that is capricious, even bizarre, but to Kircher (as well as to his contemporaries) its meaning was both broader and simpler, as the 'most free and unfettered method of composition' that displayed the invention and ingenuity (*ingenium*) of the composer. According to Kircher, the *stylus phantasticus* was used in fantasias, toccatas, ricercars and sonatas. As an example he gives Froberger's *Fantasia supra Ut, re, mi, fa, sol, la* (FbWV 201), a piece in strict four-part counterpoint which appears in its entirety elsewhere in the *Musurgia*.

Two of Kircher's other styles are relevant to the present discussion, even if he does not relate them to instrumental music: the *stylus ecclesiasticus* (church style) and the *stylus canonicus* (canonic style). Like Morley and Praetorius, Kircher does not include in his scheme instrumental settings of sacred or secular melodies, or intabulations. Perhaps he considered such derivative genres as not showing much *ingenium* (a prejudice not uncommon among modern scholars). Yet his citing of Froberger's hexachord-based fantasia as an example of the *stylus phantasticus* is itself revealing. This work certainly exhibits fantasy and *ingenium*, but it also demonstrates the composer's craft by overcoming self-imposed technical obstacles. No one is born with the ability to make the hexachord subject pass with unflinching elegance through seven different contrapuntal hoops, with multiple diminutions, inversions, chromaticism and other tricks of the polyphonic trade. Fantasy and craft both are present to some degree in almost all music: in fact, like the *inventio* and *elaboratio* of oratory, they are necessary ingredients to any successful composition. However, in some works one or the other, or sometimes both, are foregrounded as central to the basic character of

---

61 Bianconi, *Music in the Seventeenth Century*, pp. 48, 50.

the piece. Furthermore, both fantasy and craft are, for different reasons, closely associated with the instrumental solo tradition. The point will become clearer still in the discussion of different instrumental genres below.

Music of fantasy (fantasia, toccata, prelude)

According to Morley, the fantasia was the 'most principal and chiefest' kind of instrumental music, wherein (my emphasis)

> a musician taketh a point [contrapuntal subject or idea] *at his pleasure* and wresteth and turneth it *as he list* [i.e., as he is inclined], making either much or little of it *according as shall seem best in his own conceit*. In this may be more art than shown in any other music because the composer is tied to nothing, but that he may add, diminish, and alter *at his pleasure* . . . Other things you may use *at your pleasure*, as bindings [suspensions] with discords, quick motions, slow motions, Proportion, and *what you list*.[62]

Praetorius must have agreed with this description because he appropriates several phrases almost verbatim in his paragraph on the fantasia and *capriccio* (see above). Morley refers seven times to the musician's freedom to proceed at will; this clearly represents a defining quality for the fantasia, and it is also why he values the genre so highly. He is a bit vague, however, about the source of the musician's ideas and decisions, referring merely to 'his pleasure' and 'his conceit'. Praetorius calls it 'his head', and Kircher talks about 'ingenium'; in other words, it is that mysterious, innate source that today we might call the artist's imagination or, indeed, his fantasy.

Morley was thinking primarily about ensemble works ('music of parts'), but his description of spontaneous twists and turns is even more apt for solo fantasias, with their strong roots in improvisation. The notated fantasias and other works of Praetorius's *praeludia* category, such as the toccata and the *capriccio*, aim to preserve this improvised quality, to which the player can contribute by performing them with appropriate freedom. Echoing (probably unknowingly) Morley's 'quick' and 'slow' motions, Frescobaldi, in his prefaces on toccata performance, writes that the player must now hold back 'as if suspended in the air', and now rush forward.[63] Likewise, Purcell uses for his ensemble fantasias the vivid terms 'drag' and 'away'.

For the purest keyboard examples of Morley's type of fantasia, one can do no better than go back to some of Byrd's, almost all dating from the sixteenth century.[64] For example, his Fantasia in A may start with dignified imitative

---

62 Morley, *A Plain and Easy Introduction to Practical Music*, p. 196.
63 Hammond, *Girolamo Frescobaldi: a Guide to Research*, p. 188.
64 For the concept of the fantasia in early keyboard music, see Dirksen, *The Keyboard Music of Jan Pieterszoon Sweelinck*, pp. 327–36.

counterpoint in the Renaissance manner, but there is no predicting what comes next.[65] In one section, a multitude of new voices seemingly keeps entering, stretching out an imitative point beyond all proportion. In others, trumpet fanfares and marches make themselves heard, and chord progressions drum out syncopated rhythms. Often in Byrd's fantasias a jolly popular tune will appear out of nowhere, or there may be hints of galliards, jigs and so forth. During this constant flow of new ideas, the only overall organising principle seems to be to ratchet up the excitement a notch with each section by means of shorter note-values or faster metres. This undisciplined, exuberant manner has disappeared by the time we get to the refined fantasias of Orlando Gibbons, with their smooth polyphonic flow, as in the well-known *Fantazia of foure parts* included in *Parthenia, or The Maydenhead of the First Musicke that ever was Printed for the Virginalls* (London, 1612/13). Craftsmanship is beginning to assert control.

As we learn from Praetorius, both the 'preludial' and the free pieces by seventeenth-century composers carried a number of different names other than fantasia, such as toccata, prelude, ricercar, canzona, fugue or *capriccio* (he does not mention the English voluntary or the Spanish *tiento*). These genres are, at least in principle, distinguished somewhat by style and structure, although composers do not always agree on where the distinctions lie. Some types look back to earlier vocal genres: ricercars tend to be rather 'grave' contrapuntal pieces in the old motet style, whereas canzonas, while also contrapuntal, are lighter, with quicker rhythms, in the vein of earlier French chansons. However, neither could be mistaken for a literal transcription or intabulation. With the exception of the toccata and the prelude, all these genres are for the most part still rooted in imitative polyphony, the 'high style' of the Renaissance, and have more or less close connections with similarly named ensemble pieces. Toccatas and preludes exhibit the imitative style only intermittently if at all, and rarely at their beginnings. Some conclude with a prolonged imitative section which may or may not be marked as a separate movement (most often called a 'fuga'); this becomes fairly standard in the later seventeenth century, but there are earlier examples.[66]

Toccatas are generally unique to solo instruments. Almost all are for members of either the keyboard or the lute family,[67] and they are among those

---

65 No. 13 (Neighbour a1) in W. Byrd, *Keyboard Works I*, ed. A. Brown, 'Musica britannica', 27, rev. edn (London, 1976). For Byrd's keyboard fantasias, see Neighbour, *The Consort and Keyboard Music of William Byrd*, pp. 221–58.

66 Silbiger, 'The Roman Frescobaldi Tradition', p. 81; Silbiger, *Italian Manuscript Sources of 17th-Century Keyboard Music*, pp. 45–6.

67 There is a *Toccata del Signor Oratio Bassani* for *viola bastarda* (Paras, *The Music for the Viola Bastarda*, p. 108), and some fanfares for solo trumpet called 'Toccata' in Girolamo Fantini's *Modo per imparare a sonare di tromba* (Frankfurt [*recte* Florence], 1638). Monteverdi's use of the term for the opening music in *Orfeo* probably is related to the latter usage.

instruments' most idiomatic works. 'Toccata' is derived from the Italian 'toc-care' (to touch), referring to a physical act rather than to any musical qualities. We have seen that Maugars singled out for praise Frescobaldi's improvising of toccatas, and, more than for any of his other works, the performance of his printed toccatas provides the illusion of improvisation. But another kind of illusion also operates here. Frescobaldi himself gives a hint when, in his rec-ommendation not to maintain a rigid beat but to vary it according to the affect of the music, he refers to the performance style of 'modern madrigals'. For all that Frescobaldi's toccata style is rooted in keyboard improvisations on poly-phonic madrigals,[68] he probably is referring here more to the new monodies, such as those in Caccini's *Le nuove musiche*, the madrigals of which, Caccini said, were to be performed freely according to the affects of the words. Of course, Frescobaldi's toccatas do not sound the least bit like Caccini's monodies, nor could they. Compensating for the evanescent tone of the harpsichord, they provide a continuous torrent of sound. Chords, suspensions and arpeggiations give way to sweeping scales, capricious figurations, fleeting points of imita-tion, prolonged trills, and other often quite novel textures so as to avoid, in the composer's words, 'leaving the instrument empty'.[69] The listener is subjected to constant surprise, with outbursts of passion, desire, joy, distress, anger, and even shock, when harsh dissonances suddenly impinge upon the ear. As with contemporary monodies, toccatas can focus on different conceits. To take a few examples from the *Secondo libro di toccate* of 1627, one toccata may start with 'bitter tears' (*Toccata prima*), another with 'sweetest sighs' (*Toccata undecima*).[70] *Toccata nona* is unmatched for finger-twisting virtuosity, a dizzying succession of innovative keyboard effects at the end of which the composer addresses the exhausted player with the note 'Not without effort does one reach the end'.[71] Yet a few of the toccatas in the *Secondo libro*, expressly intended for organ, are of quite a different character. Two exploit an idiomatic resource unique to the medium: the sustained pedal point supporting an ecstatic web of floating voices and harmonies.

In parallel with Frescobaldi, his Roman colleague Giovanni Girolamo Kapsberger (*c.* 1580–1651), from a German family but born in Venice, was working out quite similar toccatas on the lute and chitarrone, one of many examples of harpsichordists and lutenists inspiring each other and trying to adapt the special effects of the other instrument. For instance, Frescobaldi

68 Silbiger, 'From Madrigal to Toccata'.

69 Hammond, *Girolamo Frescobaldi: a Guide to Research*, p. 189.

70 Compare these openings with Caccini's 'Queste lagrim'amare' and 'Dolcissimo sospiro', nos. 2 and 3 in *Le nuove musiche*, in G. Caccini, *Le nuove musiche (1602)*, ed. H. W. Hitchcock, 'Recent Researches in the Music of the Baroque Era', 9 (Madison, WI, 1970), pp. 62, 67. *Toccata prima* also opens with an imitation of one of Caccini's vocal *affetti*, the *ribattuta di gola*.

71 For a more extended discussion of this piece, see Judd, 'Italy', pp. 289–90.

seems to have emulated Kapsperger's special kinds of arpeggios, including the non-sequential, back-and-forth variety natural on the chitarrone with its re-entrant tunings.[72] On the keyboard, the younger Michelangelo Rossi tried to surpass Frescobaldi in chromatic and textural shock-tactics with a set of quite dramatic essays in the genre (c. 1630).[73] However, a perhaps more important and certainly more influential change in conception came from the north, from the German Froberger.

Froberger's toccatas begin very much like Frescobaldi's, in an improvisatory manner, with chords, arpeggiations and sweeping scales. Nevertheless, as they proceed one senses that the inspiration of the moment is becoming some-what subordinated to longer-range planning. Style and character do not change as often, and the rhapsodic introduction is usually followed by several quite extended fugal sections with related subjects but successively faster note-values that result in increasingly intense levels of excitement, very much like the sec-tions of a variation-canzona (see below).[74] Although his toccatas are still the product of fantasy, it is a fantasy that has a clear sense of direction towards more distant goals.

Froberger's procedures are stretched to much larger dimensions in the north German organ preludes of the late seventeenth century (some of them still called toccatas), the most magnificent specimens of which are by Dieterich Buxtehude (c. 1637–1707). Much fantasy is displayed both in original and unusual musical ideas and in formal structures, but the outlines of Froberger's scheme are usually still visible, with free sections introducing (and often terminating) fugal ones. Many of the free sections are highly dramatic and include virtuoso manual and pedal solos or extended pedal points. The fugues, which may or may not be motivically related, at times assume appreciable length and complexity. For this reason, the fugues are nowadays regarded as movements distinct from the preludes (hence 'Prelude and Fugue'), but in the sources they clearly form part of the preludes, something that is still true of Bach's organ preludes, if not of his *Well-Tempered Keyboard*. But if Frescobaldi's toccatas appear to be keyboard responses to contemporary monodies, Buxtehude's preludes can be seen as reflections of later vocal forms: the newly fashionable recitative–aria sequence. The drama of the mercurial free sections as well as their preparatory function has much in common with that of operatic recitative, whereas the extended, stable fugues, with their more fixed affects, play a role similar to arias.[75]

---

72 Coelho, 'Frescobaldi and the Lute and Chitarrone Toccatas of "Il Tedesco della Tiorba"'.

73 Judd, 'Italy', pp. 293–5; Silbiger, 'Michelangelo Rossi and his *Toccate e correnti*'.

74 See, for example, the discussion of the fourth toccata from the *Libro secondo* (FbWV 110) in Butt, 'Germany and the Netherlands', pp. 187–8.

75 Snyder, *Dieterich Buxtehude*, p. 256.

French lutenists and harpsichordists cultivated a special type of prelude, the *prélude non mesuré*, which was notated in a manner unlike that of any other music of the period.[76] The genre seems to have originated among lutenists in the 1630s and persisted in the harpsichord repertory until the early eighteenth century, still being used by Rameau in his *Premier livre des pièces de clavecin* (1706). Although precise in pitch, it is indefinite in rhythm, indicating neither metre nor fixed note-values, but employing instead various suggestive graphic devices. In its earliest, purest form, exemplified by the preludes of Louis Couperin, only semibreves are used, along with free-floating, sometimes quite extended diagonal slurs. Later composers such as Lebègue, D'Anglebert and Elisabeth-Claude Jacquet de la Guerre (1665–1729) devised their own systems to give the player more guidance, differentiating some pitches with other note-values and connecting beams which may or may not have their usual metrical significance. The precise placements and spacing on the page can also provide important visual cues; as a result, these preludes do not fare well in modern edition.

Some such preludes use a mixture of unmeasured and measured notation. Also, some of the longer unmeasured preludes, including those by Louis Couperin, may include extended imitative sections in measured notation, thus creating a form not unlike that of Froberger's toccatas. Couperin's *Prélude à l'imitation de Mr. Froberger* opens with a rendering in unmeasured notation of the beginning of Froberger's *Toccata prima* (FbWV 101); other allusions to Froberger have been detected elsewhere in Couperin's preludes.[77] Comparison of the two versions provides useful clues as to the interpretation of Couperin's notation, while also suggesting a freer reading of Froberger's. Similarly, Couperin's drawn-out arpeggiation of what Froberger notates simply as a chord at the beginning of his toccata is instructive. But beyond that, the two versions suggest that Froberger's toccatas and Couperin's preludes may not have sounded as different as they look on the page.

One other special class of prelude should be noted. As we have seen, Praetorius made a distinction between *praeludia* that served to introduce something and those that stood by themselves. Even if the terminological distinction (e.g., with toccatas and *praeambula* belonging to the first group) does not hold up with any consistency, one can nevertheless divide the *praeludia* into 'short' and 'long' preludes, defined principally according to whether they divide into subsections with distinctly different styles or maintain the same style throughout. The short preludes usually either serve as an introduction to another piece or

---

76 For a fuller discussion, see D. Moroney, 'Prélude non mesuré', in Sadie and Tyrrell (eds), *The Revised New Grove Dictionary of Music and Musicians*, xx: 294–6.

77 Ledbetter, *Harpsichord and Lute Music in 17th-Century France*, pp. 92, 94 (exx. 27, 29).

group of pieces (e.g., a set of dances), or appear in principle to be intended for this purpose, often being provided in a modally ordered set. They may carry designations such as 'toccata' and 'prelude', or have special titles not usually found with long preludes, such as *intonazione*, *intrada*, *arpeggiata* and *tastata*.

Short preludes appear to be among the earliest autonomous instrumental solo pieces (i.e., not drawing on vocal material). They date back to the fifteenth century and often retain signs of their original purposes, trying out the instrument and setting the key. Among notable examples are the preludes in the English virginal repertory, including the examples by Byrd, Bull and Gibbons in *Parthenia*, and the short toccatas that introduce the Mass movements in Frescobaldi's *Fiori musicali*. French unmeasured preludes also include a distinct 'short' variety. Some English fantasias are preceded by a short *praeludium*, thus showing the combination of a 'short' with a 'long' prelude.[78] One particular type of short prelude is of interest because of its eighteenth-century offspring: a regular arpeggiation pattern of even note-values to be applied to a succession of changing harmonies (which may just be notated as chords). Examples are found in the early seventeenth-century lute repertory, e.g., the *Toccata arpeggiata* from Kapsberger's *Libro primo d'intavolatura di chitarrone* (Venice, 1604);[79] later examples include preludes to late seventeenth-century dance suites by Zachow, Kuhnau and Fischer. There is also a little-known but quite attractive set of twelve preludes in different keys (*c.* 1682) by Johann Heinrich Kittel (1652–82).[80]

Music of craft (fantasia, capriccio, fugue, chorale variation)

According to Pietro della Valle (1640),

> Counterpoint . . . has for its aim not only the foundations of music, but perhaps even more, the ingenuity [*artificio*] and the most detailed subtleties of this art. These are fugues forwards and backwards, simple or double, imitations [echoes], canons and *perfidie* [ostinato cantus firmi], and other elegances like these, which, if used at the right time and place, adorn music marvelously . . . And experience teaches us that the frequent use of these musical devices is much more suited to instrumental music than to vocal, especially when an instrument plays solo.[81]

---

78 For example, nos. 12–13 in Byrd, *Keyboard Music I*, and no. 2 in J. Bull, *Keyboard Music I*, ed. J. Steele and F. Cameron, 'Musica britannica', 14 (London, 1960).

79 Coelho, 'Frescobaldi and the Lute and Chitarrone Toccatas', pp. 146–7.

80 In J. H. Baron (ed.), *The Brasov Tabulature (Brasov Music Manuscript 808): German Keyboard Studies 1680–1684*, 'Recent Researches in the Music of the Baroque Era', 40 (Madison, WI, 1982), pp. 1–13.

81 Strunk, *Source Readings in Music History, Revised Edition*, iv: *The Baroque Era*, p. 37. The concept of 'artificio' is difficult to render in modern English; see Durante, 'On *Artificioso* Compositions at the Time of Frescobaldi', p. 211 n. 2.

Although one can quite easily understand the admiration by contemporaries for seventeenth-century musicians who displayed their fantasy, putting crafts-manship on display seems more problematic. The fact that some music can, or even must, be enjoyed with the mind as well as with the heart is not a notion that finds much resonance nowadays. But things clearly were different in the seventeenth century, at least among discerning listeners. This, at least, seems suggested by Pietro della Valle, and also by the Roman composer Romano Micheli:

> It is true that those who compose skilled and graceful compositions are worthy men; because this is a skill which is acquired in a few years, they are considered worthy men but ordinary musicians. The most outstanding are instead those who, not being satisfied to compose perfect music, also want to understand the most profound studies of music, that is canons of different kinds and other special skills, which are not so easily acquired in such a short time.[82]

Thus there is a large body of works, particularly from the earlier years of the seventeenth century, in which craft and ingenuity are foregrounded, some-times to the extent of linking to Hermetic doctrines, with the purpose solely of demonstrating contrapuntal skill without thought of performance. Most, though not all, are compositions for solo keyboard. This may be because the solo performer was more likely to reach a receptive audience: a small group of pupils or admirers, a discerning patron, or even just the player himself. Also, of all solo instruments a keyboard is best able to manage the performance of complex counterpoint. It is probably for this reason that Della Valle favours the display of contrapuntal artifice in solo instrumental music, especially given that vocal music was now moving in different directions.

As we have seen already in the case of Froberger's hexachordal fantasia as an example (for Kircher) of the *stylus phantasticus*, the composer need not let the fantasy flow unfettered but could pit it against a self-imposed restraint (*obbligo*). Among more unusual *obblighi* in Frescobaldi's works are never to move by step, and to resolve all suspensions upwards.[83] More common are the imposition of a cantus firmus, with the additional challenge of writing canonically; an ostinato based on solmization syllables; echoes; and the contrapuntal development of one or more subjects, preferably with the usual devices of inversion, diminution and augmentation.

---

82 From the preface to Micheli's *Musica vaga ed artificiosa* (Venice, 1615), given in Durante, 'On *Artificioso* Compositions at the Time of Frescobaldi', pp. 200, 213 n. 11.

83 *Recercar ottavo, obligo di non mai di grado*, in G. Frescobaldi, *Recercari, et canzoni franzese* (Rome, 1615; repr. Farnborough, 1967), p. 32; *Capriccio ottavo cromatico di ligature al contrario*, in G. Frescobaldi, *Il primo libro di capricci* (Rome, 1624), p. 57 (in G. Frescobaldi, *Opere complete*, ed. E. Darbellay *et al.*, 8 vols (Milan, 1976–), iv: 58).

Cantus-firmus setting was one of oldest techniques of both improvised and composed counterpoint; it formed the basis of compositional instruction during much of Western music history. English composers developed a tradition of writing ambitious keyboard compositions on certain plainchant melodies. Far from being primarily works of abstract counterpoint, they are full of playful figuration, and their execution demands a high level of dexterity. These plainchant settings no longer served any liturgical purposes: in fact, some of the chants themselves had long been out of use and in some cases are misnamed. Many of these pieces are thought to have been written primarily for harpsichord, which might account for frequent passages with rapid note repetitions. Some are quite long, with frequent changes of texture and, less often, of metre.

John Bull (d. 1628) displayed his compositional virtuosity and fantasy in a dozen settings of an old favourite, the *In nomine* (the chant is the Sarum antiphon 'Gloria tibi Trinitas'). Through the course of each piece he successively introduces new ideas in the counterpoint, often of an increasingly brilliant nature: canons, scales running back and forth over the keyboard, syncopations, changes of metre, polyrhythms and so forth. One of his *In nomines* starts in 11/4 (4/4+4/4+3/4) and has a concluding section in which two measures of 6/4 alternate with one measure in 9/8 (the three measures are thus equivalent to 33/8).[84] Certainly, these are works on which performers are to cut their teeth. As if to show that Bull had not exhausted all the possibilities of the *In nomine*, Thomas Tomkins wrote a half dozen more.

Such sophisticated instrumental cantus-firmus techniques were transmitted by Sweelinck to Germany, where they found immediate application in the organ settings of hymns and chorales. Among the most stunning examples in the entire chorale-variation repertory are two gigantic variation-sets by Matthias Weckmann (who trained under two Sweelinck students): *Es ist das Heil uns kommen her* and *O lux beata Trinitas*. Each lasts approximately 30 minutes, which is too long for liturgical use. The variations present a compendium of cantus-firmus procedures, ranging from strict canons and six-part counterpoint with double pedal to lengthy fantasias on motives derived from the melody (e.g., the sixth variation of *Es ist das Heil*, which alone requires some twelve minutes). The fourth variation of *O lux beata Trinitas* is itself a mini-variation set with four variations, each with a counterpoint of fast-running passages: the first with a solo in the bass, the second with a solo in the treble, the third with a canon at the octave in the bass, and the final one with a canon at the octave in the treble. The complexity and extraordinary dimensions of these two works have

84 Bull, *Keyboard Music I*, no. 28.

invited theological interpretations, for example, seeing *O lux beata Trinitas* as a representation of the cosmos.[85]

Somewhere between cantus-firmus settings and fugal pieces fall those based on the so-called *ostinato* cantus firmus (the technique was called 'perfidio' in the seventeenth century) consisting of a short subject (usually a sequences of four to six pitches) named after the corresponding solmization syllables and repeated throughout the piece. In some pieces, the sequence moves to different pitch levels corresponding to different hexachords, or becomes a subject for imitative development as well as cantus-firmus treatment. The most famous of these subjects is the hexachord itself – *ut, re, mi, fa, sol, la* – and its use as subject has a history going far back into the Renaissance. The list of those who wrote keyboard fantasies (and often more than one) on this *obbligo* reads like a 'Who's Who' of leading keyboard composers, including Byrd, Bull, Sweelinck, Frescobaldi and, of course, Froberger. Each of these fantasias is a showpiece of contrapuntal craft as well as of ingenious novelties, prompted by the existence of its many distinguished predecessors. Among the more notable essays on this subject is one by Bull which transposes the hexachord (*ut* to *la* and back to *ut*) to the six steps of the whole-tone scale from G to E♯ (written as F), and thence to the six whole-tone steps from A♭ to F♯, concluding with five statements back in G (= F×).[86] This piece can only be realised on a keyboard with a cyclical temperament that permits enharmonic exchange.

In his usual iconoclastic fashion, Frescobaldi introduces several new twists to this subgenre. The first two pieces in the *Primo libro di capricci* (1624) are ostensibly devoted respectively to the hexachord and to its retrograde. Unlike his predecessors, he treats the subject in these pieces more often imitatively than as a cantus firmus, and aside from submitting it to various changes of metre and tempo, he introduces intermediary chromatic steps into the subject. The second *capriccio* begins, innocently enough, with the hexachord descending from E, but when it reaches the lowest step, a G♯ rather than a G is sounded, giving the unprepared listener a jolt. By introducing chromatic steps into the hexachord, Frescobaldi also refers to another famous subject: the so-called chromatic tetrachord.[87] Although a comparative novelty at the beginning of the century, it would soon become a commonplace, and eventually a cliché. Like the hexachord, it can be used either going down (D–C♯–C–B–B♭–A), or, slightly less commonly, going up. However, unlike the hexachord, it usually travels in only one direction within a piece. Probably the most famous

85 Davidsson, *Matthias Weckmann*, pp. 123–60.   86 Bull, *Keyboard Music I*, no. 15.

87 See Williams, *The Chromatic Fourth During Four Centuries of Music*. Williams prefers the term 'chromatic fourth' so as to avoid confusion with the Greek chromatic tetrachord (a descending minor third followed by two descending semitones).

composition to make the descending chromatic tetrachord its principal subject is Sweelinck's powerful *Fantasia chromatica*.[88] This is about the same length
as the Byrd fantasia discussed above but shows an entirely different conception,
and certainly not one of *ad hoc* improvisation. If Byrd's fantasia seems like a
pleasant peregrination, Sweelinck's is more like a purposeful journey; from the
moment it begins, the listener is pulled with seeming inevitability towards the
conclusion. Some of this effect is no doubt due to the single-minded subject
itself, with its strong cadential progression. But more of it has to do with the
carefully planned course of the work, in which the subject continues to assert
itself with few moments of reprieve. The piece is laid out in three parts. In the
first, the chromatic subject is stated sixteen times in different registers on the
first and fifth scale-degrees (and later, also the second), working systematically
through various permutations with two countersubjects. In the second section, the subject functions as an ostinato cantus firmus, first in minims, then
in semibreves, and finally in crotchets with rapid counterpoint in semiquavers
and then sextuplet semiquavers. In the third, the subject, still in crotchets,
falls over itself in *stretto*, then, in accelerated motion, recalls one of the opening
countersubjects, and finally, with relentless intensity, hammers again and again
in quavers over the final cadence. After this, a final flourish quickly brings the
excitement to an end.

Frescobaldi, too, was a fond user of the subject, probably as much for its
musical potential as for its affective connotations. The subject of his *Recercar
cromatico post il Credo* of the *Messa delli apostoli* is, however, a startling variant.
It begins with a chromatic ascent, A–B♭–B, but then abruptly drops down a
fourth, to continue with a chromatic descent, F♯–F–E. Beethoven's contemporary Anton Reicha (1770–1836) was so intrigued by this subject that he wrote a
'Fugue-fantasy' on it (op. 33 no. 4), and much later it inspired György Ligeti's
Musica ricercata, no. 11 (1951–3).

The chromatic tetrachord also came into fashion in fantasias for lute, an
instrument for which playing any kind of contrapuntal texture represents a
tour de force. Dowland wrote two notable 'fancies' on the subject: one entitled
Farewell, with the fourth ascending, and a *Forlorne Hope Fancy*, with the fourth
descending. These titles point to the common association of the subject with
sadness or even lament. *Forlorne Hope* is notable for some very striking harmonies and for its ending, in which the chromatic line continues its descent for
an octave and a half (not entirely by chromatic steps), perhaps portraying the
melancholy artist sinking into ultimate despair. Sadness also pervades *Farewell*,
in which when the second voice enters, the first alludes to the composer's

---

88 Dirksen, *The Keyboard Music of Jan Pieterszoon Sweelinck*, pp. 384–99.

celebrated 'Flow my tears'. This very personal outpouring, full of augmented chords, seems to have the character of a *tombeau* (see below), perhaps one the composer wrote for himself.

Through much of the seventeenth century, keyboard players continued to display their craft and their fantasy in extended, often multi-sectional imitative works labelled in various ways according to style and nationality. There existed no fixed forms for these genres; each invented its own formal procedure, which is where the fantasy came in; the craft entered with the contrapuntal execution of that procedure. However, two devices should be mentioned for creating cohesive larger forms, each of which allowed an almost infinite number of different realisations. The first was the use of several (as many as four) subjects which in principle could be combined in invertible counterpoint, as at the opening of Sweelinck's *Fantasia chromatica*. These subjects could be introduced one at a time or in various combinations, thus defining different sections. As an ultimate demonstration of skill, all subjects could be combined in the final section. The second device was the introduction in successive sections of variations of a subject, these being rhythmic (including augmentation and diminution) or melodic (including inversion and the use of the arcane technique of *inganni*), or both.[89] The first of these devices was originally more associated with the ricercar and the fantasia, the second with the canzona (e.g., the 'variation-canzona') and the *capriccio*. However, such distinctions were not consistently maintained, and often the two devices were freely combined. Sections with homophony or passage-work might further enrich these pieces, occasionally blurring the boundaries of the fantasia/fugue with the prelude/toccata. In some countries, an additional element was introduced by calling upon the organ's registration resources, for example, in the Spanish *tiento* by setting off a solo voice through split registration, or in the German organ *fuga* by employing the pedal as an independent, powerful bass.

Music of devotion (toccate per l'elevazione, *chorale preludes*)

There is a distinct group of organ pieces aimed not primarily at the display of fantasy and craft – although that is always a factor – but, rather, at the evocation of spiritual fervour and devotion. These works, which rely strongly on the employment of various technical devices and the sonorities of the instruments, include music of rare beauty. Even if they might be inspired by vocal models, and

---

89 The *inganno* (deceit) involves substituting individual notes in a subject by other notes with the same solmization syllable in a different hexachord. In practice this means the substitution of a pitch a major second, a perfect fourth or a perfect fifth higher or lower, which can make the original subject difficult to recognise.

perhaps by solo string music, they have no exact equivalents in other musical repertories.

We have seen that Italian ceremonial manuals for the Catholic Mass called for something 'quiet and slow' to be played during the Elevation, a need met by a type of music (ordinarily improvised) exemplified by works entitled 'Toccate per l'elevazione' or the like. These pieces are quite different from the flamboyantly brilliant type of toccata. They present a dense texture of slow-moving voices with interlocking chains of suspensions, chromaticism, and augmented and diminished intervals, resulting in frequent dissonances and cross-relations as well as strange harmonic progressions. All this contributes to the creation of an other-worldly aura, an effect no doubt enhanced by the use of smooth, quiet registers, perhaps with a tremulant or *vox humana* (beating pipes). There are other pieces of this type that have no specific reference to the Elevation in their titles, but that might well have been used for the same or a related purpose; some are called 'Durezze e ligature' (i.e., dissonances and suspensions), 'Consonanze stravagante' (strange harmonies) and, in Spanish sources, 'Falsas'.

Frescobaldi contributed a number of quite remarkable examples. Three are included in the 1634 *Fiori musicali* (one for each of the three Masses), all in the Phrygian mode. The first, aptly called *Toccata cromaticha per le levatione* (*sic*), fits the above description because it luxuriates in slowly moving chromatic lines. But in the second, a new element is introduced. After beginning with the traditional web of slow suspensions, a solo voice emerges which soars above the texture with expressive figures of the new vocal style. More such figures are introduced in the third toccata, although here they are also shared by the lower voices. These songs of mystical rapture inevitably bring to mind the famous sculpture by Frescobaldi's Roman contemporary, Gianlorenzo Bernini's *The Ecstasy of St Teresa*.

This new texture of an active, expressive solo line supported by a slower-moving accompaniment is dramatically different from the contrapuntal fantasias in which each voice has equal weight. The difference is comparable to that between the old polyphonic motet and the new monodic style. The 'solo' voices in Frescobaldi's elevation pieces were not played on a separate manual from the 'accompaniment', which was impossible on most Italian organs. However, on those of many other countries such separation could more often be realised, and organists soon availed themselves of the possibility, creating works that set an intense, personal voice played on a telling register (say, a reed stop) against a quieter background of flutes or soft diapasons. This did not necessarily require separate manuals: the Spanish used their divided registers quite cleverly to the same effect. For example, in the quasi-imitative introduction to Correa de Arauxo's *Tiento de medio registro de tiple de decimo tono*, the three lower voices do not reach above *c'* so as not to intrude upon the higher solo register. This constraint is turned into a virtue, since it lends the accompaniment a deep, dark sound against which the solo voice, when it finally enters, soars luminously, with ecstatic flurries of notes. The roles of the two registers can also be reversed, with the 'soloist' taking the lower voice, as in Correa's *Quinto tiento de medio registro de baxones de primero tono*, also note-worthy because its last solo episode moves into a septuple proportion, i.e., 7/8 metre.[90]

The rich resources of the 'classical' organs of Louis XIV's France allowed for many distinctive realisations of the solo/accompaniment style, which became the defining feature of the *Récit*. By using separate manuals as well as pedals, the florid solo could not only be placed in the treble or bass, as in the Spanish *tientos*, but also in the alto/tenor register (*taille*). A truly breath-taking example is offered by the young François Couperin in the *Elévation: tierce en taille* of his *Messe pour les couvents* (*c*. 1690), with the solo to be played on a *tierce*, a colourful stop with a prominent 5th harmonic. Its expressive and increasingly active two-octave voice (*D–d'*), which at its climax bursts into a fanfare, suggests that the composer might have drawn inspiration from the viola da gamba playing of his colleague Marin Marais (1656–1728). Some of the later seventeenth-century English voluntaries for 'double organ' (referring to two divisions of the instrument) also contain passages in which a brilliantly florid solo on the 'Great' is set off by slower moving counterpoint on the 'Choir' (or 'Chaire'), but the divided texture is not consistently maintained. For example, in Purcell's brilliant *Voluntary for the Double Organ*, the solo appears now in the bass, now in the treble, concluding with a faster fugal section in which all voices play on the Great.

The idea of a contemplative, intimate solo/accompaniment style was hap-pily appropriated by Lutheran organists in Germany, since it provided a per-fect format for quieter chorale settings. The chorale melody, often taken on the *Rückpositif* (the pipe division closest to the congregation and hence most focussed), could be richly adorned with suitable figures, sometimes includ-ing quick scales or arpeggios that trailed off towards greater heights or depths depending on the text of the verse. The accompaniment, saturated with suspen-sions and avoided cadences, could either develop undecorated motives from the chorale in imitation, or be in a free style. The genre became popular for stand-alone settings as well as for individual verses in variation-sets, and even for segments in large chorale-fantasias. Scheidemann, who has been credited for being the first to employ the style, used it in at least one verse of most of

90 Parkins, 'Spain and Portugal', pp. 338–40.

his variation-sets. His lengthy fantasia on 'Jesus Christus, unser Heiland' is a veritable compendium of figuration techniques, applied successively to different registers from the top to the bottom of the keyboard. Later composers such as Buxtehude and Georg Böhm (1661–1733) created numerous settings of this type, which often are quite lovely, although both harmonies and figuration tend to be restrained. Fervent passions have been tamed and domesticated for this Lutheran milieu.

Music of diversion (dances, variations and programme pieces)

Dance music has always been popular among instrumentalists, but rarely as much as in the seventeenth century. Despite its low status in classifications such as those of Morley and Praetorius, the quantity of dance pieces preserved in solo keyboard sources is enormous. They form the bulk of the contents of most collections intended for domestic use, the only serious rival being the plethora of keyboard settings of well-known songs, and many of these are also dance tunes. Their preponderance is even greater in collections for non-keyboard instruments, which contain little original instrumental music that is not dance-derived. Even though the dances in solo collections may not have been intended for actual dancing, and may not reflect the most commonly practised types of the time,[91] dance music provided a ready-made vocabulary of gestures and forms, and also perhaps the *frisson* of erotic excitement that is often a subtext of dance.

Trying to survey the multitude of dance types of the period would be a rather dizzying experience. They are much more volatile and fashion-bound than other genres. They are also more subject to regional variations, even if they might propagate quickly from one place to another. Sometimes they almost entirely supplanted local genres, as happened with some of the French dance types. They also could mutate drastically in a relatively short time, as happened with the allemande towards the middle of the century. As a final complicating issue, they might develop into a number of subtypes, not necessarily distinguished by name. A near-universal factor in embracing novel dance types was (and still is) the appeal of the exotic, sometimes reflected even in the dances' names (allemande, anglaise, polonaise etc.). The four dances that played an important part in the later dance-suite (see below), the allemande, courante, sarabande and gigue, originated respectively in Germany, France, Spain and England, and thus represented four different European peoples in a colourful sequence. The lure of the Other could also come from across class boundaries, whether from above, as with the courtly minuet, or more often from below,

---

91 R. Harris-Warrick, 'Dance: Late Renaissance and Baroque to 1730', in Sadie and Tyrrell (eds), *The Revised New Grove Dictionary of Music and Musicians*, vi: 888–99.

as is evident from the popularity of peasant- and street-dance types (*branle*, chaconne).

At the top of the dance hierarchies of Morley and Praetorius stood the pavan, 'next in gravity and goodness' only to the fantasia. In fact, many English pavans from the early years of the century hardly needed to take second place in terms of weightiness and well-crafted counterpoint. In keeping with their dense contrapuntal textures, a number of keyboard pavans led a double life as works for instrumental ensemble; however, the varied repeats of each of the three strains, almost always present in the keyboard versions, do not appear in the ensemble settings. The classical models were provided by Byrd, whose set of ten pavans in *My Ladye Nevells Booke* is among the greatest treasures of the early keyboard literature. Many of the later examples by Bull, Gibbons and Tomkins are equally worthy of the genre. But no doubt the most famous and most widely emulated pavan was John Dowland's *Lachrimae* for lute. It became virtually a genre of its own, giving rise to innumerable adaptations for other forces, including famous ones for voice and for ensemble by the composer himself. Nevertheless, well before the middle of the century, the pavan had virtually disappeared. Among the last examples of this noble tradition, perhaps a *tombeau* to its memory, is Louis Couperin's mournful *Pavane* in F sharp minor.

The galliard had been the pavan's frequent companion, and often was motivically related, if not simply a variation in triple time. It also disappeared from the European scene, but lingered slightly longer than its mate. The pair that by the middle of the century had taken their place in the dance hierarchy was the allemande and courante. Both had been around since the sixteenth century, but they drastically changed character with the assumption of their new roles. The allemande in particular took over some of the gravity and complexity of the pavan, while at the same time losing much of its dance character. Among the first keyboard examples to exhibit this new manner at its fullest were the contemplative allemandes of Froberger, although, as with Froberger's other dances, it probably owed much to French lute and possibly keyboard precedents. It is not always possible to determine in retrospect the direction of influence between Froberger and his French colleagues; it likely went in both directions.

In sheer numbers, courantes surpass allemandes by a wide margin; in fact, the courante could be regarded as the dance of the seventeenth century in the way the minuet was to become that of the eighteenth and the waltz of the nineteenth. The sources contain entire series of courantes, and certain courantes, such as *Lavignonne*, became international favourites, appearing in collections virtually everywhere in Europe. The courante was also the richest in subtypes, which went well beyond a simple division into a French 'courante' and an Italian 'corrente' (besides, the language of a title is usually a poor predictor of the type). Both Italy and France had straightforward courantes with a strong triple beat, and more complex courantes with frequent hemiolas; the later seventeenth-century French courantes were among the subtlest and most complex of all the dances.

In early seventeenth-century sources, dances such as pavans either appear alone or paired with galliards, but before long it became common to group larger numbers of dances of different types together. Nevertheless, these dance sequences should not be understood in terms of the familiar eighteenth-century German dance-suite, i.e., a multi-movement composition observing a standard order (if with slight flexibility). The seventeenth-century situation is more complex and variable, defying easy generalisation. Many sequences found in the sources do follow to some extent elements of what would become the 'standard order', beginning with an allemande, followed by a courante (often more than one) and a sarabande. Somewhere further on in the sequence (although less regularly), a gigue might appear. But one also encounters other schemes, and some sequences hardly seem to follow any pattern at all. More important, often it is not clear to what extent the sequence was in fact intended to be performed as such – or at least, was conceived by the composer as a single 'work' – and to what extent it was just a convenient way of grouping pieces in the same key. The latter seems to be more often the case in France, and remains so into the eighteenth century. Froberger's short groupings of three or four dances in a standard order clearly were written as unified compositions; sometimes the dances were even musically related, as in the Partita, FbWV 601.[92] On the other hand, in several anthology manuscripts – including the Parville MS (University of California, Berkeley, Music Library) and Babell MS (London, British Library, Add. MS 39569) – the dances of a sequence are by different composers, brought together from diverse sources by the compiler. Rarely are dance sequences headed by designations such as 'Suite' or 'Partita'. The long sequences in D'Anglebert's *Pièces de clavecin* (1689), which include, in addition to the usual dances in their standard order, arrangements of arias and other pieces from Lully's operas, were surely not intended to be performed at one sitting.

Among the most exciting new dance types to make their way into seventeenth-century keyboard, lute and guitar collections were the chaconne and the passacaglia. Variation dances were not new – the *passamezzo* pavan,

---

92 In his later years, Froberger came to prefer the order allemande–gigue–courante–sarabande, but this was disregarded in posthumous editions; see Silbiger, 'Tracing the Contents of Froberger's Lost Autographs', p. 17; J. J. Froberger, *Neue Ausgabe sämtlicher Clavier- und Orgelwerke*, ed. S. Rampe (Kassel, 1993–), i, pp. xxxi–xxxii.

much in vogue during the sixteenth century, survived for some decades – but the unprecedented seamless linking, allowing the creation of continuous pieces of any length, contributed to the rapidly rising popularity of the two new genres. Neither the instrumental solo chaconne nor the solo passacaglia was generally on a strict ground bass, except for a strain that developed late in the century in Germany. In most areas, there was some understanding about the distinction between the two types: the chaconne was more upbeat, faster and more often in the major, although such distinctions were not universally maintained.[93]

One of the most brilliant pieces of this type – probably the longest dance piece of the period – was Frescobaldi's *Cento partite sopra passacaglie* ('100 sections on the *passacaglie*'), which includes a continuous succession of different passacaglia and chaconne styles, with a courante *en passant*. The French often employed a *rondeau* form for these genres; a fine example is Louis Couperin's *Passacaille* in C major.[94] The impressive ground-bass variation sets of Buxtehude and his German contemporaries, most of them conceived for organ, largely moved away from any dance character. Symptomatic of this transformation was Buxtehude's incorporation of a chaconne section into a prelude (BuxWV 137).

Instrumental settings of popular songs and dances (with or without additional variations) form a genre not recognised by Morley and the other classifiers, probably because they were considered to be derivative or too low down the scale to deserve mention. Nevertheless, the variation-sets of the English virginal repertory are among the all-time high points of the art of variation. They are unsurpassed in the almost infinite variety of ways in which the composers dressed up their often simple tunes. Several features set these works apart from later theme-and-variation sets. Frequently, they do not stick mechanically to a single procedure for each variation but introduce variation within the variation. Ideas often are picked up from a preceding variation – for instance, the treble figuration is moved to the bass or vice versa – or successive variations may be connected by smooth linkages. Compared with later sets, the variations are quicker to abandon the harmony of the 'theme' to support it by fresh chord progressions. The texture is often saturated with imitation, and the figuration usually moves to shorter note-values or triple divisions. These techniques all contribute to making the sets sound more like cohesive, continuously developing compositions rather than a succession of short pieces that replay the same progression over and again. This applies equally to Sweelinck's delightful and oft-performed variation sets, which clearly owe much to English models.

---

93 Silbiger, 'Passacaglia and Ciaccona'.   94 Gustafson, 'France', p. 140.

During the second half of the century, variations on popular songs and basses gradually began to give way to variations on original themes (often called 'air' or 'aria') and grounds, although the genre seems not to have appealed to the best composers as much as before. Perhaps the more harmony-based techniques were less challenging. The English continued to cultivate the ground-bass variation, which always had been popular among them. The Germans directed most of their variation efforts towards the passacaglia, while the French concentrated on adding variations, called *doubles*, to their dance compositions, and occasionally to the dances of others. Louis Couperin wrote *doubles* on dances by Chambonnières, Hardel and Lebègue, and d'Anglebert wrote one on a courante by Chambonnières. Variations on popular sacred songs, such as on Lutheran chorales in Germany and on Christmas carols in France (*noëls*), continued to thrive.

Frescobaldi's *Aria detta La Frescobalda* may represent a pioneering effort of a new variation genre: that of distinct (not linked) variations on an original theme in which each variation has an individual character, often including dance types. An unusually fanciful example is Alessandro Poglietti's (d. 1683) *Aria allemagna con alcuni variationi sopra l'età della Maestà Vostra* ('German air with some variations on the age of Your Majesty', i.e., Empress Eleonore, the young bride of Emperor Leopold I).[95] Most of the twenty variations (the number corresponds to the empress's age) have titles referring to their special character, including folk instruments from various parts of Europe, such as the Dutch flageolet, the Bohemian bagpipe, the Bavarian shawm and the Hungarian fiddle, as well as various dance acts such as a tightrope dance, Polish swordplay and an old women's cortège. Bernardo Pasquini considered one of his variation sets on an original theme enough of a novelty to draw attention to it in the title, *Variazione d'invenzione*. This set appears to pay homage to Frescobaldi, since it includes eight variations based on ideas from his works, while the theme itself echoes the *Aria detta La Frescobalda*.[96]

Pieces that in one sense or another could be regarded as programme music are fairly rare. Most popular were battle pieces, perhaps not inappropriate for the century that lived through the Thirty Years War. They even were introduced in church services; Banchieri recommends the performance of a *battaglia* at Easter to symbolise Christ's victory over death.[97] Most of them are cobbled together from conventional set-pieces depicting marching troops and galloping horses, fanfares, drum rolls, battle noises, and songs of victory. Although some fine composers contributed to the genre, among them Byrd, Frescobaldi and

---

95 In Poglietti's 'Rosignolo' autograph, Vienna, Österreichische Nationalbibliothek, Musiksammlung, MS 19248 (Silbiger *et al.* (eds), *17th-Century Keyboard Music*, vi).

96 Silbiger *et al.* (eds), *17th-Century Keyboard Music*, vii, p. viii.   97 Judd, 'Italy', p. 246.

Cabanilles, battle pieces tend to be denigrated by modern commentators. There are also more or less realistic imitations of other sounds, such as bells (Byrd's *The Bells* and Lebègue's *Les cloches*) and bagpipes (in pieces called *Pastorale* or *Piva*). A large number of English (keyboard and lute) and French (mostly lute) pieces have titles naming a person, usually (one presumes) a patron or friend, but whether such a piece is a 'portrait' of the named person or merely a homage is hard to determine. Tobias Hume's *Ayres* 'for the Viole De Gambo alone' (London, 1605) contains, in addition to a detailed battle portrayal, many other pieces with playful and sometimes suggestive titles, among them a sequence including *My mistresse hath a prettie thing*, *She loves it well*, *Hit it in the middle* and *Tickell, tickell*.

A few composers attempted to represent more elaborate narratives in music. Among them is Poglietti, who wrote a dance suite on the Hungarian rebellion of 1671, with an attack and flight (Toccatina), imprisonment (Allemande), trial (Courante), sentence (Sarabande), chaining (Gigue), beheading, lament (Passacaglia) and funeral bells. However, the works offering the most detailed musical depictions for keyboard are surely the *Musicalische Vorstellung einiger Biblischer Historien* ('Musical representations of some biblical tales') of Johann Kuhnau (1660–1722) published in 1700. Drawing upon a wide range of musical genres and topoi from opera, oratorio and instrumental music – including recitative, aria, chorale setting, lament and *battaglia* – they present Old Testament stories with uncommon musical realism, among them the combat of David and Goliath, Saul cured by David, and Jacob's wedding and his death and burial.

Music of grief and mourning (laments and tombeaux)

This small but very special group of works stand out for their personal expression of artists' deeply felt emotions. Of course, laments also constituted an important contemporary vocal genre, equally noteworthy for its expression of intense feelings. However, vocal laments are generally perceived as the feelings of the poet, or more often, of the dramatic character in whose voice the words are placed, rather than of the composer. But in an instrumental lament it is the composer's and/or the performer's grief that we hear.[98] This is given further emphasis by the fact that in a commemorative lament (see below), it usually is not a mythical personage who is being mourned but someone with whom the artist had a close relationship: a patron, teacher, family member or colleague, with those for fellow musicians being by far the most numerous. Indeed, such

---

98 The issue of who is lamenting, and how sincerely, was discussed by Jonathan Gibson with reference to Marais's *Tombeau pour Mr de Lully* in ' "The Cries of Nature in Mourning" '.

personal relationships, except perhaps those with a patron, suggest that the grief is real rather than feigned; what other reason would there be to write the work?

We have already encountered some of John Dowland's mournful pieces, to which one should add his *Semper Dowland semper dolens* ('Always Dowland, always in sorrow'). While Dowland's sorrows seem to be the result of generalised melancholy, the French lutenists created a genre that responded to a specific cause: the death of a person held dear. In imitation of a literary genre serving the same purpose, they were called *tombeaux* – literally 'tombs' or 'tombstones' – being considered the musical equivalent of an inscription commemorating the deceased.[99] The earliest known example in the French lute repertory was written by Ennemond Gaultier (1575–1651) for his colleague Mezangeau (*c.* 1639). Many more were produced by harpsichordists, lutenists, guitarists and viola da gamba players through the first decades of the eighteenth century, after which the genre rapidly went out of fashion.[100] The early *tombeaux* often seem to contain echoes of Dowland's *Lachrimae* pavan, including the descending fourth and other falling figures as well as pedal points (appearing in Dowland at the opening of the third strain), and they were also often cast in the form of a slow dance – most often an allemande – suggesting the heavy tread of a funeral procession. There is even an example of a little suite written in memory of the lutenist Henri de L'Enclos in which the allemande (*Tombeau de Monsr. de Lenclos*) was contributed by Ennemond Gaultier (it opens with the A–G–F–E 'Lachrimae' motive), and the courante (*La consolation aux amis du S^r. Lenclos*) and sarabande (*La resolution des amis du s^r. Lenclos sur sa mort*) by Denis Gaultier (*c.* 1600–1672).[101]

Tombeaux were not necessarily in minor keys: indeed, two of the finest French harpsichord examples are not. Jean-Henri D'Anglebert paid homage to his older colleague and (probably) former teacher in the *Tombeau de Mr. de Chambonnières* that concludes his *Pièces de clavecin* (1689). Cast in the form of a very slow galliard ('fort lentement'), it is a deeply moving work with an air of resignation that transcends all grief. Louis Couperin's *Tombeau de Mr. de Blancrocher* is a curious piece that appears to incorporate some programmatic episodes, although no programme has survived. The lutenist Charles Fleury, Sieur de Blancrocher,

---

99 Vocal laments for departed colleagues go back to a much earlier time, and in the late sixteenth and early seventeenth centuries an instrumental commemorative genre, the Dumpe, enjoyed some popularity in England. There are also works that one could consider *tombeaux* by implication, such as John Bull's fantasia on a theme by Sweelinck ('Fantasia op de fuge van m. Jan pieterss'), dated shortly after Sweelinck's death, and Thomas Tomkins's 'A sad paven: for these distracted tymes', dated shortly after the beheading of Charles I.

100 Vendrix, 'Le tombeau en musique en France à l'époque baroque'.

101 D. Gaultier, *La Rhétorique des dieux*, ed. D. J. Buch, 'Recent Researches in the Music of the Baroque Era', 62 (Madison, WI, 1990), pp. 70–72.

had died in 1652 after falling down stairs, and Couperin is thought to depict this tragic accident.

Fleury's sudden death provoked several *tombeaux* by other composers, including Denis Gaultier and François Dufaut (before 1604–before 1702), and also one by Froberger, who happened to be visiting the lutenist when the accident occurred. Although the *tombeau* was, and remained, largely the domain of French composers, Froberger made the genre his own as a vehicle for venting his personal sorrows and for writing some of the most expressive music of the entire century. The *Tombeau sur la mort de monsieur Blancheroche* (FbWV 632), like Couperin's, appears to introduce programmatic elements: imitations of lute textures and techniques, funeral bells, and at its end, a two-octave descent towards the bottom of the keyboard. Its language is, however, less restrained and more impassioned. Froberger also wrote a *Lamento* (FbWV 612) on the death (1654) of the 21-year-old son of his patron, Emperor Ferdinand III, and three years later, a *Lamentation* (FbWV 633) on the passing of the emperor himself. The *Lamento*, in C major, takes the place of the allemande in the last of the suites of the *Libro quarto* (MS, 1656), dedicated to the emperor. It is followed by a gigue, courante and sarabande which also formed part of the memorial, to judge by the symbolism of the decoration in the manuscript (cross, funeral wreath, mourning crêpe and smoking urn). At the end, there is a scale which, unlike the one in Blancrocher's *tombeau*, ascends upwards for three octaves; in the manuscript its destination is illustrated by a representation of heaven in the form of clouds, sun rays and cherubs. The *Lamentation* for Ferdinand III, in F minor (a key still rare in keyboard music, and producing some grating sounds in tunings of the period), is the longest and by far the most impassioned of Froberger's *tombeaux*, probably reflecting the intensity of the loss to the composer of his benefactor of many years. It is full of startling harmonic shifts, harsh chords and intervals, and other extreme rhetorical gestures, virtually without respite until the final slow upward arpeggio in F major.

Froberger wrote a few other programmatic pieces in the *tombeau* vein, although not commemorating a death; like the *tombeaux* discussed above, they are usually accompanied by instructions that they must be played slowly and freely, or without a (strict) beat. They include a *Plainte* 'made in London to drive away melancholy' (FbWV 630) and a 'Meditation on my future death, which is played slowly with discretion' (FbWV 611a). The latter appears in a manuscript of Weckmann's, and probably was among the pieces that Froberger had sent to Weckmann after the two first met in Dresden.[102] Although for a

---

102 See J. Mattheson, *Grundlage einer Ehren-Pforte* (Hamburg, 1740), ed. M. Schneider (Berlin, 1910; repr. Kassel, 1969), p. 396.

poet a meditation on his own death would not have been so remarkable, we know of no earlier composer who in his music shared with the world (or at least, with a friend and colleague) such highly personal thoughts.

Bibliography

Annibaldi, C., 'La didattica del solco tracciato: il codice Chigiano Q.IV.29 da *Klavierbüchlein* d'ignoti a prima fonte frescobaldiana autografa'. *Rivista italiana di musicologia*, 20 (1986), 44–97

'Frescobaldi's Early Stay in Rome (1601–1607)'. *Recercare*, 13 (2001), 97–124

Anthony, J. R., *French Baroque Music: from Beaujoyeulx to Rameau*. Rev. edn, London, 1978

Apel, W., *The History of Keyboard Music to 1700*. Bloomington, IN, 1972

Baak Griffioen, R. van, *Jacob van Eyck's 'Der fluyten lust-hof' (1644–c1655)*. Utrecht, 1991

Bianconi, L., *Music in the Seventeenth Century*, trans. D. Bryant. Cambridge, 1987

Bishop, W. H., 'Translation of Maugars' *Response faite a un curieux sur le sentiment de la musique d'Italie*'. *Journal of the Viola da Gamba Society of America*, 8 (1971), 5–17

Bonta, S., 'The Uses of the *Sonata da chiesa*'. *Journal of the American Musicological Society*, 22 (1969), 169–74

Braun, W., *Die Musik des 17. Jahrhunderts*, 'Neues Handbuch der Musikwissenschaft', 4. 2nd edn, Laaber, 1996

Brooks, B., 'Etienne Nau, Breslau 114 and the Early Seventeenth-Century German Violin Fantasia'. *Early Music*, 32 (2004), 49–72

Buelow, G. J., 'Protestant North Germany'. In Price (ed.), *The Early Baroque Era*, pp. 185–205

Butt, J., 'Germany and the Netherlands'. In Silbiger (ed.), *Keyboard Music Before 1700*, pp. 147–234

Coelho, V., 'Frescobaldi and the Lute and Chitarrone Toccatas of "Il Tedesco della Tiorba"'. In Silbiger (ed.), *Frescobaldi Studies*, pp. 137–56

Davidsson, H., *Matthias Weckmann: the Interpretation of his Organ Music*, i. Stockholm, 1991

Demuth, N. (ed.), *An Anthology of Musical Criticism*. London, 1947

Dirksen, P., *The Keyboard Music of Jan Pieterszoon Sweelinck: its Style, Significance and Influence*. Utrecht, 1997

Dirksen, P. (ed.), *The Harpsichord and its Repertoire: Proceedings of the International Harpsichord Symposium, Utrecht 1990*. Utrecht, 1992

Durante, S., 'On *Artificioso* Compositions at the Time of Frescobaldi'. In Silbiger (ed.), *Frescobaldi Studies*, pp. 195–217

Edler, A., 'Organ Music within the Social Structure of North German Cities in the Seventeenth Century'. In P. Walker (ed.), *Church, State, and Studio: Music and its Contexts*, 'Studies in Music', 107. Ann Arbor, 1990, pp. 23–41

Fuller, D., 'French Harpsichord Playing in the 17th Century – after Le Gallois'. *Early Music*, 4 (1976), 22–6

'"Sous le doits de Chambonniere"'. *Early Music*, 21 (1993), 191–202

Gibson, J., '"The Cries of Nature in Mourning": Temporality and Aesthetics in Marais's Elegy for Lully'. Paper presented at the annual meeting of the Society for Seventeenth-Century Music, Winston-Salem, NC, April 2003

Gillies, M., 'A Conversation with Bartók: 1929'. *Musical Times*, 128 (1987), 555–9

Gustafson, B., 'France'. In Silbiger (ed.), *Keyboard Music Before 1700*, pp. 90–146

Hammond, F., *Girolamo Frescobaldi: a Guide to Research*. New York, 1988

Judd, R., 'Italy'. In Silbiger (ed.), *Keyboard Music Before 1700*, pp. 235–311

Krüger, L., 'Johann Kortkamps Organistenchronik: Eine Quelle zur Hamburgischen Musikgeschichte des 17. Jahrhunderts'. *Zeitschrift des Vereins für Hamburgische Geschichte*, 33 (1933), 188–213

Ledbetter, D., *Harpsichord and Lute Music in 17th-Century France*. Bloomington, 1987

Massip, C., 'Paris, 1600–61'. In Price (ed.), *The Early Baroque Era*, pp. 218–37

Monson, C., 'Elizabethan London'. In I. Fenlon (ed.), *The Renaissance: from the 1470s to the End of the 16th Century*, 'Man and Music', 2. Basingstoke and London, 1989, pp. 304–40

Moore, J. H., 'The Liturgical Use of the Organ in Seventeenth-Century Italy'. In Silbiger (ed.), *Frescobaldi Studies*, pp. 351–83

Neighbour, O. W., *The Consort and Keyboard Music of William Byrd*. London, 1978

Noske, F., *Sweelinck*, 'Oxford Studies of Composers', 22. Oxford, 1988

Paras, J., *The Music for the Viola Bastarda*. Bloomington, 1986

Parkins, R., 'Spain and Portugal'. In Silbiger (ed.), *Keyboard Music Before 1700*, pp. 312–57

Price, C. (ed.), *The Early Baroque Era: from the Late 16th Century to the 1660s*, 'Man and Music', 3. Basingstoke and London, 1993

Rampe, S., 'Abendmusik oder Gottesdienst? Zur Funktion norddeutscher Orgelkompositionen des 17. und frühen 18. Jahrhunderts, i: Die gottesdienstlichen Aufgaben der Organisten'. *Schütz-Jahrbuch*, 25 (2003), 7–70

Rasch, R., 'Johann Jakob Froberger and the Netherlands'. In Dirksen (ed.), *The Harpsichord and its Repertoire*, pp. 121–41

Rasch, R., and Dirksen, P., 'The Huygens–Froberger–Sybilla Correspondence'. In Dirksen (ed.), *The Harpsichord and its Repertoire*, pp. 233–45

Riedel, F. W., *Quellenkundliche Beiträge zur Geschichte der Musik für Tasteninstrumente in der 2. Hälfte des 17. Jahrhunderts*. Kassel, 1960

Das Musikarchiv im Minoritenkonvent zu Wien: Katalog des älteren Bestandes vor 1784. Kassel, 1963

Seiffert, M., 'Matthias Weckmann und das Collegium musicum in Hamburg'. *Sammelbände der Internationalen Musik-Gesellschaft*, 2 (1900–1901), 76–132

Silbiger, A., *Italian Manuscript Sources of 17th-Century Keyboard Music*, 'Studies in Musicology', 18. Ann Arbor, 1980

'The Roman Frescobaldi Tradition: 1640–1670'. *Journal of the American Musicological Society*, 33 (1980), 42–87

'Michelangelo Rossi and his *Toccate e correnti*'. *Journal of the American Musicological Society*, 36 (1983), 18–38

'Is the Italian Keyboard Intavolatura a Tablature?'. *Recercare*, 3 (1991), 81–104

'Tracing the Contents of Froberger's Lost Autographs'. *Current Musicology*, 54 (1993), 5–23

'From Madrigal to Toccata: Frescobaldi and the *Seconda prattica*'. In J. Knowles (ed.), *Critica musica: Essays in Honor of Paul Brainard*. Amsterdam, 1996, pp. 403–28

'Passacaglia and Ciaccona: Genre Pairing and Ambiguity from Frescobaldi to Couperin'. *Journal of Seventeenth-Century Music*, 2 (1996) <http://www.sscm-jscm.org/jscm/v2/no1/Silbiger.html>

Keyboard Music Before 1700. 2nd edn, New York, 2003

Silbiger, A. (ed.), *Frescobaldi Studies*. Durham, NC, 1987

Snyder, K. J., *Dieterich Buxtehude: Organist in Lübeck*. New York, 1987

Spring, M., *The Lute in Britain: a History of the Instrument and its Music*. Oxford, 2001

Strunk, O., *Source Readings in Music History, Revised Edition*, iv: *The Baroque Era*, ed. M. Murata. New York and London, 1998

Suchoff, B., 'The Impact of Italian Baroque Music on Bartók's Music'. In G. Ránki (ed.), *Bartók and Kodály Revisited*, 'Indiana University Studies on Hungary', 2. Budapest, 1987, pp. 183–95

Taminga, L., 'Music for Two Organs in Italy'. In P. Pellizzari (ed.), *Musicus perfectus: studi in onore di Luigi Ferdinando Tagliavini*. Bologna, 1995, pp. 237–66

Tollefsen, R. H., 'Jan Pietersz. Sweelinck: a Bio-Bibliography, 1604–1842'. *Tijdschrift van de Vereniging voor Nederlandse Muziekgeschiedenis*, 22 (1971), 87–125

Tyler, J., and Sparks, P., *The Guitar and its Music from the Renaissance to the Classical Era*. Oxford, 2002

Vendrix, P., 'Le tombeau en musique en France à l'époque baroque'. *Recherches sur la musique française classique*, 25 (1987), 105–38

Williams, P., *The Chromatic Fourth During Four Centuries of Music*. Oxford, 1997

14

Form and gesture: canzona, sonata and concerto

GREGORY BARNETT

On 1 January 1700, Arcangelo Corelli (1653–1713) published his *Sonate a violino e violone o cimbalo*, op. 5, in Rome. The collection stood as a landmark for violinist–composers of his time and well after, and further enhanced Corelli's international fame, which had been established by four earlier collections of trio-sonatas published during the 1680s and 1690s. Together with Giuseppe Torelli (1658–1709) and Antonio Vivaldi (1678–1741), Corelli would also establish the concerto as a genre of lasting importance.[1] Their success represents the apogee of Italianate instrumental genres of the late sixteenth and seventeenth centuries, which had spread through northern Europe to German provinces, England and even, by the 1690s, to France.

Contemporary comment reveals not just how popular such instrumental genres were to their admirers, but also how vividly expressive. In 1656 the Jesuit polymath Athanasius Kircher described hearing at an *accademia* a small ensemble of two violinists (Salvatore Mazzella and Michelangelo Rossi) and a theorbo player (Lelio Colista, whose compositions Kircher admired):

> They played with such blending of harmony, with such unusual extractions of uncommon intervals that as a result, although I can confess that in music I have investigated outstanding things, I nevertheless do not remember that I have experienced anything similar. For while they were mixing the diatonic with the chromatic, and these with the enharmonic, it is impossible to state how much the unusual minglings of these *genera* stirred my mind's emotions . . .
> While they stroked the strings in a pure manner and with a subtle drawing of

---

1 The definitive bibliographical resource for Italian instrumental music of the seventeenth century is Sartori, *Bibliografia della musica strumentale italiana stampata in Italia fino al 1700*. For an overview of seventeenth-century Italian composers of instrumental ensemble music, see Apel, *Italian Violin Music of the Seventeenth Century*, ed. Binkley, a translated and expanded version of Apel's *Die italienische Violinmusik im 17. Jahrhundert*, 'Beihefte zum Archiv für Musikwissenshaft', 21 (Wiesbaden, 1983). Apel and Binkley's volume provides over 60 composer-based entries. Each includes a brief biographical summary and discussion of the music, and a listing of works with RISM citations, location of original sources, and modern editions. An appendix added by Binkley lists over 80 additional names. This appendix is a useful addition to an already handy text, although readers should be aware of some errors of spelling, the inclusion of non-Italian composers whose names were italianized in print – such as Giovanni Federico Maestro (Meister), Giovanni Ravenscroft, Giovanni Rosenmiller (Rosenmüller), Giovanni Giacomo Valther (Walther) – and the listing of anonymous composers as specific names (e.g., 'N. N. Romano', 'N. N. Veneziano').

the bow, they seemed among themselves to be provoking the spirits of a leaping heart. Sometimes with the somewhat sad disdain of a murmuring sound, they aroused an emotion towards something gloomy and mournful – you would say that you were attending a tragic play.

In due course from a rather sad modulation they carried me little by little from relaxed figures into rapid, intense passages full of joy and dancing with such force that they were close to overwhelming me with a kind of raving madness. From there, in alternating passages rising up into something tumultuous and full of violent ferocity, they incited the mind to battles and combats. When the attack had finally subsided into something characteristic of a rather sweet affection, they summoned heavenly devotion suitable of compassion and disdain for the world.[2]

Kircher was an uncommonly receptive listener, but he was by no means unique: Roger North, the English aristocrat and musical amateur, similarly described a variety of images suggested to him by each movement of Italianate sonatas.[3] Throughout the century, composers for instrumental ensembles demonstrated their interest in stirring the listener's imagination in like fashion, and their efforts to that end produced diverse and sometimes unexpected features in their music. The *stile moderno* composers drew on the technique of the division virtuosos, but also found inspiration in the *seconda pratica* and in the new text-based expression of monody; sonata composers of the late Seicento drew more upon an expanding repertory of expressive topoi; and the Austro-German virtuosos exemplify what became known as the *stylus phantasticus* by defying expectation through ingenious formal plans, an unprecedented level of technique, and a love of programmatic representation.

Ensemble instrumental music followed patterns of dissemination similar to those of vocal genres – opera, cantata, oratorio – that began in Italy and spread further to mingle with non-Italian musical traditions. The expressive aims and means of instrumental music, however, may seem vaguer to us than in the case of those genres. This results, most obviously, from the absence of a text. But it is also due to the fact that instrumental music was discussed relatively little by theorists: accounts of the *prima* and *seconda pratica*, of the *concertato* and *a cappella* styles, and of the *stile rappresentativo*, bypass canzonas, sonatas, concertos and sinfonias altogether. The use of genre designations, moreover, seems haphazard and ill-defined by comparison with the later and more familiar practice of the eighteenth and nineteenth centuries. Thus the theorist Angelo Berardi, writing in 1689, appears to mix the meanings of 'concerto' and 'sinfonia' in a brief mention of violin music by Corelli which had been published as 'sonatas':

2 Kircher, *Itinerarum exstaticum* . . . (Rome, 1656), p. 45. I am grateful to Professor Robert Barnett for his help with the translation.
3 Wilson (ed.), *Roger North on Music*, pp. 117–18.

The *concerti* of violins and of other instruments are called 'sinfonie', and are held in high regard nowadays – particularly those of Signor Arcangelo Corelli, a celebrated violinist called *Il Bolognese*, the new Orpheus of our times.[4]

This is not carelessness: Berardi uses the word 'concerto' not in the modern, genre-based sense, but in its older meaning referring to a group of instruments working 'in concert', i.e., together.[5] Berardi calls 'sinfonia' that which Corelli himself had named 'sonata' because the theorist prefers the more grandiose Greek-derived term (also found as 'simfonia') instead of the past participle of the Italian *sonare* (to sound).[6] But Berardi's 'sinfonia' is not symphonic in the modern sense, or even in the early eighteenth-century one: it involves instruments sounding together in a pleasing manner but says nothing about scoring, or about what is being sounded (something similar applies to Giovanni Gabrieli's or Heinrich Schütz's 'symphoniae sacrae', where 'instruments' can also include voices).

There are innumerable examples through the century where seeming generic labels mean something else (e.g., the outcome of an action rather than a specific thing), where they seem interchangeable, or where they might mean almost nothing at all: Adriano Banchieri's *Ecclesiastiche sinfonie dette canzoni in aria francese* (Venice, 1607) contains texted four-part 'sinfonias, called canzonas' that, in fact, may be sung as notes or played as canzonas; and Giovanni Battista Riccio's *Il secondo libro delle divine lodi . . . con alcune canzoni da sonare* (Venice, 1614), includes not canzonas but sonatas (*a2, a4*), as does Giovanni Battista Bassani's *Sinfonie a due, e tre instromenti*, op. 5 (Bologna, 1683). This apparent confusion has commonly been viewed as a sign of transition from a fixed set of sixteenth-century instrumental genres (although terms are no less ambivalent here) to a fixed set of eighteenth-century ones. But in fact, these terms often provide distinct information. 'Canzona',[7] or 'canzona (alla) francese', refers to

---

4 A. Berardi, *Miscellanea musicale* (Bologna, 1689), p. 45.

5 Boyden, 'When is a Concerto not a Concerto?'; Piperno, '"Concerto" e "concertato" nella musica strumentale italiana del secolo decimosettimo'.

6 Berardi, who was *maestro di cappella* at S. Maria in Trastevere in Rome towards the end of his life, follows the usage of the Roman composers Alessandro Stradella ('sinfonia') and Lelio Colista ('simfonia'), or at least the manuscript sources that preserve their music for violins and bass. The broader generic issues are discussed in Newman, *The Sonata in the Baroque Era*.

7 The word-form varies: canzon, canzona (plural: 'canzone', which is rarely found), canzone (plural: 'canzoni'). The term is usually anglicised to 'canzona' (plural: 'canzonas'). The principal studies of the canzona for instrumental ensemble are Crocker, 'An Introductory Study of the Italian Canzona for Instrumental Ensembles and its Influence upon the Baroque Sonata'; Bartholomew, *Alessandro Raverij's Collection of 'Canzoni per sonare'*; Sumner, 'The Stylized Canzone'; Dell'Antonio, *Syntax, Form, and Genre in Sonatas and Canzonas*. Modern editions and detailed introductions to individual collections from the canzona repertory are provided in J. Ladewig (ed.), *Italian Instrumental Music of the Sixteenth and Early Seventeenth Centuries* (New York and London, 1980–). One might argue that composers gradually dropped the modifiers *alla francese* or *francese* as they created works that were less indebted to the thematic material of the chanson and more inspired by its rhythms, texture and structure.

a compositional model, the French chanson; 'sonata', by contrast, concerns the instrumental medium. Thus it is not inconsistent to find both terms in juxtaposition, as in Marco Uccellini's *Sonate over canzoni* for violin and continuo, op. 5 (1649). Banchieri's title, a more elaborate but still common formulation, joins function and location – 'sinfonias for the church' – with compositional type ('called *canzoni alla francese*').

Finally, it is worth noting that other types of cross-overs are apparent in repertories that have, perhaps unfortunately, been kept separate in this book. It may be necessary to distinguish between solo and ensemble instrumental music, but in certain genres, at least, a given piece could be performed by way of several different media (a canzona played on the keyboard, by one or two lutenists, or an ensemble of string or wind instruments). The preface to Adriano Banchieri's *Ecclesiastiche sinfonie* suggests that keyboard players wishing to play all four parts of his canzonas should make a score or tablature of them from the partbooks. Similarly, the famous anthology compiled and intabulated for keyboard instruments by Johann Woltz in 1617 includes numerous canzonas by Italian and non-Italian composers, many of which were originally issued in partbooks for ensembles.[8] During the course of the seventeenth century, increasingly idiomatic writing tended to make instrumental works medium-specific and thus to limit the possibilities for transferring pieces from one instrument to another, or from solo to ensemble performance. Even so, scoring in this period is less central to defining a ' work', or even a genre, than it is in later centuries.

Canzoni alla francese

Of all genre designations used for instrumental music, 'canzona' is one of the most revealing because it points to a specific compositional model, the 'chanson'. Italian publications used several variations of the term: *canzoni da sonare* (Florentio Maschera, 1584), *canzoni per sonar* (Alessandro Vincenti (ed.), 1588), *canzoni francese* (Sperindio Bertoldo, 1591), *canzoni alla francese* (Adriano Banchieri, 1596), *canzonette alla francese* (Giuseppe Guami, 1601), *canzon in aria francese* (Adriano Banchieri, 1607), *canzonette d'aria francese* (Tarquinio Merula, 1615; in the dedication), and even *aria di canzon francese per sonare* (Lodovico

---

8 *Nova musices organicae tabulatura. Das ist: Ein newe art teutscher Tabulatur, etlicher ausserlesenen latinisch und teutschen Motetten und geistlichen Gesängen, auch schönen lieblichen Fugen und Canzoni alla francese* (Basle, 1617). This large collection is divided into three parts containing (i) Latin motets, (ii) German motets and sacred songs, and (iii) *canzoni alla francese*; the last includes works by Costanzo Antegnati, Adriano Banchieri, Giovanni de Macque, Florentio Maschera, Claudio Merulo and Flaminio Tresti. Compare the tablature now located in a Cistercian monastery in Pelplin (Poland), dated to the 1620s (Pelplin, Biblioteka Seminarium, 304–8), including substantial numbers of canzonas; see Sutkowski and Mischiati, 'Una preziosa fonte manoscritta di musica strumentale'.

Viadana, 1590). The genre was initially represented mostly by transcriptions, reworkings or embellishments of previously existing chansons. By the beginning of the seventeenth century, however, the term more often referred to an original composition in their vein: a lively, spirited piece in predominantly imitative texture, comprising distinct sections (some of which may be repeated or reprised) contrasted by changing points of imitation and textures. A trademark of the genre is the opening subject's dactylic (long–short–short) rhythm, which occurs frequently in the canzona repertory, but not obsessively.

The genre had eminently practical beginnings as an easy way for music publishers to provide instrumentalists with new and popular repertory, as for example when in 1588 the Venetian printer Giacomo Vincenti issued a set of partbooks containing *Canzon di diversi per sonar con ogni sorte di stromenti*, with pieces in 4–6 parts. In the dedication (dated 20 December 1587), he explains:

> Some selection of *canzoni francese per sonare* was greatly desired by many *virtuosi*, whenceforth I, having collected up to four volumes by various composers, for four, five, six, seven, and eight parts, have resolved to allow everyone to partake of them by means of my press . . .

The collection contains transcriptions and adaptations of Franco-Flemish chansons (some misattributed and misspelt) by Thomas Crecquillon, Adriano Willaert, Robert Godard and others, as well as what appear to be new compositions (lacking a French title) in the genre by the Italian composers Gioseffo Guami (1542–1611) and Claudio Merulo (1533–1604).

Most of the models for 'chanson'-based ensemble canzonas are, in fact, Franco-Flemish rather than French, save some regular favourites by Clément Janequin (*La bataille* and *Le chant des oiseaux*) and Claudin de Sermisy: chansons by Clemens non Papa, Crecquillon, Gombert, Lassus, Richafort and Willaert found particular favour. Their music has a clear structure and incisive themes capable of sustaining interest independent of any play between music and text. By contrast, chansons by French composers, with their more homophonic, chordal style, were more popular for lute transcriptions. The Italian madrigal, with its reliance on a close and often programmatic relationship between music and poetry, appears infrequently in the canzona repertory (although some do appear in instrumental arrangements), presumably because too much was lost in the removal of the text. Some canzonas are literal transcriptions of their model, as with the five-part 'On ques Amor' in Vincenti's collection (after Crecquillon's 'Oncques amour ne fut sans grand langueur', originally published in 1553). However, transcription often represented only a point of departure. Within the repertory, we find reworkings of various kinds, which might broadly be defined as embellishment either by a composer (in the manner of parody treatment) or by a performer (with profuse and virtuosic divisions, or *passaggi*).

An example that illustrates parody technique uses not a chanson but a madrigal, Palestrina's five-voice 'Vestiva i colli e le campagne intorno', reworked by Adriano Banchieri (1568-1634) in his *Canzoni alla francese a quattro voci . . . libro secondo* (Venice, 1596). Palestrina's text consists of two quatrains, probably the octave of a sonnet, each rhyming ABBA. His imitative setting focusses more on the structure of the text than on its poetic content (a typical pastoral invocation). For each line in the first quatrain, Palestrina provides a separate point of imitation (so, in musical terms, ABCD); this is repeated for the second quatrain, with an additional repeat of the final line (ABCDD). Banchieri could easily have produced a typical canzona (even with a long–short–short opening subject) just by using Palestrina's music for the first quatrain. Instead, he made several changes. First, he reduced the texture from five to four voices (although five-fold entries of an imitative subject are preserved by sounding the subject twice in the bass part at different pitch levels). More significantly, he abandoned the successive organisation of the original (ABCD, ABCDD) to create a variation scheme by reducing the number of different points of imitation, by altering the successive expositions of those he kept, and by creating structural returns to the opening (A–B–A'–x–A'–x''–A''', where 'x' represents new material). These returns are significant: a vocal madrigal generally gains its structure (i.e., how it gets from beginning through middle to end) from its text and does not always require independent musical patterning, whereas an instrumental canzona must often, instead, rely on musical repetitions and reprises to make a satisfactory whole.

If Banchieri's treatment of 'Vestiva i colli' illustrates the application of late-Renaissance parody technique to an instrumental genre, it also more generally represents the experiments in form and texture occurring within the canzona as canzona (rather than as ersatz chanson). What seem to be free instrumental canzonas appeared in print as early as 1572 with Nicola Vicentino's inclusion of a single 'canzone a 4 da sonare' in his Fifth Book of five-voice madrigals. In the early 1580s,[9] the Brescian organist and composer Florentio Maschera published an entire collection of 21 such pieces (*Libro primo de canzoni da sonare a quattro voci*), the first of its kind. From this point on until the 1620s, composers would produce canzonas in greater and greater numbers, expanding upon the established principles of thematic contrast and variation. This expansion included

---

9 The collection published in 1584 in Brescia by Vincenzo Sabbio is a reprint that contains a dedication dated 2 March 1582; the first edition may in fact date from the 1570s. See Dario Lo Cicero's introduction to the facsimile edition (Florence, 1988), and Robert Judd's to the modern edition (New York and London, 1995).

(within the first decade of the new century) the introduction of changes of metre between sections, and a broadening of the stylistic range of the new genre through a greater variety of ensembles.

Famous in this regard is Giovanni Gabrieli, organist at St Mark's, Venice, who took advantage of the exceptional body of musicians employed in the basilica to score not only vocal works but also instrumental ones for two or more separate 'choirs' that are musically distinct whether or not they were kept apart in spatial terms. His 1597 *Sacrae symphoniae* includes fourteen canzonas and two sonatas among its motets. Gabrieli's contribution, apart from the principle of polychoral scoring, lay in the manipulation of homophonic blocks of sound, creating dialogue- and echo-effects, the latter through the innovative use of contrasting dynamics (as in the well-known *Sonata pian e forte*). Composers throughout the seventeenth century would return to this idea of sonatas *a due* (*tre*, etc.) *cori* in their works for larger instrumental ensembles, and as we shall see, Gabrieli's style also influenced later sonata composers writing for smaller groups.

The second type of 'embellishment' in the canzona repertory is performer-oriented. Virtuosos on melody instruments (e.g., violin, cornett, bassoon, viola da gamba) used original chansons, arrangements and free canzonas as source material in the creation of elaborate divisions. Italian instrumentalists such as Girolamo Dalla Casa, Giovanni Bassano and Francesco Rognoni Taeggio published their *passaggi* on many of the same chansons (among a variety of other genres) found in the printed canzona repertory. In a typical example, Rognoni Taeggio's *passaggi* (1620) on Antonio Mortaro's four-part canzona *La Portia* transforms this piece of equal-voice polyphony into an extended solo for treble instrument and accompaniment by adding profuse division-style embellishment to Mortaro's upper line.[10] The boundaries between this type of embellished canzona and the emerging solo sonata are very fluid indeed.

Probably the most interesting, and certainly the best crafted, later ensemble canzonas are those by Girolamo Frescobaldi (1583–1643). They merit particular attention not only because of their exceptional quality, but also because a good number exist in two versions, affording a unique perspective on Frescobaldi's thematic variation and formal planning. Except for three canzonas that are included in the 1608 anthology published in Venice by Alessandro Raverii, Frescobaldi's ensemble canzonas are found in three retrospective collections published between 1628 and 1635. Separate and nearly identical editions of his first book of ensemble canzonas were printed in Rome in 1628: one, in

10 Francesco Rognoni Taeggio, *Selva de varii passaggi secondo l'uso moderno per cantare et suonare con ogni sorte de stromenti*, 2 vols (Milan, 1620). Mortaro's canzona was published in his *Primo libro de canzoni da sonare a quattro voci* (Venice, 1600).

parts, bears a prefatory note by Frescobaldi himself; the other, in score, was prepared for publication by his student Bartolomeo Grassi. Frescobaldi appears to have planned a second volume, but had produced only ten new compositions by 1635, when he published a collection in Venice that mixed these ten with fourteen unchanged and sixteen revised pieces from the 1628 canzonas.[11] In the process of revision, Frescobaldi introduces significant reworkings – newly composed adagios (some chromatic) and revised or substitute imitative sections – that serve to create more streamlined and clearly structured compositions where the separate sections are made to fit into a carefully paced, coherent design. He also introduces tempo designations (*adagio*, *allegro*) usually to clarify the implications of his time-signatures. This sense of the canzona as a segmented unity is reinforced in Frescobaldi's variation-canzonas, where a single motivic idea (which may or may not be manipulated by so-called *inganni*, i.e., retaining the motive's solmization but mutating through different hexachords to change the sounding pitches) can underpin a series of musical sections that nevertheless combine in an intricate design.[12]

Except for their use of the basso continuo, Frescobaldi's canzonas are conservative for their time. Their primary interest lies in counterpoint, often imitative, and not in virtuosic or particularly idiomatic writing for any specific instrument, although in a few cases the 1628 print in separate parts indicates 'violino solo, o cornetto' or just 'violino solo' in the *Canto primo* partbook (see the discussion of instrumental ensembles below). Otherwise, both 1628 prints are designed, according to their title-pages, 'per ogni sorte di Stromenti', and Frescobaldi follows the older practice of styling the partbooks generically (*Canto, Alto, Tenore, Basso*) rather than with instrument-specific designations. He also shows no preference for the trio medium (two trebles and bass) that would dominate ensemble music of the mid and late seventeenth century. His concern centres instead on the long-standing challenge of the instrumental canzona: maintaining coherence and interest in the musical sections inherited from the French chanson in abstract form without its entertaining verses. Frescobaldi's expert handling of that challenge, however, inspired no followers: the *stile moderno* sonata represented the new direction of instrumental ensemble music of the 1620s and 1630s; and variation technique held little interest for later composers, who tended towards distinct and contrasted movements within their sonatas, or cultivated reprises among the diverse sections of their

---

11 G. Frescobaldi, *Opere complete*, ed. E. Darbellay, vol. 8/1 (Milan, 2000), pp. lxxvi–lxxvii. Harper, 'Frescobaldi's Reworked Ensemble Canzonas' includes a concordance between the two Roman and one Venetian sources. See also Gallico, *Girolamo Frescobaldi*, pp. 111–26; Harper, 'The Instrumental Canzonas of Girolamo Frescobaldi'.

12 Ladewig, 'The Origins of Frescobaldi's Variation Canzonas Reappraised' gives a concise description of Frescobaldi's variation technique within the keyboard canzonas.

pieces.[13] Frescobaldi's ensemble canzonas thus stand as a high point of the genre, some of the most elegant of their kind, but also among the last.

For church and chamber

The principal cities of early canzona composition were Brescia (Costanzo Antegnati, Ottavio Bargnani, Lodovico Beretta, Floriano Canale, Cesario Gussago, Florentio Maschera, Antonio Mortaro) and Venice (Giovanni Gabrieli, Giovanni Battista Grillo, Giovanni Picchi, Giovanni Priuli, Giovanni Battista Riccio, Francesco Sponga *detto* Usper). But by the beginning of the seventeenth century, the genre was being cultivated throughout much of Italy, starting in the nearby centres of Milan (Camillo Angleria, Giovanni Antonio Cangiasi, Giovanni Paolo Cima, Nicolò Corradini, Michel'Angelo Grancini, Guglielmo Lipparino, Gasparo Pietragrua, Francesco Rognoni Taeggio, Giovanni Domenico Rognoni Taeggio, Agostino Soderini) and Bologna (Banchieri, Aurelio Bonelli), and spreading further to Rome (Paolo Quagliati, Francesco Soriano, Frescobaldi) and Naples (Giovanni de Macque, Ascanio Mayone, Giovanni Maria Trabaci). By means of Venetian and Milanese contacts with Habsburg and German centres north of the Alps, the canzona was quickly transmitted northwards. Transalpine composers such as Hans Leo Hassler, Gregor Aichinger, Johann Hermann Schein, Samuel Scheidt, Adam Jarzębski and others composed their own canzonas (see below), including them, as did Italian composers, in both secular and sacred collections.

Given its roots in the chanson, the canzona was enjoyed as chamber music, and the dedications of canzona prints often describe the musical milieu of the *accademia* or the *ridotto*. Thus Giovanni Domenico Rognoni Taeggio describes his *Canzoni à 4. et 8. voci … libro primo* (Milan, 1605) as a means to satisfy the circle of musicians frequenting the *accademia* of his patron, Prospero Lombardo:

> Having constantly been urged by many friends to send these canzonas of mine to the press, and in particular by the *virtuosi accademici* who come regularly to find recreation in the most noble *accademia* of Your Illustrious Lordship … I have been compelled to gratify them. Wishing to publish these pieces before the world, it seemed to me that I should do so under your most honoured name, both because you are the most deserving leader of the said *accademia* and because you are by nature an enthusiast for *virtuosi* …

---

13 Tarquinio Merula, Maurizio Cazzati, Marco Uccellini and Giovanni Legrenzi each wrote instrumental ensemble works – called *canzoni* by Merula, *canzoni* or *sonate* by Cazzati, and *sonate* by Legrenzi – that feature sectional repetition and the reworking of thematic material of the opening fugal section at the end of the piece. Crocker, 'An Introductory Study of the Italian Canzona for Instrumental Ensembles', pp. 444–8, refers to this type of composition as the 'canzon-sonata'.

Floriano Canale's *Canzoni da sonare a quattro, et otto voci . . . libro primo* (Venice, 1601) paints a similar picture of the musical patronage of his dedicatee, Alessandro Bevilacqua:

> The protection that Your Very Illustrious Lordship holds for *virtuosi*, and in particular for professors of music – many of whom, with the occasion of your *accademia* that in modesty you call 'ridotto', you honourably entertain in your most illustrious house – has encouraged me to dedicate to you these canzonas of mine so that I may be known to you in the future and included in your *ridotto*, and even favoured by your virtuous grace . . .

In view of the role of the madrigal in such academies and similar environments, it is not surprising to find canzonas included in madrigal collections of the period.

This changed around the turn of the seventeenth century as canzonas (when not published independently) began to be included more frequently with sacred works, usually motets, but sometimes psalms or Masses. A rough tally of mixed publications comprising vocal and instrumental music makes the point clear: in the 1590s, three prints of sacred vocal music included canzonas; in the 1600s, ten; and in the 1610s, 21 (for prints of secular vocal music, the equivalent numbers are six, one and four). Further evidence comes from the several printed collections from the first half of the seventeenth century that provide explicit or implicit instructions for using their contents in church services.[14] These embrace a variety of instrumental genres (for organ or for instrumental ensemble) for Mass and Vespers, including the toccata, ricercar, *capriccio* and canzona.[15] This suggests that instrumental music was finding a greater place in terms of both function and ornament within the liturgy and in spiritual devotions, and it squares with the tendency for larger churches to maintain significant, permanent instrumental ensembles.[16] The dedication of Innocentio Vivarino's *Il primo libro de motetti . . . con otto sonate per il violino* (Venice,

14 Adriano Banchieri, *L'organo suonarino* (Venice, 1605); Amante Franzoni, *Apparato musicale di messa, sinfonie, canzoni, motetti, et letanie della Beata Vergine, a otto voci*, op. 5 (Venice, 1613); Bernardino Bottazzi, *Choro et organo* (Venice, 1614); Stefano Bernardi, *Concerti academici*, op. 8 (Venice, 1616); Carlo Milanuzzi, *Armonia sacra di concerti, messa et canzoni*, op. 6 (Venice, 1622); Frescobaldi, *Il secondo libro di toccate, canzone, versi d'hinni, magnificat . . .* ([Rome], 1627); Tomaso Cecchino, *Cinque messe a due voci*, op. 23 (Venice, 1628); Girolamo Frescobaldi, *Fiori musicali*, op. 12 (Venice, 1635); Antonio Croci, *Frutti musicali di messe*, op. 4 (Venice, 1642); Giovanni Battista Fasolo, *Annuale*, op. 8 (Venice, 1645); Cecchino, *Note musicali per risponder con facilità e al choro per tutte le feste dell'anno con due sonate anco per il violino* (Venice, c. 1649).

15 Higginbottom, 'Organ Music and the Liturgy'; Moore, 'The Liturgical Use of the Organ in Seventeenth-Century Italy'. Note also the short-lived *canzone-motetto*, a hybrid work *a8* (in two choirs) in which the music for one choir is texted and for the other is not; examples are found in Giovanni Domenico Rognoni Taeggio, *Canzoni à 4. et 8. voci . . . libro primo* (Milan, 1605), Agostino Soderini, *Canzoni a 4. et 8. voci . . . libro primo* (Milan, 1608), and Giovanni Antonio Cangiasi, *Melodia sacra quatuor, et quinque vocibus . . . et uno cum canzon francese . . . liber secundus* (Milan, 1612). See also Vecchi, 'La canzone strumentale e la canzone-motetto a Milano nella prima metà del Seicento'.

16 As at St Mark's in Venice, S. Maria Maggiore in Bergamo, the Steccata in Parma, and S. Petronio in Bologna; see Selfridge-Field, *Venetian Instrumental Music from Gabrieli to Vivaldi*, appendix (for St Mark's); Schnoebelen, 'The Concerted Mass at S. Petronio'; Gambassi, *La cappella musicale di S. Petronio;*

1620) refers to using these motets and violin sonatas in lieu of *intermedi* in *sacre rappresentazioni*, in the Introits of Masses, and at the beginning of Vespers and elsewhere. Within the liturgy, the canzona and the sonata tended to occur at specific points, often serving to mark a moment of conclusion.[17] During the Mass, we find them after the reading from the Epistles ('dopo l'Epistola' or the like), i.e., in place of the chanted Gradual or during its *sotto voce* recitation; after the Communion; and during the 'Deo gratias' (i.e., the end of the service). During Vespers, they appear as antiphon substitutes linked to the psalms and the Magnificat (the *Sonata sopra 'Sancta Maria, ora pro nobis'* in Monteverdi's 1610 Vespers is a famous example).

The 'secular' origins of the canzona need be no more problematic for its use in church than the secular origins of many vocal models for parody Masses in the sixteenth century. Rather, it is the lively musical character of the canzona (and also, one assumes, its sectional nature that permitted alternative endings according to need) that suited and even lent meaning as an effusive and joyous response to significant moments in the liturgy. This is underscored by comparison with the free instrumental works designated for other points in the Mass. When instrumental music was used during the Offertory or the Elevation, it had different affective profiles: for the Offertory, the more severe ricercar, sometimes on a chromatic subject; during the Elevation, something mysterious and awe-inducing, such as a piece of *durezze e ligature* or similar *movimento grave* that, in Banchieri's words, should 'move to devotion' (*muovi a devotione*).[18]

The sonata

In the third volume of his *Syntagma musicum* (1619), the German composer, theorist and organologist Michael Praetorius (1571–1621) provided definitions to distinguish the canzona and sonata:

> The 'sonata à sonando' is so named because it is performed as the canzonas are, not with human voices, but solely by instruments. Very lovely [examples] of that genre are to be found in the canzonas and sinfonias of Giovanni Gabrieli and other composers. In my opinion, however, the distinction lies in this: sonatas are made to be grave and imposing in the manner of the motet, whereas canzonas have many black notes, running briskly, gayly and rapidly through them.[19]

Vanscheeuwijck, *The 'Cappella musicale' of San Petronio in Bologna under Giovanni Paolo Colonna*; Padoan, *La musica in S. Maria Maggiore a Bergamo nel periodo di Giovanni Cavaccio*.

17 Bonta, 'The Uses of the *Sonata da chiesa*'.

18 Banchieri, *L'organo suonarino*, 2nd edn (Venice, 1611), p. 99.

19 Praetorius, *Syntagma musicum* (1619), iii: 24 (= 22). I have adapted the translation from Newman, *The Sonata in the Baroque Era*, p. 23.

While it is tempting to take Praetorius at face value, it is also worth noting just how tentative he is ('In my opinion . . .'): already in the late 1610s, it was difficult to pin down the terms 'canzona' and 'sonata'. There is, however, no question that by the middle of the seventeenth century, the sonata (whether as label or as a distinct musical type) had somehow replaced the canzona as the leading genre for instrumental ensemble. Significantly, the choice of term was influenced not just by musical style but also by social and other divisions in the musical profession: in the early seventeenth century, organists and *maestri di cappella* often preferred canzonas (in name or in style), whereas ensemble instrumentalists wrote sonatas.[20] This reflects the terminological distinctions established earlier in this chapter, where 'canzona' refers to a compositional model, while 'sonata' is in some sense (the consequence of) an action. Thus the well-trained contrapuntalists demonstrated their compositional skill and rigour, while the first priority of ensemble instrumentalists was to create music for virtuoso performance. Instrumental technique versus contrapuntal design is, therefore, a significant element in the shifting priorities that accompany the disappearance of the canzona and the emergence of the sonata.

This distinction between composer- and performer-oriented styles and genres becomes clear in comparing two composers, Cesario Gussago (*fl.* 1599–1612) and Giovanni Battista Fontana (?1589–?1630), whose careers overlapped in Brescia at the church of S. Maria delle Grazie during the early decades of the century (Fontana was one of the two dedicatees of Gussago's *Sonate a quattro, sei et otto* of 1608). Gussago was a church organist (as well as a student of philosophy and theology at the University of Pavia) who appears to have spent his career in S. Maria delle Grazie; Fontana was a virtuoso violinist who moved from Brescia to Venice, Rome and Padua.[21] Each composer left a single publication of sonatas (Fontana's appeared in 1641, although he died during the plague in 1630–31), but in remarkably contrasting styles. Gussago adopted the canzona of the late sixteenth century, with imitative and/or polychoral writing for a generic ensemble. Fontana wrote virtuoso sonatas for smaller ensembles of specified instruments whose soloistic parts unfold over the harmonic accompaniment of a basso continuo.

It would be an oversimplification to claim that virtuosity replaced contrapuntal rigour from the 1610s through the 1640s. Rather, the larger impact of this change was to add a new range of styles and techniques without necessarily phasing out the old or making it redundant. It would also be inaccurate to claim that canzonas were always old-fashioned and sonatas always more

---

20 Selfridge-Field, 'Canzona and Sonata'.

21 For biographical information on Fontana, see the introduction to G. B. Fontana, *Sonate a 1. 2. 3. per il violino . . .*, ed. T. D. Dunn, 'Recent Researches in Music of the Baroque Era', 99 (Madison, WI, 2000).

'modern' (Gussago, after all, uses the term 'sonata'). Thus these competing priorities can be observed even within the range of pieces called 'canzona', as we have already seen in those canzonas focussing on virtuoso diminutions. For example, the canzonas in the bassoonist Bartolomé de Selma y Salaverde's *Primo libro de canzoni, fantasie et correnti* (Venice, 1638) are hardly canzonas in the older sense: he writes for two, three or four players (plus continuo) each of whom can display virtuosity in solo episodes or in dialogues.

Selma y Salaverde's and Fontana's use of the basso continuo is another symptom, and also cause, of change. In the first decade of the century, Giovanni Domenico Rognoni Taeggio went to the length of including a score (*partitio*) for use of the organist with the partbooks of his 1605 canzonas because the 'basso continuato' was a less satisfactory option for him and his readers. Similarly, Tarquinio Merula (1594/5–1665), in his *Il primo libro delle canzoni a quattro voci per sonare* (Venice, 1615), noted that although he had provided a continuo part for the greater ease of organists, he himself would recommend putting these canzonas in score. By the 1630s, however, the continuo was a norm, and it had an obvious impact on the use of imitative counterpoint in the old style. In sum, virtuosity, the rise of the continuo, and the pursuit of alternatives to strict counterpoint – to which one might add the notion that instrumental music might in fact have some kind of 'rhetorical' power – tended to encourage a shift from the late-Renaissance four- or five-voice canzona to the sonata for one or two instruments (cornetts, violins) and continuo, with or without a melodic bass instrument (violone or trombone).

The parallels with the move in vocal music from *a cappella* polyphony to solo songs, duets and trios are clear, and are made explicit in the preface to Adriano Banchieri's provocatively titled *Moderna armonia di canzoni alla francese. Nuovamente composta per suonare con facilità tutte le parti nell'organo, ò clavicembalo, et dentrovi (piacendo) concertare uno et dui stromenti acuto e grave*, op. 26 (Venice, 1612):

> It is clear that modern musical compositions composed for one, two, three and more voices concerted with the organ or harpsichord offer both facility and delight to the organist, singers and listeners. We can be sure that this is caused by the arrangement and affect produced by joining in a recitative style [*recitativamente*] *accenti* and *concenti* with clear and distinct harmony. I have judged that the same effect can occur in these new *canzoni alla francese* of mine, since I adopt the same invention and manner.

Banchieri's canzonas may be played on the organ alone (he publishes them in keyboard score) or, he says, by one or two soloists and organ (he mentions a violin and violone, or cornett and trombone); he had permitted similar options in his 1607 collection of canzonas (also styled 'sotto moderno stile'). In part, he follows the trend of Lodovico Grossi da Viadana's *Cento concerti ecclesiastici* (1602) to produce adaptable pieces that allow a variety of performance options. But Banchieri also has a larger and more striking ambition: he seeks to assimilate the style of modern vocal genres within his 'modern' instrumental music, and in so doing, to rival their expressive ability.

The sonata thus enters the field of the *seconda pratica* with its search for new forms of musical expression and emotional arousal. Several collections published in the first quarter of the century advertise a new approach by way of characteristic buzzwords. Salamone Rossi (1570–*c.* 1630) included a 'Sonata detta la Moderna' in his *Il terzo libro de varie sonate, sinfonie, gagliarde, brandi e corrente per sonar* (1613);[22] he was also one of the earliest composers to use a trio medium of two treble instruments (*viole da braccio*) and bass (chitarrone) which may have been a favourite in Mantua (compare some of the instrumental writing in Monteverdi's *Orfeo* and in his 1607 *Scherzi musicali*). Biagio Marini (1594–1663) published a collection of *Affetti musicali, a1–3,* op. 1 (Venice, 1618); Dario Castello issued two books of *Sonate concertate in stil moderno* (Venice, 1621, 1629). Such terms as 'affetti', 'concertato' and 'stil moderno' have obvious resonances, and in the case of the latter two, they also establish obvious oppositions – *concertato* versus *a cappella, stile moderno* versus *stile antico,* or for that matter, *seconda* versus *prima pratica* – that may or may not map directly one onto the other but which nevertheless demonstrate a striving for something new and/or different. Marini's suggestion that instrumental music be associated with the 'affetti' also reveals an ambition already articulated by Banchieri: the term or its cognates appear on the title-pages of some fifteen musical editions between 1610 and 1625, embracing secular madrigals, canzonettas, arias and duets, and sacred motets and litanies.[23] This accords significantly with the theories of poetic expression and compositional technique traded in the aesthetic expositions centring on the *stile rappresentativo* in the early part of the century: Giulio Caccini emphasises the importance of the performer moving the affections of the listener in the well-known preface to *Le nuove musiche*; the same desire is articulated in a number of Monteverdi's letters; and indeed it becomes a topos in much writing of the period.

Composers of instrumental works thus lay claim to the ability of music without text to stir the listener's emotions. This had obvious implications for performance. In the preface to his *Toccate e partite d'intavolatura di cimbalo ... libro*

---

22 Only the third edition survives (Venice, 1623), although the dedication is dated 20 January 1613; see Harrán, *Salamone Rossi*, p. 124.

23 B. Marini, *Affetti musicali, opera prima,* ed. F. Piperno (Milan, 1990), p. xxii.

primo (Rome, 1615), Frescobaldi placed at the head of his recommendations for performance the fact that

> this way of playing must not be subject to the beat, just as we see in modern madrigals which, though difficult, are made more manageable by means of the beat, taking it now languidly, now quickly, and occasionally suspending it in mid-air, according to their *affetti* or the sense of the words.

Martino Pesenti also adopted some of the rhetoric of the *seconda pratica* in justifying the affective dissonances in his *Il primo libro delle correnti alla francese per sonar nel clavicembalo, et altri s[t]romenti* (repr. Venice, 1635):

> Do not wonder at finding in some of my *correnti* ninths, sevenths, tritones, diminished fifths and similar dissonances, since by not accompanying them with the inner parts and by playing them at a quick tempo, they render beauty and *affetto* contrary to their nature.

For composers of ensemble music, 'affetto' was applied in a specific sense to moments of harmonic intensity in slow, chordal sections, with chromaticism, cross-relations, dissonances and unusual melodic movement.

Also characteristic of the *sonata concertata in stil moderno* (to use Castello's term) was virtuosity. In the preface to Castello's *Sonate concertate in stil moderno, per sonar nel organo, overo spineta con diversi instrumenti, a2–3* (Venice, 1621), the composer warned the reader of their potential difficulties:

> For the satisfaction of those who will delight in playing these sonatas of mine, it has seemed necessary to me to advise them that even though they appear difficult at first sight, one should not lack confidence to play them more than once, because this will serve as practice, and after time they will be rendered most easily because no thing is difficult for the person who delights in it. I have to declare that I could not have composed them to be easier while observing the *stile moderno*, now followed by everyone.

According to Castello, the *stile moderno* was common practice by the late 1620s. Perhaps more novel, however, was his use of the term 'concertato' (concerted). Previously, it had referred to the combining of voices and instruments in a manner producing variety of contrasts, combinations, alternations and juxta-positions. Now Castello applies it to works for instruments alone, again as if the techniques and effects of early seventeenth-century vocal music are now claimed for the sonata.

What, then, is this 'modern' music like? As Castello points out, his pieces must have required some practice and rehearsal. They are virtuosic in their heavy use of division-style *passaggi*; Castello and his contemporaries writing in the *stile moderno* often appear to have written the *passaggi* into their pieces, particularly at cadences. The *stile moderno* is also a mercurial style in its use of instrumental effects – tremolo, echo, rapid trills, quickfire exchanges between the parts, fast repeated notes (e.g., in the *concitato genere*) and slower passages focussing on the *affetto* – in often short and starkly contrasted sections also exploiting shifts of metre. Further characteristics of the *stile moderno* are the distribution of soloistic sections across the ensemble, intricate scoring by the standards of the time, descriptive terms for markings of tempo and mood (adagio, allegro, largo, più adagio, presto), and careful indications of slurrings and dynamics (*forte*, *piano*). Not all of this is new – we have already seen the precedents in earlier division-style writing and in the music of Giovanni Gabrieli[24] – but their combination and their application to small-scale ensemble music serve to make these sonatas truly 'modern'.

Not everyone went to the extremes of a Castello. When Giuseppe Scarani published a set of *Sonate concertate a due e tre voci* in 1630, he may have been jumping on a bandwagon as an advertising ploy, or to claim merit where it was not necessarily deserved.[25] Tarquinio Merula's *Canzoni overo sonate concertate… libro terzo*, a2–3, op. 12 (1637), do not exhibit Castello's flamboyance, and his overall instrumental output covers the stylistic range from the four-part canzona to the two- and three-part sonata. On the other hand, composers who never advertised the new style demonstrated it strikingly in their music. Foremost among these is Giovanni Battista Fontana, who stands next to Castello in the innovative qualities of his music, and who (given that he was already known as a virtuoso violinist in 1608, when Gussago dedicated his sonatas to him) may have been a moving force in the *stile moderno* sonata. Another contributor to this style, and an influential one, was Gabriele Sponga *detto* Usper. His modern-style three-part sonatas in his uncle's (Francesco Usper) *Compositioni armoniche* (Venice, 1619), with *concitato*, *zampogna* (bagpipes) and *lirate* (*lira da braccio*) effects, have been credited with influencing Castello. It also suggests the reliance of the new style on programmatic music, often pastoral, employed in the contemporary madrigal,[26] again revealing instrumental music's search for the expressive power normally granted to the voice.

24 Allsop, *The Italian 'Trio' Sonata*, pp. 92–3; Collins, '"Reactions against the Virtuoso"'.

25 Just what composers meant by 'concertato' in works for instrumental ensemble of the 1620s and 1630s remains unclear. Selfridge-Field (*Venetian Instrumental Music from Gabrieli to Vivaldi*, pp. 140–41) writes that Scarani 'was clearly trying to trade on Castello's success with the same title, but these sonatas are scarcely concerted'. Dell'Antonio (*Syntax, Form, and Genre in Sonatas and Canzonas*, p. 111), however, argues the contrary: 'his subtle use of counterpoint brings to the fore the novelties of the "stile moderno" in a way which is, though different, equally powerful to Castello's style'.

26 Allsop, *The Italian 'Trio' Sonata*, p. 89; Selfridge-Field, *Venetian Instrumental Music from Gabrieli to Vivaldi*, p. 135.

However, the innovations associated with the *stile moderno* by no means account for all that was new. Another characteristic of the 1620s (although there are a few earlier examples) is the use of standard bass patterns for variation-sonatas, usually drawn from popular songs – 'Madre non mi far la monaca' (also known as La monica), 'È tanto tempo hormai' (sometimes 'Le tanto . . .'), 'Quest'è quel loco' and the *Ruggiero* (a tune associated with Ariosto) – or dances (the *Bergamasca*, *Pass'e mezzo*, Romanesca, *Ballo del Granduca*).[27] Castello never composed this kind of sonata, but others writing in the modern idiom did – including Rossi, Marini, Merula and Selma y Salaverde – as well as those whose instrumental works seem unconnected with the *stile moderno*, such as Frescobaldi (whose 1635 ensemble canzonas include variations on both the *Ruggiero* and the *Romanesca*), Giuseppe Buonamente and Andrea Falconieri, or those who include instrumental pieces in a madrigal collection, such as Giovanni Valentini and Francesco Turini (both in 1621). This is part of a broader phenomenon of adding to the repertory of styles and techniques used in sonatas. From the middle of the century on, composers such as Marco Uccellini (*c.* 1603–1680), Maurizio Cazzati (1616–78), Giovanni Legrenzi (1626–90) and Giovanni Battista Vitali (1632–92) could incorporate canzona-style fugues, polychoral writing, a sampling of virtuoso techniques from the *stile moderno* sonata, and variations on a bass into their sonatas.

Most sonatas from the middle of the century on – that is, after the initial phase of the *stile moderno* sonata – tend to exhibit only moderate degrees of virtuosity. Here, however, we are possibly misled by printed sources, which favour repertories that were accessible to significant numbers of instrumentalists. There was scant point in a Venetian, Bolognese or Modenese music printer issuing instrumental music that was too difficult for the market, at least if their prints were to serve a commercial purpose rather than being, say, just 'vanity' editions for the benefit of the composer and a small circle of connoisseurs. Highly virtuosic music from the 1660s, 1670s and 1680s does survive, however, in a number of manuscript sources, the most remarkable of which is the

---

27 Wendland, '"Madre non mi far Monaca"', p. 195, points out the close similarity between *La monica* and 'È tanto tempo hormai'. The list of all the variations on these patterns would be long. Some examples are: 'La monica', Biagio Marini (1626); 'È tanto tempo hormai', Francesco Turini (1621), Salamone Rossi (1622), Giovanni Battista Buonamente (1626), Marco Uccellini (1642); 'Quest'è quel loco', Buonamente (1626), Uccellini (1642); *Ruggiero*, Salamone Rossi (1613), Buonamente (1626), Frescobaldi (1635), Merula (1637); *Ballo del Granduca*, Banchieri (1620, 1626), Buonamente (1626). The *Ballo del Granduca* originated as Emilio de' Cavalieri's 'O che nuovo miracolo' concluding the 1589 Florentine *intermedi*; see Kirkendale, *L'aria di Fiorenza, id est Il ballo del Gran Duca*. There are also some isolated examples in the instrumental repertory of variations on plainchant, such as the cantus-firmus treatment of 'Lucis Creator optime' by Scarani (1630; see Selfridge-Field, *Venetian Instrumental Music from Gabrieli to Vivaldi*, p. 141), and the canonic variations over 'Iste confessor' by Marco Uccellini in a sonata from his *Sonate, arie, et correnti a 2. e 3.* (Venice, 1642).

extant collection of instrumental music in manuscript that was the property of
the Este dukes of Modena.[28] This has a fair number of undistinguished dances
and airs, but a substantial portion contains virtuoso works for solo violin, most
with continuo accompaniment but some without, whose technical challenges
far exceed most printed *stile moderno* sonatas. Most are by Giuseppe Colombi
(1635–94), a violinist and composer who was from 1673 *capo de gl'instrumentisti*
(head of the instrumentalists) at the Modenese court and, on the death of
Giovanni Maria Bononcini in 1678, *maestro di cappella* at Modena Cathedral.

Colombi calls for complicated bowings (arpeggios, tremolos over double-
stops, staccato marks under slurs), extremely high left-hand positions extending to b''', a full octave above the first-position range of the instrument, and
double and triple stops, frequently high up the fingerboard.[29] In several movements, moreover, Colombi weaves a two-part fugal texture by means of double
stops. Also among the Estense manuscripts are chaconne variations for unaccompanied violin and for unaccompanied bass violin,[30] and works for violin in
scordatura (g, d', g', b' and g, c', e', g') that show off their triadic tunings with
triple and quadruple stops. All of this extraordinary music merits particular
attention because nothing like it occurs in the Italian violin repertory until
Corelli's famous op. 5 sonatas (1700), and it fundamentally alters our notion of
Italian violin technique during the second half of the century.

Following the printed record, historians have long assumed that while composers north of the Alps inherited the virtuosity of the *stile moderno* sonata
and developed it further, Italian violinists before Corelli showed little interest
in virtuoso technique. The Modena manuscripts prompt a different view. Yet
their dissemination appears to have extended no farther than the Estense court
itself, where Duke Francesco II seems to have created an (instrumental) *musica
segreta* parallel to the earlier Duke Alfonso II d'Este's (vocal) *musica segreta* in
Ferrara. Indeed, the duke (who played the violin and in his youth studied with
Colombi)[31] may also have wanted to take an active part in this music: several of
Colombi's sonatas exist in two versions, the second of which eliminates double
stops and transposes the higher passages down so that the range of the piece

28 Now housed in Modena, Biblioteca Estense; see Allsop, 'Violinistic Virtuosity in the Seventeenth
Century'; Suess, 'Giuseppe Colombi's Dance Music for the Estense Court of Duke Francesco II of Modena'.
On Estense patronage, see Crowther, 'A Case Study in the Power of the Purse'; Crowther, *The Oratorio in
Modena*.

29 See, for example, the sonatas in Modena, Biblioteca Estense, Mus. F.280 (nos. 2, 5, 7).

30 The instrument called for in these chaconnes would probably be recognisable today as a violoncello
or a slightly larger version of it. Two different tunings are called for in these pieces: that of the modern
'cello, and one a tone lower, a common tuning for the seventeenth-century bass violin.

31 The dedication to Duke Francesco of Colombi's *Sonate da camera a tre strumenti*, op. 5 (Bologna,
1689), mentions 'the honour of having advanced your right [arm] – born to sceptres – in gently handling
the sonorous bow'.

lies in the violin's first position, presumably for the benefit of Colombi's noble pupil.

This music may have stayed in manuscript because of its close associations with a specific patron. But even if it were available to be printed, it is hard to imagine any Italian press taking it on board. This was not just because of the music's technical difficulty (and therefore unmarketability), but also because of the limitations of printing technology. Single-impression letterpress printing from movable type was the standard mode for music-printing, including ensemble instrumental music (for the latter, we do have a few examples of engraving, produced by the engraver, theatre-set painter and violoncellist Carlo Buffagnotti in Bologna during the 1680s and 1690s, but they are unusual). Complex notations, including double stops, were not impossible to print,[32] but they created technical problems that most printers probably did not have enough interest (financial or otherwise) to solve. Not for nothing did Colombi's four prints of instrumental music, published between 1668 and 1689, contain music that was much more moderate in its demands. Something similar occurs in the case of the Bolognese violoncellist Domenico Gabrielli, whose op. 1 dances (Bologna, 1684) contrast with his much more challenging sonatas for 'cello and continuo also in the Estense manuscripts.

Ensembles

The printed violin sonatas of the mid-to-late seventeenth century therefore tend to make modest demands of their performers, with standard bowing patterns and rarely exceeding first position (with a range from g to b'', perhaps extended up to $c\sharp''$). That range increased in the 1680s, especially in some of the repertory for solo violin – Pietro Degli Antoni (1639–1720), in his *Suonate a violino solo col basso continuo*, op. 5 (Bologna, 1686), goes up to f''' – but this is still exceptional.[33] For an earlier period, the limitations on range and the tendency to avoid overly idiomatic writing encouraged, at least in principle, the transfer of pieces from one instrument to another. From the 1610s onward, however, instrumentation is specified in both canzona and sonata prints with ever greater frequency. Designations of instruments appeared at first sporadically in tables of contents, then in the designations of partbooks and on title-pages. In terms

32 The last three dances at the end of Giovanni Maria Bononcini's *Arie, correnti, sarabande, gighe, et allemande*, op. 4 (Bologna, 1671), contain double stops that the printer split between two staves 'because of the lack of suitable type'.

33 For the early history of the violin, see Boyden, *The History of Violin Playing from its Origins to 1761*; Holman, *Four and Twenty Fiddlers*, pp. 1–31. Boyden, in particular, discusses the playing technique of the instrument throughout the Baroque era.

of the composition of larger ensembles, there is a noticeable shift in the period away from textures dense in the middle (e.g., SATTB) to those focussing on outer voices (SSATB), and from a norm of five-part writing to one of four (SSB plus a middle voice).[34] This obviously relates to polarities within the Baroque style, while also perhaps being linked to a move away from instruments of the *viola da gamba* family (viols) to those of the *viola da braccio* one (the violin family). Despite some residual resistance to the violin – 'a crude and harsh instrument of and for itself, if it is not tempered and sweetened by a delicate bow', according to Francesco Rognoni Taeggio[35] – it soon became the favoured instrument for treble parts, with the cornett sometimes specified as an alternative. The recorder (*flauto*) was much less common. Bass parts (when separate from the continuo) usually call for some form of bass instrument of the *viola da braccio* family, most often the violone.[36]

The terminology can be confusing and need not always reflect different instruments: thus for the melodic bass instrument of the ensemble we find 'basso da brazzo', 'basso di viola', 'viola', 'viola da gamba', 'basso', 'bassetto', 'violoncino', 'violonlino' and, in the latter part of the century, 'violoncello'. For middle-register strings, we may find the 'violetta' or 'viola' (sometimes specified as alto or tenor). The term 'viola' can therefore occur as a bass- or middle-register designation, although Venetian sources tended to distinguish between the (lower) 'viola' and the (higher) 'violetta'. Bass wind instruments (trombone or bassoon) are specified much less frequently, although an alto or tenor trombone was sometimes indicated when the treble parts were played on the cornett. In general, however, we enter a terminological minefield that intersects with, but does not map directly onto, complex organological issues caused, in part, by a lack of standardisation in instrument-making in different geographical areas.

Basso continuo parts most often call for an organ or harpsichord. The lute, archlute and theorbo (and its equivalent, the chitarrone), although chord-playing instruments, were usually specified as melodic bass instruments and less frequently as continuo instruments by themselves.[37] The lute, and later archlute, appear to have been the preferred plucked bass instruments in Rome, while the theorbo and chitarrone were called for in north Italian publications.

---

34 Holman, '"Col nobilissimo esercitio della vivuola"'.   35 *Selva de varii passaggi* (1620), ii: 3.

36 Bonta, 'From Violone to Violoncello'; Bonta, 'Terminology for the Bass Violin in Seventeenth-Century Italy'.

37 Borgir, *The Performance of the Basso Continuo in Italian Baroque Music* is the most detailed account concerning the instrumentation of the basso continuo. The chitarrone is the specified continuo instrument in all of Salamone Rossi's prints (1607, 1608, 1613, 1622) and in prints by Alessandro Grandi (1637) and Giovanni Battista Fontana (1641).

Quite apart from the instruments themselves, the ensembles for which sonata composers wrote present some difficulty. Unlike the canzona in its early stages, the number of parts indicated on the title-pages of sonata publications does not necessarily indicate the number of separate instruments in the ensemble, the complicating factor being the basso continuo. Sonata composers were largely consistent in using designations of *a2*, *a3* etc. for the number of melodic parts, not including the basso continuo.[38] Thus Giovanni Legrenzi's *Sonate a due, e tre . . . libro primo*, op. 2 (Venice, 1655), a representative example, includes 'a2' sonatas for two violins and continuo, and 'a3' ones for two violins, violone (or sometimes bassoon) and continuo.

There are, however, curious and sometimes perplexing variations in counting a melodic or even harmonic bass in the numbering. For instance, Maurizio Cazzati's *Suonate a due violini col suo basso continuo*, op. 18 (Bologna, 1656), which are 'a2', include parts for two violins, organ continuo, and an optional ('a beneplacito') bass part for theorbo or violone – an instance of the sometimes complicating performance options offered in repertory.[39] In contrast, the only bass part in Corelli's opp. 2 and 4 trio-sonatas (Rome, 1685, 1694) is one (with figures) for violone 'or' (not 'and') cembalo. Thus Cazzati's 'a2' sonatas call for a total of three or (optionally) four instruments, while Corelli's 'a3' sonatas also call for just three. Following the principle of not counting the continuo in the numbering, the violone must count as a melody instrument and not a harmony one, in which case there is no harmonic continuo instrument in Corelli's ensemble. But then, what of the figures in that third partbook? Adding to the confusion is the thorny issue of whether a melodic instrument could be used to double the continuo bass line even when it is not specified or (in contrast to Cazzati's op. 18) provided with a separate partbook. One could argue that the often carefully worded descriptions of bass instrumentation over the course of the century imply instructions to be taken literally. But the number of prints that mark the melodic bass as optional – including Marco Uccellini's note to his *Sonate, arie, et correnti a 2. a 3. et a 4. per sonare con diversi instromenti . . . libro secondo* (Venice, 1642) that 'these arias will sound better if the basso continuo is accompanied by the violone' – is not insignificant, suggesting a certain amount of freedom with regard to the accompanying bass.[40]

An explanation for these complexities might lie in the freedom to make choices of scoring depending on the size of the performing space, which in

38 Jensen, 'Solo Sonata, Duo Sonata and Trio Sonata'. An exception is Salvadore Gandini's *Correnti et balletti alla francese, et all'italiana a 3*, op. 4 (Venice, 1655), which includes three partbooks, one each for two violins and basso continuo.

39 For a general study of optional scorings, see Mangsen, '*Ad libitum* Procedures in Instrumental Duos and Trios'.

40 Ibid., p. 34.

turn would dictate the utility of having a bass melody instrument reinforcing the continuo line, or of doing away with a harmonic continuo instrument altogether. From the 1660s on, there are numerous prints that, like Corelli's, contain a single bass partbook, labelled 'violone o spinetta', 'spinetta o violone' or, more interestingly, 'violone e spinetta o tiorba',[41] which might or might not count in the numbering of the parts in title-page designations (*a2, a3* etc.). All of these examples come from collections of dances or *sonate da camera*, and the presence of the relatively small and quiet *spinetta* suggests that composers had an intimate setting in mind in which there would be greater room for manoeuvre.[42] One assumes that larger spaces – such as churches – offered less flexibility, especially if the lower (bass) frequencies were naturally dampened by the acoustic environment; this probably explains Cazzati's option to strengthen the bass line with an added instrument.

There is a great deal more work to be done on these issues. But they already give the lie to the ubiquitous tendency (from the late nineteenth century onwards) to subsume distinct sonata types – *a2* (two treble instruments and continuo) and *a3* (two treble instruments, one bass instrument and continuo) – under the label 'trio-sonata'. Only recently have the significant stylistic differences between these two types of sonata begun to emerge.[43] The sonata *a3* is the clearer and more consistent case: from Castello on, the scoring for three melody instruments (whether or not two trebles and one bass) and continuo allowed for more intricate contrapuntal textures that composers exploited in the fugal descendants of the imitative canzona; this, incidentally, is perhaps why Corelli chose the *a3* option (minus harmonic continuo) in his opp. 2 and 4 sonatas, given that fugal techniques appear prominently therein. The sonata *a2*, particularly when scored for two treble instruments, is in one sense more progressive, prompting considerable experimentation on the part of composers. Here fugue-like expositions of a subject quickly give way to lively motivic exchange or some form of easy counterpoint and extended flourishes in thirds between the two trebles. Yet even in the *a2* sonata, the continuo line can sometimes be contrapuntally active such that it acts as a third 'melody' part and thus makes the piece tend towards a sonata *a3*, even if it is not designated as such.

41 This particular case, Orazio Pollarolo's *Correnti, balletti, gighe, allemande, arie . . . overo Suonate da camera a tre*, op. 1 (Bologna, 1673), furnishes a rare example of a single partbook specifically intended for more than one instrument.

42 Another approach to scoring for smaller performing spaces may be seen in the continuo-less scorings of dances and *sonate da camera*: Salamone Rossi (1613: 'due violini, et un chitarrone', which does play chords, but was usually used as reinforcement for a keyboard instrument); Giovanni Battista Buonamente (1626: 'due violini, et un basso di viola'); Giuseppe Colombi (1668, with partbooks for Violino I, Violino II, Viola, Basso); Giovanni Maria Bononcini (1671: 'violino e violone, o spinetta' with the admonition to use the violone); and Arcangelo Corelli (1685: 'doi violini, e violone, ò cimbalo', where the violone is the first option).

43 Allsop, *The Italian 'Trio' Sonata*, pp. 24–6.

The *sonata da camera* and the 'proper exercises of nobles'

Another distinction often made in this repertory is the one between the *sonata da camera* (for the chamber) and the *sonata da chiesa* (for the church). Although historians have accepted these terms as useful for categorising subgenres within the sonata of the second half of the seventeenth century, here, too, there are complications. The first description of these two types of sonata comes from the French theorist, Sébastien de Brossard (1655–1730), attempting to give a rational account of Italian practice in his *Dictionnaire de musique* (1703). Brossard writes of

> suites of several little pieces suitable for dancing, and composed in the same mode or key. Such sonatas usually begin with a prelude, or little sonata, which serves as preparation for all the others. Next come the *allemande*, the *pavane*, the *courante* and other dances or serious airs; then come the *gigues*, the *passacailles*, the *gavottes*, the *menuets*, the *chaconnes* and other happy airs. And all these composed in the same key or mode, and played one after the other, make a *sonata da camera*.[44]

Thus he turns the *sonata da camera* into something comparable to the French suite. Italian composers, however, used the term to describe one of two things: a single courtly dance – most commonly an *allemanda, balletto, corrente, gagliarda, giga* or *sarabanda* – of Italian or (from the 1660s) more recent French origin;[45] or (from the mid 1680s), a suite of such dances, often introduced by a prelude and perhaps intermingled with other non-dance movements, usually slow. This latter sense of the term in Italy is not so distant from Brossard's definition, which accurately lists the dances likely to be encountered except for his mention of the outdated *pavane*. However, not all such collections of dance music in this period are necessarily called 'sonatas', and likewise, not all sonatas that incorporate dance movements are necessarily for dancing (real or implied), or even for the chamber.

Late-Seicento composers remark on various circumstances for which they wrote and then published their dances. They most often refer to the dilettante's recreation in dancing, or in playing and listening to dance music. In the preface of his *Armonia capricciosa di suonate musicali da camera*, op. 1 (Milan, 1681), Tomaso Motta – composer, *maestro di ballo*, and performer on both plucked and bowed string instruments – offers a number of services to his customers, including teaching the steps that his sonatas might accompany:

---

44 S. de Brossard, *Dictionnaire de musique*, 3rd edn (Amsterdam, *c.* 1708), pp. 139–40.
45 Sparti, ' "Baroque or not Baroque – is That the Question?" '.

should you perhaps desire to have this or that *arietta* scored for two or three instruments, that is, a four-, five- or six-string mandolin, archlutes and guitars, or should you care to learn the dance steps for these sonatas, part Italian and part French, or *ciaccone alla Spagnola*, or if you have canzonettas, motets and sinfonias to transpose by number in whatever *tuono* or instrument, I would be happy to serve you privately.

In Giovanni Maria Bononcini's (1642–78) *Arie, correnti, sarabande, gighe, et allemande a violino, e violone, over spinetta*, op. 4 (Bologna, 1671), the composer notes in an effusive dedication to Obizzo Guidoni that he wrote these dances to cater to Guidoni's enthusiasm for playing the violone. There is also ample evidence for the use of dance music as a pedagogical tool, not simply in learning to dance, but also in learning to play an instrument and to compose. The pieces in Gasparo Zanetti's *Il scolaro* (Milan, 1645) are, according to its title-page, 'for learning to play the violin and other instruments. Newly published, in which are contained the true principles of *arie, passi e mezzi, saltarelli, gagliarde, zoppe, balletti, alemane* and *correnti*'. We have numerous other examples, including Giorgio Buoni's three publications of instrumental works (all Bologna, 1693) composed by his pupils in the *Concerto de' putti*, which comprise both dance and non-dance music.

The pedagogical uses of the *sonata da camera* are also apparent in the education of boys, particularly the nobility, in the context of the Jesuit colleges that sprang up in the seventeenth century.[46] The Collegio de' Nobili di Parma, founded in 1601 by Duke Ranuccio I Farnese, had a broad curriculum that included dancing, fencing and horseback riding, along with instruction in piety and letters (*nella pietà, et nelle lettere*). As Ranuccio explained, these skills were 'proper exercises of nobles and necessary to gentlemen in order to converse with others to gain reputation and commendation'.[47] At Jesuit colleges throughout Italy, the use of music centred on dancing and the playing of various instruments. Thus Paris Francesco Alghisi (1666–1733), *maestro di cappella* of the Collegio de' Nobili in Brescia, published a collection of *sonate da camera* in 1693. He refers to his dances as 'miei armonici studii' in his dedication, and as 'miei studii musicali' in his preface, which may suggest their didactic origins in the Collegio. While Francesco Giuseppe de Castro boarded at that same college, and studied with Alghisi, he, too, published a collection of *Trattenimenti armonici da camera a tre* (Bologna, 1695), dedicating them to the 'prencipe' (leader) of an 'accademia' within the college, the Accademia de' Formati. In a preface addressed 'to the

46 Brizzi, *La formazione della classe dirigente nel Sei-Settecento*, p. 26. For music, see Bizzarini, 'Diffusione della sonata a tre nella Brescia di fine Seicento'.
47 Sparti, ' "Baroque or not Baroque – is That the Question?" ', p. 84.

courteous spirit of him who delights in harmony' (*al genio cortese di chi si diletta d'armonia*), he describes the origins of these sonatas:

> Know that I have made recourse to the printing press not out of ambition to be noticed, but merely to satisfy my natural taste and delight, conceived in the practice of handling the bow on a few strings, which for my diversion has been the undertaking of a few years now. These few sonatas are the employment of the time for recreation that is conceded to me in this place that I find myself, and for interruption of the labour of studying *belles lettres* and philosophy . . .

De Castro's efforts, however, were probably neither individual nor extra-curricular, instead fulfilling an important purpose within the Collegio: seventeenth-century librettos of staged entertainments put on as gentlemanly 'academies' (*accademie cavalleresche*) within the Jesuit colleges mention dances, sometimes designating them only as Italian or French *balletti*, and sometimes giving them names according to their staged context (dances of satyrs, of drunkards, of peasants, etc.).[48] Librettos of such entertainments composed and performed by the students of the Collegio de' Nobili in Brescia survive from the period during which de Castro was a student there, and other publications largely of dances by musicians connected with the Brescian Collegio and undoubtedly with its ballet entertainments – including Giulio Taglietti (1695 and 1696; he taught violin there), Luigi Taglietti (1697; *maestro nel Collegio*) and Giacomo Cattaneo (1700; teacher of the psaltery and 'cello) – are known.

Maurizio Cazzati's *Trattenimenti per camera d'arie, correnti, e balletti, a due violini, e violone, se piace*, op. 22 (Bologna, 1660), includes some similar 'theatrical' designations for its dances – a *ballo delle dame, delle cavaglieri, de contadini, de tadeschi* [*sic*], *de satiri, de matacini, delle ombre, delle ninfe* – although Cazzati's print mentions no connection with a Jesuit college. It is worth noting that this print, like de Castro's mentioned above, uses the title 'Trattenimenti'; another example is the *Trattenimenti armonici da camera a tre* (Modena, 1700) by Giacomo Cattaneo, also mentioned above in connection with the Collegio de' Nobili in Brescia (and this print is dedicated to a later leader of the same Accademia de' Formati mentioned by de Castro). However, other collections that use this title – by Giovanni Maria Bononcini (1675), his son Giovanni Bononcini (1685), Bartolomeo Gregori (1698) and Tomaso Pegolotti (1698) – show no perceivable connection with staged entertainments. Also noteworthy is their avoidance of

---

48 Bizzarini, 'Diffusione della sonata a tre nella Brescia di fine Seicento', p. 283; Sparti, ' "Baroque or not Baroque – is That the Question?" ', p. 85.

the term 'sonata da camera', even if they are examples of the genre in anything but name.

One final example of the 'consumption' of *sonate da camera* is known to us because it touched off a minor polemic: the affair of 'Corelli's fifths', when Bolognese musicians playing through the *Allemanda* in Corelli's recently published op. 2 no. 3 (1685) noticed its consecutive fifths and decided to ask him about them.[49] The famous composer's acerbic response to these inquiries makes for entertaining reading, but in this context it is worth pointing out that Corelli, despite such solecisms, did slightly better with his dances than with his church sonatas in his career as the top-selling sonata composer of the seventeenth century.[50] Giovanni Battista Vitali, a distant second to Corelli, similarly saw his dances outsell his other works, which perhaps explains why dance music tended to find favour with contemporary music printers. In one case, the Venetian publisher Alessandro Vincenti went so far as to collect, without permission, various dances by Giovanni Battista Buonamente (*Il quinto libro de varie sonate, sinfonie, gagliarde, corrente, et ariette*, 1629), the printing of which Vincenti dedicated to the composer himself, apologising for his 'theft from love and reverence' (*furto amoroso, e riverente*). Clearly, this music was in high demand and served diverse purposes well.

The *sonata da chiesa* and the 'consideration of the divine'

The *sonata da chiesa* similarly had several functions, prominent among them the embellishment of the liturgy. Brossard defines the *sonata da chiesa*, 'which is to say, proper to the church' as beginning 'usually with a grave and majestic movement, suited to the dignity and sanctity of the place; after which comes some sort of gay and animated fugue, etc.'.[51] This might seem straightforward enough save for the fact that few composers produced collections that actually bear the title 'sonate da chiesa'. Corelli, whom Brossard cites as a model in the third edition of his dictionary (*c.* 1708), never used the term; nor did many of his contemporaries. We have already seen that composers of presumed *sonate da camera* chose other terms for their printed collections (often invoking dance-types); when publishing non-dance music, they preferred to style their collections just 'sonate' or the like. The same applies even to those

---

49 Allsop, *Arcangelo Corelli*, pp. 35–40. For the original documents, see Rinaldi, *Arcangelo Corelli*, pp. 429–44.
50 Fabbri, 'Politica editoriale e musica strumentale in Italia dal Cinque- al Settecento'.
51 Brossard, *Dictionnaire de musique*, p. 139.

who do use 'sonata da camera' (or a cognate) for their prints, such as Giuseppe Torelli (op. 4; 1687–8), Tomaso Antonio Vitali (op. 3; 1695), Antonio Veracini (opp. 2, 3; 1696) and Antonio Caldara (op. 2; 1699). Thus what we might nowadays call a 'sonata da chiesa' was often at the time referred to as just a 'sonata', whether in contradistinction to individual dances or to a 'sonata da camera' in the form of a dance suite.

When 'da chiesa' ('per chiesa' etc.) does occur, it tends to be in contexts that refer (together with 'da camera' etc.) chiefly to potential locations for the performance of different works (or sometimes, the same works) within a single collection, presumably in large part as an advertising ploy rather than with any strong generic meaning: early examples include Tarquinio Merula's *Canzoni overo sonate concertate per chiesa e camera a due et a tre . . . libro terzo*, op. 12 (Venice, 1637), Massimiliano Neri's *Sonate e canzone a quatro da sonarsi con diversi stromenti in chiesa, et in camera, con alcune correnti pure à quattro*, op. 1 (Venice, 1644), and Marco Uccellini's *Sonate, correnti, et arie da farsi con diversi stromenti sì da camera, come da chiesa, a1–3*, op. 4 (Venice, 1645). The apparent exceptions (if they are) come from the latter part of the century, including Giovanni Maria Bononcini's *Sonate da chiesa a due violini*, op. 6 (Venice, 1672), Giovanni Bononcini's *Sinfonie da chiesa a quattro, cioè due violini, alto viola, e violoncello obligato*, op. 5 (Bologna, 1687), Giovanni Battista Vitali's *Sonate da chiesa a due violini*, op. 9 (Amsterdam, 1684), and Benedetto Vinaccesi's *Sfere armoniche, overo Sonate da chiesa a due violini, con violoncello, e parte per l'organo*, op. 2 (Venice, 1692).[52]

At least until the 1680s, then, any 'sonata' could plausibly be *da chiesa*, as it were, unless it is specified to be something else (e.g., 'da camera'). However, in the last decades of the century (and thus, closer in time to Brossard) there was an apparent move towards a more precise terminology as represented by the examples cited immediately above. This is also evident in printers' and booksellers' catalogues. Giovanni Battista Vitali's *Sonate a due, tre, quattro e cinque stromenti*, op. 5 (Bologna, 1669), is advertised in Marino Silvani's catalogue (1698–9) among the 'Sonate da chiesa . . .'; the same applies to Andrea Grossi's opp. 3 and 4 (Bologna, 1682, 1685) and Giovanni Battista Bassani's op. 5 (Bologna, 1683). Something similar occurs in the case of prints identified as containing dance-types: Silvani advertised Vitali's *Correnti e balletti da camera a due violini*, op. 1 (Bologna, 1666), and Bassani's *Balletti, correnti, gighe, e sarabande, a violino e violone, overo spinetta*, op. 1 (Bologna, 1677), as 'sonate da camera' (see also

---

52 See also Domenico Zanatta's op. 1 (Venice, 1689), Giovanni Maria Ruggieri's opp. 3, 4 (Venice: 1693, 1697), Bernardo Tonini's op. 2 (Venice, 1697) and Andrea Fiorè's op. 1 (Modena, 1699).

Vitali's opp. 3 and 4 of 1667 and 1668). This may just have been one particular bookseller's shorthand: another, slightly earlier catalogue, Giacomo Monti's of 1682, tends to be more faithful to the original titles. Nevertheless, it suggests that some change was in the air.

The issue becomes a problem only if one must presume a direct correlation between a sonata's function (and performance location) and its musical form and content. There is little justification for such a presumption. Nonetheless, there is plenty of evidence that sonatas 'da chiesa' were indeed used in church. We have already seen some examples above from earlier in the century, and similar testimony attests to a continuing practice in the mid and late seventeenth century. The dedication to Cardinal Giovanni Battista Pallotta of Giovanni Antonio Leoni's *Sonate di violino a voce sola . . . libro primo*, op. 3 (Rome, 1652) refers to Pallotta's taste for instrumental music 'in the divine service and worship' (*al servitio, e culto divino*); he also says that his sonatas were written specifically for the Santa Casa of Loreto. Likewise, in his *Sonate a tre*, op. 1 (Florence, 1692), Antonio Veracini explains how sonatas enhance sacred devotions, inspiring a 'contemplation of the immortal and heavenly, then passing to the consideration of the divine'. To some extent, there is an element of special pleading here: one effective response to the widespread mistrust of 'meaningless' instrumental music was, precisely, to claim that it could be meaningful on some level (the higher the better). Yet the presence of instrumentalists in religious paintings of the period suggests that the argument was effective. Although instrument-playing angels go back a long way (in part because of references to instruments in the Psalms), in the seventeenth century the violin often becomes symbolic of a moment of divine revelation: Gioacchino Assereto's and Carlo Saraceni's paintings of St Francis in ecstasy, for example, each show an angel playing it. It is significant, too, that in neither case is there any representation of singing, suggesting that pure (instrumental) 'sound' is what matters.[53]

None of this means that the sonata (even if identified as *da chiesa*) was destined exclusively for the church: like the canzona it could be heard in a variety of sacred and secular venues, and could excite the judgement of connoisseurs as much as intimations of the divine. Perhaps the clearest evidence of the independence of function and style is the title of Giuseppe Matteo Alberti's *Concerti per chiesa, e per camera, ad uso dell'accademia, eretta nella sala del Sig. Co[nte] Orazio Leonardo Bargellini*, op. 1 (Bologna, 1713), containing 'concertos for church and for chamber, to be used in the academy'. It is a late example, but it surely reflects a flexibility operating in the period as a whole.

---

53 Dell'Antonio, 'The Eucharist and Saint Francis'.

Topoi, tonality and the churchly

If many sonatas were somehow 'churchly', this was often because of their 'serious' musical content – Brossard's grave and majestic movements followed by animated fugues, if not always in the slow–fast–slow–fast sequence often thought typical of the genre. Other features also enabled sonatas to function *da chiesa*, such as toccata-like introductions (or intonations), ricercar-based or fugal styles, and other movement types referring to 'churchly' genres beyond the sonata. These and other gestures create a field of musical topoi that do not necessarily limit the sonata to church performance, but which certainly make it appropriate for it.

Nowhere is this more obvious than in a specific type of contrapuntal writing invoking the Palestrinian ideal of *prima pratica* vocal polyphony, now canonised as the *stile antico*. The musical features that mark this topos are a ₵ time-signature, a consistently imitative texture, and a principal subject in semibreves and minims through a small melodic range and predominantly in diatonic step-wise motion. The character of such pieces invoking the *stile antico* is sometimes made explicit by composers applying the label 'a cappella' to this music:[54] it is not *a cappella* in the traditional sense (voices without instruments) but it creates a similar ethos to earlier (and modern) *a cappella* vocal music. The musical features of this topos are unmistakable in Corelli's op. 6 concertos, in the sonatas of his imitator Paolo Bellinzani, and in examples by Giuseppe Torelli, Tomaso Antonio Vitali and Giovanni Maria Ruggieri that integrate this style of imitative movement with contrapuntal flourishes more idiomatic to the violin.[55]

Composers of the late Seicento may also be seen to cultivate the characteristics of organ genres associated with particular moments in the liturgy of the Mass. The Grave movements, described by Brossard as majestic, evoke a pathetic style by virtue of their harmonic astringencies – chromaticism, dissonances and cross-relations – that is typical of the *durezze e ligature* organ pieces often used specifically to accompany the Elevation of the Host. Introductions in the style of a toccata (sometimes labelled as such)[56] present another topos that can also be linked to precise moments in the liturgy. Adriano Banchieri's *L'organo suonarino* (Venice, 1605) includes a 'Sonata, Ingresso d'un ripieno', with passagework over sustained chords, among the free instrumental pieces

54 Andrea Fiorè, *Sinfonie da chiesa a tre cioe due violini, e violoncello con il suo basso continuo per l'organo*, op. 1 (Modena, 1699), no. 8; Francesco Onofrio Manfredini, *Sinfonie da chiesa a due violini, col basso per l'organo et una viola a beneplacito*, op. 2 (Bologna, 1709), no. 2.

55 Torelli, *Sinfonie a tre e concerti a quattro*, op. 5 (Bologna, 1692), no. 1; Tomaso Antonio Vitali, *Sonate a tre*, op. 2 (Modena, 1693), no. 8; Giovanni Maria Ruggieri, *Suonate da chiesa*, op. 3 (Venice, 1693), no. 8; Paolo Bellinzani, *Dodici suonate da chiesa a tre . . . ad imitazione d'Arcangelo Corelli* (Bologna, Civico Museo Bibliografico Muscale, DD. 133; MS, 1720s), no. 1.

56 Giovanni Buonaventura Viviani, *Suonate a tre*, op. 1 (Venice, 1673), no. 9.

to be used 'per l'occasione di cinque Salmi', i.e., at the start of an Office. A more flamboyant example is Antonio Croci's 'Toccata del primo tuono per l'Introito' in his *Frutti musicali di messe*, op. 4 (Venice, 1642), where improvised-sounding *passaggi* over held bass notes (clearly intended for the organ) most closely resemble the virtuoso fanfares later found in the sonata.

Sonata composers also cultivate the style of the antiquated ricercar on a chromatic subject in their sonatas, adding another element of *stile antico* respectability by virtue of complex contrapuntal technique: Corelli's op. 1 no. 11 is a good example, and there are others, such as Giovanni Bononcini's *Sinfonie a tre istromenti*, op. 4 (Bologna, 1686) no. 4. Croci's print of liturgical organ music includes four chromatic ricercars, and although he does not specify their place in any liturgy, it is at least possible (to judge by similar examples in the keyboard repertory, e.g., by Frescobaldi in his *Fiori musicali*) that they were intended for the Offertory or Elevation.[57] A final topos even in the 'churchly' sonata is, perhaps surprisingly, dance music. Towards the end of the century, courtly dance-types appear in more and more explicit forms as sonata finales, so that several examples of the 1680s and 1690s are dances in all but name. This might seem the last kind of music to suggest churchliness, and indeed, in the Seicento there were papal proscriptions against the use of profane music in worship just as there had been in previous centuries (such proscriptions themselves become a topos).[58] There is, however, some reason for the appearance of such music at the end of the sonata. If a sonata (like the canzona) could constitute the sounded response to culminating moments (after the Epistle; after Communion; in place of the reprised antiphon after a psalm; at the *Deo gratias* of either Mass or Vespers), then a lively, tuneful triple time could indeed serve a celebratory purpose. The eventual use of dance topoi as finales of non-dance sonatas may illustrate an avant-garde or even outré development in the late-Seicento sonata, but it is no more extreme than 'operatic' Italian settings of the Gloria or militaristic settings of the *Te Deum* in France around this same time.

The influence of church practice on musical style in the sonata extends beyond topoi to issues of tonality (not in the modern sense) which may

57 Compare the 'Sonata quarta, fuga cromatica' in Banchieri's *L'organo suonarino* (again for unspecified purpose), and the ensemble 'ricercar cromatico' in Bernardino Bottazzi's *Choro et organo* (Venice, 1614), otherwise containing organ Masses.

58 The *Piae sollicitudinis* (1657) of Pope Alexander VII, for example, begins: 'We are impelled by the fervor of pious solicitude, out of Our earnest desire to promote the observance of decorum and reverence in the churches of Rome, whence examples of good works go forth into all parts of the world, to banish from them vain introductions of whatever kind, and especially musical harmonies and symphonies in which is introduced anything that is indecorous or not in accord with ecclesiastical ritual, nor free from offense of the Divine Majesty, scandal to the faithful, and hindrance of devotion and elevation of hearts to things that are above'; given in Hayburn, *Papal Legislation on Sacred Music*, p. 76.

Table 14.1 *Adriano Banchieri's eight* tuoni ecclesiastici *(Cartella musicale nel canto figurato, fermo, et contrapunto, 3rd edn (Venice, 1614), pp. 68–83)*

Tuono	Cadenza	System (♮ = *cantus durus*; ♭ = *cantus mollis*)	Corde	Modo di fugare
1	d		f, a	d, a
2	g	♭	b♭, d	g, d
3	a		c, e	a, e
4	e		[not given]	e, a
5	c		e, g	c, g
6	f	♭	a, c	f, c
7	d	♭	f, a	d, a
8	g		c, d	g, d

themselves become topical. In matters of tonal organisation, seventeenth-century Italians spoke of 'tuoni', but they applied this term variously to the eight church modes of medieval theory, to the twelve modes of Renaissance neo-classical theory, and to the eight tonalities known specifically as the *tuoni ecclesiastici* (church tones) that arose in the seventeenth century in connection with *alternatim* psalmody. The church tones are first explained in detail by Adriano Banchieri in 1614, but they represent a performance practice that predates his writings, in which organ versets were used in alternation with psalm verses sung by a choir. In short, the *tuoni ecclesiastici* are eight tonalities originally developed for the purpose of organ substitutions for, or accompaniments to, the eight psalm tones – i.e., the melodic formulas used in psalm singing – at what came to be standard transpositions. According to Banchieri, they were defined by a final (*cadenza*) on a specific pitch, a particular system (*mollis* or *durus*), lesser cadences on other pitches (*corde*), and pitches suitable for points of imitation (*modo di fugare*); these are summarised in Table 14.1 (Banchieri does not give the *corde* for *tuono* 4 presumably because of difficulties related to its 'Phrygian' characteristics). Although Banchieri wrote his instructions for organists, numerous sonata composers followed this principle,[59] sometimes arranging their sonatas according to partial or complete cycles corresponding to the *tuoni ecclesiastici* (and labelling their individual pieces according to their 'tuono'): Tarquinio Merula's *Il quarto libro delle canzoni da suonare a doi, et a tre,*

59 Barnett, 'Modal Theory, Church Keys, and the Sonata at the End of the Seventeenth Century'.

op. 17 (Venice, 1651), and Biagio Marini's *Diversi generi di sonate, da chiesa, e da camera, a due, tre, et a quattro*, op. 22 (Venice, 1655), are cases in point, matching Banchieri's scheme precisely.[60] Here, both Merula and Marini appear to have written a set of versets for *alternatim* psalmody scored for violins, violone and continuo. These pieces, smaller than a multi-movement sonata, are brief binary forms similar to aria ritornellos. Merula and Marini call them 'sinfonie', also a common term for small-scale instrumental pieces used as introductions or interludes within larger works.

Giovanni Legrenzi, by contrast, wrote full-fledged sonatas in the *tuoni ecclesiastici*. His *Sonate a due, e tre . . . libro primo*, op. 2 (Venice, 1655), comprises one group of sonatas *a2* and one *a3*, as mentioned earlier, each ordered by way of the *tuoni ecclesiastici* (but not so labelled).[61] Here the system involves transposition not just down a fifth into *cantus mollis* (adding one flat to the signature, as in Banchieri's *tuono* 2) but also up a fifth (adding one sharp). Thus in Legrenzi's sonatas *a2*, *tuono* 7 is represented by a final on D and a one-sharp signature. This expansion, and an increasing preference for transpositions even to two-flat and two-sharp systems, is clearly apparent in cycles from the second half of the century (see Table 14.2). It is also noteworthy that the prints represented in Table 14.2 variously contain a wide range of scorings (*a1* to *a8*) and, in the case of Galli and Legrenzi, collections of dances. One assumes that ordering by the *tuoni ecclesiastici* and their derivatives has now become a matter of artful display, of affective contrast, or even just of convenience, rather than relating directly to the potential function of this music.

Table 14.2 also reveals how an ordering scheme derived from the *tuoni ecclesiastici* might interact with other such (potential or actual) schemes. Giulio Cesare Arresti's op. 4 (1665) contains twelve sonatas running through some equivalent of the eight *tuoni* in ascending order (d–♮, g–♭; a–♮, e–♮; C–♮, F–♭; D–♯, G–♮), then four tonalities used in common practice that might variously represent the remaining four modes in a twelve-mode system, or else derive from the extended sequence of the *tuoni ecclesiastici* seen in Table 14.2 (d–♭, A–♯♯, E–♯♯♯, c–♭). The merging of the *tuoni ecclesiastici* and the modes, which Banchieri had also considered earlier in the century, is made clear by Giovanni Maria Bononcini, who viewed the *tuoni* as transpositions within the twelve-mode system. His treatise *Musico prattico*, op. 8 (Bologna, 1673), details (pp. 121–4) the twelve 'tuoni, ò modi' (from authentic/plagal D-modes to authentic/plagal

---

60 As we shall see, there are potential connections between the *tuoni ecclesiastici* and the traditional 'church' modes (as there are between psalm tones and modes), but one can demonstrate (by discrepancies between the two systems) that composers often used 'tuono' to refer to the *tuoni ecclesiastici* and not to modes. The most comprehensive study of the *tuoni ecclesiastici* is Dodds, 'The Baroque Church Tones in Theory and Practice'.

61 S. Bonta (ed.), *The Instrumental Music of Giovanni Legrenzi* (Cambridge, MA, 1984), pp. xiv–xv.

Table 14.2 *Church tones and the sonata*

tuono	Legrenzi (1655)	Legrenzi (1656)	Placuzzi (1667)	P. Degli Antoni (1676)	G. B. Degli Antoni (1690)	Galli (1691)	Legrenzi (1691)
1	d-♮	d-♮	d-♮	d-♮	d-♮	d-♮	d-♮
2	g-♭	g-♭	g-♭	g-♭	g-♭	g-♭	g-♭
3	a-♮	a-♮	a-♮	a-♮	a-♮	a-♮	a-♮
4	e-♮	e-♮	e-♮	e-♯	e-♮	e-♮	e-♮
5	C-♮	C-♮	C-♮	C-♮	C-♮	c-♭♭	C-♭
6		F-♭	F-♭	F-♭	F-♭	F-♭	F-♭
7	D-♯	c-♮	D-♯♯	D-♯	E-♯♯*	d-♭	D-♯
8	G-♮	G-♮	G-♮	G-♮	G-♮	C-♮	G-♮/e-♯
9		d-♮	D-♯♯	B♭-♭	E♭-♭♭	d-♮	B♭-♭/B♭-♭♭
10			C-♮	A-♯♯	b-♯♯		B♭-♭♭
11				c-♭♭			a-♮
12				E♭-♭♭			a-♮

Sources: Giovanni Legrenzi, *Sonate a due, e tre . . . libro primo,* op. 2 (Venice, 1655); Legrenzi, *Sonate da chiesa, da camera . . . a tre,* op. 4 (Venice, 1656); Gioseffo Maria Placuzzi, *Suonate a duoi, a tre, a quattro, a cinque e otto instromenti,* op. 1 (Bologna, 1667); Pietro Degli Antoni, *Sonate a violino solo,* op. 4 (Bologna, 1676); Giovanni Battista Degli Antoni, *Ricercate a violino, e violoncello, o clavicembalo,* op. 5 (Bologna, 1690); Domenico Galli, *Trattenimento musicale sopra il violoncello* (MS in Modena, Biblioteca Estense, Mus. c.81; MS, 1691); Legrenzi, *Balletti, e correnti a cinque stromenti . . . libro quinto postumo,* op. 16 (Venice, 1691).

* G sharp is not indicated in the key signature, but is written in the music itself.

C-modes), then (p. 137) explains those ordinarily used by composers (*Quali de sopradetti Tuoni vengano ordinariamente pratticati da Compositori*), giving the common 'equivalent' for each of the first eight modes in ascending order (d–♮, g–♭; a–♮, a–♮; C–♮, F–♭; d–♭, G–♮). The rather odd equivalent for mode 7 (d–♭) undoubtedly derives from Banchieri's *tuono* 7 (see Table 14.1). More typical, however, is Bononcini's (and many other composers') use of what we would recognise as A minor to represent one or both Phrygian modes: even in the Renaissance, the E-Phrygian tonality had quite strong 'A minor' tendencies because of the inability to build a permissible triad on the fifth degree (B–D–F embraces a diminished fifth), and also because of the role of the fourth and sixth degrees, rather than the fifth, in psalm-tones 3 and 4. But even Bononcini's theory does not quite match his own practice. His *Sonate da chiesa a due violini*, op. 6 (Venice, 1672), takes transpositions still further. For example, he labels as mode 11 (C-authentic) pieces in C–♮, B♭–♭♭, and D–♯♯ (respectively transposing the mode down a tone and up a tone), while F–♭ and E♭–♭♭ represent mode 12 (transposing the mode down one fifth and, inconsistently, up a minor third). Similarly, mode 9 is represented by 'B minor', and mode 10 by 'E minor' (transposing the A-authentic mode up a tone and the A-plagal mode down a fourth), and mode 1 by 'D minor' and 'C minor' (the latter transposing the mode down a tone). Mode 2, however, is in the more standard form (found throughout the period) of 'G minor' (g–♭).

By this stage, it is no longer clear whether these 'keys' (for want of a better term) really are equivalent to, or representative of, particular modes or *tuoni ecclesiastici*, or whether any implicit or explicit designation of mode or tone for each of these keys is not, in fact, just a desperate attempt to bring some kind of theoretical order to practical chaos. Yet despite the apparent confusions, it is worth noting some consequences. First, the common practice of notating these keys with a signature containing one fewer flat(s) or sharp(s) than the modern norm (e.g., g–♭ rather than g–♭♭; D–♯ rather than D–♯♯) clearly derives from traditional 'modal' transpositions, where a mode or *tuono* could be transposed down a fifth by adding one flat to the signature (d–♮ to g–♭) and up a fifth by adding one sharp (G–♮ to D–♯); the additional flat or sharp (E♭ in 'G minor'; C♯ in 'D major') would be provided by notated accidentals, or indeed might not even be included, in which case the key sounds more 'modal' than tonal. Second, even as we move away from the eight- or twelve-mode system to the two 'modes' of major–minor tonality, and also towards so-called 'equal' temperament (a scale of twelve semitones each of the same size), keys that should, in principle, 'sound' the same by virtue of transposition within an equal-tempered system (C major, D major etc.) in fact can have different qualities, and can proceed in different ways, by virtue of their separate associations with older modes or *tuoni*.

Concerto and *concerto grosso*

Much of the foregoing discussion of topoi and tonalities applies to Arcangelo Corelli's op. 6 *concerti grossi* (Amsterdam, 1714), which fall easily into line with the stylistic developments of the late-Seicento sonata save the distinction of their particular scoring. As he explains on the title-page, Corelli scores his concertos for an ensemble that contrasts an obbligato *concertino* (two violins and violoncello) with an *ad libitum* 'concerto grosso', i.e., what is now termed the *ripieno* (two violins, viola and 'basso'), each with figured-bass parts for continuo accompaniment. One can also double the parts of the *ripieno* (*che si possono radoppiare*). Thus these pieces can be performed in three ways with increasing degrees of textural contrast: by just two violins, 'cello and continuo; by a *concertino* and one-to-a-part *ripieno* (or to put it another way, with an *ensemble* comprising four violins, one viola, one 'cello and one bass plus continuo, of which two of the violinists and the 'cellist play solo as the *concertino*); and by a *concertino* and a *ripieno*, the latter with two or more players to a part. In this light, the *concerto grosso* appears to be, in essence, a sonata writ large, and with more systematic ways of exploiting contrasting sonorities. Such contrasts, however, are common even in sonatas *per se* (for example, where virtuoso passagework might alternate with more block-like homophony), and similarly, other musical ideas and procedures presented in Corelli's *concerti grossi* are not so different from earlier sonata types. To give a simple example, we find fast-tempo movements where violins move in dotted-crotchet-plus-quaver rhythms over a running bass line in quavers or semiquavers in the trio-sonatas op. 1 no. 11 and op. 4 no. 8 (where the type is identified as an 'allemanda'), as well as in the *concerto grosso* op. 6 no. 3 (also called 'allemanda'). Indeed, Corelli's *concerto grosso* idiom, with a *ripieno* offset by a *concertino*, probably derives from his use in the early 1680s of contrasted instrumental grouping in the performance of his sonatas as documented by Georg Muffat in his *Armonico tributo* (Salzburg, 1682). Corelli, moreover, is likely to have inherited this from earlier scoring practices adopted by Alessandro Stradella from the 1660s and 1670s.[62]

Of course, block contrasts of sonorities produced by pitting one ensemble against another was typical of the polychoral writing often, if wrongly, associated primarily with Venetian composers. Following Gabrieli's famous use of polychoral scoring for instruments in his first book of *Sacrae symphoniae*

---

62 Jander, '*Concerto grosso* Instrumentation in Rome in the 1660's and 1670's'.

(Venice, 1597), composers of canzonas and then sonatas exploited such textural contrast, usually in pieces for eight or more instrumentalists but sometimes applied to smaller ensembles. The sonatas in Maurizio Cazzati's *Correnti e balletti a cinque . . . con alcune sonate a 5. 6. 7. 8.*, op. 15 (Venice, 1654), illustrate the typical practice of mid-century composers: the sonatas *a5–7* treat the parts as contributing to a single texture, often focussing on fugal imitation, while the sonata *a8* is for two four-part groups of strings (violin, alto and tenor violas, violone) and alternates between massed sonorities and antiphonal effects. Similar principles underpin the larger-scale sonatas included in Francesco Cavalli's *Musiche sacre* (Venice, 1656), Gioseffo Placuzzi's *Suonate a duoi, a tre, a quattro, a cinque e otto instromenti*, op. 1 (Bologna, 1667), and Giovanni Bononcini's *Sinfonie a 5. 6. 7. e 8. istromenti*, op. 3 (Bologna, 1685).

Cazzati wrote no further polychoral sonatas, but the textures and effects of that subgenre influenced the trumpet sonatas of his *Sonate a due, tre, quattro, e cinque, con alcune per tromba*, op. 35 (Bologna, 1665), where the solo trumpet in effect substitutes for one of the two string groups. Here he was simply adapting an old formula to new circumstances: in 1657, he became *maestro di cappella* in S. Petronio, Bologna, where he had access to the trumpeters of the long-established civic ensemble, the Concerto Palatino, and needed to fill an enormous performing space. Other composers who followed Cazzati's example, writing sonatas for trumpet and strings for the Bolognese virtuosos, include Petronio Franceschini, Giuseppe Torelli, Giovanni Bononcini and Giuseppe Jacchini. Here they experimented with recapitulatory forms, drawing upon the tendency from Gabrieli onwards to use block repetitions and refrains to bring cohesion to polychoral writing. These forms, used in place of the traditional fugal movement, feature concise thematic material stated at the opening and recurring in the manner of a frame around lengthier and thematically varied phrases.

Clearly, we seem to be moving towards the solo concerto in terms both of texture (one instrument standing out from the ensemble by virtue of virtuoso writing and/or a contrasting sonority) and of structure (incipient ritornello procedures).[63] In his *Sinfonie a tre e concerti a quattro*, op. 5 (Bologna, 1692), Giuseppe Torelli (1658–1709) distinguishes the six *sinfonie* from the six *concerti* by recommending that the latter be performed with multiple players on each part. In terms of texture, the *sinfonie* contain some of Torelli's most intricate fugues, whereas the concertos (which do not have a solo part) are more homophonic or only minimally contrapuntal; the latter also contain Allegro

---

63 Talbot, 'The Concerto Allegro in the Early Eighteenth Century' is a fine account of incipient ritornello procedures in Italian concertos between 1680 and 1720.

movements that begin and conclude with the same material, and brief slow movements that sometimes amount to little more than a cadence. The concertos essentially focus on broader gestures designed for the expansive (and problematically resonant) acoustic of S. Petronio.

In this case, Torelli's use of the term 'concerto' seems to refer back to an older meaning of the word (see above), i.e., just an instrumental ensemble. However, his *Concerti musicali a quattro*, op. 6 (Augsburg, 1698), are somewhat different. Here he is more precise than in his instructions for op. 5, recommending three or four instruments on each part. But he also notes that where the upper part is marked 'solo', it should be played by just one violin.[64] In Torelli's *Concerti grossi*, op. 8, issued posthumously in 1709, one or two violin soloists (*violini di concerto*) are thematically distinguished from the ensemble, and are given separate parts. Moreover, the discursive and virtuosic character of the solo writing throws into relief the recurring thematic material played by the full ensemble. This thematic material now comprises ritornellos that begin and end the piece and also occur internally in what we would recognise as the dominant or another related key.

These particular lines of development in the instrumental concerto have been overshadowed, retrospectively, both by the Vivaldian solo concerto and its reception among German composers in the eighteenth century, and by the Corellian *concerto grosso* and its imitations by Georg Muffat and, more idiosyncratically, Handel. In short, the search for precedents for Vivaldi and Handel, and for other early eighteenth-century developments, has tended to distort the varieties apparent in late seventeenth-century concertos (whether so called or not). Indeed, the term 'concerto' applied to pieces contrasting a solo instrument with a tutti ensemble does not appear until Torelli's op. 6 of 1698, and even here it has echoes of older senses of the word (as in Torelli's op. 5). Torelli's *Concerti grossi*, op. 8, moreover, includes pieces that would now be called solo concertos even though they are part of a collection bearing the same genre designation as Corelli's otherwise dissimilar op. 6. It may, in the end, be impossible to create a clear or even useful distinction between the two genres in ways that would emerge in the following decades, and one might reasonably ask why any distinctions between the solo concerto and *concerto grosso* should matter so greatly when both are, in essence, large-ensemble works meant to celebrate large-scale events, such as important religious feasts and princely entertainments.

---

64 Torelli, however, uses solo/tutti designations in only three of the twelve concertos (nos. 6, 10, 12). See G. Torelli, *Concerti musicali, opus 6* (1698), ed. J. Suess, 'Recent Researches in Music of the Baroque Era', 115 (Middleton, WI, 2002), pp. viii–xii, for a discussion of movement types and formal structures. See also D. K. Wilson (ed.), *Georg Muffat on Performance Practice*; Maunder, *The Scoring of Baroque Concertos*.

The sonata abroad

The dissemination of the concerto to Salzburg, Passau and London in the hands of the internationally travelled Muffat and Handel constitutes just one facet of the remarkable exportation of Italian genres around the turn of the eighteenth century. The sonata, in particular, enjoyed phenomenal international success at this time. The popularity of Corelli's sonatas far exceeded that of his Italian contemporaries to judge by their printing history, and they enjoyed similar success abroad. Manuscript copies of his music survive in Spain in the archives of cathedrals in Segovia and Jaca, and in the Iberian colonies of the New World; in England they well outsold the masterly examples of Henry Purcell; and in France, Corelli was soon taken as the model of Italian music in François Couperin's *Le Parnasse, ou L'apothéose de Corelli*, a 'grande sonade en trio' included in his *Les goûts réunis* (Paris, 1724).

Corelli's success was the key to the triumph of the Italian sonata, whose dissemination stands on a par with that of the emerging *opera seria*. Referring to the years around 1700, Brossard recalls 'the rage for writing sonatas in the Italian manner' among Parisian composers, particularly organists,[65] and from the early 1690s onward, François Couperin, Elisabeth Jacquet de la Guerre, Jean-Féry Rebel and Brossard himself were composing them for an ensemble of two trebles (violins or flutes), bass (violoncello or viola da gamba) and harpsichord.[66] Published examples would follow in Paris in the first decade of the eighteenth century, starting with Jean-François Dandrieu's *Livre de sonates en trio*, op. 1 (Paris, 1705).[67] In England, some Italian sonatas were known by the end of the 1670s, so manuscripts in the Bodleian Library in Oxford would suggest, perhaps by way of the arrival of the violin virtuoso Nicola Matteis early in that decade.[68] But they were still regarded as novelties in 1683 when in London Henry Purcell published his *Sonnata's of III Parts*, for two violins,

---

65 Brossard, *Catalogue des livres de musique, théorique et prattique, vocalle et instrumentalle* (Paris, Bibliothèque Nationale, Rés. Vm⁸ 20; MS, 1724), p. 382, given in Laurencie, *L'école française de violon de Lully à Viotti*, i: 143; see also Newman, *The Sonata in the Baroque Era*, p. 363.

66 Sadie, 'Charpentier and the Early French Ensemble Sonata' discusses an earlier French sonata by Marc-Antoine Charpentier, probably composed in the mid 1680s, and scored for '2 flûtes allemandes, 2 dessus de violon, une basse de viole, une basse de violon à 5 cordes, un clavecin et un téorbe'.

67 Violinist-composers who performed and composed dances, if not sonatas, such as Pierre Caroubel, Jacques Cordier, Louis Constantin, Guillaume Dumanoir, and Michel Mazuel, were a fixture of the French court throughout the seventeenth century as members of the *Vingt-quatre Violons du Roi* or the earlier *Violons de la Chambre du Roi*. See Anthony, *French Baroque Music*, pp. 19–24, 345–60, for an overview of French instrumental ensembles and their music during the seventeenth century.

68 Stevens, 'Seventeenth-Century Italian Instrumental Music in the Bodleian Library'; Walls, 'The Influence of the Italian Violin School in 17th-Century England'. Walls (p. 577) views the Bodleian manuscripts as evidence of a Restoration-era surge in imported Italian instrumental music, but he also allows (p. 587 n. 7) that some of that collection could have come to England later, collected or copied during visits abroad by James Sherard in 1698–9.

bass, and organ or harpsichord (discussed below), in the preface of which he explained not only the Italian terms employed in the music, but also his desire 'to bring the seriousness and gravity of that [Italian] sort of musick into vogue, and reputation among our countrymen, whose humour, 'tis time now, should begin to loath the levity and balladry of our [French] neighbours'.[69]

By contrast, in German-speaking Europe the sonata, and before it the canzona, had long been known and cultivated. For much of the seventeenth century, canzonas and sonatas were taken northwards by Italian composers mostly from the Veneto who pursued careers at the court of the Habsburg emperors in Vienna (they were aggressively recruited in the first half of the century by Ferdinand II, Ferdinand III and Leopold I), further north in Dresden or Nuremberg, and as far away as Kraków and Warsaw. For instance, the Venetian keyboard player and composer (and student of Giovanni Gabrieli) Giovanni Priuli (c. 1575–1626), whose output includes instrumental canzonas and polychoral sonatas, spent parts of his career in Graz and Vienna as *Hofkapellmeister* under the Archduke Ferdinand, later the Emperor Ferdinand II. Priuli was succeeded in Vienna by another Venetian keyboard player and composer, Giovanni Valentini (1582/3–1649), who had earlier served Sigismund III in Poland.

Italian violinist–composers also pursued careers beyond the Alps and brought not only their compositions but also their virtuosic style of violin-playing. Antonio Bertali (1605–69) succeeded Valentini as *Kapellmeister* at the imperial court; the violinist Giovanni Battista Buonamente (d. 1642) was *musicista da camera* to Emperor Ferdinand II in Vienna; and Giovanni Antonio Pandolfi-Mealli was employed at Innsbruck when his virtuosic sonatas for violin and continuo were published there in 1660 (little else is known about him). Further north, Ottavio Maria Grandi, some of whose 1628 sonatas are preserved in manuscript in Wrocław, served at the Polish court of King Sigismund III in Warsaw during the first decade of the seventeenth century;[70] Biagio Marini was *Kapellmeister* for the Wittelsbach family in Neuberg from 1621 until 1649, with visits to Brussels and Düsseldorf; and Carlo Farina (c. 1604–39) was *Konzertmeister* in Dresden, but later travelled to Gdańsk and Vienna. The direction could also be reversed: as mentioned previously, northern composers went south, and over the course of the century, Hans Leo Hassler, Gregor Aichinger, Adam

---

69 The Italianate sonata may have been a novelty in Restoration England, but music, especially dances, performed by violin ensembles date to the sixteenth century. According to Holman, *Four and Twenty Fiddlers*, pp. 60–77, rebec consorts and rebecs in mixed ensembles were known at the court of Henry VIII, but these gave way from 1540 onward to string ensembles with violins. Violinists, as Holman carefully documents, were also an essential component of English court music throughout the seventeenth century, culminating in the '24 Violins' that was organised by Charles II in imitation of the French *Vingt-quatre Violons du Roi*.

70 Wrocław, Biblioteka Uniwersytecka, MS 111, compiled by the Polish violinist and composer Adam Jarzębski. Grandi's sonatas were published as *Sonate per ogni sorte di stromenti a 1. 2. 3. 4. & 6.*, op. 2 (Venice, 1628).

Jarzębski, Johann Rosenmüller, Johann Jakob Walther and Georg Muffat all spent time in Italy, whether to study or to seek professional livelihood.

The dissemination of Italian instrumental music can also be traced in several music collections associated with central and northern European cities and courts at various points in the century. These illustrate how northern musicians kept up to date with Italian musical styles, and how a network of contacts between north and south (and within the north) must have existed in order to bring together a wide range of works from different nations.[71] The Rost Codex, compiled during the 1660s to 1680s by the German copyist Franz Rost probably for use by the Margrave of Baden-Baden, contains the instrumental works of several Italians (Valentini, Bertali, Cazzati, G. B. Vitali) alongside those by German, Austrian, Polish and Czech composers.[72] The collection amassed by Karl Liechtenstein-Kastelkorn, Prince-Bishop of Olomouc from 1664 until his death in 1695, includes sonatas by Bertali, Farina, Marini, Alessandro Poglietti and Marco Uccellini. These stand alongside those of numerous composers of other nationalities, most famous among whom are the violinist Johann Heinrich Schmelzer (d. 1680), Bertali's successor as *Kapellmeister* at the imperial court, and Heinrich Ignaz Franz von Biber (1644–1704), the unparalleled violin virtuoso who was employed by Prince-Bishop Karl during the 1660s (he later moved to Salzburg). A lesser-known collection inventoried by the Frankfurt am Main violinist Johann Georg Beck (d. 1638) does not survive, but copies of his inventory do, and these show that the latest Italian violin music, much of it by *stile moderno* composers, was already known in Frankfurt in the 1630s.[73]

The German sonata and suite

The impact of Italian composers on their northern counterparts varied widely. On the one hand, the sonata became the compositional vehicle of the most talented violinists of the century in the works of Schmelzer, Biber and Walther.[74]

---

71 The most striking example of the easy dissemination of musical repertories in manuscript copies during the seventeenth century is found in the vast repertory amassed by the Swedish organist and composer Gustaf Düben (*c*. 1628–1690). Most of Düben's collection comprises vocal works, but there are also some 300 instrumental pieces by Italian, German and French composers. In 1732, the collection was donated to the library of the University of Uppsala by Düben's son Anders, where it remains today.

72 Moser, 'Eine Pariser Quelle zur Wiener Triosonate des ausgehenden 17. Jahrhunderts'.

73 I am grateful to Brian Brooks for giving me an advance copy of his 'Etienne Nau, Breslau 114 and the Early Seventeenth-Century German Violin Fantasia'. A listing of the musical items in Beck's library may be found in Epstein, 'Das Musikwesen der Stadt Frankfurt', pp. 64–7.

74 Beckmann, *Das Violinspiel in Deutschland vor 1700*, furnishes an early but useful account of seventeenth-century German and Austrian composers for the violin (from Georg Hasz to Johann Jakob Walther) and the influence of Italian virtuosos.

On the other, a much broader array of composers integrated both the sonata and its *a2* and *a3* scorings into their publications of dances.

The pavans and galliards composed in considerable number by German composers from the beginning of the seventeenth century were the product of English influence by way of Hamburg and the court of Denmark. Early examples by William Brade, Johannes Thesselius, Paul Peuerl, Johann Hermann Schein and Isaac Posch group dances in sequence, such as Thesselius's (1609) paduana–intrada–galliard, or Schein's (1617) padovana–gagliarda–courente–allemande (plus its 'tripla').[75] Such sequences may also show varying degrees of thematic connectedness between the dances, producing a variation-suite. Content and orderings will vary, however, and at times composers will not even group their dances into suites, instead allowing performers to create their own out of collections ordered only by dance-type.

The Italian influence in this repertory appears first in the introduction of the basso continuo and the reduction of the texture from four or five parts to scorings *a2* (two trebles) or *a3* (two trebles and a bass) and continuo: this is the change from Schein's 1617 suites to Johannes Vierdanck's *Erster Theil neuer Pavanen, Gagliarden, Balletten und Correnten, mit zwey Violinen und einem Violon, nebenst dem basso continuo* (Greifswald, 1637). A second Italianate influence is the use of multi-sectional, non-dance sonatas (also called 'sinfonia' or 'sonatina') as introductory movements in each suite. This change is again reflected in the titles of printed editions, as in Matthias Kelz's *Primitiae musicales seu Concentus novi harmonici. Italis dicti: Le sonate, intrade, mascarade . . .* (Augsburg, 1658) or Jakob Scheiffelhut's *Musicalischer Gemüths-Ergötzungen erstes Werck . . . Sonaten, Allemanden, Couranten, Balletten, Sarabanden und Giquen* (Augsburg, 1684). The three sonatas in Johann Pezel's *Musica vespertina lipsiaca* (Leipzig, 1669) reveal the trend: the second, for example, begins with a movement in four sections each marked 'Adagio', followed by a prelude, allemande, courante, sarabande and gigue (Pezel uses the French titles, which also starts to become something of a pattern). Johann Rosenmüller's (*c.* 1619–1684) output for instrumental ensembles – beginning with his *Paduanen, Alemanden, Couranten, Balletten, Sarabanden, mit drey Stimmen* [two trebles and bass] *und ihrem Basso pro Organo, gesetzet* (Leipzig, 1645) – neatly illustrates some of the developments discussed

---

75 For concise accounts of the German dance-suite in the early seventeenth century, see J. Schop, *Erster Theil newer Paduanen (1633)*, ed. A. Spohr, 'Recent Researches in Music of the Baroque Era', 125 (Middleton, WI, 2003), pp. x–xii; and the introduction to W. Brade, *Pavans, Galliards, and Canzonas, 1609*, ed. B. Thomas (London, 1982). The main sources are Brade, *Newe außerlesene Paduanen, Galliarden, Canzonen, Allmand und Coranten* (Hamburg, 1609); Thesselius, *Neue liebliche Paduanen, Intraden und Galliarden* (Nuremberg, 1609); Peuerl, *Neue Padouan, Intrada, Däntz unnd Galliarda* (Nuremberg, 1611); Posch, *Musicalische Ehrenfreudt. Das jst: Allerley neuer Balleten, Gagliarden, Couranten und Täntzen teutscher Arth* (Regensburg, 1618) and *Musicalische Tafelfreudt. Das ist: Allerley neuer Paduanen und Gagliarden . . .* (Nuremberg, 1621). See also Kokole, 'The Compositions of Isaac Posch'.

here within the work of a single composer. The title of his 1667 collection (*Sonate da camera cioè sinfonie, alemande, correnti, balletti, sarabande, da suonare con cinque stromenti da arco*) suggests that it is made up of *sonate da camera* each comprising a sinfonia and succeeding dances (unless Rosenmüller is just using the term to refer to each separate piece in the print). For example, the first piece therein comprises a six-section sinfonia (Grave, Allegro–Grave–Allegro, Allegro, Adagio, Allegro–Adagio, Allegro; the third and sixth sections have the same music), followed by an 'Alemanda', 'Correnta', 'Intrata', 'Ballo' and 'Sarabanda'. (Rosenmüller's use of reprised material in the sinfonia is not untypical of mid-century Italian sonatas and earlier canzonas.) The expansive sinfonia must have held Rosenmüller's interest, because his final publication of instrumental music, the *Sonate a 2. 3. 4. e 5. stromenti da arco et altri* (Nuremberg, 1682), keeps the opening sequence of non-dance movements and simply drops the dances.

The Salzburg-based Georg Muffat's (1653–1704) *Armonico tributo, cioè sonate di camera commodissime a pocchi, o a molti stromenti* (Salzburg, 1682) illustrates yet another approach to the dance-suite. Here the term 'sonata da camera' is definitely a collective one, referring to five works in the print that freely intermingle dances with non-dance movements. Thus the first sonata contains a 'Grave', 'Allegro', 'Allemanda', 'Grave', 'Gavotta', 'Grave' and 'Menuet', and the fifth an 'Allemanda', 'Adagio', 'Fuga', 'Adagio' and 'Passacaglia'. Muffat's use of dance-types that he styles as 'gavotta', 'menuet' and 'borea' reflect the French influence on him after his travels to Paris. Together with his Corellian Grave movements, we can also see an early instance in Muffat's output of the attempt to bring together Italian and French styles that he would later advertise in his *concerti grossi*, the *Ausserlesene Instrumental-Music* (Passau, 1701). The 1682 sonatas also share *concerto grosso*-type procedures, with an *a3 concertino* distinguished (by way of 'S[olo]' and 'T[utti]' markings) from a five-part *ripieno*, which may be doubled (*raddoppiate*) by extra players. Muffat provides the further options of performance *a3* by the *concertino* alone (as Corelli would do in his op. 6; see above), and *a4* and *a5* by adding middle parts to the *concertino*.

Muffat was clearly influenced by performance practices adopted by Corelli: he visited Rome in the early 1680s and noted his debt to the Italian composer in his 1701 *concerti grossi*. However, Muffat's arrangement of dances and non-dance movements is not Corellian, and it instead continues German experiments with various dance-suite arrangements. Here, in fact, the influence seems to have gone from north to south rather than the reverse, and Muffat may even have had some effect on Corelli himself.[76] There is a marked change

---

76 Here I owe a significant debt to Daverio, 'In Search of the *Sonata da camera* before Corelli'; for a counter-argument, see Mangsen, 'The "Sonata da camera" before Corelli'. See also M. Talbot, 'The Taiheg, the Pira and Other Curiosities of Benedetto Vinaccesi's "Suonate da camera a tre", Op. 1'.

Table 14.3 *Movement titles in the twelve* sonate da camera *in Corelli's op. 2 (1685)*

1 Preludio (Largo)	Allemanda (Largo)	Corrente (Allegro)	Gavotta (Allegro)
2 [none]	Allemanda (Adagio)	Corrente (Allegro)	Giga (Allegro)
3 Preludio (Largo)	Allemanda (Allegro)	Adagio	Allemanda (Presto)
4 Preludio (Adagio)	Allemanda (Presto)	Grave–Adagio	Giga (Allegro)
5 Preludio (Adagio)	Allemanda (Allegro)	Sarabanda (Adagio)	Tempo di Gavotta (Allegro)
6 [none]	Allemanda (Largo)	Corrente (Allegro)	Giga (Allegro)
7 Preludio (Adagio)	Allemanda (Allegro)	Corrente (Allegro)	Giga (Allegro)
8 Preludio (Largo)	Allemanda (Largo)	Tempo di Sarabanda (Largo)	Tempo di Gavotta (Allegro)
9 [none]	Allemanda (Largo)	Tempo di Sarabanda (Largo)	Giga (Allegro)
10 Preludio (Adagio)	Allemanda (Allegro)	Sarabanda (Largo)	Corrente (Allegro)
11 Preludio (Adagio)	Allemanda (Presto)	Giga (Allegro)	
12 Ciaccona (Largo–Allegro)			

in the Italian *sonata da camera* in the years following Muffat's visit, and three features of Corelli's 1685 *sonate da camera*, op. 2, are unprecedented or rare in previous Italian music: the use of the term 'sonata da camera' to refer collectively to a suite of movements, and not an individual dance; the frequent use of non-dance introductions (Corelli uses the term 'Preludio'); and the mixing of dance and non-dance movements (see Table 14.3). Similar trends are apparent in Corelli's op. 4 (1694) and suggest an increasingly flexible approach to the *sonata da camera* after Muffat's example.

To be sure, groupings of two to four dances related by key and sometimes by thematic material had existed in Italy prior to any potential German influence, as with Andrea Grossi's two books of *Balletti, correnti, sarabande, e gighe a tre*, opp. 1 and 2 (Bologna, 1678, 1679). With Corelli, however, the overall conception and content of the genre changes, and it is the new idea of the *sonata da camera* that immediately influenced Corelli's contemporaries, creating a reciprocal network of influences between German and Italian composers. In sum, the Italianate sonata became a part of the German suite as a multi-section or multi-movement introduction. Rosenmüller detached that introductory portion from the dances to create the free-standing sonatas of his last instrumental publication. Muffat, by contrast, intermingled the introductory sonata's movements among the dances in his suites and firmly identified the sonata itself with the complete suite. Corelli took that idea and produced a more compact version of it, comparable in length to those of his Italian predecessors, but conceived according to Muffat's example. It is this Corellian type that we find described in Brossard's *Dictionnaire*, but its history was more complex than he knew.

Looking towards the future of dance-suites for the violin, we might note one more composer of suites and sonatas, the violinist Johann Paul von Westhoff (1656–1705), who bears mentioning because of his six extraordinary suites – allemande, courante, sarabande and gigue (there are no preludes) – for the unaccompanied violin (1696). All of Westhoff's known works were written for the solo violin, both with and without continuo. The unaccompanied suites, however, are particularly striking not only for their technical challenges (all of the dances, fast and slow, feature chordal writing, some written to mimic fugal imitation), but also for the precedent they establish for the later sonatas and partitas for unaccompanied violin of Johann Sebastian Bach (1720).[77] Indeed, Bach and Westhoff overlapped in Weimar in 1703, and Bach must have known the richly polyphonic violin suites of the older composer. Moreover, the fact that both wrote non-programmatic dance-suites which do not employ *scordatura* distinguishes their suites from the violin music of the Austrian composers Schmelzer and Biber (discussed below). While Westhoff is notably more determined than Bach to incorporate multiple stops in all of his otherwise shorter and harmonically simpler movements, their common aim to create distinctive and often virtuosic repertory using courtly dances – French and Italian in Westhoff; distinctly French in Bach – places both in a long tradition of German composers of suites.

Purcell

Henry Purcell (1659–95) presents a particularly intriguing case of late-Seicento sonata reception. He acknowledged his 'just imitation of the most fam'd Italian Masters' in the preface to his first published set of sonatas of 1683, although these pieces also prompted Roger North to claim that they were 'clog'd with somewhat of an English vein'.[78] Purcell's two collections of sonatas are the *Sonnata's of III Parts: Two Viollins and Basse; to the Organ or Harpsecord* (London, 1683) and the posthumous *Ten Sonata's in Four Parts* (London, 1697).[79] He

77 Until their rediscovery by Péter Várnai in the early 1970s, Westhoff's unaccompanied suites of 1696 were unknown. For biographical information on Westhoff and a discussion of the suites, see J. P. Westhoff, *Six suites pour violon seul sans basse*, ed. P. Várnai (Winterthur, 1975). See also Aschmann, *Das deutsche polyphone Violinspiel im 17. Jahrhundert*, pp. 15–78. Aschmann surveys works written for unaccompanied solo violin up to and including J. S. Bach's sonatas and partitas, including (pp. 47–50) a single Westhoff suite published in the *Mercure galant* in January 1683.

78 Wilson (ed.), *Roger North on Music*, p. 310. For a study of these works and an assessment of the Italian influence upon them, see Tilmouth, 'The Technique and Forms of Purcell's Sonatas'; Holman, *Henry Purcell*, pp. 85–93.

79 The differing number of parts designated in the two collections is misleading because both collections include four partbooks: first violin, second violin, bass viol, and harpsichord or organ. In the 1683 sonatas

wrote them sometime during the early the 1680s, most likely before Corelli's op. 1 sonatas (published in 1681) were known in England, and well before Corelli's phenomenal appeal spawned a host of imitators among both Italian and non-Italian composers of violin music. Purcell's sonatas are in fact neither Corellian nor purely Italianate. Rather, they are fascinating hybrids, combining contrapuntal and harmonic features seen in Purcell's own fantasias with pre-Corellian Roman influences seen in manuscript sonatas circulating in England under the name of Lelio Colista but also including works by Carlo Ambrogio Lonati.[80]

North mentions the existence in England of works by 'Cazzati, Vitali, and other lesser scrapps'. However, two characteristics of Purcell's sonatas most immediately suggest a Roman, as opposed to a north Italian, influence. First is his use of the term 'canzona' to designate the fugal movement within the sonata. Composers working in and around Rome during the 1660s, 1670s and 1680s such as Lelio Colista (in his manuscript *simfonie*), Carlo Mannelli (*Sonate a tre*, op. 2, Rome, 1682) and Angelo Berardi (*Sinfonie a violino solo . . . libro primo*, op. 7, Rome, 1670) use this term in the same way, even though it is by now uncommon among the Italians.[81] A second Roman feature, seen in the *sinfonie* for two violins and bass of Colista, Lonati and Alessandro Stradella, is the use of dance-like binary-form movements in ostensibly non-dance sonatas. In Purcell, the minuet-like Largo movements of sonatas no. 1 and no. 6 (1683) and sonata no. 3 (1697), and the gigue-like Allegro of sonata no. 9 (1683) again suggest a specifically Roman trait not common in north Italian sonatas of the period just prior to Purcell's, that is, before the 1680s.

A more general characteristic of his sonatas is their striking contrapuntal sophistication: Purcell, like Roman sonata composers, wrote for three, and not two, contrapuntal parts – i.e., two violins and bass, plus continuo. His fugal movements, moreover, are compact and densely woven pieces in which he frequently includes a countersubject or a second subject. Many of these 'canzona' fugues amount to extended expositions in which the subject and countersubject are almost never absent from the texture. Purcell often expands these movements, not with sequential episodes, but with new expositions on the inverted

Purcell followed the practice predominant among Italian title-pages of describing the contrapuntal parts above the basso continuo, whereas the 1697 print simply lists the total number of parts.

80 Allsop, 'Problems of Ascription in the Roman *Simfonia* of the Late Seventeenth Century'.

81 Later Italian composers occasionally followed this practice, as with Pietro Sanmartini's *Sinfonie a due violini*, op. 2 (Florence, 1688), Giuseppe Antonio Avitrano's *Sonate a tré*, op. 1 (Naples, 1697), and Antonio Luigi Baldassini's *Sonate à tre*, op. 2 (Rome, 1699). The English lutenist and composer William Young (d. 1662) published a set of sonatas in Innsbruck in 1653 whose fugal movements are designated 'canzona', but there is little to connect these with Purcell: Young never returned to England from Innsbruck, so it is doubtful that Purcell knew his sonatas; moreover, the fugal movements of the two composers' sonatas are otherwise dissimilar.

form of the one or two subjects of the piece. His Allegro movements in triple time are similarly imitative in the Roman style. By comparison, most north Italian composers of the 1660s and 1670s – for instance, Cazzati, Legrenzi, Vitali and Giovanni Maria Bononcini – wrote fast triple-time movements to contrast with their fugues in terms of both texture and metre, employing more clear-cut phrases in homophonic texture or dialogue-like exchanges. Purcell, instead, almost always keeps to fugal imitation.

In sum, we might interpret Purcell's intricate contrapuntal style as further evidence to distance him from northern Italian sonata composers and to bring him closer to the Romans, and particularly Colista.[82] Yet much in Purcell's sonatas can also be found in his own fantasias, which are late examples of a decidedly English genre of instrumental music. Composed during the summer of 1680, they are masterpieces of contrapuntal writing that feature fugues on one, two or three invertible subjects, and that employ augmentation, diminution, inversion and stretto. Contrapuntal sophistication is therefore an innate Purcellian trait, however much it might also reflect Roman influence. No less indebted to the fantasias are the richness of harmonic language and sometimes sheer chromatic intensity of Purcell's sonatas. North may have found them 'clog'd with somewhat of an English vein' and therefore 'unworthily despised', but he still found them 'very artificiall and good musick'. Yet Purcell's published sonatas neither sold well nor inspired followers. It was instead the Corellian vogue that took hold among English sonata composers after Purcell such as John Ravenscroft, William Corbett, William Topham and James Sherard.[83]

The *stylus phantasticus*

A markedly different handling of the sonata is seen in collections by three Austro-German virtuosos who represent the height of seventeenth-century violin technique: Johann Heinrich Schmelzer's *Sonatae unarum fidium, seu a violino solo* (Nuremberg, 1664); Heinrich Ignaz Franz von Biber's 'Rosenkranz' (Rosary) sonatas (composed in Salzburg in the mid to late 1670s) and *Sonatae violino solo* (Nuremberg, 1681); and Johann Jakob Walther's (*c.* 1650–1717) *Scherzi da violino solo con il basso continuo per l'organo o cimbalo, accompagnabile anche con una viola, o leuto* (Dresden, 1676) and *Hortulus chelicus uni violino duabus, tribus et quatuor subinde chordis simul sonantibus harmonice modulanti* (Mainz, 1688). Biber's *Rosary Sonatas* for solo violin and continuo (comprising fifteen dance-suites and a final passacaglia) are today perhaps the most famous violin music

---

82 See McCrickard, 'The Roman Repertory for Violin Before the Time of Corelli', pp. 566–8, for a discussion of Colista's contrapuntal style. His works are catalogued in Wessely-Kropik, *Lelio Colista*.

83 For Corelli's influence, see Tilmouth, 'James Sherard'.

of the seventeenth century next to Corelli's op. 5. Their well-deserved fame rests on a curious programmatic design, stunning virtuoso techniques, and the unique varieties of *scordatura*. They are fantastical creations containing writing for the violin that is unmatched in its demands on the soloist save in the works of Biber's contemporary Walther, although the latter shunned extravagant tunings as 'a squeaking now on two or more strings false tuned *ad nauseam*' (so he said in the preface to his *Hortulus chelicus*).

Considered as sonatas, these works are neither fish nor fowl. Biber's *Rosary Sonatas* in fact bear no designation of genre (the title-page is missing in their manuscript) but can be categorised as dance-suites not unlike those of Muffat, even though they are programmatic. Schmelzer and Walther, both of whom use the term 'sonata', combine elements of the dance-suite, ostinato variations and programmatic pieces such that their publications are difficult to pin down. All of these collections contain at least a few dances and virtuosic variation-movements that belong to recognisable types, but they exhibit an overall freedom that results in works that are too ambitious, too unpredictably inventive, and on too large a scale to be comprehended as tidy examples in any one genre of instrumental music.

Here we also find a substantial number of picturesque and oddly programmatic works, mostly for solo violin but some for larger ensembles. Those of Schmelzer and Biber were created for masquerades and similar entertainments at the palace of the Prince-Bishop Karl Liechtenstein-Kastelkorn at Kremsier (now Kroměříž, in the Czech Republic).[84] Walther's large contribution to this genre of *bizarrerie* could well have served the same purpose at the courts of Elector Johann Georg II in Dresden or Elector Anselm Franz von Ingelheim in Mainz, where Walther was employed. Schmelzer's representational works include the *Polnische Sackpfeiffen* (Polish bagpipes), and a *Sonata violino solo representativa* (traditionally attributed to Biber but now believed to be by Schmelzer)[85] which contains violinistic imitations of the nightingale, cuckoo, frog, hen, rooster and more. Biber, undoubtedly influenced by Schmelzer, wrote the *Sonata La pastorella* (the shepherdess), the *Sonata die Pauern-Kirchfahrt genant* ('called the peasants' drive to church') and a multi-movement *Battaglia*. Walther, all of whose known music is contained in just two publications, seems to have had considerable interest in such effects, especially given the amount included in his *Hortulus chelicus*: *Galli e galline* ('Roosters and hens'), *Scherzo d'augelli con il cuccu* ('Scherzo of birds with the cuckoo'), *Gara di due violini in*

---

84 Schmelzer uses the term 'Camerdienst' (chamber service) to describe the entertainments, as well as 'Mascara' (masquerade); see Nettl, 'Die Wiener Tanzkomposition in der zweiten Hälfte des 17. Jahrhunderts', pp. 166–75, containing correspondence concerning the music of Prince-Bishop Karl.

85 Brewer, 'The Case of the Fallacious Fauna'.

uno ('Battle of two violins in one'), *Leuto harpeggiante e rossignolo* ('Strummed lute and nightingale'), and the culminating *Serenata a un coro di violini, organo tremolante, chitarrino, piva, due trombe e timpani, lira todesca, et harpa smorzata, per un violino* ('Serenade for a choir of violins, tremolo organ, small guitar, pipe, two trumpets and timpani, German bagpipes and hurdy-gurdy, [all] for solo violin').

Such curiosities find their precedents in earlier Italian sonatas: Uccellini published a sonata on the 'marriage' of a hen and a cuckoo (1642), and Merula wrote a 'hen'-piece (1637), and the broader trends may also have been transmitted by Italian violinists who travelled north. Carlo Farina published four collections of dance-suites arranged in the German style during his time in Dresden (1625–8), and among the dances of the second collection (1627) is a *Capriccio stravagante*, an extravagance of some 380 bars (in modern edition) with numerous sections in markedly contrasting styles and including an unprecedented array of violinistic effects – glissando, pizzicato, *sul ponticello, sul tasto,* tremolo and *col legno battuto* – to depict different musical instruments and animals. Even without the humorous overtones (and Farina's capriccio is exceptional for its time), a northern interest in expanded violin technique clearly was reinforced by a stream of virtuosos coming out of Italy in the early and mid seventeenth century, who must have fired the imaginations, and inspired the technique, of northern violinists.

The startling invention of the violin music of Schmelzer, Biber and Walther also demonstrates characteristics that can be traced to the *stylus phantasticus* that Athanasius Kircher associated with the sonata in his *Musurgia universalis* (Rome, 1650):

> The *phantasticus stylus* is appropriate to instruments. It is the most free and unfettered method of composition, bound to nothing, neither to words, nor to a harmonic subject. It is organised with regard to manifest invention, the hidden reason of harmony, and an ingenious, skilled connection of harmonic phrases and fugues. And it is divided into those pieces which are commonly called *Phantasias, Ricercatas, Toccatas,* and *Sonatas*.[86]

The style is 'fantastical' not just because of its inventiveness, but also because it derives from the mind's 'fantasy' and therefore, in one Neoplatonic reading, becomes emblematic of divine inspiration. Kircher's emphasis on freedom, from both a text and a cantus firmus, and on invention well suits the otherwise

---

86 The *stylus phantasticus* is one of eight that Kircher names in his chapter on musical style, 'De vario stylorum harmonicorum artificio'. The others are (pp. 581–98): *ecclesiasticus, canonicus, motecticus, madrigalescus, melismaticus, hyporchematicus (choriacus et theatralis), symphoniacus* and *dramaticus sive recitativus.* On discussions of the *stylus phantasticus* in the music of specific composers, see Riedel, 'The Influence and Tradition of Frescobaldi's Works in the Transalpine Countries'; Snyder, *Dieterich Buxtehude,* pp. 290–96; Zink, 'Athanasius Kircher's *Stylus phantasticus* and the Viennese Ensemble Sonata of the Seventeenth Century'.

uncategorisable range of techniques and forms in the music of these three virtuosos.

For example, four of the six sonatas in Schmelzer's 1664 sonatas reveal his preference for ostinato variations in multi-sectional forms that mimic other genres: the fourth sonata presents over a single ostinato pattern what is in effect a variation-suite, with a substantial opening movement, a *sarabanda* and a *giga* before concluding in a series of cadential sections. Walther's 1676 *Scherzi* is an even more diverse collection of pieces, embracing the suite, ostinato variations and programme music. Here, too, there is a sense of playing with genres: the listener cannot know what will follow from one piece to the next. The first sonata – 'Allemanda' (variations over a ground), 'Corrente', 'Sarabanda', 'Giga' – is the only suite of dances; the fifth comprises an 'aria malincon' that is varied over a ground; and the tenth is an *Imitatione del cuccu*. Added to this unpredictability is the dazzling effect of Walther's violin technique: *arpeggiando con arcate sciolte* (arpeggiations with separate bows), *ondeggiando* (rapidly alternating slurred notes across strings), staccato (whether or not under a slur), quick string-crossing over all four strings, and *style brisé* effects (but Walther does not use the term) which, in the third sonata, combine double stops against an upper pedal within a passage of echoes.[87] Division-style *passaggi* in semiquavers and demisemiquavers occur frequently, and sometimes in shorter and more furious bursts of speed under a single bow (we even find hemidemisemiquavers in the seventh, ninth and twelfth sonatas). Walther includes triple and quadruple stops in one passage in the second sonata to create an effect of accumulating voices. In order to accommodate the extended range he demands of the violin, Walther uses four clefs: G1 (the French violin clef), G2, C2, C3. He also takes the instrument up to d''' in double-stops, and even g''' for single pitches.

The pieces that Biber styles *sonatis*, *preludys*, *allemandis*, *courent[is]*, *saraband[is]*, *arÿs*, *ciacona*, *variationibus* etc. bear all the marks of a suite: the majority of the fifteen *Rosary Sonatas* include dances – allemande, courante, gigue, sarabande, gavotte – following a prelude or sonata.[88] Yet these dances are associated with the fifteen Sacred Mysteries, and the manuscript contains appropriate copperplate engravings prior to each piece. Each sonata, moreover, uses a different tuning. *Scordatura* does not originate with Biber – it was used, for example, by Biagio Marini in his op. 8 (1626; published while he was employed in Neuberg) – but Biber takes it to unique extremes. His

---

87 Aschmann, *Das deutsche polyphone Violinspiel im 17. Jahrhundert*, pp. 79–115, surveys seventeenth-century composers, mostly German and south German, whose violin music includes multiple-stops. Among these are David Cramer, Johann Vierdanck, Philipp Friedrich Böddecker, Nicolaus Bleyer, Matthias Kelz, Thomas Baltzar and Johann Fischer.

88 Chafe, *The Church Music of Heinrich Biber*, pp. 183–226.

tunings make possible a great number of chords that are otherwise unplayable on the violin;[89] they also alter the timbre of the instrument depending on the greater or lesser string tension and on the sympathetic resonances introduced by the *scordatura*. These alterations of timbre may have had programmatic significance in creating a relatively brilliant or subdued sound appropriate to the different Mysteries. This would also complement the more obviously descriptive moments in the collection: the lament in the minor mode for the Agony in the Garden; the nail-hammering dotted rhythms of the Crucifixion; and the festive trumpet-aria of the Ascension. The Resurrection, in particular, stands out because the violin quotes the chant of the Easter hymn 'Surrexit Christus hodie', playing it in octaves. The tuning in this particular piece (g, g', d', d''), also crosses over the two middle strings, producing a symbol of the Cross with the strings crossed in the pegbox and behind the bridge.[90]

All three Austro-German virtuosos seem to be rethinking the genres in which they were working, always confronting the listener with the unexpected and the unprecedented, and allowing their freedom of invention to exceed the boundaries of form. The sense of the *stylus phantasticus* in which the imagination trumps convention, and limits are surmounted, accords well with their style. In a later German example, a similar if less flamboyant freedom of style and form characterises the ensemble sonatas of Dieterich Buxtehude (*c.* 1637 – 1707) for one and two violins, viola da gamba and harpsichord.[91] The *stylus phantasticus* has also been applied by modern scholars to the improvisatory qualities of the toccata and to unorthodox fugal techniques in ensemble sonatas. Here it refers to the composer's wealth of ideas, and to novel, imaginative conceptions of genre that intrigue, surprise and awe the listener.

If the style of writing of these northern composers owes a debt to earlier Italian virtuosos and the *stile moderno* sonata, the expressive aims are often different. The musical symbols in Schmelzer, Biber and Walther are numerous, vivid and detailed. Where Italian sonata composers more frequently aimed at evoking generalised affects in their music, the Austro-German virtuosos frequently pursued literal depictions. Both strategies, however, lay claim to our imagination, and all too intrusively for some tastes. Bernard de Fontenelle's famous query 'Sonate, que me veux-tu?'[92] is the irritated reaction to the sonata of a French

---

89 C. E. Brewer (ed.), *Solo Compositions for Violin and Viola da Gamba with Basso Continuo: from the Collection of Prince-Bishop Carl Liechtenstein-Castelcorn in Kroměříž*, 'Recent Researches in the Music of the Baroque Era', 82 (Madison, WI, 1997), p. xi, points out that Biber also played the viola da gamba, whose chord-playing possibilities may have been an inspiration in his writing for the violin.

90 I would like to thank Sylvia Ouellette for demonstrating this to me.

91 Snyder, *Dieterich Buxtehude*, p. 295, notes that the improvisatory nature of Buxtehude's ensemble sonatas creates an uncertainty so that 'one does not know what form they will take – a fugue? a variation set? a dance?' See also Linfield, 'Dietrich Buxtehude's Sonatas'.

92 Although it was well known before the end of his long life (1657–1757), Fontenelle's enigmatic query has not been traced in his writings; see Newman, *The Sonata in the Baroque Era*, p. 353, for a list of the numerous sources quoting it.

man of letters roughly contemporary with Corelli. Rousseau took Fontanelle's words and used them to demonstrate the futility of musical meaning:

> To know what means all this fracas of sonatas which assaults our ears, we must do as that ignorant painter who was obliged to write under his figures: 'This is a tree; this is a man; this is a horse'.[93]

In some cases, seventeenth-century composers did just that. Otherwise, their instrumental ensemble music touched the listener by recalling the spirit of a borrowed genre, by relying on a collection of expressive topoi, by representing human emotion, or by imitating musical and non-musical sounds. These composers had an abiding interest in demonstrating affects and images in music. Fontanelle, Rousseau and others might resist, but this music clearly spoke to many who did not.

Bibliography

Allsop, P., 'Problems of Ascription in the Roman *Simfonia* of the Late Seventeenth Century: Colista and Lonati'. *Music Review*, 50 (1989), 34–44

    The Italian 'Trio' Sonata. Oxford, 1992

    'Violinistic Virtuosity in the Seventeenth Century: Italian Supremacy or Austro-German Hegemony?'. *Il saggiatore musicale*, 3 (1996), 233–58

    Arcangelo Corelli: 'New Orpheus of our Times'. Oxford and New York, 1999

Anthony, J. R., *French Baroque Music: from Beaujoyeulx to Rameau*. Rev. edn, Portland, OR, 1997

Apel, W., *Italian Violin Music of the Seventeenth Century*, ed. T. Binkley. Bloomington and Indianapolis, 1990

Aschmann, R., *Das deutsche polyphone Violinspiel im 17. Jahrhundert*. Zurich, 1962

Barnett, G., 'Modal Theory, Church Keys, and the Sonata at the End of the Seventeenth Century'. *Journal of the American Musicological Society*, 51 (1998), 245–81

Bartholomew, L., *Alessandro Raverij's Collection of 'Canzoni per sonare' (Venice, 1608)*. Fort Hays, KS, 1965

Beckmann, G., *Das Violinspiel in Deutschland vor 1700*. Leipzig, 1918

Bizzarini, M., 'Diffusione della sonata a tre nella Brescia di fine Seicento: il ruolo del Collegio de' Nobili'. In A. Colzani, A. Luppi and M. Padoan (eds), *Barocco Padano I: atti del IX convegno internazionale sulla musica sacra nei secoli XVII–XVIII*. Como, 2002, pp. 279–309

Bonta, S., 'The Uses of the *Sonata da chiesa*'. *Journal of the American Musicological Society*, 22 (1969), 54–84

    'From Violone to Violoncello: a Question of Strings?'. *Journal of the American Musical Instrument Society*, 3 (1977), 64–99

    'Terminology for the Bass Violin in Seventeenth-Century Italy'. *Journal of the American Musical Instrument Society*, 4 (1978), 5–42

---

93 J.-J. Rousseau, *Dictionnaire de musique* (Paris, 1768), p. 460. Jean le Rond D'Alembert, *De la liberté de la musique* (Amsterdam, 1759), section 38, also cites Fontanelle in the context of an assessment of Italian sonatas (in particular, by Giuseppe Tartini); see J. R. D'Alembert, *Œuvres complètes*, 5 vols (Paris, 1821–2; repr. Geneva, 1967), i: 544.

Borgir, T., *The Performance of the Basso Continuo in Italian Baroque Music*. Ann Arbor, 1987

Boyden, D., 'When is a Concerto not a Concerto?'. *Musical Quarterly*, 43 (1957), 200–232
  The History of Violin Playing from its Origins to 1761. Oxford, 1965

Brewer, C. E., 'The Case of the Fallacious Fauna: Biber, Schmelzer, and the *Sonata violino solo representativa*'. Paper presented at the annual meeting of the Society for Seventeenth-Century Music, Lancaster, PA, April 2001

Brizzi, G. P., *La formazione della classe dirigente nel Sei–Settecento: i seminaria nobilium nell'Italia centro-settentrionale*. Bologna, 1976

Brooks, B., 'Etienne Nau, Breslau 114 and the Early Seventeenth-Century German Violin Fantasia'. *Early Music*, 32 (2004), 49–72

Chafe, E., *The Church Music of Heinrich Biber*. Ann Arbor, 1987

Collins, T. A., '"Reactions against the Virtuoso": Instrumental Ornamentation Practice and the *Stile moderno*'. *International Review of the Aesthetics and Sociology of Music*, 32 (2001), 137–52

Crocker, E., 'An Introductory Study of the Italian Canzona for Instrumental Ensembles and its Influence upon the Baroque Sonata'. Ph.D. thesis, Radcliffe College (1943)

Crowther, V., 'A Case Study in the Power of the Purse: the Management of the Ducal *Cappella* in Modena in the Reign of Francesco II d'Este'. *Journal of the Royal Musical Association*, 115 (1990), 207–19
  The Oratorio in Modena. Oxford, 1992

Daverio, J., 'In Search of the *Sonata da camera* before Corelli'. *Acta musicologica*, 57 (1985), 195–214

Dell'Antonio, A., *Syntax, Form, and Genre in Sonatas and Canzonas 1621–1635*. Lucca, 1997
  'The Eucharist and Saint Francis: Images of Musical Affect and Rapture in Counter-Reformation Italy'. Paper presented at the annual meeting of the American Musicological Society, Columbus, OH, November 2002

Dodds, M., 'The Baroque Church Tones in Theory and Practice'. Ph.D. thesis, University of Rochester (1999)

Epstein, P., 'Das Musikwesen der Stadt Frankfurt'. Ph.D. thesis, University of Breslau (1923)

Fabbri, P., 'Politica editoriale e musica strumentale in Italia dal Cinque- al Settecento'. In Wulf (ed.), *Deutsch-italienische Musikbeziehungen*, pp. 25–37

Gallico, C., *Girolamo Frescobaldi: l'affetto, l'ordito, le metamorfosi*. Florence, 1986

Gambassi, O., *La cappella musicale di S. Petronio*. Florence, 1987

Harper, J., 'The Instrumental Canzonas of Girolamo Frescobaldi: a Comparative Edition and Introductory Study'. Ph.D. thesis, University of Birmingham (1975)
  'Frescobaldi's Reworked Ensemble Canzonas'. In Silbiger (ed.), *Frescobaldi Studies*, pp. 269–83

Harrán, D., *Salamone Rossi: Jewish Musician in Late Renaissance Mantua*. Oxford and New York, 1999

Hayburn, R. F., *Papal Legislation on Sacred Music*. Collegeville, MN, 1979

Higginbottom, E., 'Organ Music and the Liturgy'. In N. Thistlethwaite and G. Webber (eds), *The Cambridge Companion to the Organ*. Cambridge, 1998, pp. 130–47

Holman, P., '"Col nobilissimo esercitio della vivuola": Monteverdi's String Writing'. *Early Music*, 21 (1993), 577–90

Four and Twenty Fiddlers: the Violin at the English Court, 1540–1690. Oxford and New York, 1993

Henry Purcell. Oxford and New York, 1994

Jander, O., ʻ*Concerto grosso* Instrumentation in Rome in the 1660's and 1670's'. *Journal of the American Musicological Society,* 21 (1968), 168–80

Jensen, N. M., ʻSolo Sonata, Duo Sonata and Trio Sonata: Some Problems of Terminology in 17th-Century Italian Instrumental Music'. In N. Schiørring, H. Glahn and C. E. Hatting (eds), *Festskrift Jens Peter Larsen.* Copenhagen, 1972, pp. 73–101

Kirkendale, W., *L'aria di Fiorenza, id est Il ballo del Gran Duca.* Florence, 1972

Kokole, M., ʻThe Compositions of Isaac Posch: Mediators between the German and Italian Musical Idioms'. In A. Colzani *et al.* (eds), *Relazioni musicali tra Italia e Germania nell'età barocca: atti del VI convegno Antiquae Musicae Italicae Studiosi.* Como, 1995, pp. 87–120

Ladewig, J., ʻThe Origins of Frescobaldi's Variation Canzonas Reappraised'. In Silbiger (ed.), *Frescobaldi Studies,* pp. 235–68

Laurencie, L. de la, *L'école française de violon de Lully à Viotti.* 3 vols, Paris, 1922–4; repr. Geneva, 1971

Linfield, E., ʻDietrich Buxtehude's Sonatas: a Historical and Analytical Study'. Ph.D. thesis, Brandeis University (1984)

McCrickard, E., ʻThe Roman Repertory for Violin Before the Time of Corelli'. *Early Music,* 18 (1990), 563–73

Mangsen, S., ʻ*Ad libitum* Procedures in Instrumental Duos and Trios'. *Early Music,* 19 (1991), 29–40

ʻThe "Sonata da camera" before Corelli: a Renewed Search'. *Music and Letters,* 76 (1995), 19–31

Maunder, R., *The Scoring of Baroque Concertos.* Rochester, 2004

Moore, J. H., ʻThe Liturgical Use of the Organ in Seventeenth-Century Italy: New Documents, New Hypotheses'. In Silbiger (ed.), *Frescobaldi Studies,* pp. 351–83

Moser, H. J., ʻEine Pariser Quelle zur Wiener Triosonate des ausgehenden 17. Jahrhunderts: der Codex Rost'. In H. Zingerle (ed.), *Festschrift Wilhelm Fischer zum 70. Geburtstag überreicht im Mozartjahr 1956.* Innsbruck, 1956, pp. 75–81

Nettl, P., ʻDie Wiener Tanzkomposition in der zweiten Hälfte des 17. Jahrhunderts'. *Studien zur Musikwissenschaft,* 8 (1921), 45–175

Newman, W. S., *The Sonata in the Baroque Era.* Chapel Hill, NC, 1959

Padoan, M., *La musica in S. Maria Maggiore a Bergamo nel periodo di Giovanni Cavaccio (1598–1626).* Como, 1983

Piperno, F., ʻ"Concerto" e "concertato" nella musica strumentale italiana del secolo decimosettimo'. In W. Konold (ed.), *Deutsch-italienische Musikbeziehungen,* pp. 129–55

Riedel, F., ʻThe Influence and Tradition of Frescobaldi's Works in the Transalpine Countries'. In Silbiger (ed.), *Frescobaldi Studies,* pp. 218–32

Rinaldi, M., *Arcangelo Corelli.* Milan, 1953

Sadie, J. A., ʻCharpentier and the Early French Ensemble Sonata'. *Early Music,* 7 (1979), 330–35

Sartori, C., *Bibliografia della musica strumentale italiana stampata in Italia fino al 1700.* 2 vols, Florence, 1952–68

Schnoebelen, A., ʻThe Concerted Mass at S. Petronio'. Ph.D. thesis, University of Illinois (1966)

Selfridge-Field, E., 'Canzona and Sonata: Some Differences in Social Identity'. *International Review of the Aesthetics and Sociology of Music*, 9 (1978), 111–19

Venetian Instrumental Music from Gabrieli to Vivaldi. 3rd edn, New York, 1994

Silbiger, A. (ed.), *Frescobaldi Studies*. Durham, NC, 1987

Snyder, K. J., *Dieterich Buxtehude: Organist in Lübeck*. New York, 1987

Sparti, B., '"Baroque or not Baroque – is That the Question?", or Dance in 17th-Century Italy'. In A. Chiarle (ed.), *L'arte della danza ai tempi di Claudio Monteverdi*. Turin, 1996, pp. 73–93

Stevens, D., 'Seventeenth-Century Italian Instrumental Music in the Bodleian Library'. *Acta musicologica*, 26 (1954), 67–75

Suess, J., 'Giuseppe Colombi's Dance Music for the Estense Court of Duke Francesco II of Modena'. In M. Caraci Vela and M. Toffetti (eds), *Marco Uccellini: atti del convegno 'Marco Uccellini da Forlimpopoli e la sua Musica' (Forlimpopoli, 26–27 ottobre 1996)*. Lucca, 1999, pp. 141–62

Sumner, F., 'The Stylized Canzone'. In R. Weaver (ed.), *Essays on the Music of J. S. Bach and Other Divers Subjects: a Tribute to Gerhard Herz*. New York, 1981, pp. 165–80

Sutkowski, A., and Mischiati, O., 'Una preziosa fonte manoscritta di musica strumentale: l'intavolatura di Pelplin'. *L'organo*, 4 (1961), 53–72

Talbot, M., 'The Concerto Allegro in the Early Eighteenth Century'. *Music and Letters*, 52 (1971), 8–18, 159–72

'The Taiheg, the Pira and Other Curiosities of Benedetto Vinaccesi's "Suonate da camera a tre", Op. 1'. *Music and Letters*, 75 (1994), 344–64

Tilmouth, M., 'The Technique and Forms of Purcell's Sonatas'. *Music and Letters*, 40 (1959), 109–21

'James Sherard: an English Amateur Composer'. *Music and Letters*, 47 (1966), 313–22

Vanscheeuwijck, M., *The 'Cappella musicale' of San Petronio in Bologna under Giovanni Paolo Colonna (1674–95)*. Brussels, 2003

Vecchi, G., 'La canzone strumentale e la canzone-motetto a Milano nella prima metà del Seicento'. In M. Padoan, A. Colzani and A. Luppi (eds), *La musica sacra in Lombardia nella prima metà del Seicento: atti del convegno internazionale di studi, Como, 31 maggio–2 giugno 1985*. Como, 1988, pp. 79–97

Walls, P., 'The Influence of the Italian Violin School in 17th-Century England'. *Early Music*, 18 (1990), 575–87

Wendland, J., '"Madre non mi far Monaca": the Biography of a Renaissance Folksong'. *Acta musicologica*, 48 (1976), 185–204

Wessely-Kropik, H., *Lelio Colista: Ein Römischer Meister vor Corelli. Leben und Umwelt*. Vienna, 1961

Wilson, D. K. (ed.), *Georg Muffat on Performance Practice*. Bloomington and Indianapolis, 2001

Wilson, J. (ed.), *Roger North on Music, Being a Selection of his Essays Written during the Years c. 1695–1728*. London, 1959

Wulf, K. (ed.), *Deutsch-italienische Musikbeziehungen: Deutsche und italienische Instrumentalmusik 1600–1750*. Munich and Salzburg, 1996

Zink, G. D., 'Athanasius Kircher's *Stylus phantasticus* and the Viennese Ensemble Sonata of the Seventeenth Century'. *Schütz Society Reports*, 7/2 (Spring 1991), 7–13

Chronology

STEPHEN ROSE

1600   In England, the East India Company is founded to do trade with Far East. Publication of *L'Artusi, overo Delle imperfettioni della moderna musica* criticising modern music, including contrapuntal licences in Monteverdi's madrigals. Performance of Emilio de' Cavalieri's *Rappresentatione di Anima, et di Corpo* in Rome. Performance of Peri's *Euridice* in Florence, celebrating the marriage of Henri IV of France to Maria de' Medici. Caccini publishes a rival setting of *Euridice*.

1601   The Earl of Essex rebels against Elizabeth I and is executed for treason. More loyal is Thomas Morley who publishes *The Triumphs of Oriana*, an anthology of madrigals honouring the queen. Monteverdi appointed *maestro della musica di camera* of the Gonzaga court in Mantua.

1602   The Dutch East India Company is formed. Galileo Galilei studying oscillation and gravity. Bodleian Library opens in Oxford. Publication of Giambattista Marino's *Rime*, which prove highly popular for musical settings. Two publications promote new composing and performing styles: Viadana's *Cento concerti ecclesiastici* is one of the first collections of few-voiced motets with continuo, and Caccini's *Le nuove musiche* one of the first of solo songs with continuo. Caccini's volume has an influential preface on modern singing styles, also advocating *sprezzatura* (graceful nonchalance) in performance.

1603   On the death of Queen Elizabeth I of England, James VI of Scotland is declared James I of England, uniting the crowns of England and Scotland. Publication of Shakespeare's *Hamlet*. Publication of Monteverdi's Fourth Book of Madrigals.

1604   England and Spain make peace in the Treaty of London. First performance of Shakespeare's *Othello*. Caccini family visit Paris on request of Maria de' Medici. Dowland's *Lachrimae, or Seaven Teares* published in London. Orlande de Lassus's sons publish *Magnum opus musicum*, a posthumous 'complete edition' of his motets. Sweelinck issues the first instalment of his setting of the psalms.

1605   The Gunpowder Plot, a Catholic conspiracy to blow up Parliament, is foiled in England. Shakespeare writes *King Lear*. In Spain, Miguel de Cervantes publishes *Don Quixote*. Monteverdi's Fifth Book of madrigals is published, with a reply to Artusi. Publication of the first part of William Byrd's collection of music for the Catholic liturgical year, *Gradualia*. Christian IV of Denmark sponsors *Giardini novi* (1605–6), an Italian madrigal collection indicating the cultural ambitions of the Danish court.

1606 Pope Paul V responds to anticlericalism in Venice by placing the Venetian republic under interdict. The Habsburgs make peace with Hungary. Shakespeare writes *Macbeth*. Publication of Joachim Burmeister's *Musica poetica* in Rostock.

1607 Venetian interdict removed. First settlers arrive in Virginia. Monteverdi's *Orfeo* is performed at Mantuan court. Publication of Monteverdi's *Scherzi musicali*, in which Giulio Cesare Monteverdi amplifies his brother's response to Artusi. Gregor Aichinger's *Cantiones ecclesiasticae* is the first significant German edition to use the basso continuo. Publication of the second part of William Byrd's *Gradualia* and Agostino Agazzari's treatise on basso continuo, *Del sonare sopra 'l basso*.

1608 In the Holy Roman Empire, rival confessional alliances of the Protestant Union and Catholic League begin to be formed (–1609). The French found Québec. At Mantua, the lengthy celebrations for the wedding of Francesco Gonzaga and Margherita of Savoy include Marco da Gagliano's *Dafne* and Monteverdi's *Arianna*; *Arianna*'s lament reportedly moves the audience to tears. Frescobaldi appointed organist at St Peter's, Rome. In Paris, Pierre Ballard issues first collection of lute airs.

1609 Emperor Rudolf II grants rights to Bohemian Protestants in his Letter of Majesty. Moriscos expelled from Spain. Twelve Years Truce between Spain and the Dutch Republic (–1621). Henry Hudson, an English navigator, explores Hudson Bay and the Hudson River (–1610). Agazzari's *Sacrae cantiones* published with a preface explaining the basso continuo. First book of Sigismondo d'India's monodies, *Le musiche*, published.

1610 Henri IV of France is assassinated by a Catholic fanatic. The successor to the French throne is Louis XIII, aged nine; Maria de' Medici is regent. Galileo's *Siderus nuncio* describes his astronomical discoveries, including the moons of Jupiter and the roughness of our moon's surface. Monteverdi's *Missa . . . ac Vespere* published.

1611 Gustavus Adolphus takes up the Swedish throne. The Polish garrison is expelled from Moscow. The Authorised Version of the Bible is published in England. Peter Paul Rubens starts painting *The Descent from the Cross*. Shakespeare writes *The Tempest*. D'India joins the Turin court of the Duke of Savoy. Publication of the first fruits of Schütz's Venetian apprenticeship, his First Book of Madrigals. Publication of William Byrd's *Psalmes, Songs and Sonnets*.

1612 The Holy Roman Emperor, Rudolf II, dies and is succeeded by his brother, Matthias. Colonisation of Bermuda begins. Giovanni Gabrieli dies. Publication of Michael Praetorius's book of French dances, *Terpsichore*. John Dowland gets a post at the English court. Monteverdi is dismissed from the Mantuan court.

1613 In a major dynastic marriage, Princess Elizabeth (James I's daughter) weds Friedrich V, Elector Palatine. Among the nuptial offerings is an engraved book of English keyboard music, *Parthenia, or The Maydenhead of the First Musicke that ever was Printed for the Virginalls*. Artusi and Gesualdo die. Monteverdi appointed as *maestro di cappella* at St Mark's, Venice.

1614   Aristocratic revolt in France. Groningen University founded. Publication of Monteverdi's Sixth Book of madrigals and of Adriano Banchieri's treatise, *Cartella musicale*. Monteverdi's *Orfeo* perhaps performed in Salzburg, the first opera to be given outside Italy.

1615   Cervantes writes Part II of *Don Quixote*. Schütz summoned to the Dresden court of the Elector of Saxony. In Bologna, Banchieri founds the Accademia dei Floridi, where professional musicians can meet to hear and discuss each other's compositions and performances. Publication of Giovanni Gabrieli's second book of *Symphoniae sacrae* (posthumously), and Frescobaldi's *Recercari et canzoni* and First Book of toccatas.

1616   Protestants are increasingly being persecuted in Bohemia. Deaths of Shakespeare and Cervantes. Publication of collected works of Ben Jonson, one of the first such complete editions. Galileo attacked by the Inquisition for proposing a heliocentric universe; for the next seven years he keeps his scholarship private. Johann Hermann Schein is appointed Cantor at the Leipzig Thomasschule.

1617   War between Sweden and Poland. Louis XIII of France seizes control of government from his regent. In Heidelberg, Martin Opitz founds the Fruchtbringende Gesellschaft, a society dedicated to promoting German as a literary language. Publication of a pioneering collection of instrumental sonatas, Biagio Marini's *Affetti musicali*. *Ballet de la délivrance de Renaud* performed in Paris, with the first known use of a band of 24 violins.

1618   The Defenestration of Prague: Bohemian Protestants meet in Prague to discuss grievances and throw imperial representatives out of a window. This Protestant revolt begins the Thirty Years War. In Florence, Giulio Caccini dies and Francesca Caccini's book of monodies, *Musiche*, is published. First edition of the third volume of Michael Praetorius's *Syntagma musicum*, which introduces Italian styles of composition and performance to Lutheran Germany. Schein's *Opella nova* treats Lutheran chorales in the style of Viadana's sacred concertos.

1619   Emperor Matthias dies and is succeeded by Ferdinand II, a diehard Catholic. In Bohemia, the Protestant rebels refuse to recognise Ferdinand as Matthias's successor as King of Bohemia, fearing further persecution. Instead they elect a Protestant – Friedrich, Elector Palatine – as their leader. Economic crisis across Europe (–1622): trade stagnates and acute inflation in Germany. The first black slaves arrive in Virginia. Johannes Kepler's *Harmonices mundi* elucidates planetary motion in a Copernican universe. Monteverdi's Seventh Book of madrigals, titled *Concerto*, is published in Venice. Giovanni Francesco Anerio's arrangement of Palestrina's *Missa Papae Marcelli* is issued in Rome, and he publishes his *Teatro armonico spirituale*, containing spiritual dialogues. Stefano Landi's *La morte d'Orfeo* perhaps given in Rome. In northern Europe, three landmarks of large-scale sacred music are published: Praetorius's *Polyhymnia caduceatrix*, Schütz's *Psalmen Davids*, and Sweelinck's *Cantiones sacrae*.

1620　At the Battle of White Mountain, Catholic armies defeat Friedrich of Bohemia. Catholicism is imposed on Bohemia. The Pilgrim Fathers, Puritan dissenters seeking freedom from the Church of England, set sail on the *Mayflower* from Plymouth and land in Massachusetts. Publication of *Pratum spirituale* by Mogens Pedersøn, containing polyphonic settings of Danish psalms for Christian IV.

1621　Philip IV crowned King of Spain. Huguenot revolt in France (–1622). With the ending of the truce between Spain and the United Provinces, war resumes in the Netherlands. Fighting continues in Germany, with imperial forces taking the Palatinate from Friedrich V (–1622). The Holy Roman Empire is in financial chaos as economies struggle to fund the war. First titled newspaper, *Corante*, is launched in London. Death of Sweelinck. Dario Castello transfers the freedom of vocal monody to instrumental sonatas in his virtuoso *Sonate concertate in stil moderno*.

1622　Forcible re-catholicisation begins in Habsburg lands. Numerous peasant revolts across central Europe (–1627). Inigo Jones completes the Banqueting House, Whitehall. The Pope canonises key figures in awakening Counter-Reformation spirituality: Ignatius Loyola, Philip Neri, Francis Xavier and Teresa of Avila. Salamone Rossi's polyphonic settings of Hebrew psalms published in Venice.

1623　Fighting continues in Germany, with the Palatinate transferred to Duke Maximilian of Bavaria. Salzburg University founded. Maffeo Barberini elected Pope Urban VIII. First folio edition of Shakespeare's plays published. William Byrd and Michael Praetorius die. Schein publishes *Israelis Brünlein*, a collection of sacred madrigals. Publication of Schütz's *Historia der Auferstehung*.

1624　Richelieu becomes leading minister in France (–1642): he centralises government and curbs the rights of Protestants. An imperial army of mercenaries is raised by the military entrepreneur Albrecht of Wallenstein. Spanish forces besiege the Dutch town of Breda (–1625). Frans Hals paints *The Laughing Cavalier*. Tarquinio Merula working in Poland. Monteverdi's *Combattimento di Tancredi e Clorinda* performed in Venice. Scheidt's *Tabulatura nova* published in Hamburg.

1625　Danes invade northern Germany in defence of Protestantism. Charles I ascends the English throne and marries Henrietta Maria, sister of the French king. War between England and Spain (–1630). The jurist Hugo Grotius proposes in his *De iure belli ac pacis* that a moral 'natural law' should govern relations within and between states. The first opera by a woman, Francesca Caccini's *La liberazione di Ruggiero dall'isola d'Alcina*, is given in Florence. Schütz's book of spiritual madrigals, *Cantiones sacrae*, is published.

1626　Christian IV of Denmark is defeated by the Catholic League at Lutter, leaving northern Germany open to Catholic occupation. Anglo-French war (–1629). Huguenots revolt in western France. In Paris, publication of Jehan Titelouze's organ settings of the Magnificat. In Leipzig, Schein publishes a second book of *Opella nova*.

1627 In a series of Catholic victories, the imperial forces subjugate northern Germany, including Holstein, Mecklenburg, Pomerania and Schleswig. Richelieu besieges La Rochelle, held by rebellious Huguenots (–1628). The death of Vincenzo II Gonzaga of Mantua opens a struggle for the Mantuan succession. Kepler's *Tabulae rudolphinae* shows how to calculate the position of the planets. Schütz's music drama *Dafne* is performed for the Saxon court. Publication of Frescobaldi's Second Book of Toccatas. Florentines in Madrid present the first opera in Spanish, *La selva sin amor* with a text by Lope de Vega and music mainly by Filippo Piccinini.

1628 Imperial forces seek to control the Baltic. La Rochelle falls after a year-long siege. In England, the House of Commons complains to the king about arbitrary taxes, martial law and the billeting of troops. William Harvey describes the circulation of the blood in *De motu cordis*. Schütz travels to Venice where he meets Monteverdi. The first Italian opera in Poland, *Acis*, is staged in Warsaw.

1629 England makes peace with France, Denmark makes peace with the emperor, and Sweden concludes a truce with Poland. In France too, the Huguenots accept peace at Alais. But in Germany, imperial power reaches its peak with a provocative Restitution Edict seizing former church lands from Protestants. In England, Charles I dissolves an obstreperous Parliament and resolves to rule personally. The Massachusetts Bay Company is founded. Carissimi becomes *maestro di cappella* at the Collegio Germanico in Rome. Schütz has his first book of *Symphoniae sacrae* published in Venice. Publication of Biagio Marini's Op. 8 sonatas.

1630 Protestant Gustavus Adolphus of Sweden, alarmed by Catholic hegemony, invades Germany. John Winthrop sails from England to be Governor of the Massachusetts Bay Company in New England. Mantua is sacked by imperial troops who carry the plague. The plague then sweeps across northern Italy (–1631); one casualty is Alessandro Grandi. Rubens paints *Peace and War*. Frescobaldi publishes his *Arie musicali*.

1631 Germany is riven by war. The imperial army sacks the Lutheran city of Magdeburg with a ferocity that terrifies all of Protestant Europe. But at the Battle of Breitenfeld, a Protestant alliance led by Sweden defeats the imperial army. War of Mantuan succession ends. First performance in Rome of Stefano Landi's opera *Sant'Alessio* in 1631 or 1632.

1632 More Swedish victories in Germany, but Gustavus Adolphus dies in battle at Lützen. His heir is the six-year-old Christina. Publication of second book of Monteverdi's *Scherzi musicali*. The only English set of concertato madrigals is published, the *Madrigales and Ayres* by Walter Porter (claimed to be a pupil of Monteverdi).

1633 Fighting continues in Germany. Schütz, despairing of the decline of music at Dresden, is given leave to be *Hofkapellmeister* in Copenhagen (–1635). Pope Urban VIII condemns Galileo's views as heretical. William Laud made Archbishop of Canterbury. John Donne's *Poems* are published. *Erminia sul Giordano* with music by Michelangelo Rossi is given by the Barberini during Carnival in Rome.

1634 Swedish defeat at Nördlingen marks recovery of Catholic cause in Germany. Utrecht University founded. Frescobaldi returns to Rome to serve the Barberini family. Spectacular masques given in England include Shirley's *The Triumph of Peace* (music by William Lawes) and Milton's *Comus* (Henry Lawes).

1635 Peace of Prague between Emperor Ferdinand II and Elector of Saxony. But the emperor is still at war with Sweden, and France declares war on Spain. Publication of Frescobaldi's organ Masses, *Fiori musicali*.

1636 Habsburg armies invade France. Harvard College founded. Marin Mersenne begins issuing *Harmonie universelle* (–1637). Schütz, lamenting the decline of German choirs in the war, issues a book of few-voiced concertos to adapt to the dwindling resources, his first book of *Kleine geistliche Concerte*.

1637 Ferdinand III is declared emperor in succession to his father Ferdinand II. A Muscovite expedition to Siberia reaches the Pacific. Riots in Scotland threaten Charles I's rule and lead eventually to war (–1640). René Descartes expounds his system of reasoning ('I think, therefore I am') in *Discours de la méthode*. A court theatre opens in Warsaw. The first public opera house in Venice, Teatro S. Cassiano, opens with *Andromeda* by Benedetto Ferrari and Francesco Manelli.

1638 Fighting continues in Germany, with French and imperial armies battling over Alsace and Lorraine. Sweden continues its campaigns in Germany (–1648). Galileo's *Dialoghi delle nuove scienze* outlines a theory of mechanics. Publication of Monteverdi's Eighth Book of madrigals, the *Madrigali guerrieri, et amorosi*, with a dedication to the newly elected Emperor Ferdinand III. Schütz's opera-ballet on the Orpheus myth is given at Dresden.

1639 War breaks out between Scotland and England, forcing Charles I to recall Parliament. Monteverdi's *Arianna* is revived in Venice. Cavalli's first opera, *Le nozze di Teti e di Peleo*, is given in Venice.

1640 Riots in Portugal lead to its ceding from Spain; the new Portuguese king is João IV, a keen patron of music. Première of Monteverdi's *Il ritorno d'Ulisse in patria* in Venice.

1641 In England, the Grand Remonstrance as Parliament objects to Charles I's remodelling of government. Opening of Teatro Novissimo, Venice, with *La finta pazza* by Francesco Sacrati and Giulio Strozzi. Publication of Monteverdi's huge collection of Venetian church music, *Selva morale e spirituale*. Chambonnières starts fee-paying concerts in Paris.

1642 Civil War breaks out in England, provoked by royal heavy-handedness and religious disputes. Charles II and his supporters flee London and set up court at Oxford, which becomes a centre of musical life. In France, Richelieu dies and Cardinal Mazarin becomes chief minister. Mazarin is Italian, and his lavish patronage promotes Italian music and opera in Paris. Rembrandt paints *The Night Watch*. Several Lutherans write lamentations for war-torn Germany, including Johann Erasmus Kindermann's cries for peace in *Musicalische Friedens-Seufftzer* (Nuremberg).

1643   Louis XIII of France dies and is succeeded by the five-year-old Louis XIV under a regency. King Charles I's armies prosper in the English Civil War. In war-torn Germany, a peace conference assembles in Westphalia (–1648). Nonetheless fighting continues, with French victories over imperial armies in Alsace and Lorraine. Danish–Swedish war (–1645). In Nuremberg, a historical concert is given of music from earliest times down to the present. Marco Scacchi publishes an attack on the psalms of Paul Siefert, starting a dispute that runs until 1649. *L'incoronazione di Poppea* is staged in Venice with music at least partly by Monteverdi. Cavalli's *Egisto*, to a libretto by Giovanni Faustini, is performed. Frescobaldi and Monteverdi die.

1644   In England, the Parliamentary armies prosper, defeating the Royalists at Marston Moor. With the rise of the Puritans, church music collapses and church organs are destroyed. Pope Urban VIII dies; his successor, Innocent X, halts the lavish spending on music and opera. Descartes's *Principia philosophiae* contrasts the universe (inert matter set in motion by its creator God) with the human soul (capable of thought and self-knowledge). An early German *Singspiel* is published, Georg Philipp Harsdörffer's *Seelewig* with music by Sigmund Theophil Staden: it is a moral allegory similar to school religious dramas. Giovanni Rovetta succeeds Monteverdi at St Mark's, Venice. Publication of Barbara Strozzi's First Book of madrigals.

1645   Civil War continues in England, with Cromwell's victory at Naseby, the surrender of Royalist Oxford and beheading of Archbishop Laud. A musician to be a casualty is William Lawes in the Siege of Chester. A group of English scientists (including Robert Boyle, John Wallis, Seth Ward and Christopher Wren) begins to meet regularly in London and Oxford; similar meetings of musical connoisseurs arise with the disruption of church and court music. Swedish offensives in Germany. Cardinal Mazarin's Italophile regime in Paris sponsors a staging of Sacrati's *La finta pazza*, the first Italian opera to be given in France.

1646   First English Civil War ends with victory of Parliament. A Presbyterian church is established in England. Some musicians from the English court are exiled in France and in the Netherlands. In Lübeck, *Abendmusik* concerts are by now a regular feature. French musicians in favour at Stockholm court of Queen Christina. Luigi Rossi arrives in Paris as part of Mazarin's promotion of Italian culture. Giovanni Battista Lulli arrives in Paris as a servant. Cavalli's *Egisto* staged in Paris.

1647   In Naples, the Masaniello uprising against the Spanish. Luigi Rossi's *Orfeo* is staged in Paris in a production controversial for its expense and extravagance. Publication of Schütz's second book of *Symphoniae sacrae* in Dresden, with a preface introducing Germans to the latest Italian string techniques.

1648   The Peace of Westphalia ends Thirty Years War. Peace of Münster between Dutch republic and Spain. A musical expression of the yearning for stability is Schütz's *Geistliche Chormusic*, with its self-consciously ordered counterpoint. In England, however, the Second Civil War starts. In France, the Fronde erupts as a protest against the absolutist government; the huge cost of Rossi's

Orfeo is one of the precipitating factors. The revolt is directed against the Italian-born Cardinal Mazarin, and this xenophobia forces Italian musicians to flee Paris. Christian IV of Denmark dies and is succeeded by Friedrich III. Carissimi's *Jephte* is performed in Rome about this time.

1649   Charles I is beheaded, and England is declared a republic. The beginning of several years of harvest failure across Europe (–1652). In *Des passions de l'âme* Descartes provides a mechanical basis for the emotions. Cavalli's *Giasone* performed in Venice. Froberger travels around Europe.

1650   Most of the occupying armies leave Germany. Further uprisings in France (–1653). Power struggle in Dutch republic. Publication of Kircher's compendium of musical knowledge, *Musurgia universalis*. Publication of Monteverdi's posthumous *Messa et salmi*.

1651   After an abortive attempt by Charles II (son of Charles I) to regain power, Cromwell is triumphant and the second Civil War ends in England. Thomas Hobbes's *Leviathan* analyses the state as a human construct, created by reason and not divinely ordained. Schütz complains repeatedly to the Elector of Saxony about the desperate poverty of the Dresden court musicians. Publication of Monteverdi's posthumous Ninth Book of madrigals. In London, John Playford issues his first music publications, *A Musicall Banquet* and *The English Dancing Master*.

1652   Trading rivalries precipitate the First Anglo-Dutch War (–1654). In England, George Fox founds the Quakers, a radical religious movement rejecting social hierarchies and the physical church. Lully enters royal service. Henri Du Mont's *Cantica sacra* are the first *petits motets* to be printed in Paris. Antonio Cesti's *Il Cesare amante* given in Venice. Cesti starts service at Innsbruck (–1657).

1653   Cromwell installed as Lord Protector of England, Scotland and Ireland. Despite the Commonwealth's ban on theatre, James Shirley's masque *Cupid and Death* is performed as a court entertainment. The noble revolt collapses in France and peace resumes with Mazarin returning from exile. Peasants rebel in Switzerland.

1654   Christina of Sweden abdicates and converts to Catholicism (1655). She moves to Rome, where her palace soon becomes a centre for musical patronage. Playford publishes *A Breefe Introduction to the Skill of Musick*, the first of many primers promoting amateur music-making in England. Cesti's *La Cleopatra* (a reworking of *Il Cesare amante*) inaugurates the Komödienhaus, Innsbruck.

1655   Sweden invades Poland. Anglo-Spanish war (–1660). Johann Rosenmüller arrested on charges of pederasty and flees Leipzig. Cavalli's *Xerse* and *Erismena* given in Venice. Publication of first book of Giovanni Legrenzi's sonatas.

1656   Christiaan Huygens invents the pendulum clock. Velázquez paints *Las Meninas*. The playwright and actor-manager William Davenant stages *The Siege of Rhodes* privately in London (the now-lost music is by a consortium of composers). Christina of Sweden appoints Carissimi as *maestro di cappella del concerto di camera*. Cesti's *Orontea*, one of the most popular operas of the century, is given in Innsbruck.

1657 Emperor Ferdinand III dies. Cesti's *La Dori* is given in Innsbruck. Johann Caspar Kerll's *L'Oronte* inaugurates opera house at Munich court.

1658 Louis XIV tries to become Holy Roman Emperor but is defeated in the election by the Habsburg candidate, Leopold I. Oliver Cromwell dies and is succeeded by his son Richard, who proves ineffectual and resigns in 1659. Calderón's *El laurel de Apolo* is the first known *zarzuela* (Spanish music theatre with mix of spoken and sung dialogue).

1659 Harvests fail across Europe (–1661). France and Spain make peace at the Pyrenees. Robert Cambert and Pierre Perrin collaborate on early French music dramas, the *Pastorale d'Issy* and *Ariane*; *Ariane* is commissioned by Mazarin to celebrate the Franco-Spanish peace. In London, *Cupid and Death* is revived with music by Matthew Locke. In Bologna a long dispute begins over the propriety of contrapuntal writing in a Mass by Maurizio Cazzati.

1660 Charles II is restored to the English and Scottish thrones. Musical life transforms, with the reopening of London's theatres and the return of music to court and church. Samuel Pepys starts a diary that captures much of the excitement of the period. To seal the Peace of the Pyrenees, Louis XIV marries Maria Theresa of Spain. Cavalli is summoned to Paris to stage *Ercole amante* in honour of the wedding, but it is not ready in time and is replaced by *Xerse*; in Spain, the celebrations include *Celos aun del aire matan*, a collaboration between Juan Hidalgo and Pedro Calderón that is the first extant Spanish opera. In Christmas Vespers at Dresden, Schütz's *Historia der Geburth Jesu Christi* is performed.

1661 Mazarin dies and Louis XIV begins his personal rule of France. He appoints his favourite, Lully, as *Surintendant de la musique de la chambre*. Robert Boyle's *The Sceptical Chymist* discusses the nature of elements and describes his experiments fully so others can replicate them. The Duke's Theatre opens at Lincoln's Inn Fields, London, with a revival of *The Siege of Rhodes*.

1662 Charles II marries the Portuguese princess Catherine of Braganza. He grants a charter to the Royal Society, dedicated to scientific discovery and discussion. The Church of England is restored; the new version of the Book of Common Prayer has rubrics permitting choral music. Cavalli ends his stay in Paris by performing *Ercole amante*.

1663 The Turks declare war on the Holy Roman Empire; they advance intermittently through the Balkans until defeated at Vienna (1683). Christopher Wren designs his first building, the Sheldonian Theatre in Oxford. Publication of Legrenzi's Third Book of sonatas. Plague in Hamburg: among the musicians to die are Thomas Selle and Heinrich Scheidemann.

1664 French East India Company formed. Johann Heinrich Schmelzer's *Sonatae unarum fidium* contains the first published solo violin sonatas by a non-Italian in Germany.

1665 Second Anglo-Dutch war (–1667). Great Plague of London. Danish royal law codifies absolutist monarchy. The sickly and childless Carlos II succeeds to Spanish throne. The *Livre d'orgue* by Guillaume Gabriel Nivers establishes the styles and textures of French classical organ music.

1666   Great Fire of London destroys much of the City but finally eradicates the plague. In Bologna, the Accademia dei Floridi is refounded as the Accademia Filarmonica. An Italian troupe of singers led by Vincenzo Albrici arrives in England as part of an unsuccessful royal attempt to foster Italian opera. Leopold I marries Margarita of Spain; the union is celebrated in Vienna with Cesti's *Nettunno e Flor festeggianti*. First performances of Schütz's St Matthew and St Luke Passions, Dresden.

1667   France invades the Spanish Netherlands. Russia and Poland end thirteen years of hostilities. In Dresden, the opera house opens. Publication of Milton's *Paradise Lost*. Further celebrations of Leopold I's marriage include the allegorical *Contesa dell'aria e dell'acqua* with music by Bertali and Schmelzer. Rosenmüller's sonatas are published in Venice.

1668   Peace of Aix-la-Chapelle between Spain and France. A secret treaty offers France certain Spanish territories in the Low Countries and Italy when the childless Carlos II dies. The two-year-long marriage celebrations in Vienna culminate in Cesti's 'festa teatrale' *Il pomo d'oro*. Buxtehude made organist of the Marienkirche, Lübeck. Cavalli made *maestro di cappella* at St Mark's, Venice. In Paris, Bénigne de Bacilly's vocal treatise *Remarques curieuses sur l'art de bien chanter* describes expressive ornamentation.

1669   Publication of a satire on the Thirty Years War, *Simplicissimus* by Jakob von Grimmelshausen. Académie Royale de Musique founded in Paris to foster opera in French. Death of Cesti.

1670   In the secret Treaty of Dover, Charles II promises France that he will break his alliance with Holland. The posthumous *Pensées* of Pascal are published. Spinoza's *Tractatus theologico-politicus* expounds a rationalist theology. Lully and Molière's *comédie-ballet*, *Le bourgeois gentilhomme*, given in Paris. Publication of two books of *Pièces de clavessin* by Jacques Champion de Chambonnières.

1671   Emperor Leopold I promises neutrality if France attacks Holland. The first true French opera, *Pomone* by Pierre Perrin with music by Cambert, is given in Paris. The *tragédie-ballet* by Lully and Molière, *Psyché*, is given in Paris. The Dorset Garden theatre opens in London with a lavish stage ideal for musical extravaganzas.

1672   William of Orange elected Stadholder of the Netherlands. France invades the Netherlands (–1678); third Anglo-Dutch war (–1674). In England, the granting of limited religious freedom to Catholics leads to fears of popery. Isaac Newton describes the spectrum and refraction of light to the Royal Society. In London, John Banister begins to present concerts where admission is charged. In Venice, Antonio Sartorio's *L'Orfeo* and *L'Adelaide* are given. The Académie Royale de Musique in Paris runs into financial troubles and is taken over by Lully, who thus gains a monopoly over opera production. Schütz dies. The first zarzuela with surviving music, *Los celos hacen estrellas* (Guevara–Hidalgo), is given in Madrid.

1673   English Test Act forbids Catholics and dissenters from holding public office. Publication of Johann Theile's Matthew Passion in Lübeck. Locke's *Melothesia* contains the first English instructions on figured bass. Lully's first *tragédie en musique, Cadmus et Hermione*, is given in Paris. Robert Cambert comes to London and tries unsuccessfully to launch a French-style Royal Academy of Musick for opera. Sartorio working in Hanover (–1675).

1674 Swedes invade Germany (–1675). Carissimi dies. Lully's *Alceste* is given in Paris. The Theatre Royal opens in Drury Lane, London.

1675 French military victories and expansion cease for several years. Danish-Swedish war (–1679). The Royal Observatory in Greenwich is founded. Christopher Wren begins St Paul's Cathedral (–1709). In Germany, Philipp Spener's *Pia desideria* calls for a personal Protestant piety. London performance of *Psyche*, an anglicised version of Lully's *tragédie-ballet* with a libretto by Shadwell and music by Locke. Stradella's oratorio *S. Giovanni Battista* given in Rome.

1676 Pope Innocent XI installed. Cavalli dies. Publication of *Musick's Monument* by Thomas Mace, a treatise nostalgic for the old ways of music in England.

1677 William of Orange marries Princess Mary, the niece of Charles II of England. Pope Innocent XI bans public theatre and opera in Rome. Lully begins publishing the music of his operas. His *Isis* causes scandal when his enemies interpret it as an allegory of the king and the royal mistresses.

1678 Peace of Nijmegen ends Franco-Dutch war; France also makes peace with Spain. In England, the Popish Plot, an alleged Catholic conspiracy. Publication of the first part of John Bunyan's *Pilgrim's Progress*. René de la Salle explores Great Lakes of Canada. Stradella starts writing operas for Genoa. Hamburg opera house opens with Theile's *Adam und Eva*, an opera based on the biblical story.

1679 Northern European wars between Sweden, Denmark and Brandenburg cease. In England, the Exclusion Crisis (–1681), an attempt to bar Charles II's brother James from the succession on account of his Catholicism. The Whig and Tory parties emerge during the debates about the succession. Purcell appointed organist of Westminster Abbey at age of twenty. Johann Heinrich Schmelzer becomes Kapellmeister to the Habsburg court in Vienna. Alessandro Scarlatti's first opera, *Gli equivoci nel sembiante*, is given in Rome.

1680 France begins policy of territorial aggression (Réunions), seizing French Rhine lands. York Buildings, with a public concert room, built in London. Purcell completes his string fantasias about this time.

1681 France takes Strasbourg. Lully made *Secrétaire du roi*. Arcangelo Corelli's op. 1 trio sonatas published in Rome.

1682 French court moves to Versailles. Louis XIV begins persecuting Huguenots in France. Stradella murdered in Genoa. Rosenmüller returns to Germany and takes up post at Wolfenbüttel court. Massive polychoral music being performed in Salzburg, including the 53-part *Missa salisburgensis*. Publication of Georg Muffat's *Armonico tributo*, sonatas that can also be performed as concertos.

1683 A major Ottoman attack on the Habsburg lands culminates in the Siege of Vienna, which is relieved by a multinational Christian army. Leopold I and Carlos II of Spain join Dutch–Swedish alliance against France. John Blow's *Venus and Adonis* is given at the London court about this time. Purcell's

Sonnata's of III Parts is published. First celebration of St Cecilia's Day in London, with Purcell's ode *Welcome to all the Pleasures*.

1684   In the Treaty of Regensburg, France agrees to cease aggression. Heinrich Biber made *Kapellmeister* at Salzburg. Giuseppe Torelli moves to Bologna. Alessandro Scarlatti appointed viceregal *maestro di cappella* and music director at the Teatro San Bartolomeo, Naples.

1685   Charles II of England dies, to be succeeded by his brother James II. James's Catholicism arouses numerous protests and an unsuccessful rebellion under the Duke of Monmouth. In London, Dryden's *Albion and Albanius* is performed with music by Louis Grabu. In France, Louis XIV revokes the Edict of Nantes that had assured religious liberty for Huguenots; Huguenots flee to Holland and Berlin. Corelli's *Sonate da camera*, op. 2, is published in Rome. *Roland* by Lully is given in Versailles.

1686   Emperor Leopold, Spain, Sweden and several German principalities form the League of Augsburg to resist French aggression. Legrenzi appointed *maestro di cappella* at St Mark's, Venice. Louis XIV orders the publication of Henry Du Mont's *Grands motets* as a document of the glories of the Versailles *Chapelle*. Lully's masterpiece, *Armide*, is given in Paris. Lully's *Cadmus et Hermione* performed in London. Georg Muffat's *Modulatio organica* published.

1687   In the Battle of Mohács, the Turks are defeated by Charles of Lorraine. Pope Innocent XI secretly excommunicates Louis XIV in a dispute about clerical rights and revenues. James II lifts religious restrictions in England. Isaac Newton's *Principia mathematica* explains the laws of gravity. Elisabeth Jacquet de La Guerre's *Pièces de clavessin* published in Paris. Lully dies, ending his absolutist stranglehold on Parisian musical life.

1688   France begins war against the League of Augsburg (–1697), invading the Palatinate. Glorious Revolution in England: after a son is born to James II, the threat of a Catholic succession leads Whig lords to invite William of Orange to invade England. James II flees to France. Agostino Steffani appointed to Hanover court (–1696). Charpentier writes sacred opera *David et Jonathas* for a Jesuit college in Paris. André Raison's *Livre d'orgue* published in Paris.

1689   William and Mary receive English crown. England joins war against France (Nine Years War). Purcell's *Dido and Aeneas* performed at a Chelsea girls' school. Ducal opera house opens in Hanover with Steffani's *Henrico Leone*. Jean-Henri d'Anglebert's *Pièces de clavecin* published with a table of ornaments. Corelli's op. 3 trio sonatas published in Rome. Publication of Giovanni Battista Vitali's *Artifici musicali*, a set of sonatas using contrapuntal techniques prized by Bolognese academicians.

1690   The exiled James II invades Ireland but is defeated by William III in the Battle of the Boyne. Two treatises by John Locke are published: *Essay on Human Understanding* analyses the role of experience and intuition in human knowledge; *Treatises of Government* rejects monarchy by divine right. With the decline of court patronage, Purcell works increasingly in London theatres, writing music for plays such as Dryden's *Dioclesian*. In Paris, François Couperin publishes his *Pièces d'orgue* with a printed title-page and the music in manuscript. In Rome, the Accademia degli Arcadi is founded, fostering a pastoral fantasy-land for literary meetings. Brunswick opera house founded by Duke Anton Ulrich.

1691   John Dryden's *King Arthur* is given in London with music by Purcell.

1692   Glencoe Massacre. Witch Trials in Salem, Massachusetts. Purcell's *The Fairy Queen* given in London. Marin Marais's *Pièces en trio* published in Paris.

1693   Louis XIV sues for peace with the Spanish Netherlands. Couperin made court organist at Versailles. Charpentier's *Médée* staged in Paris. Opera house opens in Leipzig on initiative of Johann Adam Strungk.

1694   Famine in much of Europe (–1697). In England, Queen Mary dies and is buried with funeral music by Purcell among others. William III now reigns alone. Bank of England set up to handle national debt. Purcell writes D major *Te Deum* and *Jubilate*. Halle University founded. Corelli's op. 4 chamber sonatas published in Rome. Alessandro Scarlatti's *Il Pirro e Demetrio* given in Naples. The first *tragédie en musique* by a woman, Elisabeth Jacquet de la Guerre's *Céphale et Procris* is staged in Paris but to little success.

1695   William III, leading an army in the Netherlands, retakes territory from the French. Press censorship ends in England. Purcell's *The Indian Queen* is performed in London, but later that year Purcell dies at the age of 36. Unlike any previous English composer, he is widely mourned and commemorated in concerts, elegies and compositions. John Walsh starts publishing cheap engraved music in London. Johann Pachelbel becomes organist at Sebaldkirche, Nuremberg. Publication of Georg Muffat's *Florilegium primum* in Augsburg.

1696   Treaty of Turin between France and Savoy ends the wars in northern Italy. John Toland's *Christianity not Mysterious* argues that although the world was created by God it is now governed entirely by laws of science. Financial crisis leads to disbanding of orchestra and *cappella* at S. Petronio, Bologna (–1701); Torelli leaves Bologna for Germany. Giovanni Bononcini's *Il trionfo di Camilla* performed in Naples. Publication of Buxtehude's op. 2 trio sonatas in Hamburg.

1697   Treaty of Ryswick ends Nine Years War and the fighting between France and League of Augsburg; it is celebrated with many odes in London. St Paul's Cathedral is consecrated. Estienne Roger starts publishing engraved music in Amsterdam. André Campra's opera *L'Europe galante* takes Parisian audiences by storm. Reinhard Keiser arrives as music director at the Hamburg opera.

1698   A second Spanish partition treaty seeks to maintain the balance of European powers by determining the succession of the childless Carlos II. Peter the Great of Russia concludes visits to Prussia, Netherlands, England and Vienna, and begins reforms in his homeland. Publication of Georg Muffat's *Florilegium secundum* with a preface detailing bowing and ornamentation in French orchestral playing. Torelli's *Concerti musicali*, op. 6, includes two of the first solo violin concertos.

1699   Treaty of Karlowitz ends wars with Ottoman Empire. Failure of attempt to establish a Scottish colony at Darien (Central America). English navigator and buccaneer William Dampier explores coasts of Australia and New Guinea (–1701). Russia replaces Byzantine calendar with Julian. Antonio Caldara appointed *maestro di cappella* at Mantua. Publication of Pachelbel's *Hexachordum apollonis*. Henry Playford begins issuing music serials and a periodical, *Mercurius musicus*. André Campra's *La carnaval de Venise* – an exotic masquerade – is performed in Paris.

1700   Death of Carlos II renders Spanish Habsburg line extinct; his designated heir is Louis XIV's grandson. Tension between France and Austria leads to the War of Spanish Succession (1701–13). Great Northern War begins, pitting Sweden against Russia, Denmark, Poland and Saxony (–1721), disrupting culture in cities such as Hamburg. Corelli's op. 5 violin sonatas published in Rome. In London, a contest is announced for the best setting of William Congreve's masque *The Judgement of Paris*; the surprise winner (1701) is not the favourite, John Eccles, but an outsider, John Weldon. Publication of Johann Kuhnau's *Der musikalische Quack-Salber* (a satire of a German musician who tries to hide his incompetence by pretending to be Italian) and *Musicalische Vorstellung einiger Biblischer Historien* (keyboard sonatas based on Old Testament stories).

· Appendix II ·

Places and institutions

STEPHEN ROSE

Antwerp
: Formerly the major trade centre of northern Europe, Antwerp began to stagnate economically in the seventeenth century. Nonetheless its printers continued to be of international importance. Music-printing had been established there by Tielman Susato in 1543, and by 1600 the firms of Phalèse and Plantin were producing many volumes of sacred music, lute music and Italian madrigals. The city was also famed for its harpsichord makers, including the Ruckers and Couchet families. By the 1690s, however, Antwerp had been eclipsed by Amsterdam as a centre for music-publishing.

Bologna
: Under the control of a Papal legate, Bologna was a lively musical centre, with important churches, monasteries and convents. The first musical academy to be founded in the city was the Accademia dei Floridi (1615–23; associated with Adriano Banchieri), whose fleeting successors included the Accademia dei Filomusi and Accademia dei Filaschi. Longer-lived was the Accademia Filarmonica, founded in 1666. These academies were for professional musicians, giving opportunities to discuss theory, hear new pieces, and appraise performers. The Accademia Filarmonica determined taste and codified style among Bolognese musicians. Although sometimes seen as a dusty, conservative institution, its members were at the forefront of the development of the sonata and *concerto grosso*. Given its geographical position, Bologna also acted as a clearing-house for professional singers and actors freelancing across Italy.

Bologna, San Petronio
: Situated in the centre of the city, the basilica was an influential centre of vocal and instrumental music. Its ample, if at times unmanageable, acoustics encouraged polychoral music and the use of separate groups of performers. It was renowned for its instrumentalists and for the orchestra that grew up in the second half of the century. Under Maurizio Cazzati (*maestro*, 1657–71) a distinctive orchestral style arose using timbral contrasts that led to the *concerto grosso*. Another local speciality was music for trumpet and strings, for a solo trumpet sounded with clarity in the echoing building. In the 1680s Giuseppe Torelli refined his concerto style here. During 1696–1701 the orchestra was dissolved and its members took the Bolognese concerto style elsewhere.

[547]

Copenhagen, royal court	Under King Christian IV (*reg.* 1588–1648), the court was cosmopolitan, with English and German musicians complementing native Danish talent. John Dowland worked here 1598–1606, and Schütz made several visits in the 1630s and 1640s, writing some of his *Kleine geistliche Concerte II* and *Symphoniae sacrae II* for the court. Christian IV was keen to emulate Italian music, sponsoring a madrigal anthology (*Giardini novi*, 1605–6) and sending his best native musicians such as Mogens Pedersøn to study with Giovanni Gabrieli in Venice. At the end of the century the court hosted ballets by visiting Frenchmen.
Dresden, electoral court	Dresden was the seat of the Electors of Saxony. Michael Praetorius reformed the court *Kapelle* in 1612–15. From 1617 Schütz was *Kapellmeister*: he won renown for his polychoral music and music dramas, and continued a local tradition of settings of the Passion and other biblical *historiae*. From the 1630s war badly affected court music and the morale of the musicians sank to a nadir in 1651. About this time Prince Johann Georg II began hiring Italian musicians such as Vincenzo Albrici and Giovanni Andrea Bontempi, who rapidly eclipsed the Germans. Italian operas were staged and a new opera-house opened in 1667. With the accession of Friedrich August I in 1694, a glittering age for the arts began. In 1697 he converted to Catholicism, requiring the chapel to adopt a Catholic repertory and making the court even more hospitable to Italian musicians.
Florence, grand-ducal court	The musicians at the Medici court pioneered opera and solo song. Jacopo Peri set the opera *Euridice* for the wedding of Maria de' Medici to Henri IV in 1600. Two years later Giulio Caccini published the first book of solo songs with continuo, *Le nuove musiche*. These experiments were part of a trend across Italy but there were particular reasons why they came to fruition in Florence. Peri and Caccini were influenced by the discussions about the power of ancient Greek music held at the Camerata of Giovanni de' Bardi (succeeded by Jacopo Corsi). Such Classical associations appealed to the Medici, who saw their court as a new Athens. Furthermore, Caccini associated his monody with *sprezzatura* (graceful nonchalance), an attribute desirable in any courtier and again attractive to the Medici. Later, in 1621–8 Florence was ruled by female regents who favoured Francesca Caccini, and a number of music-dramas enacted the lives of saints, virgin martyrs and Old Testament heroines who were models for female rule. The court also had distinguished music in the 1690s, when Grand Prince Ferdinando de' Medici was a lavish patron of opera composers, including Alessandro Scarlatti.
Hamburg, churches	Hamburg was an immensely rich trading centre, generally unaffected by the century's wars. Its rich church music was led by organists such as Johann Adam Reincken, Heinrich Scheidemann

and Matthias Weckmann, and cantors including Thomas Selle and Christoph Bernhard.

Hamburg, opera-house

In 1678 the focus of Hamburg's musical life moved to the new opera-house on the Gänsemarkt. This was a public theatre on the Venetian model, but to placate anxious Protestant clergy many of the operas performed there were on Biblical or moralistic plots, such as the opening production of *Adam und Eva*, with music by Johann Theile. In 1695 Reinhard Keiser became music director, and in 1703–6 Handel served his operatic apprenticeship here.

Innsbruck, archducal court

Music flourished here under Archduke Ferdinand Karl in the 1650s. Antonio Cesti was musical director 1652–7, and a *Komödienhaus* opened in 1654. Operas staged here by Cesti included *La Cleopatra* (1654), *L'Argia* (for the official conversion of Christina of Sweden to Catholicism, 1655) and *Orontea* (1656). Music lapsed in 1665 with the extinction of the Tyrolean royal house and the annexation of the province by Austria.

Kassel, court

Under Moritz of Hesse (*req.* 1592–1627) the court was a centre of music. Moritz, nicknamed 'The Learned', had passions for music, drama, alchemy and philosophy; he was an amateur composer and corresponded widely with musicians. He sponsored the Venetian apprenticeship of Heinrich Schütz and hosted visits from Dowland and Hans Leo Hassler. His court had one of the first theatres in Germany, the Ottoneum (1603–6).

London, Chapel Royal

The musical chapel of the English monarchy that moved around the various royal palaces in London and environs. Although important during the reigns of James I and Charles I, it reached a peak of prestige when refounded in 1660 on the Restoration of Charles II. Now its music became a symbol of the revived church and monarchy. Promising choristers from across the country were pressed into service at the chapel, leading to a concentration of young talent that included John Blow, Pelham Humfrey and Henry Purcell. The Chapel Royal was the only place in England to use violins in service music: Charles encouraged the performance of large-scale anthems with accompaniment from members of the royal violin band, on the model of the French *grand motet*. With the accession of William and Mary in 1689, stringed instruments were generally excluded from the Chapel and its music declined.

London, King's Music

Under James I and Charles I, the court employed a violin band, and staged extravagant masques. In 1642 the royal musicians dispersed at the start of the Civil War. On the Restoration in 1660, the violin band was enlarged to 24 instrumentalists on the French model and had much music written for it by Matthew Locke. The court musicians regularly performed odes to honour the king. With the accession of William and Mary in 1689, court music declined and only a handful of odes were newly composed.

London, public concerts	London had several series of concerts and music-meetings that tapped the public market for music. John Banister began a concert series in 1672 using musicians moonlighting from their court jobs. The first purpose-built concert hall was York Buildings, where concerts began *c.* 1680. Stationers' Hall also hosted concerts, notably (from 1683) an annual celebration of St Cecilia (the patron saint of music) for which a new ode was commissioned each year. By the 1700s such concerts made London a mecca for foreign virtuosos and composers such as Nicola Cosimi, Nicola Haym, Johann Christian Pepusch, and later, George Frideric Handel.
London, theatres	On the Restoration, two rival theatre companies were formed under the patronage of King Charles II and the Duke of York respectively. Most of their plays had incidental music and songs. In 1671 the Duke's Company moved into a well-equipped theatre at Dorset Garden, ideal for musical extravaganzas. Here it staged *The Tempest* (1674) and *Psyche* (1675). In 1682 the two companies merged, and subsequent music dramas at Dorset Garden included the unsuccessful *Albion and Albanius* (1685) and a series of so-called semi-operas with music by Purcell: *Dioclesian* (1690), *King Arthur* (1691) and *The Fairy Queen* (1692). In 1695 a breakaway company began acting at Lincoln's Inn Fields, where masques with music by Daniel Purcell and John Eccles were staged.
Madrid, court	The royal chapel was conservative, dominated by Flemish personnel and musical styles. Florentines tried to introduce opera in Spanish at the court in 1627. But *La selva sin amor* was unsuccessful: there was already a rich indigenous tradition of music drama and the 'Most Catholic' King Philip IV was unwilling to stoop to imported opera. Instead, the court poet Pedro Calderón de la Barca wrote numerous court spectacles and religious dramas. He also invented the *zarzuela*, a short spoken pastoral interspersed with music. The music was usually written by Juan Hidalgo and drew on popular vernacular song.
Mantua, ducal court	Music flourished under Duke Vincenzo Gonzaga (*req.* 1587–1612). Monteverdi served here 1589–1612 (as *maestro della musica di camera* from 1601), as did Giovanni Giacomo Gastoldi (*maestro di cappella*, 1588–1609) and the virtuoso violinist Salamone Rossi. Pioneering theatrical entertainments included Monteverdi's *Orfeo* (1607) and the larger-scale dramas for the 1608 wedding of Prince Francesco Gonzaga and Margherita of Savoy: Monteverdi's *Arianna*; Marco da Gagliano's *Dafne*; and Guarini's play *L'idropica* performed with extravagant *intermedi*. Music declined with the War of the Mantuan Succession (1627–31), which culminated in the city being sacked and struck by the plague; but the city and court gradually recovered their position.
Milan	Since the rule of Cardinal Borromeo in the 1560s, Milan was known as a bastion of the Catholic Reformation. The emphasis

on religious music increased in the seventeenth century, and some of the city's convents also became famous for their performances. Opera was slow to develop: at first touring productions appeared in the Teatrino della Commedia at the court of the Spanish rulers; only in the 1670s did a tradition of local productions emerge.

Modena, ducal court
From 1598 the seat of the Este family (formerly at Ferrara). D'India worked here in the 1620s and composed his Eighth Book of madrigals for the court. In the 1680s, during the reign of Francesco II d'Este, numerous oratorios and operas were performed. In the city, the Accademia de' Dissonanti emulated the experiments with concertos made in Rome and nearby Bologna.

Munich, electoral court
From the 1560s the Electors of Bavaria won renown for their music under the direction of Orlande de Lassus. Subsequently music was badly affected by the Thirty Years War (1618–48). From the 1650s, however, court opera began to flourish in the newly opened Salvatortheater, under the direction of Johann Caspar Kerll and Agostino Steffani among others. Meanwhile the Jesuits often staged religious drama at the city's schools and churches.

Naples
Operas were given at the Teatro San Bartolomeo from the early 1650s. At first, pieces by Cavalli, Monteverdi and others were imported from Venice. In 1684 Alessandro Scarlatti became musical director and wrote about 40 operas for the theatre until his eventual departure in 1707. Opera was also a favoured entertainment of the viceroys who ruled Naples on behalf of Spain, but the short rule of each viceroy inhibited the development of musical traditions at court. The city's conservatoires were important early examples of the institution, feeding the rapidly increasing demand for virtuoso singers (particularly castratos) and instrumentalists. Francesco Provenzale, as *maestro* (1663) of the Conservatorio di Santa Maria di Loreto, and then, from 1673, of the Conservatorio della Pietà dei Turchini, was particularly influential in these contexts.

Paris, Académie Royale de Musique
A state-sponsored, privately owned opera company in Paris. There were similar academies for dance, painting and sculpture, all putting artists, writers and scholars at the service of the king. The opera privilege was originally held by Pierre Perrin. Lully took it over in 1672 and thereafter performed a *tragédie en musique* every year until 1687 in Paris and at court. On his death the Académie was taken over by his son-in-law. The repertoire consisted mainly of revivals of Lully's works and new pieces in a similar style by a small circle of composers groomed by him.

Paris and Versailles, Musique Royale
The royal musicians followed the monarch's travels between the Louvre and country residences such as St Germain-en-Laye or Fontainebleau; from 1682 the court was based at Versailles. The Musique Royale comprised the Ecurie (players of outdoor or ceremonial instruments such as trumpets and oboes), the Chambre (playing a secular repertory for the king) and the Chapelle. The

favoured court entertainment was the *ballet de cour*, a spectacle combining music, verse, dance and stage-design; the emphasis was on dance, and the *ballets* rarely had a strong narrative. Under Louis XIV, music accompanied every ceremonial event of the royal day, and the number of *ballets* and divertissements increased. Lully rose to musical power and developed a distinctive French style (rich harmonies, eloquent ornamentation, genres such as the French overture and rondeau) that contributed to senses of national identity. Lully suppressed rivals and other styles of composition, and discouraged musicians from studying abroad. Even before his death, court music had ossified into formulas favoured by the king; in the 1690s, musicians who wanted court advancement had to maintain Lullian traditions. Nonetheless from the 1670s the court was a musical magnet, attracting Germans, English and even Italians who came to learn the 'French taste'.

Paris, Vingt-Quatre Violons du Roi
One of the ensembles at the French royal court. The first record of 24 violins playing together is at the 1617 *Ballet de la délivrance de Renaud*, but only later did the band become a formal entity. It was a five-part orchestra, with six violins on the top part, six bass instruments, and three inner parts each with four players. They played at the king's command in *ballets de cour* and official ceremonies. They became renowned for the quality of their ensemble. In London, the Francophile Charles II instigated a string ensemble of similar constitution.

Puebla (Mexico)
Music flourished at the churches and cathedral of this colonial city. At the cathedral (dedicated in 1649), Gaspar Fernández and Juan Gutiérrez de Padilla built up a large library of polyphonic Masses and motets; both also wrote *villancicos* for festivals in the church year.

Rome, academies
Roman patrons and connoisseurs often held performances in private residences that could sometimes be termed 'academies'. These might be *ad hoc* gatherings or more formal meetings with pretensions to learning. The music performed typically included cantatas and, later, Corelli's chamber sonatas. Queen Christina of Sweden held a regular academy from 1656. After her death this took a more formal shape as the Accademia degli Arcadi, a gathering of literary figures who assumed pastoral personas and whose ideas influenced the course of Italian opera at the turn of the century.

Rome, oratories
Confraternities (religious societies of laymen) met in oratories for communal prayers and singing. Sometimes there were contemplative enactments of scripture. In 1600, the oratory of the Chiesa Nuova saw the performance of Emilio de' Cavalieri's spiritual drama *Rappresentatione di Anima, et di Corpo*; similar works (such as Agostino Agazzari's *Eumelio* of 1606)

were performed in Roman seminaries and colleges. In the 1640s, the Barberini cardinals encouraged performances at the oratories of S. Girolamo della Carità, SS Crocefisso at S. Marcello, and again at the Chiesa Nuova. These were the venues for Carissimi's oratorios such as *Jephte*. In the 1670s a fourth oratory became important, the Oratorio dei Fiorentini, where Stradella's *San Giovanni Battista* was given in 1675.

Rome, Palazzo Barberini   When Maffeo Barberini was elected Pope Urban VIII in 1623, his family's palaces 'ai Giubbonari' and then 'alle Quattro fontane' became renowned for their music and spectacle. In 1631–2 the Barberini established a series of opera productions with Stefano Landi's *Sant'Alessio*. This was the first of several operas on the lives of saints, a subject that legitimised the use of the secular style of opera in Rome. Opera was staged regularly at Carnival until the last great Barberini production, Luigi Rossi's *Il palazzo incantato* (1642).

Rome, Papal chapel   The Cappella Pontificia (or Cappella Sistina) was one of the greatest choirs of the world, and being appointed here was the summit of a singer's career. It sang unaccompanied (save on a very few occasions) and for the most part avoided modern styles; instead it upheld a late sixteenth-century ideal of Catholic church music, with a repertory fixed around the Palestrina style.

Rome, St Peter's Basilica   The choir of St Peter's, the Cappella Giulia, was the other major choir in Rome. The singers, like those in the Cappella Sistina, often took outside engagements in the city's private palaces and confraternities. From 1608 Frescobaldi was organist here.

Salzburg, archbishop's court and cathedral   The Archbishops of Salzburg were keen patrons of music. In 1614 Monteverdi's *Orfeo* was performed here, the first opera to be given outside Italy. In the 1680s Biber was *Kapellmeister*, and Georg Muffat spent time at the court between his trips to Paris and Rome. The cathedral, consecrated in 1628, had four choir-lofts that provided excellent opportunities for polychoral music, such as the 53-part *Missa salisburgensis* and many other imposing pieces by Biber.

Venice, St Mark's Basilica   Located at the centre of the city, the basilica was a symbol of Venice and of its doge. Its ceremonies contributed to the image of the city-republic and impressed many foreign visitors. On grand occasions, music could be polychoral (sometimes, but not always, using the choir-lofts and balconies), mixing voices and instruments, although standard musical fare was more conservative. The city recruited musicians and composers of international stature for the basilica: its *maestri di cappella* included Monteverdi (1613–43), Giovanni Rovetta (1644–68), Cavalli (1668–76) and Giovanni Legrenzi (1685–90). Musicians holding lesser posts at the basilica included Grandi, Rigatti and Rosenmüller, while many distinguished organists, singers and instrumentalists made their name there. Musicians at St Mark's often freelanced for the city's confraternities and opera-houses.

Venice, theatres

Opera at the Teatro San Cassiano began in 1637; here Benedetto Ferrari and Francesco Manelli inaugurated new modes of music-theatrical production, providing entertainment for subscribers and the ticket-buying public. In 1639 the Teatro S. Moisè and Teatro SS Giovanni e Paolo opened, and two years later the Teatro Novissimo was completed specifically for opera. In the 1640s the business was dominated by Giovanni Faustini, whose annual collaborations with Cavalli established the forms and conventions of opera for the rest of the century. By the 1660s as many as six theatres were running simultaneously, often relying on foreign visitors for custom and building up a somewhat stereotyped repertory known to appeal to audiences. In 1674 the Teatro S. Moisè reopened offering much cheaper tickets and allowing a less elite audience to attend. By this time, however, the important venues for opera were S. Salvatore, S. Angelo (from 1677) and the high-class SS Giovanni Grisostomo (from 1678).

Venice, orphanages

Venice had four *ospedali* for orphaned or destitute girls. Each orphanage had a *cappella* that staged oratorios and other musical performances to reward and attract benefactors. By training their girls for these ensembles, the *ospedali* became early conservatoires. Music in the orphanages was led by top-rank composers including Legrenzi, Rigatti, Rosenmüller, Rovetta and (from 1703) Vivaldi.

Vienna, imperial court

Ferdinand II, Holy Roman Emperor and King of Bohemia and Hungary, moved his court to Vienna in 1619. Under his rule, many Italians worked there. The *Hofkapelle* performed colossal polychoral pieces by Giovanni Priuli and Giovanni Valentini, both of whom probably knew Giovanni Gabrieli. In 1622 Ferdinand married Eleonora Gonzaga and thus opened a link with Monteverdi, formerly musician to the Gonzagas: Monteverdi dedicated his Eighth Book of madrigals to Ferdinand, and his *Selva morale e spirituale* to Eleonora. Music also prospered under Leopold I (*req.* 1652–1705), who was a keen amateur composer. Schmelzer wrote music for equestrian ballets and dance spectaculars. Operas were staged regularly with several commissions from Cesti. The wedding of Leopold to Margarita of Spain was celebrated with three years of festivals culminating in the most lavish court opera of the century, Cesti's *Il pomo d'oro* (1668).

Warsaw   The Polish royal court moved from Kraków to Warsaw at the start of
          the seventeenth century. The royal chapel had many Italian musicians; its
          directors included Giovanni Francesco Anerio and Marco Scacchi, while
          the organist Tarquinio Merula and the singer Francesco Rasi also worked
          there briefly. Opera began in 1628 with *Acis*, followed by various *drammi per
          musica* directed by Scacchi. Musical life lapsed with the Swedish invasion
          of 1655, but by the 1690s it had recovered and Italian operas were again
          being staged.

Personalia

STEPHEN ROSE

Agazzari, Agostino (*c.* 1580–1642)	Italian composer and theorist. For most of his life he worked in Siena. His sacred music includes eight-voice motets as well as small-scale settings. In *Del sonare sopra 'l basso* (1607) he offered advice on continuo playing, not only to keyboardists realising a figured bass but also to the rich array of other instrumentalists who accompanied vocal music.
Albert, Heinrich (1604–51)	German composer and poet. From 1630 he was organist at the cathedral in Königsberg. His eight books of *Arien* (1638–50) are strophic songs that can be performed by vocal ensemble or by a soloist with continuo.
Albrici, Vincenzo (1631–1690 or 1696)	Organist and composer of Italian birth. He worked for Queen Christina of Sweden in both Stockholm and Rome, for the Electors of Saxony at Dresden, and for Charles II in London. His music has the same tunefulness as Carissimi's; his sacred concertos were among the first in Germany to incorporate strophic arias.
Anerio, Giovanni Francesco (*c.* 1567–1613)	Italian composer and organist. He spent most of his career in Rome serving various cardinals. He upheld Palestrina's legacy, arranging the *Missa Papae Marcelli* for four voices, and also wrote madrigals and dialogues for the city's oratories that established prototypes for the oratorio.
Artusi, Giovanni Maria (*c.* 1540–1613)	Bolognese monk, theorist and polemicist. He studied with Gioseffo Zarlino, the codifier of sixteenth-century counterpoint, and subsequently defended traditional counterpoint, and attacked modern compositional and performance practices, in disputes with Ercole Bottrigari and Claudio Monteverdi. His criticisms of contrapuntal licence in Monteverdi madrigals opened the debate that led to Monteverdi's definition of the *seconda pratica*.
Banchieri, Adriano (1568–1634)	Italian monk, composer and writer. He worked in several monasteries in northern Italy, and in 1615 he helped found the Accademia dei Floridi in Bologna. An accomplished composer of sacred music and witty madrigal comedies, he also wrote several treatises. These are practically orientated

and explain the latest compositional and performing techniques (e.g. *Cartella musicale*, rev. edn, 1614).

Benevoli, Orazio (1605–72)
Italian composer. He worked in Rome and had links with Austrian courts. He wrote sacred music for a wide range of scorings, from solo motets to Masses for as many as 48 voices.

Bernhard, Christoph (1628–92)
German singer, composer and theorist. He trained with Schütz in Dresden and with Carissimi in Rome. He worked mainly at Dresden, with a spell in Hamburg 1663–74. His *Tractatus compositionis augmentatis* divided music into three styles depending on the relationship of words and music. His understanding of *seconda pratica* dissonance-treatment as an embellishment of a *prima pratica* consonant frame has been adopted by some musicologists.

Biber, Heinrich von (1644–1704)
Austrian violinist and composer of Bohemian birth. For much of his career he worked for the Salzburg court and cathedral. His violin sonatas exude drama and brilliance, often using *scordatura* tunings. In his *Mystery Sonatas*, each associated with one of the fifteen Mysteries of the Rosary, virtuosity melds with religious mysticism. He also wrote large polychoral Masses for Salzburg cathedral, and three operas.

Blow, John (1648/9–1708)
English composer and teacher. Conscripted as a twelve-year-old into the Chapel Royal, he later held many posts at the English court and the Chapel Royal. He was twice the organist of Westminster Abbey, the first time resigning the post to make way for the young Purcell. His prolific church music includes symphony-anthems absorbing Continental fashions, as well as full anthems that develop native traditions. He wrote little for the theatre, although his masque *Venus and Adonis* (*c.* 1683) is an all-sung drama like Purcell's *Dido and Aeneas*. Inconsistent but highly original, his achievements were surpassed only by Purcell's in Restoration London.

Bononcini, Giovanni Maria (1642–78)
Composer and theorist working at Modena. He mostly wrote instrumental music, helping redefine the sonata as a piece with several distinct movements. He was known for his counterpoint and for his compositional treatise, *Musico prattico* (1673).

Bontempi, Giovanni Andrea (1625–1705)
Italian castrato, composer, librettist and historian. He worked at Dresden, first as a singer and then as a theatre designer, where his operas included *Il Paride* (1662). In 1695 he published his *Historia musica* (primarily a work on music theory rather than, as often claimed, the first history of music in Italian).

Burmeister, Joachim (1564–1629)
German school-teacher and theorist. His *Musica poetica* (1606) is a composition manual written from a rhetorical standpoint. It analyses Lassus motets with terms taken from rhetoric, an approach revived by some twentieth-century musicologists.

Buxtehude, Dieterich (c. 1637–1707)

Organist and composer of Danish origin. For most of his life he worked at the Marienkirche in Lübeck, where his career exceeded the customary lowliness of the organist's profession. He ran the city's concert series (*Abendmusik*) and wrote much devotional music characterised by strophic arias and a melodic sweetness. His chamber sonatas and organ works are virtuosic and have a sense of dramatic fantasy as if amid an improvisation; his multi-sectional *praeludia* exemplify the north German organ writing that developed on the instruments of Schnitger. His many achievements inspired J. S. Bach to walk to Lübeck from central Germany in 1705 in order to hear him perform.

Caccini, Francesca (1587–c. 1641)

Italian singer and composer, daughter of Giulio Caccini. For most of her life she served the Medici family in Florence. She gained especial fame during the regency of 1621–8 (the regents included Grand Duchess Christine of Lorraine and Archduchess Maria Magdalena of Austria), briefly becoming the best-paid musician at the court and writing the music for entertainments representing strong female rulers. One such spectacle, *La liberazione di Ruggiero dall'isola d'Alcina* (1625), is the first known opera by a woman.

Caccini, Giulio Romolo (1551–1618)

Italian singer, teacher and composer. He trained in Rome and from the 1560s served at the Medici court in Florence. His *Le nuove musiche* (1602) was the first publication of solo songs with basso continuo; it notates vocal ornaments and includes an essay advocating *sprezzatura* (graceful nonchalance) in performance. His second book, *Nuove musiche e nuova maniera di scriverle* (1614), also explored new notations and wide vocal ranges. Caccini's monody was influenced by Neapolitan–Roman traditions of unnotated song and by Florentine debates about ancient Greek music. Caccini was proud, pushy, and in constant competition with Jacopo Peri. In 1600 he made a rival setting of Ottavio Rinuccini's *Euridice* and rushed it into print before Peri's appeared.

Calderón de la Barca, Pedro (1600–81)

Spanish priest and dramatist. The leading playwright at the Madrid court in mid century, he wrote sacred dramas and court spectacles for which Juan Hidalgo usually supplied music. He created the *zarzuela* (music theatre with a mixture of songs and spoken dialogue); he also wrote the librettos for some of the first Spanish all-sung dramas, *La púrpura de la rosa* (1659) and *Celos aun del aire matan* (1660).

Cambert, Robert (c. 1628–1677)

French composer and organist. With the librettist Pierre Perrin, he created the first French operas, including the *Pastorale d'Issy* (1659) and, after being granted the official privilege for opera, *Pomone* (1671). When Lully seized the privilege, Cambert moved to London where he set up a Royal Academy of Musick for opera.

Cardoso, Manuel (1566–1650)   Portuguese prior and composer. His Masses modify the style of Palestrina with Iberian colourings in the form of expressive harmonies.

Carissimi, Giacomo (1605–74)   Italian composer and organist. He was *maestro di cappella* at the Collegio Germanico in Rome from 1629, where his many pupils included Albrici, Bernhard, Charpentier and Kerll. His oratorios such as *Jephte* and *Judicium Salomonis* use the dramatic devices of operatic recitative (albeit at a slower pace for good effect in an ample acoustic) and aria; choruses also participate in the action and comment on events. His many secular cantatas have melodious arias, usually on the theme of unrequited love. His music was celebrated in Italy and further afield in northern Europe.

Cavalli, Francesco (1602–76)   Venetian composer, singer and organist. He was Monteverdi's colleague at St Mark's, Venice and gained the post of *maestro* there in 1668. From 1639 he was also active in the city's opera houses as a composer and impresario. In the 1640s his collaboration with impresario and librettist Giovanni Faustini produced operas such as *Egisto* (1643); other dramas to enter the repertory were *Giasone* (1649), *Xerse* (1655) and *Erismena* (1655). Most of his operas are tragicomedies, drawing inspiration from the pastoral and the *commedia dell'arte*, as well as the trend for dramas based on quasi-historical subjects. They established conventions easily recognisable by audiences, such as the lament over a descending chromatic bass, or the love-duet; his arias are smooth, lyrical and often in triple time. He was later summoned to Paris where he staged *Xerse* (1660) and *Ercole amante* (1662) to celebrate the wedding of Louis XIV and Maria Theresa of Spain. Although in later years he was overtaken by younger composers, he died wealthy and famed.

Cazzati, Maurizio (1616–78)   Italian composer. He was *maestro di cappella* at San Petronio, Bologna, until dismissed in 1671 after a long-running polemic surrounding his music. Of his immense published output, his instrumental pieces were most influential. His op. 18 sonatas (1656) promoted a four-movement plan, while his 1665 sonatas explored the Bolognese scoring for trumpet and strings.

Cesti, (Pietro) Antonio (1623–69)   Italian friar and composer. In 1643 he became organist at Volterra Cathedral and was soon also working in Venetian opera-houses. His fame as an opera composer led to commissions from the courts of Innsbruck (*L'Argia*, 1655; *Orontea*,

1656) and Vienna (*Il pomo d'oro*, 1668; the most lavish court opera of the century). He was the most celebrated Italian musician of his day, and was enviously mocked for combining the secular world of opera with the office of a friar.

Chambonnières, Jacques Champion, Sieur de (1601/2–1672)
French harpsichordist and composer. He taught and played in noble and royal circles in Paris, starting in 1641 a series of fee-paying concerts. He was later sidelined as the court became intoxicated by Lully's music. His refined dance-suites inaugurated the French classical tradition of harpsichord composition and playing, which prized delicate touch and sensitive ornamentation.

Charles II (1630–85)
King of England (1660–85). During the Commonwealth he was exiled to France, where he gained a taste for dancing and violin music. Upon his Restoration he re-established English court music on the French model, including a band of 'four-and-twenty fiddlers'. His enthusiasm for dance-rhythms and incisive violin textures encouraged the rise of such genres as the symphony-anthem. In 1666–7 he imported an Italian troupe of singers led by Albrici in the unsuccessful hope of introducing opera into London; in 1683 he tried in vain to get Lully to write an opera celebrating the restored monarchy.

Charpentier, Marc-Antoine (1643–1704)
French composer. He studied with Carissimi in Rome, and worked in several Parisian churches and noble households, notably for the devout Mademoiselle de Guise. His sacred music includes dramatic motets, bold canticles such as the *Te Deum*, and extravagantly ornamented *Tenebrae* settings. His works for the stage include incidental music, pastorals, *divertissements*, sacred operas and the *tragédie en musique*, *Médée* (1693). He upheld the French tradition of careful text declamation, but also introduced imaginative orchestration and pungent harmonies, perhaps inspired by his Italian training.

Christina, Queen of Sweden (1626–89)
Patron. She succeeded her father, Gustavus Adolphus, at the age of six and was crowned in 1650. In 1654 she converted to Catholicism, abdicated the throne, and moved to exile in Rome. Her conversion was a coup for Catholic leaders across Europe. In Rome she compensated for her lost political power with lavish patronage of the arts. Her private theatre staged operas; her library attracted scholars such as Kircher; and she gave patronage to Carissimi, Corelli and Alessandro Scarlatti.

Corelli, Arcangelo (1653–1713)
Italian violinist and composer. From a wealthy family, he led a gentrified life in Rome working for Cardinals Pamphili and Ottoboni. He was renowned for his virtuosity as a soloist and also for the high standards of his orchestral performances, in which he insisted, like Lully, on unanimity of bowing. Unusually, his reputation as a composer depended not on

opera but on a small published output of string music: church sonatas (opp. 1, 3; 1681, 1689), chamber sonatas (opp. 2, 4; 1685, 1694), solo sonatas (op. 5; 1700) and *concerti grossi* (op. 6; 1714). His music has elegance, economy and tonal clarity; he popularised such harmonic formulas as sequences, walking basses and the circle of fifths. Through his teaching and the wide dissemination of his works, he was the most influential musician in Europe at the start of the eighteenth century.

D'Anglebert, Jean-Henri (1629–91)
French keyboardist. He was probably taught by Chambonnières, whom he succeeded as royal harpsichordist in 1662. His *Pièces de clavecin* (1689) contain dances, fugues and arrangements of Lully's overtures, all exquisitely notated and with a table explaining French ornaments.

D'India, Sigismondo (c. 1582–c. 1629)
Italian singer and composer. He was from a noble family and served the Duke of Savoy in Turin (1611–23) and then the Este court in Modena. His five books of *Musiche* (1609–23) include monodies, dance-songs, airs over popular basses, and strikingly dramatic laments. His eight books of madrigals consolidate the work of Marenzio, Gesualdo and Monteverdi, culminating in a madrigal cycle based on Guarini's *Il pastor fido* (1624).

Dowland, John (1563–1626)
English lutenist and composer. Although perhaps the best lutenist of his day, he did not get a post at the English court until 1612, instead travelling to Germany and Italy in the mid 1590s and working at Copenhagen (1598–1606). His strophic ayres can be performed by a soloist with lute or as polyphony. Some are lively dances, but others share a stylised melancholy with his set of instrumental pavans, *Lachrimae, or Seaven Teares* (1604). His music was disseminated widely in Germany.

Dryden, John (1631–1700)
English poet and playwright. He wrote for the London stage and the monarchy, being Poet Laureate 1668–89. He wrote the libretto for the patriotic *Albion and Albanius* (1685; music by Louis Grabu) and worked with Purcell on *King Arthur* (1691). In the prefaces to these dramas he discussed the role of music in English plays.

Du Mont, Henry (c. 1610–84)
French composer. From 1663 he worked at the royal chapel, eventually as *maître de la musique de la reine*. His sacred music includes *petits motets*, sometimes with dialogues and echo effects; and also *grands motets* for the large vocal and instrumental forces in the royal chapel. In 1686 twenty of these *grands motets* were published on Louis XIV's command.

Durón, Sebastian (1660–1716)
Spanish organist and composer. He worked at Spanish cathedrals and then the Madrid court. His many motets show a traditional Spanish gravity; his *villancicos* (vernacular devotional works) are vividly theatrical; and his *zarzuelas*

mingle French courtly pomp, Italian arias and native Spanish dances.

Frescobaldi, Girolamo (1583–1643)
Italian organist and composer. He trained with the Ferrarese organist Luzzasco Luzzaschi and in 1608 became organist at St Peter's, Rome. He later worked in Mantua and Florence, but in 1634 he returned to Rome to serve the Barberini family. Some of his instrumental collections are highly contrapuntal (*Recercari et canzoni*, 1615; *Fiori musicali*, 1635) but his toccatas (1615, 1627) are improvisatory and invoke the expressive freedom of contemporary madrigals; he also wrote variations on popular dances. He taught Froberger, and his music was very influential, with copies being made by composers as diverse as John Blow and Johann Sebastian Bach.

Froberger, Johann Jacob (1616–67)
German keyboardist and composer. He was perhaps the first international keyboard virtuoso, studying in Rome with Frescobaldi and then working in Vienna and travelling through France, Germany, the Low Countries and England. His music is cosmopolitan, enriching the Frescobaldian toccata with Germanic fugal sections, and synthesising German and French traditions to produce some of the earliest keyboard suites. He also wrote highly personal laments and programmatic pieces.

Gabrieli, Giovanni (*c.* 1554/7–1612)
Italian composer and organist, nephew of Andrea Gabrieli (*c.* 1532/3–1585). He was associated with Lassus in Munich and then worked in Venice, chiefly at St Mark's. His two books of *Sacrae symphoniae* (1597, 1615) contain polychoral pieces distinguished by their striking harmonic successions, enveloping sonorities and climactic tuttis. The second book specifies obbligato instruments and includes sections for solo voices with continuo, producing varied structures held together by formal planning and refrains. His music was highly influential both south and north of the Alps and he taught many northerners, notably Heinrich Schütz.

Grandi, Alessandro (1586–1630)
Italian church musician. He worked at St Mark's, Venice (1617–27) and then at Bergamo. He pioneered solo motets (including attractive Song of Solomon settings) and sacred concertos using violins in a trio texture.

Hidalgo, Juan (1614–85)
Spanish harpist and composer. He worked at the Madrid court from 1630. He mainly wrote chamber songs and theatre music, especially *zarzuelas* and mythological dramas created with Calderón. He drew on Iberian secular song rather than using recitative or Italianate affective devices. His *Celos aun del aire matan* (1660) is the earliest extant all-sung opera from Spain.

Humfrey, Pelham (1647/8–1674)	English church musician. A precocious chorister, he travelled to France and Italy in the mid 1660s. Back in London he received rapid royal preferment. He pioneered the English symphony-anthem, drawing on French string writing and Italian vocal styles.
Isabella Leonarda (1620–1704)	Italian nun and composer. Of noble birth, she spent her adult life in a convent in Novara. About 200 of her pieces survive, and with seventeen printed collections she was one of the most published Italian composers of the second half of the century.
Jacquet de la Guerre, Elisabeth-Claude (1665–1729)	French keyboardist and composer. As a girl she sang and played the harpsichord at the royal court. Upon marriage she gave lessons and concerts in Paris. Her music includes the *Pièces de clavessin* (1687) and the first French opera by a woman, *Céphale et Procris* (1694).
João IV (John IV) (1604–56), King of Portugal (1640–56).	He assembled the largest music library in Europe, acquiring titles from most major music publishers. This music was not merely for the bookshelf but was also performed so that he could hear and judge it. His preference was for Palestrina and the *stile antico*, which he defended in a treatise.
Kerll, Johann Caspar (1627–93)	German organist and composer. He worked at the courts of Brussels (1647–56), Munich (1656–73) and Vienna (1673–93). He wrote toccatas in the tradition of Frescobaldi, and several operas; in 1686 he published his set of organ versets, *Modulatio organica*, along with a thematic catalogue of his other keyboard works.
Kircher, Athanasius (1601–80)	Jesuit and polymath of German birth. After his education and early travels he settled in Rome. He founded the science of magnetism, and wrote numerous treatises that embraced and organised knowledge in Christian ways. His *Musurgia universalis* (1650) is an encyclopaedia of speculative musical theory, arguing that music is a numerical science whose ratios illuminate the cosmos and God's harmonies.
Landi, Stefano (1587–1639)	Italian singer and composer. He worked for families of successive popes, in particular the Barberini. His *La morte d'Orfeo* was written for an unknown occasion around 1619; for Carnival 1632 he made a setting of *Sant'Alessio* for the Barberini private theatre.
Lawes, William (1602–45)	English composer. He worked in London theatres and at the court of Charles I. His collection of string consort music, *The Royall Concert*, includes serious pavans and fantasias alongside light-hearted triple-time dances; he also wrote solo songs. He was killed in the Siege of Chester while fighting for the king. His brother, Henry (1596–1662), was a prolific songwriter.

Legrenzi, Giovanni (1626–90)	Italian composer and organist. He worked in Bergamo (1645–56), Ferrara (1656–65) and Venice (from 1670). He wrote operas and oratorios for Venice, but was best known for his church and chamber sonatas, which explore a variety of multi-movement designs.
Leopold I (1640–1705)	Austrian archduke and (from 1658) Holy Roman Emperor. An enthusiastic patron, he made Vienna a centre for opera. His own works include music dramas and German-language comedies.
Locke, Matthew (c. 1621/3–1677)	English organist and composer. He spent part of the Civil War in the Low Countries. On the Restoration he became composer to the Private Music, which played in the king's apartments. He wrote much consort music, often intricately contrapuntal with dense harmonies. His Catholicism barred him from church posts, but he wrote for the theatre, collaborating on the masque *Cupid and Death* (1659) and the semi-opera *Psyche* (1675).
Louis XIV (1638–1715)	King of France (1643–1715); his personal rule began in 1661. He was an absolutist king whose political power was matched by the magnificence and energy of his court. He presided over writers and thinkers such as Descartes, Molière, Pascal and Racine; he created numerous *académies* to supervise intellectual and cultural life. He was a keen dancer, and most court entertainments revolved around *ballets*. His musicians, notably Lully and Henry Du Mont, created several genres and idioms that defined the nation musically: the French overture, the *tragédie en musique*, the *grand motet*, and the orchestra combining the traditional violin band and an oboe band. His court and its culture impressed the whole of Europe and were widely emulated, inspiring Leopold I of Austria and Charles II of England to similarly lavish patronage.
Lully, Jean-Baptiste (1632–87)	Musician, dancer and composer of Italian birth. From lowly origins as a Florentine miller's son, he rose to become the most powerful figure in French music. Initially a court dancer, he attracted the favour of the young Louis XIV and in 1661 became *Surintendant de la musique de la chambre du roi*. In the 1660s he worked with Molière on a series of *comédies-ballets* (e.g., *Le bourgeois gentilhomme*, 1670) and on the tragedy *Psyché* (1671). In 1672 he gained control of the Académie Royale de Musique, with a sole patent to perform opera, and thereafter staged a *tragédie en musique* each year, for example *Cadmus et Hermione* (1673), *Alceste* (1674) and *Armide* (1686). His orchestra was renowned as the best and most disciplined in Europe. He died of gangrene from a leg wound self-inflicted when beating time with a stick. He had a

stranglehold over court music and suppressed rival talents or compositional styles. He did more than anyone to establish the musical practices of Louis XIV's reign.

Marini, Biagio (1594–1663)
Italian instrumentalist. He held posts in Italy and also travelled to Germany. His instrumental music (published between 1617 and 1655) gradually introduced idiomatic string techniques and defined a trio-sonata texture. His op. 8 sonatas (1629) present an encyclopaedic collection of instrumental genres.

Mazzocchi, Domenico (1592–1665)
Italian composer. He worked for cardinals in Rome. His music includes an opera (*La catena d'Adone*, 1626), Latin dialogues for the oratories, and madrigals (1638) that look back to polyphonic traditions and the expressive intensity of Gesualdo. His brother Virgilio (1597–1646) was *maestro* of the Cappella Giulia and also worked for the Barberini family, writing operas, oratorios and motets.

Mersenne, Marin (1588–1648)
French friar, scientist and correspondent. He made important contributions to physics and astronomy but also acted as a scientific clearing-house, exchanging and sending out ideas for testing. He examined the acoustics and compositional practice of music, making an encyclopaedic compendium of musical knowledge in his *Harmonie universelle* (1636–7).

Merula, Tarquinio (c. 1594/5–1665)
Italian instrumentalist. He held church posts at Cremona and Bergamo but also served in Poland (*c.* 1624). His four books of ensemble canzonas (1615, *c.* 1631–3, 1637, 1651) increasingly explore idiomatic violin writing.

Molière (Jean-Baptiste Poquelin; 1622–73)
French playwright and actor. During the 1660s he collaborated with Lully on *comédies-ballets* for royal festivals, including *Le mariage forcé* (1664), *L'Amour médecin* (1665) and *Le bourgeois gentilhomme* (1670). After writing the tragedy *Psyché* (1671) he fell out with Lully and thereafter worked with Charpentier.

Monteverdi, Claudio (1567–1643)
Italian composer. He worked at the Mantuan court from 1590 or 1591 until his dismissal in 1612. In 1613, he was appointed *maestro di cappella* at St Mark's, Venice, but continued to freelance for Italian courts, and late in his life wrote for the new public opera-houses in Venice. His entire output comprises vocal music and encompasses sixteenth- and seventeenth-century styles; it is both sensitive to the words and skilfully structured. His early books of madrigals consolidate Renaissance techniques but his Fourth (1603), Fifth (1605) and Sixth (1614) Books take contrapuntal licences to express the text, a procedure that he justified as a *seconda pratica* when attacked by Artusi. His Seventh (1619) and Eighth Books (1638) redefine the madrigal as a vocal *concerto*, juxtaposing passages in

opposed styles and showing a strong sense of tonal centres. By contrast, his *Scherzi musicali* are light songs that influenced later styles of arias. His sacred music includes the *Missa . . . ac Vespere* (1610) with its mix of the old and new, and the vast *Selva morale e spirituale* (1640–41) compiling his Venetian church works. He was also a pioneer of music drama, writing operas for the Mantuan court (*Orfeo*, 1607; *Arianna*, 1608) and Venetian opera-houses (*Il ritorno d'Ulisse in patria*, 1640; *L'incoronazione di Poppea*, 1643).

Muffat, Georg (1653–1704)   German composer of Scottish extraction born in Savoy. He studied with Lully, and in 1682 he met Corelli in Rome. He worked in Salzburg and from 1690 in Passau. His music is an early example of *les goûts-réunis*, combining French and Italian styles; the prefaces to his publications introduced Germans to the compositional and performing styles of Corelli and Lully. His *Armonico tributo* (1682) combines Lullian dances with Corellian sonatas that can be played as concertos. His two books of *Florilegia* (1695, 1698) are suites emulating Lully's orchestral writing for the theatre.

North, Roger (1651–1734)   English amateur musician and writer. After a short legal career in London, in 1690 he retired to Norfolk. Here he began copious 'scribbling' on music and other topics. His writings document the changes in English musical life since the 1650s; he also ventured into acoustics and musical cognition with his *Theory of Sounds*.

Pachelbel, Johann (1653–1706)   German organist. He worked in Erfurt and Stuttgart, and from 1695 was organist at St Sebaldus, Nuremberg. Nowadays best known for his three-part canon over a bass, he was a central figure in the south German organ school. He made many chorale settings, and his *Hexachordum apollinis* (1699) contains sets of variations that may have influenced J. S. Bach's *Goldberg Variations*. His sacred vocal music is also well crafted.

Pepys, Samuel (1633–1703)   English civil servant. A keen amateur musician, he played several instruments and through his duties had access to court musicians. His diary (1660–69) is a unique record of music at home and in the lively culture of Restoration London.

Peri, Jacopo (1561–1633)   Florentine singer and composer. He worked at the Medici court from 1588 and also had close ties to the Gonzagas of Mantua. In the 1590s he was a member of Jacopo Corsi's circle seeking to recapture the power that the ancient Greeks had experienced in music. He wrote the music for Ottavio Rinuccini's *Dafne* (1598) and then for Rinuccini's *Euridice* (1600), the first extant opera. In *Euridice* he pioneered a sung speech where the solo voice declaims over a static bass. Later he published songs and arias in *Le varie musiche* (1609).

Playford, John (1623–*c*. 1686/7)	English publisher. In 1651 he began issuing music in London, developing the market for domestic music during the Commonwealth ban on church and theatre music. His books included psalters, didactic manuals (*A Breefe Introduction to the Skill of Musick*, 1654), collections of dance tunes (*English Dancing Master*, 1651), and catches to sing in taverns (*Catch That Catch Can*, 1652). By the 1670s he was also publishing continuo songs and tunes from the newly reopened theatres. The business was continued by his son Henry (1657–1709) but declined in the face of competition from publishers of engraved music such as John Walsh.
Praetorius, Jacob (1586–1651)	German organist. He studied with Sweelinck and in 1603 became organist at the Petrikirche, Hamburg. His chorale fantasias require a large instrument and an impressive technique.
Praetorius, Michael (?1571–1623)	German composer and theorist. From 1595 he worked at the Wolfenbüttel court but also spent periods at Kassel and Dresden. His immense printed output of over a thousand pieces is largely based on Lutheran hymns, whether in motets, *concerti* or the vast polychoral textures of *Polyhymnia caduceatrix* (1619). His three-volume treatise *Syntagma musicum* (1614–18) describes a wide range of musical instruments, and it also introduced Germans to Italian techniques of polychoral scoring and continuo playing.
Purcell, Henry (1659–95)	The greatest English composer of the century. He was trained in the Chapel Royal and held posts there, at the court, and at Westminster Abbey. From 1690, with the decline of court patronage and of opportunities for church music, he worked mainly in London's theatres. He wrote in all genres, from bawdy tavern catches to devotional meditations. His instrumental music includes erudite consort fantasias and the Italianate sonatas of 1683. His vocal music is remarkable for its rhythmic energy, respect of English declamation, and ability to highlight key words; his odes and many of his anthems establish a patriotic style in their choruses. His stage works include the fully sung *Dido and Aeneas* (1689) and the semi-operas *Dioclesian* (1690), *King Arthur* (1691) and *The Fairy Queen* (1692). He was one of the few composers of the century whose reputation continued after his death and whose music continued to be widely performed.
Quinault, Philippe (1635–88)	French dramatist. He first worked with Lully as a contributor to *Psyché* (1671); he then became Lully's regular librettist, working on numerous *tragédies en musique* including *Alceste* (1674), *Isis* (1677), *Proserpine* (1680) and *Armide* (1686). He favoured topics from mythology or the legends of chivalry, in contrast to the farces of Molière.

Rigatti, Giovanni Antonio (c. 1613–1648)	Italian church musician. He worked in Venice at St Mark's and various *ospedali* (orphanages-cum-conservatoires). He published many small-scale motets in the 1640s, as well as grand festal settings in his 1641 *Messa e salmi*.
Rosenmüller, Johann (c. 1617–1684)	The most accomplished German composer of his generation. He studied in Leipzig but in 1655 was arrested on charges of pederasty and fled to Venice, where he worked at St Mark's and the Ospedale della Pietà. In the 1680s he returned to Germany. His music is outstandingly creative, fusing Italian styles with the contrapuntal expertise of the Schütz tradition. He set many psalms and canticles in Venice, and published major collections of sonatas in 1667 and 1682.
Rospigliosi, Giovanni (1600–69; Pope Clement IX)	Patron and librettist. In the 1620s and 1630s his poetry was set by Roman composers such as Landi and Luigi Rossi. During 1644–53 he was a papal nuncio in Madrid where he stirred Spanish interest in opera.
Rossi, Luigi (?1597/8–1653)	Italian composer and keyboard player. He trained in Naples and then worked in Rome, gradually moving into French circles by working for San Luigi dei Francesi in Rome and the Barberini family. Later on he made several trips to Paris, where the extravagant staging of his *Orfeo* (1647) excited both admiration and controversy. He is also important for his numerous chamber cantatas.
Rovetta, Giovanni (c. 1595/7–1668)	Italian church musician. He worked at St Mark's, Venice, where he succeeded Monteverdi as *maestro* in 1644. He published ceremonial Masses and four books of pleasing continuo motets.
Sartorio, Antonio (1630–80)	Italian composer active in Germany. In the 1660s he wrote operas for Venice. From 1666 he was Kapellmeister to Johann Friedrich of Brunswick-Lüneburg, travelling to Venice each winter to write operas and recruit musicians for the court. In 1676 he took a post at St Mark's, Venice. His operas are on heroic themes and are memorable for their laments and trumpet arias; they include *Giulio Cesare in Egitto* (1676).
Scacchi, Marco (c. 1600–1662)	Composer and theorist of Italian birth. He worked in Poland 1621–49 and wrote in all genres of vocal music. In the 1640s he began a long polemic by criticising Paul Siefert for not respecting the distinction between sixteenth-century and modern styles.
Scarlatti, Alessandro (1660–1725)	Italian composer. He trained in Rome and moved to Naples in 1683, where he revitalised opera at the Teatro S. Bartolomeo. In 1703 he returned to Rome, but despite generous patronage was frustrated by the restrictions on opera there. He later worked in Venice and again in Naples. His operas – including *Gli equivoci nel sembiante* (1679), *La Statira* (1690), *La caduta de' Decemviri* (1697), *Tigrane* (1715) and

Griselda (1721) – are important examples of the formalism and expressive range of the genre as it moved towards the High Baroque. He wrote hundreds of cantatas for aristocratic entertainments, usually on the theme of unrequited love.

Scheidemann, Heinrich (c. 1595–1663)
German organist. He studied with Sweelinck and then became organist at the Catharinenkirche, Hamburg. His organ chorales were renowned for their melodic sweetness; he often treated the cantus firmus as an embellished solo above an accompaniment.

Scheidt, Samuel (1587–1654)
German organist and composer. He was a pupil of Sweelinck and helped transmit the styles of the English virginalists and Dutch organists to Germany. He worked in Halle, both for the city council and for the local court. His *Tabulatura nova* (1624) is the most imposing German keyboard publication of the century. It includes variations on secular and sacred tunes, and invokes styles ranging from the contrapuntal fantasia to the martial *concitato genere*. He also published many sacred concertos and consort dances.

Schein, Johann Hermann (1585–1630)
German composer and poet. From 1616 he held the prestigious post of Cantor at the Thomasschule in Leipzig. He wrote consort dances, pieces for local Lutheran services, and pastoral madrigals for local burghers. He was a German pioneer of the sacred madrigal (*Israelis Brünlein*, 1623) and the vocal concerto (*Opella nova*, 1618, 1626). Although he never visited Italy, his music is some of the most Italianate of all his German contemporaries.

Schmelzer, Johann Heinrich (c. 1620/23–1680)
Austrian violinist and composer. He worked at the Viennese court and became *Kapellmeister* in 1679. His instrumental output includes ballets and music for the allegorical pageants favoured by Leopold I. His ensemble sonatas represent the south German tradition of rich contrapuntal writing; he also published the first solo violin sonatas in Germany (1664).

Schnitger, Arp (1648–1719)
German organ builder. He worked in Stade and from 1682 in Hamburg. The most important organ builder of the century, he and his associates produced over 170 instruments. These were mainly in north German and Baltic cities, but his organs were also exported to England, Portugal, Russia and Brazil. Schnitger organs have several self-sufficient divisions, each speaking from a different part of the case. Their choruses are well blended and powerful. Such instruments inspired the music of the north German organ school as exemplified by Buxtehude.

Schütz, Heinrich (1585–1672)
German composer and teacher. He studied with Giovanni Gabrieli in Italy and from 1615 served at the Dresden court. He also spent spells in Copenhagen and Wolfenbüttel, and made another trip to Italy in 1628 where he encountered

Monteverdi. Virtually none of his secular or dramatic music survives. His sacred music is distinguished by its skilled counterpoint and attention to the meaning of words. The early music is Italianate, including the *Psalmen Davids* (1619) which uses Gabrielian polychoral techniques, a book of sacred madrigals, and several volumes of sacred concertos. After the Thirty Years War his music became increasingly austere: he advocated old-fashioned counterpoint in *Geistliche Chormusic* (1648) and wrote three archaic unaccompanied Passions in the 1660s. Despite such conservatism, he exerted a strong influence on subsequent German music through his pupils and publications.

Steffani, Agostino (1654–1728)
Composer, churchman and diplomat of Italian birth. He worked at the Munich court of the Elector of Bavaria 1667–88 and then transferred to the service of Duke Ernst August of Hanover, first as a musician and then in the late 1690s as a diplomat. In 1703 he abandoned music for political and ecclesiastical work. His chamber duets are mini-cantatas looking forward to the style of Handel; his operas are in the French manner.

Stradella, Alessandro (1639 or 1644–1682)
Italian composer. Of noble birth, he had a turbulent life coloured by shady love affairs, one of which led to his murder. He initially worked in Rome; in 1677 he left for Venice but settled in Genoa in 1678. Unusually for the period, he wrote in almost every genre, including numerous notable chamber cantatas, operas (e.g., *La forza dell'amor paterno*, 1678) and oratorios (*S. Giovanni Battista*, 1675). The exploits of his life fascinated the eighteenth and nineteenth centuries, and were the subject of operas by Louis Niedermeyer (1837) and Friedrich von Flotow (1844).

Stradivari, Antonio (c. 1644/9–1737)
Cremonese violin maker. His instruments have such tonal excellence and beautiful design that they are now thought to be among the best in the world. His sons Francesco and Omobono were also important makers.

Strozzi, Barbara (1619–77)
Italian singer and composer. She was the adopted and probably illegitimate daughter of the noble poet Giulio Strozzi. She studied with Cavalli and subsequently sang her cantatas before Venetian connoisseurs and at a special academy run by her father. With eight published collections, she was the most-published Italian cantata composer of the century.

Sweelinck, Jan Pieterszoon (c. 1562–1621)
Dutch organist, teacher and composer. He was organist at the Oude Kerk, Amsterdam (1580–1621), where the Calvinists forbade liturgical music but the city council sponsored organ recitals. His keyboard music draws on the Italian fantasia and toccata, and also on the variation sets of English

virginalists. His vocal works include chansons, a psalter (1604–21) and the overtly Catholic *Cantiones sacrae* (1619), which displays his mastery of large-scale polyphony. He was an influential teacher, particularly of north German organists such as Scheidt and Scheidemann.

Torelli, Giuseppe (1658–1709)

Italian composer. He spent his early life in Verona and then moved to Bologna; when the orchestra there was disbanded in 1696, he served at Ansbach, Berlin and Vienna. His Bolognese works include trio-sonatas, suites and concertos. His concertos (op. 6, 1689; op. 8, 1709) experiment with ritornello form and violin solos. He also wrote pieces in the Bolognese tradition for solo trumpet and strings.

Uccellini, Marco (c. 1603–80)

Italian instrumentalist. He worked in Modena and later at Parma. His output includes sonatas and dance movements, notable for their triadic themes and bold exploration of distant keys.

Viadana, Lodovico (1560–1627)

Italian composer and monk. He worked at Padua, Cremona and Bologna. His *Cento concerti ecclesiastici* (1602) helped popularise the few-voiced motet with continuo. The book has the first instructions on continuo playing; it was widely reprinted and highly influential in Italy and Germany. Two further books followed in 1607 and 1609.

Vitali, Giovanni Battista (1632–92)

Italian composer. He had links with the academies in both Bologna and Modena. His output helped establish the trio-sonata as a genre. His *Artifici musicali* (1689) is a textbook displaying techniques of instrumental counterpoint; it includes such curiosities as a passacaglia that modulates through the circle of fifths from B flat to B.

Walther, Johann Jakob (c. 1650–1717)

German violinist. He travelled to Florence and later worked in Dresden and Mainz. His *Scherzi da violino solo* (1676) and *Hortulus chelicus* (1688) are characterised by virtuoso multiple stopping and use of high positions, often to imitate animals, birds, or other musical instruments.

Index